The Prehistoric Pueblo World, A.D. 1150–1350

The Prehistoric Pueblo World,
A.D. 1150–1350

Edited by Michael A. Adler

The
University of
Arizona
Press,
Tucson

The University of Arizona Press

Copyright © 1996

The Arizona Board of Regents

♾This book is printed on acid-free, archival-quality paper.

Manufactured in the United States of America

04 03 02 01 00   6 5 4 3 2

Library of Congress Cataloging-in-Publication Data

The prehistoric Pueblo world, A.D. 1150–1350 / edited by Michael A.
Adler.

p. cm.

Based on a conference held at the Crow Canyon Archaeological
Center in Cortez, Colo., from Mar. 28 to Apr. 1, 1990. It was
organized by William Lipe and Stephen Lekson.

Includes bibliographical references and index.

ISBN 0-8165-1468-2

ISBN 0-8165-2048-8 (pbk.)

1. Pueblo Indians—Antiquities—Congresses. 2. Pueblo Indians—
Land Tenure—Congresses. 3. Pueblo Indians—Social conditions—
Congresses. 4. Land settlement patterns—Southwest, New—
Congresses. 5. Demographic archaeology—Southwest, New—
Congresses. 6. Southwest, New—Antiquities—Congresses.
1. Adler, Michael A., 1961–

E99.P9P737   1996

979'.01—dc20 95-32452

CIP

British Cataloguing-in-Publication Data

A catalogue record for this book is available from the British Library.

Publication of this book was made possible in part by a grant from
the Crow Canyon Archaeological Center, Cortez, Colorado.

Contents

Preface

The conference "Pueblo Cultures in Transition: A.D. 1150–1350 in the American Southwest" was held at the Crow Canyon Archaeological Center[1] in Cortez, Colorado, from March 28 to April 1, 1990. It was organized by William Lipe and Stephen Lekson with financial support from the Crow Canyon Archaeological Center and the Wenner-Gren Foundation. The conference was a tightly focused dialogue among a group of southwestern archaeologists interested in prehistoric trends that led to the development of the historic Pueblos. The primary goals of the conference were (1) to integrate a variety of geographically and theoretically diverse approaches to archaeological research on the Puebloan occupation of the Southwest between A.D. 1150 and 1350 (Pueblo III period), and (2) to develop and publish a new synthesis of this period of southwestern prehistory.

Conference participants were selected to ensure coverage of 12 regions of the Anasazi world, which was defined by Lipe and Lekson in their 1989 proposal to the Wenner-Gren Foundation, "Pueblo Cultures in Transition: A.D. 1150–1350 in the American Southwest," as the maximal extent of Pueblo-style architecture and ceramics during the period addressed. As defined, the area covers nearly 150,000 mi^2 (384,000 km^2). The first two days of the conference focused on each of the 12 regions. The last two days were dedicated to discussions of interpretive models and to summary presentations. The archaeologist(s) responsible for each region presented a data summary and interpretive description of his or her region. The presentations included general and specific

impressions of "what happened" in each region during the Pueblo III period.

Twenty-two scholars participated in the conference, and their contributions fall into three main categories. Most of this volume is devoted to the regional summaries. The regions embrace nearly the entire range of major topographic features, ecological zones, and prehistoric Puebloan settlement patterns in the northern Southwest. Moving in a roughly west-to-east direction, the regions and contributors are as follows: (1) southwestern Utah and the Arizona Strip, Margaret Lyneis; (2) the northern San Juan, Mark Varien, William Lipe, Michael Adler, Ian Thompson, and Bruce Bradley; (3) northeastern Arizona, Jonathan Haas and Jeffrey Dean; (4) the Hopi Region, E. Charles Adams; (5) the Flagstaff-Prescott region, Peter Pilles; (6) the Acoma Region and the eastern San Juan Basin, John Roney; (7) the central and northern San Juan Basin, John Stein; (8) the Zuni Region, Keith Kintigh and Robert Leonard; (9) the southeastern Mogollon uplands, Steve Lekson; (10) the southwestern Mogollon uplands, J. Jefferson Reid; (11) the lower Rio Grande, Katherine Spielmann; and (12) the upper Rio Grande, Patricia Crown and Timothy Kohler. Following the conference each presentation was submitted in manuscript form by the original participants and additional co-authors.

In addition to the regional papers, two presentations on paleoenvironmental reconstructions were given at the conference. Jeffrey Dean made a presentation on paleoenvironmental reconstructions and limitations during the Pueblo III period and has integrated some of this discussion

in his treatment of the Kayenta region. Carla Van West's discussion of prehistoric carrying capacity in the Mesa Verde region is included in its entirety. A topical paper by Jonathan Haas and Winifred Creamer on prehistoric conflict and warfare provides an important discussion of prehistoric interaction and population aggregation.

The final part of the volume includes summary chapters by Linda Cordell and David Wilcox, who played invaluable roles as conference discussants. Both of them rewrote their discussion summaries for the volume.

Data originally presented at the conference have been revised and are included in this volume. In preparing their written syntheses, participants were asked to divide their regions into smaller "districts" if sufficient reason existed for such subdivisions. Seventy-three districts are defined within the 12 regions. In most cases, district delineations are based upon patterning of archaeological remains, the presence of localized chronological schemes, environmental criteria, or a combination of these.

Participants were asked to provide three classes of data for each presentation. First was a list of all recorded "big" sites occupied between A.D. 1150 and 1350 in their region. The arbitrary criteria for a "big site" were that it contain 50 rooms or more (but see regional variations in chapter 1 by Lyneis and chapter 5 by Pilles), and that constituent roomblocks be no more than an easy stone's throw apart (approximately 30 to 50 meters). Included for each "big" site were all recorded site names, a room count, span of occupation, number of kivas, and in some cases, the presence of great kivas, great houses, or other extraordinary site characteristics. These site data are included in the Master Data Table (appendix).

The second contribution asked of each participant was a site distribution map for the region. These regional site location maps are included in each chapter. In some cases, authors have included regional site maps differentiating sites by occupation dates and site size. Based upon the regional summaries, a single map with all sites recorded in the master data table was then compiled (see figure 1.2).

The third class of data consisted of a set of graphs depicting overall population trends for each region or district during the Pueblo III period. Most discussants presented impressionistic graphs of trends in population and degree of aggregation for each region, but some have (understandably) not included the graphs in their chapters due to the lack of dependable population figures for each region.

The data summaries brought to the conference were admittedly preliminary assessments, useful for establishing rough estimates of the geographic distribution of population throughout the Puebloan Southwest between A.D. 1150 and 1350. These initial estimates were also useful for determining where and when population aggregation occurred. Following the conference, participants were asked to fur-

ther refine the data tables and maps. As a whole, we found that the large sites in many regions are as poorly known as the less visible small sites. But during the course of this large cooperative effort over 800 sites have been recorded. Electronic versions of the master data table and associated bibliography are available in three separate locations for use by interested scholars (see appendix).

The success of the "Pueblo Cultures in Transition" conference was a joint effort. William Lipe and Stephen Lekson provided the foundation for this volume by conceiving the idea for the gathering, raising the funds to support the conference, and coordinating the data presentations and discussions. Ian Thompson, then executive director of the Crow Canyon Archaeological Center, and the entire staff and faculty of the center provided the facilities for a very comfortable conference. Stuart Struever was also instrumental in fund raising and conference support. We would like to thank Nance and Barbara Creager, Diane and Bob Greenlee, John Hopkins, Clayton Jackson, Jr., and Stuart Patterson and Ellie Schrader for their financial support of this volume in the form of a publication subvention. Thanks also go to the Wenner-Gren Foundation for their financial support of the conference. The staff at the University of Arizona Press, including Christine Szuter (acquiring editor), Anne

Keyl (design and production manager), and Carrie House (senior designer) have been patient, accommodating, and helpful over the long course of review and publication. Linda Gregonis copy edited the volume, and her careful work has greatly improved the style and content of each chapter. Finally, the true heroes of this volume are the conference participants and their co-authors. The participants provided four stimulating days of discussion (as well as the initiation of the First and Only World Root Crop Games, won by Bill Lipe), and subsequently have endured changing editorial teams, manuscript deadlines, and revisions. Each participant has provided an insightful and enduring contribution to our knowledge of this watershed in Pueblo prehistory. Here's hoping for a similar level of collegial productivity and intellectual stimulation at the next Pueblo III conference.

Notes

1. The Crow Canyon Archaeological Center was founded in 1983 and invites members of the lay public to participate in its research under the close supervision of experienced archaeologists. Its staff includes 18 full-time and part-time archaeologists. Not only does the Center conduct scientific research in the Four Corners region but it seeks the perspective of American Indians in the region in interpreting the archaeological record there.

The Prehistoric Pueblo World, A.D. 1150–1350

"The Great Period": The Pueblo World During the Pueblo III Period, A.D. 1150 to 1350

Michael A. Adler

If we knew the relative date of the founding and abandonment of every ruin in the Southwest, it would be a comparatively simple matter, by estimating the approximate population of each, and plotting the results on a series of maps, to visualize the entire history of the Pueblo peoples. Our task, therefore, is: first, to locate all of the ruins and record their size; second, to determine the length of their occupancy, and their age relative to each other; and, third, to establish their age, not only in relative terms, but according to the years of our own calendar. This is a heavy program and one which naturally can never be completely carried out.
—A. V. Kidder, *An Introduction to the Study of Southwestern Archaeology,* [1924] 1962

Alfred Vincent Kidder's words not only evoke the grand hopes of 70 years ago, but they provide an apt summary of the research goals to which many southwestern archaeologists still aspire. Although few prehistorians would share Kidder's optimism that we might one day visualize "the entire history of the Pueblo peoples," Kidder's "heavy program" encapsulates the multiple levels of archaeological inquiry that are necessary for a clearer understanding of the regional, local, and site-level dynamics of Pueblo prehistory in the American Southwest.

More than a century of archaeological research in the Southwest has been dedicated to clarifying the links between the historic Pueblos and the innumerable prehistoric ruins spread out across the region. The extent to which historic Pueblo architectural and settlement patterns emerged during the Pueblo III period (A.D. 1150–1350 in this volume), and the prehistoric context within which these patterns did (or did not) emerge, formed the primary research focus for a working conference held between March 28 and April 1, 1990, at the Crow Canyon Archaeological Center in Cortez, Colorado. The "Pueblo Cultures in Transition: A.D. 1150–1350 in the Southwest" conference, organized by William Lipe and Stephen Lekson,

brought together 22 scholars to discuss this period in southwestern prehistory (Lipe and Lekson 1990). Over the past five years the "Pueblo Cultures in Transition" conference has become known as the "Pueblo III conference."

Several questions provided the impetus for the Pueblo III conference (Lipe and Lekson 1989; see also Cordell, chapter 16). These questions include the effect of the end of the much-debated "Chaco phenomenon" in the early twelfth century on the later Pueblo world, local and regional abandonments, variations in social integrative architecture, and changing relationships between Pueblo groups and the populations of adjacent regions such as the Hohokam and Mogollon regions.

During the conference the Pueblo Southwest was discussed on a regional basis (figure 1.1), and each participant presented an interpretive paper on his or her own areal specialty. The presentations included syntheses of settlement patterns at the regional, local, and site levels. These data have been summarized here in graphical (figure 1.2) and tabular (appendix) form. Discussions also focused on several models that seek to explain the processes of population aggregation, relocation, and regional integration in the precontact Pueblo Southwest. By the end

of the conference it was clear that although major gaps still exist in the data and explanatory models that have been brought to bear on this period of great change, the results of the conference were worthy of broader dissemination. As such, the volume serves as a data resource and a summary of ideas about prehistoric changes in Puebloan settlement and in regional interaction across nearly 150,000 mi² (384,000 km²) of the Southwest.

Before I discuss the major topics raised at the conference, several terms and word choices used throughout the volume require mention. Chronologists will recognize that the conference version of the Pueblo III period, A.D. 1150 to 1350, is not fully contemporaneous with the dates of the traditional Pueblo III period (A.D. 1100–1300) first assigned by the Gladwins (Gladwin and Gladwin 1934: figure 10) to Kidder's Pueblo III stage (Kidder 1927) and canonized by later revisions (Reed 1948). The "revisionist" Pueblo III period of A.D. 1150 to 1350 is used because it is bounded by two important watersheds in southwestern prehistory, the decline of the Chacoan regional system by about A.D. 1150, and the establishment by A.D. 1350 of a Puebloan settlement geography that closely parallels that

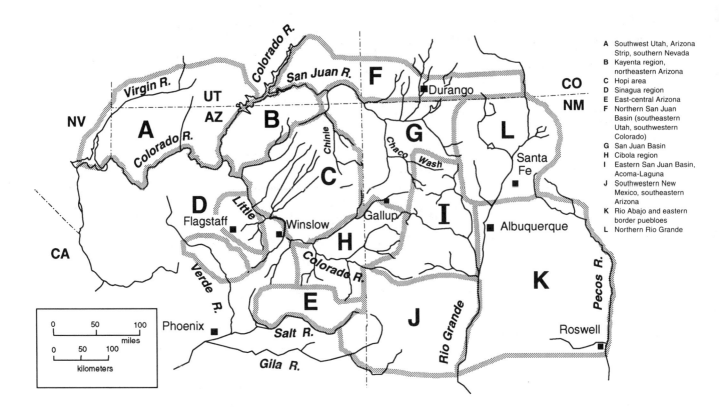

Figure 1.1. Regions discussed in this volume. In some cases, regional boundaries overlap, and authors discuss these overlapping areas in the text. Boldface letters refer to the chapter in which the region is discussed.

of the historic Pueblos.[1] Readers will also notice the fallout from the continuing terminological struggle with Chaco-related archaeological features across the Southwest, reflecting the varying interpretations of Chaco currently being debated (Doyel 1992; Judge 1991; Lekson 1991; Sebastian 1992; Vivian 1990). "Chaco-style" is a term indicating the presence of architectural and ceramic attributes common in Chaco Canyon during the height of its occupation. Wilcox (chapter 17) finds "Chaco-style" too generic, while my own inclination is that the term should lack specificity given the wide range in various examples of great house public architecture during the eleventh and twelfth centuries. A similar level of ambiguity can be found in the description of Chaco as the hub of a "regional system." Although some (including myself) envision such a system as a regional tangle of interacting communities sharing a similar architectural expression of public, integrative ar-

chitecture, others argue that the regional system was coordinated and controlled by powerful decision-making individuals living within Chaco Canyon and its important great houses.

Some authors have also chosen to use "prehistoric Pueblo" rather than the traditional, Navajo-derived term, "Anasazi." The Hopi Tribe has requested that Puebloan, rather than non-Puebloan, terms be used to identify ancestral Pueblo populations.[2] Among the authors in this volume there is certainly a consensus that twelfth-through fourteenth-century Pueblo populations across the Southwest have relatively direct ties to historic Puebloan groups, but authors were free to utilize a range of terms in their discussions.

In the following paragraphs I discuss three different scales of analytical inquiry that are central to our archaeological investigations of the Pueblo Southwest; the region, the locality, and the individual settlement. It is an archaeological tru-

ism that these "levels" of inquiry are spatially nested and conceptually interdependent (Gumerman 1994:6; McGuire et al. 1994), but because so much of our actual research is carried out at a spatially restricted scale, it is rare for an archaeological data set to include all three levels. This volume is an attempt to achieve an integration of these three spatial scales.

Pueblo III: Period, Pattern or Panacea?

The Pueblo III period took its place in chronological history as part of the Pecos Classification (Kidder 1927), the first major regional synthesis of southwestern prehistory. Kidder stated several criteria that define the Pueblo III period, including village type, architecture, sandal type, pictographs, textiles, stone and bone implements, kinds and styles of ornaments, and pottery, but it is clear that the big, sprawling pueblos and their

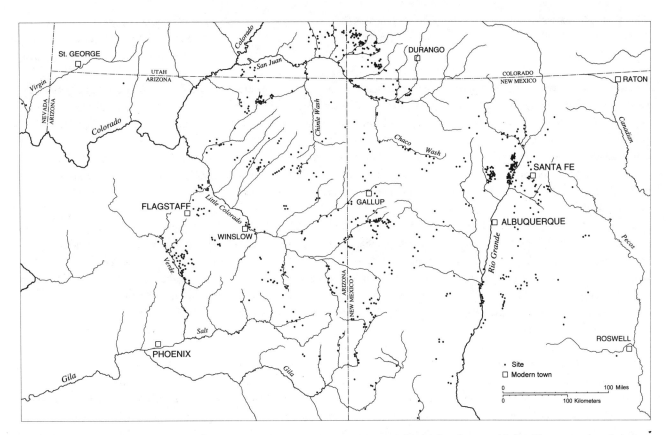

Figure 1.2. Distribution map of all large sites (50-plus rooms in most cases) in the Southwest with Pueblo occupations between A.D. 1100 and 1400. For more extensive discussions of the map and data, refer to appendix.

associated ceramic assemblages were the primary inspirations for this classificatory unit. Similarly, Kidder's contemporaries agreed that the big site criterion was the period's single most important defining factor (Gladwin 1945; Roberts 1935).

Kidder (1962) describes Pueblo III remains in glowing terms, calling this stage the "Great Period" of Puebloan cultural development. The attainments in grand architectural scale, ceramic and decorative arts, and other manufactures (cotton, especially) were, in Kidder's estimation, the results of territorial contraction, increasing aggregation, and the coalescence of defense-minded Puebloan populations into thriving, specialized communities. During the Great Period, "pressure of one sort or another had forced the Pueblos to draw together into large aggregations, where community of interest stimulated community of effort. The difficulties confronting them were sufficient to spur them

to their best endeavors, but not great enough to stunt their progress" (Kidder 1962:338–39).

Early debates over the Pecos Classification and the Pueblo III period were numerous and productive. While Roberts (1935) crowned Pueblo III the "Great Pueblo period," Harold Gladwin (1945:3) characterized Pueblo III as "a period about which it is dangerous to generalize as cultural progress was very uneven both as regards degree and time. It may be enough to say that it was a period of large pueblos and cliff dwellings." The subsequent definition of the Hohokam (Roberts 1935), Mogollon (Haury 1936), and Patayan (Colton 1945) culture areas further partitioned the Southwest into distinct research realms, each with its own terms, chronologies, and research history.

As would be expected in any areally extensive synthesis, contributors to this volume mirror the earlier debates con-

cerning the benefits and pitfalls of utilizing the Pueblo III period concept across the Pueblo Southwest. For those in the Mesa Verde and Kayenta regions, Pueblo III remains the shorthand for a period characterized by large, massed pueblo architecture, cliff dwellings, carbon-painted ceramics, and ultimate abandonment. As one moves out from the San Juan drainage, the utility of the Pueblo III label wanes (see Kintigh, chapter 9) and is replaced by local phase designations and variations in settlement and abandonment regimes. Given the large measure of late prehistoric cultural variability recorded across the Southwest, our dependence on "Pueblo III" as a period, trait-list, and archaeological shorthand for big sites is outmoded. In its stead we require multiple scales of inquiry to address this variability.

The Multiple Scales of Archaeological Inquiry

Arguments are mustered (literally with every new grant proposal) for the appropriate scale at which to examine our convoluted interpretations of southwestern prehistory. Each call for an expansion or contraction of a research realm always requires the obligatory hat-tipping to other scales of research. But as Marquardt and Crumley (1987) point out, there is no single "effective scale" of research, that scale at which patterns may be recognized and explanations for the patterns proffered. Research must be geared so that there is an appropriate fit between the questions asked, the scale of the system about which the questions are asked, and the nature of the data to be collected.

The analyses and data presented in this volume are effective on a number of different and often mutually informative scales. The conference organizers asked participants to discuss large areas, consider expansive questions, and to amass information on significant population aggregates. Though none of the participants would consider large-scale considerations to be *the* most appropriate scales at which to address the prehistoric dynamics in the Southwest, most would agree that the resulting observations and summaries address a number of appropriate scales of inquiry. In this volume, three spatial scales receive significant consideration, namely the Puebloan Southwest as a region, the locality, and the settlement. The nested, yet distinct, nature of these scales, however, has not precluded each contributor from bringing important data to bear on significant questions pertaining to each level of inquiry. By way of example, brief discussions of regional abandonment, community organization, and site layout reveal the multiple levels of explanatory potential contained in these far-reaching regional summaries and data sets.

The Region as an Effective Scale of Study

Primary aims of the Pueblo III conference were not to think about big sites alone, but to address big sites within the context of regional changes across the Southwest. David Wilcox (chapter 17) and others (F. Plog 1979, 1983; Upham 1982) have advocated archaeological inquiry at this and even larger spatial scales. Wilcox promotes a network approach to understanding the Southwest, stressing the need to conceptualize settlements and settlement clusters as "nodes" connected by various types of social and economic relationships that vary by type and intensity. Fred Plog has argued that the regional patterns in prehistoric Puebloan material culture that form the basis for chronological frameworks reflect the emergence of large-scale "provinces," that is, regional organizational systems covering about 3,800 to 6,000 mi² (10,000–15,000 km²), characterized by internal economic interdependence and probable social hierarchy. Upham (1982) has inferred similarly large regional systems, which he calls "alliances," in the late prehistoric occupation of the Upper Little Colorado region. Whether we call them "regional systems" or "alliances" or "provinces," proponents argue that these large-scale organizational entities provided the regional context within which prehistoric Pueblo groups exchanged people, information, goods and energy.

Though we must be mindful of the pitfalls of making potentially noncontemporaneous (and hence non-interacting) settlements part of a contemporaneous prehistoric interaction network, the Pueblo III conference provided us with the most comprehensive foundation yet for assessing the utility of these regional alliance and interaction models. The patchiness of our knowledge of the Pueblo world between A.D. 1150 and 1350 is evident throughout the volume, but it is unlikely that the uneven archaeological coverage of the Southwest is the primary reason for the varying spatial extent of regional settlement clusters (figure 1.2). Some settlement clusters cover much larger geographical areas than others. Many of these same clusters comprise Plog's (1983) "provinces" and Upham's (1982) "alliances." Though I am personally not yet convinced of the presence of social hierarchy within and between these clusters, the Pueblo III conference data will benefit future examinations of extant models of regional alliance in the Southwest.

One potentially fruitful avenue for assessing the fit between regional settlement pattern maps and possible prehistoric alliances rests with future work on regional abandonment,[3] a necessary chapter in every text on Puebloan prehistory. Regional changes in population density and occupation are by no means unique to the Pueblo III period. Significant regional abandonments occurred in the Pueblo I (A.D. 750–900) and Pueblo II (A.D. 900–1150) periods as well. What is apparent, however, is the progressively larger geographical scales at which regional abandonment occurred throughout Puebloan prehistory.

For example, the Pueblo I period occupation (A.D. 750–900) in southwestern Colorado and northwestern New Mexico involved several thousand individuals occupying an area of approximately 1,950 mi² (ca. 5,000 km²) (Wilshusen 1991). Schlanger and Wilshusen (1993) make a strong argument for two abandonments of the region during the Pueblo I period. Just prior to the second abandonment in the late ninth century, Pueblo I populations occupied large, aggregated villages and smaller dispersed settlements. Applying the settlement and stylistic (ceramic) criteria proposed by F. Plog (1983) and Upham (1982), this area was possibly the locus of a ninth-century province comprising multiple interacting, local communities.

The next significant regional changes involved the Puebloan occupation of the geologic San Juan Basin[4] and its centerpiece, Chaco Canyon. By about the mid-twelfth century, depending on who you debate, populations either abandoned the geologic San Juan Basin or experienced a severe disruption of the extant settlement regime. John Roney's (chapter 10) perspective that "abandonment" is too simple a term for this regional disruption is probably right. The archaeological signature is one of regional discontinuity in settlement location (movement to higher elevations), ceramics (shift to a dependence on organic-based paints), and settlement layout (abandonment or modification of existing Chacoan great houses). The extent to which this involved actual loss of population in the geologic San Juan Basin as opposed to significant reconfiguration of intact populations is debatable (McKenna 1991; Roney, chapter 10; Windes 1987). Given the consensus in some circles that Chaco Canyon and its outliers were integrated into some sort of a regional social-economic-political system, the area affected by the Chaco demise and regional reorganization may have been on the order of 8,000 to 12,000 mi² (20,720–31,080 km²). This is a significantly larger area than was affected by the Pueblo I abandonment and presumably involved the collapse of a more populous province or polity.

By the beginning of the thirteenth century the Mesa Verde tradition had expanded to cover the entire San Juan River Basin, including the former Chaco region, to create a single, large, ceramically homogeneous region (Roney, chapter 10, see also Lekson, chapter 11). Plog (1983) refers to this expanded, thirteenth-century region as the "Mesa Verde province."

The end of the thirteenth century marked the next regional abandonment in the Pueblo world. The emptying out of much of the Mesa Verde province, including the Kayenta and Four Corners regions, involved a much larger regional population and the most extensive areal abandonment to date. Encompassing approximately 23,200 mi² (ca. 60,000 km²) (Lipe 1994), the Four Corners-Kayenta aban-

donment involved tens of thousands of people (Dean, Doelle, and Orcutt 1994), most of whom were living in aggregated settlements up to the time of the abandonment. The depopulated regions included several of Plog's provinces, which not surprisingly, are best defined for the period between A.D. 1100 and 1300 (Plog 1983: table 7.2). In other words, some of the largest and most clearly defined provinces were among those abandoned.

Fish et al. (1994) convincingly argue for a link between the emergence of aggregated settlement systems and subsequent regional abandonment. Given the increasing geographical scale of regional abandonments through time, we must consider the possible role of regional political and economic systems within the suggested aggregation-and-abandonment phenomenon. As the size and prevalence of aggregated settlements increased in the Southwest, a trend clearly supported by the Pueblo III conference data (Adler 1994), more people would have been involved in each "connection" between nodes in regional networks. Aggregation may have caused increasing volatility within and among regional systems, a trend that was ultimately countered not by abandoning the aggregation strategy, but by relocating several provincial populations in more predictable environmental zones within a spatially contracted version of the protohistoric Pueblo world (Fish et al. 1994:156).

Local Level Archaeology and The Prehistoric Pueblo Community

A second important analytical focus of these chapters, the local community, involves archaeological inquiry at a smaller geographic scale than the macroregion or region. The importance of community organization within the Pueblo world, as in food-producing societies in general, is not a recent inspiration in archaeology (Chang 1958; Flannery 1972; Rohn 1971, 1977). Still, the community concept has received its most explicit definition and

use in sociology and cultural anthropology. In these fields the term refers to an ideal type of social organization based upon kinship relationships, spatial proximity of habitation areas, and the existence of various forms of social unity, including sharing of resources, risks, and a common identity (Hillery 1955).

Closer to home, archaeologists have tended to adopt Murdock's (1949; Murdock and Wilson 1972) definition in which the community represents a spatially clustered group of people who interact on a daily basis (Rohn 1971:40). To this I would add that communities serve an important role in defining, maintaining, and defending social access to important resources on the local and regional levels (Adler 1992, 1995). Specific archaeological applications of the community concept in the Pueblo Southwest have tended to rely upon spatial distributions of residential sites (Benson 1988; Biella 1979; Dykeman and Langenfeld 1987; Fowler and Stein 1987; Gilman 1988; Neily 1983; Rohn 1977) and social integrative features (Adler 1995; Adler and Varien 1994; Kintigh 1994). Resulting estimates of community geographic and demographic scale are derived from spatial proximity and the absolute number of recorded architectural features. Due to our reliance on spatial patterning of material culture in archaeological research, this spatial approach to identifying the community is necessary. But to more completely understand the community, we must recognize the wide range of spatial configurations the community can take in the archaeological record.

In a recent publication discussing prehistoric communities in the Southwest, Wills and Leonard (1994) differentiate between two major types of community studies. The first type analyzes an individual site as a single corporate unit that the authors define as a "residential community." The second community study considers a number of individual, noncontiguous sites that together comprise what Wills and Leonard (1994:xiii) call a political community. The terminology is somewhat unfortunate, given that residential (aggregated) communities often are also political communities, and "residential" describes a spatial settlement characteristic while "political" refers to a social organizational aspect of the local residential population. Their basic distinction, though, is a valid one across the Pueblo world; community populations occupied a wide range of residential configurations and utilized an equally varied repertoire of architectural spaces for community integrative activities, spaces ranging from round great kivas to enclosed rectangular plazas.

A primary focus of the conference was on the number, size, layout, and distribution of large sites, and nearly all of the contributors differentiate between the settlement—an archeological unit of residence—and the community—a conceptual level of social organization and integration. But that is where consensus on community configuration ends. For example, in those areas where population estimates were possible for Puebloan communities we find a great deal of variation. The Virgin Anasazi region and surrounding areas illustrate the lower end of the scale, where the largest twelfth-century community clusters probably housed well under 100 individuals and where there is no evidence of large-scale community integrative architecture (Lyneis, chapter 2). At the same time, a few hundred miles to the east, communities such as Guadalupe discussed by Roney (chapter 10) contained 800 rooms, great kivas, great houses, and probably housed several hundred individuals.

Each author has described changes in the spatial configuration (i.e., degree of dispersion) of residential and integrative architecture in each region, and the variations visible across time and space should give pause to those of us who continue to describe these as integrated, interacting, contemporary "communities." It is unlikely that similar social, economic and ideological strategies existed in all Puebloan communities. Kintigh (chapter 9)

raises this point in his discussion of Cibolan settlement patterns during the Pueblo III period. Archaeological survey and testing indicate no single pan-Cibolan pattern of community layout, making it difficult to define communities and calling into question whether we should be treating all communities as a single class of organizational entity in our analyses. Populations in some regions clearly depended on relatively dispersed community configurations throughout the Pueblo III and earlier periods, including the far western region (Lyneis, chapter 2), the Sinagua area around Flagstaff (Pilles, chapter 5), and the densely populated eastern portion of the geologic San Juan Basin and Acoma-Laguna regions (Roney, chapter 10). At the same time, however, large portions of the prehistoric Pueblo world transformed their earlier, dispersed communities by aggregating into larger settlements, and sometimes an entire community coalesced into a single village. We currently lack a sufficient set of organizational models to assess the degree to which the configuration of residential, integrative, and other architecture influenced the organization of the functioning social unit we classify as the community.

There is substantial diversity in the range of community configurations discussed in the volume, but there are also some interesting consistencies in the geographic scale of southwestern communities in these and other regional analyses. Community-oriented surveys indicate that many dispersed communities were not areally extensive. Estimates of "community radius," or that distance from the center of a community cluster out to the farthest sites in the cluster, range between about one and five miles (ca. 2–8 km) in the northern San Juan River Basin (Adler 1995; Varien et al., chapter 7), the eastern San Juan (geologic) Basin and Acoma-Laguna area (Roney, chapter 10) and the Cibola region (Duff 1993; Kintigh, chapter 9). Similar radii are reported for Hohokam communities during the Classic period (Fish 1995). Obvious reasons for an

upper limit on community spatial extent include transport costs of moving goods (Drennan 1984; Wilcox, chapter 17), distance to agricultural fields (Chisholm 1962), and other distance-dependent factors. Even though we struggle as a discipline with the near absence of chronological proof of site contemporaneity, future research needs to address reasons for these local-level regularities in settlement patterning and potential constraints on the geographic scale of communities.

Puebloan Settlement Layout and Community Integration

Intrasite architectural analysis has traditionally been the context within which archaeologists have addressed specific sets of activities such as storage, food processing, ritual, and material discard. Settlement layout has clearly been a significant criterion used by those defining the extent of the Puebloan Southwest. Equally critical in the Southwest, however, is the dependence on settlement layout patterns when delineating regional systems of social integration and ideology. Comparing types of community integrative architecture, when present, provides the means for determining the variability in population size, geographical scale, and social organization that existed among communities throughout the Puebloan Southwest.

The so-called Chacoan great houses are the subject of debate, particularly those located outside of Chaco Canyon proper. To date, great house outliers have been interpreted as resource outposts for supplying goods to Chaco Canyon (Kane 1993), integrative centers for dispersed communities, Chacoan-derived or not (Toll 1985; Varien et al., chapter 7), residences for community elites (Powers et al. 1983), and religious *visitas* for Chacoan or Chaco-trained priests (Bradley 1993). The criteria for elevating a structure to "great-ness" include architectural layout, masonry styles, and landscape modifications surrounding the structure (see Stein and Fowler, chapter 8). The distribution of outliers and road systems forms the basis for defining the hypothetical Chaco Regional System (Lekson et al. 1988; Wilcox, chapter 17), a very sizable piece of real estate no matter how far out you place the farthest outliers.

According to several authors in the volume, the demise of Chaco did not halt the construction of outliers. "Post-Chaco great houses" retain many of the architectural features and the general layout of the earlier great houses and, significantly, still appear to be surrounded by (or in some cases, occupied by) dispersed residential communities. More importantly, though, Chaco-style architecture was not the final format for community integrative architecture in the Puebloan Southwest. During the Pueblo III period a variety of integrative features were in use, highlighting the pervasiveness of community organization across the Southwest and the significant variety of architectural features that may have been constructed in the name of community identity and integration.

For example, Dean (chapter 3) and Adams (chapter 4) downplay Chaco's role in the western Pueblo region given the paucity of great houses there during the Pueblo II and Pueblo III periods. Instead, other distinct types of architecture served as possible integrative contexts within communities, including "spinal" room blocks in the Kayenta region (Dean, chapter 3), enclosed plazas in the Hopi region (Adams 1991, chapter 4), and "ladder" room block forms in the eastern San Juan Basin (Roney, chapter 10). These features are found in "preeminent sites" (Roney, chapter 10) and other probable community integrative centers, much in the same way that Chaco-style great houses and great kivas are believed to be the integrative hub of the dispersed communities in which they are located. This is a productive area for future research given the strong evidence for community integrative architecture in both dispersed and aggregated settlement regimes in the prehistoric Pueblo world and the apparent region-to-region variations in this archi-

tectural class. I think it is naive to consider this macroregional variation as indicative of community-level "experiments" with novel integrative systems. Social integrative activities often involve ritual, one of the most conservative forms of social action in any society. Rappaport (1979: 175) typifies ritual as the "performance of more or less invariant sequences of formal acts and utterances not encoded by the performers," highlighting ritual's formality and conservatism. A similar level of relative invariance is encoded into ritual integrative architecture within, but not necessarily shared across, regions (Adler 1990, 1993; Fowler and Stein 1990; Stein and Lekson 1992). These large site data are ripe for a series of significant comparative analyses of site layout variation across space (within and between regions) and inferred function (public, integrative space, domestic architecture, etc.). Several authors do point out the lack of obvious public architecture and large-scale integrative spaces in portions of the Puebloan Southwest, including the western reaches (Lyneis, chapter 2) and portions of the Rio Grande valley (Crown, Orcutt and Kohler, chapter 13; Spielmann, chapter 12). Given the assumed ubiquity of community organization, scholars need to address reasons for this apparent lack of integrative facilities in these parts of the Southwest.

Finally, the settlement data presented in this volume should serve to improve our current theories about southwestern culture change. This is already under way with respect to the origins and role of katsina cult beliefs. Recently, Adams (chapter 4, 1991) has argued that this religious system originated in the Little Colorado region during the late thirteenth and the early fourteenth centuries, spreading to nearly pan-southwestern proportions during a period of population relocation and aggregation, and significant climatic fluctuations. Katsina cult beliefs provided cross-cutting integrative ties that helped integrate large, socially fragile aggregated communities (but see Crown 1994). The conference data strongly support these ar-

guments and at the same time raise questions. Analysis of the data set (Adler 1995) clearly supports the increase in the size of aggregated communities after A.D. 1350. At most, the Pueblo settlements in regions abandoned prior to A.D. 1300 rarely exceed 700 rooms. Exceptions to this size limit include sites in the Zuni region (see Kintigh, chapter 9), but occupation also continued in that same region after A.D. 1350. In contrast, maximal site size for aggregated settlements occupied during the fourteenth and fifteenth centuries, many of which were not occupied during the Pueblo III period, routinely exceeds 1,000 rooms, reaching over 2,000 rooms in the Hopi Mesas, along the Rio Grande, and other portions of the Southwest.

Adams has argued that the spread of the katsina cult is archaeologically visible in site layout changes across major portions of the Southwest, particularly in the adoption of large, enclosed plazas. Others in the volume (Cordell, chapter 16; Kintigh, chapter 9; Lekson, chapter 11) point out that the front-oriented plaza pattern, as seen at sites such as Pueblo Bonito, is older in the southern portion of the San Juan River Basin. Again, this is not to dispel the arguments for the origins and spread of important macroregional ideological systems. But as large site data continue to be reworked across the Southwest we should expect to see a greater degree of temporal and spatial variability in site layouts generated as much by local and regional architectural traditions as by the adoption of a macroregional ideological system.

The Prehistoric Pueblo World: Future Research

Clearly no single scale will be sufficient for understanding the Southwest, or any large region for that matter. But as Lipe and Lekson (1990) point out, the archaeological record of large sites in the Southwest has been a curiously underutilized resource. Archaeologists are profoundly aware of how subtle patterning can be and how difficult it is to draw interpretation from faint patterns. But this does not make the interpretation of large, ostentatious settlement any easier; in fact the record is made all the more obscure by intensive occupation and multiple, overlapping activities within a limited locale.

Throughout the compilation of the conference proceedings the rallying cry has been that we need to get these regional perspectives on this important period of Pueblo change out to our colleagues. The data are already obsolete in the sense that new large sites are constantly being located and recorded in every region of the Southwest. But these data and our interpretations, like all scholarly pursuits, are works in progress. Although it is true that any progress in our understanding of Puebloan prehistory requires new and better data and improved models and methods, we must also be willing to work with partial and poor-quality data. This includes doing more of what we already do as archaeologists; conducting large- and small-scale survey (Fish and Kowalewski 1990), estimating sizes and use-lives of settlements (Adler and Varien 1994; Varien 1990), and refining existing ceramic chronologies (Hegmon 1991).

In a sense, the Pueblo Cultures in Transition Conference was a return to the early days of broad regional synthesis (Kidder 1927, 1962) and revision (Gladwin and Gladwin 1934; Roberts 1936) in southwestern archaeology. Not unlike the situation today, southwestern specialists in the early part of this century were faced with a deluge of archaeological data, and the times required broad syntheses. The data deluge continues today, though for different reasons. Cultural resource management and continued institutional research have largely replaced the museum-based excavations and surveys of the first half of the twentieth century, but the discipline of archaeology continues to produce more data than can be readily synthesized. Clearly shared across the decades, though, is the realization that major trends in settlement, subsistence, architectural layout, and stylistic motifs can be discerned across space during a relatively restricted temporal span in the Southwest. An increased understanding of these trends requires broad syntheses of spatially, temporally, and definitionally diverse data sets such as those in this volume. When the next Pueblo III conference convenes, we will all be the richer for having undertaken Kidder's "heavy program."

Acknowledgments

My thanks to Ian Thompson, Mark Varien, Bill Lipe, John Roney, Steve Lekson, and two anonymous reviewers for their insightful comments on earlier versions of this chapter. Although I take the responsibility for the factual content and personal opinions in this chapter, the inspiration to finish the chapter and volume came from the conference participants and their high-quality contributions.

Notes

1. Although the Pueblo III period was defined as A.D. 1150 to 1350 for the conference (Lipe and Lekson 1989, 1990), authors have redefined the time period and questioned its utility throughout the volume. Authors were requested to focus their discussions primarily on the period between A.D. 1100 and 1400 but were also encouraged to summarize earlier and later periods of culture change to better contextualize their observations.

2. The Hopi prefer the term *hisatsinom*, Hopi for "old ones" (Adams, personal communication 1994).

3. The Hopi tribe has formally objected to the term "abandonment" being applied to ancestral Puebloan population movements because of the implication of discontinued use and, hence, discontinued interest in formerly occupied areas. The Hopi prefer references that reflect their own concepts of long- and short-term cycles of changing land use patterns and the sanctity of ancestral sites, ideas that play a central role in religious beliefs of Hopi origins and ancestral migrations.

4. Throughout the volume we have attempted to differentiate between the geologic San Juan Basin and the hydrologic San Juan River Basin, both of which are often referred to as the "San Juan Basin." The hydrologic basin is much larger than the geologic basin because it comprises the entire San Juan River drainage, including the entire Mesa Verde region north of the San Juan River as well as the Chaco region south of the San Juan River. The geologic San Juan Basin is a structural feature of about 15,625 mi^2 (40,000 km^2) formed by surrounding monoclines, uplifts, and mesas and slopes (Fassett and Hinds 1971; Powers et al. 1983:1).

References Cited

Adams, E. Charles
1991 *The Origin and Development of the Katsina Cult*. University of Arizona Press, Tucson.

Adler, Michael A.
1990 *Communities of Soil and Stone: An Archaeological Investigation of Population Aggregation Among the Mesa Verde Region Anasazi, A.D. 900–1300*. Unpublished Ph.D. dissertation, Department of Anthropology, University of Michigan, Ann Arbor.
1993 Why Is a Kiva? New Interpretations of Prehistoric Social Integrative Architecture in the Northern Rio Grande Region of New Mexico. *Journal of Anthropological Research* 49(4):319–46.
1995 Fathoming the Scale of Mesa Verde Region Communities. In *Interpreting Southwestern Diversity: Underlying Principles and Overarching Patterns*, edited by Paul Fish and J. Jefferson Reid. Anthropological Research Papers. Arizona State University, Tempe, in press.

Adler, Michael A., and Mark D. Varien
1994 The Changing Face of the Community in the Mesa Verde Region A.D. 1000–1300. In *Proceedings of the Anasazi Symposium 1991*, compiled by Art Hutchinson and Jack E. Smith, pp. 83–98. Mesa Verde National Park Association, Mesa Verde, Colorado.

Benson, Charlotte L.
1988 *Explaining Organizational Change: Anasazi Community Patterns*. Ph.D. dissertation, Department of Anthropology, University of Washington, Seattle. University Microfilms, Ann Arbor.

Biella, Jan V.
1979 Changing Residential Patterns Among the Anasazi, A.D. 750–1525. In *Adaptive Change in the Northern Rio Grande Valley*, pp. 103–44. Archaeological Investigations in the Cochiti Reservoir, New Mexico, vol. 4, edited by Jan V. Biella and Richard C. Chapman. University of New Mexico Press, Albuquerque.

Bradley, Bruce
1993 Wallace Ruin Implications for Outlier Studies. In *The Chimney Rock*

Archaeological Symposium, edited by J. McKim Malville and Gary Matlock, pp. 72–75. General Technical Report RM-227. USDA, Forest Service, Rocky Mountain Forest and Range Experiment Station, Fort Collins.

Chang, Kwang-chih
1958   Study of the Neolithic Social Grouping: Examples from the New World. *American Anthropologist* 60:298–334.

Chisholm, Michael
1962   *Rural Settlement and Land Use: An Essay in Location*. Hutchinson University Library, London.

Colton, Harold S.
1945   The Patayan Problem in the Colorado River Valley. *Southwestern Journal of Anthropology* 1(1):114–21.

Crown, Patricia L.
1994   *Ceramics and Ideology: Salado Ceramic Pottery*. University of New Mexico Press, Albuquerque.

Dean, Jeffrey S., William H. Doelle, and Janet D. Orcutt
1994   Adaptive Stress: Environment and Demography. In *Themes in Southwestern Prehistory*, edited by George J. Gumerman, 53–87. School of American Research Seminar Series. School of American Research Press, Santa Fe.

Doyel, David E. (editor)
1992   *Anasazi Regional Organization and the Chaco System*. Maxwell Museum of Anthropology, University of New Mexico, Albuquerque.

Drennan, Robert D.
1984   Long-Distance Transport Costs in Pre-Hispanic Mesoamerica. *American Anthropologist* 86(1): 105–12.

Duff, Andrew I.L.
1993   *An Exploration of Post-Chacoan Community Organization through Ceramic Sourcing*. Unpublished Master's thesis, Department of Anthropology, Arizona State University, Tempe.

Dykeman, Douglas D., and Kristin Langenfeld
1987   *Prehistory and History of the La Plata Valley, New Mexico*. Contributions to Anthropology Series 891. San Juan County Archaeological Research Center and Library, Farmington, New Mexico.

Fassett, James E., and Jim S. Hinds
1971   *Geology and Fuel Resources in the Fruitland Formation and Kirtland Shale of the San Juan Basin, New Mexico and Colorado*. Geological Survey Professional Paper 676. USDI, U.S. Geological Survey, Washington, D.C.

Fish, Paul, Suzanne K. Fish, George J. Gumerman, and J. Jefferson Reid
1994   Toward an Explanation for Southwestern "Abandonments." In *Themes in Southwestern Prehistory*, edited by George J. Gumerman, pp. 135–64. School of American Research Seminar Series. School of American Research Press, Santa Fe.

Fish, Suzanne K.
1995   Dynamics of Scale in the Southern Deserts. In *Interpreting Southwestern Diversity: Underlying Principles and Overarching Patterns*, edited by Paul Fish and J. Jefferson Reid. Anthropological Papers. Arizona State University, Tempe, in press. Ms. 1992.

Fish, Suzanne K., and Stephen Kowalewski (editors)
1990   *The Archaeology of Regions: A Case for Full-Coverage Survey*. Smithsonian Institution Press, Washington, D.C.

Flannery, Kent V.
1972   The Origins of the Village as a Settlement Type in Mesoamerica and the Near East: A Comparative Approach. In *Man, Settlement and Urbanism*, edited by Peter J. Ucko, Ruth Tringham, and George W. Dimbleby, pp. 22–53. Gerald Duckworth, Cambridge, England.

Fowler, Andrew J., John R. Stein, and Roger Anyon
1987   An Archaeological Reconnaissance of West-central New Mexico: The Anasazi Monuments Project. Ms. in possession of the authors.
1990   The Anasazi Great House in Space and Time. Paper presented at the 55th Annual Meeting of the Society for American Archaeology, Las Vegas.

Gilman, Patricia A.
1988   Households, Communities and Painted Pottery in the Mimbres Region of Southwestern New Mexico. In *Community Structure. Proceedings of the 1988 Chacmool Conference*. University of Calgary, Alberta, Canada.

Gladwin, Harold S.
1945   The Chaco Branch, Excavations at White Mound and in the Red Mesa Valley. *Medallion Papers* 33. Gila Pueblo, Globe, Arizona.

Gladwin, Winifred, and Harold S. Gladwin
1934   A Method for Designation of Cultures and their Variations. *Medallion Papers* 15. Gila Pueblo, Globe, Arizona.

Gumerman, George J.
1994   Patterns and Perturbations in Southwest Prehistory. In *Themes in Southwestern Prehistory*, edited by George J. Gumerman, 3–10. School of American Research Seminar Series. School of American Research Press, Santa Fe.

Haury, Emil W.
1936   The Mogollon Culture of Southwestern New Mexico. *Medallion Papers* 20. Gila Pueblo, Globe, Arizona.

Hegmon, Michelle
1991   Six Easy Steps to Dating Pueblo III Ceramic Assemblages. Ms. on file, Crow Canyon Archaeological Center, Cortez, Colorado.

Hillery, George
1955   Definitions of Community: Areas of Agreement. *Rural Sociology* 20:111–23.

Judge, W. James
1991   Chaco: Current Views of Prehistory and the Regional System. In *Chaco & Hohokam: Prehistoric Regional Systems in the American Southwest*, edited by Patricia L. Crown and W. James Judge, pp. 11–30. School of American Research Press, Santa Fe.

Kane, Allen E
1993   Settlement Analogues for Chimney Rock: A Model of 11th and 12th Century Northern Anasazi Society. In *The Chimney Rock Archaeological Symposium*, edited by J. McKim Malville and Gary Matlock, pp. 43–60. General Technical Report RM-227. USDA, Forest Service, Rocky Mountain Forest and Range Experiment Station, Fort Collins.

Kidder, Alfred V.
1927   Southwestern Archaeological Conference. *Science* 68:489–91.
1962   *An Introduction to the Study of Southwestern Archaeology, with a Preliminary Account of the Excavations at Pecos*, revised edition. Yale University Press, New Haven. Originally published 1924, Papers of the Phillips Academy Southwest Expedition 1, Phillips Academy, Andover, Massachusetts.

Kintigh, Keith W.
1994   Chaco, Communal Architecture, and Cibolan Aggregation. In *The Ancient Southwestern Community: Models and Methods for the Study of Prehistoric Social Organization*, edited by Wirt W. Wills and Robert D. Leonard, pp. 131–40. University of New Mexico Press, Albuquerque.

Lekson, Stephen H.
1991 Settlement Pattern and the Chaco Region. In *Chaco & Hohokam: Prehistoric Regional Systems in the American Southwest*, edited by Patricia L. Crown and W. James Judge, pp. 31–55. School of American Research Press, Santa Fe.

Lekson, Stephen H., Thomas C. Windes, John R. Stein, and W. James Judge
1988 The Chaco Canyon Community. *Scientific American* 256(7):100–109.

Lipe, William D.
1995 The Depopulation of the Northern San Juan: Conditions in the Turbulent 1200s. *Journal of Anthropological Archaeology* 14:(2):143–69.

Lipe, William D., and Stephen H. Lekson
1989 Pueblo Cultures in Transition: A.D. 1150–1350 in the American Southwest. Proposal to the Wenner-Gren Foundation. Ms. on file, Crow Canyon Archaeological Center, Cortez, Colorado.
1990 Pueblo Cultures in Transition: Report of a Conference. Paper presented at the 55th Annual Meeting of the Society for American Archaeology, Las Vegas, Nevada.

McGuire, Randall H., E. Charles Adams, Ben A. Nelson, and Katherine Spielmann
1994 Drawing the Southwest to Scale: Perspectives on Macroregional Relations. In *Themes in Southwestern Prehistory*, edited by George J. Gumerman, pp. 239–65. School of American Research Seminar Series. School of American Research Press, Santa Fe.

McKenna, Peter J.
1991 Chaco Canyon's Mesa Verde Phase. In *Excavations at 29SJ633: The Eleventh Hour Site, Chaco Canyon, New Mexico*, edited by Frances Joan Mathien, pp. 127–37. Reports of the Chaco Center 10. USDI, Division of Cultural Research, National Park Service, Santa Fe.

Marquardt, William H., and Carole L. Crumley
1987 Theoretical Issues in the Analysis of Spatial Patterning. In *Regional Dynamics: Burgundian Landscapes in Historical Perspective*, edited by Carole L. Crumley and William H. Marquardt, pp. 1–18. Academic Press, Orlando.

Murdock, George P.
1949 *Social Structure*. The Free Press, New York.

Murdock, George P., and Susan Wilson
1972 Settlement Patterns and Community Organization: Cross Cultural Codes 3. *Ethnology* 11:254–95.

Neily, Robert
1983 *The Prehistoric Community on the Colorado Plateau, An Approach to the Study of Change and Survival in the Northern San Juan Area of the American Southwest*. Ph.D. dissertation, Southern Illinois University, University Microfilms, Ann Arbor.

Plog, Fred
1979 Prehistory: Western Anasazi. In *Southwest*, edited by Alfonso Ortiz, pp. 108–30. Handbook of North American Indians, vol. 9, William C. Sturtevant, general editor. Smithsonian Institution, Washington, D.C.
1983 Political and Economic Alliances on the Colorado Plateaus, A.D. 400–1450. In *Advances in World Archaeology*, vol. 2, edited by Fred Wendorf and Angela Close, pp. 289–330. Academic Press, New York.

Powers, Robert P., William B. Gillespie, and Stephen Lekson
1983 *The Outlier Survey: A Regional View of Settlement in the San Juan Basin*. Reports of the Chaco Center 3. USDI, National Park Service, Division of Cultural Research, Albuquerque.

Rappaport, Roy A.
1979 The Obvious Aspects of Ritual. In *Ecology, Meaning and Religion*, edited by Roy A. Rappaport, pp. 173–222. North Atlantic Books, Berkeley.

Reed, Erik K.
1948 The Western Pueblo archaeological Complex. *El Palacio* 55:(1):9–15.

Roberts, Frank H. H.
1935 A Survey of Southwestern Archaeology. *American Anthropologist* 37:1–33.

Rohn, Arthur H.
1971 *Mug House, Mesa Verde National Park, Colorado*. Archaeological Research Series no. 7-D. USDI, National Park Service, Washington D.C.
1977 *Cultural Change and Continuity on Chapin Mesa*. Regents Press of Kansas, Lawrence.

Schlanger, Sarah H., and Richard H. Wilshusen
1993 Local Abandonments and Regional Conditions in the North American Southwest. In *Abandonment of Settlements and Regions: Ethnoarchaeological and Archaeological Approaches*, ed. Catherine M.

Cameron and Steve A. Tomka, pp. 85–98. Cambridge University Press, Cambridge.

Sebastian, Lynne
1992 *The Chaco Anasazi: Sociopolitical Evolution in the Prehistoric Southwest*. Cambridge University Press, Cambridge.

Stein, John R., and Stephen H. Lekson
1992 Anasazi Ritual Landscapes. In *Anasazi Regional Organization and the Chaco System*, edited by David E. Doyel, pp. 87–100. Maxwell Museum of Anthropology, University of New Mexico, Albuquerque.

Toll, H. Wolcott
1985 *Pottery Production, Public Architecture, and the Chaco Anasazi System*. Unpublished Ph.D. dissertation, Department of Anthropology, University of Colorado, Boulder.

Upham, Steadman
1982 *Polities and Power: An Economic and Political History of the Western Pueblo*. Academic Press, New York.

Varien, Mark D.
1990 Measuring Site Uselife and Seasonality of Occupation: Accumulation Rate Studies. Paper presented at 55th annual Meeting of the Society for American Archaeology, Las Vegas, Nevada.

Vivian, R. Gwinn
1990 *The Chacoan Prehistory of the San Juan Basin*. Academic Press, San Diego.

Wills, Wirt W., and Robert D. Leonard
1994 Preface. In *The Ancient Southwestern Community: Models and Methods for the Study of Prehistoric Social Organization*, edited by Wirt W. Wills and Robert D. Leonard, pp. xiii–xvi. University of New Mexico Press, Albuquerque.

Wilshusen, Richard H.
1991 *Early Villages in the American Southwest: Cross-Cultural and Archaeological Perspectives*. Unpublished Ph.D. Dissertation, Department of Anthropology, University of Colorado, Boulder.

Windes, Thomas C.
1987 *Summary of Tests and Excavations at the Pueblo Alto Community*. Investigations at the Pueblo Alto Complex, Chaco Canyon, New Mexico, 1975–1979, vol. 1. Chaco Canyon Studies Publications in Archeology 18F. USDI, National Park Service, Santa Fe.

Chapter 2

Pueblo II–Pueblo III Change in Southwestern Utah, the Arizona Strip, and Southern Nevada

Margaret M. Lyneis

The area north and west of the Colorado River was occupied by Anasazi peoples as far west as the Muddy River of southern Nevada. These populations reached their apparent peak between about A.D. 1050 and 1150, and declined precipitously in the next 50 to 100 years. By A.D. 1175 the western half of the region, beyond the drainage of Kanab Creek, seems to have been abandoned, or very nearly so. Population appears to have declined drastically east of Kanab in the next 50 years, with House Rock Valley, Powell Plateau, Walhalla Glades and the Inner Canyon sites vacant by A.D. 1200. Sites on the South Rim show occupation until A.D. 1200 to 1225. I follow Fairley (1989) in assigning occupations between A.D. 1000 and 1150 to the Pueblo II period and post-A.D. 1150 occupations to the Pueblo III period in this region.

The most evident change across this area during the early PIII period was depopulation that followed rapidly after the population maximum. Several scholars have addressed the fate of this widespread, but well-integrated Pueblo II population. Some would like to think that they, like other Anasazi, moved in with neighbors to the east, and formed part of a "retreat." If that were the case, there should have been a bulge of population moving across the region just in advance of local abandonment. But neither population studies nor chronological control are of sufficient precision to test for this form of abandonment by relocation. If a retreat model remains untested from a population perspective, from a cultural viewpoint, Virgin Anasazi populations have not been "traced" in an eastward shift. In fact, during the crucial period of A.D. 1100 to 1200, the area east

of the Kanab Creek drainage seems to show the effects of the Kayenta expansion that began around A.D. 1050, resulting in the establishment of Kayenta populations in the Kaiparowits and Paria Plateaus, the Inner Canyon, and Walhalla Glades. Thus we have little evidence that abandonment was by eastward emigration, but can hardly consider this possibility tested, yet alone disproved.

If eastward retreat was not the mechanism of abandonment, what are the other possibilities? For the peoples of the Muddy-Virgin Lowlands and the St. George Basin, one possibility might have been northward relocation among the Fremont. Wilde (1992:51) has made a convincing argument for dating the major construction and use of the Fremont Baker site in eastern Nevada to between A.D. 1250 and 1300. Some of the Parowan Fremont structural sites are thought to have been occupied until A.D. 1200, but ceramics and architecture seem to show a continuous local development, rather than indicating an intrusion of Virgin Anasazi characteristics. Square house pits mark the latest occupation in the Parowan Fremont area (Dodd 1982:18, 38).

Another possibility is a shift to non-sedentary life that leaves no structural sites, an archaeological invisibility from which there was no rebound. If through this mechanism or another, these remnant populations re-emerged as Paiute, there is such a disjuncture in material culture that development of the Paiute out of the Virgin Anasazi seems improbable, and absorption of now-mobile Anasazi remnants by Paiutes filling the almost vacant areas seems more plausible. Huffman (1993) argues that the Virgin Anasazi of the Uinka-

ret Plateau, and by extension, other Virgin groups, practiced a mixed subsistence in which the foraging aspects were similar to the Southern Paiute who succeeded them. He contrasts the Virgin peoples with the Kayenta Anasazi to the east, who he interprets as having been more dependent on farming. His point is that the Kayenta people north of the Colorado River and the Virgin Anasazi may have responded quite differently to the troubled times of the late 1100s. The Kayenta Anasazi, with ties to their heartland, may well have retreated. In contrast, the Virgin population, with looser links to the greater Anasazi world and a more flexible subsistence system, were more likely to have assimilated with the spreading Numic speakers.

If the Virgin Anasazi were not assimilated by the Paiute or the Parowan Fremont and did not join Anasazi to the east, we are left with the possibility of catastrophic change. Widespread failure to reproduce, perhaps in the course of a return to a more mobile, collecting-dependent lifeway, may have led to physical and cultural extinction of the Far Western Anasazi populations. Such a death of the Virgin Anasazi cultural tradition is the end prescribed by Gumerman and Dean (1989:121), who have stated that "Western Anasazi settlement underwent a drastic and sudden change at the beginning of this period [A.D. 1150–1250]. Range expansion ceased, and populations withdrew from peripheral areas and returned to the Kayenta-Tusayan-Winslow nuclear areas. At the same time, the Virgin branch came to an end."

In one sense, what happened in the Arizona Strip, southwestern Utah, and southern Nevada just prior to A.D. 1150

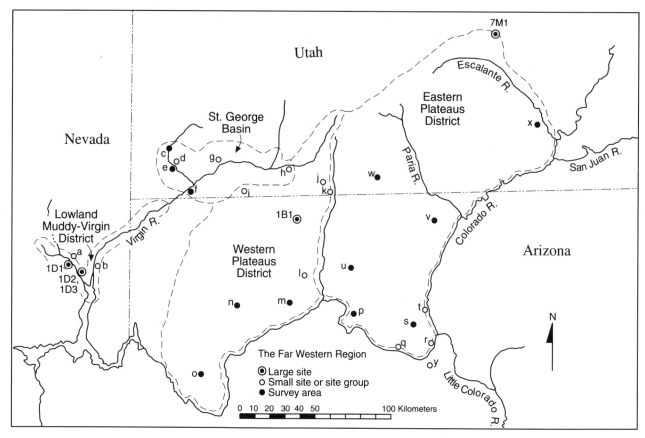

Figure 2.1. Map of the far western Anasazi region and its districts, showing locations of sites and survey localities. Large site labels correspond with those in the Appendix. Small sites and survey localities are (a) Pueblo Point, (b) the Lower Virgin River, (c) the Santa Clara River, Gunlock section, (d) Three Mile Ruin (42Ws50), (e) the Santa Clara River, Land Hills section, (f) the Virgin River, Atkinsville Inventory, (g) Quail Creek, (h) Zion National Park sites, (i) Little Creek Mountain, (j) Cottonwood Canyon Cliff Dwelling (42ka1504), (k) the Kanab site (42Ka1969), (l) the Pinenut site (AZ B:6:44[ASM]), (m) the Kanab Plateau project, (n) the Mt. Trumbull survey, (o) the Shivwits Plateau survey, (p) Powell Plateau, (q) the Bright Angel site, (r) Unkar Delta, Furnace Flats, (s) Walhalla Glades, (t) Nankoweap, (u) Ranger Pass Habitat Improvement, (v) the Paria Plateau Survey, (x) Fifty-mile Mountain, Kaiparowits Plateau, and (y) Tusayan Ruin.

is the beginning of the Pueblo III transition. If the response south and east of the Colorado River was aggregation and intensification of food production, why did populations to the north and west respond so differently? Is there evidence that intensification and aggregation were attempted in the Arizona Strip-Southwest Utah-Southern Nevada region, but were even less successful than they proved to be to the east? These questions frame the considerations that follow. There were Pueblo II populations on the plateaus and along the river valleys at the western edge, and those populations collapsed during the late twelfth and thirteenth centuries.

Following a discussion of each district I address the dynamics of the population reduction that occurred across the area, and discuss the evidence for post-A.D. 1150 occupation in the region. I include a review of the evidence for intensification of food production strategies and aggregation and discuss the structure and changing intensity of exchange in the region during the Pueblo II and Pueblo III periods.

The Region and Its Districts

Most of the region north and west of the Colorado River (figure 2.1) is usually assigned to the Virgin Branch or Virgin

Anasazi. Its eastern portion was subject to a Kayenta intrusion in A.D. 1050 or so, extending some distance north and west of the Colorado River, resulting in boundaries such as those shown by Gumerman and Dean (1989:figure 13). In any small-scale society, sharp cultural boundaries can be difficult to find in the material record. In this region, where relatively little excavation or detailed artifact analysis has been undertaken, it is difficult to know how well our cultural concepts relate to any prehistoric sense of ethnicity or boundedness. Euler (1988:195), for instance, treats the Virgin Branch as part of the Kayenta subtradition. For these reasons, I have subdivided the region into districts based on the geography of the region, rather than into cultural units.

The Arizona Strip-Southwest Utah-Southern Nevada Region includes three distinct environmental zones that created very different settings for horticulturally dependent peoples. Much of the region is part of the Colorado Plateaus, in which most Anasazi residential sites are situated at elevations of 5,000 to 7,000 ft (1,524 to 2,134 m) in pinyon-juniper and sage-flat settings. The St. George Basin, to the northwest of the western plateaus, is a unique environment intermediate in elevation between the Colorado Plateaus and the Lowland Muddy-Virgin Valleys area. Southwest of the St. George Basin, Anasazi occupation extended into the Lower Sonoran Desert along the margins of the Muddy and Virgin Rivers in southern Nevada where elevations range between 1,180 and 1,800 ft (350–550 m).

I classify both the St. George Basin and the Lowland Muddy-Virgin Valleys as districts, and have subdivided the extensive Colorado Plateaus part of the region into two districts: Western Plateaus, west of the Kanab Creek drainage; and Eastern Plateaus, including the drainage of Kanab Creek and the plateaus all the way to the Colorado River. Across the Eastern and Western Plateaus Districts, food production was dependent on rainfall and local runoff from summer precipitation. The St. George Basin and the Lowland Muddy-Virgin Valleys are at markedly lower elevations, and the low, winter-dominant precipitation characteristic of both districts does not support rainfall-dependent agriculture. Here, small-scale stream diversion, and perhaps naturally sub-irrigated areas, limited agricultural production to the margins of year-round streams.

Throughout all the districts, which together stretch roughly 150 mi (240 km) east to west, Puebloan occupation was characterized by small, dispersed settlements in Pueblo II (A.D. 900–1150) and early Pueblo III (A.D. 1150–1200) times. Prior to the mid-thirteenth century most

districts supported a substantial, but still incompletely documented, Anasazi population. In the following sections, settlement patterns and site densities are discussed for each district; this information is summarized in table 2.1.

Eastern Plateaus District

This topographically dissected region includes the Inner Canyons of the Grand Canyon from Bright Angel Creek east, and on its west margin, the drainage of Kanab Creek. Its northeastern edge is the Escalante Basin.

Structural sites have been systematically recorded for the Kaiparowits Plateau and part of the Paria Plateau (table 2.1). Annual precipitation across the district varies between 10 and 16 inches (26–42 cm) with most precipitation falling between July and September (Fowler and Aikens 1963:3).

Structural sites are found throughout the elevational gradient in this district, but there is an increase in site density as elevation increases up to a limit of about 8,000 feet (2,440 m). At Seaman Wash, structural sites are located along the drainages at the base of the Vermilion Cliffs at elevations of 5,300 to 5,800 ft (1,615–1,768 m) (table 2.1). The survey of Powell Plateau at elevations of 6,700 to 7,000 ft (2,042–2,134 m) showed a high site density for the period A.D. 1050 to 1150 (table 2.1). Of the 60 structural sites located in transect and quadrant surveys, half have more than one room (Effland, Jones, and Euler 1981:28). This may, however, be partly the result of seasonal movement of habitation sites. Schwartz, Kepp, and Chapman (1981:129) proposed that summer residents of the Walhalla Glades, which has elevations of 7,850 to 8,200 ft (2,393–2,500 m), wintered at sites on the floor of the Grand Canyon.

Western Plateaus District

This district spans an area within which both summer- and winter-dominant pre-

cipitation patterns are recorded. Annual precipitation varies with elevation, but generally ranges between 9 and 16 inches (23–41 cm). Structural sites were often situated at the interface of sagebrush and pinyon-juniper stands (Huffman et al. 1990:27, 29, 87). Archaeologically, this is the most poorly known of the four districts. The Kanab Plateau and the Mt. Trumbull area on the Uinkaret Plateau have the highest recorded site densities in the district (table 2.1). Sites exhibit a wide range of site sizes, with single and multiple room blocks present.

St. George Basin District

Dalley and McFadden (1985:3) characterize the St. George Basin as surrounded by "Pine Valley Mountains on the north, the Hurricane Cliffs on the east, the Shivwits Plateau on the south, and the Beaver Dam Mountains on the west." The district is unique in that it includes a narrow band of Mojave Desert flora that stretches eastward between the Mojave Desert to the Canyon Lands section of Utah.

The St. George Basin is a relatively low-lying district compared to the Plateau districts, and most of the Pueblo II occupation is limited to the margins of the Virgin River and its tributary, the Santa Clara River. Site densities remained fairly low throughout the district (table 2.1).

Lowland Muddy-Virgin Valleys District

The Muddy River, which drains the Moapa Valley, and the lower course of the Virgin River cut through the Lower Sonoran Desert of southern Nevada. The low elevations of the riverine environments (1,180 to 1,300 ft; 350 to 550 m) result in low rainfall and a long growing season. Annual precipitation is limited to about 4 inches (10 cm), with only about one-third falling in the summer months. At Logandale, 9 years in 10, the temperature does not drop below 32° for a 180-day growing season, and in the same

Table 2.1   Settlement Pattern and Environmental Data by District, Far Western Anasazi Region

District and Locality	Number and Type of Sites	Occupation Period (A.D.)	Survey Area (mi²)	Site Density (mi²)	Elevation (ft above sea level)	Vegetation
Eastern Plateaus						
Seaman Wash Inventory[a]	44 structural sites	1000–1150	7.9	5.6	5300–5800	pinyon-juniper, sage
Ranger Pass[b]	98 structural sites	900–1200	7.6	13.1	5800–6900	pinyon-juniper
Kaiparowits Plateau[c]	157 open architectural sites	1000–1150	21.2	7.4	5000–7000+	pinyon-juniper
Paria Plateau 1968 Survey[d]	107 open structural sites	1050–1200	approx. 63	1.7	5200–7100	pinyon-juniper, sage
Powell Plateau[e]	60 structural sites	1000–1200	2.0	30.0	6500–7600	pinyon-juniper, ponderosa
Western Plateaus						
Kanab Plateau—East[f]	unknown	900–1150	judgmental	13.9	5900–6100	sage, pinyon-juniper
Kanab Plateau—West[f]	unknown	900–1150	judgmental	10.8	5900–6100	sage, pinyon-juniper
Hancock Knolls[f]	unknown	900–1150	judgmental	15.7	5800–6000	sage, pinyon-juniper
Mt. Trumbull Survey[g]	28 structural sites	1000–1150	3.3	8.5	6300–7500	pinyon-juniper, ponderosa
Shivwits Plateau Survey[h]	16 masonry sites	900–1150	2.3	7.0	4400–6000	pinyon-juniper
Little Creek Mtn. Survey[i]	50 structural sites	900–1150	12.0	4.2	5100–5900	pinyon-juniper, sage
St. George Basin						
Gunlock Sect. Inventory[j]	11 structural sites	1000–1150	2.5	4.4	2400–3000	creosote, sage
Virgin River-Akinsville[j]	16 structural sites	1000–1150	2.0	8.0	2400–3000	creosote, sage
Santa Clara-Land Hill[j]	15 structural sites	1000–1150	3.5	4.3	2400–3000	creosote, sage
Lowland Muddy—Virgin						
Lower Virgin Valley[k]	30 structural sites	850–1150	25 RM	1.2/RM	1180–1300	creosote, bursage
Lower Moapa Valley[k]	76 structural sites	850–1150	13 RM	6/RM	1180–1300	creosote, bursage
Sand Bench, Lower Moapa[l]	32 structural sites	1000–1150	4.2 RM	7/RM	1180–1300	creosote, bursage

Notes

a. Data from McFadden, personal communications 1989, 1990.

b. Zamora and Cartledge 1981.

c. Tabulated from Gunnerson 1959a.

d. Estimates developed from Mueller et al. 1968.

e. Effland, Jones, and Euler 1981.

f. Calculated from Huffman personal communication, 1990, and Huffman et al. 1990: 96–97.

g. Moffit and Chang 1978.

h. From Wells 1991:147.

i. Wise 1986.

j. These sites are distributed linearly, along a stream edge of about the length of the stated area in km². Compiled from site records provided by Gardiner Dalley, personal communication 1989.

k. Estimate developed from data in Larson 1987.

l. Estimate developed from Alexander 1973. A "house" in this area means a habitation room and its associated storage. This is an estimate only. Sand Bench was an unusual concentration of households, and this figure should not be generalized to the Lower Moapa Valley. Surficial evidence of occupation along Sand Bench is almost continuous, and it cannot be divided into "sites" in a meaningful way.

RM. River Miles, indicates survey done along the linear stretches along the river.

span, it is 243 days between temperatures of 28° (Soil Conservation Service 1980). Thus water, rather than frost, was the primary limiting factor for far western Anasazi agriculture. Crops must have been dependent on irrigation or natural sub-irrigation, perhaps supplemented by gardening after the retreat of spring and summer floods along the Virgin River.

Structural sites are essentially restricted to the margins of these rivers' floodplains. Larson's (1987) estimates for site densities for the period A.D. 850–1150 for the lower Virgin and lower Moapa Valleys show a lower density for the Virgin than the Moapa Valley. My estimate of mid-to-late Pueblo II site density for a portion of the lower Moapa Valley shows about seven structural sites per running mile (table 2.1).

Chronology and Late Occupation of the Region

Due to the limited scope of site excavations and the paucity of tree-ring dates, chronology is not as well-controlled in this region as in the Kayenta and Northern San Juan regions to the east. Chronological frameworks have relied primarily on stylistic parallels between local ceramics and the Kayenta ceramic sequence as well as cross-dating with trade wares. Specific characteristics used to date sites include the style of design on black-on-gray and black-on-white pottery, the presence of red wares from the Kayenta and Upper San Juan regions, and the presence and frequency of corrugated pottery.

Although this region forms the western periphery of the Anasazi area, its occupation was not the result of a late, short-lived spread of Pueblo peoples. Most districts show Anasazi occupation beginning before A.D. 500. These aceramic Basketmaker II sites are small groups of pit structures or alcoves with slab-lined cists. Basketmaker III and Pueblo I sites are also found in each of the districts.

In contrast, surveys on the North Rim of the Grand Canyon have not identified significant early Anasazi occupations. In the Western Plateaus district, no Anasazi sites predating the Pueblo II period were located in the Shivwits Plateau survey area. Similarly, the Powell Plateau survey (Effland, Jones, and Euler 1981) and the Walhalla Glades surveys (Jones 1986a; Schwartz, Kepp, and Chapman 1981) in the Eastern Plateaus District did not reveal structural sites predating the tenth century A.D. At the northeast edge of the region, the Kayenta intrusion onto Fifty-mile Mountain was apparently at the expense of Fremont populations (Fowler and Aikens 1963; Gunnerson 1959a; McFadden 1988a).

Although the eleventh- and twelfth-century Anasazi occupation of the region is widespread (table 2.1), there is less certainty about presence and size of Puebloan populations during the Pueblo III period. Ambler's (1985) chronology places the beginning date for Flagstaff Black-on-white at A.D. 1165, so I have considered sites with Flagstaff Black-on-white and polychromes to date after A.D. 1150, and thus to the early Pueblo III period. This places some of the occupation on Powell Plateau, Walhalla Glades, and the Inner Canyon sites such as Bright Angel, Nankoweap, and Unkar Delta after A.D. 1150, and later than dated by the original researchers. Schwartz, Chapman, and Kepp (1980:56) used chronologies that have been superseded by Ambler's, but they do record two radiocarbon dates of A.D. 1165±85 and A.D. 1195±95. With calibration, these site occupations would be even later.

Jones dates six Grand Canyon sites, in-

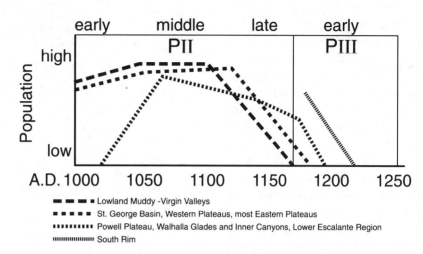

Figure 2.2.   Impressionistic population curves for the districts of the far western Anasazi region.

cluding Furnace Flats, to about A.D. 1170. Based on her interpretation of Furnace Flats, she suggests that these were among the last of the settlements occupied after the major depopulation of the region about A.D. 1150 (Jones 1986b:102, 324). Applying Ambler's dates to Fowler and Aikens' (1963) Kaiparowits assemblages pushes them back to no later than A.D. 1250. Only the identification and dating of Kiet Siel Gray ceramics support a date as recent as A.D. 1250. Two dendrochronological dates are from storage sites, one at A.D. 1143±G, and the second at 1189V (McFadden 1988b:18). To the north, a series of dendrochronological dates from the Coombs site indicated "construction activity in the A.D. 1160's or shortly thereafter" (Bannister, Dean, and Robinson 1969:12). According to Phil Geib (personal communication 1990), there is occupation in the lower Escalante Basin after the abandonment of the Coombs site. The Davis Kiva site (Gunnerson 1959b) apparently dates to the late twelfth century, but there are sites in upper Cow Canyon and Bowns Canyon that were occupied in the early thirteenth century.

A case for post-A.D. 1150 occupation west of Kanab Creek rests on thinner ground, but is gaining strength. Thompson (in Walling et al. 1986) identified some Flagstaff-style ceramics at sites at Quail Creek in the St. George Basin, and radio-

carbon dates (uncalibrated) include three that are between A.D. 1170 and 1270.

Thus, although significant depopulation did occur after A.D. 1150, the far western Anasazi lands were not completely abandoned after this date. Part of the difficulty in locating Pueblo III period sites may rest with the current ceramic-based chronological scheme. As Westfall has pointed out, the Pinenut site has yielded a cluster of four dates between A.D. 1245 to 1290, and one from A.D. 1360. Westfall (1987:95, 185) has argued that post-twelfth century occupation at Pinenut lacks diagnostic pottery because the regional abandonment by the Kayenta caused the breakup of exchange networks and the subsequent absence of post-A.D. 1150 Kayenta sherds at the site.

Changing Population, Environment and Agricultural Intensification

The impressionistic population history for each of the districts (figure 2.2) shows a similar curve, a rise from previous levels to a peak in Pueblo II times, followed by a precipitous decline and subsequent abandonment. Aikens (1966:55) has pointed out that the Virgin region shared the characteristic of Pueblo II population growth with the Kayenta, and subsequent authors have agreed that Pueblo II was the population maximum for the Virgin Anasazi.

Small-scale intensification of agriculture may well have accompanied the Pueblo II regional population increase. In the Eastern Plateaus District, there are water control devices in some locations, perhaps associated with the later occupations in the area. Those on Walhalla Glades are well-known (Jones 1986a; Schwartz, Kepp, and Chapman 1981:72). In the vicinity of the Pinenut site, there are control systems such as serial check dams and terraces (Westfall 1987:28), although they have not been directly dated. Not far away, McFadden's (personal communication, 1990) work on Seaman Wash recorded a shift from the occupation of deep soil locations during the early Pueblo II, indicating dry-farming, to site location on drainages with greater runoff potential during the late Pueblo II period. On the southern Shivwits Plateau in the Western Plateaus District, Wells (1991:74) has reported such agricultural features as check dams, terraces, and fields cleared of rock.

In the Moapa Valley, the population buildup was primarily in the lower valley and may have been associated with increased use of irrigation (Clark 1984: 111–12). Myhrer (1986) found indirect evidence of agricultural intensification in the artifact assemblages of Pueblo II sites in the valley.

The Dynamics of Western Anasazi Community Patterns

Pueblo II–Pueblo III times saw rapid change, most evident in apparent population, which I discussed previously, and in exchange, which is summarized later. Community patterns during this time are highly variable. Across the region, the "dispersed household," with its habitation room and associated storage facilities spatially separated from similar structural sites, seems to have been the fundamental residence unit. Few areas have been surveyed and analyzed with an eye to testing for clustering of these seemingly independent households, but Jones's

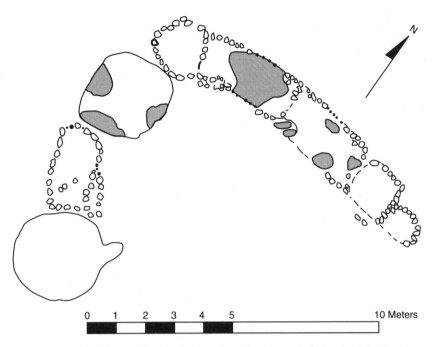

Figure 2.3. Site plan of Pueblo Point, a Pueblo II household in the Muddy River Valley of southern Nevada (after Olson 1979:321).

(1986a:436) nearest neighbor analysis of Walhalla Glades site distributions indicates a clustered settlement pattern. As we learn more about the region, clustering of households may prove to have been the more often used pattern. Whether or not they were organized into dispersed communities, these households were not socially isolated. All required social and economic links that provided marriageable partners, food, and other resources. The following discussion of community patterns is framed by three questions. First, were multifamily residential communities, even if seasonal, part of the general pattern? Second, are site size differences due to chronological change, site function, population immigration, or a mixture of these? Finally, is the presence of kivas in the region primarily associated with the Kayenta intrusion or with changing patterns of social integration?

Western Plateaus, St. George Basin, and the Lowland Muddy-Virgin Valleys

By A.D. 1000, the basic residential unit of the household was well-established. Residential sites consisted of at least one habitation room and its storerooms. These are particularly well-known through excavations in the St. George Basin and the Lowland Muddy-Virgin Valleys (Dalley and McFadden 1985, 1988; Lyneis 1986; Walling et al. 1986). In the Western Plateaus, the large number of sites with four to seven rooms recorded on survey are probably the same kind of household-level settlement. In these sites, the contiguous storerooms formed a gently curved room block. Together with the habitation room, sometimes attached to the room block, other times constructed separately, the structures created an informal courtyard for the household. Occasionally two or more household room blocks were grouped together. The household continued to be the basic residential pattern through Pueblo II times. Pueblo Point is an example from the lower Muddy River Valley (figure 2.3).

Although most Early Pueblo II households were dispersed, the Mecca site in the Western Plateaus District (Allison 1988: 17–27) probably housed a sizeable aggregated community (figure 2.4). The site is estimated to include 80 to 100 rooms, based on visible wall-lines, with a high ratio of storage rooms to habitation rooms. Of the three areas included in the site, "Area B, the central part of the site, is the largest of the three sections. It is composed of a linear room block, about 100 m long and 20 m wide, that runs in a generally north-south direction. Rows of rooms surround four open areas, two of which are open to the east" (Allison 1988:20). Allison interprets the construction to have been primarily jacal, with upright slabs supporting the bases of the walls.

In mid-Pueblo II times, an outsized site existed at Main Ridge (figure 2.5), perhaps the largest of the sites in the extensive zone of Anasazi occupation in the Lower Moapa Valley popularly known as "Lost City" (Gumerman and Dean 1989: 118; Shutler 1961) The site was excavated by Mark Raymond Harrington between 1924 and 1926. Main Ridge is a cluster of 44 "houses" that included more than 203 rooms. Of these, at least 20 were multiroom households of conjoined habitation and storage rooms. Recent collections from the surviving parts of the site indicate that all 14 of the multiroom households that remain were at least roughly contemporaneous, and they include 124 rooms, 18 of which were habitation rooms. One hundred six were storerooms or were functionally unidentified. This suggests a minimum community size of 14 households, and it probably included 21 households. Despite the apparent large size of the community, it was simply a concentration of households, each maintaining distinct storage. There is no evidence of any form of community facilities such as a formal plaza or communal structure (Lyneis 1992).

Though the Mecca and Main Ridge sites seem to be anomalies, other apparent multihousehold sites have been located whenever surveys are done in the Western Plateaus, St. George Basin and Lowland Muddy-Virgin Valleys. Generally called "C-shaped" or "crescent" pueblos, examples have been excavated in the Lowland Muddy-Virgin Valleys,

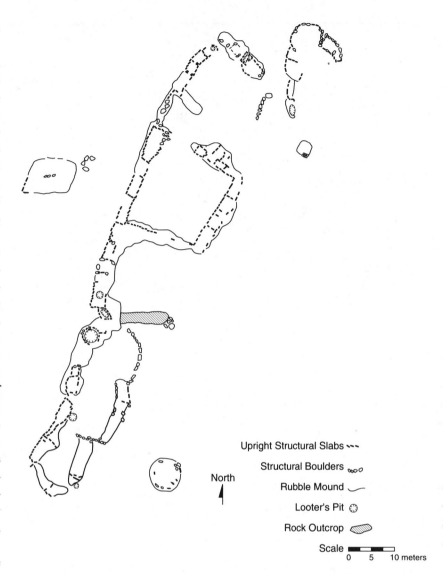

Figure 2.4. Area B of the Mecca site, AZ B:1:68 [BLM], showing the outlines of rooms arranged around plazas (after Allison 1988:figure 9).

including Mesa House (figure 2.6) and House 47 (figure 2.7) and House 89 (Lyneis 1986). Similar sites have been found in the St. George Basin—Three Mile Ruin (Aikens 1965), for example—as well as on the Western Plateaus (Allison 1988; Moffit and Chang 1978; Wells 1991:68; Wise 1986). Archaeologists in the area sometimes apply these terms to sites that might have housed only one or two households, but some of them are the largest sites in the districts. Aikens (1965) excavated about half of Three Mile Ruin, exposing 3 habitation rooms and 9 storage rooms, suggesting that the site may have

been made up of about 25 rooms, perhaps 6 of which were habitation rooms.

Several suggestions can be made regarding the role of the large C-shaped or circular pueblos. They might have been seasonal (presumably winter) residences of groups of families that dispersed to field locations for the horticultural season. If so, we should expect close contemporaneity between these sites and smaller, more dispersed household sites, with differences in ceramic associations consistent with functional differences rather than chronological ones. If, on the other hand, they represent late Pueblo II aggregations of year-

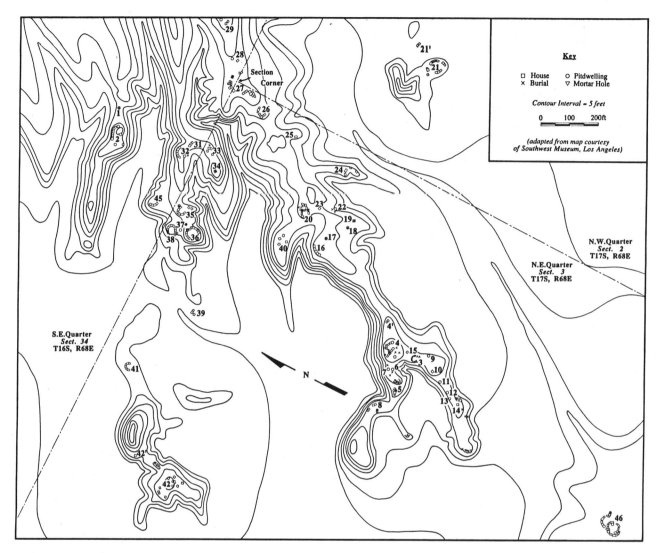

Figure 2.5. Plan of the Main Ridge site, 26Ck2148. Based on *Pueblo Grande de Nevada Map,* courtesy of the Southwest Museum, Los Angeles (adapted from Lyneis 1992:figure 3).

round residences, we would expect few or no contemporaneous single-household sites. I have suggested (Lyneis 1986:71) that Mesa House represents some pooling of resources by families in a lineage. And at House 47 (figure 2.7), also in the Lower Moapa Valley, lines of storerooms are detached from a row of habitation rooms, further indicating a loosening of ties between individual families and their stored reserves. Westfall (1986:20) has suggested that these arcuate pueblos served as ceremonial sites within which food storage and redistribution helped the expanding population face an increasingly diminished resource base.

However we eventually come to understand these large residential sites, they still represent small-scale communities relative to the aggregated settlements discussed elsewhere in this volume. Room counts from the largest C-shaped and circular sites can approach 50 to 70 rooms, but that does not bring them to the true scale of 50- to 70-room pueblos found elsewhere. At least in the Muddy River Valley, these sites have large numbers of small storage rooms. Larson and Michaelsen (1990:table 3) list House 47 as having 54 rooms. The plan of House 47 (figure 2.7) shows clear superposition of some of these rooms, although it also shows that

only part of the site was excavated. Mesa House (figure 2.6) has 33 formal rooms enclosing its courtyard, but only 3 to 5 of these were habitation rooms, the rest being small storerooms. Other "rooms" at the site that run the count to 84 are detached, and only 3 had walls and fireplaces. For the western Anasazi region, population estimates based on the number of habitation rooms only suggest that most of the settlements housed no more than three to five families.

Eastern Plateaus District

In the Eastern Plateaus District in mid-
to late Pueblo II and early Pueblo III
times, architectural layouts were more linear and rectilinear, contrasting with the
dominant curvilinear pattern of the Western Plateaus and Lowland Muddy-Virgin
Valleys. The plan of site GC212/212A from
Walhalla Glades (figure 2.8) is a good example. In addition to different site layouts,
Eastern Plateau rooms tended to be larger
than those on contemporaneous sites in
the western districts. On Walhalla Glades,
the average room size in excavated early
Pueblo III sites is 7.7 m² (Schwartz, Kepp,
and Chapman 1981:67). Bright Angel
Pueblo (Schwartz, Marshall, and Kepp
1979) and Unkar Delta (Schwartz, Chapman, and Kepp 1980) also have predominantly large rooms, as do late Pueblo II
sites on the Kaiparowits Plateau (Fowler
and Aikens 1963; Gunnerson 1959a). The
pattern of large room size characteristic
of the southern and eastern margin of
the Eastern Plateaus District is reflected
on Powell Plateau as well, where average size for all rooms in various localities
ranges from 7.1–12.0 m² (Effland, Jones,
and Euler 1981:table 9).

Site layout and room-size differences
may be due in part to the immigration of
Kayenta populations into the Eastern Plateaus District about A.D. 1050. With the
exception of the final occupation of the
lower Escalante Basin, Kayenta people apparently occupied the area until the end
of the Anasazi era. The appearance of
Kayenta populations north and west of
the Colorado River in the Paria and Kaiparowits Plateaus is thought by Ambler,
Fairley, and Geib (1985) to have been an
extension of Kayenta migration into the
northeastern Navajo Mountain and Paiute
Mesa localities. According to McFadden
(1988a, 1988b), this expansion onto the
Kaiparowits Plateau was at the expense of
Fremont people. Geib (1990) makes similar arguments for the Glen Canyon area.

The Kayenta intrusion extended as far
north as the Coombs site in the upper

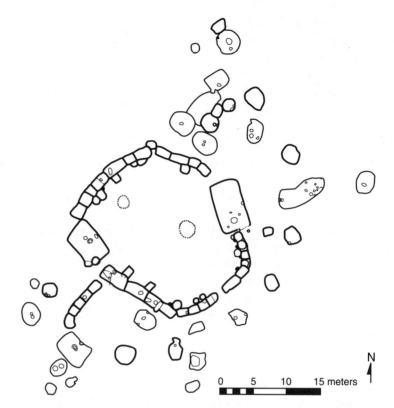

Figure 2.6. Plan of Mesa House, a late Pueblo II site in the lower Muddy River Valley (after Hayden 1930:figure 1; courtesy of the Southwest Museum, Los Angeles).

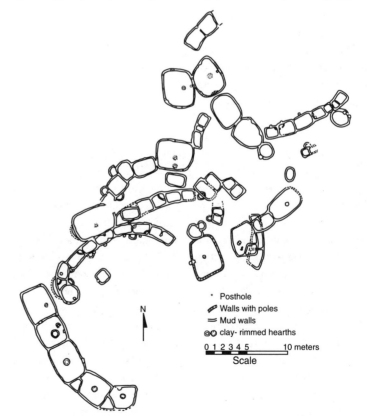

Figure 2.7. Plan of House 47, a late Pueblo II site in the lower Muddy River Valley (after Shutler 1961:plate 30).

part of the Escalante Basin near Boulder, Utah. The Coombs site remains something of an anomaly (Lipe 1970). The site contains a diverse range of ceramics, including Kayenta pottery, locally made Kayenta-style pottery, ceramics attributed to the Virgin Anasazi, and Fremont types. Coombs site architecture is no less diverse, including a series of semi-subterranean pit structures on the south side and a complex of contiguous rooms that roughly frame a courtyard on the northwest side of the site. Its northeast quadrant includes a remarkably rectilinear room complex, Structure A, to the end of which were attached some poorly defined rooms with rounded outlines (figure 2.9). Of the structures at the Coombs site, the strict linearity of Structure A looks most particularly Kayenta in style.

The excavators considered the three forms of architecture to have been in use at the same time (Lister, Ambler, and Lister 1960:5). They originally dated the occupation between A.D. 1075 and 1275, but subsequent refinements in regional ceramic chronology indicate that the Coombs site was not occupied during the thirteenth century. A series of tree-ring dates, six of them from pit houses, supports the excavators' interpretation of general contemporaneity of the several architectural forms at the site, and "indicates construction activity in the A.D. 1160s or shortly thereafter" (Bannister, Dean, and Robinson 1969). Only one instance of superposition, that of Structure J over two pit structures, Structures N and O (Lister, Ambler, and Lister 1960:87–92), contradicts the apparent contemporaneity of the three structural forms at the site. Even if the occupation was more sequential than simultaneous, the Coombs site still could have housed a large community by regional standards. The northwest courtyard group was a large room block in itself, comprised of 33 rooms, 15 of which were probably habitation rooms.

Not all architectural variation can be directly attributed to Kayenta immigrants. In the western part of the Eastern Plateaus

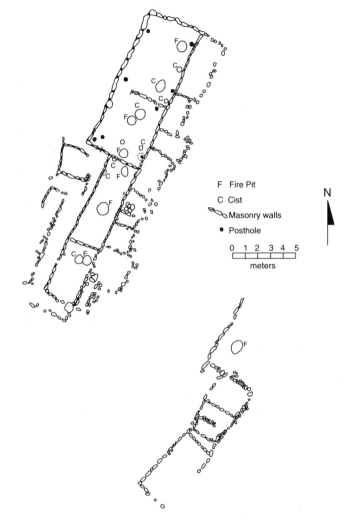

F Fire Pit
C Cist
⟲ Masonry walls
• Posthole

N

0 1 2 3 4 5
meters

Figure 2.8. Plan of GC212/212A, Walhalla Glades (from Schwartz, Kepp, and Chapman 1981:figure 43; adapted from map by Rachel Conine).

District, specifically the Seaman Wash area, McFadden (personal communication 1990) has observed contrasts between early and mid-to-late Pueblo II sites. The early Pueblo II sites were predominantly curvilinear jacal room blocks, while the mid- to late Pueblo II sites were mostly linear masonry room blocks (table 2.2). McFadden does not, however, note an increase in room size.

Despite the contrast in site plans, when one looks at room counts and other estimators of size, sites in the Eastern Plateaus District show the same general patterns as the western districts. The Eastern Plateaus supported many small, dispersed, one to two family households. There are a few larger sites, none of which exceeds

25 rooms. The largest one recorded on Powell Plateau (Effland, Jones, and Euler 1981:26) is 15 rooms, and the largest site reported by Jones (1986a, 428) for Walhalla Glades is 9 rooms. One large site on Walhalla Glades (GC215) has 18 rooms divided into four room blocks (Schwartz, Kepp, and Chapman 1981:63). There are also suggestions in the data from Walhalla Glades and Powell Plateau that there was some small-scale aggregation in early Pueblo III times. On the South Rim, a degree of aggregation is indicated by increased site size from A.D. 1100 to 1225 (Effland, Jones, and Euler 1981:17; Haury 1931).

In sum, the nature of aggregation in the Eastern and Western Plateaus Dis-

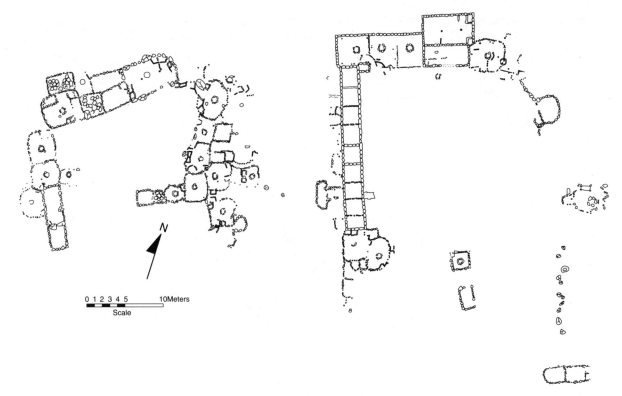

Figure 2.9.   Plan of the Coombs site with pit structures omitted (after Lister, Ambler, and Lister 1960:figure 3).

trict is generally small-scale. It reflects a tendency for some of the largest sites to show use into early Pueblo III times, and very little evidence that the smallest sites were still in use. Similar patterns have been noted previously for Powell Plateau and Kanab Plateau. On Paria Plateau, small pueblos are the most common type of Pueblo II site, while evidence of early Pueblo III occupation is concentrated at large pueblos (table 2.3).

The Question of Kivas in the Far West

A common theme throughout this volume is the increasing use of socially integrative architecture associated with increasing settlement size throughout the Puebloan Southwest. Traditionally, one of the distinctions of the Virgin Anasazi has been the lack of kivas in the region, and the presence of kivas in the far west is commonly attributed to the intrusion of kiva-building Kayenta populations.

The kivas at Unkar Delta (Schwartz,

Table 2.2   Changing Community Patterns at Seaman Wash.

Site Type	Early PII	Early and Late PII	Late PII	Total
Light (jacal) roomblocks				
light	5	1	4	10
light curvilinear	7	1	8	16
light linear	1	1	0	2
light with pithouse	1	0	0	1
Masonry roomblocks				
masonry	0	0	5	5
masonry curvilinear	0	0	7	7
masonry linear	0	1	13	14
Multiple roomblocks	1	2	1	4

Note: Data provided by Douglas McFadden, personal communications 1989, 1990.

Chapman, and Kepp 1980) and the possible above-ground kivas on Powell Plateau mentioned previously are both in the area of the Kayenta intrusion and interestingly, are square or rectangular. Additional poorly known cases suggest that circular, subterranean structures that functioned as kivas may have had a wider distribution. Wise (1986:326) notes that kivas are associated with unit pueblos in the Little Creek Mountain area at the very western

edge of the Western Plateaus. Cautionary use of Wise's data, and most other information from the Eastern and Western Plateaus Districts, is prudent given that these interpretations are based on survey data and the presence of a depression associated with a room block.

At least two excavated pit structures in the region may have served as kivas. Schroeder (1955:63–66) describes a kiva from ZNP-3, one of the Zion National Park

Table 2.3   Changing Community Patterns on Paria Plateau

Site Type	Early and Mid-to-Late Pueblo II	Mid-to-Late Pueblo II	Mid-to-late Pueblo II and Early Pueblo III	Early and Mid-to-Late Pueblo II and Early Pueblo III	Not Dated
Large pueblos (16+ rooms)	2	3	1	11	0
Medium pueblos (6–15 rooms)	8	5	4	16	7
Small pueblos (1–5 rooms)	19	25	4	9	44

Note: Data from Mueller et al. 1968:61.

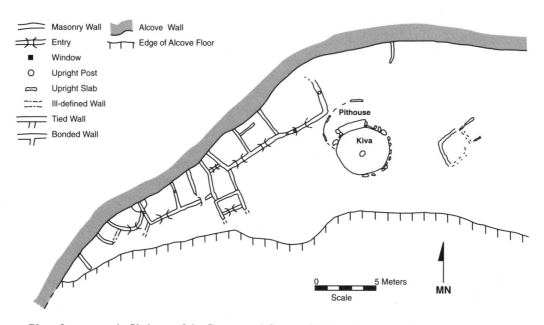

Figure 2.10.   Plan of structures in Shelter A of the Cottonwood Canyon Cliff Dwelling (after Tipps 1989:figure 11).

sites in Parunuweap Canyon. This site, apparently Early Pueblo II in its ceramic associations, has a circular layout that includes contiguous storerooms and three living rooms. The kiva—called "kiva-like" in one place (Schroeder 1955:15)—is just a few meters south of an opening in the south side of the circle, and may well have been a special room associated with the early Pueblo II occupation.

The best documented instance of a kiva is at the Cottonwood Canyon Alcove site, 42Ka-1504 (figure 2.10), which is about 6 miles (9.5 km) northwest of the Kanab site. The site consists of a 12-room block built against the back wall of the rockshelter and a round, deep, masonry-lined kiva with a central hearth and a recessed, slab-lined bench on the north side. Dates from one radiocarbon sample, tree-ring

dates, and associated ceramics suggest a construction date between A.D. 1090 and 1140. Tipps (1989:191) does not attribute the kiva to Kayenta immigrants, and cites architectural data that suggest construction by local Virgin Anasazi occupants.

The presence of kivas farther west, especially in the St. George Basin and the Lowland Muddy-Virgin Valleys, remains to be demonstrated. Rafferty's (1989:571) identification of a kiva in the lower Moapa Valley at the multicomponent Steve Perkins site (26CK-2072) probably refers to a pit structure interpreted to be preceramic in date by the excavators at the site (Olson 1979:317). Charcoal from the structure's hearth yielded a date of A.D. 655 (Myhrer 1989:24–27, 92).

At this point the question of kivas in the far west is limited by definitional prob-

lems and by our understanding of how such structures would have functioned within the local Anasazi communities. It is notable that the possible kivas identified to date tend to be at the larger sites, generally those with at least 5 to 15 rooms. So far all of them are in the Plateaus Districts, but the Cottonwood Canyon Alcove kiva indicates that they are not limited to the area of the Kayenta intrusion.

Extra-regional Exchange and Interaction

In mid-to-late Pueblo II times, ceramic evidence indicates that there was a high degree of interaction among far western Anasazi communities and that there may have been two large interaction networks within the region. The Eastern Plateaus District maintained strong ties with the Kayenta heartland to the east, forming an "eastern" network. To the west during the tenth and eleventh centuries the Western Plateaus and Lowland Muddy-Virgin Valleys were closely linked. The eastern and western networks were not isolated, however, because the presence of eastern red wares in the western region indicates some level of interconnection.

It is widely accepted that from A.D. 1050 to 1250, the intrusive Kayenta communities north and west of the Colorado River maintained close relationships with the Kayenta heartland. Black-on-white ceramics from the area are readily classified into the Kayenta Series, and some authors, Effland, Jones, and Euler (1981: 46) for instance, assume that this indicates the ceramics were imported directly from the Kayenta region.

Less well-known is the evidence for intensive exchange between the Western Plateaus District and the Lowland Muddy-Virgin Valleys. Here, too, the ceramic evidence is presumably the most apparent indicator of an exchange network that involved many materials. Moapa Gray Ware is present in assemblages in the Muddy-Virgin Lowlands from Basketmaker III-Pueblo I times through Pueblo II times (Larson 1987:89). Tempered with crushed olivine-rich nodules found in the vicinity of Mt. Trumbull and Tuweep, Moapa Gray Ware was produced on the Uinkaret Plateau and exchanged westward, across the Shivwits Plateau into the Lowland Muddy-Virgin Valleys. This intraregional exchange intensified in middle Pueblo II times, coincident with the apparent peak of population size and dispersion in the two districts. In middle Pueblo II times about 39 percent of all pottery recovered at Main Ridge on the Muddy River was produced in the Western Plateaus region. This large quantity of intrusive pottery included plain jars and painted and plain bowls of Moapa Gray Ware and jars of a newly defined type, Shivwits Plain, which was apparently pro-

duced on the Shivwits Plateau (Lyneis 1988, 1992).

As mentioned previously, the western exchange network was not isolated from the Kayenta-linked network east of Kanab Creek. Tsegi Orange Ware and andesite-tempered San Juan Red Ware reached the Lowland Muddy-Virgin District in small quantities, as did Black Mesa Black-on-white (Lyneis 1988, 1992). The regional distributional data indicate that there is a marked drop-off in the frequency of red ware at about Kanab Creek, with most sites to the east having 5 percent or more red ware, and sites to the west having 3 percent or less (Lyneis 1988). These data indicate that the two exchange networks were linked, but were two networks, not one.

The intensity of exchange between the Lowland Muddy-Virgin Valleys and the Western Plateaus District drops precipitously in late Pueblo II times, at least as indicated by ceramics. Shivwits Plain does not reach the Muddy River sites, and Moapa Gray Ware is rare. Instead, sand-tempered ware, presumably locally produced, is augmented by two varieties of paddle-and-anvil-thinned pottery, one a Lower Colorado Buff Ware, the other an unclassified brown ware (Lyneis, Rusco, and Myhrer 1989:22–26). A realignment, as well as a reduction, of exchange relationships is indicated for late Pueblo II sites in the Moapa Valley, just prior to abandonment.

Despite the decreased intensity of east-west intraregional exchange, red ware from outside the region continued to reach the Muddy River sites in late Pueblo II times. The quantity may have decreased, however. Although the Pueblo II occupation at the Steve Perkins site included 2.9 percent red ware, less than 2.0 percent red ware was recovered at the Late Pueblo II sites, Mesa House and Adam 2 (Myhrer 1989; Hayden 1930; Lyneis, Rusco, and Myhrer 1989:29).

The data from the region, although admittedly sketchy, are consistent with non-centralized exchange networks of the scale

proposed by Effland, Jones, and Euler, who characterize it as "non-institutionalized redistribution" (1981:48) and "intra- and intercommunity exchange" (1981:46). These extensive interregional exchange networks were clearly enabled by the significant but dispersed population across the region between the tenth and thirteenth centuries and the resulting accessibility of extralocal ceramics, ornaments, and other exchange items. Throughout the region, sites were situated for access to farmland, not to maximize other aspects of their economy. The volume of ceramic exchange between the Lowland Muddy-Virgin Valleys and the Western Plateaus District indicates that exchange was a deeply embedded part of their economy, and probably involved subsistence resources on a substantial scale, taking advantage of the sharp contrasts between the two districts in kinds of food products and their seasonality. Given the small scale of the communities, and the likelihood that they were relatively egalitarian, numerous small communities were apparently the backbone of exchange that spanned 300 miles.

Not all would agree with this scenario. Wilcox (1990) suggests a rather different picture, one of an established pre-A.D. 1050 connection between Anasazi of the Moapa Valley and Chaco, an arrangement interdicted by the northward Kayenta expansion and a resulting increase in the intensity of economic activity across the region. Wilcox's suggestion raises the issue of whether the flow of commodities across the region north and west of the Colorado River was quickened by the economic pull of more complex centers that were essentially external to it, but does not discount the model of loosely connected, relatively egalitarian communities previously discussed.

The dynamics of the exchange networks within the region does indicate that changes in regional interaction relationships preceded local depopulation. In the Lowland Muddy-Virgin Valleys the flow of red ware from the east continued until late in the sequence, but apparently at a diminished rate, indicating that exchange connections were not broken. At the same time the flow of gray ware ceases, and the southern Nevada people looked to the south for an alternate supply (Lyneis 1992:88). In the eastern Plateaus, archaeologists have interpreted late ceramic assemblages at Furnace Flats in the Grand Canyon (Jones 1986b) and the Pinenut site in the Kanab Creek drainage (Westfall 1987) as evidence of continuing occupation after the breakup of the Kayenta-anchored exchange network.

Regional Depopulation

Larson's (1987; Larson and Michaelsen 1990) studies of the Moapa and lower Virgin Valleys may be the only formal work on population increase and decline that has been done within the region. For the region as a whole, the timing of the decline shifts from west to east, being about 50 years earlier in the Lowland Muddy-Virgin Valleys than it is on the North Rim and in the Inner Canyon. The South Rim was apparently the last area to be abandoned. The final, Horsefly Hollow phase occupation of the lower Escalante Basin in the first half of the thirteenth century may be a repopulation of the area from both Kayenta and Mesa Verdean areas, as it was across the Colorado River on the Red Rock Plateau (Lipe 1970).

As in other parts of the Southwest, the major question addresses the conditions surrounding the local and regional processes of depopulation during the twelfth and thirteenth centuries. With populations at their peak in Pueblo II times, imbalance between population and natural resources seems the most reasonable explanation for the depopulation that followed, particularly in the Plateau Districts where agriculture was clearly marginal. Westfall (1987) and Jones (1986b) have explicitly discussed the implications of the paleoclimatic model developed by Dean et al. (1985). Each of them deals with sites in

the Eastern Plateaus District that appear to have been inhabited after A.D. 1150. Westfall correlates an abandonment of the Pinenut site with deteriorating hydrological conditions from A.D. 1150 to 1200, and its late reoccupation with a period of higher water tables and aggradation from 1200 to 1275 (Westfall 1987:185; but see Wilcox 1988 for a different interpretation of the site's sequence). Jones (1986b:335) argues that the reciprocal exchange network postulated by Effland, Jones, and Euler (1981) worked well in the period of great spatial variability in dendroclimate (A.D. 1050–1150), but would not have been sufficient to handle the reduced variability plus drought that begins at A.D. 1150.

The reconstruction of climatic variability by Dean et al. (1985) is less applicable farther west, because it does not include samples from the area and because as is the case at present, rainfall distribution is more winter-dominant. Dean (1988:figure 5.1) illustrates the regional shift in seasonality of rainfall in the Southwest, contrasting Kanab's biseasonal pattern with locales to the south and east, which have a summer-dominant pattern. The same seasonal shift operates at a smaller scale across the Plateaus District, which is astride the monsoon boundary. The boundary shifts from year to year, making for great unpredictability of essential summer rainfall (Rose 1989:35). The quantity of annual precipitation across the region is also highly elevation-dependent. Most of the Western Plateaus District is at lower elevations than the well-populated portions of the Eastern Plateaus District, however, and the combination of lower total rainfall due to elevation with proportionally less of it falling in the summer must have made rainfall-dependent horticulture riskier in the Western Plateaus than in the Eastern Plateaus.

The occupants of the Lowland Muddy-Virgin Valleys, where annual precipitation is about 4 inches per year, were never dependent on rainfall for their crops. Larson (1987; Larson and Michaelsen 1990) has

attempted a dendrohydrological reconstruction of Virgin River flows. Although it must be regarded as preliminary (see Rose 1989:41–42), it shows a "period of prolonged drought between A.D. 1120 and A.D. 1150" (Larson and Michaelsen 1990:224).

Regional drought would surely have affected the flow of the Virgin River, but the abandonment of the Moapa Valley does not seem so easily explained. The Muddy River rises from springs in the upper Moapa Valley, and flows 30 miles (45 km) to its confluence with the Virgin River, which today is drowned by the waters of Lake Mead. The springs release water captured far to the north, and during the historic period they have maintained an even flow, little influenced by changes in precipitation. There is no reason to think that the Muddy River did not flow during the climatic changes of A.D. 1100 to 1250. Though data are not currently available for the local paleohydrology, it is possible that changing hydrology of the Virgin or the Colorado Rivers could have initiated headward erosion of the Muddy River's course. An incised channel would have dried up subirrigated areas and made small-scale diversion for irrigation impossible. In addition, the floodplain in the Moapa Valley is subject to occasional severe flooding when heavy rains fall in one or several of the large wash systems that feed into the river. Finally, salinization of fields may have plagued Anasazi farmers, much as it has over the past century of modern agriculture in the area (Soule 1981).

In addition to the plethora of local environmental stresses that might have had a role in the depopulation of the Moapa Valley, we also need to keep a regional perspective on abandonment. It may have been the populations of the lower Virgin Valley and the Shivwits Plateau to the east who encountered difficulties. Material remains indicate that the Muddy River people were closely linked to these eastern populations. Relocation of their eastern neighbors would have left the Muddy

River peoples isolated, so these western Anasazi may have chosen to join them in relocating elsewhere rather remain isolated in the Moapa Valley.

Interregional Migration

Whether interregional migration was a mechanism for the depopulation of the northern Southwest is a key issue in coming to understand this large-scale phenomenon. The region north and west of the Colorado River was home to a large Anasazi population in Pueblo II times. Some archaeologists are inclined to think that the intrusive Kayenta Anasazi of the Eastern Plateaus District returned to the heartland area (Ambler, Fairley, and Geib 1985:23–24), contributing to the thirteenth- and fourteenth-century demographic, organizational, and subsistence changes discussed by other authors in this volume. Those who work south and east of the Colorado River seem to assume that the Virgin Anasazi were not involved in this retreat, leaving them to some other fate. Evidence to the contrary, that substantial Virgin Anasazi populations moved to the east, is hard to garner. We might expect to see a population bulge, moving as a wave across the region just prior to abandonment. Or, if we think the Virgin Anasazi could undergo such large-scale disruption and retain their social identity, we would expect to see some Virgin Anasazi cultural characteristics show up late in the Eastern Plateaus District.

If population shifted to the east by joining communities, we do not yet see it in the data. My impression is that the population maximum in the Eastern Plateaus District is perhaps 50 years later than the maximum in the Lowland Muddy-Virgin Valleys. If this proves to be the case with more intensive investigations in the region, we still must look at several explanations in addition to an influx from the west. The sites that are the evidence for the population maximum in the Eastern Plateaus District are precisely those that

look, in their architecture, to be of Kayenta or Kayenta-influenced style. In coming to understand the population maximum of the Eastern Plateaus District, archaeologists will need to distinguish among the effects of migration from the west, local population growth, and continued flow of Kayenta Anasazi into the Eastern Plateaus District from the Kayenta heartland.

Summary

At about A.D. 1100, population across the region was at, or close to, its maximum, but the Anasazi occupation of the region was no short-lived affair. Sites of the Basketmaker II period are found all the way to the region's southwestern edge in southern Nevada, and there are structural sites from Basketmaker III, Pueblo I, and earlier Pueblo II periods.

In the period from A.D. 1050 to 1200, the basic unit of settlement was the household, consisting of the living and storage rooms, at least some of them contiguous, of one or two families. "Dispersed" best describes the overall settlement pattern across the far western reaches of the Anasazi world. Sites were situated to maximize access to land the Anasazi could cultivate, whether in the sagebrush and pinyon-juniper zones of the Colorado Plateaus, or along the permanent streams of the St. George Basin and Lowland Muddy-Virgin Valleys. When large-scale surveys and spatial analysis are done, we will probably find that clustering of these dispersed households is more common than can be demonstrated at present, and that each cluster is probably best understood as a socially interdependent community. Because the present convention in archaeology is to record each dispersed household settlement as a site, we will continue to find small sites in the region, with most containing 10 or fewer rooms.

Larger sites are found, but they are not unique to the A.D. 1050 to 1200 period, for large sites occur earlier, at least sporadically. Larger late sites from the Muddy

River Valley and Three-Mile Ruin in the St. George Basin are arranged to almost fully enclose a common courtyard. They would have housed at least three to five families, and their layouts suggest that the households may have shared food reserves.

If aggregation did occur during the A.D. 1100 to 1250 period in this region it was on a much smaller scale than what occurred across the rest of the Puebloan Southwest. Some sites are large for the region, but they do not exceed site sizes achieved previously. More common, perhaps, at least on the plateaus, is the non-use at that time of sites of the smallest structural size, one or two rooms. This results in a higher percentage of late sites being "large", but large means seven or so rooms. Sites with 20 rooms or more are rare.

At about A.D. 1050 to 1100, the communities across the region were linked by exchange networks for which ceramics are the best indicator. The Eastern Plateaus sustained ties with the Kayenta heartland. The Lowland Muddy-Virgin and Western Plateaus Districts maintained a high degree of interaction, if not integration. The two networks were not isolated, however. Northern San Juan and Kayenta red wares moved west through them to the communities of the Muddy River. The western network changed about A.D. 1100, and after that time little utilitarian pottery from the Uinkaret and Shivwits Plateaus reached southern Nevada, although the flow of red ware seems to have continued. In the Eastern Plateaus District, trade with the Kayenta heartland was maintained until serious depopulation set in. Some settlements, such as Furnace Flats and the Pinenut site, may have persisted after the Kayenta-based network collapsed.

Depopulation seems to have begun in the west and proceeded rapidly to the east. Based on ceramic seriation, the Lowland Muddy-Virgin Valleys seem to be empty of Anasazi by A.D. 1160, the St. George Basin and the Western Plateaus by A.D. 1175 or so. The year A.D. 1175 may be a good date for depopulation of much of the Eastern Plateaus District as well, but occupation in the Inner Canyons and lower Escalante Basin apparently continued until close to A.D. 1200. Sites on the South Rim, such as Tusayan Ruin, were occupied a little longer, perhaps until A.D. 1225. Lipe (1970) viewed the thirteenth-century Horsefly Hollow phase, which extends into the lower Escalante Basin, as a reoccupation after a settlement hiatus.

There is a zone of late Pueblo II–early Pueblo III occupation, known almost entirely from site survey, that includes the Kanab Creek drainage and areas east, in which the more rectilinear architecture has a taint of Kayenta characteristics to an eye accustomed to late Pueblo II Virgin Anasazi architecture. What it means in terms of ethnicity or interaction with other communities remains to be learned. It is not, however, easily interpreted as evidence of eastward shift of Virgin Anasazi.

The processes involved in the regional depopulation remain to be explained, and for the most part, there are not yet data for testing ideas about them. It is generally assumed that population identified as intrusive Kayenta Anasazi along the southeast margin was absorbed into Pueblo III Kayenta populations east of the Colorado River. Farther west, we can only speculate about the fate of the population. It is clear that the major trends in settlement, migration, and abandonment in the far western Anasazi realm were influenced by, and ultimately influenced, similar trends in that area probably known to the Virgin Anasazi as the "far eastern" realm.

Acknowledgments

The area north and west of the Colorado River is the least understood of the regions of Anasazi occupation, for there have been few excavations and no large-scale, funded projects. Many archaeologists are working in the area now, and

thinking about what the unfolding prehistoric record means. I am grateful to them for sharing data, insights, manuscripts, and comments, many of which are cited in this chapter. My own first-hand knowledge is primarily of sites in the Lowland Muddy-Virgin Valleys, and the contributions of others have been essential to the preparation of this manuscript. My special thanks go to James Allison, Arizona State University; Gardiner Dalley, Cedar City District, Bureau of Land Management (BLM); Marietta Davenport, Kaibab Ranger District, U.S. Forest Service (USFS); Helen C. Fairley, Grand Canyon National Park; Phil Geib, Navajo Nation Archaeology Department, Northern Arizona University Branch Office; Jim Huffman, Northern Arizona University; Aline LaForge, St. George District, BLM; Douglas McFadden, Kanab Resource Area, BLM; Keith Myhrer, Las Vegas District, BLM; Carl J. Phagan, Northern Arizona University; Richard A. Thompson, Museum of Southern Utah, Southern Utah State University; Deborah A. Westfall, Abajo Archaeology; and David R. Wilcox, Museum of Northern Arizona. In addition, I thank Dorothy House of the library of the Museum of Northern Arizona for expediting the loan of a copy of the report of the 1968 survey of the Paria Plateau.

References Cited

Aikens, C. Melvin
  1965 *Excavations in Southwest Utah.* University of Utah Anthropological Papers No. 76. University of Utah Press, Salt Lake City.
  1966 *Virgin-Kayenta Cultural Relationships.* Anthropological Papers No. 79. University of Utah Press, Salt Lake City.
Alexander, Larry
  1973 Muddy River Survey. Two notebooks, on file, Archaeology Laboratory, Department of Anthropology, University of Nevada, Las Vegas.
Allison, James R.
  1988 *The Archaeology of Yellowstone Mesa,* *Mohave County, Arizona.* Technical Series no. 88–24. Museum of Peoples and Cultures, Brigham Young University, Provo.
Ambler, J. Richard
  1985 Northern Kayenta Ceramic Chronology. In *Archaeological Investigations Near Rainbow City, Navajo Mountain, Utah,* edited by Phil R. Geib, J. Richard Ambler, and Martha Callahan. Submitted to Martell and Associates, Kansas City, Kansas, by Department of Anthropology, Northern Arizona University, Flagstaff.
Ambler, J. Richard, Helen C. Fairley, and Phil Geib
  1985 Kayenta Anasazi Utilization of Canyons and Plateaus in the Navajo Mountain District. Paper presented at the Second Anasazi Symposium, Farmington, New Mexico.
Bannister, Bryant, Jeffrey Dean, and William J. Robinson
  1969 *Tree-ring Dates from Utah S-W.* Laboratory of Tree-Ring Research, University of Arizona, Tucson.
Clark, Jeanne Wilson
  1984 *Prehistoric Settlement in the Moapa Valley.* Anthropological Papers No. 19. Nevada State Museum, Carson City.
Dalley, Gardiner F., and Douglas A. McFadden
  1985 *The Archaeology of the Red Cliffs Site.* Cultural Resource Series No. 17. USDI, Bureau of Land Management, Salt Lake City.
  1988 *The Little Man Archaeological Sites: Excavations on the Virgin River Near Hurricane, Utah.* Cultural Resource Series No. 23. USDI, Bureau of Land Management, Salt Lake City.
Dean, Jeffrey S.
  1988 Dendrochronology and Paleoenvironmental Reconstruction on the Colorado Plateaus. In *The Anasazi in a Changing Environment,* edited by George J. Gumerman, 119–67. Cambridge University Press, Cambridge.
Dean, Jeffrey S., Robert C. Euler, George J. Gumerman, Fred Plog, Richard H. Hevley, and Thor N. V. Karlstrom
  1985 Human Behavior, Demography, and Paleoenvironment on the Colorado Plateaus. *American Antiquity* 50: 537–54.
Dodd, Walter A., Jr.
  1982 *Final Years Excavations at the Evans*

Mound. Anthropological Papers 106. University of Utah Press, Salt Lake City.

Effland, Richard W., Jr., Ann Trinkle Jones, and Robert C. Euler
  1981   *The Archaeology of Powell Plateau: Regional Interaction at Grand Canyon.* Monograph No. 3. The Grand Canyon Natural History Association, Prescott, Arizona.

Euler, Robert C.
  1988   Demography and Cultural Dynamics on the Colorado Plateaus. In *The Anasazi in a Changing Environment*, edited by George J. Gumerman, pp. 192–229. Cambridge University Press, Cambridge.

Fairley, Helen C.
  1989   Culture History. In *Man, Models and Management: An Overview of the Arizona Strip and the Management of its Cultural Resources*, edited by Jeffrey H. Altschul and Helen C. Fairley, pp. 85–152. Submitted to the USDA Forest Service and the USDI Bureau of Land Management by Statistical Research, Tucson; Plateau Archaeology, Flagstaff; and Dames and Moore, Phoenix.

Fowler, Don D., and C. Melvin Aikens
  1963   *1961 Excavations, Kaiparowits Plateau.* Anthropological Papers No. 66 (Glen Canyon Series No. 20). University of Utah Press, Salt Lake City.

Geib, Phil R.
  1990   Early Formative (BMIII-PI) Occupation of Glen Canyon. Paper presented at the 63rd Annual Pecos Conference, Blanding, Utah.

Gumerman, George J., and Jeffrey S. Dean
  1989   Prehistoric Cooperation and Competition in the Western Anasazi Area. In *Dynamics of Southwest Prehistory*, edited by Linda S. Cordell and George J. Gumerman, pp. 99–148. Smithsonian Institution Press, Washington, D.C.

Gunnerson, James H.
  1959a   Archeological Survey of the Kaiparowits Plateau. In *The Glen Canyon Archeological Survey*, Part II, by Don D. Fowler, James H. Gunnerson, Jesse D. Jennings, Robert H. Lister, Dee Ann Suhm, and Ted Weller, pp. 319–469. Anthropological Papers No. 39. University of Utah Press, Salt Lake City.
  1959b   *1957 Excavations, Glen Canyon Area.* Anthropological Papers No. 43.

University of Utah Press, Salt Lake City.

Harrington, Mark Raymond
  1937   Some Early Pit Dwellings in Southern Nevada. *The Masterkey* 11(4): 122–24.
  1942   Black Dog Cave. *The Masterkey* 16(5):173–74.

Haury, Emil W.
  1931   Kivas of the Tusayan Ruin, Grand Canyon, Arizona. *Medallion Papers* 9. Globe: Gila Pueblo.

Hayden, Irwin
  1930   Mesa House. *Southwest Museum Papers* 4(2):26–92.

Huffman, Jim
  1993   *Between River and Rim: Subsistence Systems in Grand Canyon, Arizona.* Unpublished Master's thesis, Department of Anthropology, Northern Arizona University, Flagstaff.

Huffman, Jim, Carl J. Phagan, Gregory Haynes, and Timothy W. Burchett
  1990   *Archaeological Survey on the Kanab Plateau: 1989–90 Annual Technical Report.* Northern Arizona University Archaeology Report No. 1044, prepared for Division of Resources Management and Planning, Grand Canyon National Park, Grand Canyon, Arizona.

Jones, Ann Trinkle
  1986a   Agricultural Systems in the Grand Canyon: Walhalla Glades. *Western Anasazi Reports* 3:405–41. Cedar City, Utah.
  1986b   *A Cross Section of Grand Canyon Archeology: Excavations at Five Sites along the Colorado River.* USDI, National Park Service, Western Archeological and Conservation Center, Tucson.

Larson, Daniel O.
  1987   *An Economic Analysis of the Differential Effects of Population Growth and Climatic Variability Among Hunters and Gatherers and Food Producers.* Unpublished Ph.D. dissertation, Department of Anthropology, University of California, Santa Barbara.

Larson, Daniel O., and Joel Michaelsen
  1990   Impacts of Climatic Variability and Population Growth on Virgin Branch Anasazi Cultural Developments. *American Antiquity* 55:227–49.

Lipe, William D.
  1970   Anasazi Communities in the Red Rock Plateau, Southeastern Utah. In *Reconstructing Prehistoric Pueblo Soci-*

eties, edited by William A. Longacre, 84–139. University of New Mexico Press, Albuquerque.

Lister, Robert H., J. Richard Ambler, and Florence C. Lister
  1960   *The Coombs Site* Part 2. Anthropological Papers No. 41. University of Utah Press, Salt Lake City.

Lyneis, Margaret M.
  1986   A Spatial Analysis of Anasazi Architecture A.D. 950–1150, Moapa Valley, Nevada. *Kiva* 52:53–74.
  1988   Ceramic Production and Exchange Among the Virgin Anasazi. Paper presented at the 53rd Annual Meeting of the Society for American Archaeology, Phoenix.
  1992   *The Main Ridge Community at Lost City: Virgin Anasazi Architecture, Ceramics and Burials.* Anthropological Papers No. 117. University of Utah Press, Salt Lake City.

Lyneis, Margaret M., Mary K. Rusco and Keith Myhrer
  1989   *Investigations at Adam 2 (26CK2059): A Mesa House Phase Site in the Moapa Valley, Nevada.* Anthropological Papers No. 22. Nevada State Museum, Carson City.

McFadden, Douglas
  1988a   Kaiparowits Revisited. UPAC *News* 6(3–4):11–2. Salt Lake City.
  1988b   *A Cultural Resource Management Plan for Fiftymile Mountain.* USDI, Bureau of Land Management, Escalante Resource Area, Cedar City District, Cedar City, Utah.

Moffitt, Kathleen, and Claudia Chang
  1978   The Mount Trumbull Archaeological Survey. *Western Anasazi Reports* 1:185–250. Cedar City, Utah.

Mueller, James W., Gregory J. Staley, Gayle G. Harrison, Ronald W. Ralph, Carla A. Sartwell, and Ronald C. Gauthier
  1968   *The Paria Plateau Survey, Report 1968 Season: Archaeological Inventory of Indian Ruins Located in Coconino County.* Museum of Northern Arizona, Flagstaff. Submitted to USDI, Bureau of Land Management, Arizona Strip District, St. George, Utah.

Myhrer, Keith
  1986   *Evidence for an Increasing Dependence on Agriculture During Virgin Anasazi Occupation in the Moapa Valley.* Unpublished Master's thesis, Department of Anthropology, University of Nevada, Las Vegas.
  1989   Basketmaker and Puebloan Occu-

pation at the Steve Perkins Site, Moapa Valley, Southern Nevada. Ms. on file, USDI, Bureau of Land Management, Las Vegas District, Las Vegas, Nevada.

Olson, Kathryne
1979   An Attribute Analysis of Muddy River Ceramics. *Western Anasazi Reports* 2:303–64. Cedar City, Utah.

Rafferty, Kevin
1989   Virgin Anasazi Sociopolitical Organization, A.D. 1 to 1150. In *The Sociopolitical Structure of Prehistoric Southwestern Societies*, edited by Steadman Upham, Kent G. Lightfoot, and Roberta A. Jewett, 557–80. Westview Press, Boulder.

Rose, Martin R.
1989   Present and Past Environmental Conditions. In *Man, Models and Management: An Overview of the Arizona Strip and the Management of its Cultural Resources*, edited by Jeffrey H. Altschul and Helen C. Fairley, pp. 7–52. Submitted to the USDA Forest Service and the USDI Bureau of Land Management by Statistical Research, Tucson; Plateau Archaeology, Flagstaff; and Dames and Moore, Phoenix.

Schroeder, Albert H.
1955   *Archeology of Zion Park*. Anthropological Papers No. 22. University of Utah Press, Salt Lake City.

Schwartz, Douglas W., Richard Chapman, and Jane Kepp
1980   *Archaeology of the Grand Canyon: Unkar Delta*. Grand Canyon Archaeological Series 2. School of American Research Press, Santa Fe.

Schwartz, Douglas W., Jane Kepp, and Richard C. Chapman
1981   *The Archaeology of the Grand Canyon: The Walhalla Plateau*. Grand Canyon Archaeological Series, Vol. 3. School of American Research Press, Santa Fe.

Schwartz, Douglas W., Michael P. Marshall, and Jane Kepp
1979   *Archaeology of the Grand Canyon: The Bright Angel Site*. Grand Canyon Archaeological Series, Vol. 1. School of American Research Press, Santa Fe.

Shutler, Richard Jr.
1961   *Lost City: Pueblo Grande de Nevada*. Anthropological Papers No. 5. Nevada State Museum, Carson City.

Soil Conservation Service
1980   *Soil Survey of Virgin River Area, Nevada-Arizona*. USDA, Soil Conservation Service, Washington, D.C.

Soule, Edwin Charles
1981   *Agriculture, Aridity, and Salinity in the Prehistoric Moapa Valley*. Unpublished Ph.D. dissertation, Department of Anthropology, University of California, Riverside.

Tipps, Betsy L.
1989   *Cultural Resource Investigations Near Kanab, Utah: Excavation and Structural Stabilization at Cottonwood Canyon Cliff Dwelling*. Cultural Resources Report 421-1-8821. Submitted to the USDI, Bureau of Land Management, Kanab Resource Area Office, Kanab, by P-III Associates, Salt Lake City.

Walling, Barbara A., Richard A. Thompson, Gardiner F. Dalley, and Dennis G. Weder
1986   *Excavations at Quail Creek*. Cultural Resource Series no. 20. USDI, Bureau of Land Management, Salt Lake City.

Wells, Susan J.
1991   *The Shivwits Plateau Survey: Archeology at Lake Mead National Recreation Area*. Publications in Anthropology 56. USDI, National Park Service, Western Archeological and Conservation Center, Tucson.

Westfall, Deborah
1986   Life in the Land of Little Water: The Prehistory of the Arizona Strip. In The Arizona Strip: Splendid Isolation. *Plateau* 57 (2):18–21.

1987   *The Pinenut Site: Virgin Anasazi Archaeology on the Kanab Plateau of Northwestern Arizona*. Cultural Resource Series No. 4. USDI, Bureau of Land Management, Phoenix.

Wilcox, David R.
1988   Review of The Pinenut Site: Virgin Anasazi Archaeology on the Kanab Plateau of Northwestern Arizona. *Utah Archaeology 1988* 1:68–70.

1990   Factors Affecting the First Appearance of Sinagua Villages. Paper presented at the 54th Annual Meeting of the Society for American Archaeology, Las Vegas, Nevada.

Wilde, James D.
1992   Finding a Date: Some Thoughts on Radiocarbon Dating and the Baker Fremont Site in Eastern Nevada. *Utah Archaeology 1992* 5(1):39–53.

Wise, Karen E.
1986   Prehistoric Settlement Patterns and Site Plans on Little Creek Mountain. *Western Anasazi Reports* 3:273–339.

Zamora, Elaine, and Thomas R. Cartledge
1981   Ranger Pass Habitat Improvement Project Cultural Resource Survey, North Kaibab Ranger District, Kaibab National Forest.

Chapter 3

Kayenta Anasazi Settlement Transformations in Northeastern Arizona, A.D. 1150 to 1350

Jeffrey S. Dean

Since the late 1800s, the archaeological remains west of the Lukachukai-Chuska Mountains have been recognized as being different from those in the Chaco and Mesa Verde areas to the east (Kidder 1917; Kidder and Guernsey 1919; Prudden 1903). During the ensuing century, the western materials were sorted into a variety of typological categories: Kayenta, Tusayan, Winslow, Virgin, Sinagua, Cohonina, Cerbat, Patayan, and so on. This chapter is limited to the "western Anasazi" (Gumerman and Dean 1989) and is focused on the Kayenta branch (figure 13.1) and, for limited purposes, the related Virgin and Tusayan branches.

Archaeologically, the Kayenta branch is distinguished from its eastern counterparts by differences in ceramics, architecture, site structure, settlement pattern, interareal interactions, social organization, and rates of development. A voluminous literature details the differences between Kayenta and eastern Anasazi ceramics (Beals, Brainerd, and Smith 1945:87–150; Breternitz, Rohn, and Morris 1974; Colton 1955, 1956; Colton and Hargrave 1937; Hawley 1950; Smith 1971), and this topic need be discussed no further. Post-A.D. 1150 Kayenta branch architecture (Dean 1969; Lindsay 1969) is distinguished from its eastern counterparts by the rarity of elaborate masonry and roof beam treatments, the prevalence of simple masonry and jacal construction, a characteristic method of granary closure, a unique living room feature (the "entry-box"), the persistence of residential pit houses throughout the sequence, a wider variety of kiva forms and features (Kidder 1924:69; Kidder and Guernsey 1919:201;

Smith 1952a), and the absence of great kivas and biwall and triwall structures.

That Kayenta pueblos are smaller than their eastern Anasazi counterparts is exemplified by the fact that the 50-room lower limit adopted for the "Pueblos in Transition" conference eliminates most of the Kayenta sequence from consideration. Sites this large do not appear in the Kayenta area until after A.D. 1250, and, even then, the largest of these villages were dwarfed by enormous pueblos in southwestern Colorado (Varien et al., chapter 7) and the Zuni area (Kintigh, chapter 9). Kayenta site layouts also exhibit less partitioning than do eastern Anasazi sites, lacking the kiva-focused room groups of Mesa Verde (Fewkes 1911; Rohn 1965, 1989) and the dual divisions of Chaco (Vivian 1970, 1990; Wendorf 1956).

Functional differentiation of sites is less evident in the Kayenta than in the Mesa Verde area, where specialized ceremonial and administrative sites occur (Rohn 1989), and in the Chaco area, where various residential, ceremonial, economic, administrative, and communications sites are found (Vivian 1990). The Chacoan pattern of core units surrounded by satellite communities is not evident in the Kayenta area before A.D. 1250.

The Kayenta area lacks anything comparable to the networks of roads, trails, and signaling stations that linked Chaco Canyon to its far-flung outliers. Interaction between Kayenta site clusters appears to have been restricted to visual communication and the exchange of material goods with no apparent dominance-subordinance relationships (but see Haas and Creamer, chapter 14). Interaction

with other Anasazi (Virgin, Tusayan, Mesa Verde, Chaco) and non-Anasazi (Fremont, Cohonina, Sinagua, Mogollon, Hohokam) populations was restricted primarily to low-level trade in material items, the principal manifestation of which is the occurrence of Kayenta pottery in these foreign areas.

Considerable time lags separated Kayenta developments from those in the eastern Anasazi area. On the western fringes of the Kayenta area, the Basketmaker II lifeway may have persisted until A.D. 700 (Harlan and Dean 1968:380–81), 150 years longer than it did in the eastern Anasazi area. Kayenta Pueblo I cultural manifestations are more similar to Basketmaker III patterns than to those of the Pueblo II period, just the reverse of the eastern Anasazi situation. Large sites and hierarchical settlement configurations did not develop until A.D. 1250, some 300 years after they had appeared in Chaco Canyon and the Mesa Verde region.

Temporal and Spatial Systematics

An argument could be made that the Kayenta area diverged from the eastern Anasazi area as early as the late Archaic period (2000–1000 B.C.). Certainly by the inception of the Basketmaker II period (1000 B.C.–A.D. 550), consistent differences are evident, a situation that prevailed until the end of the Kayenta sequence around A.D. 1300. The geographic extent of the Kayenta branch, that is, the range of Kayenta ceramics and architectural forms, varied considerably through time. A heartland area bounded by the San Juan and Colorado Rivers on the north and west

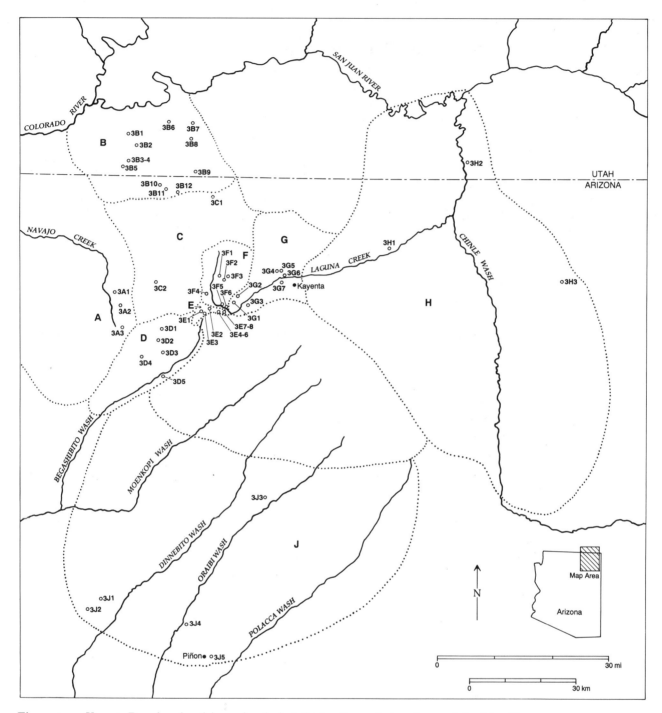

Figure 3.1. Kayenta Branch and outlying archaeological districts. Letter designations as defined in table 3.1.

and the extremities of Black Mesa on the south and east exhibited strong Kayenta affiliations at all times. Maximum expanse was achieved during the Pueblo II period (A.D. 1000–1150) when Kayenta ceramics occurred well north of the San Juan River (where they mixed with Mesa Verde pot-tery), beyond the Colorado River (especially if the Virgin branch is considered to be Kayenta), south to the Little Colorado River (especially if the Tusayan and Winslow branches are lumped with the Kayenta), and east into the Lukachukai Mountains. By A.D. 1250, this range had shrunk to discrete pockets of settlement in the Laguna Creek, Marsh Pass, Klethla Valley, and Navajo Mountain localities.

Archaeologists have devised a number of space-time schemes to systematize the material embodiments of Kayenta prehistory. Table 3.1 and figure 3.1 summarize

Table 3.1   Archaeological Districts in the Kayenta Area, A.D. 1150–1300

District Name and Letter[1]	Data Rating[2]	Comments
Lower Laguna and Chinle Valleys (H)	IV	No systematic survey of most of the area. Few large sites except cliff dwellings in Chinle and Walker Creek drainages. Important as the locus of intense interaction between Kayenta and Mesa Verde populations; Mesa Verde incursions into Kayenta area.
Monument Valley to Nakai Canyon	IV	No systematic surveys except in Monument Valley and along San Juan River. Sparsely occupied area throughout Kayenta prehistory. No large sites known, a few medium-sized cliff dwellings in Tsegi haa ts'osi, Oljato Wash, Nakai Canyon. Medium-sized open sites in uplands. Monument Valley depopulated after A.D. 1250.
Kayenta Valley (G)	I	Intensive survey by Lindsay and Miller on Tyende Mesa and Haas and Creamer's Kayenta Warfare Project. Several large (50+ room) central pueblos with numerous satellite habitations. Valley level system. Heavy occupation until end of Tsegi phase.
Tsegi Canyon (F)	I	Intensive systematic surveys by Rainbow Bridge-Monument Valley Expedition, Kayenta Warfare Project, Andy Christenson. Only possible central pueblos are open sites near the mouth of the canyon. Two large, three medium, and many small cliff dwellings. Heavy occupation until end of the Tsegi phase.
Long House Valley (G)	I	Intensive, systematic survey by Long House Valley Project. Five large to medium central pueblos, each with numerous satellite sites. Valley-level organization linked with the Kayenta Valley system but not with Klethla Valley system. Heavily populated until the end of the Tsegi phase.
Shonto Plateau (C)	III	Localized surveys by Stein (MNA), Baker (Navajo Nation), and Ambler (NAU). Large areas unstudied. A few large sites; a couple of central pueblos; mostly medium to small habitation sites and small limited activity loci. Apparently, population was low to moderate throughout the PIII period. Population may have declined during the Tsegi phase.
Klethla Valley (D)	I	"Strip" surveys in connection with highway (U.S. 160) and railroad (BM & LPRR); intensive survey by Kayenta Warfare Project. Transition period population concentrations near Tuba City and Black Mesa Junction. Both these areas depopulated by Tsegi phase when population concentrated between Tonalea and Thief Rock. Large central pueblos with satellite sites, large habitation sites, and pit house villages all present. Occupied until the end of the Tsegi phase.
Rainbow Plateau, Paiute Canyon, Mesa (B)	I	Systematic Survey by Amsden (Gila Pueblo), Glen Canyon Project (MNA), and NAU. Sparsely populated during Transition period; large population increment in Tsegi phase. Large central pueblos with satellite sites, large habitation sites, pit house villages all present. Large scale site intervisibility. Period of heaviest construction predates that of Tsegi-Marsh Pass area by a decade. Later dates from cliff dwellings than open sites. Population may have declined during the Tsegi phase.
Navajo Canyon, White Mesa, Kaibito Plateau (A)	III	Systematic but localized surveys of Navajo Canyon by Breternitz, Euler, and Miller (MNA), White Mesa by Miller and Czaplicki (MNA), and BM & LPRR right-of-way across the Kaibito Plateau (MNA). Entire area occupied during Transition period; Kaibito Plateau abandoned by Tsegi phase. Population density low except locally, especially in Navajo Canyon. Large central pueblo with line of sight to Klethla Valley and into Navajo Canyon, perhaps to Navajo Mountain. Occupied throughout the Tsegi phase.
Interior Black Mesa (J)	IV	No large-scale surveys; local surveys in connection with Joint Use Area, coal mining, and road construction. Gap between this area and northern Pueblo III period sites. Large central pueblos with satellite sites. Occupied into the Pueblo IV period (post A.D. 1300).

Notes

1. The letter in parentheses after the district name corresponds with the letter in the "site ID" column in the appendix, which lists the large sites in the Kayenta area. For example, 3A1, Inscription House (see appendix), is located in the Navajo Canyon, White Mesa, Kaibito Plateau District, labeled with an (A). Note that the Monument Valley to Nakai Canyon District has no letter. This is because no large sites are located in the district, and hence no letter designation exists in the appendix for the district.

2. Codes, which range from I to IV, refer to extent of survey coverage in the Kayenta region, with "I" indicating the highest level of intensive survey coverage, and "IV" indicating the least amount of survey coverage.

the geographic parameters of this material by identifying ten localities, or zones, that can be differentiated on the basis of either archaeological content or the nature of the available archaeological data. Figure 3.2 presents chronological breakdowns that have been devised to segment the archaeological sequences in these zones between A.D. 975 and 1425. Most of the local sequences are characterized in combinations of Pecos Classification, phase, and period categories. For the zones around Navajo Mountain, Ambler's (1983, 1985a, 1985b) phase system is used to more finely divide the continuum. A few zones yielded enough data to reflect post-A.D. 1100 population trends (figure 3.3).

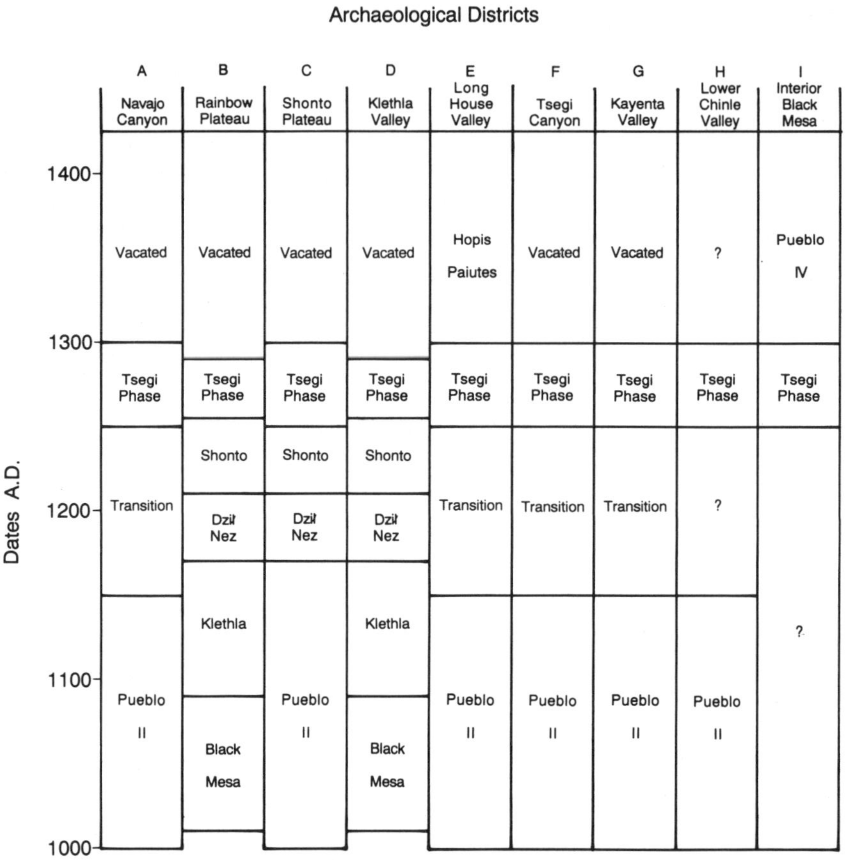

Puebloan Prehistory in the Kayenta

Post-A.D. 1150 Kayenta prehistory cannot be fully comprehended simply in terms of that interval because societies of that period were products of centuries of evolution. Developments during the period of interest were shaped by the reactions of existing adaptive systems to social and environmental conditions and relationships. Therefore, the target interval must be put in the context of the long sequence of behavioral adaptations that preceded it by briefly characterizing Kayenta branch prehistory prior to A.D. 1150, material that is more fully covered elsewhere (Gumerman and Dean 1989).

Pre-A.D. 1150 Kayenta Branch

Following a poorly documented and apparently limited Paleoindian utilization, the Kayenta area was sparsely occupied by Archaic populations. By 1000 B.C., the introduction of maize horticulture marked the transition to the Basketmaker II stage, which exhibits two sequent settlement configurations (Smiley 1985, 1993; Smiley, Parry, and Gumerman 1986). The first, which predates A.D. 150, was characterized by the occupation of lowland and upland rock shelters, the widespread use of unlined and slab-lined cists for storage

Archaeological Districts

Figure 3.2. Chronological sequences in the Kayenta Branch archaeological districts, A.D. 1000 to 1400.

and burial, the near absence of true domiciliary structures, and a rich assemblage of perishable and durable artifacts. This is the classic Basketmaker II occupation of Grand Gulch (Matson 1991; Pepper 1902; Prudden 1897), the Tsegi-Marsh Pass locality (Guernsey and Kidder 1921; Kidder and Guernsey 1919; Lockett and Hargrave 1953; Smiley 1985, 1993), Navajo Mountain (Lindsay et al. 1968), and Canyon de Chelly (E. Morris 1925; A. Morris 1934). The subsequent pattern, which postdates A.D. 150 (Smiley 1985, 1993), involved true pit houses combined with surface and subterranean storage facilities into small, open hamlets. This pattern has been documented primarily in upland localities on Black Mesa (Nichols and Smiley 1985; Smiley 1985, 1993), Cedar Mesa (Matson 1991; Matson, Lipe, and Haase 1988), and Paiute Mesa. Major differences in settlement configuration, architecture,

and artifacts distinguish Kayenta Basketmaker II from contemporary eastern Anasazi patterns exemplified by the Durango rockshelters and open sites (Biggs 1967; Morris and Burgh 1954) and the Navajo Reservoir Los Pinos phase (Eddy 1961).

Technological innovations (including ceramics, the ground stone ax, and the bow), new settlement layouts, and increased reliance on farming marked the Basketmaker III pattern, which emerged by A.D. 600 in the eastern Kayenta area and sometime after A.D. 700 in the west. Small pit house hamlets (Daifuku 1961; Sebastian 1985) continued from the preceding period. At the same time, large, structured pit house villages developed. The largest of these, Juniper Cove (Haury 1928), included nearly 100 structures and the only great kiva presently known for the Kayenta branch. Settlement was concentrated along the margins of lowland valleys

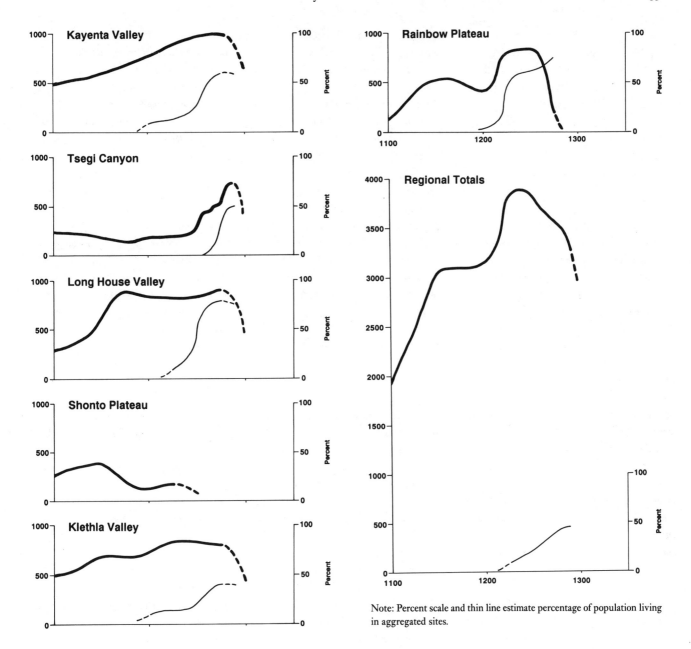

Note: Percent scale and thin line estimate percentage of population living in aggregated sites.

Figure 3.3.   Population trends in selected Kayenta branch archaeological districts, A.D. 1100 to 1350.

and canyons and along upland drainages on central and southern Black Mesa and the Shonto Plateau. Kayenta settlement probably resembled that of the eastern Anasazi more closely during the Basketmaker III period than at any other time.

The transition to the Pueblo I period around A.D. 850 was marked more by changes in settlement location and ceramic design than by major alterations in architecture and site configurations. Pit house form and features are virtually identical to those of the Basketmaker III

period, and associated surface storage units differ little from their predecessors. Great kivas disappeared from the Kayenta architectural repertoire. Pit house-storage units were grouped into numerous hamlets (Green et al. 1985) and a few large villages, such as Alkali Ridge (Brew 1946), one underneath Valley View Ruin on the rim of Black Mesa (Haas and Creamer 1993:76–77), and several along Laguna Creek east of Marsh Pass (Taylor 1954). Site structure ranged from the highly patterned arrangement of pit houses and

surface rooms at Alkali Ridge to the haphazard agglomerations of pit house-storage units in the Laguna Creek sites. The Pueblo I period marked the reoccupation of upland localities, such as northern Black Mesa, that had been vacated during Basketmaker III times. Lowland settlement moved away from the margins of the valleys onto the floodplains themselves. The continuity between Kayenta Basketmaker III and Pueblo I settlement contrasts sharply with developments in the eastern Anasazi area where Pueblo I settlement had already begun to evolve toward later Pueblo II and Chacoan configurations.

The beginning of the Kayenta Pueblo II period (A.D. 1000–1150) was marked by a sudden and radical change in settlement. The pit house sites of the Pueblo I period were replaced by "unit pueblos," each consisting of a block of masonry and jacal surface living and storage rooms fronted by a subterranean structure and a trash mound. The largest of these sites possess fewer than 30 rooms, and most are much smaller. Pit houses were succeeded by subterranean structures that, whether they served only religious functions or combined domestic and ceremonial uses, are recognized as kivas on the basis of their architecture. Many sites also possess a semisubterranean grinding room situated between the kiva and room block. The Pueblo I pattern of aggregated communities gave way to a configuration in which unit pueblo "homesteads" were distributed widely throughout the area. During this interval, Kayenta populations achieved their greatest geographic range, expanding beyond the San Juan and Colorado Rivers on the north and west, and to the Little Colorado River on the south. If the Virgin branch is included, the range can be extended into southern Nevada (see Lyneis, chapter 2). The Pueblo II period, like Pueblo I, was terminated by major settlement transformations throughout the Kayenta domain, which brings us to the target period of this volume.

Transition Period:
A.D. 1150–1250

Between A.D. 1150 and 1250, the dispersed, small, relatively autonomous homesteads that dotted the Pueblo II landscape evolved into the large, aggregated, interdependent communities of the Tsegi phase. By the beginning of the Transition period, the range expansion that had characterized the preceding 300 years had ceased, abandonment of peripheral areas had begun, and the population had begun concentrat-

ing in the heartland. Except for outliers, such as the Coombs site (Lister 1959) and the Tusayan Ruin (Haury 1931), Kayenta peoples vacated the areas north and west of the San Juan and Colorado Rivers and around the Grand Canyon. Much of the Virgin Anasazi region was abandoned (Lyneis, chapter 2), and the Kayenta presence in the Chinle drainage waned. Occupation of Monument Valley (Neely and Olson 1977:72–73) and the San Juan and Colorado River gorges (Adams, Lindsay, and Turner 1961; Long 1966) diminished toward the end of the period. This spatial contraction appears to have involved a straightforward withdrawal from the perimeter toward the center. Population curves in many core localities (figure 3.3; Gumerman and Dean 1989:108, figure 15) exhibit increments that probably reflect the absorption of immigrants from the peripheries.

Important settlement rearrangements also occurred in the Kayenta heartland. Except around Navajo Mountain, uplands were virtually abandoned as loci of permanent habitation, as northern Black Mesa, large areas of the Shonto Plateau, and lesser highlands were vacated. Populations began to aggregate in localities favored by arable land and water. In the Navajo Mountain uplands, sites were concentrated along alluviated drainages and near dune areas. Except for Navajo and Paiute Canyons, the western lowlands were not heavily occupied. The opposite elevational trend prevailed in the eastern part of the Kayenta heartland where the most favorable agricultural conditions occurred in the lowlands. The alluviated Laguna Creek, Long House, and Klethla valleys became foci of settlement as did the lower, heavily duned southwestern flanks of the Shonto Plateau. Settlement changes also occurred within inhabited districts. In the eastern lowlands, a generalized convergence of settlement on suitable agricultural localities, which were being progressively diminished by rapidly changing alluvial and hydrologic conditions, began. This adjustment included movement

toward the upper reaches of the drainages as well as the concentration of sites near pockets of arable land (Dean 1990; Dean and Lindsay 1978; Dean, Lindsay, and Robinson 1978).

A major result of these settlement shifts was the development of "empty" areas between population centers. The abandonment of northern Black Mesa created a large uninhabited zone between the eastern communities and the populations of central and southern Black Mesa. Similar gaps developed on the Shonto Plateau and between the Klethla Valley and Long House Valley settlements. Despite the increasing isolation of Kayenta groups, interaction among the centers was high as indicated by strong similarities in ceramic design and the exchange of ceramic raw materials and finished products (Ambler 1983; Geib and Callahan 1987).

Important changes in habitation site configuration accompanied the settlement shifts of this period. The "unit pueblo" site type typical of the Pueblo II period was augmented by at least two new community forms. One new type, the plaza pueblo, may represent the coalescence of two or more unit pueblos. Plaza pueblos consisted of a masonry room block or room blocks facing an open or enclosed plaza containing one or more kivas (figure 3.4a). Occasionally, pit houses rather than masonry rooms flanked the plaza. Toward the end of this period, sites of this type became quite large in terms of area and height of rubble mound, although the number of rooms in any one site never exceeded 50. The other new site type, the pit house village, consisted of scattered pit houses associated with surface and subterranean storage facilities and isolated kivas (figure 3.4b; Anderson 1980:7, figure 4; Bannister, Dean, and Robinson 1968:71). Semisubterranean grinding rooms and surface use areas also are sometimes present. Due to insufficient excavation, the range of variation in this type of site remains obscure.

In addition to the foregoing formal layouts are site configurations governed by situational factors. Principal among these are ledge sites (Ambler, Lindsay, and Stein 1964:43–53, figures 31–38), cliff dwellings (Klesert 1982), slump boulder sites, and walled-up crevices (Neely and Olson 1977:figures 5 and 7).

Based on limited excavation, the three main site types appear to occur in different proportions in different zones. Unit and plaza pueblos are more abundant in the Marsh Pass and Navajo Mountain localities, while pit house villages seem to be concentrated in the Klethla Valley and southern Shonto Plateau (Haas and Creamer 1993), and on central Black Mesa (Linford 1982). Future excavations, however, are likely to alter this perception.

Tsegi Phase:

A.D. 1250–1300

Tsegi phase settlement represents the culmination of trends set in motion at the beginning of the Transition period. Peripheral areas continued to be vacated, and settlement density grew in the core localities. By the beginning of the Tsegi phase, Monument Valley was virtually abandoned as a place of permanent residence (Neely and Olson 1977:72), and the canyons draining northward into the San Juan and Colorado Rivers were used seasonally, mainly in a logistic manner, as habitation was concentrated in the uplands around Navajo Mountain. In the Chinle drainage, Kayenta "influence" continued to wane while the Mesa Verde presence grew.

Continued population contraction widened the gaps between the Kayenta people and their neighbors on all sides. Paradoxically, interaction with some of these neighbors increased at this time. Virtual identity in ceramic design (Smith 1962, 1971) and a few imported vessels indicate that the people of the Kayenta heartland remained in contact with Tusayan peoples to the south. Even more distant southern connections, perhaps mediated by Tusayan groups, are indicated by the occurrence of Kayenta White Ware and White

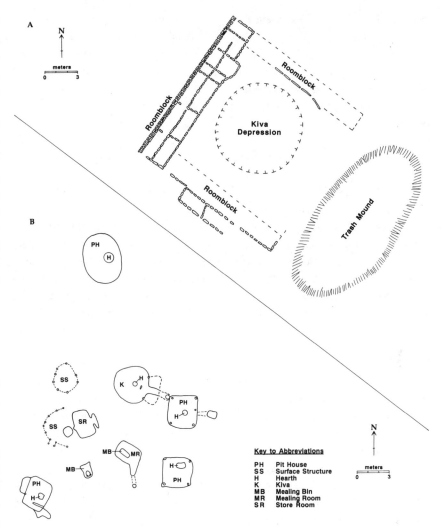

Figure 3.4. Transition period (A.D. 1150–1250) site configurations: (a) plaza site (NA 12062) in Long House Valley; (b) pit house village (Hard Floor Site, NA 9460) on the Shonto Plateau.

Mountain Red Ware pottery in areas of opposite affiliation, the addition of white outlining to some Kayenta polychromes, and Kayenta or Tusayan migrations to Point of Pines (Haury 1958; Lindsay 1987) and the San Pedro Valley (Di Peso 1958; Lindsay 1987, 1992).

Considerable evidence testifies to interaction with Mesa Verdean groups. Mesa Verde ceramics are the most abundant extralocal pottery in Tsegi phase sites, although Kayenta ceramics are not equally abundant in Mesa Verde sites. The existence in Tsegi phase sites of novel architectural forms that originated in the Mesa Verde area also attest to contact between these peoples. Kiva pilasters (Dean 1969:98; Morss 1927:32), towers at Poncho House (Guernsey 1931:plates 38, 39), Ruin 8 (Kidder and Guernsey 1919:57–58, plate 18), and Kiet Siel (Dean 1969:138–39), "mask-like" aperture arrangements at Poncho House (Gaede and Gaede 1977:figure 6), and the Mesa Verde style masonry and doorway closure in a granary at Kiet Siel (Dean 1969:125–26) exemplify these forms.

The conduit of Mesa Verde-Kayenta interaction was the natural corridor between the two areas formed by the Chinle Valley. Several late thirteenth-century cliff dwellings in the Chinle Valley have Mesa

Verdean architectural forms executed in Kayenta masonry styles. Except for Poncho House (Neely and Olson 1977:69–70), these sites appear to be dominated by Mesa Verde ceramics. In contrast, painted textiles from Painted Cave have Kayenta ceramic designs (Haury 1945:plates 10–12). Poncho House likely was pivotal in the transmission of trade items and architectural ideas from Mesa Verdean populations into the eastern Kayenta area.

In the Kayenta heartland, settlement trends that began during the Transition period continued into the Tsegi phase. Substantial upland settlement persisted only on the Rainbow Plateau and Paiute Mesa, and both these localities were depopulated before the end of the phase (figure 3.3; Ambler, Fairley, and Geib 1983: figures 5–6). Paiute Canyon was abandoned shortly after A.D. 1250 (Ambler, Fairley, and Geib 1983:figure 3.3), while Navajo Canyon was occupied throughout the phase.

In the eastern Kayenta area, the relocation of settlements toward the upper reaches of lowland drainages and aggregation into large sites intensified. These processes account for the concentration of settlements in Long House Valley (Dean, Lindsay, and Robinson 1978), Tsegi Canyon (Dean 1969), the southern Shonto Plateau (Haas and Creamer 1993), and the Kayenta and Klethla Valleys (Haas and Creamer 1993). Limited survey on central Black Mesa suggests a similar pattern of large settlements along major drainages. Farther south, aggregation occurred in the Hopi area (Smith 1971) and along the Little Colorado River (Adams, chapter 4, 1991:171–74; Hays, Adams, and Lange 1991). These rearrangements intensified the concentration of settlements in the diminishing number of localities favorable for large-scale agriculture under worsening fluvial and climatic conditions.

These settlement shifts widened the gaps between population centers. A major break comprising most of the Shonto Plateau separated the Tsegi-Marsh Pass and Navajo Mountain centers, and a 15-km gap opened between the Tsegi-Marsh Pass and Klethla Valley centers (Haas and Creamer 1993:85). Additional southward withdrawal increased the space between groups on central Black Mesa and their heartland cohorts. The size of the separation, if any, between central Black Mesa groups and the Tusayan branch communities south of the mesa is unknown.

As during the Transition period, the spatial disjunctions between Kayenta settlement clusters did not hinder interaction between the various loci. Minor differences in ceramic designs and type frequencies, architectural features, and community pattern do not negate the evidence for the widespread sharing of items and ideas. Visual interlocality communication systems were inaugurated or elaborated during this interval. Upland communities around Navajo Mountain are linked in a line-of-sight network of sites focused on Thumb Rock Pueblo on Paiute Mesa. Communication between the Klethla Valley and central Black Mesa may have been effected through the Valley View site (Haas and Creamer 1993:76–77, figure 4–22) on the north rim of the mesa. Long House Valley appears to have been visually connected with the Kayenta Valley (Haas and Creamer 1993), where a string of sites along Laguna Creek could have linked these groups with Chinle Valley populations. Visual linkages have yet to be established between the Navajo Mountain, Marsh Pass, and Klethla Valley centers.

Settlement shifts within the inhabited areas are local reflections of a general Tsegi phase concentration in dwindling prime farming areas. Population curves estimated by Ambler, Fairley, and Geib (1983: figures 3–5) reflect changes in settlement distributions in the Navajo Mountain locality. In the eastern area, a concentration of communities around arable lands in the upper end of the Laguna Creek drainage is evident (Haas and Creamer 1993). Between A.D. 1250 and 1286, nearly 700 people moved into the sparsely populated Tsegi Canyon and established at least 20 villages ranging in size from one or two households to more than 100 individuals (Dean 1969:194). In Long House Valley, the shift of residential loci continued toward the lower end of the valley where arable land is most abundant (Dean, Lindsay, and Robinson 1978; Harrill 1982: 138–47, figure 8).

The Tsegi phase is characterized by considerable morphological and functional differentiation of sites and architectural units within sites. Ten different types of structures are denoted by attributes indicative of their use: living rooms, granaries, storerooms, grinding rooms, courtyards, plazas, galleries, kivas, ceremonial annexes, and towers (Dean 1969:26–34, 1970:153–55; Lindsay 1969:141–80). The basic structural component of habitation sites is a grouping of functionally differentiated chambers called the room cluster (Dean 1969:34–35, 1970:155–57; Lindsay 1969:156–57). Typically, this unit consists of one or two living rooms, 1 to 12 storage chambers, and occasionally a grinding room, all grouped around an unroofed courtyard that provides access to the rooms. Sometimes two or more room clusters share a single courtyard to produce a courtyard complex (Dean 1969: 35; Lindsay 1969:157). In some open loci, groups of room clusters and kivas form discrete units within larger sites as at Segazlin Mesa (Lindsay et al. 1968: 231–63), Pottery Pueblo (Stein 1984), and Long House.

These structural units form four types of residential sites. To Lindsay's (1969: 243–46) plaza and courtyard types must be added pit house villages (Ambler 1985a: 51) and ad hoc forms dictated by the peculiarities of the building sites. Although four types can be conceptualized, to some extent they grade into one another. For example, a courtyard site consisting of a single room cluster and a kiva has the form of a small plaza site, which in turn could be classified as a unit pueblo, and the point at which a pueblo with pit houses becomes a pit house village is indefinite.

Plaza pueblos consist of masonry room

blocks or pit houses flanking one to four sides of a partially or wholly enclosed plaza that contains one or more kivas. Although strongly patterned, plaza pueblos vary considerably in size, complexity, and ground plan. Sizes range from fewer than 10 to more than 300 rooms. The simplest form, which occurs in large and small sites, includes a single plaza surrounded by masonry and jacal rooms and sometimes, as at Neskahi Village (Hobler 1974), pit houses. Red House and Yellow House on the southern flank of Navajo Mountain have two plazas each, while Long House has at least six bounded plazas. This variability is due in part to adjustments to the peculiarities of the construction loci and in part to factors that enter when construction is physically unconstrained. Plaza sites are oriented between 90 and 180 degrees with the main room block at the back. Every plaza site that has been investigated is composed of room clusters.

Courtyard pueblos lack formal plazas. Instead, room clusters and courtyard complexes are grouped around single or multiple courtyards, oriented along "streets" or linear open areas, or arranged to conform to the space available. Lacking the unifying influence of plazas, courtyard sites exhibit a wide range of variation in size, complexity, and layout. The largest courtyard sites, Pottery Pueblo (Stein 1984) and Kiet Siel, have around 150 rooms, while the smallest have only one or two room clusters, as at Lolomaki (Dean 1969:160–61, figure 42). Complexity varies from the simplicity of Lolomaki to the street arrangement of Kiet Siel and the noncontiguous courtyard complexes at Pottery Pueblo. Courtyard site ground plans range from the linear arrangements of most cliff dwellings and the Segazlin Mesa sites to the comparatively amorphous layout of Pottery Pueblo. Courtyard pueblo kivas are associated with courtyard complexes, as at Segazlin Mesa and Pottery Pueblo, or with the village as a whole, as in the Tsegi Canyon cliff pueblos. The secular activities performed in the plazas of plaza sites probably were confined to the courtyards of courtyard sites, while the "streets" and other public areas of the latter may have taken on some of the plazas' public functions.

No Tsegi phase pit house villages have been intensively studied. Indeed, only one excavated Tsegi phase pit house has been described (Ambler and Olson 1977:23–24, figures 24 and 25), a small, squarish structure with a ramp entry and an entrybox. Fairly large sites apparently consisting of scattered pit houses and a few masonry surface structures have been discovered in the Klethla Valley (Haas and Creamer 1993) and near Navajo Mountain. The two Klethla Valley sites that have been tested, Thief and Kin Klethla (Haas and Creamer 1993:78–85, figures 4–23 to 4–26), have more than 40 pit houses each, and the latter has a substantial masonry component as well.

Many sites are ad hoc constructions, the layouts of which were adjusted to the spatial constraints of the locations in which they were built. Ledges, low overhangs, slump boulders, crevices, and bedrock features commonly determine the forms of these sites.

As Ambler (1985a:51) points out, the different kinds of sites are not uniformly distributed in space. Plaza pueblos and courtyard sites occur everywhere but are differentially distributed relative to terrain features. Plaza pueblos tend to occur on eminences ranging from steep-sided buttes to bajadas or hill crests with little topographic relief. The main room block usually is situated on the highest point with the plaza sloping away to the south-southeast. Courtyard sites often are situated on eminences steeper and less accessible than those chosen for plaza sites. Open courtyard sites appear to be more numerous in the Navajo Mountain locality than in the east, but this could be an artifact of sampling. All cliff dwellings are courtyard sites if only because rock shelters cannot accommodate plazas. Pit house sites seem to be concentrated in the Klethla Valley, a continuation of a long local tradition; they also occur around Navajo Mountain and in Long House Valley (Bliss 1960). Ad hoc sites occur everywhere.

Analyses of cliff dwellings fostered the conclusion that the localized village represented the highest level of Tsegi phase social organization (Dean 1969, 1970). Subsequent research has revealed additional levels of social integration. In Long House Valley, Tsegi phase sites were organized into a "hierarchical" settlement system (Dean 1990; Dean, Lindsay, and Robinson 1978:33; Effland 1979) that seems to be characteristic of the eastern Kayenta valleys (Haas and Creamer 1993) and western uplands. In this system, individual residential sites representing two or possibly three levels of complexity are spatially and structurally associated to form multisite communities. Other spatial relationships and communication linkages integrate these communities into even larger interactional systems.

The lowest organizational level comprises small-to-medium habitation sites located adjacent to plots of arable land. Such sites range in size from 1 to about 10 room clusters and include plaza pueblos, courtyard pueblos, and pit house sites. No matter how small, these sites have evidence for the full range of secular and ceremonial activities (Dean, Lindsay, and Robinson 1978:29; Haas and Creamer 1993:37–47). All possess room clusters and their associated domestic functions. Artifacts and trash specify a full array of procurement, maintenance, use, consumption, and discard behaviors. Even the smallest usually have kivas, and the number of kivas generally is proportional to site size. Though commonly situated above the valley floors and footed on bedrock, there is nothing defensive about either the locations or features of these sites. They seem to represent functionally self-contained, relatively autonomous social units ranging from one to several households.

A higher level of social integration may be indicated by larger residential sites, which range from 50 to 100 rooms, where the necessity to coordinate more people may have generated greater organizational complexity. Nothing but size, however, distinguishes these from the smaller pueblos, and both may be equivalent members of a single, variable class of habitation site.

The highest single-site organizational level is represented by a few "central pueblos" (Dean 1990:184–85; Dean, Lindsay, and Robinson 1978:33) that appear to have had special, extra-residential functions related to the maintenance of communities composed of several habitation sites. Central pueblos have all the attributes diagnostic of a full range of secular and ceremonial activities: domestic rooms of all types, room clusters, courtyard complexes, plazas and room blocks, kivas and other ceremonial structures, and the artifacts and debris indicative of the same activities that were performed at the residential sites. Inadequate sampling prohibits determining whether central pueblos exhibit artifact type or attribute differences from the habitation sites. Central pueblos do not have numbers of imported items disproportionate to their sizes or burials richer than those associated with residential pueblos. Central pueblos and residential sites exhibit no consistent size relationships: some central pueblos are smaller than some of the (hierarchically subordinate) residential sites with which they are associated.

Despite the similarities between residential sites and central pueblos, the latter have several attributes that clearly demarcate them from the former. Most central pueblos are plaza sites, the most notable possible exception to this generalization being Pottery Pueblo (Stein 1984). All central pueblos (except Pottery Pueblo) have "spinal" room blocks constructed of double faced masonry, a technique absent from residential pueblos. Other units of the pueblo are situated with reference to these "structures of orientation" (Lindsay 1969:245). The evidence available indicates that spinal room blocks did not have a single, uniform function. Those in the Navajo Mountain area contained both living rooms and granaries, while those in Long House Valley seem to have been communal (food) storage structures. Spinal room blocks are similar in construction and layout to the "ladder" buildings discussed by Roney (chapter 10), but we currently lack the data to assess functional similarities between the two architectural forms.

Most central pueblos have reservoirs for the capture and storage of domestic water (Kidder and Guernsey 1919:plate 23a). Some central pueblos have features designed to limit or regulate access to the interior plazas. Features such as ramps, corridors, crosswalls, and restricted entries (along with the sites' massive walls and elevation above the surrounding countryside) have been interpreted as defensive arrangements (chapter 14, Haas 1986, 1989; Haas and Creamer 1993). It is equally probable that these elements served to control access to sacred precincts within the pueblos and to channel ceremonial observances and other communal activities. Taken together, the features that distinguish central pueblos specify extra-village functions related to the maintenance of multisite communities. Among such functions are the storage, protection, and distribution of community water and food supplies, community integration, intercommunity relations, and possibly refuge in times of strife.

Habitation sites and central pueblos are grouped into localized communities that represent a still higher level of integration. Each of these communities consists of a number of residential sites clustered around a single central pueblo situated on an eminence overlooking the cluster. In Long House Valley, the clusters are spatially discrete and include from 3 to 15 habitation sites each (Dean 1990:figure 46). The total number of rooms in the Long House Valley clusters covaries with the area of associated arable land (Harrill 1982). The structural, size, and spatial relationships within each cluster suggest that the residential sites, despite a recognizable degree of independence, were organized into a community by activities and deliberations that took place in the central pueblos. Sparse occupation of the lands between the clusters suggests that these multivillage communities probably were fairly autonomous and perhaps competed with one another for access to or control of vital subsistence and other resources.

Despite the fissive effects of competition, evidence exists for an even higher level of social interaction. The four central pueblos adjacent to the floor of Long House Valley—Long House, Tower House, NA 11980, and NA 11958—are situated so as to be mutually intervisible; each site can be seen from the other three. There can be little doubt that clear lines of sight were important variables in locating central pueblos (Haas and Creamer 1993: 30–31, figures 2–6 and 2–7). The visual connections among these sites are best explained as a means of facilitating communication among the four Long House Valley communities. Communication may have been necessitated by the potential of conflict with groups from outside the valley or by the need to coordinate activities, perhaps ritual observances, at all four sites. Whatever its function, intervisibility implies valley-wide communication and cooperation, and the effort expended to achieve intervisibility strongly suggests coordination of activities on the scale of the entire valley. Similar visual connections among central pueblos in the Kayenta and Klethla Valleys (Haas and Creamer 1993) and around Navajo Mountain reveal comparable intercommunity interaction networks throughout the Kayenta area.

Haas and Creamer (1993) have found central pueblos located so as to suggest connections between Long House Valley and the Kayenta Valley to the east. Interestingly, there appears to be no corresponding westward linkage with the Klethla Valley. The potential line-of-sight connection through Valley View Pueblo (Haas and Creamer 1993:76–77) suggests a link between the Klethla Valley community and the interior of Black Mesa. Thus, a strong case can be made for a fifth (or sixth) interactional level joining adjacent communication systems. Further research may document even broader regional communications linkages.

Settlement systems similar to those in the eastern Kayenta valleys existed in the Navajo Mountain uplands. Central pueblos such as Yellow House, Red House, Upper Desha Pueblo, and Pottery Pueblo (or, possibly, Neskahi Village) are surrounded by "lower order" satellite communities and are joined by unobstructed lines of sight into two (or possibly only one) communications networks.

Settlement in the eastern and western canyons appears to have been less structured than that of the western uplands and eastern valleys. Although sites of all sizes up to about 150 rooms occur in the canyons, they are rarely clustered into groups. Rather, individual, functionally complete sites are situated near drainage confluences where the conjunction of land and water favors farming. A few cliff dwellings, notably Kiet Siel, might have served as loci of some activities, principally ceremonial, that were shared with the inhabitants of nearby, subordinate sites. Lacking the attributes of central pueblos, cliff dwellings seem to have functioned as residential loci where the full range of secular and ceremonial activities was performed. The severely limited vistas from most rockshelters precluded line-of-sight communication. Although the residents of canyons undoubtedly interacted with one another, it more likely was by foot than by eye, as attested by the many trail systems traversing the canyons. Hierarchical settlement systems probably existed only in attenuated form, if at all, in the confined environs of the canyons.

Abandonment of the Kayenta Area

As part of the general Anasazi exodus from the San Juan drainage, the Kayenta area was vacated sometime between A.D. 1290 and 1300. This event brought an end to the Tsegi phase and with it the Kayenta branch as an archaeological entity in northeastern Arizona. The reasons for the general Anasazi abandonment of the Four Corners area and the Kayenta component of that population dislocation have been debated for decades. Whatever the causes of the former, it seems likely that local and extralocal environmental and social factors, acting simultaneously, exerted decisive "push-pull" effects that determined the fate of the latter (Dean 1966, 1969: 194–96, 1987, 1991; see also Varien et al., chapter 7). Without going into detail, it is probable that unfavorable fluvial and climatic conditions, high population densities, and prevailing levels of technology and sociocultural integration combined to create adaptive circumstances favoring either a substantial reduction in social complexity or the translocation of the existing social system to an environmental setting in which it could be maintained. Such an environment existed in the Hopi Mesas area (Hack 1942) where, at the same time, social mechanisms that facilitated the acceptance of immigrants (Eggan 1950:123–33), the inception of new religious concepts connected with the katsina cult (Adams 1991, chapter 4), and increasing social complexity acted as attractive forces. Thus, the "push" of deteriorating conditions at home coupled with the "pull" of enticing new cultural developments among closely related Tusayan groups probably stimulated the Kayenta people to move south to the middle Little Colorado drainage. At some point, when the homeland population decreased to levels supportable under the deteriorating environmental conditions, the positive pull factors would have assumed primacy over the negative push factors.

Post-A.D. 1300 Kayenta "Extensions"

Although the Kayenta branch, as a geographically discrete unit, ceased to exist after the late thirteenth-century exodus from the heartland, recognizable echoes of the tradition continued to reverberate through the Southwest. The clearest persistence of Kayenta ceramic, architectural, and organizational principles into the post-A.D. 1300 era occurred among the closely related Tusayan groups of the middle Little Colorado drainage, which were being transformed by a complex interplay of cultural and demographic forces into recognizable prototypes of later Hopi patterns. The Peabody Museum's work on Antelope Mesa (Brew 1937, 1939, 1941; Smith 1952b, 1971, 1972, 1992) and the Arizona State Museum's Homol'ovi Project (Adams 1989, 1991; Adams and Hays 1991) document the continuities between late Pueblo III Kayenta and early Pueblo IV "Proto-Hopi" manifestations.

A second, more limited, occurrence of Kayenta-inspired elements exists on the Defiance Plateau and Hopi Buttes areas where some late thirteenth- and early fourteenth-century black-on-white and polychrome pottery exhibits designs derived from Kayenta prototypes (Colton 1956). These ceramics, however, occur in sites (such as Klagetoh, Kin Tiel, and Bidahochi Pueblo) that have little in common with Kayenta architecture. Due to the dearth of excavation data, the nature of the relationship of these groups to Kayenta populations is at present indeterminate.

Equally interesting are apparent Kayenta (or Tusayan) affiliations with areas far south of the western Anasazi homeland. The best known of these intrusions is, of course, the late thirteenth-century Kayenta (or Tusayan) immigration into Point of Pines (Haury 1958; Lindsay 1987; Reed 1958). Distinctive architectural features and local copies of Tsegi Orange Ware polychrome designs—the Maverick Mountain series—mark the presence at the Point of Pines Ruin of immigrants from the north. Kayenta-derived materials also occur in the Safford Valley in the form of abundant Maverick Mountain pottery (Alexander J. Lindsay, Jr., personal communication) and a "ceremonial" cache on Bonita Creek (Wasley 1962) that closely resembles a cache from Sunflower Cave in Marsh Pass (Kidder and Guernsey 1919:145–47).

Even farther south, in the middle San Pedro Valley, are two pueblos that possess ceramic traits and architectural features indicative of Kayenta affiliation. The Reeve Ruin (DiPeso 1958; Gerald 1975) yielded quantities of Tucson Polychrome, an indigenous type with Kayenta-inspired (Maverick Mountain) designs (Lindsay 1992), and sherds from perforated-rim plates, a form that originated in the Kayenta area during Pueblo II times. Even more significant is the only known occurrence of entryboxes outside the Kayenta area. Across the San Pedro River, the Davis site (Gerald 1975) possesses a rectangular kiva similar to the Hopi-style kivas that developed after A.D. 1300 north of the Gila River.

The major fourteenth-century social, religious, and ideological changes that transformed the Anasazi into recognizable predecessors of the modern pueblo groups (Adams 1991) effectively severed the thread of continuity between the Kayenta pattern and later Puebloan manifestations. Nevertheless, there can be little doubt that Kayenta immigrants formed an important increment to the populations of the middle Little Colorado River Valley that later evolved into the modern Hopis. The Kayenta legacy, however attenuated, is still to be found in that area.

Kayenta and Chaco

The foregoing summary of Kayenta branch prehistory provides a basis for assessing the relationship of the Kayenta Anasazi to the Chacoan regional system that waxed and waned in the San Juan Basin between A.D. 850 and 1200. The "Pueblos in Transition" conference was convened specifically to consider the regional consequences of the collapse of the Chacoan system after A.D. 1150. Attention was focused on the period between A.D. 1150 and 1350 when prehistoric Pueb-

loan societies were transformed from configurations dominated by the Chacoan system into patterns recognizably ancestral to the modern Pueblos (Lipe and Lekson 1990:3). The strength of the Chacocentric paradigm is exemplified by the opening words of the application for conference support to the Wenner-Gren Foundation: "In the late A.D. 1000s, the entire Pueblo world was dominated by a regional sociocultural system centered in Chaco Canyon, New Mexico" (Lipe and Lekson 1989:2). It is my view that not only was the Kayenta corner of the Pueblo world not dominated by the Chacoan regional system, its prehistory cannot be understood in terms of a Chaco dominance model of Anasazi culture development. In other words, the Kayenta Anasazi remained basically independent of Chacoan influence. Their cultural trajectory was the result of responses to other historical, sociocultural, and environmental factors.

There is no archaeological indication that the Kayenta Anasazi were incorporated into or even interacted systematically with the Chacoan system. Undoubtedly, the Kayentans knew of the Chacoan polity, but it clearly had minimal impact on their daily lives. One has but to consider the vast organizational differences between Kayenta and Chaco to appreciate this point. Around A.D. 850, when the distinctive Chacoan site pattern was emerging, the Kayenta Anasazi lived in relatively unstructured pit house villages that lacked great kivas. From A.D. 850 to 1000, when the Chacoan configuration was evolving in the San Juan Basin, the Kayenta pattern remained little changed from that of the Basketmaker III period. Between A.D. 1000 and 1150, when the Chacoan regional system expanded to its maximum extent and "power," Kayenta populations were dispersed across the countryside in small "unit pueblo" hamlets that bore no resemblance to the immense, complex, and aggregated Chacoan communities. Even after A.D. 1150, Kayenta society remained less complex than the northern and southern successors of the Chacoan system.

The Kayenta area lacks the distinctive architectural forms and site layouts that are thought to signify Chacoan hegemony. Chaco-style "great houses," some with great kivas and road segments, exist on the eastern and northern margins of the Kayenta area but are absent from the heartland. "Great houses" occur in the Puerco West and Chinle valleys, on the southeastern flank of Black Mesa, and in southeastern Utah (Stein 1989; Stein and Fowler, chapter 8). The Chinle Valley and Black Mesa great houses (Gilpin 1989) seem to date late in the Chacoan sequence, to have been only briefly occupied, and to have had little discernible effect on nearby Kayenta populations who continued to reside in small, dispersed hamlets (Adams, chapter 4). Perhaps the most telling architectural indicator of Kayenta independence is the complete absence of great kivas, a key element in models of the Chacoan system.

Material culture likewise indicates little Kayenta interaction with the Chacoan regional system. Small quantities of Pueblo II Kayenta pottery occur in Chacoan sites. Conversely, only minuscule amounts of Chacoan pottery are found in the Kayenta area. Even the Kayenta use of the Dogoszhi black-on-white ceramic design style, a hallmark of "classic" Chacoan pottery design (Neitzel 1994:216; Neitzel and Bishop 1990), does not indicate strong Chacoan influence. Although the Dogoszhi style is anomalous in terms of the Kayenta black-on-white ceramic design tradition, the style occurs earlier and persists longer in Tusayan Black-on-red, a Tsegi Orange Ware type (Colton 1956).

Despite the Kayenta peoples' apparent freedom from direct Chacoan control, the two subtraditions do have some things in common. These commonalities reside primarily in the synchroneity of important sociocultural developments in each area. The change from localized pit house villages to scattered "unit pueblo" hamlets in the Kayenta area coincides roughly with the beginning of Chacoan regional expansion around A.D. 1000. Similarly, the demise of the Kayenta "unit pueblo" settlement pattern around A.D. 1150 is roughly coeval with the cessation of Chacoan expansion. Thus, the Kayenta Pueblo II period conforms closely to the period in which the Chacoan system grew to its maximum extent. These coincidences could denote linkages between Chaco and Kayenta that differed from the mechanisms used to incorporate other groups into the regional system. Conversely, these correspondences could be fortuitous or outcomes of external forces that affected both groups. The Chacoan collapse and Kayenta settlement transformations of around A.D. 1150 are but two examples of important sociocultural changes that occurred throughout the Southwest at this time. These changes include widespread population movements, the abandonment of many upland areas, the attenuation of the Virgin branch, and the end of the Hohokam Sedentary period. That these events coincided with major environmental changes (Dean et al. 1985; Euler et al. 1979; Plog et al. 1988) suggests that natural as well as behavioral variables may have contributed to the synchronisms between Chaco and Kayenta. Whatever the causes of these coincidences, the differences between Kayenta and Chaco are too great to allow Kayenta prehistory to be explained in terms of the rise and fall of the Chacoan system.

The fact that Kayenta prehistory cannot presently be explained solely in terms of the dynamics of the "Chaco phenomenon" does not mean that efforts to discover and explore relationships between Kayenta and Chaco should be abandoned; indeed, they should be intensified. Strengthening the case for a lack of influence would be just as important as a demonstration of close ties between the two. The former outcome would give rise to numerous interesting questions, such as why Chaco failed to exert an influence west of the Chinle drainage concomitant to its apparent dominance farther east, and how a disjunction between the two groups was maintained. Such issues can

be attacked only through research focused on several important points. What, for example, was the true nature of the Chacoan regional system? Despite a plethora of opinions, we are still far from a satisfactory understanding of the considerable variability in sites assigned to the system and of the behavioral meaning of this variability. Do the Chaco-style great houses on the eastern margin of the Kayenta area represent colonists or proselytizers from the Chaco core area, expansion from secondary centers (such as those along the Puerco River), or local groups attempting through emulation to share in the benefits of the Chacoan system? Finally, research is necessary to elucidate the interrelationships between the inhabitants of the western "great houses" and adjacent Kayenta groups.

Conclusions

Post-Chacoan sociocultural developments in the Kayenta area were outcomes of interactions among many conditions and variables (Gumerman and Dean 1989). Important conditions were the nature of Kayenta society, which was the result of a unique evolutionary history, and the "stable" aspects (Dean 1984) of the environment, which entailed several different habitats with differing resource and subsistence potentials. Important variables fall into four broad categories: behavioral, demographic, environmental, and historical (Dean 1988; Dean et al. 1985). The first of these provides societies with reservoirs of alternative behaviors that allow them to adapt to changed environmental or social circumstances (Dean 1995). Important demographic variables include the total number of people and their local densities. The spectrum of environmental variability is divided into low frequency (base periodicities ≥ 25 years) and high frequency (base periodicities < 25 years) domains (Dean 1984, 1988; Dean et al. 1985).

The Kayenta Anasazi brought into the post-Chacoan era a culture that was the result of a particular history of develop-

ment that spanned the preceding 2,000 years. This history involved behavioral adaptations not only to social and environmental conditions and changes, but also to a particular sequence of interactions with other inhabitants of the Southwest, including other Anasazi groups and the Sinagua, Cohonina, Fremont, and Hohokam. The Kayenta Anasazi responded to the environmental, demographic, and social transformations of the post-A.D. 1150 period primarily in terms of the culture that had evolved in response to this unique history. Thus, the results of the Kayenta adaptation to post-Chacoan circumstances were contingent (Gould 1989: 284–85) on their previous history, current sociocultural capacity, and prevailing external conditions.

Kayenta society was characterized by a degree of simplicity that, while inhibiting the development of complex social systems such as those exhibited by the eastern Anasazi, endowed it with the flexibility to adjust rapidly and effectively to changing environmental and social conditions. The basic social unit throughout the Kayenta sequence was the extended family household that occupied a residential complex consisting of a dwelling (pit house or living room), separate storage facilities (cists or storerooms), and outdoor work areas. The Kayenta Anasazi displayed remarkable flexibility in combining extended families into larger social units —such as the fairly large Basketmaker III, Pueblo I, and Tsegi phase villages—or in disaggregating the larger units into isolated households or small hamlets, as during Basketmaker II, Pueblo II, and the Transition period. Larger social units of whatever period seem to have been composed of relatively autonomous, economically equivalent households. Hierarchical organizations of increasingly larger social units developed only during the Tsegi phase, and even then households behaved fairly independently of one another (Dean 1969:191, 1970). Thus, aggregation and disaggregation appear to have been key organizational aspects of Kayenta response to changing physical and social circumstances.

Compared to the eastern Anasazi region, the environment of the Kayenta area is marginal for agriculture. The sandy soils of the Kayenta heartland are less productive than the clay soils of the San Juan Basin or the loess of southwestern Colorado. Rainfall is too meager and too variable to sustain dry farming (Dean 1969: 14–16; Hack 1942:23), and ditch irrigation is possible in only a few localities. Prehistoric agriculture was limited to places where geologic, topographic, and hydrologic factors united soil with sufficient water, either in the form of high alluvial groundwater levels or favorable surface runoff conditions. As a result of these circumstances, Kayenta societies had less productive and less stable subsistence bases than those of the eastern Anasazi.

The marginality of the Kayenta environment was exacerbated by major fluctuations in the amount of arable land that accompanied the rise and fall of alluvial water tables, the deposition and erosion of floodplain sediments, and seasonal and annual variations in precipitation (Dean et al. 1985:figure 1; Plog et al. 1988:figure 1). By and large, the Basketmaker III period was characterized by fluvial conditions conducive to alluvial farming, and precipitation would have played only a minor role in agricultural production. In contrast, falling water tables and floodplain erosion between A.D. 750 and 925 reduced the amount of farmable floodplain and increased dependence on rainfall. These factors, coupled with a comparatively small population, allowed Kayenta Pueblo I peoples to aggregate in favorable localities near their floodplain fields.

The Pueblo II period settlement dispersal occurred during what was perhaps the least stressful environmental interlude in the last two millennia, when low frequency (fluvial) and high frequency (climate) conditions were good for farming in every habitat throughout the Kayenta area. Freed of low frequency constraints on field and settlement location, the population abandoned the aggregated settlement configuration that had characterized the Pueblo I period and dispersed to small hamlets scattered widely across the landscape.

The shift to the organizational variability of the Transition period (A.D. 1150–1250) coincided with important environmental changes. A secondary fluvial degradation and a prolonged drought terminated the salubrious conditions that had permitted farming nearly anywhere in the Kayenta area. The scattered population began to concentrate in localities suitable for farming under the altered conditions. Resulting increases in local population densities and the sizes of social units created an unprecedented variety of community configurations. In Long House Valley, a brief relaxation of environmental constraints after A.D. 1180 allowed a transitory settlement redispersal (Effland 1979). The respite was brief, however, and the renewal of low and high frequency stress after A.D. 1250 stimulated further behavioral adjustments.

The distinctive Tsegi phase settlement configurations are best explained as local organizational responses to population aggregations caused by the decreased amount of arable land and reduced rainfall. These changes undoubtedly led to competition for suitable farmland, and to the development of mechanisms for establishing and enforcing communities' claims to such resources. Whether this competition led to overt conflict (Haas 1986, 1989; Haas and Creamer 1993 and this volume, chapter 14) is debatable, but the increased potential for strife certainly would have affected Tsegi phase settlement. In addition, sharply increased local population densities and community sizes created a wide range of social problems relating to the allocation of resources (particularly farmland), coordination of activities, and resolution of disputes. The combination of internal social stress and competition, even conflict, with other groups probably was responsible for the hierarchical settlement configurations that developed throughout the area after A.D. 1250. Although resembling, on a much lower scale, the earlier Chacoan system, no evident connection can be made between the two.

Although the abandonment of a site or a region often is viewed as a "failure" of the social system, such is not always the case. Before the modern Pueblo communities were fixed in place by European colonial fiat, frequent movement was an integral component of Puebloan adaptive behavior, and these "sedentary" societies were characterized by a high degree of mobility. Within this context, the Kayenta Anasazi withdrawal from the San Juan drainage does not necessarily signify a failure of the Tsegi phase adaptive system. Rather, it probably represents the preservation of a threatened social system by transferring it to an area where environmental and social conditions allowed it to perpetuate itself (Dean 1966, 1969). The inability of the Tsegi phase system to survive conditions similar to those weathered by Pueblo I groups 400 years earlier probably is due to the greater population densities and more complex and rigid social arrangements of the later groups, which could not be sustained in the reduced post-A.D. 1250 environmental circumstances (Dean 1987). In order to maintain the complex social relationships that had evolved by the Tsegi phase, the system was moved to the Hopi Mesas area where unique environmental conditions favored agriculture during periods of depressed alluvial water tables and channel incision (Hack 1942). Other important factors in this transference were the ability of the Hopi area populations to absorb immigrants into the existing social system (Eggan 1950:123–33) and the development of novel socioreligious principles that promised greater social and environmental control (Adams 1991).

In conclusion, the sociocultural transformations that marked the transition from the dispersed Kayenta Pueblo II settlement pattern into the recognizably proto-Hopi configuration that prevailed in the middle Little Colorado River drainage after A.D. 1350 probably are not directly related to the rise and demise of the Chacoan regional system. This is not to say that, despite little direct evidence for Chacoan influence on the Kayenta Anasazi, the latter were totally unaffected by the eastern Anasazi colossus. It is obvious, however, that the Kayenta population as a whole was not stimulated to emulate (Renfrew and Cherry 1986) the eastern Anasazi groups. Nor does the Kayenta Pueblo II period dispersed settlement pattern seem to be a predictable response to aggressive recruitment or expansion by the Chacoan system. Rather, it seems more reasonable to infer that, for whatever reasons, the Chacoan regional system neither included nor greatly affected the Kayenta Anasazi. Kayenta sociocultural developments between A.D. 1150 and 1350 can best be understood in terms of the behavioral responses of a flexible, fairly simple society to two primary factors— steadily growing population and major low and high frequency environmental fluctuations—and a secondary factor—interactions with neighboring populations including the eastern Anasazi.

References Cited

Adams, E. Charles
    1989   The Homol'ovi Research Program. *Kiva* 54:175–94.
    1991   *The Origin and Development of the Pueblo Katsina Cult.* University of Arizona Press, Tucson.
Adams, E. Charles, and Kelley Ann Hays (editors)
    1991   *Homol'ovi II: Archaeology of an Ancestral Hopi Village, Arizona.* Anthropological Papers No. 55. University of Arizona Press, Tucson.
Adams, William Y., Alexander J. Lindsay, Jr., and Christy G. Turner II
    1961   *Survey and Excavations in Lower Glen Canyon, 1952–1958.* Bulletin No. 36. Museum of Northern Arizona, Flagstaff.
Ambler, J. Richard
    1983   Kayenta Craft Specialization and Social Differentiation. In *Proceedings of the Anasazi Symposium 1981*, edited by Jack E. Smith, pp. 75–82. Mesa Verde Museum Association, Mesa Verde National Park.
    1985a   *Navajo National Monument: An Archaeological Assessment.* Archaeological Series No. 1. Northern Arizona University, Flagstaff.
    1985b   Northern Kayenta Ceramic Chronology. In *Archaeological Investigations Near Rainbow City, Navajo Mountain, Utah*, edited by Phil R. Geib, J. Richard Ambler, and Martha M. Callahan, pp. 28–68. Archaeological Report No. 576. Northern Arizona University, Flagstaff.
Ambler, J. Richard, Helen C. Fairley, and Phil R. Geib
    1983   Kayenta Anasazi Utilization of Canyons and Plateaus in the Navajo Mountain District. Paper presented at the Second Anasazi Symposium, Bloomfield, New Mexico.
Ambler, J. Richard, Alexander J. Lindsay, Jr., and Mary Anne Stein
    1964   *Survey and Excavations on Cummings Mesa, Arizona and Utah, 1960–1961.* Bulletin No. 39. Museum of Northern Arizona, Flagstaff.
Ambler, J. Richard, and Alan P. Olson
    1977   *Salvage Archaeology in the Cow Springs Area.* Technical Series No. 15. Museum of Northern Arizona, Flagstaff.
Anderson, Keith M.
    1980   *Highway Salvage on Arizona State Highway 98: Kayenta Anasazi Sites Between Kaibito and the Klethla Valley.* Arizona State Museum Archaeological Series No. 140. University of Arizona, Tucson.
Bannister, Bryant, Jeffrey S. Dean, and William J. Robinson
    1968   *Tree-Ring Dates from Arizona C-D: Eastern Grand Canyon-Tsegi Canyon-Kayenta Area.* Laboratory of Tree-Ring Research, University of Arizona, Tucson.
Beals, Ralph L., George W. Brainerd, and Watson Smith
    1945   *Archaeological Studies in Northeast Arizona.* University of California Publications in American Archaeology and Ethnology, Vol. 44, No. 1. University of California Press, Berkeley and Los Angeles.
Biggs, Robert W.
    1967   Progress Report 1966 Excavations of Basket Maker II Sites North of Durango, Colorado. Ms. on file, Department of Anthropology, University of Colorado, Boulder.
Bliss, Wesley L.
    1960   Impact of Pipeline Archaeology on Indian Prehistory. *Plateau* 33(1): 10–13.
Breternitz, David A., Arthur H. Rohn, and Elizabeth A. Morris
    1974   *Prehistoric Ceramics of the Mesa Verde Region.* Ceramic Series No. 5. Museum of Northern Arizona, Flagstaff.
Brew, John Otis
    1937   The First Two Seasons at Awatovi. *American Antiquity* 3:122–37.
    1939   Preliminary Report of the Peabody Museum Awatovi Expedition of 1937. *American Antiquity* 5:103–114.
    1941   Preliminary Report of the Peabody Museum Awatovi Expedition of 1939. *Plateau* 13(3):37–48.
    1946   *Archaeology of Alkali Ridge, Southeastern Utah.* Papers of the Peabody Museum of American Archaeology and Ethnology Vol. 21. Harvard University, Cambridge.
Colton, Harold S.
    1955   *Pottery Types of the Southwest: Tusayan Gray and White Wares, Little Colorado Gray and White Wares; Wares 8A, 8B, 9A, 9B.* Ceramic Series No. 3A. Museum of Northern Arizona, Flagstaff.
    1956   *Pottery Types of the Southwest: San Juan Red, Tsegi Orange, Homolovi Orange, Winslow Orange, Awatovi Yellow, Jeddito Yellow, and Sichomovi Red Wares; Wares 5A, 5B, 6A, 6B 7A, 7B, 7C.* Ceramic Series No. 3C. Museum of Northern Arizona, Flagstaff.
Colton, Harold S., and Lyndon L. Hargrave
    1937   *Handbook of Northern Arizona Pottery Wares.* Bulletin No. 11. Museum of Northern Arizona, Flagstaff.
Daifuku, Hiroshi
    1961   *Jeddito 264: A Report on the Excavation of a Basket Maker III-Pueblo I Site in Northeastern Arizona With a Review of Some Current Theories in Southwestern Archaeology.* Reports of the Awatovi Expedition No. 7. Papers of the Peabody Museum of American Archaeology and Ethnology Vol. 33, No. 1. Harvard University, Cambridge.
Dean, Jeffrey S.
    1966   The Pueblo Abandonment of Tsegi Canyon, Northeastern Arizona. Paper presented at the 31st Annual Meeting of the Society for American Archaeology, Reno.
    1969   *Chronological Analysis of Tsegi Phase Sites in Northeastern Arizona.* Papers

of the Laboratory of Tree-Ring Research No. 3. University of Arizona Press, Tucson.

1970   Aspects of Tsegi Phase Social Organization: A Trial Reconstruction. In *Reconstructing Prehistoric Pueblo Societies*, edited by William A. Longacre, pp. 140–74. University of New Mexico Press, Albuquerque.

1984   Environmental Aspects of Modeling Human Activity-Locating Behavior. In *Theory and Model Building: Refining Survey Strategies for Locating Prehistoric Heritage Resources: Trial Formulations for Southwestern Forests*, edited by Linda S. Cordell and Dee F. Green, pp. 8–20. Cultural Resources Management Report No. 5. USDA, Forest Service, Southwest Region, Albuquerque.

1987   Prehistoric Behavioral Response to Abrupt Environmental Changes in Northeastern Arizona. Paper prepared for the Conference on Civilization and Rapid Climate Change, Calgary Institute for the Humanities, University of Calgary, Calgary.

1988   A Model of Anasazi Behavioral Adaptation. In *The Anasazi in a Changing Environment*, edited by George J. Gumerman, pp. 25–44. Cambridge University Press, Cambridge.

1990   Intensive Archaeological Survey of Long House Valley, Northeastern Arizona. In *The Archaeology of Regions: A Case for Full-Coverage Survey*, edited by Suzanne K. Fish and Stephen A. Kowalewski, pp. 173–88. Smithsonian Institution Press, Washington, D.C.

1991   Social Complexity and Environmental Variability in Northeastern Arizona. Paper presented at the 24th Chacmool Conference, Calgary.

1995   *Environmental Risk and Economic Response in the Prehistoric Southwest*, edited by Joseph A. Tainter and B. Bagley Tainter. Santa Fe Institute Studies in the Science of Complexity. Addison-Wesley, Reading, Massachusetts, in press.

Dean, Jeffrey S., Robert C. Euler, George J. Gumerman, Fred Plog, Richard H. Hevly, and Thor N. V. Karlstrom

1985   Human Behavior, Demography, and Paleoenvironment on the Colorado Plateaus. *American Antiquity* 50: 537–54.

Dean, Jeffrey S., and Alexander J. Lindsay, Jr.

1978   Special Use Sites in Long House Valley, Northeastern Arizona: An Analysis of the Southwestern Anthropological Research Group Data File. In *Limited Activity and Occupation Sites: A Collection of Conference Papers*, edited by Albert E. Ward, pp. 109–117. Contributions to Anthropological Studies No. 1. Center for Anthropological Studies, Albuquerque.

Dean, Jeffrey S., Alexander J. Lindsay, Jr., and William J. Robinson

1978   Prehistoric Settlement in Long House Valley, Northeastern Arizona. *In Investigations of the Southwestern Anthropological Research Group: An Experiment in Archaeological Cooperation: The Proceedings of the 1976 Conference*, edited by Robert C. Euler and George J. Gumerman, pp. 25–44. Museum of Northern Arizona, Flagstaff.

DiPeso, Charles C.

1958   *The Reeve Ruin of Southeastern Arizona: A Study of a Prehistoric Western Pueblo Migration Into the Middle San Pedro Valley*. Amerind Foundation Publication No. 8. Amerind Foundation, Dragoon, Arizona.

Eddy, Frank W.

1961   *Excavations at Los Pinos Phase Sites in the Navajo Reservoir District*. Papers in Anthropology No. 4. Museum of New Mexico, Santa Fe.

Effland, Richard Wayne, Jr.

1979   *A Study of Prehistoric Spatial Behavior: Long House Valley, Northeastern Arizona*. Ph.D dissertation, Arizona State University, Tempe. University Microfilms, Ann Arbor.

Eggan, Fred

1950   *Social Organization of the Western Pueblos*. University of Chicago Press, Chicago.

Euler, Robert C., George J. Gumerman, Thor N. V. Karlstrom, Jeffrey S. Dean, and Richard H. Hevly

1979   The Colorado Plateaus: Cultural Dynamics and Paleoenvironment. *Science* 205:1089–1101.

Fewkes, Jesse Walter

1911   *Antiquities of the Mesa Verde National Park: Cliff Palace*. Bureau of American Ethnology Bulletin 51. U.S. Government Printing Office, Washington, D.C.

Gaede, Marc, and Marnie Gaede

1977   100 Years of Erosion at Poncho House. *The Kiva* 43:37–48.

Geib, Phil R., and Martha M. Callahan

1987   Ceramic Exchange Within the Kayenta Anasazi Region: Volcanic Ash-Tempered Tusayan White Ware. *The Kiva* 52:95–112.

Gerald, Rex Ervin

1975   *Drought Correlated Change in Two Prehistoric Pueblo Communities in Southeastern Arizona*. Ph.D dissertation, Department of Anthropology, University of Chicago. University Microfilms, Ann Arbor.

Gilpin, Dennis

1989   Great Houses and Pueblos in Northeastern Arizona. Paper presented at the 1989 Pecos Conference, Bandelier National Monument.

Gould, Stephen Jay

1989   *Wonderful Life: The Burgess Shale and the Nature of History*. W. W. Norton, New York.

Green, Margerie, Keith Jacobi, Bruce Boeke, Helen L. O'Brien, Elizabeth S. Word, Richard L. Boston, Heather B. Trigg, Gilbert D. Glennie, and Melissa Gould

1985   Arizona D:11:2030. In *Excavations on Black Mesa, 1983: A Descriptive Report*, edited by Andrew L. Christenson and William J. Parry, pp. 223–59. Center for Archaeological Investigations Research Paper No. 46. Southern Illinois University, Carbondale.

Guernsey, Samuel James

1931   *Explorations in Northeastern Arizona: Report on the Archaeological Fieldwork of 1920–1923*. Papers of the Peabody Museum of American Archaeology and Ethnology Vol. 12, No. 1. Harvard University, Cambridge.

Guernsey, Samuel James, and Alfred Vincent Kidder

1921   *Basket-Maker Caves of Northeastern Arizona: Report on the Explorations, 1916–1917*. Papers of the Peabody Museum of American Archaeology and Ethnology Vol. 8, No. 2. Harvard University, Cambridge.

Gumerman, George J., and Jeffrey S. Dean

1989   Prehistoric Cooperation and Competition in the Western Anasazi Area. In *Dynamics of Southwest Prehistory*, edited by Linda S. Cordell and George J. Gumerman, pp. 99–148. Smithsonian Institution Press, Washington, D.C.

Haas, Jonathan
1986 The Evolution of the Kayenta Anasazi. In *Tsé Yaa Kin: Houses Beneath the Rock*, edited by David Grant Noble, pp. 14–23. Exploration. School of American Research, Santa Fe.
1989 The Evolution of the Kayenta Regional System. In *The Sociopolitical Structure of Prehistoric Southwestern Societies*, edited by Steadman Upham, Kent G. Lightfoot, and Roberta A. Jewett, pp. 491–508. Westview Press, Boulder.

Haas, Jonathan, and Winifred Creamer
1993 Stress and Warfare Among the Kayenta Anasazi of the Thirteenth Century A.D. *Fieldiana: Anthropology* n.s. 21. Field Museum of Natural History, Chicago.

Hack, John T.
1942 *The Changing Physical Environment of the Hopi Indians of Arizona.* Reports of the Awatovi Expedition No. 1. Papers of the Peabody Museum of American Archaeology and Ethnology Vol. 35, No. 1. Harvard University, Cambridge.

Harlan, Thomas P., and Jeffrey S. Dean
1968 Tree-Ring Data for Several Navajo Mountain Region Sites. In *Survey and Excavations North and East of Navajo Mountain, Utah, 1959–1962*, by Alexander J. Lindsay, Jr., J. Richard Ambler, Mary Anne Stein, and Philip M. Hobler, pp. 379–82. Bulletin No. 45. Museum of Northern Arizona, Flagstaff.

Harrill, Bruce Gilbert
1982 *Prehistoric Agricultural Adaptation and Settlement in Long House Valley, Northeastern Arizona.* Ph.D. dissertation, Department of Anthropology, University of Arizona, Tucson. University Microfilms, Ann Arbor.

Haury, Emil W.
1928 *The Succession of House Types in the Pueblo Area.* Unpublished Master's thesis, University of Arizona, Tucson.
1931 Kivas of the Tusayan Ruin, Grand Canyon, Arizona. *Medallion Papers* No. 9. Gila Pueblo, Globe, Arizona.
1945 *Painted Cave, Northeastern Arizona.* Amerind Foundation Publication No. 3. Amerind Foundation, Dragoon, Arizona.
1958 Evidence at Point of Pines for a Prehistoric Migration from Northern Arizona. In *Migrations in New World Culture History*, edited by Ray-

mond H. Thompson, pp. 1–6. Social Science Bulletin, no. 27. University of Arizona Press, Tucson.

Hawley, Florence M.
1950 *Field Manual of Prehistoric Southwestern Pottery Types* (revised edition). University of New Mexico Bulletin, Anthropology Series, Vol. 1, No. 4. University of New Mexico, Albuquerque.

Hays, Kelley Ann, E. Charles Adams, and Richard C. Lange
1991 Regional Prehistory and Research. In *Homol'ovi II: Archaeology of an Ancestral Hopi Village, Arizona*, edited by E. Charles Adams and Kelley Ann Hays, pp. 1–9. Anthropological Papers No. 55. University of Arizona Press, Tucson.

Hobler, Philip M.
1974 The Late Survival of Pithouse Architecture in the Kayenta Anasazi Area. *Southwestern Lore* 40(1):1–44.

Kidder, Alfred Vincent
1917 Prehistoric Cultures of the San Juan Drainage. *Proceedings of the Nineteenth International Congress of Americanists Held at Washington, D.C., December 27–31, 1915*, edited by F. W. Hodge, pp. 108–113. Washington, D.C.
1924 *An Introduction to the Study of Southwestern Archaeology, with a Preliminary Account of the Excavations at Pecos.* Papers of the Phillips Academy Southwestern Expedition No. 1. Yale University Press, New Haven.

Kidder, Alfred Vincent, and Samuel James Guernsey
1919 *Archaeological Explorations in Northeastern Arizona.* Bureau of American Ethnology Bulletin 65. U.S. Government Printing Office, Washington, D.C.

Klesert, Anthony
1982 Standing Fall House: An Early Puebloan Storage and Redistribution Center in Northeastern Arizona. *The Kiva* 48:39–61.

Lindsay, Alexander J., Jr.
1969 *The Tsegi Phase of the Kayenta Cultural Tradition in Northeastern Arizona.* Ph.D dissertation, University of Arizona, Tucson. University Microfilms, Ann Arbor.
1987 Anasazi Population Movements to Southeastern Arizona. *American Archaeology* 6:190–98.

1992 Tucson Polychrome: History, Dating, Distribution, and Design. In *Proceedings of the Second Salado Conference*, edited by Richard C. Lange and Stephen Germick, pp. 230–37. Occasional Paper 1992. Arizona Archaeological Society, Phoenix.

Lindsay, Alexander J., Jr., J. Richard Ambler, Mary Anne Stein, and Philip M. Hobler
1968 *Survey and Excavations North and East of Navajo Mountain, Utah, 1959–1962.* Bulletin No. 45. Museum of Northern Arizona, Flagstaff.

Linford, Laurence D. (editor and assembler)
1982 *Kayenta Anasazi Archaeology on Central Black Mesa, Northeastern Arizona: The Piñon Project.* Papers in Anthropology No. 10. Navajo Nation Cultural Resource Management Program, Window Rock, Arizona.

Lipe, William D., and Stephen H. Lekson
1989 Pueblo Cultures in Transition: A.D. 1150–1350 in the American Southwest. Application for Conference Award to the Wenner-Gren Foundation for Anthropological Research by Crow Canyon Archaeological Center, Cortez.
1990 Southwestern Pueblo Cultures in Transition: Report of a Conference. Paper presented at the 55th Annual Meeting of the Society for American Archaeology, Las Vegas, Nevada.

Lister, Robert H.
1959 *The Coombs Site.* Anthropological Papers No. 41. University of Utah Press, Salt Lake City.

Lockett, H. Claiborne, and Lyndon L. Hargrave
1953 *Woodchuck Cave: A Basketmaker II Site in Tsegi Canyon, Arizona*, edited by Harold S. Colton and Robert C. Euler. Bulletin No. 26. Museum of Northern Arizona, Flagstaff.

Long, Paul V., Jr.
1966 *Archaeological Excavations in Lower Glen Canyon, Utah, 1959–1960.* Bulletin No. 42. Museum of Northern Arizona, Flagstaff.

Matson, R. G.
1991 *The Origins of Southwestern Agriculture.* University of Arizona Press, Tucson.

Matson, R. G., William D. Lipe, and William R. Haase IV
1988 Adaptational Continuities and Occupational Discontinuities: The Cedar Mesa Anasazi. *Journal of Field Archaeology* 15:245–64.

Morris, Ann Axtell
  1934   *Digging in the Southwest*. Doubleday, Doran, New York.
Morris, Earl H.
  1925   Exploring in the Canyon of Death. *National Geographic Magazine* 48: 291–300.
Morris, Earl H., and Robert F. Burgh
  1954   *Basket Maker II Sites Near Durango, Colorado*. Publication 604. Carnegie Institution of Washington, Washington, D.C.
Morss, Noel
  1927   *Archaeological Explorations on the Middle Chinlee, 1925*. Memoirs No. 34. American Anthropological Association, Menasha, Wisconsin.
Neely, James A., and Alan P. Olson
  1977   *Archaeological Reconnaissance of Monument Valley in Northeastern Arizona*. Anthropology Research Report No. 3. Museum of Northern Arizona, Flagstaff.
Neitzel, Jill E.
  1994   Boundary Dynamics in the Chacoan Regional System. In *The Ancient Southwestern Community: Models and Methods for the Study of Prehistoric Social Organization*, edited by Wirt W. Wills and Robert D. Leonard, pp. 209–240. University of New Mexico Press, Albuquerque.
Neitzel, Jill E., and Ronald L. Bishop
  1990   Neutron Activation of Dogoszhi Style Ceramics: Production and Exchange in the Chacoan Regional System. *Kiva* 56:67–85.
Nichols, Deborah L., and F. E. Smiley
  1985   An Overview of Northern Black Mesa Archaeology. In *Excavations on Black Mesa, 1983: A Descriptive Report*, edited by Andrew L. Christenson and William J. Parry, pp. 49–81. Center for Archaeological Investigations Research Paper No. 46. Southern Illinois University, Carbondale.
Pepper, George H
  1902   The Ancient Basket Makers of Southeastern Utah. *American Museum Journal* 2(4) supplement: 1–26.
Plog, Fred, George J. Gumerman, Robert C. Euler, Jeffrey S. Dean, Richard H. Hevly, and Thor N. V. Karlstrom
  1988   Anasazi Adaptive Strategies: The Model, Predictions, and Results. In *The Anasazi in a Changing Environment*, edited by George J.

Gumerman, pp. 230–76. Cambridge University Press, Cambridge.
Prudden, T. Mitchell
  1897   An Elder Brother to the Cliff-Dwellers. *Harper's New Monthly Magazine* 95:56–62.
  1903   The Prehistoric Ruins of the San Juan Watershed in Utah, Arizona, Colorado, and New Mexico. *American Anthropologist* 5:224–88.
Reed, Erik K.
  1958   Comment on "Evidence at Point of Pines for a Prehistoric Migration from Northern Arizona" by Emil W. Haury. In *Migrations in New World Culture History*, edited by Raymond H. Thompson, pp. 7–8. Social Science Bulletin No. 27. University of Arizona, Tucson.
Renfrew, Colin, and John F. Cherry (editors)
  1986   *Peer Polity Interaction and Socio-Political Change*. Cambridge University Press, Cambridge.
Rohn, Arthur H.
  1965   Postulation of Socio-Economic Groups from Archaeological Evidence. In *Contributions of the Wetherill Mesa Archeological Project*, assembled by Douglas Osborne, pp. 65–69. Memoirs No. 19. Society for American Archaeology, Salt Lake City.
  1989   Northern San Juan Prehistory. In *Dynamics of Southwest Prehistory*, edited by Linda S. Cordell and George J. Gumerman, pp. 149–77. Smithsonian Institution Press, Washington, D.C.
Sebastian, Lynn
  1985   *Archeological Excavation along the Turquoise Trail: The Mitigation Program*. Office of Contract Archeology, University of New Mexico. Albuquerque.
Smiley, Francis Edward, IV
  1985   *The Chronometrics of Early Agricultural Sites in Northeastern Arizona: Approaches to the Interpretation of Radiocarbon Dates*. Ph.D dissertation, Department of Anthropology, University of Michigan, Ann Arbor. University Microfilms, Ann Arbor.
  1993   Early Farmers in the Northern Southwest: A View from Marsh Pass. In *Anasazi Basketmaker: Papers from the 1990 Wetherill-Grand Gulch Symposium*, edited by V. M. Atkins, pp. 243–54. Cultural Resource Series No. 24. USDI, Bureau of Land Management, Salt Lake City.

Smiley, F. E., IV, William J. Parry, and George J. Gumerman
  1986   Early Agriculture in the Black Mesa/Marsh Pass Region of Arizona: New Chronometric Data and Recent Excavations at Three Fir Shelter. Paper presented at the 51st Annual Meeting of the Society for American Archaeology, New Orleans.
Smith, Watson
  1952a   *Excavations in Big Hawk Valley, Wupatki National Monument, Arizona*. Bulletin No. 24. Museum of Northern Arizona, Flagstaff.
  1952b   *Kiva Mural Decorations at Awatovi and Kawaika'a With a Survey of Other Wall Paintings in the Pueblo Southwest*. Reports of the Awatovi Expedition, No. 5. Papers of the Peabody Museum of American Archaeology and Ethnology Vol. 37. Harvard University, Cambridge.
  1962   Schools, Pots, and Potters. *American Anthropologist* 64:1165–78.
  1971   *Painted Ceramics of the Western Mound at Awatovi*. Papers of the Peabody Museum of American Archaeology and Ethnology Vol. 38. Harvard University, Cambridge.
  1972   *Prehistoric Kivas of Antelope Mesa, Northeastern Arizona*. Reports of the Awatovi Expedition, No. 9. Papers of the Peabody Museum of American Archaeology and Ethnology Vol. 39, No. 1. Harvard University, Cambridge.
  1992   One Man's Archæology. *Kiva* 57: 101–191.
Stein, John R.
  1989   The Chaco Roads: Clues to an Ancient Riddle? *El Palacio* 94(3): 4–17.
Stein, Mary Anne
  1984   *Pottery Pueblo: A Tsegi Phase Village on Paiute Mesa, Utah*. Ph.D dissertation, Department of Anthropology, Southern Methodist University, Dallas. University Microfilms, Ann Arbor.
Taylor, Walter W.
  1954   An Early Slabhouse Near Kayenta, Arizona. *Plateau* 26:109–116.
Vivian, R. Gwinn
  1970   An Inquiry into Prehistoric Social Organization in Chaco Canyon, New Mexico. In *Reconstructing Prehistoric Pueblo Societies*, edited by William A. Longacre, pp. 59–83. University of New Mexico Press, Albuquerque.

1990   *The Chacoan Prehistory of the San Juan Basin*. Academic Press, San Diego.

Wasley, William W.

1962   A Ceremonial Cave on Bonita Creek, Arizona. *American Antiquity* 27: 380–94.

Wendorf, Fred

1956   Some Distributions of Settlement Patterns in the Pueblo Southwest. In *Prehistoric Settlement Patterns in the New World*, edited by Gordon R. Willey, pp. 18–25. Viking Fund Publications in Anthropology No. 23. New York.

Chapter 4

The Pueblo III–Pueblo IV Transition in the Hopi Area, Arizona

E. Charles Adams

For the purposes of this chapter, the Hopi area is defined as bounded by the Little Colorado River Valley on the south and west, southern Black Mesa and the Moen-kopi Wash area on the north, and the Hopi Buttes on the east (figure 4.1). This 6,300 mi² (16,320 km²) area has been divided into four districts based on per-ceived differences in land use and occu-pation between A.D. 1150 and 1350. These districts are: the Middle Little Colorado River, Hopi Mesas, Moenkopi, and the Hopi Buttes (figure 4.1). Together these four areas comprise less than half (44 per-cent) of the Hopi area. The remainder is either poorly documented from an ar-chaeological standpoint or was virtually unoccupied during the 200-year period of interest. For example, the 30-mile-wide strip east of the Little Colorado River ap-pears to have been used only seasonally after A.D. 1150.

Taken as a whole the Hopi area, with the exception of southern Black Mesa, falls into the Great Basin Desert Grassland province of the Upper Sonoran Life Zone (Gumerman 1969). Elevation ranges from 1,220 meters at the confluence of Moen-kopi Wash with the Little Colorado River, to 2,134 meters on Black Mesa. Precipita-tion and vegetation are strongly correlated with elevation. Along the Little Colorado River precipitation ranges from 5.9 to 8.8 inches (150–225 mm) per annum rising to over 11.8 inches (300 mm) per annum on southern Black Mesa. In the vicinity of the Hopi villages annual precipitation ranges from 8.8 inches (225 mm) on Third Mesa to 10.8 inches (275 mm) on Antelope Mesa (Adams 1979). Thus, arid desert condi-tions prevail over much of the area, giving way to semiarid conditions on Black Mesa

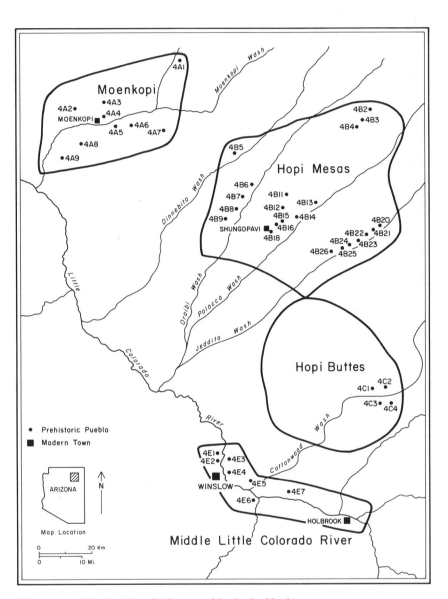

Figure 4.1. Site locations for large pueblos in the Hopi area.

and the eastern Hopi Buttes. In western parts of the area trees occur only along major water courses, such as the Little Colorado River, where cottonwood is the most common type. In contrast, juniper ranges from sparse to dominant on the

mesas in the Hopi Buttes and on top of Black Mesa.

Where such arid conditions prevail, arable land gives way to water as the most critical resource. Springs are com-mon throughout the area and dictated prehistoric habitation site locations in the Moenkopi, Hopi Mesa, and Hopi Buttes districts. Moenkopi Wash and the Little Colorado River provide linear water sources that supersede nearby springs in settlement preference.

Several authors in this volume discuss the influences of Chaco culture on Puebloan populations succeeding the demise of this regional system about A.D. 1150. At present no Chaco-style great houses, great kivas, or descendent architecture are known in the Hopi area as defined in this chapter, although several Chaco or post-Chaco sites are discussed by Stein and Fowler (chapter 8) in the Pueblo Colorado and related drainages just east of the Hopi Mesas. It seems likely that eleventh- or twelfth-century occupants of the Hopi area were at least aware of, if not marginal participants in, the Chaco regional system. The minimal participation by residents of the Hopi area in the Chaco system may have been due to the area's aridity and resultant marginal productivity and low population. Although occupants of the Hopi area seem to have been little affected by prehistoric events to the east, they were profoundly influenced by events of the late thirteenth century, also known as the Great Drought. The exact cause or causes of the abandonment of the Four Corners region by the Anasazi around A.D. 1275 to 1300 is beyond the scope of this chapter (see Van West, chapter 15), but the impacts of the resulting emigration on the Hopi area occupants are undeniable. Colton (1974) and I (Adams 1981, 1985) have detailed the settlement changes in the Hopi district in the late thirteenth century A.D., and Gumerman (1988) and I (Adams 1989b) have discussed these changes for the Hopi Buttes and the middle Little Colorado River (Homol'ovi) areas.

The Hopi Mesas and Homol'ovi districts were apparent recipients of immigrants, a phenomenon that caused local populations to increase substantially. This resulted in the establishment of new settlements, the several-fold increase in size of existing settlements, and the reconfigura-

Table 4.1 Chronological Chart for the Hopi Area by District.

	Middle Little Colorado River	Hopi Mesas	Moenkopi Wash	Hopi Buttes
1400	--------	--------	--------	--------
			Jeddito	
1350	Homol'ovi	Jeddito	--------	Pueblo IV
1300	--------	--------	unoccupied	--------
	Tuwiuca	Huckovi		unoccupied?
1260	--------			
1250	unoccupied?	--------		
1225	--------			
1200		Tusayan	Klethla	McDonald
	McDonald			
1150	--------	--------	--------	--------

tion of settlement layouts. The organizational requirements needed to cope with these changes are considered in the conclusions to this chapter. The prehistoric use and occupation of each of the four districts are next considered in some detail before moving on to a synthetic treatment of the area and interpretation of the database.

Middle Little Colorado River Valley District

The settlement and culture history of this area have recently been summarized by Lange (1989), Adams (1989b), Adams and Hays (1991), and Adams, Stark, and Dosh (1993) under the auspices of the Homol'ovi Research Program (HRP), Arizona State Museum (appendix and table 4.1). Extrapolation from the 15.4 mi[2] (40 km[2]) data set of HRP to the broader area on the map bears some risks. Within the area dominated by the river environment, an area with low annual precipitation (<9.8 in [250 mm]), a paucity of wood, and almost no arable land on sur-

rounding mesa tops, the pattern found by HRP should hold, as discussed later.

The area was sparsely settled between A.D. 1100 and 1225–1250 (Pueblo III period) by small groups of people occupying pit house settlements on gravel terraces overlooking the Middle Little Colorado River. Establishing contemporaneity of pit house occupation is difficult and cannot be dealt with in any detail. Ceramic assemblages associated with the pit house settlements in the Middle Little Colorado River district are dominated by Walnut Black-on-white, which has been variously dated at A.D. 1070–1160 to 1200–1250 (Colton and Hargrave 1937; Douglass 1988; Downum and Sullivan 1990; Wood 1987). Dates of A.D. 1130 to 1225 are used here as a compromise that best reflects tree-ring dated proveniences. The pit house settlements were hamlet-size (less than 30 pit houses), each containing 10 to 20 pit houses. Tree-ring dated pottery, superposition of structures and trash, and radiocarbon dates indicate these terrace settlements were occupied intermittently during the Pueblo III period. Given that occupation of individual pit houses is typically 10 to 20 years (Ahlstrom 1985), I assume less than half of the pit houses were occupied at any one time.

Subsurface information on this occupation is best understood from AZ J:14:36 (ASM), a pit house hamlet excavated by Lisa C. Young in 1987, 1988, and 1990 (Young 1989, 1990). At AZ J:14:36, three late pit structures and numerous other features were excavated (figure 4.2). Two jacal surface rooms associated with this occupation were also documented and tested. Two of the pit houses were small, deep, rectangular structures about 2.5 m on a side and 1.5 m deep. Notable features included a rectangular, stone-lined hearth and a ventilator system. One nonresidential pit structure was partly excavated. It was a 15 m-wide, 1 m-deep, circular structure, probably unroofed when in use (Young 1989). A similar structure, in the form of an equally large depression, was present in an adjacent hamlet believed to be contemporaneous with the occupation of AZ J:14:36. This suggests that the large pit structures may not have been intervillage, but rather were intravillage, integrative structures. It is equally plausible that the structures were not in use at the same time.

Settlement was concentrated along the river. It was sparse, dispersed, and could have been seasonal, based on the pit house architecture. Consequently, total population and population density were very low. No Pueblo III settlements are known in this area that even approach 50 rooms or the equivalent in pit houses. More work might reveal settlement "clusters," however, that are equivalent to 50-room pueblos. For example, the six settlements recorded in the Homol'ovi study area are clustered because of the patchy nature of resources in the area, and could comprise 20 to 50 pit houses. The population estimate for the 15.4 mi² (40 km²) Homol'ovi area (given five individuals per pit structure) could range up to just over five persons per square mile (two people per square kilometer); however, given the

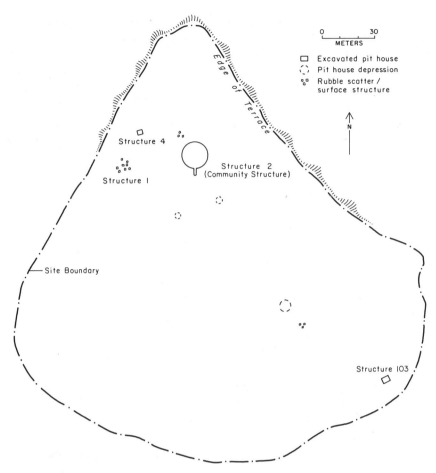

Figure 4.2.   Plan view of AZ J:14:36 (ASM), a Pueblo III pit house hamlet typical of the Middle Little Colorado River district.

short duration of pit house occupation, population density was probably less than three persons per square mile (one person per square kilometer).

These trends changed substantially between A.D. 1260 and 1280. The area seems to have been abandoned by the pit house occupants, but even if there was a small indigenous population, it was overwhelmed by immigrants from the north, southeast, and possibly southwest based on the sudden influx of nonlocal ceramics and architectural forms, as well as new settlement configurations. These settlers built large, aggregated pueblos. Homol'ovi IV was the first to be established and was occupied between about A.D. 1260 and 1280. This 150-room settlement was built by immigrants from the Hopi Mesas or Hopi Buttes areas. Homol'ovi III, dating between A.D. 1280 and 1300, had a great

kiva for a settlement of about 50 rooms. This and other contemporary settlements at Homol'ovi I, Chevelon, Jackrabbit, and Cottonwood Creek appear to have been constructed by immigrants from the upper Little Colorado region. Continued aggregation after A.D. 1300 at Homol'ovi I, Chevelon, Cottonwood Creek, and Jackrabbit resulted in agglomerated, multistory pueblos surrounding small, interior plazas. All of the settlements are located along the river (appendix and figure 4.1).

Founded after A.D. 1330, Homol'ovi II has over 1,000 rooms, whereas Homol'ovi I and Chevelon are each about half this size (figure 4.3). The existence of a single large pueblo that was twice the size of any other may signal its political dominance over the others. The Homol'ovi II occupants were almost certainly immigrants from the Hopi Mesas, possibly from Antelope

Mesa, as inferred from neutron activation analysis source characterization of Hopi yellow ware pottery (Bishop et al. 1988). With the arrival of the Homol'ovi II occupants there is a shift in the ceramic signature of the area from locally produced Winslow Orange Wares and traded White Mountain Red Wares to Jeddito Yellow Wares. Thus, the construction of Homol'ovi II probably represents a shift in political control of the Homol'ovi area from one directed from the southeast in the vicinity of the upper Little Colorado River villages to one directed from the north in the vicinity of the Hopi Mesa villages. The area was abandoned between A.D. 1400 and 1425.

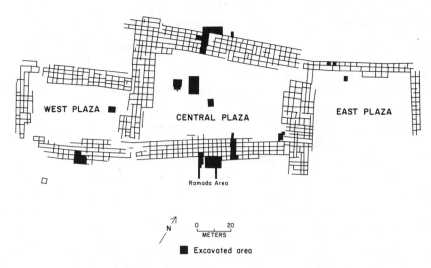

Figure 4.3. Plan view of Homol'ovi II (AZ J:14:14 (ASM)), a large Pueblo IV plaza-oriented pueblo in the Middle Little Colorado River district.

Hopi Mesas District

The archaeology of this district has been summarized by Adams (1981), Brew (1979), Colton (1974), and Ellis (1974). Three sites in this area, Blue Gap, Kiit Siili, and Lamb Springs, have been termed "Tsegi great houses" by Gilpin (1989). But the first two have 21 and 10 rooms, respectively, making them too small for this database, and neither has evidence of a great kiva or interior or enclosed plaza. Although Lamb Springs has a plaza, its attribution as a great house can also be questioned. The term "Tsegi great house" is a misnomer because the Tsegi phase postdates great house architecture by a century. Great kivas were not present in the Hopi Mesas district and it is questionable whether great houses were ever present; however, the Tse Chizzi great house is just under 13 miles (20 km) from the Jeddito Valley pueblos, suggesting close proximity between the western margins of the Chaco regional system and the Hopi Mesas district (Gilpin 1989).

Settlement between A.D. 1100 and 1250 was generally dispersed along major drainages or mesa edges near springs. The four largest settlements dating to this period contain between 40 and 100 rooms. All had associated open spaces, but none had enclosed plazas as large or formalized as those in the later settlements. Probably 90 percent or more of the population continued to reside in various settlement types equivalent to 10- to 20-room pueblos.

After A.D. 1250 (but possibly as early as A.D. 1200) this pattern changed. The upland areas were abandoned and populations aggregated into villages on the four mesas where the historic Hopi villages are located. By A.D. 1300 most of the villages had over 100 rooms and Awatovi possibly had 300 (appendix and figure 4.1).

Population and aggregation in these Hopi villages increased rapidly during the "Great Drought" period (A.D. 1275–1300). Fourteen settlements were established during the last few decades of the thirteenth century, with 12 surviving to about A.D. 1400, and 9 past A.D. 1400 (Adams, Stark, and Dosh 1993; Colton 1974). By A.D. 1350 village sizes ranged from 100 to 800 rooms, with the largest being Awatovi. The 14 settlements averaged 250 rooms, although fourteenth-century settlement size is difficult to estimate because of the lengthy occupation of many of the pueblos (appendix). The distribution of the seven largest settlements, each having 400 to 800 rooms, is interesting; two each were present at Antelope, First, and Second Mesas, and one was present at Third Mesa (Adams, Stark, and Dosh 1993). Awatovi and Oraibi were the largest settlements during the thirteenth and fourteenth centuries.

A study of settlement layout within the large villages reveals a pattern first noticed at Homol'ovi. That is, a large aggregated room block was established at most villages (e.g., Awatovi, Kawaika-a, Sikyatki) between A.D. 1250 and 1300. A plaza was added by the beginning of the fourteenth century or a little later. A second influx of people occurred between A.D. 1350 and 1400 at which time the original pueblo was sometimes abandoned and multiple plaza settlements, bordered by room blocks on three to four sides, replaced it. The early fourteenth-century pueblos were probably half the size of the later occupations at these sites. For example, the western mound at Awatovi contained about 300 rooms and this was replaced by a settlement estimated at 800 rooms. Thus, the relatively dispersed settlement pattern that characterized the area before A.D. 1250 was replaced by an aggregated pattern between A.D. 1250 and 1350 which in turn was superseded by a highly aggregated, even nucleated, pattern sometime after A.D. 1350. Of the four districts discussed here, the Hopi Mesas district was the only one populated by Pueblo people much after A.D. 1400.

Moenkopi District

The settlement pattern in the Moenkopi district was partially documented by Colton during his Museum of Northern Arizona surveys when he recorded Old Moenkopi and Posewlelena (figure 4.1). The remaining pattern was recorded by Adams (1989d) in conjunction with work done for a Navajo-Hopi Land Claims Case.

Between A.D. 1100 and 1250, settlement was highly dispersed into small pueblos of 10 to 35 rooms (table 4.1). No great house architecture is known or expected. Settlements were closely associated with springs or seasonal water sources. Whether some of these sites were seasonal cannot be known without some excavation. In comparison to the other districts, perhaps excepting the Hopi Buttes, population density was very low, certainly less than one person per square kilometer. On the basis of incomplete data, settlements appear to have been separated by distances of at least 3 miles (5 km). By A.D. 1250 year-round Pueblo occupation of the area had ceased, and the district may have had only seasonal use until the 1870s. It is possible that Old Moenkopi, which was established by A.D. 1400, had permanent occupants, but such was not the case when the settlement was visited by historic Spanish, Mexican, and U.S. groups in the eighteenth and nineteenth centuries. The district certainly constituted part of the Hopi sustaining area, probably from A.D. 1250 on.

Hopi Buttes District

The present understanding of Hopi Buttes district occupation is still based on Gumerman's earlier work (1969) and his recent update (1988). In the area where Gumerman focused his research, Pueblo III (A.D. 1100–1250) occupation was highly dispersed and consisted of small settlements containing ten or fewer rooms (appendix and table 4.1). The Plaza site, which Gilpin (1989) calls a "Hopi Butte great house," consisted of seven rooms, a rectangular great kiva, and a second smaller kiva. This site was probably a ritual center for the dispersed local population, but it is unlikely it functioned as a great house within the Chaco regional system. The Plaza site is not included in the database list.

Outside Gumerman's area, Hough (1903) and Gilpin (1989) have documented other large settlements. One, Malpais Springs, is also termed a "Hopi Butte great house" by Gilpin and consists of 36 rooms dispersed in several units over a mesa top. Whether Malpais Springs participated in any Chaco regional system is highly problematical, although it was contemporary with other great houses. It is unlikely that either Malpais Springs or the Plaza site were Chaco great houses or functioned in that role in the Chaco regional system.

Because of poor survey coverage, I can only suggest that aggregation occurred after A.D. 1250 in the eastern Hopi Buttes area. The site of Bidahochi Southwest dates between A.D. 1250 and 1300 and contained at least 100 rooms (see appendix). Other comparable sites may also be in the area. Only two sites are known to date after A.D. 1300, Bidahochi and Bidahochi Southeast (see appendix). Both villages had enclosed plazas, with Bidahochi likely containing twice the number of rooms as Bidahochi Southeast.

Settlements in the western Hopi Buttes district were highly dispersed because of the aridity of the land and paucity of water, which occurred only as springs. The eastern Hopi Buttes were better watered, especially along the lower Pueblo Colorado-Cottonwood Wash, where the large pueblos are located. Site placement was dictated by the location of springs and arable land conducive to runoff farming.

After A.D. 1250, the western buttes were abandoned and population seems to have aggregated into larger villages in the eastern buttes. Population in the western area peaked about A.D. 1200, according to Gumerman (1988). Though available data allow only an educated guess at this point, it appears that Eastern Buttes population peaked in the thirteenth or early fourteenth century.

Discussion

In the foregoing discussion I highlighted several patterns of settlement in the Hopi area. These include: (1) the use of great kivas as integrative devices in the southern and eastern parts of the area from A.D. 1100 to 1300; (2) a trend toward aggregation between A.D. 1200 and 1300 that accelerates in the fourteenth century; (3) the replacement of great kivas and generalized establishment of plaza-oriented villages after A.D. 1200 to 1250 with enclosed plazas postdating A.D. 1250 to 1300; and (4) possible settlement hierarchy, with one or more smaller sites associated with each large settlement. These large settlements may prove to have been central places within the various Hopi area districts. District-level central places after A.D. 1250 include Homol'ovi II for the Middle Little Colorado River, Bidahochi for the Hopi Buttes, and Awatovi in the Hopi Mesas area (although each mesa may have had its own central place—Koechaptevela/Sikyatki, Old Shungopavi, and Oraibi). Settlement in the Moenkopi district was too sparse and poorly known to detect a central place, if one existed.

Patterns of contact, alliance, and exchange have been discussed with respect to the great house phenomena (A.D. 1050–1150) by Lekson et al. (1988) and Gilpin (1989) and for the Pueblo IV period (A.D. 1275–1400) by Adams (1985) and Adams, Stark, and Dosh (1993). The period A.D. 1125–1150 to 1250–1275 is less well understood and is probably critical as a transition between the great house and Pueblo IV patterns (cf. Kintigh 1990).

The work on the great houses suggests that the Puerco River and Pueblo Colorado districts east of the Hopi area were linked to the Chaco regional system (Gilpin 1989). The four districts in the Hopi area appear to lie outside this system, although their occupants must have been aware of, and possibly in contact with, the participants in the regional system. During the heyday of great house construction (A.D. 1050–1150), the Little Colorado, Hopi Buttes, and Moenkopi districts were all sparsely occupied by a residentially dispersed population, although the presence of a major watercourse dictated a somewhat linear settlement grouping in the Little Colorado district. The Hopi Mesas district had several smaller pueblos comparable in size to the great houses but not visibly involved in the great house system.

In the San Juan Basin and its upland peripheries the great houses seem to have encouraged, inspired, or stimulated settlement clustering (see Stein and Fowler, chapter 8). Although the great houses themselves were generally under 50 rooms, they usually were located at the center of dispersed communities that contained populations several times larger than the potential resident population at the great house. Perhaps herein lay the seeds for later aggregation.

The enclosed plaza settlement pattern that characterizes post-A.D. 1250 sites is not obviously related to the great house sites or particularly to late twelfth-or early thirteenth-century settlement patterns in the Hopi area. Elsewhere (Adams 1991) I have argued that enclosed plazas are a southern pattern and are not indigenous to the area. In the Mogollon area during the twelfth and thirteenth centuries, enclosed plazas replaced great kivas. The post-A.D. 1300 sites in the Little Colorado, Hopi Buttes, and Hopi Mesas districts all had enclosed plazas. Detailed studies of plaza construction and use at Hopi and Homol'ovi indicate the enclosed plazas were additions to existing room aggregates. This suggests that the concept of enclosed plazas as integrative structures had become part of the organizational fabric of the Hopi area. These enclosed plazas replaced great kivas, based on the twelfth- and thirteenth-century Mogollon patterns. The enclosed plaza pattern is clearly related to the ability of post-A.D. 1250 settlements to sustain population aggregation.

A great deal of change is evident in the settlement patterns of groups occupying the Hopi area between A.D. 1150 and 1350. In every district but the Hopi Mesas, mid-twelfth century settlement patterns consisted of dispersed habitation sites focused on water sources. These settlements were short-lived, having slight to moderate accumulations of trash, with low resident populations. Settlements averaged about five households, based on data gathered from pit house-dominated occupations in the Hopi Buttes and Middle Little Colorado River Valley districts. Small pueblos averaging 20 rooms characterize the Moenkopi area and would also have housed about five households. Populations of 25 to 50 people per habitation settlement were typical. Clearly, such a small population could not be sustained without interactions with neighboring settlements, involving exchange, marriage, and other interdependent relationships.

Incomplete data from the Moenkopi district suggest a spacing of 3 miles (5 km) or more between settlements. No intervillage integrative structures are visible in the architecture. This is not the case in the Hopi Buttes area, where the Plaza site has been postulated by Gumerman (1969) and Gumerman and Skinner (1968) as an integrative center for locally dispersed communities. Both a great kiva and a plaza-like area enclosed by a wall were present. In the Homol'ovi area, AZ J:14:36 (Young 1989) had a large circular structure that probably served as a community or intersite integrative structure.

Neither the Plaza site nor AZ J:14:36 resemble great houses or Chaco-inspired sites that have commonly been termed "outliers." Integrative structures were present in the Anasazi and Mogollon areas as early as late Basketmaker period (A.D. 600–700) and there is no need to invoke the Chaco integrative system to explain their presence after A.D. 1150 in the Hopi area.

By the mid-thirteenth century the Hopi Mesas area had numerous small pueblos. Although pueblos with integrative archi-

tecture would be expected in such a dispersed settlement pattern, none have been recorded. This is noteworthy because the Tse Chizzi great house, which has two associated great kivas and was presumably established about A.D. 1100, is only 7.7 miles (12.3 km) from the Jeddito Valley pueblos and 18.8 miles (30 km) from those on First Mesa. It is possible, therefore, that one or more of the large pueblos at the Hopi Mesas is built over a great house or similar integrative structure.

It is also possible that the Hopi pueblos lay outside the Chaco system or were organized into a competing system. An enormous amount of research needs to be completed before an effective argument can be mustered to support any organizational claim. Given the temporal depth and the spatial breadth of great kivas in the region, it seems likely that these and other integrative facilities played a part in the organization of twelfth-century communities on the Hopi Mesas.

Changes that began sweeping across the Anasazi world between A.D. 1150 and 1250 as a result of the collapse of the Chaco system either did not occur in the Hopi area or we cannot yet measure them. Data are simply too incomplete to make supportable claims, with the following exceptions. In the Moenkopi district the pattern of scattered, small pueblos is attenuated between A.D. 1200 and 1250. With the exception of the seasonally used Moenkopi pueblo, the area is never again occupied by Pueblo people. Gumerman and Skinner's (1968) discussion of the Hopi Buttes area pertains equally today as it did then. The A.D. 1150 to 1250 period (McDonald phase) is characterized by a dispersed pattern of small pit house sites integrated through communal construction and use of great kiva architecture, such as the Plaza site. The western Hopi Buttes were abandoned by A.D. 1250. In contrast, the post-A.D. 1250 occupation of the eastern Hopi Buttes was characterized by aggregation into a few large pueblos focused along the Pueblo Colorado Wash.

Settlement patterns in the Middle

Little Colorado River and Hopi Mesa districts continued along those established by A.D. 1150. In the Middle Little Colorado River district, small habitation sites were dominated by pit house architecture. At Hopi, small pueblos were focused along the edges of mesa tops near springs.

Local ceramic traditions continued to distinguish the areas between A.D. 1150 and 1250 with Hopi and Moenkopi occupants manufacturing Tusayan tradition ceramics consisting of both white ware and orange ware decorated ceramics. The Hopi Buttes and Homol'ovi area populations manufactured Little Colorado White Ware, importing a few Tsegi Orange Wares from the north and Alameda Brown Wares from the southwest. There is little evidence of their having imported White Mountain Red Wares from the south. These patterns suggest that a political boundary of sorts (the populations are too small to be called polities) bisected the Hopi region into the Hopi-Moenkopi area and the Hopi Buttes-Middle Little Colorado River area. The Hopi-Moenkopi half had exchange links to the north and possibly the east, whereas exchange relationships in the Hopi Buttes-Middle Little Colorado area were oriented south and west (cf. Douglass 1988). This pattern of political separation continued into the fourteenth century.

The post-A.D. 1250 period was one of enormous change in the Hopi area. Aggregated settlement patterns began to dominate the landscape. Population aggregation in the eastern Hopi Buttes, Hopi, and Middle Little Colorado River districts corresponded with the switch from white ware decorated ceramics to orange wares. Early decorated orange ware styles resemble those depicted on the white wares.

Although the pre-A.D. 1250 ceramic decorative and architectural styles of the Hopi area bear more similarity to those located to the north, by A.D. 1275 this pattern shifted and became stylistically more diffuse. Pinedale-style designs became co-dominant with Tusayan style designs in the Middle Little Colorado River pueblos after A.D. 1280. Even in the eastern Hopi Buttes and on the Hopi Mesas, White Mountain Red Ware patterns of decoration became part of the stylistic repertoire of the potters. Elsewhere (Adams 1989c), I have argued for immigration of White Mountain Red Ware-manufacturing populations into the Homol'ovi area of the Middle Little Colorado River Valley district in the late thirteenth century. This would help explain the greater impact of Pinedale-style designs on the local Homol'ovi ceramic tradition than on those farther north.

The reduced number and subsequent replacement of decorated white wares by decorated orange wares and later by yellow wares was a pattern that swept through the Hopi area between A.D. 1250 and 1300. Although it is clear that different clays were being used, this change is basically technological. The replacement of wood with coal as the pottery firing fuel is probably the principal reason the people on the Hopi Mesas used oxidizing atmospheres to fire all of their pottery by A.D. 1300. Coal produced a hotter fire, was locally available at Hopi (Hack 1942), and saved wood fuel. Coal was also used to heat homes. In general, then, coal represents significant progress in harnessing energy. Hack (1942) discovered several coal mines near Awatovi and Kawaika-a. Matters of coal ownership and exploitation and organization of coal-mining labor may prove significant in explaining Awatovi's impressive size (800 rooms) compared to other nearby settlements by the early fourteenth century.

The accelerated change from the pre-A.D. 1250 pattern of dispersed settlement in the Hopi area was due at least in part to population immigration. The origin of these immigrants was from the north, east, and west into the Hopi Mesas district, from the south and north into the Middle Little Colorado River district, and probably locally or from the north into the Bidahochi pueblos of the eastern Hopi Buttes area. The Hopi Buttes population, although always low, may have been sufficient to populate the two post-A.D. 1300 Bidahochi pueblos.

Areas preferred by the new immigrants were those with large, dependable water sources and adequate arable land. Every post-A.D. 1250 pueblo was located near either a spring or a permanent river such as the Little Colorado. Arable land capable of being watered by irrigation or runoff also characterized the valleys below the Hopi Mesas, the Pueblo Colorado Wash below Bidahochi, and the Little Colorado River Valley of Homol'ovi.

Although these areas may have been choice relocation spots for immigrants because of low indigenous populations, continuity in local ceramic traditions indicate that changes were not due solely to the influx of massive populations from as far north as the Four Corners. The process that seems most operative is one of aggregation. Although there is no denying that populations did immigrate into the Hopi area, especially the Middle Little Colorado River Valley district (Adams 1989c), the large number of dispersed pueblos on the landscape at the Hopi Mesas could probably account for the majority of the population in the aggregated pueblos.

Elsewhere, I (Adams 1989a, 1989b, 1991) have presented a model that attempts to explain this aggregation. The forces causing aggregation during the late thirteenth century were a combination of decreasing resources and increasing population. These stresses required populations to reorganize or face substantial population reduction through warfare and/or starvation. Exact causes of the almost total depopulation of the Four Corners during the last quarter of the thirteenth century are still debated. It is clear, however, that the abandonment corresponds with major changes in the environment characterized by degradation of floodplains and a prolonged drought (Dean et al. 1985; but see Van West, chapter 15). The principal response was emigration. Colton (1974) has detailed settlement change in response to immigration for the Hopi Mesas district, and my colleagues and I (Adams 1989b; Adams, Stark, and Dosh 1993; and Lange 1989) have done the same for the Middle Little Colorado River district. In 1993 we (Adams, Stark, and Dosh 1993) presented a detailed account of settlement pattern and pueblo size change throughout the Hopi area for the thirteenth and fourteenth centuries.

The indigenous inhabitants of the Hopi region were faced with two challenges in the late thirteenth century, a degrading environment and immigrating populations competing for even more limited resources. Four choices can be considered as appropriate responses to such a situation. First, Puebloan communities could disperse, resorting to different adaptive strategies for survival (Upham 1984). Second and third, population could be maintained at a level equal to production of food through either natural processes (starvation) or cultural processes, such as infanticide or warfare (Adams 1989a). Fourth, populations could opt for organizational changes. In the Hopi area, none of the first three choices was apparently made because population certainly increased. Population aggregation and the formation of large pueblos suggests the fourth choice was made.

For the fourth choice, more production or energy had to be obtained from local resources to support the expanding population and make aggregation a reasonable solution. This could be accomplished through intensifying food production on existing lands, expanding into new lands, or exchanging with other communities (see, for example, Upham 1982).

All three of these strategies were ultimately used by the occupants of the aggregated pueblos. Intensified use of spring-fed agricultural terraces probably originated at this time, and expansion into previously unutilized lands occurred in the Homol'ovi pueblos area as a result of stream degradation (Adams 1989b; Kolbe

1991; Lange 1989). Increased agricultural production was undertaken by intensifying water management techniques such as runoff and stream irrigated floodplain agriculture. Prior to impact by Anglo-American culture, half of historic period Hopi agriculture was based on runoff-managed water (Hack 1942). Among other researchers, Upham (1982) and I (Adams 1989a) have stressed the significant increase in exchange associated with settlement aggregation. Within the individual districts of the Hopi area where nearest settlements were always within about 6.3 mi (10 km), exchange of food to mitigate localized shortages would have been feasible.

Thus, intensification and diversification of subsistence options occurred in the A.D. 1250–1350 period in association with settlement aggregation. These strategies were apparently successful in the long run, because we see the continuation of aggregated pueblo life with its dependence on diverse intensive agricultural practices into the historic period. At the same time we do have archaeological evidence of localized failures, such as in the Hopi Buttes (Bidahochi) and Middle Little Colorado River Valley (Homol'ovi) districts where once successful communities were abandoned between A.D. 1350 and 1425.

The questions that remain are: What was the organizational framework that was successfully adopted and what was its basis? I have suggested elsewhere (Adams 1981, 1989a, 1989b, 1991) that the significant alterations in settlement layout, change in room-to-kiva ratio, and adoption of katsina iconography all had roots in the sociopolitical shifts designed to promote and maintain aggregation in pueblos. The effectiveness of those organizational changes is inferred from room count estimates. By A.D. 1350, on the average, pueblos were 500 percent larger than those occupied 100 years earlier (Adams, Stark, and Dosh 1993).

Between A.D. 1250 and 1300 pueblos be-

gan to have plazas enclosed by rooms. The kivas were located within these enclosures. The enclosed plazas, if modern pueblos can serve as analogs, served as integrative spaces to stage public ceremonies, much as their architectural predecessor, the great kiva, did. The private aspect of the ceremonies, where ritual knowledge was maintained and controlled, took place in the smaller kivas. Today, ownership and use of kivas is controlled by the most powerful social groups in Hopi society. This control of ritual was probably the source of power for prehistoric Pueblo leaders as well. For example, katsina iconography appeared on ceramics, in rock art, and on kiva walls during the fourteenth century in the Hopi area (Adams 1991). The katsina symbols on pottery and rock art, both visible to the general public, were single figures or occasional renderings of scenes. In the sacred, controlled domain of the kiva, however, the iconography became extraordinarily complex depicting ceremonies and sacred altars (Smith 1952). This suggests that ritual knowledge was being controlled by smaller groups within the community and was not available to the general public.

Development of such ritual-based leadership during the fourteenth century is a predictable outcome of mechanisms being employed by prehistoric Pueblo people to cope with subsistence stress. Status differentiation has been a noted characteristic of Pueblo culture in both the eastern and western Pueblo. Rewards reaped by the most powerful groups at Hopi today include not only the prestige that goes with the control of ceremonies and ceremonial knowledge, but also access to and use of the best agricultural lands (Bradfield 1971; Levy 1992).

If the types of status differentiation that we see in current Pueblo society expanded to something like its present form during the fourteenth century, what gave rise to such a system? Did the Chaco integrative system of the A.D. 1050 to 1150 period require status differentiation that formed the basis for a fourteenth-century form, or was some other system responsible for its development? Although details needed to trace the roots of inequality to the fourteenth-century aggregated settlements are still sketchy, at least two plausible scenarios can be addressed with data from the Hopi area.

Stein and Fowler (chapter 8), Roney (chapter 10), and Kintigh (1990) have been able to trace remnants of the Chaco system beyond its collapse about A.D. 1150. Significant research relevant to this issue has been done in the upper Little Colorado River drainages along the Puerco River in Arizona and the Zuni River. Following the collapse of the Chaco regional system, outliers in the upper Little Colorado River seem to have maintained great kivas, great houses (a contiguous, multistoried room block), and road segments. Enclosed plaza spaces are also present, but site layouts rarely exhibit the use of rooms to completely surround the plazas. Stein and Fowler argue that by A.D. 1250 rooms began to be used to surround these enclosures, and eventually this layout may have been transformed into the enclosed plazas of fourteenth-century villages. Kintigh (1990) notes a related pattern in that post-A.D. 1150 sites with great kivas differed from their Chaco predecessors. These post-Chaco great kivas were apparently unroofed and were much larger than their Chaco-era counterparts.

Most of these post-Chaco sites with great house-great kiva architecture were surrounded by a community of pueblos and probably served as community integrative centers. Presumably, community leaders either lived in these post-Chaco great houses or performed integrative rituals in these structures derived from the Chaco legacy. Over time it appears that the previously dispersed inhabitants of the local pueblos moved their primary residences into these increasingly plaza-oriented integrative centers. Kintigh (1990) has identified pueblos that seem to have had both the large unroofed great kiva and the population housed in a plaza-oriented pueblo.

Given this type of organization, it is not unreasonable to postulate that the roots of aggregated pueblos oriented around central plazas lie in Chaco great house architecture. These arguments are based solely on architectural and some settlement data, however, which leads to the second model for the development of the fourteenth-century aggregated pueblos. This model considers enclosed plazas as a transformation of great kiva integrative architecture within the milieu of thirteenth-century demographic and cultural changes.

Paul S. Martin and his Chicago Field Museum field schools of the 1950s and early 1960s excavated a sequence of sites ranging from the Reserve area of west-central New Mexico to the upper Little Colorado River Valley, especially Hay Hollow Valley and the Vernon area near Springerville (Longacre 1964). I (Adams 1991) constructed a developmental sequence using data from these excavations, specifically features: the rectangular kiva, the great kiva, and the enclosed plaza. Between about A.D. 1100 and 1250 in the upper Little Colorado River area, the primary community integrative architectural form was the great kiva. Although in some areas the Chaco-style circular great kiva was present, throughout most of the area the earlier circular great kiva was replaced by a rectangular form. This large public ceremonial structure was apparently complemented by smaller private ceremonial "rooms" within the associated pueblo room blocks. By the early thirteenth century the ceremonial rooms became formalized with benches. These rooms were attached to the south side and ends of the pueblos, or were separated from the pueblos altogether. Throughout this period, pueblos grew slowly, but by about A.D. 1250 pueblo size began to increase more rapidly, with Broken K Pueblo (Hill 1970) an excellent example. Broken K had a well-developed rectangular plaza within which were located the ceremonial rooms, or rectangular kivas. There was no associated great kiva. Between A.D. 1250 and 1300 the great kiva

was phased out, seemingly replaced by the enclosed plaza. Its function as integrative architecture was probably also replaced by the enclosed plaza.

Several lines of evidence point to the upper Little Colorado River area as the source of the organizational strategies that supported population aggregation. These include the stylistic influence from the upper Little Colorado area into the Hopi area after A.D. 1200, the immigration of people from the area to Homol'ovi about A.D. 1280 (Adams 1989c), the impact of upper Little Colorado katsina iconography in the Hopi area after A.D. 1300, and the clear continuity of architecture in the upper Little Colorado River area mimicked in the Hopi area. Whether these strategies were originally employed by Hopi area village leaders attempting to cope with resource base loss and population increase and competition increase is debatable. Looking at layout change between A.D. 1250 and 1300, one would conclude that in the pueblos of the Homol'ovi and Hopi Mesas areas these organizational decisions did not include the enclosed plaza integrative model.

About A.D. 1280, a great kiva was built at Homol'ovi III (Adams 1989c). Contemporaneous pueblos, including Homol'ovi I and Chevelon in the Middle Little Colorado River district and Awatovi and Kawaika-a on Antelope Mesa in the Hopi district, each consisted of a large, multistoried, agglomerated room block. Apparently within this room block were one or more small, informal plazas; "informal" in the sense that they were irregular in form and seemingly unplanned in the development of the pueblo unit. Between A.D. 1300 and 1350 in the Homol'ovi and Hopi districts, formalized plazas enclosed by room blocks were added to all of the pueblos. These were formal in the sense that they had a regular, predictable form and were clearly pre-planned in the construction of the pueblo. Homol'ovi II, which was probably constructed in the 1330s, was a pre-planned pueblo surrounding three formal plazas. Given that Homol'ovi II was built by immigrants from the Hopi Mesas, formalized enclosed plazas were predominant in both districts in the early 1300s. Homol'ovi II also had a preponderance of katsina iconography in its pottery, rock art, and possibly even in one kiva with murals (Pond 1966).

The dating of enclosed plazas to the fourteenth century in the Hopi area and their earlier appearance to the southeast in the Upper Little Colorado River area argue for the origin of this layout pattern in the south rather than the east. The absence of intermediate forms from the Chaco system dating after A.D. 1200–1250 makes it difficult to see the continuity of this architectural style in the fourteenth-century enclosed plaza layout.

Summary

Enormous changes in settlement plan and organization occurred in the Hopi area beginning in the late thirteenth century. These changes caused a transformation in the earlier (A.D. 1150–1250) dispersed pattern of small settlements that were probably integrated by some suprasettlement community organization. These communities generally built oversized structures, often termed "great kivas," as their primary integrative architecture.

After A.D. 1250, regional settlement patterns and village layouts changed. Organizational structures maintained by village leaders were used to manage subsistence stress brought on by an episode of severe drought and environmental degradation. But with the arrival of immigrants from the north who could compete for limited land sources already under the control of indigenous inhabitants, the existing leadership had to make a choice.

Options probably included open competition for resources (warfare) or the use of existing cooperative systems to integrate the immigrants. Absorbing the immigrants allowed continued control of the land resources and ensured that the leadership would retain the best farm lands. There were, however, no existing structures to integrate the new populations into the pueblos. The great kiva structure was inadequate. Instead, the community was organized around enclosed plazas, a design that replaced the great kiva and may have had its origin in compound structures to the south or the great house layouts of the Chaco era. Like the earlier great kiva, the plaza was used for village integration involving public ritual activities. The evolving small kiva form was used for the planning of the public rituals and performance of private rituals that could be controlled by the village leadership.

The organization of Pueblo society changed rapidly between A.D. 1150 and 1350 from one based primarily on kinship and a reliance on many small kivas to one based on sodalities, fewer kivas, and increased reliance on plazas as public ritual places. The katsina cult, which originated during this period, symbolizes this development. The cult was developed as an integrative ritual based not in kinship, but in cross-kinship social organization. Kinship terms aside, Pueblo leadership intensified and formalized ritual behavior in order to harness the social power required to organize and support the increasingly larger social systems created by fourteenth-century population aggregation.

Thus, the significance of the transition from the Pueblo III to Pueblo IV period is the transformation of Pueblo culture from the dispersed, kinship-based settlement system so common within the Anasazi world to the aggregated settlement system that characterized all Pueblo habitations at Spanish contact. This transition involved significant changes in social organization and leadership within the village unit. This evolution of more highly integrated social networks facilitated the organization of labor and the control of land necessary to support aggregated settlements. With these systems in place, a stable aggregated community could be maintained, a pattern that has lasted to the present day.

Acknowledgments

I would like to thank the organizers, Bill Lipe and Steve Lekson, for inviting me to the PIII conference. Special thanks to the Crow Canyon Archaeological Center for hosting the conference. Thanks also to the other conference participants for their helpful comments on the oral presentation of my paper. Ron Beckwith drafted figures 4.1 and 4.2. Mike Adler, Carla Van West, and two anonymous reviewers provided constructive comments on earlier versions of this chapter that have much improved it. Nevertheless, I take sole responsibility for any errors or oversights.

References Cited

Adams, E. Charles

1979   Cold Air Drainage and Length of Growing Season on the Hopi Mesas. *The Kiva* 44:285–97.

1981   A View from the Hopi Mesas. In *The Protohistoric Period in the North American Southwest*, A.D. 1450–1700, edited by David R. Wilcox and W. Bruce Masse, pp. 321–55. Anthropological Research Papers No. 24. Arizona State University, Tempe.

1985   The Archaeology of the Southern Black Mesa to Central Little Colorado River Valley Area. Paper presented at the symposium "Anasazi Update, Current Research Report," Arizona Archaeological Council, Flagstaff.

1989a   The Case for Conflict during the Late Prehistoric and Protohistoric Periods in the Western Pueblo Area of the American Southwest. In *Cultures in Conflict: Current Archaeological Perspectives*, edited by Diane Clair Tkaczak and Brian C. Vivian, pp. 103–11. The Archaeological Association of Calgary, Calgary.

1989b   The Homol'ovi Research Program. *Kiva* 54(3):175–94.

1989c   Homol'ovi III: A Pueblo Hamlet in the Middle Little Colorado River Valley, Arizona. *Kiva* 54(3):217–30.

1989d   *Hopi Use, Occupancy, and Possession of the Indian Reservation Defined by the Act of June 14, 1934: An Archaeological Perspective.* Report prepared for the 1934 Case Litigation. The Hopi Tribe, Kykotsmovi, Arizona.

1991   *The Origin and Development of the Pueblo Katsina Cult.* University of Arizona Press, Tucson.

Adams, E. Charles, and Kelley Ann Hays

1991   *Homol'ovi II: Archaeology of an Ancestral Hopi Village, Arizona.* Anthropological Papers No. 55. University of Arizona Press, Tucson.

Adams, E. Charles, Miriam T. Stark, and Deborah S. Dosh

1993   Ceramic Distribution and Ceramic Exchange: Jeddito Yellow Ware and Implications for Social Complexity. *Journal of Field Archaeology* 20:3–21.

Ahlstrom, Richard V. N.

1985   *The Interpretation of Tree-Ring Dates.* Unpublished Ph.D. dissertation, Department of Anthropology, University of Arizona, Tucson.

Bishop, Ronald L., Veletta Canouts, Suzanne P. De Atley, Alfred Qoyawayma, and C. W. Aikens

1988   The Formation of Ceramic Analytical Groups: Hopi Pottery Production and Exchange, A.D. 1300–1600. *Journal of Field Archaeology* 15:317–37.

Bradfield, Maitland M.

1971   *The Changing Pattern of Hopi Agriculture.* Occasional Paper 30. Royal Anthropological Institute of Great Britain and Ireland, London.

Brew, J. O.

1979   Hopi Prehistory and History to 1850. In *Southwest*, edited by Alfonso Ortiz, pp. 514–23. Handbook of North American Indians, Vol. 9, William C. Sturtevant, general editor. Smithsonian Institution, Washington D.C.

Colton, Harold S.

1974   Hopi History and Ethnobotany. In *Hopi Indians*, edited by David A. Horr. Garland, New York.

Colton, Harold S., and Lyndon L. Hargrave

1937   *Handbook of Northern Arizona Pottery Wares.* Bulletin No. 11. Museum of Northern Arizona, Flagstaff.

Dean, Jeffrey S., Robert C. Euler, George J. Gumerman, Fred Plog, Richard H. Hevly, and Thor N. V. Karlstrom

1985   Human Behavior, Demography, and Paleoenvironment on the Colorado Plateaus. *American Antiquity* 50:537–54.

Douglass, Amy A.

1988   *Prehistoric Exchange and Sociopolitical Development: The Little Colorado Whiteware Production-Distribution System.* Unpublished Ph.D. dissertation, Department of Anthropology, Arizona State University, Tempe.

Downum, Christian E., and Alan P. Sullivan, III

1990   Description and Analysis of Prehistoric Settlement Patterns at Wupatki National Monument. In *The Wupatki Archeological Inventory Survey Project: Final Report*, compiled by Bruce A. Anderson, pp. 5-1–5-90. USDI, National Park Service, Southwest Cultural Resources Center, Santa Fe.

Ellis, Florence H.

1974   The Hopi: Their History and Use of Lands. In *Hopi Indians*, edited by David A. Horr, pp. 25–277. Garland, New York.

Gilpin, Dennis

1989   Great Houses and Pueblos in Northeastern Arizona. Paper presented at the 1989 Pecos Conference, Los Alamos, New Mexico.

Gumerman, George J.

1969   *The Archaeology of the Hopi Buttes District, Arizona.* Unpublished Ph.D. dissertation, Department of Anthropology, University of Arizona, Tucson.

1988   *The Archaeology of the Hopi Buttes District, Arizona.* Center for Archaeological Investigations, Research Paper No. 49. Southern Illinois University, Carbondale.

Gumerman, George J., and S. Alan Skinner

1968   A Synthesis of the Prehistory of the Central Little Colorado River Valley, Arizona. *American Antiquity* 33:185–99.

Hack, John T.

1942   *Prehistoric Coal Mining in the Jeddito Valley, Arizona.* Papers of the Peabody Museum of American Archaeology and Ethnology, No. 35(2). Harvard University, Cambridge.

Hill, James N.

1970   *Broken K. Pueblo: Prehistoric Social Organization in the American Southwest.* Anthropological Papers No. 18. University of Arizona Press, Tucson.

Hough, Walter

1903   *Archaeological Field Work in Northeastern Arizona: The Museum Gates Expedition, 1901.* Annual Report for 1901. U.S. National Museum, Washington, D.C.

Kintigh, Keith W.

1990   Chaco, Communal Architecture, and Cibolan Aggregation. Paper presented at the Second Southwest Symposium, Albuquerque.

Kolbe, Thomas

1991   *Fluvial Changes in the Little Colorado River, Northeast Arizona, and their*

Effect on the Settlement Patterns at Homolovi III, a P-IV Floodplain Hamlet. Unpublished Master's thesis, Department of Quaternary Studies, Northern Arizona University, Flagstaff.

Lange, Richard C.

1989   A Survey of Homolovi Ruins State Park. *Kiva* 54(3):195–216.

Lekson, Stephen H., Thomas C. Windes, John R. Stein, and W. James Judge

1988   The Chaco Canyon Community. *Scientific American* 259(1):100–109.

Levy, Jerrold E.

1992   *Orayvi Revisted: Social Stratification in an "Egalitarian" Society.* University of Arizona Press, Tucson.

Longacre, William A.

1964   A Synthesis of Upper Little Colorado Prehistory, Eastern Arizona. In Chapters in the Prehistory of Arizona, II, assembled by Paul S. Martin, pp. 201–15. *Fieldiana: Anthropology* Vol. 55.

Pond, Gordon G.

1966   A Painted Kiva near Winslow, Arizona. *American Antiquity* 31:555–58.

Smith, Watson

1952   *Kiva Mural Decorations at Awatovi and Kawaika-a, with a Survey of Other Wall Paintings in the Pueblo Southwest.* Papers of the Peabody Museum of American Archaeology and Ethnology No. 37. Harvard University, Cambridge.

Upham, Steadman

1982   *Polities and Power: An Economic and Political History of the Western Pueblo.* Academic Press, New York.

1984   Adaptive Diversity and Southwestern Abandonment. *Journal of Anthropological Research* 40(2):235–56.

Wood, J. Scott

1987   *Checklist of Pottery Types for the Tonto National Forest.* The Arizona Archaeologist No. 21. Arizona Archaeological Society, Phoenix.

Young, Lisa C.

1989   Preliminary Investigations at AZ J:14:36, A Pit House Village in Homolovi Ruins State Park, Arizona. Ms. on file, Arizona State Museum Archives, University of Arizona, Tucson.

1990   Archaeological Excavations of AZ J:14:36: 1990 Field Season. Ms. on file, Arizona State Museum Archives, University of Arizona, Tucson.

Chapter 5

The Pueblo III Period along the Mogollon Rim:
The Honanki, Elden, and Turkey Hill Phases of the Sinagua

Peter J. Pilles, Jr.

In the prehistoric past, the region south of the Anasazi world in northern Arizona was occupied by a people known as the Sinagua. Their realm was divided into two major regions: the Northern Sinagua on the south and east sides of the San Francisco Peaks, and the Southern Sinagua in the Verde Valley. Separating them was an extensive, virtually unoccupied, band of high ponderosa pine forest (figures 5.1 and 5.2). Combined, this Sinagua world comprised about 3,346 mi² (8,700 km²).

To the north and northeast, Anasazi populations occurred along the Little Colorado River while the Cohonina lived to the north and northwest. In this area, in what is now Wupatki National Monument and the surrounding areas, ceramic assemblages create a confusing picture of what has been called a "frontier," in which people of all three groups co-existed, sometimes on the same sites.

The Northern Sinagua realm had considerable environmental diversity, ranging from the tundra zone at 12,000 feet (3,658 m) on top of the San Francisco Peaks, through an open ponderosa pine forest between elevations of 6,500 and 7,300 feet (1,982 and 2,226 m), through an extensive pinyon-juniper forest below 6,500 feet (1982 m), into the desert scrub and grasslands below 5,400 feet (1,646 m), and reaching its lowest elevations on the Little Colorado River at 4,200 feet (1,280 m). This region totals about 1,000 mi² (2,600 km²).

The vacant ponderosa pine forest to the south follows the Mogollon Rim, a giant escarpment that cuts diagonally across the state of Arizona. Almost completely dominated by rugged basalt bedrock, most of the soils in the forest were too thin, and the growing season too short, for agriculture. This ponderosa forest zone was likely used for hunting, but despite considerable archaeological survey in this forest zone, evidence of use is almost absent. This vacant ponderosa pine country occupies about 1,308 mi² (3,400 km²).

The Southern Sinagua region consisted of the upper and middle segments of the Verde Valley, between Perkinsville on the north and the confluence with the East Verde River on the south. Its western margin was the Black Hills, while the Mogollon Rim formed the eastern boundary. The Verde Valley includes two major environmental zones: the Verde Uplands are primarily pinyon-juniper forests, based on soils derived from basaltic substrate, while the Verde Lowlands consist of grasslands and creosote flats growing primarily on limestone-derived soils. The major characteristic of the Verde Uplands is its elaborate canyon system. To the west, this consists of the spectacular Red Rock sandstone canyons around Sedona, and on the east are steep sided, rugged canyons that cut for miles into the Mogollon Rim.

As the name suggests, the Sinagua (Spanish for "without water") region had limited water. Scattered springs were the only perennial water sources for the Northern Sinagua. Because of the limited water sources, the Sinagua became masters of water conservation and manipulation. They created numerous small, shallow reservoirs near their villages by scraping away the thin soil and overlying rocks down to the limestone bedrock. In addition to these individual family catchments, large communal reservoirs were made in identical fashion.

The Southern Sinagua, however, could rely upon the permanent water resources of the Verde River, as well as a number of perennial tributary streams on the east side of the valley, such as Oak Creek, West Clear Creek, and Beaver Creek, which are fed by springs along the base of the Mogollon Rim. Unlike the Northern Sinagua, no prehistoric reservoirs have yet been identified in the Verde Valley.

Sinagua Phase System

Early literature on the Sinagua region used the Pecos Classification System to refer to the various time periods identified in the area. In 1939, however, specific phase systems for the Northern and Southern Sinagua were created by Harold S. Colton (1939). These were modified by later researchers (Breternitz 1960:20–25; Fish and Fish 1977:11–18; Pilles 1979, 1981:8–14, 1988; Wilson 1969:351–506) and figure 5.3 correlates the Sinagua phase systems with the Hohokam and Anasazi chronologies.

The time period of interest for this chapter, the Anasazi Pueblo III Period, corresponds with the Honanki phase of the Southern Sinagua and both the Elden and Turkey Hill phases of the Northern Sinagua. The Honanki phase (A.D. 1150–1300) is named after the largest cliff dwelling of the Red Rocks Country (Colton 1939: 44). For the Northern Sinagua, early to middle Pueblo III times are represented by the Elden phase (A.D. 1150 to 1250), for which Elden Pueblo is the type site. The late Pueblo III period, or Tsegi phase, is represented by the Turkey Hill phase (A.D. 1250–1300), and Turkey Hill Pueblo is the type site for this phase.

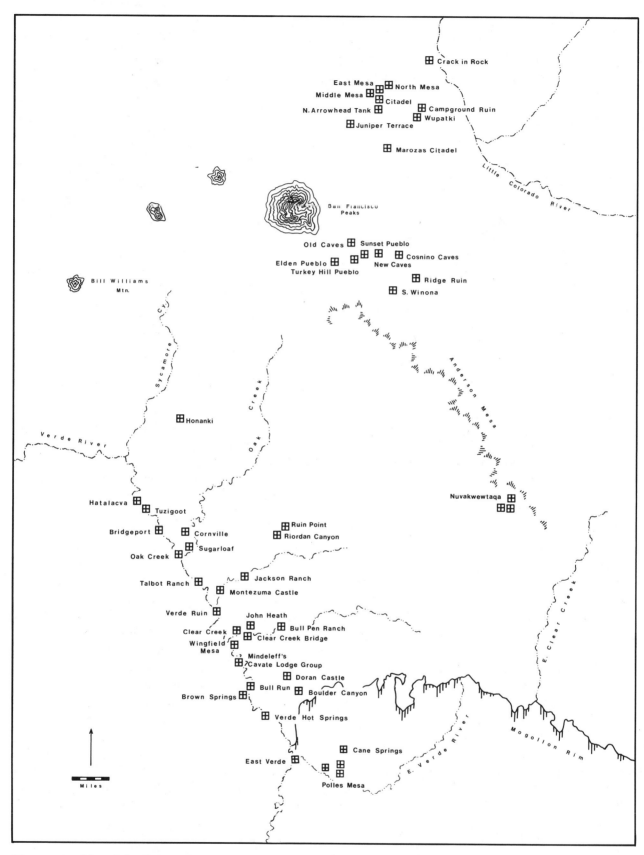

Figure 5.1. Map of the Sinagua region, with large sites (here defined as 20 rooms or more) dating between A.D. 1150 and 1300 plotted. Refer to appendix for site information.

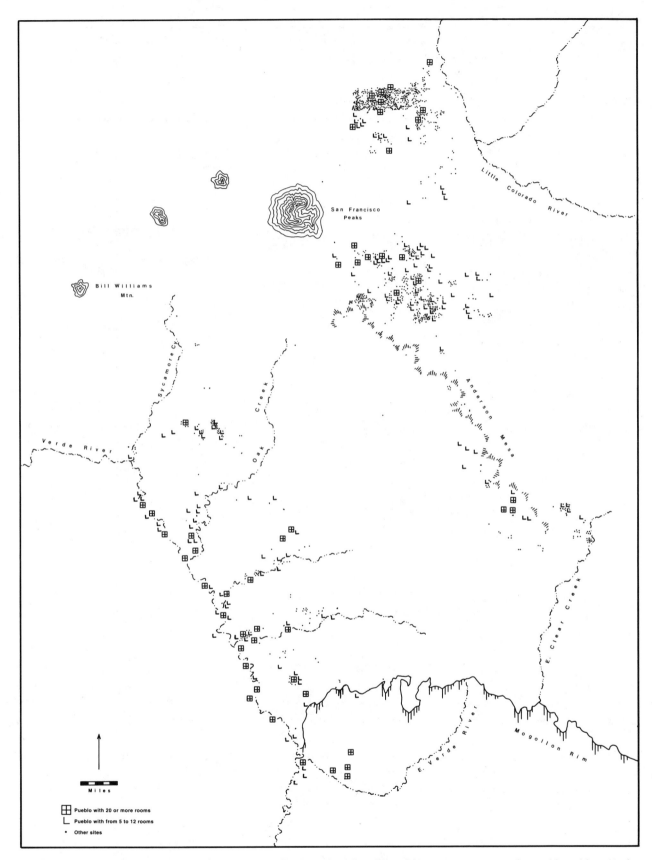

Figure 5.2. All Sinagua sites, A.D. 1150–1350. Note the clustering of pueblos with 5 to 12 rooms near the pueblos with more than 20 rooms.

Dating of the Sinagua Phases

Assignment of Sinagua sites to a specific phase is quite difficult, and sometimes impossible, without excavation. Unlike the relatively abundant and well-dated ceramics found on Anasazi sites, Sinagua sites are characterized by paddle-and-anvil produced plain wares and red wares that changed little through time. Temper distinctions and surface treatment are the attributes upon which types are based, but temporal distinctions based on the local ceramics alone are seldom precise enough to be useful. In general, fine-tempered Rio de Flag Brown is typical prior to the initial eruption of Sunset Crater in A.D. 1064. The plethora of temper types used after 1064, although useful for determining the localities where ceramics were made, are not helpful for making temporal distinctions, because they lasted unchanged until the end of the Sinagua sequence in A.D. 1400. There are some indications that red ware and smudged pottery becomes more abundant through time, but this has not yet been quantified in sufficient detail to be useful. Seriation of the plain ware types has been used in the Nuvakwewtaqa-Chavez Pass locality (Henderson 1979:31–32) but has not yet been attempted in other areas.

Hence, dating of Sinagua phases is typically based upon intrusive ceramics. An early to middle Pueblo III Anasazi assemblage, dominated by Flagstaff and Walnut Black-on-white ceramics, identifies the Elden phase, while a Tsegi phase assemblage, dominated by Tusayan Black-on-white, Tusayan and Kayenta varieties, identifies sites of the Turkey Hill phase. The Honanki phase, however, is represented by the total Pueblo III period ceramic assemblage.

Although the dating for these ceramics and sites excavated in the Northern Sinagua Region is well grounded in tree-ring studies (Downum 1988:336–497; Robinson, Harrill, and Warren 1975), tree-ring dating has not been very successful in the

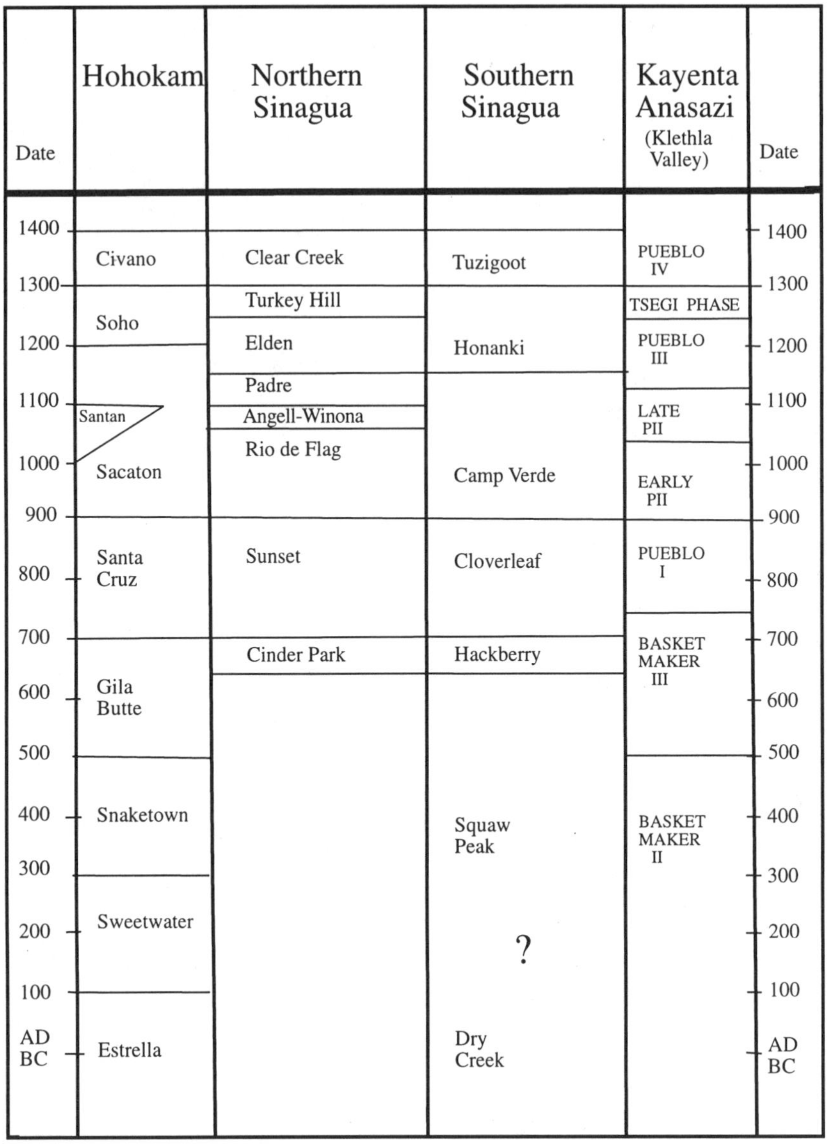

Date	Hohokam	Northern Sinagua	Southern Sinagua	Kayenta Anasazi (Klethla Valley)	Date
1400	Civano	Clear Creek	Tuzigoot	PUEBLO IV	1400
1300	Soho	Turkey Hill		TSEGI PHASE	1300
1200		Elden	Honanki	PUEBLO III	1200
1100	Santan	Padre		LATE PII	1100
		Angell-Winona			
1000	Sacaton	Rio de Flag	Camp Verde	EARLY PII	1000
900					900
800	Santa Cruz	Sunset	Cloverleaf	PUEBLO I	800
700		Cinder Park	Hackberry	BASKET MAKER III	700
600	Gila Butte				600
500					500
400	Snaketown		Squaw Peak	BASKET MAKER II	400
300					300
200	Sweetwater		?		200
100					100
AD BC	Estrella		Dry Creek		AD BC

Figure 5.3. Chronological phase system for the Sinagua region, compared with the chronological systems commonly used in the Anasazi and Hohokam regions.

Verde Valley (Bannister, Gell, and Hannah 1966:vi–viii; Breternitz 1977:37–38).

Dating of survey sites depends on the number of intrusive sherds that can be identified on the surface of the ground. Because most Sinagua sites are small and have very few diagnostic ceramics, assigning them to a specific phase is very difficult. For example, of 7,900 sites inventoried by the Coconino National Forest in the Sinagua region, only 41 percent (3,200) are datable. During the survey of Walnut Canyon National Monument, only 168 of 242 sites recorded could be dated

(69 percent) (Bremer 1989). In the Anderson Mesa area, 42 percent of the sites had no decorated ceramics at all, and, of those that did, only a few decorated sherds were present (Henderson 1979:30). Consequently, synthetic studies such as the present one are difficult, and smaller sites, due to their lack of ceramics, are likely underrepresented.

Regional syntheses are also hampered by the survey coverage of the region examined by this chapter, about 3,346 mi² (8,700 km²). Approximately 75 percent of the region has been covered by sample surveys of varying intensity, and only about 33 percent has been investigated with systematic survey. Various locations within the Coconino National Forest have undergone intensive survey, such as the east side of the San Francisco Peaks, numerous blocks in the ponderosa zone, and other blocks of 1 to 2 mi² (2–5 km²) areas surrounding several of the largest sites in the Verde Valley and Flagstaff areas. Elden and Turkey Hill phase sites were found to be absent from many of these blocks in the Flagstaff area and provided only negative data for this synthesis.

Casual "windshield" surveys and anecdotal information suggest that many of the gaps in survey coverage of the Verde Valley will eventually be found to contain significant numbers of Honanki phase sites. Although many more Elden and Turkey Hill phase sites will be found in the Flagstaff area, the overall site patterns and distributions described in this chapter will probably not differ significantly from the information presently available.

The "Pueblo III" Sinagua Data Base

The data base used for this study consists primarily of the archaeological survey files of the Coconino National Forest, which includes the survey information recorded by the Museum of Northern Arizona since 1916. Survey data for national monuments within the study area were obtained from publications summarizing the National Park Service surveys of those monuments. These consist of Tuzigoot (Tagg 1986), Montezuma Castle and Montezuma Well (Wells and Anderson 1988), Walnut Canyon (Bremer 1989), and Wupatki (Downum and Sullivan 1990). These monuments were completely surveyed and the reader is referred to those reports to obtain more detailed information about site types, distributions, and patterns not covered in this chapter.

From these sources, 1,835 sites could be dated to the A.D. 1150 to 1300 time period and form the data base used for

this study. Because many sites contain more than one architectural unit as well as various other features, these individual components were used as units of analysis, rather than using "sites" as individual cases. Hence, a total of 2,067 components were used for this study.

A common convention used throughout this volume is that regional summaries focus on sites containing 50 or more rooms (but see Lyneis, chapter 2). In the Sinagua region, however, the scale of population aggregation apparent during the A.D. 1150 to 1300 period falls well below this arbitrary size limit. Consequently, the Sinagua region sites summarized in the appendix contain all those recorded sites with 20 or more rooms. Most of the pueblos listed in the appendix continued to be occupied after A.D. 1300 and achieved their greatest size, often 50 or more rooms, during the Tuzigoot and Clear Creek phases.

Given the increases in settlement size during and after the thirteenth century, an erroneous picture of Pueblo III site and population size would have resulted had their final, Pueblo IV, sizes been used in this study. Consequently, an estimate was made of Pueblo III period settlement size in one of two ways. When ceramic counts for a site were available, generally survey counts, an estimate of the number of rooms present during the Pueblo III period was made, based upon the percentage of Pueblo III period pottery found at the site. For example, if 30 percent of the survey or excavated ceramic counts for a 100-room Tuzigoot phase pueblo were of Pueblo III types, it was estimated that the Honanki phase size of that site was 30 rooms.

When no sherd counts were available, but pueblo layout and room sizes indicated more than a single period of occupation, an estimate of 20 rooms was arbitrarily assigned to those sites unless room size classes suggested another figure. This is based on a previous study of Pueblo IV Sinagua pueblos where an apparent size distinction between early and late Tuzigoot phase room sizes was noted (Pilles 1986). Examination of the plans for a few

multicomponent pueblos in the Verde Valley where room sizes and sherd counts are available suggests this approach works reasonably well.

Only a single Tuzigoot phase pueblo —namely Tuzigoot—has been excavated sufficiently to evaluate this approach. Tuzigoot was completely excavated by Caywood and Spicer (1935:38–40), who estimated the pueblo growth through time based on ceramics, construction on older deposits, and wall abutments. Later, tree-ring dates were obtained for those building periods (Hartman 1976:47–48) that suggest the Honanki phase size of Tuzigoot was about 33 rooms before it reached its maximum size of about 92 rooms. Using the Pueblo III period sherd counts (Caywood and Spicer 1935:48) for the site, this approach would suggest a Honanki phase component of about 43 rooms, rather than the 33 estimated by Caywood and Spicer.

Although there are problems with this approach, given the limited data presently available for the large pueblos, it is thought that the results are reasonable enough for the purpose of comparing the relative sizes of the large pueblos during the A.D. 1150 to 1300 period and their distributions with other contemporaneous sites. Table 5.1 shows the total number of rooms reported for the 50 Sinagua large pueblos included in this data summary and the number of rooms estimated to have been occupied during the Pueblo III period. In order to place the Pueblo III period Sinagua site distributions in perspective, a brief summary of Sinagua prehistory prior to this time is now presented.

Sinagua Settlement and Population Through Time

The Early Sinagua, A.D. 650–900

The first sedentary agriculturalists appeared in the Flagstaff and Verde Valley areas around A.D. 650 to 725. In the north, sites dating to this time are rare, but they occur in several localities (Colton 1946: 261; Wilcox 1987; Wilson 1969:371). In the Verde Valley, although a few have been reported in the lowlands, they are more common in the uplands (Fish and Fish 1977:12; Breternitz 1960:21). Population density was probably low based on the small number of sites from this period that have been reported.

The next 200 years, from A.D. 700 to 900, saw a small increase in the number of sites, suggesting local growth. Explanations of the growth have implicated Hohokam migration into the Verde Valley during this time. More recent work (Fish, Pilles, and Fish 1980) suggests that, although some Hohokam may have been in the valley, population growth cannot be attributed solely to Hohokam colonists, as previously suggested. Some sites have been found in the Verde Lowlands, although most from this period have been recorded in the Verde Upland zone. In the Flagstaff area, Sunset phase sites do occur, contrary to earlier arguments (Plog 1989: 267–68). Most settlements are found in the ponderosa pine-pinyon-juniper fringe country, north and northeast of Flagstaff, particularly in the Cinder Hills, Juniper Terrace, Deadman Wash, and Baker Ranch localities. The greatest concentration of these appears to be in the Cinder Hills locality, where most sites have been covered by volcanic ash from the eruptions of Sunset Crater, although this has not precluded their recognition and recent excavation (Bradley 1994). Typical village plans resemble those of the Anasazi of the Winslow area in having three or more pit houses built in an arc around a communal work and storage area. At the larger sites, a community pit house is also present that likely served as a community center for smaller pit house clusters in the area.

The Middle Period Sinagua,
A.D. 900–1150

During the A.D. 900 to 1150 period, several phases have been identified in the Northern and Southern Sinagua regions.

Table 5.1 Site Size Comparisons Between Number of Total Rooms Constructed at the Site and the Estimated Number of Rooms Occupied Between A.D. 1150 and 1300

Site Name	Total Rooms	Total PIII Rooms	Site Name	Total Rooms	Total PIII Rooms
Clear Creek	150	70	Brown Springs	80	20
John Heath	100	20	Bull Run	50	20
Montezuma Castle A	57	20	Jackson Ranch	30	21
Riordan Canyon	53	25	Verde Hot Springs	42	20
Tuzigoot	92	43	East Verde	38	20
Oak Creek	52	24	Hatalacva	60	28
Sugarloaf	65	20	Old Caves	80	50
Bridgeport	237	32	Nuvakwewtaqa North	100	20
Cornville	70	20	Nuvakwewtaqa Southeast	252	20
Talbot Ranch	165	20	Nuvakwewtaqa Southwest	685	20
Doran Castle	100	20	Polles Mesa (TNF 40)	30	20
Boulder Canyon	44	20	Polles Mesa (NA6362)	36	31
Mindeleff's Cavate Lodge	29	20	Spring Creek	30	20

This has been traditionally suggested to have been a time when considerable population increase occurred, due to numerous migrations into the region, supposedly to exploit the improved agricultural productivity of the Flagstaff area following the initial eruptions of Sunset Crater in 1064 and 1066. Although past interpretations have suggested that Hohokam populations migrated into the Verde Valley to expand trade markets and exploit this new "frontier" for the benefit of the Hohokam heartland of the Salt River Valley, it is now thought that this migration paradigm has been overemphasized and that most of the developments at this time were the result of indigenous change with little inmigration (Fish, Pilles, and Fish, 1980; Pilles 1979). In the Northern Sinagua region, populations were most numerous along the margins of the San Francisco Peaks, perhaps due to the increased moisture availability around the peaks during this period of overall drier conditions (Hevly et al., 1979:499–501; Pilles 1979:463). Pit house sites increased in size and number, and there is evidence for formal community organization and village structure. Typically, smaller sites containing three or more pit houses clustered around a single larger site containing eight or more pit houses. The larger central site was often associated with a com-

munity room-pit house or a ball court. Masonry structures are definitely part of the architectural pattern of this period. These include masonry-lined pit houses, field houses, and surface rooms on large and small pit houses sites. In the Verde Valley, sites are found in both upland and lowland settings, but are most numerous in the lowland zone. A dichotomy of architectural styles is also present and further distinguishes the upland sites from those in the lowlands. Large, circular and sub-square pit houses with ramp entries, identical to those found in the Flagstaff area, occur in the Verde Uplands, while shallower pit houses in a variety of shapes are more common in the Verde Lowlands. These include a few Hohokam-style "houses in pits," as well as large community pit houses in some villages.

"Pueblo III" Sinagua:
The Elden and Honanki Phases, A.D. 1150–1300

One obvious difference between the Sinagua and Anasazi regions can be seen during the Pueblo III period. Although it was during the Pueblo II period that the Anasazi occupation reached its greatest geographic extent across the rest of the Southwest, the most widespread occupation of the Flagstaff and Verde Valley regions occurred during the Elden and Honanki phases, concurrent with the Anasazi Pueblo III period. As with the Anasazi, however, this was also the time when the Sinagua experienced their greatest cultural florescence.

During the Elden and Honanki phases, the Sinagua occupied four primary, separate geographic areas: Flagstaff, the Verde Valley, Anderson Mesa, and Wupatki (figure 5.1). It has been suggested that this expansion and population growth was largely due to changes in climate and moisture availability (Pilles 1978:128–31, 1979). This is best seen in the Flagstaff and Verde Valley areas, where dramatic settlement pattern shifts are evident. Such shifts are not seen in the Wupatki area and survey data are inadequate at the present time to determine if there were major shifts in the Anderson Mesa area. Overall, in the Flagstaff area, there was a movement to lower elevations. With the exception of a few sites, notably Elden Pueblo, Turkey Hill Pueblo, and Old Caves Pueblo, all of which are in the ponderosa zone around the margins of Doney Park, the majority of the population appears to have moved to the pinyon-juniper zone, north and east of Flagstaff. In the pinyon-juniper zone, site densities range from 60 to 80 sites per square mile.

In general, the entire pinyon-juniper zone on the east side of the San Francisco Peaks was heavily occupied at this time, with the exception of the deep cinder fall zone from Sunset Crater, where virtually no post-eruptive sites are recorded. Once the north and south edges of the deep cinder fall zone are reached, sites appear regularly and frequently, extending north into the Deadman Wash-Wupatki localities and ending in the dry desert of the Moenkopi Sandstone plains of the Little Colorado River Valley. Sites extend eastward for about 5 miles (8 km) past Canyon Padre, where the elevation decreases and the pinyon-juniper forest gives way to grassland. Only a small number of sites are recorded in the pinyon-juniper country to the southeast, along Anderson Mesa. This

is believed to be due largely to spotty survey coverage rather than an actual absence of Elden phase sites. Survey gaps may also explain a lack of Elden phase sites in the pinyon-juniper zone north of the San Francisco Peaks, but it is more likely that this absence is real, perhaps due to soil conditions in that area. Soils north of the Peaks are derived from basalt and are much less suitable for agriculture than are the limestone-derived soils found in the pinyon-juniper country northeast and east of the Peaks.

In the Verde Valley, late twelfth- and thirteenth-century populations expanded into the canyons at higher elevations. In the Verde Valley, survey data is much more limited and geographically sketchy than for the Flagstaff area, although available data seems to portray a fairly clear picture. Sites are generally restricted to the immediate streamside environs of the Verde Lowlands and the canyons of the Verde Uplands, with virtually no sites recorded in the creosote and grasslands of the Verde Lowlands. Of particular interest are pockets of Honanki phase occupations in the uplands, away from permanent water sources, such as in the Hackberry Basin, Boulder Canyon, and Cedar Flat localities. Survey data are particularly lacking in the canyon country of the Red Rocks and Mogollon Rim areas. It is virtually certain, however, that future surveys will record numerous Honanki phase sites in those areas.

There is little information available about population distributions along Anderson Mesa except in the Chavez Pass locality. There, the situation seems to be the same as that in the Wupatki area. Although there was an increase in the number of sites, there was no movement out of the localities occupied during earlier periods (Henderson 1979:43–46; Downum and Sullivan 1990:5-14–5-15).

What factors explain these site distributions? The most obvious explanation, suggested by several researchers, is that there was an increase in available moisture after A.D. 1070 (Pilles 1978:128–31; 1979:

468–69; 1981:13; Hevly et al. 1979:499–501). Although site survey coverage in the Verde Valley is not yet sufficient to consider overall settlement pattern changes, data for the Flagstaff region are sufficiently abundant to clearly show shifts in the major settlement pattern that seem to reflect major shifts in climatic conditions. The same may hold true for the Verde Valley, where increased moisture availability in the canyons likely improved spring and seep productivity, and attracted populations into the canyons, where they remained for about the first decade of the Great Drought of A.D. 1276 to 1299.

Distribution of Site Types, A.D. 1150–1300

For this study, the 2067 components of the 1835 Sinagua site types have been divided into 12 component types for analytical purposes: scatters, cavates, pit houses, 1- to 2-room pueblos, 3- to 4-room pueblos, 5- to 8-room pueblos, 9- to 12-room pueblos, 13- to 20-room pueblos, 20-plus-room pueblos, agricultural sites, rock art sites, and other. Their distributions within the four major areas of this study are shown in table 5.2.

Field Houses

As is evident, small sites containing one to four rooms are the most common site class recorded across the entire Sinagua region. Although some were clearly habitations, most were seasonally utilized field houses (Pilles 1978). Some differences are apparent, however, in the distribution of seasonally utilized sites across the four areas. In the Verde Valley, although still the most numerous site type in the area, the frequency of this site type relative to other sites (32 percent) is the lowest of the four areas. This is due to the numerous riparian zones in the Verde that offer more abundant and productive agricultural locations than the other Sinagua areas. Because of this, more habitation sites in the Verde Lowlands were located closer to field

Table 5.2   Distribution of Site Components and Sizes Across the Four Major Areas within the Sinagua Region

	Cavate	Scatters	Pit House	1–2 rooms	3–4 rooms	5–8 rooms	9–12 rooms	13–20 rooms	>20 rooms	Agri-cultural	Petro-glyph	Other	Totals
Verde Valley	44	14	11	91	29	31	21	25	29	13	34	44	386
Wupatki	0	7	17	290	377	0	57	38	9	6	1	17	819
Flagstaff	26	41	104	339	83	58	19	11	7	22	2	27	739
Anderson Mesa	1	9	7	39	18	5	5	0	5	11	4	11	115
Total count	71	71	139	759	507	94	102	74	50	52	41	99	2059
Percentage of total	3.4	3.4	6.7	36.8	24.6	4.6	5.0	3.6	2.4	2.5	2.0	4.8	99.8

locations than in the Flagstaff, Anderson Mesa, or Wupatki areas. Further evidence of this is evident in the Verde Uplands. There, away from the riparian zones, the pattern is identical to the rest of the Sinagua region. For example, data from the Bald Hill Locality, along the Mogollon Rim, show that 1- to 4-room field houses made up 46 percent of the sites recorded there (Wells 1981:34–37).

Habitation Sites

The most striking difference between Sinagua site classes and those discussed elsewhere in this volume is that "very large" pueblos found in many of the Anasazi regions are virtually absent in the Sinagua region between A.D. 1150 and 1300. In the Sinagua region, 20-plus-room sites are considered to be "very large," and make up only 2 percent of the sites assigned to this time period (table 5.2). The largest, at 102 rooms, is Wupatki. It was not until the subsequent Clear Creek and Tuzigoot phases, the culmination of the process of Sinagua aggregation, that "very large" pueblos were more common. Additional, undiscovered, 20-plus-room pueblos dating to the twelfth and thirteenth centuries undoubtedly exist in the Sinagua region, most likely in the Verde Valley, Anderson Mesa, and Flagstaff areas. Those localities most likely to contain as yet unrecorded pueblos of this size are in the Verde Uplands, along Deadman Wash south of Wupatki National Monument, and the Angell Locality, 20 miles (32 km) east of Flagstaff.

As mentioned previously, the number of rooms constructed and used during the A.D. 1150 to 1300 time period was estimated for those pueblos that continued to be occupied after A.D. 1300. Most of the large pueblos fall into this category. Of the 50 pueblos listed, only 19 appear to have been occupied solely during the Pueblo III period. With the exception of Honanki, in the Verde Valley, these 19 pueblos are all in the Flagstaff or Wupatki areas. The Flagstaff and Wupatki areas were virtually abandoned by A.D. 1300, although occupation continued in much larger pueblos in the Verde and Anderson Mesa areas until A.D. 1400.

Four site plans can be delineated within the current sample of large Sinagua pueblos. These include massed room blocks, plaza-oriented pueblos, courtyard-oriented pueblos, and clustered room blocks. Assignment of Sinagua sites into one of these four architectural layout categories can be found in the appendix.

Massed Room Block Pueblos

Massed room block pueblos are the most typical pueblo plan (n = 28) for the entire Sinagua region for all time periods. As these pueblos grew, individual rooms or blocks of rooms were simply added onto existing rooms. Elden Pueblo is an example of this type of site (figure 5.4). Several of these pueblos, such as Elden and Turkey Hill, also have small pueblos with one to four rooms constructed within 50 m of the main pueblo that distinguishes them from the class of clustered room block sites.

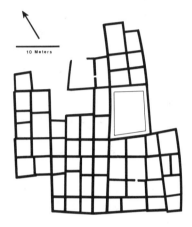

Figure 5.4. Elden Pueblo site plan, showing massed roomblock architectural layout.

Plaza-oriented Pueblos

Plaza-oriented pueblos occur, but are relatively infrequent (n = 10). A plaza orientation is more typical of Anasazi or, in compound form, of Salado pueblos. It is significant that most of the plaza-oriented sites occur in the northern and southern ends of the study area. In the Wupatki area, ceramics on these sites indicate affiliation with Kayenta, rather than Sinagua, populations. The plaza-oriented sites in the southern end of the Verde Valley are closest to the Salado area, and ceramics on these sites indicate Sinagua occupations with closer trade associations with the Salado area than are probable for other sites in the Verde. The Sugarloaf Ruin is one of these plaza-oriented pueblos in plan (figure 5.5), although functionally it likely belongs with the courtyard-oriented pueblos. Crack-in-Rock Pueblo, a Kayenta site, is difficult to fit into the pueblo plan

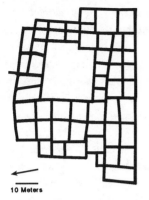

Figure 5.5. Sugarloaf Ruin site plan, showing plaza-oriented architectural layout.

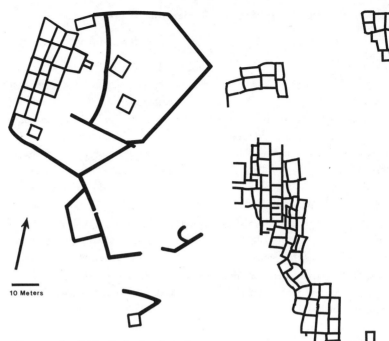

Figure 5.6. Ridge Ruin site plan, showing courtyard-oriented architectural layout.

Figure 5.7. Tuzigoot Ruin site plan, showing clustered room architectural layout. Open areas may have served as plazas, but were not architecturally defined as in the plaza- and courtyard-oriented sites.

types. Its plaza is delineated by walls as well as rooms, giving it a courtyard-like appearance. Additional isolated rooms are scattered below it, so it could be included in the clustered room block class of site types as well.

Courtyard-oriented Pueblos

Courtyard-oriented pueblos are rare (n = 3) and usually represent particularly important sites in the Sinagua regional system, as will be discussed later. Ridge Ruin (figure 5.6) is the classic example of this type of pueblo. Rather than having open spaces defined by blocks of rooms, as is the case with plaza-oriented pueblos, walls define the courtyards. Courtyard pueblos in the Sinagua region typically have two courtyards, with the inner courtyard containing a massed room block or several architectural units, including other pueblos, rooms, kivas, community rooms, and pit houses. Although few in number, courtyard pueblos occur throughout the entire Sinagua region. In the Deadman Wash and Wupatki localities, courtyard-like sites are more numerous than in other areas. The proximity of these localities to others occupied by the Cohonina suggests a relationship may exist between these courtyard sites and similar sites recently described for the Sitgreaves Mt. area (Samples and Wilcox 1992), where they are also rare.

Clustered Room Block Pueblos

Clustered room block pueblos occur at only two locations during the Honanki phase, with the third, North Mesa, located in the Wupatki area. These are at Tuzigoot and Hatalacva, two sites located only 1.5 miles (2.4 km) apart. Tuzigoot (figure 5.7) is the best example of this pueblo type, where several massed room block pueblos were constructed in close proximity to each other. The open spaces between these room blocks may have served as plazas; however, these possible communal areas were not formally defined as was the case with plaza sites. In all cases, individual pueblos were used for permanent habitation, and may represent the separate abodes of different social groups.

Cavate Sites

Unlike the other large pueblos listed in the appendix, Cosnino Caves is not a pueblo but is a grouping of cavates, naturally occurring caves that have been modified for

occupation. Besides expanding the size of the small naturally formed caves by smoothing the cave walls, occupants of these cavate domiciles also hollowed storage pits or small rooms into the cave walls. Walls were usually constructed across the mouths of the cavates to form these cliffside rooms.

Other cavate sites are found in the Flagstaff and Verde Valley areas, such as those at Clear Creek Ruins and Mindeleff's Cavate Lodge Group. These sites either cannot be dated to the A.D. 1150 to 1300 time period, or they occur in small, separated groups that could be considered as separate sites. Consequently, they are not classified as a contiguous population unit, as are the pueblos listed in the appendix. Similarly, Cluster 2 at Walnut Canyon (Bremer 1989:98) and Horseshoe Mesa at Wupatki (Downum and Sullivan 1990:5–39), are not included in the appendix because they are clusters of individual "sites."

Site Type Summary

As is evident from the architectural layout assignments (appendix), the preferred Sinagua domicile was a small pueblo containing from 5 to 12 rooms, or secondarily, one with 13 to 20 rooms. Wing walls occur on many of these small, massed room block pueblos, particularly in the Wupatki area; they may be a single wall running off the pueblo or two curved walls that frame an outside activity area. Wing walls tend to shelter the activity area from the prevailing southwesterly winds and may have supported brush walls or a ramada-like roof.

It is important to point out, however, that although pueblos were the most numerous habitation architectural form, pit houses continued to be an important part of the Sinagua settlement regime during the period under consideration. This is particularly significant in the Flagstaff area, where pit houses represent 14 percent of all sites occupied during this time, considerably more than in any of the other Sinagua areas. Often, pit houses and surface pueblos were occupied contemporaneously on the same site, as was likely the situation where cavates co-occurred with pueblos. Whether small pueblos represent seasonally utilized structures, storage, habitation, or a range of all of these functions, remains to be determined.

Regardless of the plan of the pueblo, Sinagua rooms are larger than typical Anasazi rooms, averaging about 16 to 20 m² in floor area. A partial explanation for this may be that Sinagua pueblos seldom have specialized storage rooms. Rooms in Sinagua sites were multipurpose, requiring a larger area within which habitation and storage could be facilitated. Reports from excavated sites do mention the presence of clusters of large storage jars in rooms.

Settlement Patterns

The Northern Sinagua Area

Elden and Turkey Hill phase settlement patterns in the Flagstaff and Anderson Mesa areas appear to be the same, although Anderson Mesa has the least survey data for any of the four areas under consideration. Observation of site distributions in these areas (figure 5.2) suggests three major settlement types: (1) isolated large pueblos, (2) isolated 5- to 12-room pueblos, and (3) clustered 5- to 12-room pueblos. Spacing between the 5- to 12-room pueblos, whether isolated or clustered, is about one-half to two miles (1 to 3 km). These pueblos generally have a number of additional support sites scattered around them, including field houses and other limited activity sites indicated by artifact scatters. Although figure 5.2 shows a number of 5- to 12-room pueblos that occur without satellite support sites, this is likely due to lack of survey or lack of temporally sensitive ceramics being recognized at sites in their vicinity. Although most of the large pueblos at Wupatki have contemporaneous support sites around them, this does not seem to be the case in the Flagstaff area, although this may be due to lack of survey or inability to date small sites in the vicinity. Ridge Ruin and New Caves, for example, are exceptions to this. Ridge Ruin has a few contemporaneous pit house sites, as well as two earlier ball courts, near it. New Caves may be unique in the Flagstaff area because it contains sites that illustrate both patterns, including a large 20-plus-room pueblo and a cluster of 5- to 12-room pueblos, each with a number of supporting satellite sites.

This pair of disparate patterns, one in which people have aggregated into large pueblos, and another in which social units appear to have maintained their physical independence in separate small pueblos, even to the point of building separate pueblos in close proximity, raises questions about the contemporaneity of these two settlement regimes. Rather than two contemporaneous, but disparate patterns,

could this be the archaeological fallout created by the process of aggregation taking place within the Elden phase? From survey data, it is impossible to refine the dating for these sites any finer than the 100 years comprising the Elden phase, but a progression from isolated small pueblos, to clusters of small pueblos, to large aggregated pueblos, does seem to be one logical interpretation of these data. If these sites do represent stages of population aggregation, rather than contemporaneous communities, it further indicates that population levels during the Elden phase were significantly smaller than usually thought.

This interpretation is not without its problems. Based on the location of the 20-plus-room pueblos in the Flagstaff area, this scenario would require a movement of people from the pinyon-juniper zone back into the ponderosa zone, reversing the general population trend that started between about A.D. 1066 and 1100. This differs from the usual interpretation that populations moved from the pinyon-juniper country east of Flagstaff to join the large pueblos of Anderson Mesa after A.D. 1250. Nonetheless, movement of Sinagua populations to higher elevations nearer the San Francisco Peaks and Anderson Mesa, where moister microclimate conditions could be found, would be a likely response to increased drought conditions after A.D. 1200. This would be particularly true if soil fertility had been depleted by intensive and extensive use of the limited arable soils that occur in the pinyon-juniper zones (Pilles 1978: 130–31).

Supporting evidence for a return of the Sinagua to the ponderosa zone may be indicated at Elden Pueblo and Turkey Hill Pueblo, where blocks of rooms were successively added on to the pueblos in the latter part of their occupations, particularly after A.D. 1250. The construction of blocks of rooms, rather than individual rooms, could be interpreted as groups of people moving into the pueblo, rather than the result of in situ population growth at each pueblo.

In any event, it is evident that most of the Elden phase is represented by dispersed, rather than aggregated, settlements. In order to examine population densities and the distribution of social units over the area, it is necessary to change our focus of examination from individual sites to clusters of sites that formed dispersed communities prior to or during the occupation of the large, 20-plus-room pueblos. If such community clusters could be defined, the number of settlements equivalent to the 20-plus-room pueblos listed in the appendix would be greatly expanded. Considerably more intensive surveys of large blocks of lands are needed before this can be accomplished.

To help define these dispersed communities, it would be useful to know the territory occupied by each community. Several intensive surveys form the basis for a set of community estimations. Ridge Ruin and its Elden phase pit house sites are contained within a 180-acre (73 ha) area, and the Elden phase sites at New Caves are within a 300-acre (121 ha) area. Based upon his survey of Walnut Canyon National Monument, Bremer (1989:48–51) identified likely settlement clusters using a minimal spacing tree statistical analysis. It is difficult to say how "typical" these settlement clusters may be for other localities, given the unique topographic situation of the canyon and rim environments. In addition, some clusters were represented by only one or two sites, and others likely extended outside the survey area, beyond the boundaries of the monument. For those completely contained within the monument, Bremer identified cluster sizes of 11, 21, 30, 38, 248, and 372 acres (5, 9, 12, 15, 100, and 150 ha) that contained 4, 6, 5, 4, 35, and 84 sites, respectively. The largest of these clusters may, however, represent two clusters of approximately 135 acres (55 ha) and 116 acres (47 ha) (Bremer 1989:88–89, 99).

Fairly complete surveys have also been completed around several of the 20-plus-room pueblos, specifically Elden Pueblo, Turkey Hill Pueblo, Old Caves Pueblo, Ridge Ruin, and New Caves. By utilizing natural topographic boundaries, such as ridge lines and mesa edges, it can be suggested that the immediate sustaining area for these communities might have ranged between 9 and 10.5 mi² (23 and 27 km²).

The Verde Valley

Because most of the large Honanki phase sites continued to be occupied into the Tuzigoot phase, settlement patterns are basically the same as those previously described for the Tuzigoot phase (Pilles 1981:14, 1986). Settlement patterns in the Verde Valley are dominated by linear site distributions corresponding to the Verde River, its perennial tributary systems, and the steep canyons of the Red Rocks country near Sedona. Along the perennial waterways, sites are spaced about 1.8 miles (2.9 km) apart with no other contemporaneous sites between them. These linear arrangements may have linked lowland and upland resource zones into larger communal networks. Unlike the Flagstaff area, however, there are several locations where 20-plus-room pueblos as well as 13- to 20- room pueblos occur in close proximity. Examples include Tuzigoot, Hatalacva, Talbot Ranch, Spring Creek Ruin, and the lower end of the Verde Valley, north of the East Verde River. Several 20-plus-room pueblos are also associated with satellite support sites and with 5- to 12-room pueblos, such as Honanki, Montezuma Well, and Clear Creek Ruins.

Nonlinear patterns similar to those found in the Flagstaff and Anderson Mesa areas are evident outside the river and stream valleys in the Verde Uplands. In these upland settings there are several large, isolated, 20-plus-room pueblos such as Doran Castle and Boulder Canyon, isolated 5- to 12-room pueblos, and 5- to 12-room pueblos with satellite support sites, as well as isolated field houses, scatters, and agricultural sites that are likely related to unrecorded 5- to 12-room pueblos in the vicinity.

As is the case with the Flagstaff area, it cannot be determined whether the various classes of site size and type are due to diverse strategies pursued within a single, contemporaneous settlement regime, or are the remains of successively more aggregated settlement strategies being used through time. It is tempting to suggest the 5- to 12-room pueblos in the uplands represent early stages in the aggregation process, culminating with the 20-plus-room pueblos in both the lowlands and uplands. As with the Flagstaff sites, movements to other locations with more reliable water sources would have been a likely response to drier climatic conditions toward the end of the Honanki phase. In the Verde Valley, however, movement would have likely been to the river and stream sides at lower elevations, or to the vicinity of permanent springs in the uplands.

Settlement Patterns and Social Complexity

In describing Sinagua settlement patterns during the Honanki, Elden, and Turkey Hill phases, several pueblo layout patterns and two pueblo size classes can be identified. Explanations for these classes have been offered, suggesting either a rapid aggregation process over 100 years or a disparate pattern of large aggregated pueblos occupied contemporaneously with dispersed settlement clusters. This latter settlement pattern, which mixed large and small settlements across the same landscape, forms the basis for the following discussion of Sinagua social complexity.

It has previously been suggested that the different size classes and settlement plans of pueblos noted for the Northern Sinagua area might reflect different social levels within the society, specifically a four-tiered settlement hierarchy (Gratz and Pilles 1979; Fish, Pilles, and Fish 1980:171). In addition to the observed differences in potentially contemporaneous settlement sizes, burial patterns studied by Hohmann (1982:75) led him to postulate that Sinagua society changed from a limited stratified society into a hierarchically organized society functioning at a chiefdom level during the early portion of the Elden phase.

The large, courtyard-oriented pueblos have several characteristics that suggest they were regional centers, including site location on a hill or ridge top along a likely prehistoric trade route, a higher incidence of trade ceramics and luxury goods than found at contemporaneous sites, association with a ball court, a community room, inner and outer courtyards formed by walls, and a Hohokam-like pit house located inside the inner courtyard. Of the 20-plus-room pueblos included in this summary (see appendix), Nuvakwewtaqa SE and SW, Ridge Ruin, Clear Creek Ruins, Wupatki, Sugarloaf, Juniper Terrace, Old Caves, and New Caves are considered to have served as central places or "chief villages," although a few lack clear evidence for all of the characteristics listed here.

The famous Magician's Burial from Ridge Ruin has been identified as a high status individual, specifically, a *Qualeetaqa* of the *Motswimi* Society, that is, a war chief (McGregor 1943:295; Pilles 1987: 115–16). This is significant, as it suggests the presence of clan and society organizations in the Sinagua during the Elden phase. Other possible indicators of status include nose plugs, carved shell bracelets, carved and painted bone hair pins, wands tipped with conch shells, unique pottery vessels, and staffs. When found with burials, such items were associated with older men. This contrasts with the most elaborate burials found in the Anasazi region, which tended to be those of older women. Individuals with wands and other items previously noted are also seen in petroglyphs in scenes depicting leadership, if not authority.

The presence of specialized community architecture, such as kivas, ball courts, community rooms, and "dance plazas" further suggests that sociopolitical hierarchy probably influenced the use of architectural space among the Sinagua. These same types of communal architecture are found throughout the entire Sinagua region and most can be traced from the earliest beginnings of the Sinagua.

Sinagua kivas are square or rectangular in shape and have a raised bench across one end. Most are subterranean with the bench oriented to the north; however, others occur as specialized rooms within pueblos. Community rooms are usually rectangular, although some, such as the "amphitheater" at Wupatki, are circular. In the Flagstaff, Verde Valley, and Anderson Mesa areas, they occur at the large pueblos and pit house sites (figure 5.4), but in the Wupatki and Deadman Wash areas, they are also found at smaller pueblos containing 5 to 8 rooms (e.g., Anderson 1990:2–5, 2–29). At least 31 community rooms have been identified in A.D. 1150 to 1300 period sites. The smallest ones are 35 to 63 m² in size, although most range between 100 and 300 m² in size.

Fish, Pilles, and Fish (1980:160–61) list the ball courts found in the Sinagua region and suggest that although most date between A.D. 1000 and 1150, use of some ball courts extended past A.D. 1150, such as at Sacred Mountain in the Verde Valley, and at Wupatki, Juniper Terrace, Old Caves, and Nuvakwewtaqa in the north.

"Dance plazas" are large subtriangular or rectangular areas, outlined by masonry walls, large rocks, and berms of earth. One example at New Caves covers 670 m² and the other example, at Clear Creek Ruins, is estimated to be 1,200 m². Both were constructed a short distance from the main pueblo, similar to the location of ball courts at other sites.

That some centralized form of authority was present is also suggested by the persistence of settlement locations through time. When areas are surveyed around the large pueblos and the community clusters of smaller pueblos, earlier pit house sites are invariably found in the vicinity. This suggests a long-term continuity of communities and perhaps somewhat stable and culturally recognized territorial boundaries that lasted 200 or more years (Bremer 1989:109).

Other researchers, however, disagree with concepts of a stratified Sinagua society. Kamp and Whittaker (1990:116–118) suggest that simpler, less centralized, levels of organization are indicated by architectural and artifactual data recovered in excavations. Although their analysis provides an alternative interpretation of the data, it does not obviate the fact that the test implications for demonstrating a "chiefdom level" of organization are met in the Sinagua area (Gratz and Pilles 1979). Whether a complex chiefdom level of organization is present or not, many lines of evidence indicate Sinagua society was certainly more complex than is typically suggested in the literature.

Summary

From the beginning of the Sinagua regional tradition, a close interaction between population movements, environmental zones, and climatic change can be documented. This is most evident during the Elden, Turkey Hill, Honanki, and Tuzigoot phases, which correspond roughly to the Pueblo III period across the Anasazi world. During times of increased available moisture, Sinagua populations moved into areas that had not been previously occupied, presumably due to a lack of water. In the Northern Sinagua region, this involved a movement to the lower pinyon-juniper zone, while in the Verde Valley, movement was into the canyons of the Red Rock and Mogollon Rim. Around A.D. 1250, there was another major shift, apparently in response to increasingly drying conditions, that caused the Northern Sinagua to retreat back to the higher elevations in the ponderosa pine forest near the San Francisco Peaks, and to the higher mesa country of Anderson Mesa. In the Verde Valley, the areas along the river, its perennial streams, and permanent springs became the primary locales of occupation.

Analysis of site distributions indicates significant differences between site size and settlement patterns in the Sinagua region and surrounding Anasazi regional traditions. Sinagua settlements were considerably smaller than those recorded across the northern Southwest during the same time period. Sinagua population aggregation was represented by either 5- to 12-room pueblos or 20-plus-room pueblos during this time. Pit house villages were also present and a variety of smaller support sites, notably field houses, were numerically the most abundant site type during this period of time.

Given the comparison with the rest of the Anasazi world, the period of most apparent population aggregation in the Sinagua region was the fourteenth century. During the Clear Creek and Tuzigoot phases (between A.D. 1300 and 1400), many of the pueblos founded between A.D. 1150 and 1300 expanded considerably in size, and many other aggregated pueblos were also established. Concomitant with the aggregation process, there is also evidence for the development of clans, societies, and high-status individuals.

The difficulty of dating Sinagua sites from surface remains and inadequacies of survey information limit our ability to determine whether the settlement data result from a contemporaneous population organized into a hierarchical chiefdom, or whether the settlement hierarchy was the result of diachronic change in settlement size associated with increasing aggregation over a 100-year time span characterized by considerable environmental stress. It is hoped that summaries such as this, coupled with the observations presented by others in this volume, will form the basis for investigations that can shed light on this formative period of culture change in the American Southwest.

References Cited

Anderson, Bruce A.
1990   The Wupatki Archeological Inventory Survey Project: Final Report. Professional Paper No. 35. USDI, National Park Service, Southwest Regional Office, Division of Anthropology, Santa Fe.

Bannister, Bryant, Elizabeth A. M. Gell, John W. Hannah
1966   Tree-Ring Dates from Arizona N-Q: Verde-Showlow-St. Johns Area. Laboratory of Tree-Ring Research, University of Arizona, Tucson.

Bradley, Ronna J.
1994   Before the Sky Fell: The Pre-eruptive Sinagua of the Flagstaff Area. Across the Colorado Plateau: Anthropological Studies for the Transwestern Pipeline Expansion Project, Vol. 12. Office of Contract Archeology and Maxwell Museum of Anthropology, University of New Mexico, Albuquerque.

Bremer, J. Michael
1989   Walnut Canyon: Settlement and Land Use. The Arizona Archaeologist No. 23. Arizona Archaeological Society, Phoenix

Breternitz, Cory D.
1977   Dendrochronology and Archaeology of Six Sites in the Verde Valley, Central Arizona. Ms. on file, USDA, Coconino National Forest Supervisor's Office, Flagstaff.

Breternitz, David A.
1960   Excavations at Three Sites in the Verde Valley, Arizona. Bulletin No. 34. Museum of Northern Arizona, Flagstaff.

Caywood, Louis R., and Edward H. Spicer
1935   Tuzigoot: The Excavation and Repair of a Ruin on the Verde River Near Clarkdale, Arizona. USDI, National Park Service, Office of Southwestern National Monuments, Coolidge, Arizona.

Colton, Harold S.
1939   Prehistoric Culture Units and their Relationships in Northern Arizona. Bulletin No. 17. Museum of Northern Arizona, Flagstaff.
1946   The Sinagua: A Summary of the Archaeology of the Region of Flagstaff, Arizona. Bulletin 22. Museum of Northern Arizona, Flagstaff.

Downum, Christian E.
1988   "One Grand History": A Critical Review of Flagstaff Archaeology, 1851 to 1988. Unpublished Ph.D. dissertation, Department of Anthropology, University of Arizona, Tucson.

Downum, Christian E., and Alan P. Sullivan, III
1990   Settlement Patterns. In The Wupatki Archeological Inventory Survey Project: Final Report, compiled by Bruce A. Anderson, pp. 5-1–5-89. Professional Paper No. 35. USDI, National Park Service, Southwest Regional Office, Division of Anthropology, Santa Fe.

Fish, Paul R., and Suzanne K. Fish
1977   Verde Valley Archaeology: Review and Prospective. Research Paper No. 8. Museum of Northern Arizona, Flagstaff.

Fish, Paul R., Peter J. Pilles, Jr., and Suzanne K. Fish
1980   Colonies, Traders and Traits: The Hohokam in the North. In Current Issues in Hohokam Prehistory: Proceedings of a Symposium, edited by David E. Doyel and Fred Plog, pp. 151–75. Anthropological Research Papers No. 23. Arizona State University, Tempe.

Gratz, Kathleen E., and Peter J. Pilles, Jr.
1979   Sinagua Settlement Patterns and Organizational Models: A Trial Survey. Paper presented at the Annual Meeting of the Southwestern Anthropological Society, Santa Barbara.

Hartman, Dana
1976   Tuzigoot: An Archaeological Overview. Research Paper No. 4. Museum of Northern Arizona, Flagstaff.

Henderson, T. Kathleen
1979   Archaeological Survey at Chavez Pass Ruin, Coconino National Forest, Arizona: The 1978 Field Season. Ms. on file, USDA, Coconino National Forest Supervisor's Office, Flagstaff.

Hevly, Richard H., Roger E. Kelly, Glenn A. Anderson, and Stanley J. Olsen
1979   Comparative Effects of Climatic Change, Cultural Impact, and Volcanism in the Paleoecology of Flagstaff, Arizona, A.D. 900–1300. In Volcanic Activity and Human Ecology, edited by Payson D. Sheets and Donald K. Grayson, pp. 487–523. Academic Press, New York.

Hohmann, John C.
1982   Sinagua Social Organization: Inferences Based Upon Prehistoric Mortuary Practices. The Arizona Archaeologist 17. Arizona Archaeological Society, Phoenix.

Kamp, Kathryn A., and John C. Whittaker
1990   Lizard Man Village: A Small Site Perspective on Northern Sinagua Social Organization. The Kiva 55(2): 99–125.

McGregor, John C.

1941   *Winona and Ridge Ruin, Part I. Archi-
        tecture and Material Culture.* Museum
        of Northern Arizona Bulletin 18.
        Flagstaff.

1943   Burial of an Early American Magi-
        cian. *Proceedings of the American
        Philosophical Society* 86(2):270–98.

1962   The Two Kivas Site. Ms. on file,
        Museum of Northern Arizona,
        Department of Anthropology,
        Flagstaff.

Pilles, Peter J., Jr.

1978   The Field House and Sinagua
        Demography. In *Limited Activity
        and Occupation Sites: A Collection of
        Conference Papers*, edited by A. E.
        Ward, pp. 119–33. Contributions
        to Anthropological Studies 1. Cen-
        ter for Anthropological Studies,
        Albuquerque.

1979   Sunset Crater and the Sinagua:
        A New Interpretation. In *Volcanic
        Activity and Human Ecology*, edited
        by Payson D. Sheets and Donald K.
        Grayson, pp. 459–85. Academic
        Press, New York.

1981   The Southern Sinagua. *Plateau*
        53(1):6–17.

1986   New Developments in the Pueblo IV
        Period in the Verde Valley. Paper
        presented at the 59th Annual Meet-
        ing of the Pecos Conference, Payson,
        Arizona.

1987   Hisatsinom: The Ancient People.
        In *Earth Fire: A Hopi legend of the
        Sunset Crater Eruption*, edited by
        Ekkehart Malotki with Michael
        Lomatuway'ma, pp. 105–20,
        Northland Press, Flagstaff.

1988   Contributing author in *Historical
        Dictionary of North American Archae-
        ology*, edited by Edward Jelks and
        Juliet C. Jelks. Greenwood Press,
        New York.

Plog, Fred

1989   The Sinagua and their Relations. In
        Dynamics of Southwest Prehistory,
        edited by Linda S. Cordell and
        George J. Gumerman, pp. 263–
        91. Smithsonian Institution Press,
        Washington, D.C.

Robinson, William J., Bruce G. Harrill,
Richard L. Warren

1975   *Tree-Ring Dates from Arizona H-
        I: Flagstaff Area.* Laboratory of
        Tree-Ring Research, University of
        Arizona, Tucson.

Samples, Terry, and David R. Wilcox

1992   Permit Report to Kaibab National
        Forest on Work of the 1990
        MNA/NAU/Oberlin Archaeologi-
        cal Field School and Subsequent
        Studies during 1991. Ms. on file,
        USDA, Kaibab National Forest
        Supervisor's Office, Williams.

Tagg, Martyn D.

1986   *The Tuzigoot Survey and Three Small
        Verde Valley Projects: Archeological
        Investigations in the Middle Verde
        Valley, Arizona.* Publications in
        Anthropology No. 40. USDI, National
        Park Service, Western Archeological
        and Conservation Center, Tucson.

Wells, Susan Joyce

1981   *An Archaeological Survey of the
        Bald Hill Locality, Mogollon Rim,
        North Central Arizona.* Unpublished
        Master's thesis, Department of
        Anthropology, University of Arizona,
        Tucson.

Wells, Susan J., and Keith M. Anderson

1988   *Archeological Survey and Architectural
        Study of Montezuma Castle National
        Monument.* Publications in Anthro-
        pology No. 50. USDI, National Park
        Service, Western Archeological and
        Conservation Center, Tucson.

Wilcox, David R.

1987   Archaeological Investigations of the
        1986 MNA/NAU Archaeological Field
        School on the Coconino National
        Forest. Ms. on file, USDI, Coconino
        National Forest Supervisor's Office,
        Flagstaff.

Wilson, John Philip

1969   *The Sinagua and their Neighbors.*
        Unpublished Ph.D. Dissertation,
        Harvard University, Cambridge.

Chapter 6

A Demographic Overview of the Late Pueblo III Period in the Mountains of East-Central Arizona

J. Jefferson Reid, John R. Welch, Barbara K. Montgomery, and María Nieves Zedeño

The late Pueblo III period (A.D. 1250–1300) in the mountains of east-central Arizona has long been recognized as one of transition from pit houses, cobble surface rooms, and small pueblos to the large masonry pueblos that mark the last prehistoric occupation. The shift in site characteristics is the most visible manifestation of widespread cultural and behavioral changes that took place around A.D. 1300. In few places is this transition as dramatic or as well documented as in the Grasshopper Region. In presenting a picture of population dynamics in the Arizona mountains, we focus in this chapter on the Grasshopper Region, incorporating settlement, ceramic, and ethnographic information from other areas to strengthen our arguments. We begin with a brief discussion of geography and relevant archaeological fieldwork, move to a discussion of our research orientation, and then describe the late Pueblo III period settlement pattern and system. Last, we infer processes of late Pueblo III period population dynamics based on settlement and ceramic data, and we employ ethnography to summarize the prehistoric reconstructions.

In this chapter we utilize a rough cultural chronology that is based upon the original Pecos Classification. Our use of Pueblo II period (A.D. 900–1150), Pueblo III period (A.D. 1150–1300), and Pueblo IV period (A.D. 1300–1540) pertains exclusively to the absolute dates assigned to each period. Also, we use "region" rather than "district" in our discussion because this term best fits the current nomenclature used by archaeological research projects in east-central Arizona.

Geography and Fieldwork

The geographic boundaries of the study area are the Mogollon Rim on the north, the upper reach of the Black River on the east, the Black and Salt Rivers on the south, and Cherry Creek on the west (figure 6.1). Significant fieldwork information requires a short, southern extension to include Point of Pines. This broad area includes the entire White Mountain Apache Reservation (2,600 mi², 6,743 km²) and portions of the San Carlos Reservation and the Tonto National Forest. Within this mountainous domain three areas of intensive archaeological research, Forestdale, Point of Pines, and Grasshopper-Q Ranch, form a data triangle (figure 6.1). Because few sites in the Arizona mountains contained 50 or more rooms during the latter half of the thirteenth century, these areas provide a critical point of comparison to the settlement in surrounding regions.

The Forestdale Valley is a narrow valley (1.31 mi², 3.4 km²) immediately below the Mogollon Rim at an elevation of 6,494 feet (1,980 m). Emil Haury surveyed the valley during the 1931 reconnaissance that led to the recognition and definition of the Mogollon culture (Haury 1936, 1986). Haury returned to Forestdale in 1939 to direct the University of Arizona Field School excavation of Bluff, Bear, and Tla Kii villages (Haury 1985). The late Pueblo III period site AZ P:16:9 (ASM) has 40 to 50 rooms and the Pueblo IV period pueblo ruin of Tundastusa contains approximately 200 rooms. Both were tested by Haury.

Point of Pines provides critical information on large, late thirteenth-century masonry pueblos and populations. The region is an area of roughly 174 mi² (450 km²) around Circle Prairie, a large upland basin at an elevation of 6,000 feet (1,830 m). The long history of occupation of the region from late Archaic times (2000 B.C.) until abandonment of the mountains around A.D. 1400 is well documented by Haury's field school excavations (see Haury 1989:114–121, 125 for a summary of culture history and bibliography). Of particular relevance are Turkey Creek Pueblo (Lowell 1989, 1991), a 335-room masonry ruin, and the Kayenta intrusion (Maverick Mountain phase) at the 800-room Point of Pines Pueblo (Haury 1958; Lindsay 1987).

The adjacent Grasshopper and Q Ranch regions comprise upland plateaus separated by steep canyons. The Q Ranch region (180 mi², 466 km²) is known from survey and excavation by Arizona State University Field School in the Vosberg Valley (Cartledge 1976, 1977; Chenhall 1972; Morris 1970) and the University of Arizona's Cholla Project (Reid 1982). In addition, the Cholla Project provided survey and excavation information along a 220-kilometer transect from the Little Colorado River to south of Lake Roosevelt (figure 6.1).

The Grasshopper Region (320 mi², 830 km²) is subdivided into the Grasshopper Plateau (85 mi², 220 km²), drained by the seasonally flowing Salt River Draw, and the Cibecue Valley, drained by the perennially flowing Cibecue Creek. One important late thirteenth-century occupation within the region is at Chodistaas, an 18-room pueblo located one mile (1.6 km) north of Grasshopper Pueblo

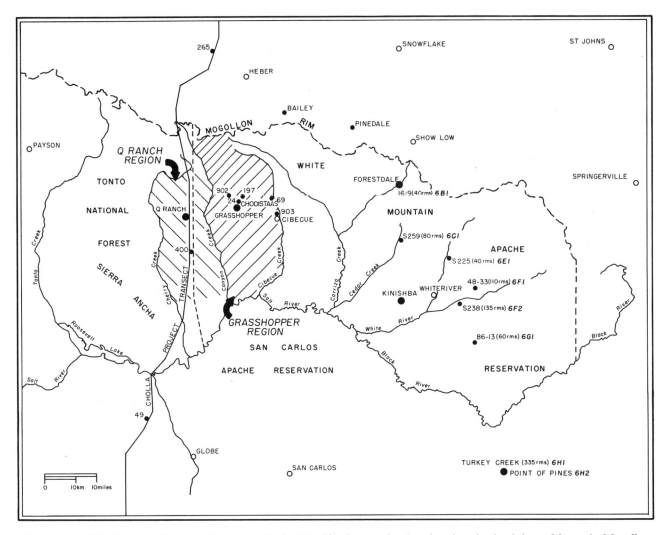

Figure 6.1.   Distribution of large settlements (with site identification numbers) and regions in the Arizona Mountain Mogollon area. Some of the sites shown do not exceed 50 rooms, but they are included to supplement the settlement pattern discussion in this chapter. Site data for those settlements containing 50 or more rooms during the Pueblo III period are listed in the appendix.

(Crown 1981; Montgomery 1992; Montgomery and Reid 1990; Reid 1989:77–79; Zedeño 1994).

Much of the archaeological work over the past 30 years in the Grasshopper Region has been on the large, fourteenth-century Grasshopper Pueblo. Tuggle's (1970) research was the first systematic survey of the region. Full-coverage survey of 180 mi² (466 km²) and many additional miles of transects over broken country have resulted in the discovery of 779 sites and 713 artifact scatters in the Grasshopper Region. No Pueblo III period site of 50 rooms or more—the lower limit of sites considered in this volume—has been

recorded in either the Q Ranch or Grasshopper region.

The Grasshopper and Q Ranch regions never witnessed the consistent occupation that characterized mountain "hot spots" of local resource abundance such as Forestdale, Point of Pines, and probably the region around Kinishba. Kinishba Pueblo, excavated by Byron Cummings (1940) as part of his 1930s field school and restoration program, is in the center of the "Mogollon triangle" defined by these same regions. Although assigned by Cummings to the Great Pueblo period (Pueblo III), most of his excavations clearly focused on the portion of Kinishba occu-

pied during the fourteenth century. Except for the early reconnaissance by Spier (1919), there is little information for the late thirteenth century from this critical area, though a number of pueblos larger than 50 rooms have been recorded.

These mountain regions are part of the vastly larger circum-Sonoran uplands, a biotic and physiographic province of rugged, mostly semiarid regions receiving 8 to 19 inches (20–50 cm) of precipitation annually (Shreve 1951). The uplands are characterized by heavily dissected terrain, high topographic relief, and generally thin but variable soil and vegetation cover. This rugged relief and large number of moisture-collecting summits over 6,560 feet (2,000 m) support a high water table and abundant springs. The territories of all 12 groups that form the basis for the ethnographic comparison discussed later include tracts above 3,280 feet (1,000 m) and at least 1,000 meters in elevational difference within each territory. Like the prehistoric inhabitants of the Arizona mountains, these ethnographic groups each have access to a diverse array of canyon, steppe, and forest biomes. Compared to the Colorado Plateaus physiographic province, the Arizona uplands have more favorable precipitation and temperature regimes, more diverse but thinner soils, higher biomass levels, and much more water. Climatic, physiographic, and biotic similarities give a basic structure to the uplands as well as a set of common themes linking the effective environment (see Steward 1955) to the adaptive strategies of the 12 ethnographic case studies discussed later in this chapter (Welch 1990).

Research Perspectives

Conceptualizing Settlements

Our thinking about the distribution of populations and their use of landscapes is informed by excavation and extensive artifact analysis in addition to conventional survey information. This perspective produces an emphasis on activities rather than morphological categories.

We abandoned the conventional settlement dichotomy of habitation and limited activity sites when it became apparent that in the mountains this two-class typology failed to characterize the variability in the accumulating survey data. Cholla Project researchers developed a six-class typology to describe the range of settlement variability as a function of activity performance (Whittlesey and Reid 1982). Because the Cholla sites included no large pueblos and limited excavation data, we view this analysis as provisional and, thus, assign preliminary descriptive labels (Class A through F) rather than functional labels to activity categories represented at settlements. One revelation of the analysis of Pueblo II and III period sites along the Cholla Project's 137-mile (220-km) axis was that activities at settlements were variable, occupation was more often temporary than permanent, and populations were highly mobile prior to A.D. 1300. In addition, the material record indicates a significant degree of cultural or ethnic heterogeneity. Our typology forced us to think of settlement dynamics in terms that differ from much of the current archaeological literature. Rather than conceptualizing settlement as a series of static behaviors through space and time, prehistoric occupation occurred as ever-changing sets of activities at many localities spread over a landscape much larger than that investigated by most archaeological projects.

Following Winters (1969:110) we find it useful to distinguish between settlement pattern, the location and distribution of settlements in relation to the natural environment, and settlement system, the set of settlement strategies utilized by a population throughout a normal cycle of annual activities.

Conceptualizing Social Organization

It is now commonly accepted in archaeology that Service's (1962) evolutionary sequence of organizational levels—band, tribe, chiefdom, state—does not adequately depict the varied developmental trajectories followed by human sociopolitical systems. Alternative approaches to understanding organizational complexity have been proposed by cultural ecologists (Netting 1990), comparative ethnologists (Jorgensen 1980, 1987), and Old World archaeologists specializing in the rise of civilization (Johnson 1982, 1983, 1989). Each has combined broad ethnographic surveys with detailed analyses in an effort to explain the conditions under which different sociopolitical forms arise and operate. Particularly relevant to our thinking is Jorgensen's (1980) massive, computer-assisted analysis of the relationships among critical variables in 172 western North American societies, each evaluated in terms of cultural configuration at the time of European contact. Jorgensen examines the relationships between environmental zone, resource distribution, residential mobility, population aggregates, raiding, property ownership, decision making, and a variety of social organizational forms. His work is rich in the discussion of variables relevant to archaeological reconstructions and provides an approach helpful to the investigation of prehistoric sociopolitical organization. Because the analysis is confined to societies of aboriginal western North America, including the Southwest, the results are demonstrably more relevant to the Arizona mountain population than are other world areas from which ethnographic models often are derived for archaeological application. A brief discussion of Jorgensen's terminology is useful.

Jorgensen identifies three broad categories of political-economic-territorial units in western North America: (1) residential kinship groups, (2) bands and villages, and (3) tribes and districts (Jorgensen 1980:211–19). Residential kinship groups, the simplest and most common organization, had no formal ties with any other group and might be described as lacking political organization. The importance of this basal social unit underscores the significance of household analysis in Grasshopper research (see Ciolek-Torrello 1984, 1985; Ciolek-Torrello and Reid 1974; Montgomery 1991; Reid and Whittlesey 1982; Rock 1974).

Bands and villages consist of several residential kin groups that recognize common leadership, common territory, and no jurisdiction beyond the local organization. Band organizations characterize mobile hunters and gatherers in mountainous regions with access to two or more biotic life zones. Villages, on the other hand, have greater interannual residential stability, due in part to a more intensive exploitation of a single biotic life zone. Villages also demonstrate a much broader range of organizational complexity than bands, ranging from the sociopolitically simple to the complex.

Districts are political units comprising two or more villages, while tribes are the more mobile counterparts of districts, being composed of several bands.

The utility of Jorgensen's nomenclature is that it does not imply a unilineal evolutionary sequence as Service (1962) does. Instead, Jorgensen provides a flexible framework that recognizes a group's capacity to alter its demographic-organizational configuration in response to stress or opportunity. Although Jorgensen shows that organization and subsistence strategy do not develop in lockstep (see Netting 1990), he does observe that the variables that best account for socio-political configurations are closely linked to subsistence strategy and territory. Of particular note are the considerable environmental and social limitations on the development of organizational complexity above the level of residential kinship group. We utilize Jorgensen's approach in our discussion of twelfth- and thirteenth-century regional population dynamics.

Pueblo II and Early Pueblo III Period Settlement: Background for Change

A settlement analysis for this period (roughly A.D. 900–1200) is available for the Q Ranch Region investigated as part of the Cholla Project (Reid 1982; Tuggle 1982; Whittlesey and Reid 1982). Inferences based on the Q Ranch data may be extrapolated to the adjacent Grasshopper Region.

Settlement Pattern

The Q Ranch sites are small, with 5 to 10 pit houses, two to three low-walled cobble structures, or a combination of pit house and cobble structures. The sites are located throughout a variety of landforms

and environmental zones, though habitation sites are generally absent in the elevations above 6,400 feet (1,951 m), where only lithic scatters occur. The habitation sites are highly variable in the density and absolute number of surface artifacts.

Visual evaluation of site distributions suggests seemingly random placement within or near soils that are inferred to be of horticultural importance. This distribution contrasts with the pattern of site clustering around focal settlements that is common in the eastern mountains at Forestdale and Point of Pines. Gardening is inferred but we currently lack any quantitative data on its contribution to the diet. Habitation camps are characterized by evidence for food storage and preparation, including grinding, primary reduction and production of flakes for expedient tools or blanks for further modification, and maintenance and processing activities.

Hunting was an important subsistence activity. Specialized localities reflect hunting, butchering, and equipment maintenance, including tool retouch and resharpening, as well as other specialized procurement and processing tasks. Localities for specialized plant food processing are absent, so all plant food grinding apparently occurred at habitation camps. The overall pattern is one of part-time habitation of settlements and specialized use of particular areas for resource procurement.

Settlement System

Throughout the Pueblo II and early Pueblo III periods there appears to have been an emphasis on temporary settlement occupations and hunting. Based upon the settlement data and a cluster analysis of stone tools (Graybill and Reid 1982) from the region, the archaeological record appears to have been created by mobile populations of hunter-gatherer-gardeners exploiting the upland resources (especially animal and mineral) of the Q Ranch Region and the plant resources of the desert

areas to the south along the Salt River. There is no evidence in surface collections for plant cultivation, though the location of sites near diabase soil throughout the occupation of the region suggests horticulture as a subsistence activity (see Cartledge 1976, 1977; Tuggle 1982; Wood 1980).

We find evidence at this time of different ethnic groups using the mountains. Red-on-buff and micaceous plain ware pottery, carbon-painted white ware pottery, and the exploitation of steatite resources occurred during the Pueblo II period (A.D. 900–1150). In contrast, during the subsequent early Pueblo III period there was an absence of the "desert items" and a shift in the northern source of black-on-white ceramics (Tuggle, Kintigh, and Reid 1982; Zedeño 1994). The remains at Walnut Creek Village in the Q Ranch Region (Morris 1970; Whittlesey 1982) and Bear Village in the Forestdale Valley (Haury 1985) can be interpreted to represent either sequential occupations by different ethnic groups or ethnic coresidence (Reid 1989:67, 73–74). The broader picture, however, is of flexible group membership consistent with highly mobile residential kinship groups exploiting different life zones (Jorgensen 1980). There is no evidence to suggest temporary aggregates of kin groups into band or village organizations (as defined by Jorgensen 1980) in the Grasshopper or Q Ranch regions before A.D. 1250.

In summary we see a pattern of isolated settlements, located near garden plots, occupied intermittently by a mobile population of autonomous residential kin groups relying on a subsistence of hunting, gathering and gardening. The absence of settlements clustered around a focal settlement contrasts with the long-term pattern of such clusters farther east at Forestdale and Point of Pines. Joint use of the mountains by different ethnic groups accounts for many of the seemingly enigmatic patterns in the archaeological record.

Late Pueblo III Period Settlement

Grasshopper and Q Ranch Regions

The Grasshopper and Q Ranch regions provide information on events and processes that may have occurred earlier at Point of Pines and other eastern mountain regions. The regional pattern is for sites to cluster on the Grasshopper Plateau and the Cibecue Creek Valley, and the Campbell Creek area of Q Ranch. Individual sites are located on terraces above creeks, on the pediment overlooking the Cibecue Valley, and on moderately high landforms such as prominent ridge and hill tops. There is no evidence for the construction of cliff dwellings in the Grasshopper area, though some were begun in the Sierra Anchas (Ciolek-Torrello and Lange 1990).

Sites include sherd scatters, small cobble or cobble and slab pueblos of 1 to 10 rooms, and slab-masonry pueblos of 1 to 30 rooms. The cobble rooms have low walls and may be either contiguous or separate. The slab rooms represent a variety of forms from low to high walls, and are constructed as contiguous-walled room blocks as well as isolated rooms. Larger sites have contiguous rooms and often contain a plaza bounded by a wall or defined by surrounding room blocks.

Intensive survey coverage of the area around Grasshopper Pueblo has revealed a spatial clustering of sites adjacent to agricultural soil with the largest settlements functioning as focal settlements. Three settlement clusters have been proposed—one at Chodistaas, one at Grasshopper Spring, and one at Grasshopper Pueblo (see Tuggle 1970:89–104). This same pattern of settlement clusters occurs in the Cibecue Valley, Oak Creek Valley, and Campbell Creek (Q Ranch). The arrangement is a local expression of the long-term pattern of settlements dispersed around a focal settlement. In the eastern mountains focal settlements generally contain a great kiva (Haury 1985), while those in the

Grasshopper and Q Ranch regions commonly have a plaza or courtyard.

Beginning in the A.D. 1280s there was a rapid increase in site density in the Grasshopper Region. This increase resulted from immigration into the region by populations from above the Mogollon Rim and perhaps the desert below. Associated with the increase in site density is a decrease in residential mobility by the inhabitants of the region. We suspect that these settlement shifts were a product of the relocation of populations associated with the widespread demographic shifts on the Colorado Plateaus (Dean and Robinson 1982).

Compared to surrounding regions, the late thirteenth- and early fourteenth-century aggregation into large pueblo communities in the Grasshopper and Q Ranch regions occurred relatively late. In the eastern part of the White Mountain Apache Reservation there are pueblos of up to 100 rooms occupied during the late thirteenth century. To the north, above the Mogollon Rim, Pinedale Pueblo has produced tree-ring dates in this period and serves as the type site for the Pinedale phase (see Kintigh, chapter 9). To the west, in the Sierra Ancha, tree-ring dates on cliff dwellings suggest thirteenth-century beginnings for population aggregation (Ciolek-Torrello and Lange 1990). Finally, there is evidence from the southwest in the Tonto Basin that fairly large communities were occupied during the thirteenth century. Ceramics and community layout plans indicate the presence in the mountains of indigenous, mountain people as well as people from plateau areas.

Population movement into the Grasshopper Region and the build up of aggregated communities outside of the region had two major effects on the local settlement structure (Reid 1989:77–81). First, the traditional pattern of residential mobility was interrupted, resulting in more permanent occupation of settlements. We think that this occurred in the A.D. 1280s at the height of the Great

Drought (Montgomery and Reid 1990). Second, increased population density and the presence of displaced populations increased the competition for resources and created an atmosphere of social and economic uncertainty. For residential kinship groups in small pueblo communities of the Grasshopper Region this competition would have been heightened by the presence of increasingly aggregated communities in the surrounding area. Social uncertainty may have reached the level of real threats through raiding. All three of the excavated settlements dating to this period, Chodistaas, Grasshopper Spring, and AZ P:14:197 (ASM), show evidence of burning. Population aggregation into large pueblo communities in the Grasshopper Region and at Point of Pines may well relate to the need for greater protection of people and provisions.

Point of Pines Region

Lowell (1989, 1991) has brought into sharp focus a special case of late Pueblo III period aggregation in the Point of Pines region. Based upon field notes and records from excavations at Turkey Creek Pueblo in the 1950s (Haury 1989; A. Johnson 1965), Lowell reconstructed social groups at this 335-room masonry ruin. Her analysis of architecture (314 excavated rooms), fixed floor features, and artifacts revealed four social units (Lowell 1989:188). The basic unit, the household, utilized three types of rooms, habitation, special activity, and storage. Households were grouped into suprahousehold units that Lowell interprets as residential kinship groups. The residential kinship group comprised nuclear and extended families. These groups are recognized architecturally by long walls that divide the pueblo into about 21 such groups. Lowell estimates an average of 16 rooms per group, with a range of 8 to 30 rooms. The third group was the moiety, identified by architectural features that distinguish the northern rooms from the southern rooms.

The fourth grouping, the village itself, was unified by the single great kiva.

Lowell (1989:192–94) explains aggregation as a coming together of similar social groups to form the large pueblo village. The long-lived mountain pattern of small settlements dispersed around a focal community marked by a great kiva gave rise to a pueblo community through the coalescence of extant social groupings. The suprahousehold units identified at Turkey Creek were most probably architecturally and functionally equivalent to the isolated sites that characterize Pueblo II and III period settlement in the Point of Pines region (see Olson 1959).

Although the mechanics of aggregation are clear for Turkey Creek, the reasons for terminating the ceremonial-community pattern dating back to Crooked Ridge Village (Wheat 1954) must be inferred. The heavy emphasis on storage rooms at Turkey Creek leads us to suggest that aggregation occurred to protect food provisions and people, a response consistent with Turkey Creek's defensibility (Lowell 1989:188–92).

Models for Late Pueblo III Period Demographic Change in the Arizona Mountains

Explaining social phenomena through the use of the prehistoric record is a complicated process. Accordingly, we have developed a number of procedures that can be considered part of research protocol for work at Grasshopper. Relevant here is that the method of multiple working hypotheses is most efficacious when accompanied by several researchers pursuing a number of independent lines of evidence. We first discuss a settlement model of population interaction in the Grasshopper Region, then move on to a ceramic-based approach to the region. Both of these models are then discussed in relation to ethnographic data from upland populations in the greater American Southwest.

A Settlement Model for the Grasshopper Region

The Pueblo II and early Pueblo III (A.D. 900–1250) pattern of mobile residential kin groups subsisting by hunting, gathering, and gardening was augmented in the latter half of the thirteenth century by kin groups periodically coming together in settlements clustered around a focal settlement with a plaza or courtyard. This late thirteenth-century pattern fits the band as defined by Jorgensen (1980).

During the late thirteenth century, population movement into the mountains by nonlocal people disrupted established patterns of mobility and resource use. Demographic pressure and resource competition increased social and economic tension. By the A.D. 1280s, at the height of the Great Drought, residential mobility had decreased in response to population packing.

The reconfiguration of territorial rights and rescheduling of procurement patterns required a renegotiation of resource procurement rules and social structural relationships. One result may have been an increasing emphasis on food production due to dwindling resources and growing conflict potential (Welch 1991).

Continued immigration of displaced persons and the establishment of villages (see Jorgensen 1980) in areas surrounding the Grasshopper Region increased real and perceived threats to the smaller communities of the Grasshopper Plateau and Cibecue Valley. Burned settlements of small kin groups suggest a breakdown of conventional modes of maintaining order. Site destruction also demonstrated to victims and bystanders alike the inadequacy of a settlement system of small, dispersed, and vulnerable residential kinship groups.

The Cibecue Valley, which had been occupied extensively during the thirteenth century, was abandoned as aggregation began on the Grasshopper Plateau around A.D. 1300. People living in the communities on the eastern flank of the Grass-

hopper Plateau may have continued to use the valley for farming. Abandonment of this well-watered valley for the upland Grasshopper Plateau, which lacks permanent surface water, suggests that this movement was not driven by a need to improve local hydraulic conditions for agriculture. It is conceivable that the inhabitants of the Cibecue Valley, potentially immigrants from above the Mogollon Rim (see Montgomery and Reid 1994), carried a more advanced agricultural technology and a stronger commitment to maize cultivation when they moved onto the Grasshopper Plateau.

The formation of villages on the Grasshopper Plateau beginning around A.D. 1300 was initially in response to threats against people and provisions. Population aggregation and the emergence of village structure forced organizational solutions to permit cooperation among divergent residential kinship groups of similar and dissimilar ethnic traditions. The community decision-making hierarchy was most probably structured by restricted sodalities. The prominence of the Arrow Society at Grasshopper Pueblo (Reid 1989; Reid and Whittlesey 1982, 1990) in a sodality hierarchy is consistent with a settlement configuration stressing defense (Jorgensen 1980:226–40).

A Ceramic Model for the Mountains of East-Central Arizona

Because ceramics from emergent village farmer contexts carry a wealth of behavioral information (Reid, Montgomery, and Zedeño 1989), we now present a separate but complementary ceramic-based model so that it may be closely examined without the distractions of other discussions. Our ceramic model is divided into two sets of observations and behavioral inferences. The first is based on the frequency distribution of brown pottery, orange-gray pottery, and Salado Red pottery. The second set derives from a compositional analysis of ceramics (Zedeño 1994) from Chodistaas (Crown 1981; Montgomery 1992; Montgomery and Reid 1990, 1994; Reid 1989).

Observations on Undecorated Ceramics. Cholla Project analysis convinced us that ceramic assemblages could vary measurably according to settlement function and occupation duration (see Plog 1980). To assure a level of analytical control of functional variability, the ceramic distributions represented in figure 6.2 were taken from surface collections of sites with the same layout plan, in this case surface rooms with a plaza-courtyard. Also enhancing assignment consistency is the fact that Montgomery participated in the classification of ceramics from all sites, Zedeño in all but three sites.

Most conspicuous in figure 6.2 is that the Grasshopper Plateau represented by Chodistaas (24) and two other sites (902, 197) differs quite dramatically from the Cibecue Valley (69, 903) in the frequency of brown and orange-gray corrugated pottery (Montgomery and Reid 1994; Zedeño 1994). Furthermore, brown pottery occurs to the west of Grasshopper, whereas orange-gray pottery occurs to the east, especially toward the northeast. In the absence of comparable data, we only can suspect that orange-gray pottery decreases as one moves south from Site 8613 toward Point of Pines (see figure 6.1).

On the basis of undecorated ceramics one may observe that the Cibecue Valley sites (69, 903) are more similar to Forestdale (16:9) than they are to the Grasshopper Plateau sites (24, 197, 902) (see Montgomery and Reid 1994). Chodistaas (24), on the other hand, is nearly identical in undecorated ceramics to the Q Ranch site (400) and a site (49) south of the Salt River. The frequency of Salado Red in these three sites (24, 49, 400) is of special interest in linking Chodistaas (24) undecorated ceramics to the southwest. In contrast, the frequencies of decorated ceramics, essentially the

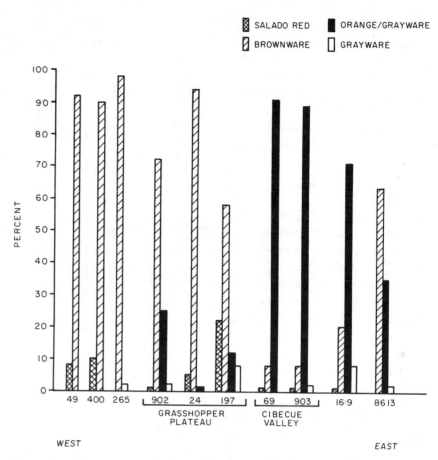

Figure 6.2. Percentages of various types of utility wares tabulated on settlements in the study area, displayed from west to east. Site numbers correspond to those in figure 6.1. Because not all sites displayed contain more than 50 rooms, some are not listed in the appendix.

Cibola White Wares, are similar in most sites investigated regardless of the marked differences in undecorated ceramics (figure 6.3). The frequency distribution of undecorated ceramics is consistent with the notion that people with a southern connection occupied the mountains alongside people with a northern connection.

Observations on Chodistaas Ceramics. Zedeño's (1994) analysis establishes the data for these observations as well as stringent conditions for upgrading ceramic-based arguments of past behavior. She examines technological, stylistic, and compositional attributes of the nearly 300 Chodistaas whole and reconstructible vessels to develop the methodology for identifying ceramics made locally from those

made elsewhere. The observations presented here are based on the local-nonlocal assignment of ceramics resulting from her analysis.

Locally manufactured wares from Chodistaas include brown corrugated, Salado Red Corrugated, and brown plain. The red plain, a nonlocal ware, is almost identical to Inspiration Red (Doyel 1978), which further emphasizes the southerly orientation previously noted. The highly variable paste of the orange-gray ware suggests a number of different manufacturing localities to the east of the Grasshopper Plateau, perhaps centering on the Cibecue Valley where the orange-gray ware predominates (Montgomery and Reid 1994; Zedeño 1994).

The decorated vessels allow for a different set of observations (table 6.1). Salado White-on-red is the only securely identified, locally produced decorated ceramic. McDonald Painted Corrugated could be locally produced, but it is more probable that it came from other mountain areas to the east. The two White Mountain Red Ware vessels (St. Johns Polychrome) certainly originated to the northeast, beyond the mountains.

Of special interest are Cibola White Ware and Roosevelt Red Ware (Pinto Black-on-red and Polychrome). Except for two locally made vessels, the Cibola White Ware vessels recovered from Chodistaas were manufactured outside the Grasshopper Region, most probably to the north on the Colorado Plateau (Zedeño 1994; see also Plog 1980; Tuggle, Kintigh, and Reid 1982).

Roosevelt Red Ware (Pinto Black-on-red and Polychrome), which occurs late in the occupation of Chodistaas (Montgomery and Reid 1990; Reid et al. 1992), presents a different pattern. Of 16 vessels assayed, 13 with either sherd and sand temper or only sand temper and one with diabase temper could be matched to local clays and to local wares, while two vessels with sherd temper are inferred, by the same criteria, to have been manufactured elsewhere (Zedeño 1994).

A provisional interpretation of the Cibola White Ware–Roosevelt Red Ware pattern is that people with the white ware technology may have developed Roosevelt Red Ware (Reid et al. 1992) and, upon moving to the mountains, perhaps even to Chodistaas, began making Roosevelt Red Ware locally. Quite apart from the specific behavioral mechanisms that may have operated to produce the patterns observed for Chodistaas ceramics, it is clear to us that the ceramic data are consistent with general interpretations of demographic trends and changes as the product of population movement.

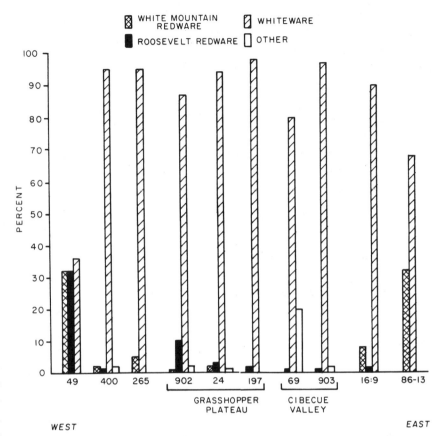

Figure 6.3. Percentages of various types of decorated ceramics on settlements in the study area, displayed from west to east. Site numbers correspond to those in figure 6.1. Because not all sites displayed contain more than 50 rooms, some are not listed in the appendix.

Ethnography as Summary

Our interpretations of the settlement and ceramic prehistory of the mountains during the late Pueblo III (A.D. 1250–1300) period can be summarized and strengthened with ethnographic data from the circum-Sonoran uplands (table 6.2). Placing the archaeological observations in this context adds human substance, further broadens the region under study, and strengthens the prehistoric pattern by documenting a settlement history dominated ethnographically by rancheria horticulture, with village farming making a cameo appearance only in the late Pueblo III and Pueblo IV (A.D. 1300–1540) periods (Welch 1990). Significant parallels in subsistence, settlement, and social organizational strategies can be found between the ethnographic record and our models describing prehistoric occupation of the Arizona mountains.

The environmental consistency of the circum-Sonoran uplands corresponds with fundamental similarities in food resource use. For example, although considerable variation exists in the proportions of the food categories used (table 6.2), upland groups generally rely more on wild plants than any other food category; they obtain these resources from various microenvironments. Also, upland horticulturists employ a more flexible and diverse range of subsistence activities than do their lowland neighbors (Pennington 1980:189). Dunnigan (1983:219) sees this flexibility as a means by which contemporary native groups cope with periods of food scarcity.

Wild plants typically contribute more to diet in the uplands than game, cultivated plants, trading, and raiding. Lists of over 100 regularly exploited, edible species are common in many ethnographies, and agave seems to be the single most widely eaten plant staple (Bennett and Zingg 1935; Castetter and Opler 1936; Gentry 1963; Gifford 1932, 1936; Pennington 1963, 1969, 1980). The variety of species gathered for medicinal and manufacturing applications is also impressive. The secondary benefits of plant food gathering, which account for its persistence among agriculturalists, include increasing dietary diversity, eliminating crop predators, maintaining traditional medicine, and generally promoting group solidarity (Caballero and Mares 1985).

Though the literature is inconsistent regarding the antiquity and importance of cultigens, food production is more important to settlement patterning than to diet in the 12 upland societies summarized in table 6.1 (compare Gifford 1940; Jorgensen 1980, 1983; Winter 1974). Cultivated plots range in elevation from 2,463 feet (750 m) to at least 6,560 feet (2,000 m) (Gifford 1932; Kennedy 1978). Service (1969:824) suggests that the size and density of the settlements are both dependent on local agricultural potential.

Upland horticulturists maximize water availability by locating fields along drainages or on slopes where soils are underlain by less permeable bedrock. Though bottom lands are frequently the only places where soil has the opportunity to accumulate, this alluvium is most susceptible to simple, highly productive irrigation and to damaging erosion following heavy rains (Gentry 1963:73–74; Hinton 1983:317).

Western Apache cultivation, aptly labeled "desultory" by Haury (1985:401), is typical of upland food production (see Graves 1982). Cultivation is embedded in their seasonal round of wild food exploitation. The size of Apache farm plots, typically about an acre, is determined by the area that could be planted in one day.

Table 6.1 Chodistaas Decorated Vessels by Room and Ware (Zedeño 1994: Table 4.1).

Room	Cibola White Wares	Roosevelt Red Wares	White Mountain Red Wares	Painted Corrugated	Total	Percentage of total
1	2	—	—	2	4	(3.54)
2	2	1	3	—	1	(4.42)
3	6	3	—	3	12	(10.62)
4	2	3	—	2	7	(6.19)
5	5	3	—	2	10	(8.85)
6	6	5	—	2	13	(11.50)
7	4	6	1	1	12	(10.62)
8	5	7	—	2	14	(12.39)
9	7	—	—	—	7	(6.19)
10	—	—	—	—	—	
11	2	3	—	2	7	(6.19)
13	2	3	—	1	6	(5.31)
14	4	1	—	2	7	(6.19)
15	3	2	1	—	6	(5.31)
16	2	—	—	—	2	(1.77)
17	—	—	—	—	—	
Test pit 1	—	1	—	—	1	(0.88)
Total	51	40	2	20	113	(99.97)
Total (in percentage)	(45.2)	(35.4)	(1.77)	(17.7)	(100.0)	

Table 6.2 Population Densities, Environmental Data, and Subsistence-diet Information for Historic Cultures in the Circum-Sonoran Region in the American Southwest

Group	Population per km²	Frost-free Days per Year	Residence Moves per Year	Subsistence-diet Percentage Cultivated Plants	Percentage Wild Plants	Percentage Game
Northern Tepehuan	1.0	X	2–5	X	X	X
Tarahumara	1.2	X	2–3	35–55	25–35	10–25
Warihio	0.3	190	4–10	5–20	45–60	30–40
Upland Lower Pima	0.6	185	2–6	30–45	30–45	15–30
Opata[1]	1.0	200	1–2	35–60	20–35	X
Eudave/Jova	0.9	X	1–2	0–40	25–35	15–30
Chiricahua Apache	< 1.0	185	3–7	5–10	35–45	30–40
San Carlos Apache	< 1.0	165	2–6	15–25	35–45	20–35
White Mtn. Apache	1.1	140	2–3	20–35	30–45	25–30
Tonto Apache	X	150	3–6	10–20	35–55	25–35
Cibicue Apache	1.0	145	2–4	20–30	30–45	20–30
Yavapai	0.2	185	3–10	5–20	35–60	20–35
Combined Average	0.8	170	4	30	45	25

Notes
1. Data particularly suspect.
X-Data missing.
Many values estimated or interpolated.
(Sources: Basso 1983; Gentry 1963; Goodwin 1937, 1942; Hinton 1983; Jorgensen 1980, 1987; Khera and Mariella 1983; Opler 1941, 1983; Pennington 1963, 1983a, 1983b; Winter 1974.)

After planting, the Apache might return only to divert water to the plants once or twice, and then to harvest crops if any were available. Western Apache farming involves investing enough to make substantial yields possible without overtaxing the land, obviating other subsistence possibilities or attempting to guarantee success. Buskirk (1986:226–27) claims that this noncommittal strategy includes deliberate underexploitation of their territories' agricultural potential.

Circum-Sonoran upland populations employ a ranchería pattern of loosely integrated, mostly nuclear, family households. A typical Tarahumara ranchería might, for example, control territory within a 9.3 mile (15 km) radius (Pennington 1983a: 278), a pattern similar to that of the Northern Tepehuan. Most of the groups have either one or two home bases, places to which they habitually return, usually near plots of good land. Settlements are widely spaced and population densities are generally low. Merrill (1983:290) notes that this dispersion has caused "considerable variation in language, worldview, ritual, settlement patterns, subsistence strategies, dress, and many other domains."

The frequency of settlement moves varies with the number and location of the most reliable staple food sources. This creates considerable settlement pattern variation between and within culture groups. With the possible exception of the Opata and the late prehistoric Pueblo agriculturalists, all upland populations change residence at least once seasonally to facilitate exploitation of the full range of accessible microenvironments. Western Apache and Tarahumara, as well as others with access to good agricultural land, might move only twice a year. People in adjacent territories lacking deep, well-watered, alluvial deposits could relocate as many as six times annually (Buskirk 1986). Few descriptions of sites with different seasonal functions are available, but caching of food and implements as well as temporary abandonment of tools, such as ground stone, have been documented (Graham 1990).

Cultivation plot locations are the most important single determinant of settlement placement. Upland horticulturalists display a "tethered nomadism" (Taylor 1964) in that soil and water concentrations keep them returning to plant, not so much because their survival depends on it, but because it is a good chance at high yields through low labor inputs. Among the Tarahumara, Northern Tepehuan, and upland Lower Pima, the success of the highland summer harvest influences mobility. Good corn harvests obviate the need to descend to lower elevations to plant the less productive and more unreliable canyon winter crop (Pennington 1980:308, 1983b; Merrill 1983:291). Low yields, a frequent occurrence due to drought and flood, often prompt visits to generous kin and friends, to neighbors of different cultural and subsistence traditions (ethnic coresidence), or to seldom-traveled territories in search of wild foods. Throughout the circum-Sonoran uplands, raiding seems to be a fairly common last option to alleviate food shortages.

Conclusion

Survey and ceramic data combine with ethnography to form a consistent demographic picture of the Grasshopper Region prior to the late Pueblo III period. The late Pueblo III period (A.D. 1250–1300) is best understood in terms of demographic processes that created the conditions for aggregation into the pueblo communities characteristic of the thirteenth-century occupation of the Arizona mountains. The failure of these aggregated agricultural communities during the late fourteenth century left the mountains open to the reintroduction of a typical circum-Sonoran upland adaptation pursued historically by the Western Apache.

Use of different data categories illustrates a secure approach to reconstructing prehistory. Settlement data permit identifying adjustments to the local Grasshopper landscape and tracking subsequent accommodations to changing social and environmental conditions. Ceramics provide access to broad stretches of prehistoric landscape where the movement of people and pots may be meaningfully mapped. The high resolution data of the Grasshopper Region permit variables and processes to be isolated and studied and illustrate anew the value of strong cases of the prehistoric record for developing the necessary conceptual tools for understanding the past. Ethnography serves as a check on the reasonableness of reconstructions as well as a ready means of putting real people back into the pages of prehistory.

References Cited

Basso, Keith H.
1983   Western Apache. In *Southwest*, edited by Alfonso Ortiz, pp. 462–501. Handbook of North American Indians, Vol. 10, William C. Sturtevant, general editor. Smithsonian Institution, Washington, D.C.

Bennett, Wendell C., and Robert M. Zingg
1935   *The Tarahumara, an Indian Tribe of Northern Mexico*. University of Chicago Press, Chicago.

Buskirk, Winfred
1986   *The Western Apache: Living With the Land Before 1950*. University of Oklahoma Press, Norman.

Caballero N., Javier, and Christina Mares S.
1985   Gathering and Subsistence Patterns Among the P'urhepecha Indians of Mexico. *Journal of Ethnobiology* 5(1): 31–47.

Cartledge, Thomas R.
1976   Prehistory in the Vosberg Valley, Central Arizona. *Kiva* 42:95–104.
1977   *Human Ecology and Changing Patterns of Co-Residence in the Vosberg Locality, Tonto National Forest, Central Arizona*. Cultural Resources Report No. 17. USDA, Forest Service, Southwest Region, Albuquerque.

Castetter, Edward F., and Morris E. Opler
1936   *The Ethnobiology of the Chiricahua and Mescalero Apache*. Bulletin 297, Biological Series 4(5). University of New Mexico, Albuquerque.

Chenhall, Robert G.
1972   *Random Sampling in an Archaeological Survey*. Unpublished Ph.D. dissertation, Department of Anthropology, Arizona State University, Tempe.

Ciolek-Torrello, Richard S.
1984   An Alternative Model of Room
        Function From Grasshopper Pueblo,
        Arizona. In *Intrasite Spatial Analysis
        in Archaeology*, edited by Harold J.
        Hietala, pp. 127–53. Cambridge
        University Press, New York.
1985   A Typology of Room Function
        at Grasshopper Pueblo, Arizona.
        Journal of Field Archaeology 12:
        41–63.

Ciolek-Torrello, Richard S., and J. Jefferson Reid
1974   Change in Household Size at
        Grasshopper. *Kiva* 40:39–47.

Ciolek-Torrello, Richard S., and Richard C.
Lange
1990   The Gila Pueblo Survey of the
        Southeastern Sierra Ancha. *Kiva* 55:
        127–54.

Crown, Patricia L.
1981   *Variability in Ceramic Manufacture
        at the Chodistaas Site, East-Central
        Arizona.* Ph.D. dissertation, Depart-
        ment of Anthropology, University
        of Arizona, Tucson. University
        Microfilms, Ann Arbor.

Cummings, Byron
1940   *Kinishba, a Prehistoric Pueblo of
        the Great Pueblo Period.* Hohokam
        Museums Association, Tucson.

Dean, Jeffrey S., and William J. Robinson
1982   Dendrochronology of Grasshopper
        Pueblo. In *Multidisciplinary Research
        at Grasshopper Pueblo, Arizona*,
        edited by W. A. Longacre, Sally J.
        Holbrook, and Michael W. Graves,
        pp. 46–60. Anthropological Papers
        No. 40. University of Arizona Press,
        Tucson.

Doyel, David E.
1978   *The Miami Wash Project: Hohokam
        and Salado in the Globe-Miami Area,
        Central Arizona.* Contributions
        to Highway Salvage Archaeology
        in Arizona No. 52. Arizona State
        Museum, University of Arizona,
        Tucson.

Dunnigan, Timothy
1983   Lower Pima. In *Southwest*, Hand-
        book of North American Indians,
        vol. 10, edited by Alfonso Ortiz, pp.
        217–29. William C. Sturtevant, gen-
        eral editor. Smithsonian Institution,
        Washington, D.C.

Gentry, Howard Scott
1963   *The Warihio Indians of Sonora-
        Chihuahua: An Ethnographic Survey.*
        Bulletin No. 186, Anthropological
        Papers No. 65. Bureau of American
        Ethnology, Washington, D.C.

Gifford, Edward W.
1932   The Southeastern Yavapai. *Uni-
        versity of California Publications in
        American Archaeology and Ethnology*
        29(3):177–252.
1936   Northeastern and Western Yavapai.
        *University of California Publica-
        tions in American Archaeology and
        Ethnology* 34(4):247–354.
1940   Culture Element Distributions,
        XII: Apache-Pueblo. *University of
        California Anthropological Records*
        4(1):1–207.

Goodwin, Grenville
1937   The Characteristics and Function
        of Clan in a Southern Athapaskan
        Culture. *American Anthropologist*
        39(3):394–407.
1942   *The Social Organization of the West-
        ern Apache.* University of Chicago
        Press, Chicago.

Graham, Martha
1990   Periodically Abandoned Residence
        Among the Tarahumara: Settlement
        Organization and Assemblage Vari-
        ability. Paper presented at the 55th
        Annual Meeting of the Society for
        American Archaeology, Las Vegas,
        Nevada.

Graves, Michael W.
1982   Apache Adaptation to the Moun-
        tains. In *The Q Ranch Region*, pp.
        193–215. Cholla Project Archaeology,
        Vol. 3, edited by J. Jefferson Reid.
        Arizona State Museum Archaeo-
        logical Series No. 161. University of
        Arizona, Tucson.

Graybill, Donald A., and J. Jefferson Reid
1982   Cholla Project Chipped Stone Iden-
        tification Procedures. In *Introduction
        and Special Studies*, pp. 27–34. Cholla
        Project Archaeology, Vol. 1, edited
        by J. Jefferson Reid. Arizona State
        Museum Archaeological Series
        No. 161. University of Arizona,
        Tucson.

Haury, Emil W.
1936   *The Mogollon Culture of Southwestern
        New Mexico.* Medallion Papers
        No. 20. Gila Pueblo, Globe, Arizona.
1958   Evidence at Point of Pines for a
        Prehistoric Migration From North-
        ern Arizona. In *Migrations in New
        World Culture History*, edited by
        Raymond H. Thompson, pp. 1–8.
        University of Arizona Bulletin 29(2).
        University of Arizona Press, Tucson.
1985   *Mogollon Culture in the Forestdale Val-
        ley, East-Central Arizona.* University
        of Arizona Press, Tucson.

1986   The Mogollon Culture of South-
        western New Mexico. In *Emil W.
        Haury's Prehistory of the American
        Southwest*, edited by J. Jefferson Reid
        and David E. Doyel, pp. 305–404.
        University of Arizona Press, Tucson.
1989   *Point of Pines, Arizona, A History of
        the University of Arizona Archaeo-
        logical Field School.* Anthropological
        Papers No. 50. University of Arizona
        Press, Tucson.

Hinton, Thomas B.
1983   Southern Periphery: West. In *South-
        west*, edited by Alfonso Ortiz, pp.
        315–328. Handbook of North Ameri-
        can Indians, Vol. 10. William C.
        Sturtevant, general editor. Smith-
        sonian Institution, Washington,
        D.C.

Johnson, Alfred E.
1965   *The Development of Western Pueblo
        Culture.* Unpublished Ph.D. disserta-
        tion, Department of Anthropology,
        University of Arizona, Tucson.

Johnson, Gregory A.
1982   Organizational Structures and Scalar
        Stress. In *Theory and Explanation
        in Archaeology: The Southampton
        Conference*, edited by Colin Renfrew,
        Michael J. Rowlands, and Barbara
        Abbott Seagraves, pp. 389–421.
        Academic Press, New York.
1983   Decision-Making Organization and
        Pastoral Nomad Camp Size. *Human
        Ecology* 11(2):175–199.
1989   Dynamics of Southwestern Pre-
        history, Far Outside—Looking In.
        In *Dynamics of Southwestern Pre-
        history*, edited by Linda S. Cordell
        and George J. Gumerman, pp. 371–
        89. Smithsonian Institution Press,
        Washington, D.C.

Jorgensen, Joseph G.
1980   *Western Indians.* W. H. Freeman, San
        Francisco.
1983   Comparative Traditional Eco-
        nomics and Ecological Adaptations.
        In *Southwest*, edited by Alfonso
        Ortiz, pp. 684–710. Handbook of
        North American Indians, Vol. 10,
        William C. Sturtevant, general
        editor. Smithsonian Institution,
        Washington, D.C.
1987   Toward an Explanation of Political
        Society and Subsistence Resources in
        Aboriginal Western North America.
        In *Themes in Ethnology and Culture
        History*, edited by Leland F. Donald,
        pp. 175–226. Archana Publications,
        Meerut, India.

Kennedy, John G.

1978   *The Tarahumara of the Sierra Madre: Beer, Ecology, and Social Organization.* AHM Publishing, Arlington Hts., Illinois.

Khera, Sigrid, and Patricia S. Mariella

1983   Yavapai. In *Southwest*, edited by Alfonso Ortiz, 38–54. Handbook of North American Indians, vol. 10, William C. Sturtevant, general editor. Smithsonian Institution, Washington D.C.

Lindsay, Alexander, Jr.

1987   Anasazi Population Movements to Southeastern Arizona. *American Archaeology* 6(3):190–198.

Lowell, Julie C.

1989   Flexible Social Units in the Changing Communities of Point of Pines, Arizona. In *Households and Communities*, edited by A. Scott MacEachern, David J. W. Archer, and Richard D. Garvin, pp. 186–195. Proceedings of the Twenty-First Annual Conference of the Archaeological Association of the University of Calgary, Alberta, Canada.

1991   *Prehistoric Households at Turkey Creek, Arizona.* Anthropological Papers No. 54. University of Arizona Press, Tucson.

Merrill, William L.

1983   Tarahumara Social Organization, Political Organization, and Religion. In *Southwest*, edited by Alfonso Ortiz, pp. 290–305. Handbook of North American Indians, vol. 10, William C. Sturtevant, general editor. Smithsonian Institution, Washington, D.C.

Montgomery, Barbara K.

1991   Changes in Household Organization. Paper presented at the Annual Meeting of the Southwest Anthropological Association, Tucson.

1992   *Understanding the Formation of the Archaeological Record: Ceramic Variability at Chodistaas Pueblo, Arizona.* Ph.D. dissertation, Department of Anthropology, University of Arizona, Tucson. University Microfilms, Ann Arbor.

Montgomery, Barbara K., and J. Jefferson Reid

1990   An Instance of Rapid Ceramic Change in the American Southwest. *American Antiquity* 55:88–97.

1994   The Brown and The Gray: People, Pots, and Population Movement in East-Central Arizona. Paper presented at the 59th Annual Meet-

ing of the Society for American Archaeology, Anaheim.

Morris, Donald H.

1970   Walnut Creek Village: A Ninth-Century Hohokam-Anasazi Settlement in the Mountains of Central Arizona. *American Antiquity* 35:49–61.

Netting, Robert McC.

1990   Population, Permanent Agriculture, and Polities: Unpacking the Evolutionary Portmanteau. In *The Evolution of Political Systems*, edited by Steadman Upham, 21–61. Cambridge University Press, Cambridge.

Olson, Alan P.

1959   *An Evaluation of the Phase Concept in Southwestern Archaeology: As Applied to the Eleventh and Twelfth Century Occupations at Point of Pines.* Unpublished Ph.D. dissertation, Department of Anthropology, University of Arizona, Tucson.

Opler, Morris E.

1941   *An Apache Life-way.* Chicago: University of Chicago.

1983   The Apache Culture Pattern and its Origins. In *Southwest*, edited by Alfonso Ortiz, pp. 368–392. Handbook of North American Indians, vol. 10, William C. Sturtevant, general editor. Smithsonian Institution, Washington, D.C.

Pennington, Campbell

1963   *The Tarahumar of Mexico, Their Environment and Material Culture.* University of Utah Press, Salt Lake City.

1969   *The Tepehuan of Chihuahua, Their Material Culture.* University of Utah Press, Salt Lake City.

1980   *The Pima Bajo.* 2 Vols. University of Utah Press, Salt Lake City.

1983a   Northern Tepehuan. In *Southwest*, edited by Alfonso Ortiz, pp. 306–14. Handbook of North American Indians, vol. 10, William C. Sturtevant, general editor. Smithsonian Institution, Washington, D.C.

1983b   Tarahumara. In *Southwest*, edited by Alfonso Ortiz, pp. 276–89. Handbook of North American Indians, vol. 10, William C. Sturtevant, general editor. Smithsonian Institution, Washington, D.C.

Plog, Stephen

1980   *Stylistic Variation in Prehistoric Ceramics.* Cambridge: Cambridge University Press.

Reid, J. Jefferson

1989   Grasshopper Perspective on the Mogollon of the Arizona Mountains. In *Dynamics of Southwestern Prehistory*, edited by Linda S. Cordell and George J. Gumerman, pp. 65–97. Smithsonian Institution Press, Washington, D.C.

Reid, J. Jefferson (editor)

1982   *Cholla Project Archaeology.* Arizona State Museum Archaeological Series No. 161. University of Arizona, Tucson.

Reid, J. Jefferson, and Stephanie M. Whittlesey

1982   Households at Grasshopper Pueblo. *American Behavioral Scientist* 25(6):687–703.

1990   The Complicated and the Complex: Observations on the Archaeological Record of Large Pueblos. In *Perspectives on Southwestern Prehistory*, edited by Paul E. Minnis and Charles L. Redman, 184–95. Westview Press, Boulder.

Reid, J. Jefferson, Barbara K. Montgomery, and M. Nieves Zedeño

1989   The Birth of Roosevelt Redware: Ceramic Theory Beyond Taxonomy. Paper presented at the Arizona Archaeological Council Fall Meeting, Phoenix.

Reid, J. Jefferson, Barbara K. Montgomery, M. Nieves Zedeño, and Mark A. Neupert

1992   The Origin of Roosevelt Red Ware. *Proceedings of the Second Salado Conference, Globe, Arizona, 1992*, edited by Richard C. Lange and Stephen Germick, pp. 212–15. Occasional Paper, Arizona Archaeological Society, Phoenix.

Rock, James T.

1974   The Use of Social Models in Archaeological Interpretation. *Kiva* 40:81–91.

Service, Elman R.

1962   *Primitive Social Organization: An Evolutionary Perspective.* New York: Random House.

1969   The Northern Tepehuan. In *Ethnology*, edited by Evon Z. Vogt, pp. 822–29. Handbook of Middle American Indians, Vol. 8, Robert Wauchope, general editor. University of Texas Press, Austin.

Shreve, Forrest

1951   *Vegetation of the Sonoran Desert.* 2 vols. Carnegie Institution, Washington, D.C.

Spier, Leslie

1919   Ruins in the White Mountains,

Arizona. *Anthropological Papers of the American Museum of Natural History* 18(5):363–87.

Steward, Julian D.
1955   *A Theory of Culture Change.* University of Illinois Press, Urbana.

Taylor, Walter W.
1964   Tethered Nomadism and Water Territoriality: An Hypothesis. In *Proceedings of the 35th International Congress of Americanists* 2:197–203. Mexico, D.F.

Tuggle, H. David
1970   *Prehistoric Community Relationships in East-Central Arizona.* Ph.D. dissertation, Department of Anthropology, University of Arizona, Tucson. University Microfilms, Ann Arbor.
1982   Settlement Patterns in the Q Ranch Region. In *The Q Ranch Region*, pp. 151–64. Cholla Project Archaeology, Vol. 3, edited by J. Jefferson Reid. Arizona State Museum Archaeological Series No. 161. University of Arizona, Tucson.

Tuggle, H. David, Keith W. Kintigh, and J. Jefferson Reid
1982   Trace Element Analysis of White Wares. In *Ceramic Studies*, pp. 22–38. Cholla Project Archaeology, Vol. 5, edited by J. J. Reid. Arizona State Museum Archaeological Series No. 161. University of Arizona, Tucson.

Welch, John R.
1990   Seasonality and Adaptive Strategy in the Circum-Sonoran Uplands. Paper presented at the 55th Annual Meeting of the Society for American Archaeology, Las Vegas.
1991   From Horticulture to Agriculture in the Late Prehistory of the Grasshopper Region, Arizona. In *Mogollon* v, edited by Pat Beckett, pp. 75–92. COAS, Las Cruces, New Mexico.

Wheat, Joe Ben
1954   *Crooked Ridge Village, Arizona w: 10:15.* University of Arizona Bulletin 25(3). Social Sciences Bulletin No. 24. University of Arizona Press, Tucson.

Whittlesey, Stephanie M.
1982   Examination of Previous Work in the Q Ranch Region: Comparison and Analysis. In *The Q Ranch Region*, pp. 123–50. Cholla Project Archaeology, Vol. 3, edited by J. Jefferson Reid. Arizona State Museum Archaeological Series No. 161. University of Arizona, Tucson.

Whittlesey, Stephanie M., and J. Jefferson Reid
1982   Analysis of Interassemblage Variability and Settlement System Reconstruction. In *The Q Ranch Region*, pp. 176–92. Cholla Project Archaeology, edited by J. Jefferson Reid. Arizona State Museum Archaeological Series No. 161. University of Arizona, Tucson.

Winter, Joseph C.
1974   *Aboriginal Agriculture in the Southwest and Great Basin.* Ph.D. dissertation, Department of Anthropology, University of Utah, Salt Lake City. University Microfilms, Ann Arbor.

Winters, Howard D.
1969   *The Riverton Culture.* Illinois State Museum Reports of Investigations No. 13. The Illinois Archaeological Survey, University of Illinois, Urbana.

Wood, J. Scott
1980   The Gentry Timber Sale: Behavioral Patterning and Predictability in the Upper Cherry Creek Area, Central Arizona. *Kiva* 16:99–119.

Zedeño, María Nieves
1994   *Sourcing Prehistoric Ceramics at Chodistaas Pueblo, Arizona.* Anthropological Papers No. 58. University of Arizona Press, Tucson.

Chapter 7

Southwestern Colorado and Southeastern Utah Settlement Patterns:
A.D. 1100 TO 1300

Mark D. Varien, William D. Lipe, Michael A. Adler,
Ian M. Thompson, and Bruce A. Bradley

In this chapter we examine settlement patterns in southwestern Colorado and southeastern Utah between A.D. 1100 and 1300. We have divided this area into 13 districts (figure 7.1). The central districts in this area are also referred to as the "central Mesa Verde area." Most of the sites discussed here are in these central districts. The westernmost districts extend beyond the Mesa Verde region and include sites with predominantly Kayenta or Virgin Branch pottery for at least part of the period considered. The eastern district also has pottery and residential architecture that differ from traditions characterizing the center of the Mesa Verde region.

In Colorado the region is bounded on the south by the state line and in Utah by the San Juan River. Although many consider the Mesa Verde region to include the part of New Mexico that lies north of the San Juan River, that area, the Totah region (McKenna and Toll 1992; Stein and McKenna 1988), is treated here as a district in the San Juan region (see Stein and Fowler chapter 8).

Following a presentation of our analytical methods, we examine settlement pattern cycles before A.D. 1100. Next we look south of the San Juan River to assess the impact of trends in the Chaco drainage on settlement patterns north of the river

in the late eleventh and early twelfth centuries. That is followed by a discussion of changing settlement patterns—cycles of population dispersion and aggregation—beginning in A.D. 1150 and culminating in the abandonment of the region by A.D. 1300. Finally, we present a synthesis of recent research into the causes of that abandonment.

Data assembled for the region discussed in this chapter includes an inventory of all known sites that contain more than 50 rooms. The density of known sites varies from area to area across the region. One possible explanation for this is that the intensity of archaeological research has

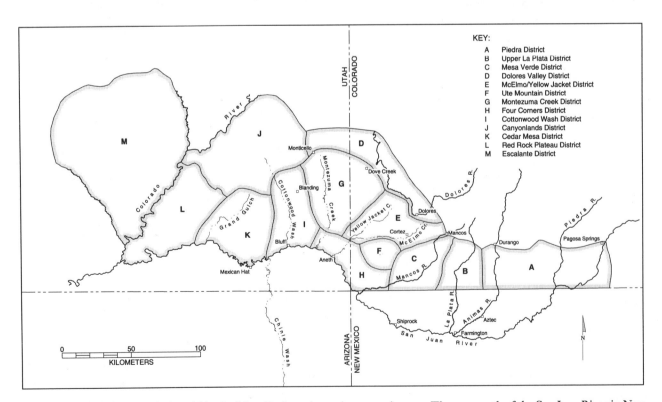

Figure 7.1. District boundaries within the Mesa Verde region and areas to the west. The area north of the San Juan River in New Mexico is covered in chapter 8.

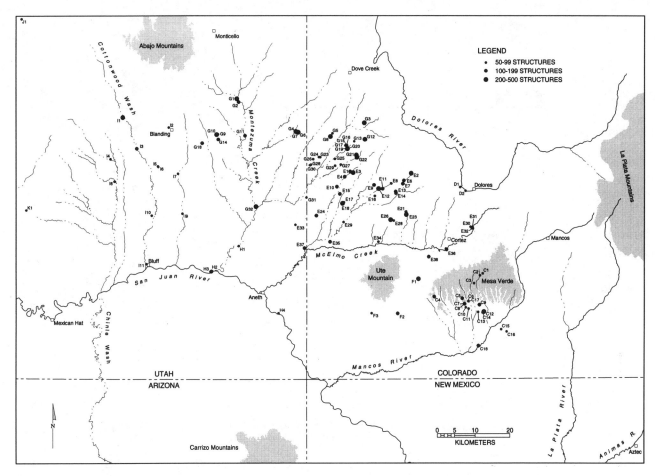

Figure 7.2.   Sites larger than 50 rooms in the Mesa Verde region (sites are preceded by 7 in app.), A.D. 1100–1300.

varied from area to area within the region and areas where research has been most intense are where the greatest number of known sites are located. Areas where little or no research has been conducted may contain sites that remain unknown.

Analytical Methods

After reviewing previous schemes that subdivided the Mesa Verde region (Gillespie 1976; Eddy, Kane, and Nickens, 1984), we concluded that the specific goals of this chapter would be better addressed by creating 13 new districts (figure 7.1). Our purpose was to define areas within which there appears to be a similar occupational history and intensity of data recovery. Landforms and drainage systems were also considered in drawing the district boundaries. In the center of the Mesa

Verde region, where there is greater homogeneity in the occupational history, we created three districts. This was done to avoid creating districts with uneven intensity of archaeological research or that were too large to analyze for variation. These arbitrarily defined Mesa Verdean central districts are the McElmo-Yellow Jacket, the Montezuma Creek, and the Cottonwood-Recapture Districts. The distribution of large sites within each of the thirteen districts is illustrated in figure 7.2, and data for each site are summarized in the master data base (appendix).

The first interpretive problem in building the master data base was estimating the period of site occupation. The second problem was estimating site size. The confidence for these estimates varies from site to site. Excavated sites with large samples of tree-ring dates provide the best chronological and size estimates. These excavated

sites serve as a standard for evaluating the chronology and size of unexcavated sites. Of the sites in our inventory, more than 75 percent have been visited by at least one of the authors of this chapter. Maps or site forms are available for about 80 percent of the sites, providing a reasonably consistent means for estimating size and period of occupation. For sites with no map or site form, data was collected from other archaeologists who had visited these unrecorded or previously destroyed sites. Finally, we flew over much of the region and observed and photographed a large percentage of the sites from the air.

Four dating estimates for each site were originally in the master data base, including a beginning, ending, core, and peak date. The beginning date is often difficult to determine because earlier components can be obscured by later occupations. Core dates refer to the period of major occu-

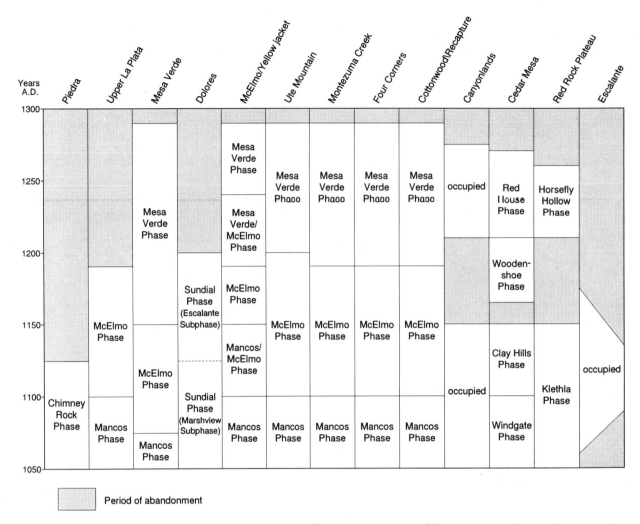

Figure 7.3.   Phase chronologies within the Mesa Verde region. Chart adapted from the following sources: Piedra (Eddy 1977); Mesa Verde (Hayes 1964); Dolores (Robinson et al. 1986); Ute Mountain (Fuller 1988c); Cedar Mesa (Matson, Lipe, and Haase 1988); and Red Rock (Lipe 1970). The remaining phase assignments adapted by Varien from a number of sources and by talking with archaeologists who have worked in each area.

pation. Well documented sites have the most accurate core dates. Some sites have what appear to be discrete major occupations separated by periods of little use or abandonment. Ceramic dating indicates that many sites have long occupational histories, but discrete components could not be defined on the basis of these surface remains. These sites got longer core dates. In such cases the core date brackets the major occupation, but the intensity of the occupation may vary within that core date. Due to space limitations, only the beginning and ending dates are included here (see appendix).

Breaking down the A.D. 1100 to 1300

period into 50-year blocks roughly corresponds to recognized periods. Between A.D. 1100 and 1150 the presumed Chaco phenomenon reached its greatest extent and began its decline. Though the nature of Chacoan influence in the Mesa Verde region is beyond the scope of this chapter —and continues to be the topic of debate among many southwestern archaeologists —we can say that Mesa Verde settlements during this time included great houses and associated dispersed communities of smaller houses. The A.D. 1150 to 1200 period was characterized by extended periods of drought (see Van West, chapter 15), including what may have been

the most significant period of dry years during the Puebloan occupation of the Mesa Verde region. The A.D. 1200 to 1250 period represents the beginning of the Mesa Verde phase, while A.D. 1250 to 1300 represents the final period of occupation. Figure 7.3 shows chronologies that have been developed for the individual districts.

When available, tree-ring dates were used to assign sites to chronological periods. Where tree-ring dates were not available, pottery and architecture were used to date sites. Sites with a predominance of Mancos Black-on-white and McElmo Black-on-white pottery were placed in the A.D. 1100 to 1150 period. Sites lacking Mancos but with McElmo Black-on-white pottery present were assigned to the A.D. 1150 to 1200 period. Sites where McElmo Black-on-white and Mesa Verde Black-on-white pottery are present are considered to be post A.D. 1200. When Mesa Verde Black-on-white is more common than the McElmo variety, we placed the site after A.D. 1250.

Adler and Varien (1994) have recently summarized some of the architectural trends in the Mesa Verde region between A.D. 1000 and 1300 and they propose that site location and site layout are temporally sensitive in the region. These trends are the basis for architectural dating of large sites and they are briefly described here. Sites with great house characteristics were assigned to the A.D. 1100 to 1150 period. Between A.D. 1150 and 1250, large sites consisted of clusters of room blocks and associated kivas, which we call multiple room block sites (Adler 1990). Sites assigned to the post A.D. 1250 period, although still comprised of multiple-kiva room blocks, were more tightly clustered than the earlier sites (see figure 7.4). Enclosing walls were more common, the sites were frequently located on canyon rims and at the heads of canyons, and they were often built around springs. Because surface pottery is sparse on many of these canyon-head and canyon-rim sites, site location and site layout played a more important role than pottery in assigning sites to this period.

The remains of collapsed buildings at many Mesa Verde sites retain surface details that allow accurate mapping of room blocks and kivas. The accuracy of these maps has been confirmed at sites where excavation has taken place (for example, Sand Canyon Pueblo, figure 7.4). These surface remains provide the basis for the estimates of room and kiva counts given in the master data base (appendix) and figure into district population estimates as well (figure 7.5). The number of rooms was subjectively estimated by comparing the size of rubble mounds at unexcavated sites to the size of rubble mounds at excavated

sites with known room counts. These estimates should only be considered as approximations of the absolute number rooms actually present at sites; however, as a relative measure of site size they are believed to be fairly accurate. At sites where accurate counts of kiva depressions can be made we multiplied the number of kivas by six (see Lipe 1989) to get a conservative estimate of the number of rooms present. On sites where kiva depressions were not as clear, the area of the rubble mound was used to make a rough estimate of the number of structures present.

Site size and period of occupation were used to create the 50-year period distribution maps (figures 7.6–7.9). Clearly these estimates are approximations and are more useful as relative, rather than absolute, comparisons of site size and occupation, because significant variability exists in the normative sequence of architectural changes at the large sites described here.

For most Mesa Verde region sites a general rule applies: the bigger the site the more complicated its occupational history. Typically, sites in the Cottonwood-Recapture and western Montezuma Creek districts have both Pueblo I and Pueblo III occupations. In the McElmo-Yellow Jacket district and the eastern portion of the Montezuma Creek district, many sites have both Pueblo II and Pueblo III components. On most sites there is not enough surface evidence to determine (at least with a quick reconnaissance) if these components represent continuous use or a series of occupations separated by periods of site abandonment.

To avoid "overfilling" these figures we placed sites only on the map representing the 50-year period when we estimated that the site reached its maximum size. We called this the site's "peak date." The exceptions to this are four sites that have distinct architectural complexes that clearly date to different periods. These sites—Yellow Jacket, Mitchell Springs, Lancaster, and Yucca House—are the only four sites that appear on more than one site distribution map. Because many sites

have pottery indicative of occupation during several periods, these site distribution figures are likely to be more underfilled than overfilled.

Site layout varied during each period, which led to problems in defining site boundaries. Through time, unit pueblos become less dispersed and more tightly clustered (Fetterman and Honeycutt 1987; Kuckelman and Morris 1988; Neily 1983; Adler 1988, 1990). As a result of this clustering, it is sometimes difficult to decide whether separate room blocks should be considered to be several individual sites or to be a single multiple room block site. We relied on the proximity of the room blocks in deciding whether to define these clusters as a single aggregated site. Multiple room blocks were defined as aggregated sites if the room blocks were within approximately 25 meters of one another, and if the dating criteria indicated the room blocks were contemporaneous. Figure 7.4 shows some of the variation present in large site layout.

Focusing on sites has its limitations. One goal of this research is to address questions of community organization, but in most cases the concepts of site and community cannot be used synonymously. In some cases a large site may have housed an entire community, while in other cases a large site may have served as the center for a community that included dispersed smaller sites. Clear definition and recognition of communities and their geographical boundaries will ultimately provide a better picture of the cultural landscape than maps dotted with sites. Future intensive surveys should provide additional information about the dispersed communities that surround each large site.

A significant effort was made to assess the types of public architecture associated with large sites (see master data base). By public architecture we mean structures or features that required organized, suprahousehold labor to construct and facilities interpreted to have functioned as community integrative structures (Flannery and Marcus 1976). These include great kivas, biwall and triwall structures, great houses, and "roads." Not consistently included in this inventory of public architecture are earthworks, reservoirs, enclosing walls, and plazas—features worthy of consideration but poorly recorded in the regional literature.

While visiting sites we recognized a set of cultural features that are not well described in our area and which do not fit easily into descriptive categories. We began to refer to these features collectively as AWUF: architecture with unknown function (Thompson et al. 1991). The features include earthworks, low stone walls or stone alignments (some of which enclose or connect room blocks), cliff edge plazas enclosed by room blocks and low stone walls, stone features that protrude from these stone walls, stone circles, rectangular stone boxes, and circular structures that enclose the tops of cracks in cliff faces at canyon rim sites. These features have been documented at numerous sites in the region and are probably present at other sites. In her master's thesis, Susan Kenzle (1993) examines a particular type of AWUF, low enclosing walls, and addresses the role these features may have played in defining social boundaries within and between communities.

Finally, we estimated the changes in absolute and relative population density through time for each district (figure 7.5). These estimates were derived from the most reliable survey data available for each district. When no recent survey information was available, reconnaissance level observations were used or comparisons were made to adjacent districts with reliable survey data. It should be noted that the district-wide estimates of population density are based upon pedestrian surveys of localities within districts, localities that are often characterized by good agricultural soils and are therefore the areas where settlement was most dense. If the population density of less arable lands surrounding these densely settled localities within districts had been included, it would substantially reduce the population

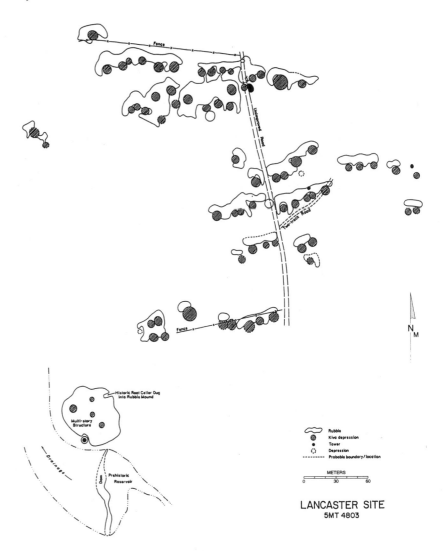

Figure 7.4. Examples of site plans illustrating differences in site size and the layout of architectural features. The Lancaster Ruin is shown on the left; Wallace Ruin, Sand Canyon Pueblo, and Goodman Point Ruin are on the right. (Maps used with permis-

density estimates for that district. Where possible we have charted the differing population estimates for a given district in order to display the likely range of population counts that can be estimated for the region as a whole (figure 7.5).

The Big Picture: Settlement and Community Organization

Pre-1100

The first village-sized aggregates that meet the 50-room threshold appeared in the Mesa Verde region beginning in the late A.D. 700s and they continued to be constructed through the 800s. Some of these villages included several hundred rooms. Sites such as Alkali Ridge Site 13 (Brew 1946), Badger House (Hayes and Lancaster 1975), and the Dolores sites (Lipe et al. 1988; Kane 1986b, 1988) are well known, but there are many other unexcavated or lesser known sites that are in the same size range (Fuller 1988a, 1988b; Wilshusen, 1991; Wilshusen and Blinman 1992). Across the region as a whole, Pueblo I sites appear well represented in the Piedra, Animas, and LaPlata drainages in the east, and in the Mesa Verde, McElmo-Yellow Jacket, Monte-

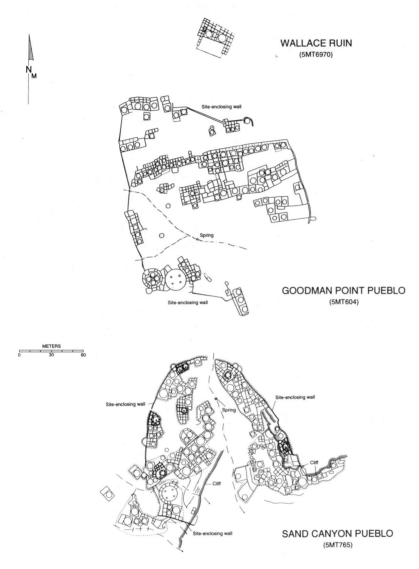

WALLACE RUIN
(5MT6970)

Site-enclosing wall

Spring

GOODMAN POINT PUEBLO
(5MT604)

Site-enclosing wall

METERS
0   30   60

Site-enclosing wall

Site-enclosing wall

Spring

Cliff

Cliff

Site-enclosing wall

SAND CANYON PUEBLO
(5MT765)

sion of the following: Lancaster Ruin, Mark Chenault; Wallace Ruin, Bruce Bradley; Goodman Point Ruin and Sand Canyon Pueblo, Crow Canyon Archaeological Center.)

zuma Creek, Upper Dolores Valley, and Cottonwood-Recapture areas in the central part of the region. Whether there is a substantial Pueblo I occupation in the Ute Mountain District is not clear, but that seems probable. There are also several clusters of PI sites along the San Juan River near Aneth and Bluff, Utah, as well as in the lower elevations of the Montezuma, Recapture, and Cottonwood drainages. This distribution does not extend to the western districts. Although Pueblo I sites are common in Comb Wash and on the eastern slopes of Cedar Mesa, they are very rare in the central and western Cedar Mesa (Matson, Lipe, and Haase 1988) and

to our knowledge do not occur in the Canyonlands, the Red Rock Plateau, or the Escalante Districts.

Although the total area occupied during the eighth and ninth centuries is large, occupation within the region was spotty at any given time. This pattern appears to be the result of settlement clustering in certain locales that were separated by hinterlands with few or no settlements. The distribution of occupied locales seems not to be highly constrained by environmental factors (but see Petersen 1988), because settlement clusters range in elevation from 6,800 to 7,000 ft (2,073–2,134 m) in the Dolores Valley and adjacent Dolores rim

to below 4,600 feet (1,402 m) on the San Juan River.

Temporally, these occupation areas apparently began as loosely defined, low-density clusters of small Basketmaker III or early Pueblo I households or hamlets. These areas (or at least portions of them) underwent population increase—rapidly and with inmigration in the Dolores case (Schlanger 1985, 1988)—and large hamlets and then villages composed of multi-household room blocks were developed because of that increase. In the resulting villages, there is some architectural evidence of ritual intensification, but little or no evidence of social hierarchy (Orcutt, Blinman, and Kohler 1990; Wilshusen 1986, 1989; but see Kane 1989). These Pueblo I villages were apparently short-lived, and alternating periods of occupation and abandonment may have occurred within their relatively short use lives (Schlanger and Wilshusen 1993). Supra-annual residential mobility appears to have been an important aspect of the Pueblo I adaptation. After a brief period of population aggregation these settlement clusters were largely abandoned by A.D. 900 (Kohler 1992), a sequence similar to the Pueblo III pattern described later.

Although this scenario of rapid population buildup, aggregation, and ritual intensification followed by rapid population decline appears to have been played out repeatedly during the ninth century (Wilshusen 1991; Schlanger and Wilshusen 1993), it was not entirely simultaneous over the whole area. This process occurred in the Durango and Alkali Ridge clusters during the late eighth century or early ninth century (Fuller 1988a; Brew 1946), during the early to middle ninth century in the southern portion of the Mesa Verde District (Wilshusen and Blinman 1992), and during the last half of the ninth century in the Dolores District (Kane 1986b, 1989; Schlanger 1985, 1988). Researchers from the Dolores Archaeological Project (Kohler et al., 1986; Kohler and Matthews 1988; Kohler 1992; Orcutt, Blinman, and Kohler 1990) have proposed an explanatory model that argues that these communities were committed to low intensity farming and foraging. Communities reaped the best resources from newly settled lands, and in the process of doing so experienced population growth that led to village life. Aggregation was an epiphenomenon of an organizational solution to problems engendered by that growth. Chief among these problems was competition for increasingly scarce resources, and aggregation became a means of reducing the potential conflict over these resources. Resource depletion and (perhaps) the social instability of these aggregated settlements then led to abandonment, dispersal of the community, the settlement of new lands, and the re-initiation of the aggregation cycle.

The Dolores model assumes that on a regional or macroregional scale, there was plenty of room for everybody, and that community clusters did not get in each other's way as they move around. The processes that resulted in aggregation appear to be density dependent. For such processes to work in an environment that has plenty of room requires some kind of spatial constraint on settlement. This could have been provided by the social definition of community territories, with core areas and hinterlands; such bounding would have been enhanced by warfare or the threat of warfare. Alternatively, Petersen has argued that drier than normal conditions during the Pueblo I period circumscribed those locations where successful farming could take place (Petersen 1986a, 1986b, 1987a, 1987b, 1988). Whether the Pueblo I models for community mobility could work for the late Pueblo II and Pueblo III periods, when regional population was probably higher and there was less room to move around, is discussed next. We argue that Adler's (1990) in situ model for the development of village size aggregates better describes events in later periods, at least in the central districts of the Mesa Verde region.

Pueblo I period aggregation came to an end about A.D. 900. With few ex-

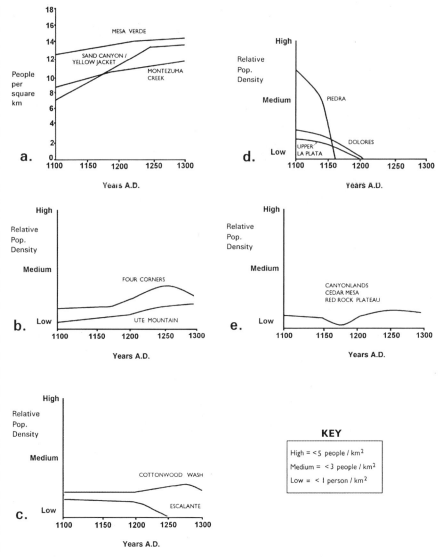

Figure 7.5. Population density estimates in the various Mesa Verde region districts. District estimates are adapted from various sources: Mesa Verde (Hayes 1964; Rohn 1977), Sand Canyon-Yellow Jacket (Adler 1992; Fetterman and Honeycutt 1987), Piedra (Eddy 1977), Dolores (Schlanger 1988).

ceptions, the archaeological record of the tenth century and, to some extent, the early eleventh century, is difficult to find in the Mesa Verde region. It is possible that this is at least in part the product of ceramic dating problems (Blinman 1994) or the result of early sites being obscured by later occupations (Hayes 1964), but we do not think these are the primary reasons for the perceived scarcity of sites from this period. We think that population was in fact low, almost certainly lower than it had been during the eighth and ninth centuries. We have few data on community patterns for the tenth and early eleventh centuries, but we think that communities probably were small and composed of dispersed habitations, and that the individual habitations were also small. The unit pueblo (Prudden 1903), a redundant architectural complex consisting of a kiva and several surface rooms, was probably the typical habitation.

The Mesa Verde region was not totally depopulated during the tenth and early eleventh centuries. A few occupation sites

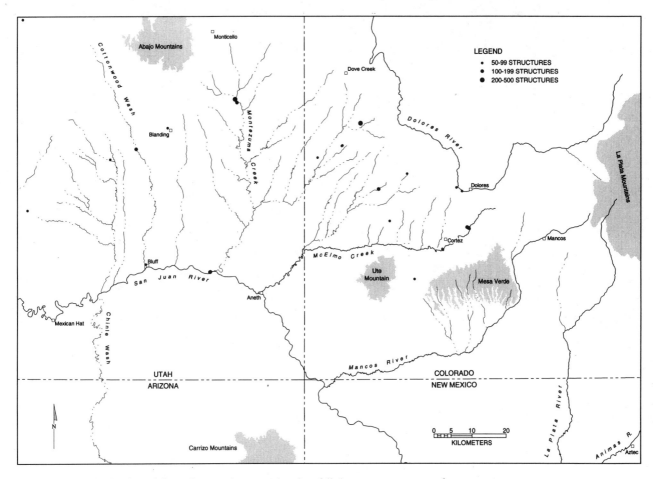

Figure 7.6. Distribution of sites whose peak occupation date falls between A.D. 1100 and 1149.

can be assigned to this period in the eastern, central, and Cedar Mesa districts, but no examples of similar occupations have been found to the west of eastern Cedar Mesa. There appear to be a number of small early Pueblo II settlements on White Mesa, south of Blanding, Utah, in the Cottonwood-Recapture District (Davis 1985). Tree-ring dated sites from the tenth century in the central Mesa Verde region are extremely rare compared to earlier and later periods; the few that are known are in the Ackmen-Lowry, Negro Canyon, Mesa Verde, and Mancos Canyon areas (Robinson and Cameron 1991). Adler (1990, 1992) believes that a dispersed community with a great kiva was established in the Sand Canyon locality in the late tenth century. And Farmer (1977:284) reports a great kiva dating to this time in Mancos Canyon. Based on available information, the low

point of population was probably in the early tenth century, with regional population levels rebounding through the late tenth and eleventh centuries.

It is interesting to speculate on what happened to the Pueblo I period populations: if population declined during the tenth century, where did the occupants of the large, aggregated Pueblo I villages go? A partial answer is that some of these early villagers stayed on in small settlements throughout the Mesa Verde region, reproduced, and kept at least some communities going. A second scenario may be that some or most communities dwindled in place due to adaptive failure because of environmental problems, with child and adult mortality increasing to the point that it outstripped reproductive rates. A third possibility, and one more appealing to us, is that at least some of the Pueblo I period populations from the Mesa Verde region

ended up in the Chaco drainage, where population grew rapidly in the early tenth century (Vivian 1990). The influx of Puebloan groups already experienced in village aggregation and ritual intensification on the community level may have provided at least some of the impetus for the development of the large tenth and eleventh-century communities in Chaco Canyon.

A.D. 1100 to 1150

By the early twelfth century, population appears to have rebounded to relatively high levels again throughout the Mesa Verde Region (figures 7.5 and 7.6). In the central part of the region, surveys show a steady increase in numbers of sites, and probably in population, during the eleventh century. The western districts—Cedar Mesa, the Red Rock Plateau, Canyonlands, and Escalante—were

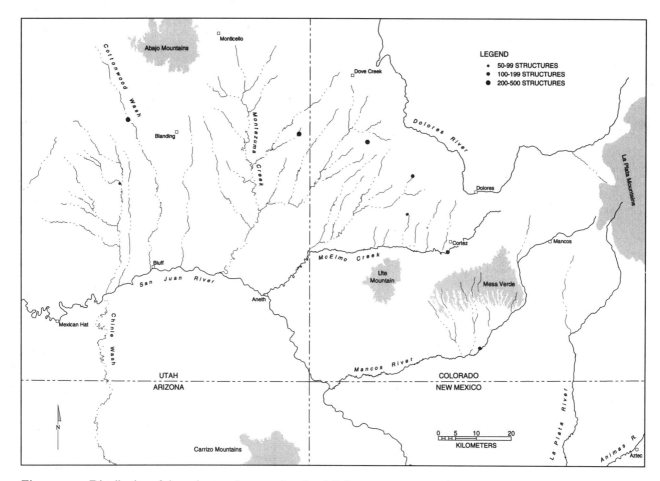

Figure 7.7.   Distribution of sites whose peak occupation date falls between A.D. 1150 and 1199.

also resettled in the late eleventh or early twelfth centuries (Lipe 1970; Matson, Lipe, and Haase 1988). In the Red Rock Plateau and Escalante Districts, these new settlers seem to be largely from the Kayenta area (Lipe and Huntington 1969). Even on Cedar Mesa and in the southern Canyonlands there is a strong Kayenta element in the pottery of this period (Lipe 1981; Lipe and Lindsay 1983).

The population increase in the Mesa Verde region during the late eleventh and early twelfth centuries may relate to the prolonged episode of relatively high amounts and equable distribution of rainfall documented for the San Juan drainage during that time (Sebastian 1988). Climatic conditions may also have made much of the Mesa Verde region more attractive for low-intensity farming (Petersen 1988).

A pattern of highly dispersed com-

munities composed of small habitation units seems to have been established during the eleventh century (Kuckelman and Morris 1988; Kent 1991). Dispersed communities persist in some districts through the Pueblo III period (Matson, Lipe, and Haase 1988). Larger sites, including great houses, began to appear in the central Mesa Verde area by the end of the eleventh century (Bradley 1988b).

In the Piedra district, there was a large early twelfth-century population cluster in the Stollsteimer Mesa-Chimney Rock area in the Piedra drainage (Eddy 1977). Though not shown on the map for the A.D. 1100–1149 time period, one and perhaps two Chaco-style great houses were associated with this cluster. In addition to scattered hamlets and single-household habitations, there was a densely settled village of large "above-ground pit houses" with very thick masonry walls.

Although there is a Mesa Verde element in the associated pottery, it appears to be predominantly San Juan in affiliation (David Breternitz, personal communication 1990). The habitation architecture also differs substantially from that of the central Mesa Verde area farther west. The Piedra populations may have had stronger relationships with the Largo-Gallina area to the south.

The Dolores Valley area that had been so heavily settled during the ninth century appears to have had little permanent population during and after the early twelfth century. A few small habitations and seasonal sites have been recorded, but these sites probably relate to the settlements in the McElmo drainage just to the south. Three settlements with examples of public architecture (Emerson Ruin, Reservoir Village, and Escalante Ruin) are found on the elevational divide between

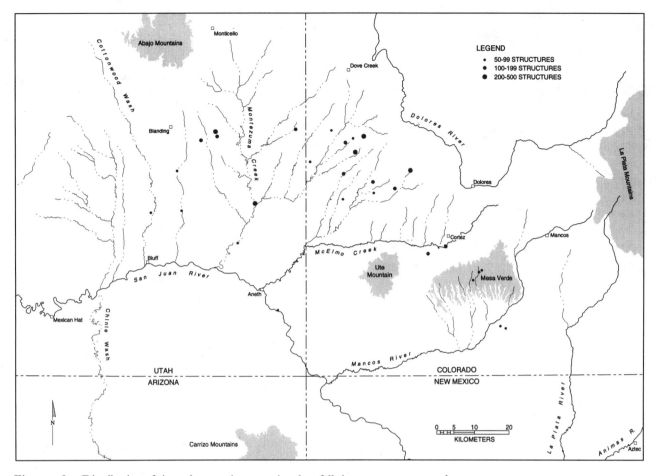

Figure 7.8.   Distribution of sites whose peak occupation date falls between A.D. 1200 and 1249.

the upper Dolores and McElmo watersheds (Eddy, Kane, and Nickens 1984; Fewkes 1919; Hallasi 1979). Each may have been the integrative center for small, dispersed settlements in the area.

In the central Mesa Verde region (McElmo-Yellow Jacket, Montezuma Creek, and Cottonwood-Recapture districts), habitation sites dating to the late eleventh and early twelfth centuries are numerous. Many individual habitation sites are single-kiva unit pueblos or "Prudden units" (Prudden 1903; Lipe 1989) that tend to cluster along low ridges in mesa top environs (Adler 1990; Fetterman and Honeycutt 1987). These clusters of unit pueblos are generally widely dispersed, so that community boundaries are often difficult to perceive, especially in transect-based surveys. Indeed, the identification of communities is based largely on the presence of a great house, frequently ac-

companied by a great kiva. Archaeologists have begun to identify road segments in many parts of the Mesa Verde region; these appear to be associated with some of the great houses of this period though few linkages between sites have been confirmed. Some of the road segments may relate to post-A.D. 1150 sites, and perhaps, even to earlier pre-A.D. 900 communities (personal communication, Dale Davidson and Winston Hurst 1990).

The number of aggregated sites recorded for this period (figure 7.6) is in good part a product of the number of great houses, many of which meet the 50-room criterion. In the absence of great houses, most communities in this period would not have a site that would meet the size criterion, because room blocks in this period were not large enough or tightly enough aggregated to qualify. This community pattern is interesting in relation to the

Pueblo I patterns discussed earlier. The Pueblo II communities generally appear to have maintained a dispersed pattern even as the regional population density (probably) grew beyond Pueblo I period levels. The distribution of settlement appears to have been more widespread and uniform during late Pueblo II times than was the case during the late Pueblo I period. Perhaps there was less social or environmental circumscription of community space.

Structures that we refer to as Chaco-style great houses exhibit a great deal of architectural variation, though they do share at least one characteristic, namely their large size relative to other structures in the vicinity. Some great houses meet most or all of the criteria researchers have used for labeling sites as Chacoan outliers, including but not limited to Chaco-style masonry, large, massed buildings, blocked-in kivas, associated great

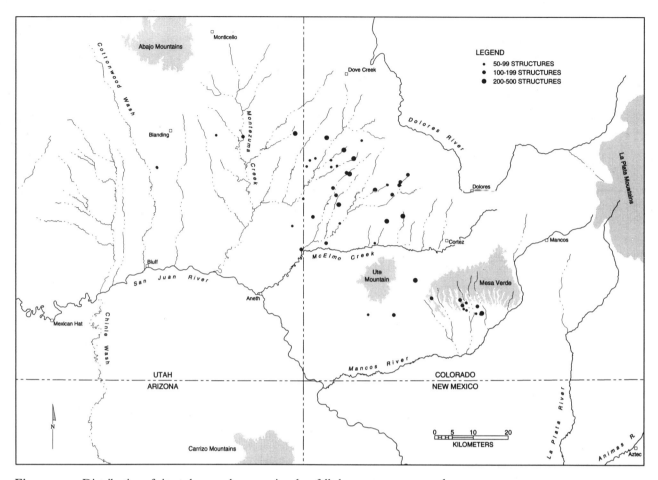

Figure 7.9   Distribution of sites whose peak occupation date falls between A.D. 1250 and 1300.

kivas, earthen berms, and road segments (Marshall et al. 1979; Powers, Gillespie, and Lekson 1983). Wallace Ruin (Bradley 1974, 1988b), Yucca House (Marshall et al. 1979), and Lowry Ruin (Martin 1936) are examples. Many of the great house sites in the Mesa Verde region do not appear on this map because they have less than 50 rooms. We think that, regardless of size, these great houses were significant as central elements of public architecture within the surrounding dispersed communities. Marshall, Doyel, and Breternitz (1982: 1227) consider this type of public architecture to be a defining characteristic of a "Bonito style" architectural tradition that had considerable time depth and regional distribution.

In most or all cases with which we are familiar, great house structures were built within existing settlement clusters

or communities, rather than having had communities form around them (Marshall et al. 1979; Van West, Adler, and Huber 1987; Adler 1990). It appears that the establishment of great houses, most of which do not predate A.D. 1080, was not a major factor in attracting Puebloan peoples to the Mesa Verde region after the population low point in the tenth century. Despite our belief that dispersed communities were present before the introduction of great house architecture, we recognize that demographic trends in relation to great houses need much more testing and investigation.

Although most great houses are associated with a community of dispersed unit pueblos, there are notable exceptions. Reservoir Village (Kane 1986a) and the Ansel Hall site (Guthe 1949) are comprised of a substantial concentration of

closely spaced room blocks. The latter has a large number of small (one to three kivas) separate room blocks, as well as a possible great house, a small great kiva, and probable other "public architecture." Taken as a whole, the number of individual room blocks at Ansel Hall make it one of the largest Chaco-era settlements in the Mesa Verde region.

Not all areas with relatively dense settlement show evidence of great house architecture. Mesa Verde is one example (Hayes 1964; Rohn 1977). Far View Ruin is a possible great house, although construction and occupation of this site clearly continues into the early thirteenth century. There also are areas where there seem to be more than one great house per community. The Lakeview group includes great houses at Wallace Ruin (Bradley 1988b) and Haynie Ruin, as well as a great kiva at the Ida Jean site (Brisbin and Brisbin 1977). All of these structures are located within an area of about 1 square kilometer.

There are notable gaps in the distribution of great houses. One gap separates the Chimney Rock community in the east and the main distribution of great houses to the west, and a similar gap separates the main concentration of great houses in the central area from the Et Al. site on Cedar Mesa.

The Cedar Mesa and Red Rock Plateau surveys (Matson, Lipe, and Haase 1988; Lipe 1966, 1970) indicate that the Pueblo population density was low, ranging from a high of 1.5 persons per square kilometer in central Cedar Mesa to much lower in the Red Rock Plateau area. In these areas, community clusters are very poorly defined in all periods (though on Cedar Mesa this could be partly an artifact of quadrat survey) and the individual settlement unit is generally a single family household. Aggregation even at the level of the two or three household unit pueblo was rare in all periods. The Et Al. site is not associated with an obvious cluster of nearby small habitations, although numerous small habitations of this period are thinly distributed within a radius of several kilometers around the site.

In the Canyonlands District, the Fable Valley site is an early twelfth-century aggregate that probably exceeds our 50-room threshold. Although larger than surrounding dispersed settlements, this site does not have Chaco-style great house architectural characteristics. Kayenta and Mesa Verde style pottery is present, and the site may be associated with a brief but extensive intrusion of Kayenta settlement into the western part of the Mesa Verde region during the late eleventh century (Lipe 1970, 1981; Matson, Lipe, and Haase 1988). Overall, the majority of the early twelfth-century population probably did not live in aggregated settlements. Many people, particularly the inhabitants of the drier portions of the region, may

have lived in dispersed communities that lacked a great house community center.

In general, we would expect that by the early twelfth century, communities in the central area of the Mesa Verde region had established territorial claims to dependable water sources and the best arable lands. Under most climatic regimes, however, there was probably still ample habitable land outside the more heavily settled community core areas. In the prevailing mode of dispersed settlement, it should have been relatively easy for communities to fission or for households to establish new homesteads outside established farming areas.

Another characteristic of early twelfth-century Puebloan occupation that we cannot quantify but that we subjectively support is that a larger amount of interregional exchange occurred in the Mesa Verde region during this period than in later times. It is not clear if this was related to the presence of some type of supracommunity, supraregional political, or religious organization, or whether it was due to the more uniform distribution of people over the Four Corners landscape. We are not arguing that a very large amount of interregional exchange can be documented even for this period, only that more extralocal resources were being moved across the landscape relative to the post-A.D. 1150 periods.

A.D. 1150 to 1199

Our map of the central Mesa Verde region in the late twelfth century (figure 7.7) shows fewer but larger dots compared with the map for the previous half-century (figure 7.6). The area in which the dots occur is also smaller. Except for the Coombs site, aggregated sites were confined to the central part of the Mesa Verde region, with no aggregates east of the Mesa Verde proper or west of upper Comb Wash. Although the aggregates for this period were larger on average than in the previous period, the total room count for the aggregates

was lower than in the previous period because there were fewer larger sites.

It is unclear whether these changes reflect yet another dip in regional population levels during the late twelfth century. Population decreases are possible for the eastern and western peripheries. The Piedra and Upper LaPlata Districts seem to have had very low populations at this time, a condition that continued through the thirteenth century (Eddy 1977; Adams 1975). In the central area, the easternmost portion of the McElmo-Yellow Jacket District probably lost population in the late twelfth century, though it was not completely depopulated. To the west, Matson, Lipe, and Haase (1988) make a case for a possible occupation hiatus on Cedar Mesa during the late twelfth century, and Lipe (1966, 1970) makes a stronger case for a depopulation of the Red Rock Plateau during this time. The Canyonlands District may also have had few or no Anasazi residents in the late twelfth century, although it never had very many. In the Escalante District, people at the Coombs site (Lister 1959; Lister et al. 1960; Lister and Lister 1961) apparently bucked the trends by building new structures at the site in the 1160s. The nine (mostly v and vv) tree-ring samples from the Coombs site date between A.D. 1129v and 1169+vv, with six of the nine falling after 1158. Lipe thinks that the predominance of Kayenta tradition Sosi and Dogoszhi style pottery from the site indicates that the occupation peaked in the early twelfth century, but there is no question that there was significant activity at the site in the later half of the twelfth century.

The Coombs site (R. Lister 1959; Lister, Ambler, and Lister 1960; Lister and Lister 1961; see also Lyneis, chapter 2) is something of an anomaly. With several room blocks and a combined total of 83 excavated surface rooms and pit structures, it is far and away the largest single settlement in our area west of Cottonwood Wash. It is not clear whether there was a contemporaneous dispersed community of small habitations in the area surrounding the Coombs site. Although the bulk of the Coombs site ceramics are clearly in the Kayenta tradition, substantial amounts of Fremont pottery found at the site indicate fairly intensive exchange and interaction with Fremont populations (Lister and Lister 1961). The distinctive Coombs Variety pottery also shows up in small frequencies in predominantly Kayenta sites many kilometers away in the Upper Glen Canyon area (Lipe et al. 1960; F. Lister 1964), indicating frequent interaction with other Kayenta Branch populations.

In the central Mesa Verde area north of McElmo Creek, occupation clearly continues through the late twelfth century, but we are currently unable to assess the possibility of a population decline during this period. There are almost no sites with tree-ring dates in the A.D. 1150 to 1180 interval (Robinson and Cameron 1991). All or most of our assignments of site occupations to this period are based on assessment of surface pottery, and we are not yet sure that this period has a clear ceramic signature. Archaeological surveys in the central Mesa Verde area (all of which share our problems of dating sites to this period) indicate either population stability or gradual increase during the late twelfth century. If we take these survey results at face value, they suggest that if people were leaving the San Juan Geologic Basin, the Virgin Branch territory, or the extreme eastern and western parts of our study area during the severe drought of the middle and late twelfth century, they apparently were not coming in large numbers to the central Mesa Verde area. Or, if they were, their numbers were only sufficient to stabilize or slightly augment a locally declining population.

As previously described, large aggregates of the late twelfth century are likely to be made up of multiple, closely spaced, often parallel aggregates of Prudden units. The aggregates appear to have numerous outlying habitation sites that are not part of the densely settled central locus. Other

communities remain entirely dispersed, lacking a central aggregate big enough to show up on one of our maps. In general, the individual room blocks, even those outside a village-sized aggregate, appear to be larger than in the previous period. Habitation sites with two to three kivas are more common than during prior periods. Larger room blocks also occur, especially in the village-sized aggregates.

A.D. 1200 to 1300

Between A.D. 1200 and 1250 there appears to have been an overall increase in population density, size, and degree of settlement aggregation, at least in the central area, and there was a dramatic increase in site size and number (figure 7.8). This may be due in part to our difficulty in recognizing sites occupied during the last half of the twelfth century. It is also due in part to our use of "peak" dates for the figures, because many of the sites assigned to the thirteenth-century occupation were probably settled during the late twelfth century. While on the topic of site counts, we need to keep in mind that the entire Mesa Verde region may have been abandoned by the mid-1280s, making the last occupational period (A.D. 1250–1300) shorter, with a higher average momentary population relative to the first half of the century.

The Piedra and the Upper LaPlata districts continued to be unpopulated through the thirteenth century (Eddy 1977; Adams 1975; Mobley-Tanaka 1990). The western districts (with the probable exception of Escalante) were repopulated during the thirteenth century at a low density of settlement. As previously noted, the central area apparently experienced population growth, at least during the early thirteenth century.

Survey data that incorporate both small and large sites indicate that there were probably significantly more people in our study area during the early thirteenth century than during the late twelfth century, and that a larger fraction — though probably not the majority — were living

in large (50-plus-room) villages (Hayes 1964; Rohn 1977, 1989; Chandler, Reed, and Nickens 1980; Neily 1983; Kuckelman 1986; Fetterman and Honeycutt 1987; Fuller 1987, 1988c; Adler 1988, 1990). The trend toward increasing aggregation continues through the late thirteenth century, especially in the central area. Many of the small mesa top habitations, associated with what are today the best agricultural soils, appear to have been abandoned as year-round habitations by about A.D. 1250 (Adler and Varien 1994; Varien 1990; Varien, Kuckelman, and Kleidon 1992). A limited number of small habitations outside the main aggregated sites were constructed during this last period of occupation (Varien, Kuckelman, and Kleidon 1992), nearly all of which are situated at the base of cliffs, talus slopes, and locations inside the canyons.

In the less densely populated areas to the west, some aggregation occurs, but even the largest thirteenth-century settlements do not reach the 50-room level. The Moon House complex on Cedar Mesa, which dates predominantly to the 1250s and 1260s, is the largest aggregated Pueblo III settlement recorded in this district (Bloomer 1989). Still, it has less than 40 rooms distributed among three spatially discrete, contemporaneous complexes.

Cliff dwellings became well established during the thirteenth century (Hayes 1964; Rohn 1977) and stand-alone towers at canyon-head springs are common by A.D. 1250 (Winter 1975, 1976, 1977, 1984). Cliff dwellings reached their highest frequency in the Mesa Verde District, while canyon-head towers are more prevalent in the western part of the McElmo drainage. In general, as the thirteenth century wore on, mesa tops increasingly gave way to canyon rims or canyon heads as locations for settlements. Many of the largest of the canyon-oriented sites enclose springs or are located adjacent to a dependable water supply. These are probably the same springs that served earlier, more dispersed mesa top communities, but during the late thirteenth century, people apparently wanted to live closer to reliable water sources. The increased dependence on cliff dwellings and tower complexes also reflect this emphasis on canyon edges and dependable water sources although this does not explain the occurrence of these specific architectural forms.

Although not all thirteenth-century sites are in easily defended locations, there does seem to be a clear increase in use of such locations during this time. Cliff dwellings and sites built atop rock prominences often have walls designed to channel and restrict site access. "Loophole" apertures in walls that front the site or that flank entrances are also common, possibly to shield site occupants as they checked the affiliation and intentions of visitors. Walls enclosing all or parts of sites also became common (Kenzle 1993). Indisputable evidence of conflict is rare during this and other centuries (but see Haas and Creamer, chapter 14), but recent excavations in the Sand Canyon locality indicate that some violent conflict occurred (Lightfoot and Kuckelman 1994).

Given the paucity and equivocal nature of evidence for violent deaths in the archaeological record, a case can be made based on more indirect evidence that raiding or feuding, or at least anxiety over the possibility of hostilities, was more common in the thirteenth century—and particularly in the late thirteenth century—than earlier. In general, there is little evidence of interregional exchange during the thirteenth century in comparison to earlier centuries. It is our impression that this trend continued through the thirteenth century. By the late thirteenth century, site assemblages from the central Mesa Verde districts contain virtually no shell or imported pottery (White Mountain Red Ware or Tsegi Orange Ware). Local exchange at the intercommunity level may also have decreased. Neily (1983) compared site assemblages from settlements on Squaw and Bug Points in the Montezuma Creek drainage and concluded that, through time, site assemblages became more different from one another. He argued from this evidence that neighboring communities engaged in less exchange and became more independent of one another. At the same time, however, we should point out that detailed similarities in ceramic design styles are maintained throughout the central Mesa Verde region, indicating that interaction and communication continued to be intense over this large area throughout the thirteenth century.

As pointed out earlier, several changes in settlement pattern occurred during the thirteenth century. Construction that required suprahousehold labor, including settlement-enclosing walls, large biwall or triwall structures, D-shaped buildings, reservoirs, and AWUFs apparently became more common. The canyon-head clusters of towers (Thompson 1993) may also fall into this category. Plazas, though perhaps not as formal as those enclosed by villages in the Cibola, Little Colorado, and Mogollon areas, were present at some of the larger sites (figure 7.4). At late canyon-rim architectural complexes, low walls defined cliff top plazas and enclosed buildings, possibly representing new forms of public architecture (Kenzle 1993; Kelly, Lipe, and Varien 1994). These low complexes were often associated with more extensive residential architecture built at the base of canyon rims and on talus slopes.

Over the course of the thirteenth century the prevailing large-site pattern of multiple, parallel room blocks composed of redundant kiva-and-room units (Adler 1990; Lange et al. 1986; Rohn 1984) gave way to a greater variety of community patterns. These range from multistoried pueblos contained in a single structure to loose aggregates of several room blocks of varying sizes and architectural composition. In all cases, the average ratio of rooms to kivas remains low (generally less than five rooms per kiva), and the kiva-based habitation unit apparently remained the primary architectural building block within the village. Although modular in layout we stress that there was still considerable variation in both room-to-kiva ratios and the spatial redundancy of the kiva-based units. The occurrence of settlement-enclosing walls, the greater frequency of public architecture and the possible appearance of functionally specific sets of rooms (e.g. possible storage complexes) in some villages distinguish the later aggregates from those occupied in the late twelfth and early thirteenth centuries (Bradley 1986, 1987, 1990, 1992, 1993; Kleidon and Bradley 1989).

We interpret these changes in community patterning as an indication that Puebloan communities were experimenting with organizational schemes meant to counter the fragility of large village aggregates. Similar periods of experimentation are proposed for the Cibola (Kintigh, chapter 9) and Hopi (Adams, chapter 4) regions. Given that the Mesa Verde region communities were likely comprised of more or less independent low-level social segments represented by suites of kivas and associated surface rooms, the social fragility of the these villages would have required some form of community-level integration. These experiments in integration may be rooted in social or resource-based competition with other communities, or in problems recognized during a long history of unstable community organization.

Our studies of thirteenth-century community organization in the Sand Canyon locality (in the Yellow Jacket-McElmo District), though still in progress, have not produced evidence of institutionalized social hierarchy or marked socioeconomic inequality within Sand Canyon Pueblo or between this large settlement and its smaller satellite sites (Lipe 1992). Subtle differences show up in the latter comparison, such as differences in ceramic vessel size and distribution of faunal remains within sites (Driver 1993; Huber 1993), but there is little material evidence for the presence of a well-differentiated elite.

There may, however, have been important inequalities between community members that fall short of the establishment of institutionalized elites. Marked differences may have existed between the authority of individuals within the community based on their gender, age, or lineage affiliation, and these inequalities may have created divisive tensions requiring changes in community organization within the region (Bender 1990; Brumfiel 1992). As one example, the largest variation in site size in the Sand Canyon locality occurred during the late twelfth and early thirteenth centuries when some households were living in multiple room block sites while other households were living in unit pueblos with a single kiva (Adler 1990). These dramatic size differences between coresidential groups may have also meant differences in the ability to organize labor and access to the best productive resources (e.g., arable land and dependable water supplies). The debate in the Southwest over social complexity has traditionally treated inequality as an either-or phenomenon and, unfortunately, focused on whether elites were present or absent. The position taken here is that even though inequality in Mesa Verde region communities may not have been fully institutionalized, there may still have been important differences in the social relations of production. We need to remain open to archaeological evidence of these differences, as they may represent an important catalyst for change within these communities.

Changes in Mesa Verde area community patterns may have set the stage for acceptance of a different set of strategies in community organization, the same strategies that appear to have swept through the Rio Grande and Western Pueblo areas during the late thirteenth and early fourteenth centuries (Adams 1989; Lipe 1989; and elsewhere in this volume). In these more southerly areas, the appearance and spread of formal plaza-oriented spatial organization, the replacement of numerous smaller kivas by a few larger kivas, and the florescence of the katsina cult (Adams 1991) may be the archaeological signatures left by experiments in community

organization. In contrast to the apparent insularity of the late thirteenth-century communities of the Mesa Verde region, it appears that interlocality and interregional exchange were becoming very well developed to the south of the Four Corners area. If Mesa Verde people adopted or contributed to these changes, however, it was only after they left the Mesa Verde region and resettled farther south.

Population Aggregation

As mentioned earlier, the 50-room threshold serves as an arbitrary analytical boundary meant to focus our attention on the larger class of settlements. The value of the boundary lies not in its defined magnitude, but in its distinction between larger aggregated settlements and the smaller unit pueblo settlements that are so common across the Southwest during the prehistoric period. Village aggregation has been attributed to a number of processes, each of which is addressed throughout this volume (see especially Cordell, chapter 16).

We assert that both demographic change and community histories were influential in settlement pattern trends that, by the end of the thirteenth century, resulted in the almost wholesale movement of Mesa Verde region populations into large, aggregated villages. Aggregation puts more people into closer proximity for longer periods of time compared to earlier periods when settlement dispersal was the rule. Although the shift to aggregation had potentially detrimental effects—increased crowding, less sanitary conditions, and more pressure to share resources—the benefits of aggregation included a larger group within which labor and defense concerns could be shared. We hasten to point out that the process of village aggregation did not invent community organization. Instead we believe that community organization was central to Puebloan survival during periods of aggregation and dispersal. Existing, dispersed communities invented, and in the central Mesa Verde

region, twice returned to, aggregated village life between the ninth and thirteenth centuries.

Our use of the term "community" follows Adler's (1990) cross-cultural research on communities in politically nonstratified societies. Within these societies the community plays several roles, including the definition of both land use territories and associated resource access rights for local populations within the broader regional system. We define the community as a social organization that defines access to necessary natural resources, provides a level of social identity for its constituent households, and serves as a significant decision-making entity above the level of the primary household unit. This organizational perspective encompasses communities that are dependent upon a wide range of settlement strategies, including dispersed and aggregated settlements (see also Wills and Leonard 1994:xiii).

The demographic scale of agricultural communities varies widely in the ethnographic record, but there are some notable regularities. There does, for instance, seem to be an upper limit to the population size of communities in politically nonstratified societies. In world-wide and regional cross cultural samples, the size of the community rarely exceeds 1500 people (Adler 1990). The presence of a demographic limit for tribal communities is supported by others (Forge 1972; Kosse 1990, 1995), including Steve Lekson (1985, 1988), who places the upper limit at about 2,000 people. This ceiling probably results from limitations faced by nonstratified communities in integrating a larger number of people in the absence of a strongly hierarchical social framework.

Aggregation and Community

Traditionally, archaeologists have defined communities based largely upon the spatial clustering of sites (Rohn 1977) or by the presence of a single aggregated site. Although spatial relationships between settlements certainly play an important part in community interaction, we also seek to consider how people were integrated into communities and what types of activities were organized at the social scale of the community. Toward this end we identify a number of archaeological proxies for community level integration in the Mesa Verde region, all of which are embodied in public architectural features. These include great kivas, biwall and tri-wall structures, great houses, and "roads" or linear earthen features. We do not yet include reservoirs, enclosing walls, and plazas in this inventory of public architecture, but future research should probably consider their worth as proxies for community integration.

During the early twelfth century, great kivas and Chaco-style great houses served as the predominant community integrative facilities. Throughout this period, community members resided primarily in small, dispersed residential sites surrounding these community integrative facilities. Seldom were these small domestic sites constructed close enough to great houses and great kivas to be considered part of the same archaeological "site."

We are certainly not the first to suggest that great houses and great kivas served as the integrative focus for dispersed communities (Fowler, Stein, and Anyon 1987; Marshall, Doyel, and Breternitz 1982; Marshall et al. 1979; Powers, Gillespie, and Lekson 1983). As we have already stated, great house construction was incorporated into the architectural repertoire of Mesa Verde communities that were already in place prior to the great house building boom of the late eleventh and early twelfth centuries. Our compilation of probable great houses in the region shows that they are spaced fairly regularly across the central area of the Mesa Verde region, generally four to eight kilometers apart (Adler 1994). This indicates that the extant communities had established boundaries before the great houses were constructed (Adler 1992). Estimat-

ing the number of people in these dispersed communities requires large-scale, comprehensive survey coverage, a relatively rare commodity in the Mesa Verde region. In at least one large-scale survey in the McElmo-Yellow Jacket District (Adler 1990, 1992), estimates of momentary population for two probable twelfth-century communities—Casa Negra and Goodman Point—range from 75 to 350 people per community (Adler 1990).

The question of whether the great houses we observe in the Mesa Verde region indicate a "Chacoan presence" linking the Mesa Verde area with a single religious, economic, or political system centered in the San Juan Geologic Basin, or whether they represent a general architectural style that simply reaches its architectural apogee in Chaco Canyon (Fowler and Stein 1990), goes beyond the scope of this chapter. We should, however, note the possibility that some Mesa Verde great houses may represent local attempts to conform to pan-Puebloan concepts of community integrative architecture. It does not appear that great house construction was a defensive measure because the primary residential site during the eleventh and twelfth centuries was a small, dispersed settlement that left the occupants open to raiding. Future research should focus on evidence of possible conflict in order to assess whether the dispersed community pattern was supported by some sort of "pax Chaco," a religious or political system that may have had sufficient influence on an intercommunity level to dampen social conflict and reduce resource competition.

Communities and Regional Organization

We believe that by the end of the eleventh century the central area of the Mesa Verde region was carved up into many community territories, setting the stage for the process of population aggregation so evident during the twelfth and thirteenth

centuries. Referred to earlier as the in situ model of community aggregation, the model proposes that by the early twelfth century, communities in the central Mesa Verde region had established their territorial claims to good water sources and areas of good land. In the late twelfth century and throughout the thirteenth century the extant communities underwent significant contraction in the spatial dispersion of residential sites, as evidenced by increases in average habitation (room block) size through the late Pueblo II period (Adler 1988, 1990; Fetterman and Honeycutt 1987). We hasten to add that this model does not propose that all changes were local, or that we exclude any consideration of population immigration, long-distance exchange, or macroregional interaction in our explanation (see Wilcox, chapter 17). Instead, the in situ nature of the model refers to the important roles played by existing community boundaries and populations in the process of population aggregation.

By the mid-twelfth century, not only did the pace of population aggregation quicken, but the organizational role of great houses began to change. Though post-Chacoan great houses and great kivas remained important as community integrative features in the Zuni region in the late twelfth and early thirteenth centuries (Fowler, Stein, and Anyon 1987; Kintigh 1994), public architecture appears to be quite variable in form and use in the Mesa Verde region during this period. Indeed, there is evidence that the great kiva at Lowry was remodeled during this time (Ahlstrom, Breternitz, and Warren 1985). During a visit to Yucca House, Keith Kintigh noted that the site was similar in form to post-Chacoan settlements in the Zuni region, for example the Hinkson site. Given that the A.D. 1150 to 1200 period is the interval for which we have least control over chronology and demography, we should remain open to the possibility that sites like Yucca House have components that date to this period. We consider it likely that Chacoan period great houses continued to play an important role in the ritual landscape of the post-Chacoan communities, but also think it probable that facilities such as great kivas, large, open unroofed kivas (see Kintigh, chapter 9) and other structures were part of the repertoire of Puebloan public architecture during this time.

Although diversity is likely in public architecture during the late twelfth and early thirteenth centuries, the characteristics of residential architecture remained more constant. Refuse continued to be placed in front of each habitation unit rather than in a common site midden, and burials were placed primarily in these same refuse areas. The relentless modularity of the community spatial organization suggests that the kiva group or the room block unit continued to be the strongest and most durable level of social organization, with the encompassing community present but in a socially more fragile form (Lipe 1989; Lipe and Hegmon, 1989). As with the earlier occupations in the region, any evidence for economic or political stratification is not striking enough to show up in the fuzzy picture we have of the communities that date to this period. The lack of evidence for economic or political stratification is not surprising given the relatively small size of the communities under consideration. If our perceptions of the demographic scale of these communities are not wildly in error, none of the intensively studied communities in the region would have exceeded 1,500 people, and the great majority of communities contained considerably fewer than one thousand people.

As described previously, the trend toward community aggregation continues throughout the thirteenth century, resulting in the construction of multiple large settlements, some with several hundred rooms and scores of kivas. It is significant that many of the largest thirteenth-century settlements surround fresh water springs at canyon-head locations, indicating the value of these domestic water sources to the communities. This does not mean that water was unimportant to earlier, dispersed communities. Earlier great houses and great kivas are often located in close proximity (often less than 0.5 km) to these same springs. The thirteenth-century communities aggregated immediately adjacent to water, but this follows a long history of locating community integrative facilities near this same important resource.

Although we argue that the community framework within which thirteenth-century settlement aggregation occurred had long been in place throughout the Mesa Verde region, the in situ model as presented still needs to explain why the dispersed pattern gave way to the aggregated villages when it did. As noted, the model presented here is similar in some respects to models developed by Dolores Project researchers (Kohler et al. 1986; Kohler and Matthews 1988; Kohler 1992; Orcutt, Blinman, and Kohler 1990) that address community aggregation during the Pueblo I period in the region. In the Dolores models, communities underwent population growth and subsequently aggregated as one means of decreasing conflict over arable land, hunting areas, and other important resources. The in situ model and the Dolores models suggest that communities utilized bounded territories within which a variety of natural resources were claimed and exploited.

The Dolores models emphasize environmental conditions that circumscribed where farming communities could have located, thereby limiting mobility options. Schlanger (1988) suggests that water control technology developed after A.D. 1000 allowed the inhabitants to break free from these constraints posed by fluctuations in precipitation. It is our opinion that the degree to which fluctuations in precipitation dictated the location of farming communities has been overstated. Van West's (1994 and chapter 15) research shows that some agricultural productivity could have been sustained even in the driest years, and the research of Wilshusen (Wilshusen and Blinman 1992; Wilshusen and Schlanger 1993; Wilshusen 1991) and Lightfoot (Lightfoot and Etzkorn 1993) show that settlements were located outside of the area predicted by the Dolores environmental model.

Environmental circumscription certainly influenced broad geographical limits for successful food production, but we also need to more fully appreciate the relationship between increasing aggregation and the decreased or complete inability of individuals, households, and communities to relocate into unsettled lands once necessary resources had been depleted. Based upon the large number of settlements located throughout the Mesa Verde region from the eleventh century on, we believe that the cultural landscape became increasingly crowded, and that constraints on residential movement led in part to the increasing aggregation of residential space. Increased population necessarily decreased the range of mobility options.

The increased "packing" of community territories within the central area necessitated changes in mobility and agricultural production strategies. It is no coincidence that the evidence for permanent agricultural features (field houses, check dams, contour terraces, and reservoirs) increases dramatically in the region during the late twelfth and the thirteenth centuries. Limited mobility was counteracted by increasing investment in available agricultural lands. Increasing investment in agricultural features would have made residential moves a progressively more expensive proposition. This contrasts to the pre-aggregation, great house period when dispersed households resided on the best arable lands and apparently relocated residences relatively often rather than investing in labor intensive agricultural strategies.

An increasingly "crowded" landscape does not depend solely on the number of people present at any one time. Cross-cultural research into land tenure systems among agricultural societies (Adler 1990, 1992; Netting 1990) has established that land use histories significantly constrain mobility options at the household and community levels. Populations, particularly those dependent upon food-producing subsistence systems, retain rights to lands, residential sites, and other resources for varying amounts of time after the time the resource was last actively used. In the case of the Mesa Verde region, the longer the region was occupied, the more its own history of occupation and land use constrained the mobility options of its people and communities. The cultural landscape was a mosaic of socially negotiated spaces, filled with potential symbols of ownership, including abandoned structures, burials in abandoned sites, and agricultural features. The history of land use and its obvious symbols probably served to restrict the area that was open to new settlement. One significant strategy for living in such a landscape, delimited as it was by natural and cultural constraints, was to bring community members into a central residential site. Agricultural activities would have required travel to and from distant fields, but the return benefit would be closer proximity to other (communal) resources such as water, shared labor, and mutual deterrence of outside threats to life and livelihood.

The process of aggregation was not simply the inevitable result of increasingly larger populations "settling in" and filling up the landscape. The change in settlement also occurred within a context of increasingly intensive utilization of necessary resources and higher potential for conflict. Canyon-rim settings provided the opportunity to manage surface runoff (hence the prevalence of reservoirs and water catchment facilities on and around the large, late sites) and utilize springs for pot-watering. The increase in number and type of water-catchment and diversion features linked with agricultural fields also occurs late in the Mesa Verde region occupation (Adler 1990; Rohn 1963, 1977).

Our proposal that the process of population aggregation was part of the entrenchment of already defined communities into increasingly immobile organizational entities investing increasing amounts of labor into their food production and water conservation strategies also ties into the carrying capacity conundrum raised by Van West (1994 and chapter 15). Van West's research indicates that agricultural carrying capacity would not have been exceeded in the Mesa Verde region at any point in the occupation of the area. Even during the worst years of drought there should have been sufficient arable land to support the estimated population in the region. This assumes, however, that a boundary-free landscape existed, one in which each person, household or community would have had equal access to productive resources each year. If, as we propose, community boundaries had become increasingly inflexible over time in the Mesa Verde region, the lack of mobility and dispersal may have obliterated the ability of entire communities to sustain themselves for too many unproductive years in a row within their community territories. We noted earlier that data from excavated and surface contexts point to an overall decrease in the amount of extralocal materials on the latest and most highly aggregated of the settlements in the central areas of the region. Excessive investment in a single locale may have spelled disaster for fixed communities, particularly during the environmental perturbations of the late thirteenth century.

Abandonment

In a recent survey of tree-ring cutting dates, Lipe (1994) documented the rapidity with which building activity terminated in the northern Mesa Verde region in the late thirteenth century. In southeastern Utah, beam-cutting declined rapidly in the 1260s, with only a few dates after A.D. 1265. In the Sand Canyon locality (McElmo-Yellow Jacket District), there was a sharp decrease in the early 1270s, with no dates later than A.D. 1277. On the Mesa Verde proper, there was a burst of building activity in the early

1270s, followed by a decline in the late 1270s, with the latest date at A.D. 1280. A large enough number of sites and projects are covered by the existing tree-ring record to give us confidence that abandonment followed the last cutting dates by relatively few years, and that the northern Mesa Verde region had probably lost most or all of its population by the middle A.D. 1280s.

Movement at scales ranging from the household to the regional population was not unusual for ancestral Puebloan groups in the Mesa Verde region (see e.g., Schlanger and Wilshusen 1993; Wilshusen and Schlanger 1993), and was probably a common way of solving, or at least avoiding, a variety of environmental and social problems. What is unusual about the abandonment of the northern San Juan and the whole Four Corners area in the late thirteenth century, however, is the evidently large number of people involved, the rapidity with which it occurred, the distances that the emigrants must have moved, and the apparent completeness of the depopulation that resulted.

How large a population was involved in this rapid population decline or abandonment in our study area? Our survey of the existing data on Mesa Verde region site sizes and distributions has convinced us that Rohn's (1983, 1989) interpretations of population history are generally correct—there were large populations in the northern Mesa Verde area in the thirteenth century, and the population probably reached its peak at that time. Alternative interpretations (e.g., Lipe 1978, 1983) that populations peaked in the early twelfth century and then gradually declined throughout the late twelfth and thirteenth centuries find less support in the most current data sets.

Rohn (1989) suggests that 30,000 people may have inhabited the area between the Mesa Verde proper and Blanding, Utah, during the thirteenth century. The post-1250 sites we have identified, though numerous, will not account for a population in the several tens of thousands. Although there undoubtedly are many more such sites that have yet to be recorded, we doubt that there are enough of these to account for a post-A.D. 1250 population as high as Rohn's estimate. Estimates in the thousands, rather than tens of thousands, are also reasonable, but the regional survey data are not adequate to provide an empirical test of this proposition.

The timing of the population peak is also poorly defined, but given recent research in the Sand Canyon locality, our best guess would have populations at their maximum between A.D. 1250 and 1280. Having said this, it is clear from the data we have compiled here that a sizable population still occupied the area after A.D. 1250. Tree-ring data show that a significant amount of building was still going on in many parts of the region in the A.D. 1260s and early 1270s (Schlanger, Lipe, and Robinson 1993). Over 50 sites exceeding the 50-room cutoff contain evidence of occupations between A.D. 1250 and 1280, and together total over 6,000 rooms. This probably represents a population between 5,000 and 10,000.

The demographic and chronological data indicate a rate of depopulation that cannot be accounted for by a gradual decline resulting from a slight excess of death over birth rates. Consequently, either catastrophic decline or emigration seem the more likely explanation for this final phase. What caused this rapid and apparently complete depopulation—one that has generated hundreds if not thousands of undergraduate term papers and countless media evocations of a sublime and impenetrable mystery? There seem to us to be several reasonable possibilities.

Decisions to leave an area involve an assessment of economic and social conditions in the current location ("push" factors) relative to conditions in the potential relocation area ("pull" factors). Changes in either or both could eventually trigger a move (Lipe 1986). It is possible that local stresses were in themselves sufficient to make people look for settlement alter-

natives farther south. On the other hand, there may also have been developments in the Rio Grande area or in the Western Pueblo area that helped alter the balance as well. We first consider the "push" factors.

Pushed Around:
Adaptive Problems Related to
Environmental Change

The "Great Drought" of A.D. 1276 to 1299 does have a striking correlation with the final depopulation of the central Mesa Verde region, though as noted, abandonment may have begun earlier in the western part of the region. Van West's (1994 and chapter 15) recent tree-ring based model of effective soil moisture and crop productivity in southwestern Colorado indicates, however, that the area as a whole could support a very large population of maize farmers, even in drought years, although some communities may have had difficulties in some years. As argued previously, restrictions on movement associated with aggregation, community claims to unused farmland, land tenure rules, and warfare would undoubtedly have magnified the effects of drought on particular households and communities.

Petersen (1986, 1987a, 1988) has suggested that the onset of the first pulse of the Little Ice Age in the mid-thirteenth century may have shortened growing seasons enough to make dry farming in the higher elevation uplands much riskier in southwestern Colorado. Specifically, summer precipitation may have declined because the circulation pattern associated with the Little Ice Age may have weakened the summer monsoons that have always been variable in strength in the northern San Juan. Petersen (1986a, 1987a, 1988) found pollen evidence of a decline in summer moisture in southwestern Colorado.

Dean (1993) recently reported some exciting new evidence from analysis of tree-ring series that suggests a significant decrease in the predictability of rainfall in the Four Corners occurred between ca.

A.D. 1250 and 1450. Such a change in predictability may have affected not only the practice of agriculture but also the religious systems related to rainfall and crop success.

There is also evidence that a cycle of arroyo cutting began in the Four Corners area during the Pueblo III period (Hack 1942; Euler et al. 1979; Dean et al. 1985); this would have affected settlements dependent on floodplain farming. Arroyo cutting may have had less of an impact on Mesa Verde region occupants because the majority of settlements in the area appear to have been dependent on rainfall agriculture practiced in mesa top settings.

Given the large populations we have posited for the thirteenth century, it is also likely that the option of taking up full-time foraging as a response to crop failure would not have been available to more than a small fraction of the population. Furthermore, the use of foraged resources as a "fall-back" strategy to supplement cultigens in poor crop years may also have been constrained by population density and the depletion of nondomesticated resources due to generations of exploitation. Hence, the thirteenth-century populations of the northern Mesa Verde area may have been more dependent on maize for their survival than were earlier populations, and hence more vulnerable to environmental variability that affected food production.

Although the adaptive problems discussed earlier must have posed challenges, the Pueblo inhabitants of the region were resourceful and resilient farmers. Furthermore, the area is environmentally variable, and it is hard to believe that at least some areas would not have remained productive even under worst-case scenarios. Even in an extremely dry year there is more precipitation in the Mesa Verde uplands than in the San Juan Geologic Basin or at Hopi during a good year of precipitation. Anecdotally, the summer of 1989 was the driest on modern record in southwestern Colorado, yet the majority of commercial wheat and pinto bean dry farmers obtained at least partial crops.

More Push Factors:
Social Sources of Stress

Like other parts of the southwest, the Mesa Verde region was likely not a peaceful haven for Puebloan populations. Haas and Creamer (chapter 14) argue that intercommunity warfare increased during the Pueblo III period over the entire Four Corners area. Kenzle (1993) recently assembled evidence on walled Pueblo III period settlements in the northern San Juan area, and shows that many of the walls have characteristics that make them suitable for use as defensive structures, although they likely served other functions as well. Lightfoot and Kuckelman (1994) have recently assembled data on human remains encountered at Sand Canyon Pueblo and the Castle Rock site, both of which were abandoned in the mid to late 1270s. On the basis of several lines of evidence, they argue that warfare was a factor in the deaths of a number of individuals coincident with abandonment of Castle Rock, and that warfare may have been involved in some deaths during the latest part of the occupation at Sand Canyon Pueblo. Similar patterns in which numerous human remains are associated with abandonment or terminal occupations are not present, however, in other large late sites, such as Mug House (Rohn 1971) and Long House (Cattanach 1980), which were abandoned in the late thirteenth century at Mesa Verde.

If intercommunity warfare was common in the area in the late thirteenth century, as seems probable, it may have reinforced the trends toward community integration and boundedness discussed previously. This in turn would have curtailed household movement as a way of solving both social and adaptive problems. Recent research by Kohler and Van West (1996) is relevant here. Using Van West's model of agricultural productivity in southwestern Colorado, they identified patterns of spatial and temporal variability in maize production under which it would be beneficial for households to share food with other households, and other patterns of variability in production under which it would be disadvantageous for them to share. They assumed that food sharing would be more likely in aggregated settlements and thus predicted when household aggregation or dispersion would be favored as an economic strategy. In the 400 years they consider, the period A.D. 1272 to 1288 has the strongest prediction for household dispersion. But households did not disperse locally during those years in the northern San Juan area—instead, settlements remained aggregated until they were abandoned, and their occupants moved out of the region entirely. The data are somewhat equivocal on whether movement out of the area was by household groups or by entire communities.

Pull Factors in
Regional Abandonment:
Outside Attractions

There is a strong correlation between the distribution of summer rainfall and maize agriculture in western North America, including the Southwest. It also appears to be the case that the areas that experienced population growth during the late thirteenth and early fourteenth centuries were ones that today have more reliable summer rainfall than does the northern San Juan. If climatic shifts during the thirteenth century affected the amount or predictability of summer monsoonal precipitation in the northern Southwest, this may have made areas to the south of the northern San Juan drainage relatively more attractive for subsequent settlement.

The center of gravity of population in the Pueblo world also shifted south because of the collapse of the Chacoan system in the early twelfth century. The period of the "great abandonment"—the late thirteenth century—was not only one of contraction in the north, but of considerable expansion of the Puebloan world to the south. We need to focus on the latter as well as the former—they are both part of what may be the same large-scale geographic and cultural shift.

In searching for social or cultural evidence that might have a bearing on the San Juan abandonment, it is worth noting that among the characteristics of Mesa Verdean culture that did not survive the movement to the south were some that were probably involved with religious symbolism and practice. For example, the small San Juan household level kiva disappears after the late thirteenth century. The kivas of the Rio Grande, Mogollon Rim, and Western Pueblo areas–all of which grew in population during the late thirteenth and fourteenth centuries—are larger, much fewer in number, and evidently served larger groups (Lipe 1989). The front-oriented settlement plan (Reed 1956) that characterized the whole San Juan drainage for centuries, with its rigorous adherence to a north-south or northwest-southeast axis, also gave way to an inward-looking settlement plan focused on formal plaza spaces. It seems likely that the strong directional patterning in San Juan settlement planning and kiva architecture was an expression of religious symbolism. It also appears that some of the forms of thirteenth-century civic architecture in the Mesa Verde area disappeared, including free-standing towers and multistoried D-shaped buildings.

As Puebloan populations moved out of the Mesa Verde area to settle in or near existing communities farther south, they would undoubtedly have accepted new cultural forms in order to promote their social acceptance and integration. But perhaps these communities had religious ideologies and practices that were part of the attraction for the immigrants from the north. Adaptive failures or social stresses experienced in the Mesa Verde area may have weakened the power of existing religious practice there. Furthermore, it is unlikely that ideologies, symbols, and rituals encountered in the Rio Grande or other areas were totally unrelated to those already practiced in the northern San Juan. The forms being practiced by existing Pueblo communities farther south may have been seen by the Mesa Verde people as providing an opportunity for spiritual revitalization. The part of the Pueblo Southwest that continued to be occupied after the late thirteenth century experienced remarkable cultural dynamism during the fourteenth century. Developments reflecting that dynamism include the widespread establishment of the katsina cult (Adams 1991), the emergence of the Salado phenomenon (Crown 1994), and the appearance of extensive trade networks (Upham 1982; Graves, Longacre, and Holbrook 1982). These developments appear to have happened a few decades too late to have themselves been instrumental in attracting immigrants from the north. In fact, they are often considered to be responses to the problems of integrating new populations (Eggan 1950; Adams 1989, 1991). Continued work on the roots of these developments, however, should consider whether their initial stages might have occurred early enough to have contributed in some way to attracting migrants from the Four Corners area.

Summary

In this chapter we have presented our perspectives on Pueblo III settlement patterns in the northern Mesa Verde Region. As reflected in our discussion, two phenomena have long dominated Pueblo III Mesa Verde region research, namely the aggregation of population into large sites and the abandonment of the region. A more complete understanding of these phenomena require an appreciation of settlement dynamics before and during the focal centuries of this volume.

We have developed two themes in particular. First, we argue that to best understand Pueblo III settlement, we must understand the early settlement "roots"

of this tradition. Along these lines, it is clear that population aggregation was not a one-shot experiment in the Mesa Verde region. Village aggregation occurred on a large scale during the ninth century, and models proposed to explain this early period of aggregation are complementary to and in contrast with our in situ model of community aggregation.

Second, we argue that community structure provided an important form of social organization and local integration prior to and during the A.D. 1100 to 1300 period. A critical organizational function performed by communities was to regulate access to resources. Especially important was access to arable land. Pueblo II dispersed communities were characterized by small habitation sites located on what are today the most productive arable soils. The development of land tenure systems in these dispersed communities was achieved in part by people living on or nearby the land they farmed. These dispersed communities appear to have been well established by the early eleventh century. During the late eleventh century, great house public architecture appeared and functioned as some type of integrative center for these communities.

Small Pueblo II habitation sites were probably occupied by one or two households, and these residential units formed the building blocks for the larger community. Larger, multiple-household habitation sites became increasingly common through time. In addition, these multiple-household habitations were grouped into increasingly larger clusters. By the beginning of the Pueblo III period it is the clusters that dot the dispersed community landscape. Multiple-household clusters represent a type of middle range aggregation that, we believe, was important in organizing the economic activities of individual households. We also believe that such clusters, when present in dispersed communities, were analogous to the discrete room block groups that comprised the larger, aggregated sites so common during the Pueblo III period.

The multiple-household clusters represent middle-range organizational units as well as middle-range aggregation.

In contrast to Lekson's (1990) arguments concerning the ephemeral occupational histories of most prehistoric Puebloan communities, this analysis posits that "deep sedentism" started early at the community level (though not at the level of individual sites) in the central Mesa Verde Region, and that it was in large part a response to high population densities and relatively stable agricultural resources. Lekson's model of widespread community mobility is congruent with the model for Mesa Verde region Pueblo I aggregation proposed by Kohler and his colleagues (Kohler et al. 1986; Kohler and Matthews 1988; Kohler 1992). This type of community mobility may better fit Pueblo III settlement dynamics in areas outside of the central Mesa Verde region where population densities were lower and resources less abundant.

After A.D. 1200, settlement moved away from the mesa tops, and the direct association of habitation sites with the best agricultural soils no longer existed. This is true for both relatively small sites and the large aggregated sites. Securing a domestic water source appears to have been a central concern, as many of the large sites surround a spring at the head of a canyon. Abandoned mesa top habitations may have continued to be used as limited activity sites (e.g., field houses), but small sites were increasingly located toward the canyon rims, at the base of cliffs, on talus slopes, in alcoves, or on terraces inside the canyon in the mid-to-late thirteenth century.

Perhaps this shift in site location was a response to environmental or social conditions that eventually resulted in the abandonment of the Mesa Verde Region, but as yet we do not understand the connection between these events. It is clear that construction of new sites, both large and small, continued to take place decades after the shift in settlement pattern occurred. Construction appears to be common through the early A.D. 1270s, making the drop-off in construction in the late A.D. 1270s all the more dramatic.

The association of aggregation with overall population increase and the general pattern of the largest aggregates occurring in the most densely populated areas supports Adler's (1990) density-dependent model of village formation. Limitations on arable land is an important factor in this process even in light of arguments that agricultural carrying capacity would not have been reached in most areas (Van West, chapter 15). Though there is a great deal of arable land in the central Mesa Verde region, the critical variable was not simply how much arable land was available in particularly bad years, but whether community members had the social ties that bound them to the most productive lands.

Because relatively high population densities had been maintained for several generations, wild game and perhaps other nondomesticated resources were probably significantly depleted by the late thirteenth century, at least in the vicinity of the central areas. These nonagricultural resources might also have been as important a set of factors in limiting settlement than was arable land. The heavy reliance on turkeys displayed at late sites was probably a response to depletion of game (Munro 1994). Still, viewing wild resources as a limiting factor has its problems. The Mesa Verde region is on the edge of a vast nonagricultural area that could have been accessed by relatively short hunting and foraging trips. On the other hand, attempts by communities to preserve hinterlands as foraging areas closer to home may have helped maintain high population densities in central areas. If such hinterlands were adjacent or shared, there may have been inter-community competition or conflict for access to their increasingly scarce wild resources. Furthermore, if warfare became endemic for whatever reason, it would probably inhibit away-from-home foraging and especially, long-distance hunting.

Warfare alone might provide the compression of central territories required to promote density-dependent processes based on competition for arable soil.

Environmental degradation clearly put a stress on Mesa Verde region communities in the late thirteenth century, but it is difficult to explain the rapid, complete, and permanent abandonment that took place solely in terms of environmental change. Understanding changes in the organization of the Pueblo world outside of the Mesa Verde Region may have had an equally important role in explaining the disappearance of the Mesa Verde region occupants.

The "Pueblo Cultures in Transition" conference, where the seeds for this volume were planted, was energized by the attempt to better understand this larger context, wherein prehistoric Puebloan culture could be viewed as something more than regional manifestations of unique culture histories. We hope that this chapter makes a contribution to that greater understanding, and that these data and interpretations contribute to the developing picture of the social and environmental changes that, by the end of the Pueblo III period, transformed the Puebloan world.

Acknowledgments

The data base we assembled is largely the result of the efforts of our colleagues working in the Mesa Verde region. Many sites were located as the result of our colleagues pointing them out to us. Every time we approached a colleague for information, they provided assistance and encouragement. The spirit of cooperation that made this chapter possible reminded each of the authors how genuinely fun and rewarding archaeology can be.

The following people generously contributed information about sites in the area considered in this chapter: Larry Agenbroad, Jim Allison, Kristie Arrington, Victoria Atkins, Bill Davis, Mark Chenault, Dale Davidson, Doug Bowman, Dave Breternitz, Doug Dykeman, Jerry Fetterman, Steve Fuller, Larry Hammack, Alden Hayes, Linda Honeycutt, Winston Hurst, Peter Kakos, Jim Kendrick, Susan Kenzle, Todd Metzger, Jeannie Mobley-Tanaka, Neal Morris, Arthur Rohn, Charmaine Thompson, Debbie Westfall, Joe Ben Wheat, Richard Wilshusen, and Dean Wilson. Kristie Arrington was particularly helpful in locating sites and providing site forms for sites on BLM land. Arthur Rohn provided detailed information on sites near Yellow Jacket and Lowry Pueblos, and he commented on an earlier draft of this chapter. Mark Chenault and Susan Kenzle both generously shared site maps. Several anonymous reviewers also provided detailed and helpful comments on an earlier draft of the chapter. Finally, we would like to thank Neal Morris for drafting the figures in this chapter. We appreciate the help of each of these individuals, and recognize that many would disagree with some of our interpretations. To anyone we may have forgotten, our sincere apologies.

We also relied on scores of reports and site forms prepared by numerous archaeologists working in the region. We regret that we cannot recognize each of these colleagues individually; however, we gratefully acknowledge their collective efforts. Any success this project achieves is largely due to the skill and dedication they bring to the profession.

References Cited

Adams, E. Charles
  1975   *Causes of Prehistoric Settlement Systems in the Piedra District, Colorado.* Unpublished Ph.D. dissertation, Department of Anthropology, University of Colorado, Boulder.
  1989   Changing Form and Function in Western Pueblo Ceremonial Architecture from A.D. 1000 to A.D. 1500. In *The Architecture of Social Integration in Prehistoric Pueblos,* edited by William D. Lipe and Michelle Hegmon, pp. 155–60. Occasional Papers No. 1. Crow Canyon Archaeological Center, Cortez, Colorado.
  1991   *The Origin and Development of the*

Pueblo Katsina Cult. University of Arizona Press, Tucson.

Adler, Michael A.

1988   *Archaeological Survey and Testing in the Sand Canyon Pueblo/Goodman Point Ruin Locality, Montezuma County, Colorado, 1987 Field Season*. Crow Canyon Archaeological Center, Cortez, Colorado. Report submitted to the Bureau of Land Management, San Juan Resource Area Office, Durango, Colorado.

1990   *Communities of Soil and Stone: An Archaeological Investigation of Population Aggregation Among the Mesa Verde Region Anasazi, A.D. 900–1300*. Unpublished Ph.D. dissertation, Department of Anthropology, University of Michigan. University Microfilms, Ann Arbor.

1992   The Upland Survey. In *The Sand Canyon Archaeological Project: A Progress Report*, edited by William D. Lipe and Michelle Hegmon, pp. 11–23. Occasional Papers No. 1. Crow Canyon Archaeological Center, Cortez, Colorado.

1995   Fathoming the Scale of Mesa Verde Region Communities. In *Interpreting Southwestern Diversity: Underlying Principles and Overarching Patterns*, edited by Paul Fish and J. Jefferson Reid. Anthropological Papers. Arizona State University, Tempe, in press.

Adler, Michael A., and Mark D. Varien

1994   The Changing Face of the Community in the Mesa Verde Region A.D. 1000–1300. In *Proceedings of the Anasazi Symposium 1991*, compiled by Art Hutchinson and Jack E. Smith, Mesa Verde National Park Association, Mesa Verde, Colorado.

Ahlstrom, Richard V. N., David A. Breternitz, and Richard L. Warren

1985   New Tree-Ring Dates from Lowry Ruin. *The Kiva* 51(1):39–42.

Bender, Barbara

1990   The Dynamics of Nonhierarchical Societies. In *The Evolution of Political Systems: Sociopolitics in Small-Scale Sedentary Societies*, edited by Steadman Upham, pp. 247–63. Cambridge University Press, Cambridge.

Blinman, Eric

1994   Adjusting the Pueblo I Chronology: Implications for Culture Change at Dolores and in the Mesa Verde Region at Large, In *Proceedings of the Anasazi Symposium 1991*, compiled by A. Hutchinson and Jack E. Smith, Mesa Verde National Park, Mesa Verde, Colorado.

Bloomer, William

1989   *Moon House: A Pueblo III Period Cliff Dwelling Complex in Southeastern Utah*. Unpublished Master's thesis, Department of Anthropology, Washington State University, Pullman.

Bradley, Bruce A.

1974   Preliminary Report on Excavations at Wallace Ruin. *Southwestern Lore* 40(3 & 4):63–71.

1986   *Annual Report of Test Excavations at Sand Canyon Pueblo (5MT765)*. Crow Canyon Archaeological Center, Cortez, Colorado. Report submitted to the Bureau of Land Management, San Juan Resource Area Office, Durango, Colorado.

1987   *Annual Report of Test Excavations at Sand Canyon Pueblo (5MT765)*. Crow Canyon Archaeological Center, Cortez, Colorado. Report submitted to the Bureau of Land Management, San Juan Resource Area Office, Durango, Colorado.

1988a   *Annual Report on the Excavations at Sand Canyon Pueblo, 1987 Field Season*. Crow Canyon Archaeological Center, Cortez, Colorado. Report submitted to the Bureau of Land Management, San Juan Resource Area Office, Durango, Colorado.

1988b   Wallace Ruin Interim Report. *Southwestern Lore* 54(2):8–33.

1990   *Annual Report of the 1989 Excavations at Sand Canyon Pueblo (5MT765)*. Crow Canyon Archaeological Center, Cortez, Colorado. Report submitted to the Bureau of Land Management, San Juan Resource Area Office, Durango, Colorado.

1992   Excavations at Sand Canyon Pueblo. In *The Sand Canyon Project: A Progress Report*, edited by William D. Lipe, pp. 79–97. Occasional Papers No. 2. Crow Canyon Archaeological Center, Cortez, Colorado.

1993   Planning, Growth, and Functional Differentiation at a Prehistoric Pueblo: A Case Study for SW Colorado. *Journal of Field Archaeology* 20: 23–42.

Brew, J. O.

1946   *Archaeology of Alkali Ridge, Southeastern Utah*. Papers of the Peabody Museum of American Archaeology and Ethnology, Vol. 21. Harvard University, Cambridge.

Brisbin, Joel M., and Charlotte J. Brisbin

1977   Excavations at the Ida Jean Site. Ms. on file, Crow Canyon Archaeological Center, Cortez, Colorado.

Brumfiel, Elizabeth M.

1992   Distinguished Lecture in Archeology: Breaking and Entering the Ecosystem—Gender, Class, and Faction Steal the Show. *American Anthropologist* 94:551–67.

Cattanach, George S., Jr.

1980   *Long House, Mesa Verde National Park, Colorado*. Publications in Archeology No. 7H. USDI, National Park Service, Washington, D.C.

Chandler, Susan M., Alan D. Reed, and Paul R. Nickens

1980   *Ecological Variability and Archaeological Site Location in Southwestern Colorado: The Class III Cultural Resource Inventory of the Bureau of Land Management's Sacred Mountain Planning Unit*. USDI, Bureau of Land Management, Montrose District, Montrose, Colorado.

Crown, Patricia L.

1994   *Ceramics and Ideology: Salado Polychrome Pottery*. University of New Mexico Press, Albuquerque.

Davis, William A.

1985   *Anasazi Subsistence and Settlement on White Mesa, San Juan County, Utah*. University Press of America, Lanham, Maryland.

Dean, Jeffrey S.

1993   Paleoenvironmental Variability in the American Southwest During the Last 2000 Years. Paper presented at the 58th Annual Meeting of the Society for American Archaeology, St. Louis.

Dean, Jeffrey S., Robert C. Euler, George J. Gumerman, Fred Plog, Richard H. Hevly, and Thor N. V. Karlstrom

1985   Human Behavior, Demography, and Paleoenvironment on the Colorado Plateaus. *American Antiquity* 50: 537–54.

Driver, Jonathan C.

1993   Social Complexity and Hunting Systems in Southwestern Colorado. Paper presented at the 1993 Chacmool Conference, Calgary, Alberta.

Eddy, Frank W.

1977   *Archaeological Investigations at Chimney Rock Mesa, 1970–72*. Memoirs

No. 1. Colorado Archaeological Society, Boulder.

Eddy, Frank W., Allen E. Kane, and Paul R. Nickens

1984 *Southwest Colorado Prehistoric Context: Archaeological Background and Research Directions*. Office of Archaeology and Historic Preservation, Colorado Historical Society, Denver.

Eggan, Fred

1950 *Social Organization of the Western Pueblos*. University of Chicago Press, Chicago.

Euler, Robert C., George J. Gumerman, Thor N. V. Karlstrom, Jeffrey S. Dean, and Richard H. Hevly

1979 The Colorado Plateaus: Cultural Dynamics and Paleoenvironment. *Science* 205:1089–1101.

Farmer, T. Reid

1977 *Salvage Excavations in Mancos Canyon, Colorado, 1975*. Unpublished Master's thesis. University of Colorado, Boulder.

Fetterman, Jerry, and Linda Honeycutt

1987 *The Mockingbird Mesa Survey, Southwestern Colorado*. Cultural Resource Series no. 22. USDI, Bureau of Land Management, Denver.

Fewkes, Jesse W.

1919 *Prehistoric Villages, Castles, and Towers of Southwestern Colorado*. Bureau of American Ethnology Bulletin No. 70. Smithsonian Institution, Washington, D.C.

Flannery, Kent V., and Joyce Marcus

1976 Evolution of the Public Building in Formative Oaxaca. In *Cultural Change and Continuity: Essays in Honor of James Bennett Griffin*, edited by Charles E. Cleland, pp. 205–21. Academic Press, New York.

Forge, Anthony

1972 Normative Factors in the Settlement Size of Neolithic Cultivators (New Guinea). In *Man, Settlement, and Urbanism*, edited by Ruth Tringham, George W. Dimbley and Peter J. Ucko, 363–76. Duckworth, London.

Fowler, Andrew P., John R. Stein, and Roger Anyon

1987 *An Archaeological Reconnaissance of West-Central New Mexico: The Anasazi Monuments Project*. Report submitted to the State of New Mexico Office of Cultural Affairs, Historic Preservation Division, Santa Fe.

Fowler, Andrew P., and John R. Stein

1990 The Anasazi Great House in Time and Space. Paper presented at the 55th Annual Meeting of the Society for American Archaeology, Las Vegas.

Fuller, Steven L.

1987 *Cultural Resource Inventories for the Dolores Project: Dove Creek Canal Distribution System and Dawson Draw Reservoir*. Four Corners Archaeological Project Report No. 7. Complete Archaeological Service Associates, Cortez, Colorado.

1988a *Archaeological Investigations in the Bodo Canyon Area, La Plata County Colorado*. UMTRA Archaeological Report No. 25. U.S. Department of Energy, Washington, D.C.

1988b *Cultural Resource Inventories for the Animas-La Plata: The Wheeler and Koshak Borrow Sources*. Four Corners Archaeological Project Report No. 12. Complete Archaeological Service Associates, Cortez, Colorado.

1988c *Cultural Resource Inventories for the Dolores Project: The Ute Irrigated Lands Survey*. Four Corners Archaeological Project Report No. 13. Complete Archaeological Service Associates, Cortez, Colorado.

Gillespie, William B.

1976 *Culture Change at the Ute Canyon Site: A Study of the Pithouse-Kiva Transition in the Mesa Verde Region*. Unpublished Master's thesis, Department of Anthropology, University of Colorado, Boulder.

Graves, Michael W., William A. Longacre, and Sally J. Holbrook

1982 Aggregation and Abandonment at Grasshopper Pueblo. *Journal of Field Archaeology* 9:193–206.

Guthe, Alfred K.

1949 A Preliminary Report on Excavations in Southwestern Colorado. *American Antiquity*, 15 (2):144–54.

Hack, John T.

1942 *The Changing Physical Environment of the Hopi Indians of Arizona*. Papers of the Peabody Museum of American Archaeology and Ethnology, Vol. 35, No. 1. Harvard University, Cambridge.

Hallasi, Judith A.

1979 Archaeological Investigation at the Escalante Site, Dolores, Colorado, 1975–76. In *The Archeology and Stabilization of the Dominguez and Escalante Ruins*, by Alan D. Reed, Judith A. Halasi, Adrian S. White, and David A. Breternitz, pp. 197–

425. Cultural Resource Series No. 7. Bureau of Land Management, Colorado State Office, Denver.

Hayes, Alden C.

1964 *The Archaeological Survey of Wetherill Mesa, Mesa Verde National Park, Colorado*. Archaeological Research Series No. 7-A. USDI, National Park Service, Washington, D.C.

Hayes, Alden C., and James A. Lancaster

1975 *Badger House Community, Mesa Verde National Park*. Publications in Archaeology No. 7E. USDI, National Park Service, Washington, D.C.

Huber, Edgar K.

1993 *Thirteenth Century Pueblo Aggregation and Organizational Change in Southwestern Colorado*. Unpublished Ph.D. dissertation, Department of Anthropology, Washington State University, Pullman.

Kane, Allen E.

1986a Prehistory of the Dolores River Valley. In *Dolores Archaeological Program: Final Synthetic Report*, compiled by David A. Breternitz, Christine K. Robinson, and G. Timothy Gross, pp. 353–435. USDI, Bureau of Reclamation, Engineering and Research Center, Denver.

1986b Social Organization and Cultural Process in Dolores Anasazi Communities, A.D. 600–900. *In Dolores Archaeological Program: Final Synthetic Report*, compiled by David A. Breternitz, C. K. Robinson and G. Timothy Gross, pp. 633–61. USDI, Bureau of Reclamation, Engineering and Research Center, Denver.

1988 McPhee Community Cluster Introduction. In *Dolores Archaeological Program: Anasazi Communities at Dolores: McPhee Village*, compiled by Allen E. Kane and C. K. Robinson, pp. 2–59. USDI, Bureau of Reclamation, Engineering and Research Center, Denver.

1989 Did the Sheep Look Up? Sociopolitical Complexity in 9th Century Dolores Society. In *The Sociopolitical Structure of Prehistoric Southwestern Societies*, edited by Steadman Upham, Kent G. Lightfoot, and Roberta A. Jewett, pp. 307–61. Westview Press, Boulder.

Kelley, Jeffrey, William D. Lipe, and Mark D. Varien

1994 Thirteenth Century Canyon-Rim Architectural Complexes in the

Mesa Verde Region. Poster Session, 59th Annual Meeting of the Society for American Archaeology, Anaheim.

Kent, Susan
1991   Excavations at a Small Mesa Verde Pueblo II Anasazi Site in Southwestern Colorado. *Kiva* 57(1): 55–75.

Kenzle, Susan
1993   *Prehistoric Architecture: A Study of Enclosing Walls in the Northern Southwest.* Unpublished Master's Thesis, Department of Anthropology, University of Calgary, Alberta.

Kintigh, Keith W.
1994   Chaco, Communal Architecture, and Cibolan Aggregation. In *The Ancient Southwestern Community: Models and Methods for the Study of Prehistoric Social Organization*, edited by Wirt H. Wills and Robert D. Leonard, pp. 131–40. University of New Mexico Press, Albuquerque.

Kleidon, James H. and Bruce A. Bradley
1989   *Annual Report of the 1988 Excavations at Sand Canyon Pueblo (5MT765).* Crow Canyon Archaeological Center, Cortez, Colorado. Report submitted to the USDI, Bureau of Land Management, San Juan Resource Area Office, Durango, Colorado.

Kohler, Timothy A.
1992   Field Houses, Villages, and the Tragedy of the Commons in the Early Northern Anasazi Southwest. *American Antiquity* 57:617–35.

Kohler, Timothy A., and Meredith H. Matthews
1988   Long-Term Anasazi Land Use and Forest Reduction: A Case Study from Southwest Colorado. *American Antiquity* 53:537–64.

Kohler, Timothy A., Janet D. Orcutt, Eric Blinman, and Kenneth L. Petersen
1986   Anasazi Spreadsheets: The Cost of Doing Agricultural Business in Prehistoric Dolores. In *Dolores Archaeological Program: Final Synthetic Report*, compiled by David A. Breternitz, C. K. Robinson, and G. Timothy Gross, 525–38. USDI, Bureau of Reclamation, Engineering and Research Center, Denver.

Kohler, Timothy A., and Carla Van West
1996   The Calculus of Self Interest in the Development of Cooperation: Sociopolitical Development and Risk Among the Northern Anasazi. In *Evolving Complexity and Environmental Risk in the Prehistoric Southwest*, edited by Joseph A. Tainter and Bonnie Bagley Tainter. Proceedings of Santa Fe Institute Studies in the Science of Complexity. Addison-Wesley, Reading, Massachusetts, in press.

Kosse, Krisztina
1990   Group Size and Societal Complexity: Thresholds in the Long-Term Memory. *Journal of Anthropological Archaeology* 9:275–303.
1995   Settlement Size and Complexity. In *Interpreting Southwestern Diversity: Underlying Principles and Overarching Patterns*, edited by Paul Fish and J. Jefferson Reid. Arizona State University Anthropological Papers. In press.

Kuckelman, Kristin A.
1986   *Cultural Resource Inventory for the Towaoc Canal Project: Highline Ditch, Lower Hermana Lateral, Rocky Ford Laterals, and Portions of the Upper Hermana and Lone Pine Laterals.* Four Corners Archaeological Project, Report No. 8. Complete Archaeological Service Associates, Cortez, Colorado.

Kuckelman, Kristin A., and James N. Morris
1988   *Archaeological Investigations on South Canal.* Four Corners Archaeological Project Report No. 11. Complete Archaeological Service Associates, Cortez, Colorado.

Lange, Fred, Nancy Mahaney, Joe Ben Wheat, and Mark L. Chenault
1986   *Yellow Jacket: A Four Corners Anasazi Ceremonial Center.* Johnson Books, Boulder.

Lekson, Stephen H.
1985   Largest Settlement Size and the Interpretation of Socio-Political Complexity at Chaco Canyon. *Haliksa'i* 4:68–75.
1988   The Idea of The Kiva in Anasazi Archaeology. *The Kiva* 53:213–53.
1990   Sedentism and Aggregation in Anasazi Archaeology. In *Perspectives on Southwestern Prehistory*, edited by Paul E. Minnis and Charles L. Redman, pp. 333–40. Westview Press, Boulder, Colorado.

Lightfoot, Ricky R. and Mary C. Etzkorn
1993   *Descriptive Archaeology.* The Duckfoot Site, Vol. 1. Occasional Papers, No. 3. Crow Canyon Archaeological Center, Cortez, Colorado.

Lightfoot, Ricky R., and Kristin A. Kuckelman
1994   Warfare and the Pueblo Abandonment of the Mesa Verde Region. Paper presented at the 59th Annual Meeting of the Society for American Archaeology, Anaheim, California.

Lipe, William D.
1966   *Anasazi Culture and Its Relationship to the Environment in the Red Rock Plateau Region, Southeastern Utah.* Ph.D. dissertation, Department of Anthropology, Yale University, New Haven. University Microfilms, Ann Arbor.
1970   Anasazi Communities in the Red Rock Plateau, Southeastern Utah. In *Reconstructing Prehistoric Pueblo Societies*, edited by William A. Longacre, pp. 84–139. University of New Mexico Press, Albuquerque.
1978   The Southwest. In *Ancient Native Americans*, edited by Jesse D. Jennings, pp. 327–41. San Francisco: W. H. Freeman.
1981   Mobile Pots or Potters: Kayenta Ceramics in Southeastern Utah. Paper presented at the Symposium on Kayenta Archaeology, 46th Annual Meeting of the Society for American Archaeology, San Diego.
1983   The Southwest. In *Ancient Native Americans*, edited by Jesse D. Jennings, 421–93. W. H. Freeman, San Francisco.
1986   Modeling Dolores Area Cultural Dynamics. In *Dolores Archaeological Program: Final Synthetic Report*, compiled by David A. Breternitz, C. K. Robinson, and G. Timothy Gross, pp. 439–67. USDI, Bureau of Reclamation, Engineering and Research Center, Denver.
1989   Social Scale of Mesa Verde Anasazi Kivas. In *The Architecture of Social Integration in Prehistoric Pueblos*, edited by William D. Lipe and Michelle Hegmon, pp. 53–71. Occasional Papers No. 1. Crow Canyon Archaeological Center, Cortez, Colorado.
1992   Summary and Concluding Comments. In *The Sand Canyon Archaeological Project: A Progress Report*, edited by William D. Lipe, pp. 121–33. Occasional Papers No. 2. Crow Canyon Archaeological Center, Cortez, Colorado.
1994   The Depopulation of the Northern San Juan: Conditions in the Turbulent 1200s. Paper presented at the 4th Southwest Symposium, Arizona State University, Tempe, Arizona.

Lipe, William D., Timothy A. Kohler, Mark D. Varien, James N. Morris, and Ricky R. Lightfoot
1988   Synthesis. In *Dolores Archaeological Program: Anasazi Communities at Dolores: Grass Mesa Village*, compiled by William D. Lipe, James N. Morris, and Timothy A. Kohler, pp. 1213–1276. Denver, Colorado: Bureau of Reclamation, Engineering and Research Center.

Lipe, William D., and Michelle Hegmon
1989   Historical and Analytical Perspectives on Architecture and Social Integration in the Prehistoric Pueblos. In *The Architecture of Social Integration in Prehistoric Pueblos*, edited by William D. Lipe and Michelle Hegmon, pp. 15–34. Occasional Papers No. 1. Crow Canyon Archaeological Center, Cortez, Colorado.

Lipe, William D., and C. Frank Huntington
1969   Centrographic Indices: Some Methods for Analyzing Complex Areal Distributions in Archaeology. *The Kiva* 35(1):29–54.

Lipe, William D., and Alexander J. Lindsay, Jr.
1983   Pueblo Adaptations in the Glen Canyon Area. Paper presented at the 1983 Anasazi Symposium, Farmington, New Mexico.

Lipe, William D., Floyd Sharrock, David Dibble, and Keith Anderson
1960   *1959 Excavations, Glen Canyon Area.* Anthropological Papers No. 49. University of Utah Press, Salt Lake City.

Lister, Florence C.
1964   *Kaiparowits Plateau and Glen Canyon Prehistory: An Interpretation Based on Ceramics.* Anthropological Papers No. 71. University of Utah Press, Salt Lake City.

Lister, Robert H.
1959   *The Coombs Site.* Anthropological Papers No. 41(1). University of Utah Press, Salt Lake City.

Lister, Robert H., J. Richard Ambler, and Florence C. Lister
1960   *The Coombs Site*, Part II. Anthropological Papers No. 41(2). University of Utah Press, Salt Lake City.

Lister, Robert H., and Florence C. Lister
1961   *The Coombs Site*, Part III, *Summary and Conclusions.* Anthropological Papers No. 41(3). University of Utah Press, Salt Lake City.

Marshall, Michael P., John R. Stein, Richard W. Loose, and Judith E. Novotny
1979   *Anasazi Communities of the San Juan Basin.* Public Service Company of New Mexico and Historic Preservation Bureau, Planning Division, Department of Finance and Administration of the State of New Mexico, Santa Fe.

Marshall, Michael P., David E. Doyel, and Cory D. Breternitz
1982   A Regional Perspective on the Late Bonito Phase. In *Bis Sa'ani: A Late Bonito Phase Community on Escavada Wash, Northwest New Mexico*, edited by Cory D. Breternitz, David E. Doyel, and Michael P. Marshall, pp. 1127-1240. Papers in Anthropology No. 14. Navajo Nation, Window Rock, Arizona.

Martin, Paul S.
1936   *Lowry Ruin in Southwestern Colorado.* Report No. 23(1). Field Museum of Natural History, Chicago.

Matson, R. G., William D. Lipe, and William R. Haase, IV
1988   Adaptational Continuities and Occupational Discontinuities: The Cedar Mesa Anasazi. *Journal of Field Archaeology* 15:245–64.

McKenna, Peter J. and H. Wolcott Toll
1992   Regional Patterns of Great House Development among the Totah Anasazi, New Mexico. In *Anasazi Regional Organization and the Chaco System*, edited by David E. Doyel, pp. 133–46. Maxwell Museum of Anthropology, University of New Mexico, Albuquerque.

Mobley-Tanaka, Jeannette L.
1990   *Prehistoric Community and Community Interaction at Chimney Rock, Colorado.* Unpublished Master's thesis, Department of Anthropology, University of Colorado, Boulder.

Munro, Natalie D.
1994   *Implications of Intensification: An Investigation Into Turkey Production in Southwest Colorado.* Unpublished Master's Thesis, Department of Anthropology, Simon Fraser University, Burnaby, British Columbia.

Neily, Robert B.
1983   *The Prehistoric Community on the Colorado Plateau: An Approach to the Study of Change and Survival in the Northern San Juan Area of the American Southwest.* Ph.D. dissertation, Southern Illinois University, Carbondale. University Microfilms, Ann Arbor.

Netting, Robert McC.
1990   Population, Permanent Agricul-
ture and Politics: Unpacking the Evolutionary Portmanteau. In *The Evolution of Political Systems*, edited by, Steadman Upham, pp. 21–61. Cambridge University Press, Cambridge, England.

Orcutt, Janet D., Eric Blinman, and Timothy A. Kohler
1990   Explanations of Population Aggregation in the Mesa Verde Region Prior to A.D. 900. In *Perspectives on Southwestern Prehistory*, edited by Paul E. Minnis and Charles L. Redman, pp. 196–212. Westview Press, Boulder.

Petersen, Kenneth L.
1986a   Climatic Reconstruction for the Dolores Project. In *Dolores Archaeological Program: Final Synthetic Report*, compiled by David A. Breternitz, C. K. Robinson, and G. Timothy Gross, pp. 311–25. USDI, Bureau of Reclamation, Engineering and Research Center, Denver.

1986b   Resource Studies, In *Dolores Archaeological Program: Final Synthetic Report*, compiled David A. Breternitz, C. K. Robinson, and G. Timothy Gross, pp. 469–91. USDI, Bureau of Reclamation, Engineering and Research Center, Denver.

1987a   Reconstruction of Droughts for the Dolores Project Area. In *Dolores Archaeological Program Supporting Studies: Settlement and Environment*, compiled by Kenneth L. Petersen and Janet D. Orcutt, pp. 89–102. USDI, Bureau of Reclamation, Engineering and Research Center, Denver.

1987b   Summer Warmth: A Critical Factor for the Dolores Anasazi. In *Dolores Archaeological Program Supporting Studies: Settlement and Environment*, compiled by Kenneth L. Petersen and Janet D. Orcutt, 61–71. USDI, Bureau of Reclamation, Engineering and Research Center, Denver.

1988   *Climate and the Dolores River Anasazi: A Paleoenvironmental Reconstruction from a 10,000-Year Pollen Record, La Plata Mountains, Southwestern Colorado.* Anthropological Papers No. 113. University of Utah Press, Salt Lake City.

Powers, Robert P., William B. Gillespie, and Stephen H. Lekson
1983   *The Outlier Survey: A Regional View of Settlement in the San Juan Basin.* Reports of the Chaco Center

No. 3. USDI, National Park Service, Albuquerque.

Prudden, T. Mitchell
1903   The Prehistoric Ruins of the San Juan Watershed in Utah, Arizona, Colorado, and New Mexico. *American Anthropologist* 5:224–88.

Reed, Erik K.
1956   Types of Village Plan Layouts in the Southwest. In *Prehistoric Settlement Patterns in the New World*, edited by Gordon R. Willey, pp. 11–17. Viking Fund Publications in Anthropology No. 23. Wenner-Gren Foundation for Anthropological Research, New York.

Robinson, Christine K., G. Timothy Gross, and David A. Breternitz
1986   Overview of the Dolores Archaeological Program. In *Dolores Archaeological Program: Final Synthetic Report*, compiled by David A. Breternitz, Christine K. Robinson, and G. Timothy Gross, pp. 3–50. USDI, Bureau of Reclamation, Engineering and Research Center, Denver, Colorado.

Robinson, William J., and Catherine M. Cameron
1991   *A Directory of Tree-Ring Dated Prehistoric Sites in the American Southwest*. Laboratory of Tree-Ring Research, University of Arizona, Tucson.

Rohn, Arthur H.
1963   Prehistoric Soil and Water Conservation on Chapin Mesa, Southwestern Colorado. *American Antiquity* 28(4): 441–55.
1971   *Mug House, Mesa Verde National Park, Colorado*. Archaeological Research Series No. 7-D. USDI, National Park Service, Washington, D.C.
1977   *Cultural Change and Continuity on Chapin Mesa*. Regents Press of Kansas, Lawrence.
1983   Budding Urban Settlements in the Northern San Juan. In *Proceedings of the Anasazi Symposium, 1981*, edited by Jack E. Smith, pp. 75–80. Mesa Verde Museum Association, Mesa Verde National Park.
1984   Lowry Settlement District. National Register of Historic Places Inventory Nomination Form. Document on file, USDI, Bureau of Land Management, San Juan Area Resource Office, Durango, Colorado.
1989   Northern San Juan Prehistory. In *Dynamics of Southwest Prehistory*, edited by Linda S. Cordell and

George J. Gumerman, pp. 149–77. Smithsonian Institution Press, Washington, D.C.

Schlanger, Sarah H.
1985   *Prehistoric Population Dynamics in the Dolores Area, Southwestern Colorado*. Ph.D. dissertation, Department of Anthropology, Washington State University, Pullman. University Microfilms, Ann Arbor.
1988   Patterns of Population Movement and Long-Term Population Growth in Southwestern Colorado. *American Antiquity* 53:773–93.

Schlanger, Sarah H., William D. Lipe, and William Robinson
1993   An Atlas of Occupation and Abandonment Across the Northern Southwest. Poster Session, 58th Annual Meeting of the Society for American Archaeology, St. Louis.

Schlanger, Sarah H., and Richard H. Wilshusen
1993   Local Abandonments and Regional Conditions in the North American Southwest. In *Abandonment of Settlements and Regions: Ethnoarchaeological and Archaeological Approaches*, edited by Catherine M. Cameron, and Steve A. Tomka, pp. 85–98. Cambridge University Press, Cambridge, England.

Sebastian, Lynne
1988   *Leadership, Power, and Productive Potential: A Political Model of the Chaco System*. Unpublished Ph.D. dissertation, Department of Anthropology, University of New Mexico, Albuquerque.

Stein, John R., and Peter J. McKenna
1988   *An Archaeological Reconnaissance of a Late Bonito Phase Occupation Near Aztec Ruins National Monument, New Mexico*. USDI, National Park Service, Southwest Cultural Resources Center, Santa Fe.

Thompson, Ian M.
1993   *The Towers of Hovenweep*. Mesa Verde Museum Association, Mesa Verde National Park.

Thompson, Ian M., Mark D. Varien, Susan Kenzle, and Rina Swentzell
1991   Prehistoric Architecture With Unknown Function. In *Anasazi Architecture and American Design*, edited by B. H. Morrow and V. B. Price. University of New Mexico Press, Albuquerque, in press.

Upham, Steadman
1982   *Polities and Power: An Economic

and Political History of the Western Pueblo*. New York, Academic Press.

Van West, Carla R.
1994   *Modeling Prehistoric Climatic Variability and Agricultural Production in Southwestern Colorado: A G.I.S. Approach*. Reports of Investigations No. 67. Crow Canyon Archaeological Center, Cortez, Colorado.

Van West, Carla R., Michael A. Adler, and Edgar K. Huber
1987   *Archaeological Survey and Testing in the Vicinity of Sand Canyon Pueblo, Montezuma County, Colorado, 1986 Field Season*. Crow Canyon Archaeological Center, Cortez, Colorado. Report submitted to USDI, Bureau of Land Management, San Juan Resource Area Office, Durango, Colorado.

Varien, Mark D.
1990   Measuring Site Uselife: Accumulation Rate Studies. Paper presented at the 55th Annual Meeting of the Society for American Archaeology, Las Vegas.

Varien, Mark D., Kristin A. Kuckelman, and J. H. Kleidon
1992   The Site Testing Program. In *The Sand Canyon Archaeological Project: A Progress Report*, edited by William D. Lipe, 45–67. Occasional Papers No. 2. Crow Canyon Archaeological Center, Cortez, Colorado.

Vivian, R. Gwinn
1990   *The Chacoan Prehistory of the San Juan Basin*. Academic Press, New York.

Wills, Wirt H., and Robert D. Leonard (editors)
1994   *The Ancient Southwestern Community: Models and Methods for the Study of Prehistoric Social Organization*. University of New Mexico Press, Albuquerque.

Wilshusen, Richard H.
1986   The Relationship Between Abandonment Mode and Ritual Use in Pueblo I Anasazi Protokivas. *Journal of Field Archaeology* 13:245–54.
1989   Unstuffing the Estufa: Ritual Floor Features in Anasazi Pit Structures and Pueblo Kivas. In *The Architecture of Social Integration in Prehistoric Pueblos*, edited by William D. Lipe and Michelle Hegmon, pp. 89–111. Occasional Papers No. 1. Crow Canyon Archaeological Center, Cortez, Colorado.

1991   *Early Villages in the American Southwest: Cross Cultural and Archaeological Perspectives.* Unpublished Ph.D. Dissertation, Department of Anthropology, University of Colorado, Boulder.

Wilshusen, Richard H. and Eric Blinman

1992   Pueblo 1 Village Formation: A Re-evaluation of Sites Recorded by Earl Morris on Ute Mountain Ute Tribal Lands. *Kiva* 57:251–69.

Wilshusen, Richard H., and Sarah H. Schlanger

1993   Late Pueblo 1 Population Movement in the Northern Southwest: The Big Picture. Paper presented at the Fifth Anasazi Symposium, Farmington, New Mexico.

Winter, Joseph C.

1975   *Hovenweep 1974.* Archaeological Report, No. 1. San Jose State University, California.

1976   *Hovenweep 1975.* Archaeological Report, No. 2. San Jose State University, California.

1977   *Hovenweep 1976.* Archaeological Report, No. 3. San Jose State University, California.

1984   The Towers at Hovenweep: Theories of Use and a History of Tower Research. In *Insights Into the Ancient Ones*, edited by Joanne H. Berger and Edward F. Berger, pp. 73–80. Cortez Printers, Cortez, Colorado.

Chapter 8

Looking Beyond Chaco in the San Juan Basin and Its Peripheries

John R. Stein and Andrew P. Fowler

The archaeological remains of the San Juan Basin are often cited as some of the most intriguing remnants of indigenous American architecture. For approximately four centuries, concluding abruptly at the close of the thirteenth century, the San Juan Basin was center stage for a cycle of monumental construction. Although the specific geographic focus of these architectural developments was the seemingly unaccommodating environs of Chaco Canyon, the overall scale of the endeavor encompassed much of, and perhaps even defined, the region we know as the old Anasazi world.

But this volume is not about Chaco. The temporal period selected for investigation specifically excludes the major developments at Chaco. For the purposes of this chapter, however, we must include a discussion of Chaco.

Of the ghosts that haunt the monuments of Chaco Canyon, it is the legacy of our intellectual forefathers that we find most vexing. In 1927, after little more than a decade of intensive work in southwestern ruins, a group of southwestern archaeologists gathered at the ruins of Pecos Pueblo and formalized a classification of "culture stages" (Kidder 1927). The Pecos Classification was and is a unilineal evolutionary construct describing "stages of culture" (or "culture time") independent of real time.

In the Pecos Classification scheme, Pueblo Bonito (Kidder 1924, 1927) is compared with ruins such as Keet Siel and Cliff Palace as archetypes of the Great Pueblo or Great Period (Pueblo III) culture stage. Pueblo Bonito and Cliff Palace are described as the highest achievements of the period and are identified with a "Chaco Culture" and a "Mesa Verde Culture," respectively.

In 1929, Douglas placed Pueblo Bonito and Cliff Palace into real time, demonstrating that Pueblo Bonito was more ancient than Cliff Palace by a matter of centuries. This discovery created a paradox whereby Pueblo Bonito, as the preeminent building of the Great Pueblo Period (Pueblo III), was found to be contemporary with the small sites of an earlier stage of culture (Pueblo II). In the course of scientific inquiry, contradictions between theory and fact normally result in a critical reexamination of theory. By 1929, however, the Pecos Classification was already an entrenched and institutionalized dogma of Anasazi archaeology. Rather than question the validity of the Pecos Classification, archaeologists instead sought to explain the early Pueblo III occupation at Chaco as an anomaly. The assumptions of the Pecos Classification continue to determine the content and direction of our research.

Since the time that Douglas blew a big hole in the Pecos Classification, Anasazi archaeology has been focused on the task of patching it. Accordingly, the term "Chaco Phenomenon" has been used to describe the accelerated progression of a single "advanced" component of the Anasazi cultural milieu through the developmental stages of "culture," an idea that promotes the rise and fall of a "Chaco Culture" and conveniently ameliorates problems with real time and culture time. But does it make sense? We think not.

There is another explanation for the monumental structures of Chaco Canyon, one that is faithful to the forces that predictably shape the built environments of traditional societies. In our explanation of developments in Chaco Canyon, the great houses are but elements of a larger planned architectural composition which functioned in the ritual, not the residential, realm. We suggest that Pueblo Bonito was not a pueblo, that Chaco Canyon was never a proto-urban center of culture and commerce, and that the canyon population, the so-called Chacoans, resided in smallish but otherwise normal communities spaced along the length of the canyon. There is no argument that the monumental architecture of Chaco Canyon is magnitudes larger than a contemporary Anasazi dwelling; however, the "mystery" of Chaco is a reference to our discomfort with the empirical reality of the scale and timing of the Chaco monuments, contrasted with our expectations based on the Pecos Classification. We caution that the idea of a "Chaco Phenomenon" is an artifact of the Pecos Classification.

Problems with Pueblo Bonito and the Pueblo III Period

The Pueblo III period is shorthand for a "culture stage." Pueblo Bonito is the archetype for this stage. Carefully stated intentions cannot justify using "Pueblo III period" as a reference for real time, because the term cannot be separated from its implied and intended meaning. If, as we suggest, Pueblo Bonito is not a pueblo, then we find ourselves searching for prehistoric people within an Escher-like illusion, a strange loop of logic.

What would be the consequences of ignoring the real-time/culture-time enigma? To do so would be to endorse and consequently promote the content of a suite of

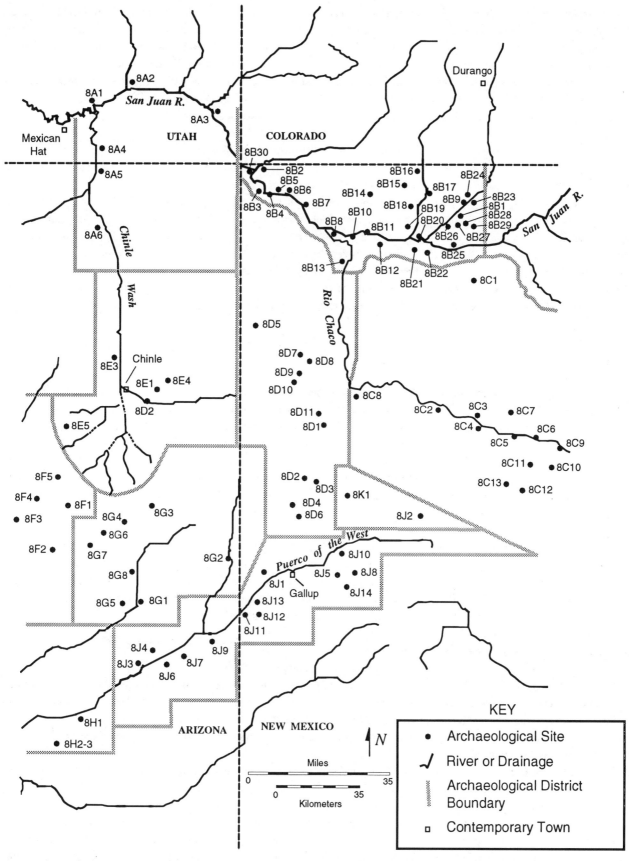

Figure 8.1. San Juan Basin and peripheral areas: districts and large settlements in the central San Juan Basin with occupations between A.D. 1100 and 1300 (Drafted by Michael Adler).

related assumptions still firmly rooted in the "culture time" of the Pecos Classification. Primary among these assumptions is the notion that "big architecture" may be used as a direct proxy for population, and by extension that "big architecture" equals complexity in the social organizational sense. The Pecos Classification is dwelling oriented; it recognizes only residential architectural functions, and it measures the levels of culture in architectural scale.

Elsewhere (Fowler and Stein 1992) we have described three parallel traditions of the Anasazi architectural vernacular: the household residence; the great house, which functions to integrate a community of households; and the great-great house(s), which function to integrate a region of communities. These traditions share a common architectural vocabulary, which is expressed in variations in scale. In this scheme the community-level and regional structures are primarily ritual, not residential. Only the architecture of the common dwelling can legitimately serve as a direct proxy for population. Even then, it is not quite that simple.

From our work in the Anasazi area, we have found that residential and integrative architectural forms evolve uniformly through the periods of the old Anasazi world, a pattern recognizable from the seventh through the close of the thirteenth centuries. One very important aspect of this pattern is what we interpret as a rigid social and political structure that defined and maintained the boundaries of the old communities from at least Basketmaker times on.

During the histories of the old Anasazi communities, there are uniform cycles of relocating and replacing the community-level integrative facilities and refocusing the community. We know of no exceptions to this pattern in the central Anasazi area. A clear result of these uniform cycles of retirement and renewal is a suite or "set" of temporally sequential facilities within each community. This pattern is truncated with the abandonment of every

community in this area at the close of the thirteenth century.

Construction of Pueblo Bonito and the other principal structures of the Chaco Complex began in the early ninth century. We interpret these developments as the initial construction of the regional center, although the importance of the place may vastly antedate the archaeologically visible evidence. We do know that construction of the Chaco Complex did not cease at A.D. 1150 but continued at a less visible scale until the middle of the thirteenth century and possibly later.

In the early decades of the twelfth century, there is a clear break in the construction of ritual centers at the community and regional levels. In each community this is marked by the construction of a totally new facility. Often, but not always, the site for new construction is some distance from the old center. We have argued (Fowler and Stein 1992) that the regional facility at Chaco was similarly retired at this time and that the new center was constructed along the Rio Animas in the Totah district. This change in the middle of the twelfth century is sufficiently dramatic to suggest an economic collapse and abandonment, but the physical evidence for such a disruption simply is not there. The old communities, including those in Chaco Canyon and the San Juan Basin, continue to move forward in lockstep, with no evidence of disruption; no "Chacoans" were displaced by the "Chaco Collapse."

We suggest that the "Chaco Collapse" was a planned renewal of ritual facilities undertaken on a community and a regional scale. Such an effort suggests the end of one age and the beginning of another. We have chosen to use the term "ritual retirement" rather than "abandonment" for several reasons. The old facilities retained the principal architectural elements of even older landscapes and incorporated the older "abandoned" state as important elements of the expanded ritual landscape. In the same fashion, the facilities replaced in the early twelfth century often show

evidence of special, presumably ritual, use or embellishment at a time when those same buildings essentially lay in ruins. Finally, the old and new facilities are consistently connected by earthen umbilicals, sometimes called Chacoan roads.

Time and Architecture

One of the characteristics of Anasazi archaeology which gave rise to the Pecos Classification is the synchronous shifting of ceramic style and architectural form on a regional scale. This shifting has traditionally been interpreted in a framework of "culture time." We suggest instead that we are witnessing the cycles of "ritual time," as described here.

The McElmo Phase:
A.D. 1100–1150

The McElmo phase is described by Vivian and Mathews (1965) based on their work at Kin Kletso in Chaco Canyon, but this distinct horizon is apparent throughout the central Anasazi area. The McElmo phase is a period of intense construction activity. It is erroneously recognized as the last major construction effort in the Chaco Complex. Our story begins somewhat arbitrarily in the middle of the twelfth century, since we do not know exactly when construction and use of the McElmo style of structures actually concluded.

The Post-Chaco Phase:
A.D. 1150–1250

Little is known of the period following the McElmo phase. Because there was no allowance for such a phase in the Pecos Classification, we refer to the century between A.D. 1150 and 1250 as the Post-Chaco Interval or the Post-Chaco Era (Fowler and Stein 1992; Fowler, Stein and Anyon 1987). The events of this period are clearly evidenced in the ceramic and architectural record at the community level, particularly in the larger communities such as those in Manuelito Canyon, where we first recognized the period. The architecture of the Post-Chaco period great houses is sufficiently similar to the Chaco Era constructions that many have been mistaken for Chaco Era great houses. Nevertheless, some characteristics of these landscapes make them easily identifiable: they are very "busy" compared with those of the preceding period, in that they are heavily modified by "roads" and residential-scale structures that cluster around the great house. The great kivas of this period are generally larger than those of the Chaco Era. Finally, although the landscapes of this period have a highly developed earthen component, the earthen barrier that enclosed the Chaco Era great house is often replaced by a massive masonry wall. Because of this preference for utilizing masonry to delineate space, we refer to the community ritual landscapes of this period as "walled compounds." Three examples are illustrated: Holmes Group in the Totah (figure 8.2), Atsee Nitsaa in the Rio Puerco subarea (figure 8.2), and Reservoir Ruin (CM 100) (figure 8.3) in the Central San Juan Basin.

At the regional scale, this phase is more difficult to identify. The tri-wall structure at Pueblo del Arroyo (figure 8.4) is considered a late McElmo phase construction (Lekson 1984a:223), but it may date to this period. Construction of tri-walled structures may also have been undertaken at Aztec during this period (Lekson 1984b; Fowler and Stein 1992:120). McKenna and Toll (1992:138) place the initial construction of Aztec East (figure 8.4) in the Post-Chaco period.

The Big House Period:
A.D. 1250–1300

We name this period after Big House in Manuelito Canyon. This period is identified by the selection of new sites for the construction of a new form of great house throughout the San Juan Basin and its peripheries. These structures have tra-

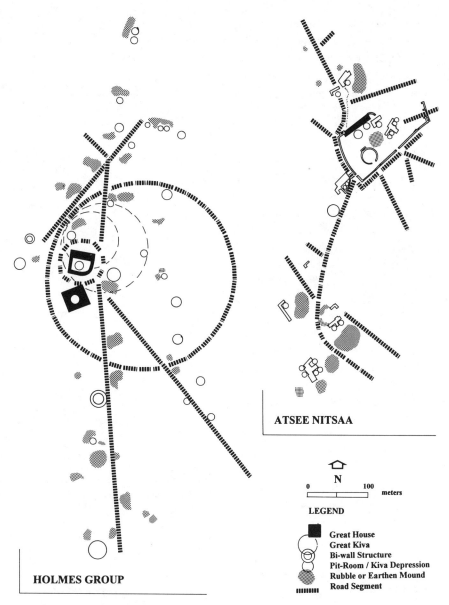

ATSEE NITSAA

HOLMES GROUP

N
0   100   meters

LEGEND
◼ Great House
◯ Great Kiva
◉ Bi-wall Structure
◯ Pit-Room / Kiva Depression
▦ Rubble or Earthen Mound
▥ Road Segment

Figure 8.2. Community ritual landscapes (A.D. 1150–1250). Sites illustrated are the Holmes Group and Atsee Nitsaa.

ditionally been called "pueblos," but we prefer the term "compounds" because these buildings exhibit the design and architectural vocabularies attributed to Anasazi sacred architecture. Compounds reinterpret the architectural elements of the earlier form of great house (the walled compound) and integrate these elements into the mass of a single structure. These are planned buildings constructed with a great deal of care and attention to detail. Large or small, the "compound" is essen-

tially an elevated platform with a sunken central court (or courts).

With the exception of Pueblo Bonito (figure 8.4), which is shown as a comparison for scale, all of the structures illustrated in figures 8.3 through 8.7 are of the compound type, each illustrated to the same scale and orientation. Though the source maps for these structural footprints are by no means a uniform archive, there is a clear regularity of layout and consistency in overall scale. In the central

Anasazi area, Kin Tiel (figure 8.5), Big House (figure 8.5), Crumbled House (figure 8.6), and Flora Vista are the largest thirteenth-century structures that we interpret as community-level facilities. At the regional level, Big House period construction of great houses and remodeling of key architectural elements appear to have occurred at both Aztec and Chaco (figure 8.4). McKenna and Toll (1992: 138) suggest substantial construction of Aztec East in the thirteenth century. We wonder if the massive thirteenth-century structures at Flora Vista might not be a component of a larger regional ritual landscape (Aztec Complex) rather than a community-focused integrative facility. At Chaco Canyon, Tom Windes (personal communication) has suggested that Hillside Ruin (figure 8.4) is a thirteenth-century great house. To this we would add the remodeling of the principal great kivas of the Chaco Core and the "Chetro Ketl Field," which we suggest is not an agricultural field but the layout for a thirteenth-century great house that was never completed.

It is apparent from figures 8.4 and 8.5 that Big House and Kin Tiel, structures we interpret as community facilities, are comparable in scale to Pueblo Bonito and Aztec East, the largest of the structures that we interpret as regional facilities. There are sufficient differences in the structure and character of the built environments of the community and regional centers, however, to make these assignments credible. Several of these community structures are tethered by earthen umbilicals (roads) to the earlier ritual landscapes. This reinforces the inference that compounds are the final manifestation of the community-level ritual facility, i.e., that they are temple architecture.

This certainly raises a question: If compounds aren't residential pueblos, where was everybody in the thirteenth century? Perhaps there was an aggregation of the population into a new architectural type that combined the residential function of the "small house" and the sacred/integra-

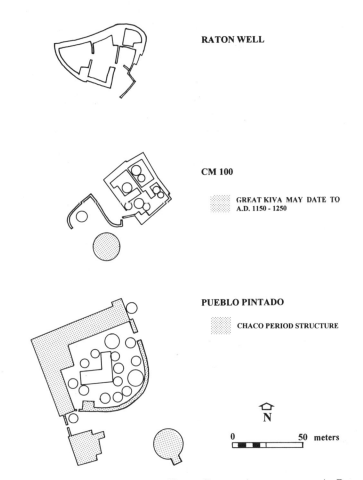

RATON WELL

CM 100

GREAT KIVA MAY DATE TO
A.D. 1150 - 1250

PUEBLO PINTADO

CHACO PERIOD STRUCTURE

N

0   50 meters

Figure 8.3. Compound sites near Chaco Canyon (A.D. 1250–1300): Raton Well, Reservoir Ruin (CM 100), and Pueblo Pintado.

tive function of the "big house." But even in structures such as Big House and Kin Tiel, with architectural footprints that are sufficiently large to argue for local community aggregation, the bulk of the architecture is invested in the mass of a great kiva, court, and perimeter wall, features that we normally do not equate with residential functions. For this reason, we argue that the population remained dispersed in single-family residential units archaeologically much less visible than the community centers.

Archaeological Districts

Having established our perceptions of the development of the social landscape, we now proceed to a description of the regional archaeological record. The greater portion of the central Anasazi area lies

within Navajo country, where Anasazi ruins, as remnants of the Fourth World, are regarded as important features of the Navajo sacred landscape. The ruins are spiritually dangerous places if not treated with the proper respect and are avoided by most as a matter of teaching and tradition. Respect for the places of the old ones, favorable factors of climate, and low population density have left the prehistoric landscape in a remarkable state of preservation.

The region we discuss in this chapter is coherent both historically and archaeologically. Historically, the central Anasazi area is the arena of research within which archaeologists have attempted to explain the monumental architecture of Chaco Canyon. In fact, Chaco Canyon is as well known or better known from the outside than it is from the inside. The idea of a

"Chaco Culture" was forged in large part by Harold S. Gladwin's work along the Rio Puerco of the West and the Red Mesa Valley (Gladwin 1945), well south and west of the canyon itself, and by Earl Morris's extensive excavations at Aztec Ruins and the La Plata Valley (Morris 1928, 1939), far to the north. From an archaeological perspective, the central Anasazi area is rather like a prehistoric "Three Corners," where the Mesa Verde, Cibola, and Tusayan cultural traditions overlap. For these reasons, the central Anasazi area is an appropriate scale at which we can illustrate a pattern of community and regional evolution, and establish a context for the construction of big sites of the eleventh through thirteenth centuries.

We have divided our area of interest into nine subareas (figure 8.1), determined in part by geographical boundaries and in part by the character of the archaeological remains.

The Central San Juan Basin

Following Marshall et al. (1979:21–22), the San Juan Basin is a geologic feature bounded on the north by the San Juan River, on the south by the Dutton Plateau and Lobo Mesa, on the east by the Nacimiento Uplift, and on the west by the Chuska Mountains. Our central San Juan Basin includes the upper and middle drainage of the Chaco River, Chacra Mesa and the canyon, the area to the south and west of Chacra Mesa known as the basin floor, and the Chaco Plateau below Gallegos Mesa.

The central San Juan Basin is desolate. Underlain by vast deposits of coal, the region is dissected by badlands of eroded coal shales and remnants of sandstone caprock. The Anasazi occupation of the central basin is concentrated in the Chaco Core and in the basin floor south of the canyon. In the sage plains and badlands to the north and east of Chaco Canyon (Chaco Plateau), Anasazi settlement is restricted or missing (Lekson 1984a).

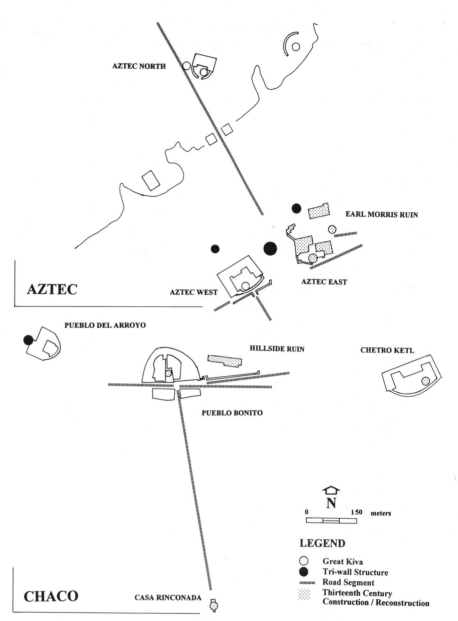

Figure 8.4.   Regional architecture: Aztec and Chaco Canyon.

Principal references to the archaeological literature of the central San Juan Basin include Hayes (1981), Judd (1954, 1959, 1964), Pepper (1920), Vivian and Mathews (1965), Lekson (1984a), Lekson et al. (1983), Windes (1987), McKenna and Truel (1986), Lister and Lister (1981), Vivian (1990), and Sebastian (1992). In contrast to the intensive efforts in Chaco Canyon itself, extensive regional reconnaissance has also been conducted (e.g., Gladwin 1945; Marshall et al. 1979; Powers, Gillespie, and Lekson 1983; Kincaid 1983; Nials, Stein, and Roney 1987; Fowler, Stein, and Anyon 1987; Fowler and Stein 1992; Breternitz, Doyel, and Marshall 1982; Donaldson 1983; Jacobson and Roney 1985; Sebastian and Altschul 1986; Harper et al. 1988; Marshall and Sofaer 1986; Windes 1993; Marshall 1994).

We identify twelve locations in the central basin with components in the mid-twelfth century or later. Thus, this list excludes early twelfth century (McElmo period) construction. Great houses such as Bis Sa'ani, Bee Burrow, Tse Lichii, Pierres, Kin Kletso, New Alto, Casa

Chiquita, Tsin Kletzin, and Wijiji were constructed entirely during the McElmo period. This was also a period during which substantial additions were made to existing structures in the core area of the Chaco Complex.

We have assigned two structures to the Post-Chaco period (AD 1150–1250). Reservoir Ruin (CM100) (figure 8.3) is described by Jacobson and Roney (1985). It contains a low enclosing wall, a great kiva, "roads," and a cluster of associated structures, suggesting a walled compound characteristic of this period (Fowler and Stein 1992). The second building is constructed on the upper ledges of Fajada Butte (Ford 1993), in the vicinity of a 230 m long "ramp" which ascends 95 vertical meters to the top of the butte. There is no sure way of associating this unnamed structure with the ramp. Because of the clear association with Mesa Verde Black-on-white, we lean toward placing this structure in the middle to late thirteenth century as a more or less typical "pinnacle" structure.

Eleven locations, including the Fajada Butte location, are assigned to the middle to late thirteenth century (the Big House period). Most of these structures are compounds constructed on the tops and sides of elevated landforms such as isolated pinnacles and buttes. One structure is contained within the plaza of Pueblo Pintado (figure 8.3) (Marshall et al. 1979:81–86).

There is evidence for extensive modification and "new construction" within the core development at Chaco Canyon during the thirteenth century. Construction efforts include remodeling of Great Kiva A at Pueblo Bonito, the Great Sanctuary at Chetro Ketl, and possibly the Great Kiva at Casa Rinconada. Hillside Ruin (Judd 1964; Tom Windes, personal communication) may be a thirteenth-century great house constructed between Pueblo Bonito and Chetro Ketl (figure 8.4). Finally, the "Chetro Ketl Field" (Loose and Lyons 1976; Richard Loose, personal communication 1991) was constructed during the thirteenth century. We interpret this

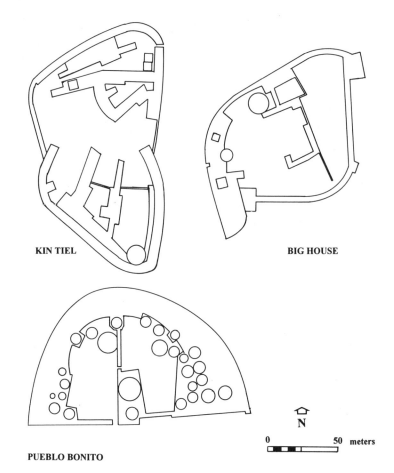

KIN TIEL

BIG HOUSE

PUEBLO BONITO

N

0   50 meters

Figure 8.5. Scale comparisons of large Anasazi structures in the Chaco and Post-Chaco periods.

unique feature as a foundation of a never-completed great house.

Communities of small extended family dwellings are found in dispersed but well-bounded clusters that focus on a central, community-level integrative structure. These are very small communities, but they are numerous, relatively undisturbed, and very visible in the McElmo period and earlier. Tom Windes (1993) recognizes six communities within or adjacent to the Chaco River from Pueblo Pintado to Peñasco Blanco, including Bis'a'ani, Padilla Well, Bonito/South Gap, Fajada Gap, Chaco East, and Pueblo Pintado. To these we would add the possibility that the Escavada/Greasy Hill complex was a discrete community. North of Chaco Canyon, Anasazi settlement is limited. The Pierre's Ruin Complex and Twin

Angels may not be communities per se but instead special architecture associated with the construction of the Great North Road. Numerous clusters of structures that focus on a great house may be found in the basin floor south and west of the canyon. These include Kin Klizhin, Upper Kin Klizhin, Bee Burrow, Greenlee, Lake Valley, Kin Bineola, Indian Creek, Whirlwind Lake, Escalon, Grey Hill Spring, and Great Bend. South and east of the canyon below the scarp of Chacra Mesa are located Mesa Pueblo, El Castillejo (figure 8.8), and Kin Nazhin, all "large" thirteenth-century structures. Evidence of Anasazi settlement east of Chaco Canyon and north of the scarp of Chacra Mesa ends abruptly at Raton Well (figure 8.3). There has now been sufficient archaeological investigation in the area to suggest that this is a real boundary. Neverthe-less, the relationship between Raton Well, Reservoir Ruin (CM 100) (figure 8.3), and the thirteenth-century component in the plaza of Pueblo Pintado (figure 8.3) re-mains problematic. Our tentative scenario is that these structures are partial sets of integrative facilities used by two distinct communities.

It is difficult to estimate numbers of residential units within communities from surface survey. Bis'a'ani (Breternitz, Doyel, and Marshall 1982), which may be the only Anasazi community to be completely excavated, consists of 19 or 20 units. Windes (1993:379) reports 40 houses in the Fajada Gap community dur-ing its maximum occupation and approxi-mately 60 residences (total) for Chaco East (1993:459–463). Jacobson and Roney (1985) describe 40 or so houses asso-ciated with Reservoir Ruin (CM 100) and Marshall (1994:J 1–18) describes approxi-mately 60 residential sites comprising the Escalon–El Llano community. Windes (1993:378) speculates that the population of an individual Chaco Canyon commu-nity was never more than several hundred persons. This figure is reasonable and per-haps even generous for communities out-side the canyon as well.

According to Windes (1993) and McKenna (1991), we may characterize the early twelfth century as a period of both extensive occupation (reoccupation?) of existing structures as well as substantial new construction, both at a community level and within the Chaco Complex. In the Chaco East community, for example, 15 to 20 new house sites of 15 to 25 rooms each were constructed in an area of 40 or so housemounds associated with a predominantly Red Mesa Black-on-white (tenth to early eleventh century) ceramic assemblage. The Chaco East great house was apparently no longer in use during the McElmo period, since the earlier struc-tures address it, while the McElmo struc-tures do not. A major reoccupation of the East community appears to have occurred

in the thirteenth century, as evidenced by new construction on earlier housemounds and reuse of the great house. To a greater or lesser extent, this scenario may be ap-plied to many of the communities in the central basin.

Lobo Mesa

The northern footslopes of the Lobo Mesa–Dutton Plateau form the inner southern rim of the central San Juan Basin. From the vantage of Chaco Canyon, the imposing form of Hosta Butte and gaps formed by Borrego, Wheat Grass, Satan, and Dalton Passes comprise a familiar and presumably significant sky-line.

General references for the archaeology of the Lobo Mesa include Marshall et al. (1979), Nials, Stein, and Roney (1987),

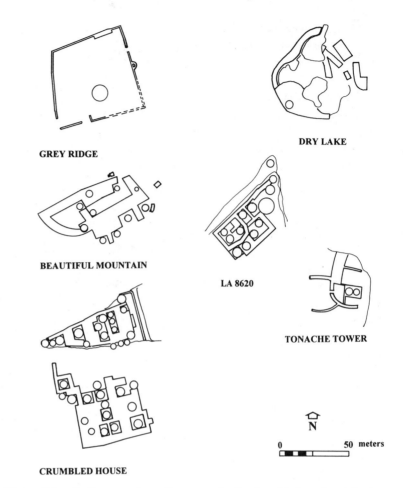

Figure 8.6. Scale comparison of compounds, San Juan Basin and peripheries.

Powers, Gillespie, and Lekson (1983), and Marshall (1994).

Six discrete communities are located along the length of the base of Lobo Mesa: Bluewater Spring, Kin Ya'a, Muddy Water, Dalton Pass, Standing Rock, and Peach Springs. Components dating to the Post-Chaco period are known from Muddy Water (Marshall et al. 1979:207–214), and Peach Springs (Powers, Gil-lespie, and Lekson 1983:363). Marshall (1994:348–377) describes approximately 46 "sites" that form the core cluster of the Standing Rock community. He found significant evidence that the occupation of the community and the use of the great house continued until the latter decades of the twelfth century.

There are no known thirteenth-century compounds in the Lobo Mesa district. Such structures may exist higher up on the footslopes of the mesa—or on the mesa top, for that matter. Very little in the way of archaeological work has been undertaken there. One intriguing possibility is that the Coyote Canyon road was a link between Peach Springs and Grey Ridge Compound. A similar "road" departs from the Muddy Water complex in the direction of the mesa.

Chuska Slope

The Chuska Slope district is essentially the eastern footslopes of the Chuska Range between the San Juan River and the Rio Puerco of the West. This region is known, perhaps inappropriately, as the Chuska Valley. The northern and southern sections of the Chuska Slope differ in both environment and archaeology. The southern section, in the vicinity of Twin Lakes and Tohatchi is very well watered and supported a super-community of dispersed settlement in the Grey Ridge–Tohatchi Flats vicinity. North of Tohatchi the northern footslopes are within the mountain's rain shadow and are extremely arid. Settlement in this area is concentrated in the major drainages at the very base of the mountain. A super-community at Newcomb and Skunk Springs appears to have been supported by extensive irrigation works collecting runoff from locations high on the mountain.

The archaeology of the northern area is known primarily from the reconnaissance survey conducted by Peckham and Wilson (1967) and Harris, Schoenwetter, and Warren (1967) in association with the Navajo Indian Irrigation Project. This work concentrated on the area between Naschitti and Shiprock. Marshall et al. (1979) report on several of the Chuska Valley communities. Reconnaissance south of Naschitti has been conducted by Marshall and Sofaer (1986) and by Fowler, Stein, and Anyon (1987). Peckham and Wilson (1967) documented numerous habitation sites and great kivas at the Skunk Springs, Tocito, Mitten Rock, and Peña Blanca (Sanostee) localities. Subsequent

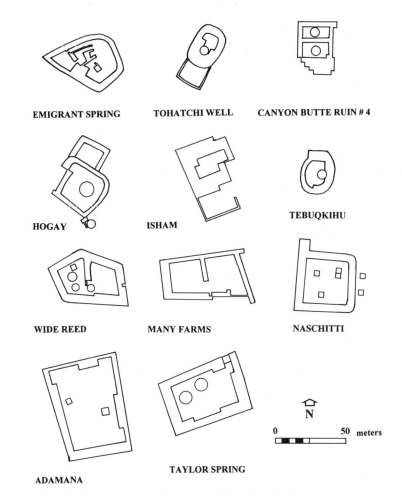

Figure 8.7.   Scale comparison of compounds, San Juan Basin and peripheries.

studies have identified two and possibly three great kivas at Newcomb (Marshall et al. 1979), a thirteenth-century compound at Beautiful Mountain (figure 8.6) (Dykeman 1990), and a great house with associated community at Cove (Paul Reed, personal communication 1994). We recognize seven communities on the northern section of the Chuska Slope: Naschitti (figure 8.7), Skunk Springs–Crumbled House (figure 8.6), Newcomb–Dry Lake (figure 8.6), Tocito–Beautiful Mountain (figure 8.6), lower Sanostee–CGP 56 (figure 8.8), Mitten Rock, and Cove.

Along the southern section of the Chuska Slope, within a broad embayment formed by the western tip of Lobo Mesa, is an area we call Tohatchi Flats. Tohatchi Flats contains a super-community stretching from Tolakai to Tohatchi and from the base of the mountain to Coyote

Canyon. A number of great houses, great kivas, and compounds are known from the area, including Tolakai, Grey Ridge (figure 8.6), Red Willow–Los Rayos, Figueredo, Nakaibitoh, Twin Lakes, Tohatchi Basketmaker village, Tohatchi Well (a bi-wall structure and compound) (figure 8.7), and Grey Ridge Compound. These locations contain community integrative architecture dating from the sixth and seventh centuries to the close of the thirteenth century. Our guess is that at least three communities are represented. Of these, Twin Lakes is clearly a Post-Chaco great house and great kiva. Tolakai and Red Willow may date to this period as well. The Grey Ridge Compound and Tohatchi Well stand out as thirteenth-century construction. Grey Ridge Compound is one of the larger compounds (figure 8.6), but it contains only three rooms. Tohatchi

Well (figure 8.7) is one of the smallest of the compound structures. The suggestion that this building contains thirty rooms (appendix) is probably an exaggeration. We expect to find at least one more thirteenth-century compound in the Tohatchi Flats community.

Totah

The Totah district, which derives its name from the Navajo term for "rivers coming together," is described by McKenna and Toll (1992) as the region that includes the major drainages of the Animas, San Juan, and La Plata Rivers. For convenience, we have stretched the western boundary of the Totah district to the New Mexico state line, which includes the confluences of the Mancos and Chaco Rivers with the San Juan River.

Our use of the Colorado–New Mexico state line as the northern boundary of the district appears quite arbitrary, but the major Anasazi settlement of the Animas and La Plata Rivers occurs in New Mexico.

Early descriptions of the archaeology of the Totah region are offered by W. H. Holmes (1878), Warren K. Moorehead (1908), and T. Mitchell Prudden (1903, 1918). The work of Earl Morris at Aztec (Morris 1928) and in the La Plata Valley (Morris 1939) remains a primary source of information on the region. Recent archaeological surveys and syntheses of Totah archaeology include Dykeman and Langenfeld (1987), Germic (1985), Irwin-Williams and Shelly (1980), McKenna and Toll (1992), and Stein and McKenna (1988).

The Totah was a densely populated region, but site visibility is poor in comparison with the San Juan Basin. Unfortunately, many of the archaeology sites in the Totah have been or are currently being destroyed by development. We have identified thirty large structures within the period of interest. These range from the "Old Indian Racetrack" to Aztec East.

Like Chaco Canyon, the "big sites"

of the Totah served to integrate populations at both regional and community scales. Structures such as the Old Indian Racetrack, Kello Blancett, Flora Vista, Salmon, and the structures of the Aztec complex may be architectural elements of a regional center constructed on the scale of Chaco (figure 8.4). Centers such as Holmes Group (figure 8.2) and Morris 41 on the La Plata River are large and complex and presumably functioned as community facilities.

We cannot begin to guess the number of communities represented by our list of "big sites" in the Totah. A string of thirteenth-century compounds are spaced along the rim overlooking the south bank of the San Juan. A number of late buildings are similarly spaced along the La Plata. These settlements, as well as the intensive developments along the Animas, all suggest a highly structured and densely populated regional occupation during the period under consideration.

Middle San Juan–Lower Chinle Wash

The lower Chinle Wash and its confluence with the San Juan River comprise the core of this district. The boundaries as drawn delineate a region of spectacular desolation. The area lies between the San Juan River to the north, Round Rock to the south, Monument Valley and the eastern slopes of Black Mesa to the west, and the Carrizo and Lukachukai Mountains to the east. In addition to the lower Chinle Wash, the district incorporates lower Laguna Creek, Walker Creek, Teec Nos Pos, Gothic, Saltwater, and Tsitah Washes.

As with much of the region described in this chapter, archaeology began early in this district (Jackson 1878; see also Gaede and Gaede 1977). Surveys and limited excavations were numerous (Guernsey 1931; Guernsey and Kidder 1921; Kidder and Guernsey 1919; Morss 1927; Prudden 1903). The region was repeatedly traversed by Earl Morris and the Bernheimer expeditions in the 1910s and

CGP 56

MESA TIERRA

EL CASTILLEJO

N

0   50 meters

Figure 8.8. Small compounds on pinnacles in the San Juan Basin.

1920s, but documentation of the results of these forays is limited. Findings of the government-sponsored Rainbow Bridge–Monument Valley Expedition were reported by Hargrave (1935) and Beals, Brainerd, and Smith (1945). Adams (1951) and Neely and Olson (1977) provide detailed overviews of the region. During the past decade much of the archaeological work in the district has been clearance-oriented, and with exceptions (e.g., Gilpin 1989), it remains an unsynthesized corpus of "gray" literature.

Anasazi settlement east of the confluence of the San Juan River and Chinle Wash was concentrated along the principal drainages north of the San Juan (Varien et al., chapter 7). In comparison, the region to the south of the river was sparsely populated between the eleventh and thirteenth centuries.

South of the San Juan River, Teec Nos Pos was apparently the core of a small Anasazi community, with a great house–great kiva complex dating to the Chaco and Post-Chaco periods. Poncho House is among the largest of the known cliff dwellings (Neely and Olson 1977:31–32). Promontory Ruin is an unusual cliff structure because it is composed primarily of kivas. Though it falls well short of the 50-room cutoff for "big sites," this structure was most likely not a residential site but rather the integrative focus of a larger, dispersed Pueblo III period community situated in the locality. Ford House and Waterfall Ruin are reported as modest-sized cliff structures.

The Chinle Wash appears to have been a boundary area between Kayenta populations to the west and the Chaco–Mesa Verde groups to the north, east, and south. Prior to the thirteenth century, the architecture and material culture of the local populations are strongly reminiscent of those found in the Kayenta region to the north and northwest. In contrast, architecture and material culture from the thirteenth-century occupations show the distinctive characteristics common in the Mesa Verde region to the north and east.

Upper Chinle–Canyon de Chelly

This region is in the vicinity of Chinle, Arizona, where several drainages (Bala-kai, Cottonwood, Nazlini, Monument, de Chelly, Black Rock, and del Muerto) converge to form the Chinle. The Cottonwood and Balakai Washes drain the eastern slopes of Balakai Mesa, and the Nazlini, de Chelly, and del Muerto systems drain the Sonsela and Tunitcha sections of the Chuska Range. The district can be subdivided into four distinct geographic settings: the deep, narrow canyons of the de Chelly and del Muerto systems; the high, open plain of Beautiful Valley; the valley of the upper Chinle south of Round Rock; and the base of the Chuska Range along Lukachukai Creek.

The archaeology of de Chelly and del Muerto Canyons has been and continues to be the focus of intensive study (De Harport 1959; McDonald 1976; Mindeleff 1895, 1897; D. Morris 1986; E. Morris

1925, 1926, 1938, 1941), while the contrary holds true for the remainder of the district. Coverage from clearance-oriented surveys has been spatially extensive, but these data remain to be synthesized.

The archaeological remains of Canyons de Chelly and del Muerto remain remarkably well preserved due to the shelter of the canyon walls. Although a great deal of architecture was constructed in the nooks and crannies of the canyon, many of these structures were used as storage spaces. Cliff dwellings are present in the canyon, but they are few in number and small in size. Many of these structures were constructed in the Chaco Era or earlier (Scott Travis, personal communication 1991). Mummy Cave is the preeminent thirteenth-century structure in the canyon system, as well as being one of the largest known "cliff dwellings." Elsewhere (Fowler and Stein 1992) we have described White House, Antelope House, and Mummy Cave as a "set" of community integrative facilities, implying that a single community occupied the canyon system.

Beyond the canyon rim, communities are located along the Chinle and its tributaries. Basketmaker period great kivas and Chaco Era great houses are known from the Lukachukai and Round Rock vicinities. Examples of thirteenth-century compounds may be found at Salina Springs and Many Farms (figure 8.7), where we expect that earlier forms of community architecture will ultimately be found (Gilpin 1989).

Defiance Plateau

This district focuses on Black Creek and the Wide Ruin and Upper Pueblo Colorado Washes above 6,000 ft (1,829 m) in elevation, essentially the entire length of Black Creek. The southern boundary of the district roughly parallels the valley of the Rio Puerco of the West, while the Arizona–New Mexico state line defines the eastern boundary. The northern boundary of the district corresponds to

the crest of a topographic fin that extends from the eastern scarp of the Black and Balakai Mesas. To the north of this fin, Nazlini Wash drains northward to the Chinle. To the south, Black Creek, Wide Ruin, and Pueblo Colorado Washes drain southward to the Rio Puerco. From its origin in the vicinity of Crystal, New Mexico, to where it joins the Rio Puerco west of Lupton Gap, Black Creek stretches a distance of approximately 50 miles. The region is a high pinyon-juniper woodland grading into ponderosa forest (Benallie 1993; Eck 1994; Fehr et al. 1982; Gilpin 1987, 1989; Mount 1974).

From a ceramic perspective, this district can be linked with the Rio Puerco pattern, or what Reed (1944) describes as the "Kin Tiel focus." The definition of this focus is based on the pottery at Big House in Manuelito Canyon and the architecture of Kin Tiel (Wide Ruin), the preeminent building in the district (figure 8.5). The district is somewhat of a crossroads of ceramic traditions. From east to west, pre-A.D. 1150 ceramic assemblages grade from a predominantly Cibola association in the Black Creek Valley into a mixed Cibola, Little Colorado, and Tusayan-Kayenta association farther west. The ceramics of the "Kin Tiel focus" are the northern expression of the Tularosa (Cibola) pattern.

Twelve big sites are recorded in this region. Slippery Rock, Hunters Point, and Ganado are identified as Chaco Era great houses–great kivas. Judging from its architecture, Sunrise Springs fits this group as well. Kinlichee and Sunrise Springs are unusually massive structures that are interpreted as great houses of the Post-Chaco phase. Both of these structures are located on prominent elevated landforms, and each appears to contain an elevated circular kiva encased in a massive enclosure. Kinlichee is a true bi-wall structure, while Sunrise Springs is a towerlike mass associated with a nearby great kiva.

Four structures (Wide Reed Ruin, Cornfields, Klagetoh, and Kin Tiel) are examples of thirteenth-century compounds. Kin Tiel is one of the largest thirteenth-century structures recorded in any part of the Anasazi world. When first observed by the Mindeleff brothers in 1881 (Mindeleff 1891), walls of core-and-veneer masonry faced with dressed blocks still stood three stories high. Photographs of the structure illustrate large rooms with galleries of doorways in the style of the Chaco era great house. The structure is shaped like a butterfly, with the wings centered on an intermittent wash and active spring. Fewkes (1904) and Hargrave (1931) conducted excavations at Kin Tiel. Based upon Hargrave's work, the construction dates for the two rectangular kivas are A.D. 1275 and 1276.

Rio Puerco of the West and Painted Desert

The Rio Puerco of the West has its headwaters in the Pinedale Valley high on Lobo Mesa, west of the continental divide. The river flows westward to its confluence with the Little Colorado River at Holbrook, Arizona, a distance of approximately 125 mi (201 km), and its drainage forms the heart of the Rio Puerco of the West district. At a point roughly 60 mi (100 km) above this confluence, the high, rolling grasslands suddenly fall away into the spectacular landscape of the Painted Desert. This district also includes the lower reaches of Leroux Wash and its confluence with the Little Colorado River.

This area of physiographic transition marks a significant change in the number and density of Chaco Era and Post-Chaco period great houses and their associated communities. The Cottonwood Seep great house rests on this cusp. To the northeast of Cottonwood Seep are the remains of the Navajo Springs–Chambers supercommunity, which exhibit great house architecture of classic proportions. To the west, while the density of Anasazi settlement is diminished, the characteristic pattern of public and residential architectural forms is present in the Anasazi sites of the Painted Desert.

The archaeology of the district began with the late-nineteenth-century observations of Abert (U.S. Army, Corps of Topographical Engineers, 1962) and Bandelier (1892). Archaeological references include Bice (1990); Copeland (1988); Ferg (1978); Fowler, Stein, and Anyon (1987); Gladwin (1945); Graves (1990); Hough (1903); Isham (1985); Jones (1986); Lee (1966); Marshall et al. (1979); Powers, Gillespie, and Lekson (1983); Reed (1938); Roberts (1939, 1940); Sant and Marek (1994); Warburton (1990); Warburton and Graves (1992); Wasley (1960); and Wendorf, Fox, and Lewis (1956). Syntheses of Rio Puerco archaeology are provided by Fowler, Stein, and Anyon (1987); Gladwin (1945); and Gumerman and Olson (1968).

We estimate that at least seventeen communities can be identified in the Rio Puerco–Painted Desert district. Many of these are large communities with clearly delineated integrative architecture for the Chaco, Post-Chaco, and Big House periods. From east to west, we find communities at Pinedale, Church Rock–Springstead, Iyanbito, Fort Wingate–Penned-Up Horse Canyon, Heaton Canyon, Tseyatoh, Bread Springs, Manuelito, Whitewater, Houck–Isham, Sanders–Emigrant Springs, Navajo Springs–Rocky Point, Chambers–Taylor Spring, Cottonwood Seep, Dead Wash–Adamana, Canyon Butte, and Sundown. Some of these are shown in figure 8.7.

The archaeological remains of the district are very visible and for the most part intact. This clarity of the remains of the old communities has allowed for detailed description of community structure (Fowler, Stein, and Anyon 1987). Many examples of Chaco Era, Post-Chaco period, and Big House period landscapes may be found within this district.

Conclusion

As discussed in the introductory material and explained in the section on the central San Juan Basin, the issues surrounding the identification of population size are complex. Confounding these issues are architectural forms ("big sites") that are not primarily residential in function, as well as dramatic differences in the visibility of small sites between the earlier (Chaco) and later (Post-Chaco) periods.

Since Anasazi buildings are constructed to serve a variety of functions, they may be expected to exhibit a variety of configurations. The number of rectangular aboveground cells in Anasazi structures cannot be used as a measure of settlement population size since we cannot expect "rooms" to have equal meaning from structure to structure or even from room to room within a structure. Compare, for example, the Taylor Spring compound (figure 8.7) with the Grey Ridge Compound (figure 8.6). Both structures satisfy the critical requirements for the compound building type, and they are similar in spatial scale. Taylor Springs is composed of two hundred rooms; Grey Ridge has only four.

Above-grade rectangular "rooms" should not be used as a direct proxy for population. The bigger the structure, the more cautious we should be about making such measurements. A community-level integrative facility may serve as a proxy for a community, a regional-level integrative facility may serve as a proxy for a region, and a small site may serve as a proxy for a household. Even in the smallest examples of Anasazi architecture, room counts and "kiva" counts will yield significantly different impressions of population size.

We are concerned that many of the assumptions surrounding the construction, use, and disuse of the Chaco Complex are unfounded. We propose that the major structures of the Chaco Complex are examples of regional integrative architecture and that, as such, these structures are not simply residential "pueblos." We find the population of Chaco Canyon living in communities not unlike any other in the central Anasazi area, and like their counterparts, these communities appear to have survived into the twelfth century. If the Chaco Complex was never really occupied, then "abandonment" suggests some very different circumstances and consequences. In fact, there is good evidence for thirteenth-century construction in the Chaco complex, including construction of and planning for entirely new great houses. We contend that this construction may be maintenance activity since the primary functions of the regional center appear to have been relocated to the Totah and Aztec East.

We have illustrated a number of examples of twelfth- and thirteenth-century architecture in order to demonstrate a consistency in scale and form over a wide region. We interpret these structures as examples of community integrative architecture and suggest that, occupied or not, they were located, designed, and constructed under very structured circumstances by and for the members of pre-existing communities. We strongly disagree that structures of this type represent sudden aggregations of formerly unaligned populations.

Southwestern archaeologists have traditionally relied on patterns of architecture and ceramics to tell time and identify people in the old Anasazi World. But after a tremendous burst of activity in the McElmo period there is a significant change in the pattern. In his summary of the history of research and current status of the "Mesa Verde phase" in Chaco Canyon, McKenna (1991) describes the period as one of low visibility owing to the reuse of existing structures, limited duration of occupations, discontinuation of the use of external "middens," and masking by the high visibility of the remains of earlier periods. He cites problems such as a traditional lack of interest in the period and a consequent lack of methodological vigilance by researchers in the Chaco. He discusses the discrepancy between population estimates derived from counting square rooms and those derived from counting round rooms. McKenna concludes that "Its consistent 'background' presence and variability belie the ephemeral, transient status or minor presence often assigned to the period" and that the

perceived reduction in population may be "more apparent than real" (McKenna 1991:131, 133).

Finally, we emphasize the fact that the Pueblo III Era Anasazi communities tethered themselves to their own ancestral communities by integrating aspects of earlier ritual architecture into the new, compound-oriented structures. The significance of the plaza space within these later, larger sites is tied into the subsequent emergence of the katsina cult (Adams, chapter 4), and the compound layout is certainly a primary form of pueblo layout utilized across the post-thirteenth-century Anasazi world. Throughout all of the change, though, we must appreciate the constant ties between the ancestral and the living in the ritual landscape of the Anasazi community.

Acknowledgments

The archaeology of the San Juan Basin is the product of innumerable scholars working together over the past century. Individuals influential in our perceptions of this region include Mike Marshall, Steve Lekson, John Roney, and numerous others. Our particular thanks to Mike Adler and June-el Piper for editing assistance in preparing this document. The interpretations are only partly ours, the mistakes are our own.

References Cited

Adams, William Y.
    1951   Archaeological and Culture History of the Navajo Country: Report on Reconnaissance for the Pueblo Ecology Study. Ms. on file, Museum of Northern Arizona, Flagstaff.
Bandelier, Adolf F.
    1892   Final Report of Excavations Among the Indians of the Southwestern United States. Part 2. Papers of the Archaeological Institute of America, American Series No. 4. Archaeological Institute of America, Cambridge, Massachusetts.
Beals, Ralph L., G. W. Brainerd, and Watson Smith
    1945   An Archaeological Survey of Northeast Arizona. Publications in American Archaeology and Ethnology No. 44. University of California, Berkeley.
Benallie, Larry, Jr.
    1993   An Archaeological Survey of the Klagetoh to Kintiel Water Line System: 91 Scattered Homesites with Septic Tank and Drainfield Systems. NNAD 89-343. Navajo Archaeology Department, Window Rock.
Bice, Richard A.
    1990   The Vidal Great Kiva, Near Gallup, New Mexico: Summary Status Report of the Archaeological Society of New Mexico Field School. Albuquerque Archaeological Society Press, Albuquerque.
Breternitz, Cory Dale, David E. Doyel, and Michael P. Marshall.
    1982   Bis Sa'ani: A Late Bonito Phase Community on Escavada Wash, Northwest New Mexico. Navajo Nation Papers in Anthropology No. 14. Navajo Nation Cultural Resource Management Program, Window Rock.
Copeland, James M.
    1988   Archaeological Survey: Residential Power Line Extensions Along the Puerco River Valley and Adjacent Areas, Church Rock, McKinley County, New Mexico. Cultural Resource Management Program Report No. 87-212. Navajo Nation, Window Rock.
De Harport, D. L.
    1959   An Archaeological Survey of the Canyon of de Chelly, Northeastern Arizona: A Puebloan Community Through Time. Unpublished Ph.D. dissertation. Department of Anthropology, Harvard University, Cambridge, Massachusetts.
Donaldson, Marcia
    1983   Cultural Resource Inventory Along the Proposed Continental Divide Pipeline, Southwestern Colorado and Northwestern New Mexico. Office of Contract Archaeology, University of New Mexico, Albuquerque.
Dykeman, Douglas D.
    1990   Room for a View: Chaco Canyon from the Chuska Slope. Paper presented at the 55th Annual Meeting of the Society for American Archaeology, Las Vegas.
Dykeman, Douglass D., and Kristen Langenfeld
    1987   Prehistory and History of the La Plata Valley, New Mexico: An Overview. Ms. on file, Office of Cultural

Affairs, State Historic Preservation Office, State of New Mexico.

Eck, David C.

1994   *The Anasazi of Wide Ruin Wash and the Hopi Buttes in Across the Colorado Plateau.* Anthropological Studies for the Transwestern Pipeline Expansion Project. Office of Contract Archaeology and the Maxwell Museum of Anthropology, University of New Mexico, Albuquerque.

Fehr, Russell T., Klara B. Kelley, Linda Popelish, and Laurie E. Warner

1982   *Prehistoric and Historic Occupation of the Black Creek Valley, Navajo Nation.* Navajo Nation Papers in Anthropology 7. Window Rock.

Ferg, Alan

1978   *The Painted Cliffs Rest Area: Excavations Along the Rio Puerco, Northeastern Arizona.* Contributions to Highway Salvage Archaeology in Arizona No. 50. Arizona State Museum, Tucson.

Fewkes, Jesse W.

1904   Two Summers' Work in Pueblo Ruins. *22nd Annual Report of the Bureau of American Ethnology, 1900–1901.* Smithsonian Institution, Washington, D.C.

Ford, Dabney

1993   Architecture on Fajada Butte. Appendix H in *The Spadefoot Toad Site: Investigations at 29S7629, Chaco Canyon, New Mexico.* Reports of the Chaco Center, Number 12. Branch of Cultural Research, Division of Anthropology, National Park Service, Santa Fe, New Mexico.

Fowler, Andrew P.

1986   *Archaeological Reconnaissance of Selected Ruins on the Navajo Indian Reservation.* Cultural Resource Management Program Report No. 86-123. Navajo Nation, Window Rock.

Fowler, Andrew P., and John R. Stein

1992   The Anasazi Great House in Space, Time and Paradigm. In *Anasazi Regional Organization and the Chaco System,* edited by David E. Doyel, pp. 101–122. Anthropological Papers No. 5. Maxwell Museum of Anthropology, Albuquerque.

Fowler, Andrew P., John R. Stein, and Roger Anyon

1987   An Archaeological Reconnaissance of West-Central New Mexico: The Anasazi Monuments Project. Draft report on file, Office of Cultural

Affairs, New Mexico Historic Preservation Division, Santa Fe.

Gaede, Marc, and Marnie Gaede

1977   100 Years of Erosion at Poncho House. *The Kiva* 43(1):37–48.

Germic, Stephen

1985   *An Archaeological Reconnaissance Along the San Juan and Lower Mancos Rivers, Northwestern New Mexico.* Northern Arizona Archaeological Reports No. 748. Northern Arizona University, Flagstaff.

Gilpin, Dennis

1987   Current Research on Large, Thirteenth and Fourteenth Century Sites in the Black Mesa, Pueblo Colorado Valley, Chinle Valley, and Defiance Plateau Region of the Navajo Indian Reservation, Apache and Navajo Counties, Arizona. Paper presented at the 1987 Pecos Conference, Pecos, New Mexico.

1989   Great Houses and Pueblos in Northeastern Arizona. Paper presented at the 1989 Pecos Conference, Bandelier National Monument, New Mexico.

Gladwin, Harold S.

1945   *The Chaco Branch: Excavations at White Mound and in the Red Mesa Valley.* Medallion Papers No. 33. Gila Pueblo, Globe, Arizona.

Graves, Donna K.

1990   Navajo Springs: An Examination of the Great House and Surrounding Community. Unpublished master's thesis, Department of Anthropology, Northern Arizona University, Flagstaff.

Guernsey, Samuel J.

1931   *Peabody Explorations in Northeast Arizona: Report on the Archaeological Field Work of 1920–1923.* Papers of the Peabody Museum of American Archaeology and Ethnology 12(1). Harvard University, Cambridge, Massachusetts.

Guernsey, Samuel J., and Alfred Vincent Kidder

1921   *Basketmaker Caves of Northeastern Arizona.* Papers of the Peabody Museum of American Archaeology and Ethnology 8(2). Harvard University, Cambridge, Massachusetts.

Gumerman, George J., and Alan P. Olsen

1968   Prehistory in the Puerco Valley, Eastern Arizona. *Plateau* 40(4): 113–27.

Hargrave, Lyndon L.

1931   Excavations at Kin Tiel and Kokopnyama. *Smithsonian Mis-*

cellaneous Collections 82:80–120. Smithsonian Institution, Washington, D.C.

1935   Archaeological Investigations in the Tsegi Canyons of Northeastern Arizona in 1934. *Museum Notes* 7(7):25–28. Museum of Northern Arizona, Flagstaff.

Harper, R. A., M. K. Swift, B. J. Mills, J. M. Brandi, and J. C. Winter

1988   The Casa Mero and Pierre's Outliers Survey: An Archaeological Class III Inventory of the BLM Lands Surrounding the Outliers. Office of Contract Archaeology, University of New Mexico, Albuquerque.

Harris, A. J., James Schoenwetter, and A. H. Warren

1967   *An Archeological Survey of the Chuska Valley and the Chaco Plateau, New Mexico. Part 1: Natural Science Studies.* Research Records No. 4. Museum of New Mexico, Albuquerque.

Hayes, Alden C.

1981   A Survey of Chaco Canyon. In *Archeological Surveys of Chaco Canyon, New Mexico,* edited by Alden C. Hayes, David M. Brugge, and W. James Judge, pp. 1–68. Chaco Canyon Studies, Publications in Archeology No. 18A. USDI, National Park Service, Washington, D.C.

Holmes, William H.

1878   Report on the Ancient Ruins of Southwestern Colorado, Examined During the Summers of 1875 and 1876. In *Tenth Annual Report of the United States Geological and Geographical Survey of the Territories,* edited by F. V. Hayden, pp. 383–408. U. S. Government Printing Office, Washington, D.C.

Hough, Walter

1903   *Archaeological Field Work in Northeastern Arizona: The Museum-Gates Expedition of 1901.* Annual Report for 1901. U.S. National Museum, Washington, D.C.

Irwin-Williams, Cynthia, and Phillip H. Shelly

1980   *Investigations at the Salmon Site: The Structure of Chacoan Society in the Northern Southwest.* Vols. 1–4. Report to Funding Agencies. Eastern New Mexico University, Portales.

Isham, Dana

1985   *Archeological Survey of the Allentown-Sanders Power Line, Phase II.* Cultural Resource Management

Program Report No. 85-171. Navajo Nation, Window Rock.

Jackson, William H.

1878   *Report on the Ancient Ruins Examined in 1875 and 1877. Tenth Annual Report of the U.S. Geological and Geographical Survey of the Territories, 1876.* U.S. Government Printing Office, Washington, D.C.

Jacobson, Louann, and John R. Roney

1985   Chaco Mesa Pueblo III, Thematic Group: Chacra Mesa Pueblos, Thematic Nomination to the National Register of Historic Places. Ms. on file, Office of Cultural Affairs, State Historic Preservation Division, State of New Mexico, Santa Fe.

Jones, Anne Trinkle

1986   *Pueblo Period Archaeology at Four Sites, Petrified Forest National Park: Data Recovery Along the Mainline Road.* Western Archaeological and Conservation Center Publications in Anthropology 38. National Park Service, Tucson.

Judd, Neil M.

1954   The Material Culture of Pueblo Bonito. *Smithsonian Miscellaneous Collections* 147(1). Smithsonian Institution, Washington, D.C.

1959   Pueblo del Arroyo, Chaco Canyon, New Mexico. *Smithsonian Miscellaneous Collections* 138. Smithsonian Institution, Washington, D.C.

1964   The Architecture of Pueblo Bonito. *Smithsonian Miscellaneous Collections* 147(1). Smithsonian Institution, Washington, D.C.

Kidder, Alfred Vincent

1924   *An Introduction to the Study of Southwestern Archaeology, with a Preliminary Account of the Excavations at Pecos.* Papers of the Phillips Academy Southwestern Expedition No. 1. Phillips Academy, New Haven, Connecticut.

1927   Southwestern Archaeological Conference. *Science* 66:489–491.

Kidder, Alfred Vincent, and Samuel J. Guernsey

1919   *Archaeological Explorations in Northeastern Arizona.* Bureau of American Ethnology Bulletin No. 65. U.S. Government Printing Office, Washington, D.C.

Kincaid, Chris

1983   *Chaco Roads Project Phase 1: A Reappraisal of Prehistoric Roads in the San Juan Basin.* USDI, Bureau of Land Management, Albuquerque.

Lee, Thomas A., Jr.

1966   An Archaeological Reconnaissance of the South Eastern Portion of the Navajo Reservation. Unpublished master's thesis, Department of Anthropology, University of Arizona, Tucson.

Lekson, Stephen H.

1984a   *Great Pueblo Architecture of Chaco Canyon.* Chaco Canyon Studies, Publications in Archaeology No. 18B. USDI, National Park Service, Division of Cultural Research, Albuquerque.

1984b   Dating the Hubbard Tri-wall and other Tri-wall Structures. *Southwestern Lore* 49(4):15–23.

Lekson, Stephen H., Peter J. McKenna, Jeffrey S. Dean, and Richard L. Warren

1983   *The Architecture and Dendrochronology of Chetro Ketl, Chaco Canyon, New Mexico.* Reports of the Chaco Center, No. 6. USDI, National Park Service, Albuquerque.

Lister, Robert H., and Florence C. Lister

1981   *Chaco Canyon Archaeology and Its Archeologists.* University of New Mexico Press, Albuquerque.

1990   *Aztec Ruins National Monument: Administrative History of an Archeological Preserve.* Professional Papers No. 24. USDI, National Park Service, Southwestern Cultural Resources Center, Santa Fe.

Loose, Richard W., and Thomas R. Lyons

1976   The Chetro Ketl Field: A Planned Water Control System in Chaco Canyon. In *Remote Sensing Experiments in Cultural Resource Studies: Non-Destructive Methods of Archaeological Exploration, Survey and Analysis,* assembled by T. R. Lyons, pp. 133–156. Report of the Chaco Center No. 1. National Park Service, University of New Mexico, Albuquerque.

Marshall, Michael P., and Ronna J. Bradley

1994   El Llano–Escalon and Standing Rock Communities in Across the Colorado Plateau. Anthropological Studies for the Transwestern Pipeline Expansion Project, vol. 9: *A Study of Two Anasazi Communities in the San Juan Basin,* edited by Ronna J. Bradley and Richard B. Sullivan, pp. 313–381, app. J–K. Office of Contract Archaeology and the Maxwell Museum of Anthropology, University of New Mexico, Albuquerque.

Marshall, Michael P., and Anna Sofaer

1986   Solstice Project Investigations in the Chaco District, 1984 and 1985, the Technical Report. Ms. in possession of the authors.

Marshall, Michael P., John R. Stein, Richard W. Loose, and Judith E. Novotny

1979   *Anasazi Communities of the San Juan Basin.* Public Service Company of New Mexico, Albuquerque, and State of New Mexico, Historic Preservation Bureau, Planning Division, Santa Fe.

McDonald, James A.

1976   *An Archaeological Assessment of Canyon de Chelly National Monument.* Publications in Anthropology No. 5. USDI, National Park Service, Western Archeological and Conservation Center, Tucson.

McKenna, Peter J.

1991   Chaco Canyon's Mesa Verde Phase. In *Excavations at 29SJ633: The Eleventh Hour Site, Chaco Canyon, New Mexico,* edited by Frances Joan Mathien, pp. 127–137. Reports of the Chaco Center, Number 10. Branch of Cultural Research, Division of Anthropology, National Park Service, Santa Fe, New Mexico.

McKenna, Peter J., and H. Wolcott Toll

1992   Regional Patterns of Great House Development Among the Totah Anasazi, New Mexico. In *Anasazi Regional Organization and the Chaco System,* edited by David E. Doyel, pp. 133–143. Anthropological Papers, No. 5. Maxwell Museum of Anthropology, Albuquerque.

McKenna, Peter J., and Marcia L. Truell

1986   *Small Site Architecture of Chaco Canyon.* Chaco Canyon Studies, Publications in Archeology No. 18D. USDI, National Park Service, Southwestern Cultural Resources Center, Santa Fe.

Mindeleff, Cosmos

1895   Cliff Ruins of Canyon de Chelly, Arizona. *American Anthropologist* 89(2):153–174.

1897   The Cliff Ruins of Canyon de Chelly, Arizona. *Bureau of American Ethnology, 16th Annual Report.* Smithsonian Institution, Washington, D.C.

Mindeleff, Victor

1891   A Study of Pueblo Architecture, Tusayan and Cibola. *Bureau of American Ethnology 8th Annual*

Report. U.S. Government Printing Office, Washington, D.C.

Moorehead, Warren K.
1908 Ruins at Aztec and on the Rio la Plata, New Mexico. *American Anthropologist* 10(2):243–255.

Morris, Don P.
1986 *Archeological Investigations at Antelope House.* USDI, National Park Service, Washington, D.C.

Morris, Earl H.
1925 Exploring the Canyon of Death. *National Geographic* 48(3):263–300.
1926 Notes on Excavations at Canyon de Chelly: Season–1926. Photocopy on file, USDI, National Park Service, Western Archeological Center, Tucson.
1928 *The Aztec Ruin.* Anthropological Papers No. 26. American Museum of Natural History, New York.
1938 Mummy Cave. *Natural History* 42(2):127–138.
1939 *Archaeological Studies in the La Plata District.* Publication No. 519. Carnegie Institution of Washington, Washington, D.C.
1941 Prayer Sticks in Walls of Mummy Cave Tower, Canyon del Muerto. *American Antiquity* 6(3):227–230.

Morss, Noel
1927 *Archaeological Explorations on the Middle Chinlee, 1925.* Memoirs No. 34. American Anthropological Association, Washington, D.C.

Mount, James
1974 Wide Reed Ruin. Ms. on file, Hubbell Trading Post National Historic Site, Ganado, Arizona.

Neely, James A., and Alan P. Olson
1977 *Archaeological Reconnaissance of Monument Valley in Northeastern Arizona.* Research Paper No. 3. Museum of Northern Arizona, Flagstaff.

Nials, Fred, John R. Stein, and John Roney
1987 *Chaco Roads in the Southern Periphery: Results of Phase II of the BLM Chaco Roads Project.* Albuquerque, Bureau of Land Management.

Peckham, Stewart, and John P. Wilson
1967 Archaeological Survey of the Chuska Valley and the Chaco Plateau, New Mexico. Part 2: Survey. Ms. on file, Laboratory of Anthropology, Museum of New Mexico, Santa Fe.

Pepper, George H.
1920 *Pueblo Bonito.* Anthropological Papers No. 27. American Museum of Natural History, New York.

Powers, Robert, William B. Gillespie, and Stephen H. Lekson
1983 *The Outlier Survey: A Regional View of Settlement in the San Juan Basin.* Reports of the Chaco Center, No. 3. USDI, National Park Service, Division of Cultural Research, Albuquerque.

Prudden, T. Mitchell
1903 The Prehistoric Ruins of the San Juan Watershed in Utah, Arizona, Colorado and New Mexico. *American Anthropologist* (n.s.) 5:224–28.
1918 A Further Study of Prehistoric Small House Ruins in the San Juan Watershed. *Memoirs of the American Anthropological Association* 5(1):3–50.

Reagan, Albert
1928a Further Notes on the Archaeology of the Navajo Country. *El Palacio* 25(1): 35–36.
1928b The Small and Semi-Pueblo Ruins of the Painted (and Shiny Painted) Ware Series in the Cornfields–Hopi Volcanic Buttes Field, in the Navajo Country, Arizona. *El Palacio* 25(1): 14–17.
1928c The Small House Ruins of the Slab-House and Black-on-White Pottery Series in the Cornfields–Hopi Volcanic Buttes Field, in the Navajo Country, Arizona. *El Palacio* 25(2).
1928d Some Notes on the Archaeology of the Navajo Country. *El Palacio* 24(4): 334–46.

Reed, Erik K.
1938 Archaeological Report: Proposed Anasazi National Monument, Manuelito, New Mexico. Ms. on file, USDI, National Park Service, Southwest Regional Office, Santa Fe.
1944 The Abandonment of the San Juan Region. *El Palacio* 74(3):61–74.

Roberts, Frank H. H., Jr.
1939 *Archaeological Remains in the Whitewater District, Eastern Arizona.* Part 1: *House Types.* Bureau of American Ethnology, Bulletin No. 121. U.S. Government Printing Office, Washington, D.C.
1940 *Archaeological Remains in the Whitewater District, Eastern Arizona.* Part 2: *Artifacts and Burials.* Bureau of American Ethnology Bulletin No. 126. U.S. Government Printing Office, Washington, D.C.

Sant, Mark B., and Marianne Marek
1994 *Excavations at Early Puebloan Sites in the Puerco River Valley, Arizona: The N-2007 Project.* Zuni Archaeology Program Report No. 271. Research

Series No. 8. Zuni Archaeology Program, Zuni Pueblo.

Sebastian, Lynne
1992 *The Chaco Anasazi: Sociopolitical Evolution in the Prehistoric Southwest.* Cambridge University Press, Cambridge.

Sebastian, Lynne, and Jeffrey H. Altschul
1986 Settlement Pattern, Site Typology and Demographic Analyses: The Anasazi, Archaic and Unknown Sites. *In* Archaeological Survey at Chaco Culture National Historic Park, edited by Robert B. Powers. Ms. on file, Branch of Cultural Research, Division of Anthropology, National Park Service, Santa Fe, New Mexico.

Stein, John R., and Peter J. McKenna
1988 An Archeological Reconnaissance of a Late Bonito Phase Occupation Near Aztec Ruins National Monument, New Mexico. Ms. on file, USDI, National Park Service, Southwest Cultural Resources Center, Santa Fe.

U.S. Army, Corps of Topographical Engineers
1962 *Abert's New Mexico Report, 1846–1847.* Horn and Wallace, Albuquerque. Originally published in 1848.

Vivian, R. Gordon, and Tom W. Mathews
1965 *Kin Kletso: A Pueblo III Community in Chaco Canyon, New Mexico.* Technical Series No. 6(1). Southwest Parks and Monuments Association, Globe, Arizona.

Vivian, R. Gwinn
1990 *The Chacoan Prehistory of the San Juan Basin.* Academic Press, San Diego.

Warburton, Miranda
1990 Archaeological Research at the Navajo Springs Great House. Paper presented at the 55th Annual Meeting of the Society for American Archaeology, Las Vegas.

Warburton, Miranda, and Donna K. Graves.
1992 Navajo Springs, Arizona: Frontier Outlier or Autonomous Great House? *Journal of Field Archaeology* 19(1):51–69.

Wasley, William W.
1960 Salvage Archaeology on Highway 66 in Eastern Arizona. *American Antiquity* 26(1):30–42.

Wendorf, Fred, Nancy Fox, and Orian L. Lewis
1956 *Pipeline Archaeology: Reports of Salvage Operations in the Southwest on El Paso Natural Gas Company*

Projects, 1950–1953. Laboratory of Anthropology, Santa Fe.

Windes, Thomas C.

1987   *Summary of Tests and Excavations at the Pueblo Alto Community*. Investigations at the Pueblo Alto Complex, Chaco Canyon, New Mexico, 1975–1979, vol. 1. Chaco Canyon Studies, Publications in Archeology No. 18F. USDI, National Park Service, Santa Fe.

1993   *The Spadefoot Toad Site: Investigations at 29SJ629, Chaco Canyon, New Mexico*. Reports of the Chaco Center, Number 12. Branch of Cultural Research, Division of Anthropology, National Park Service, Santa Fe, New Mexico.

Chapter 9

The Cibola Region in the Post-Chacoan Era

Keith W. Kintigh

The A.D. 1150 to 1350 period saw some of the most dramatic social changes in the prehistory of the Cibola region. During this time, the population left dispersed settlements and small communities characteristic of Chacoan times and aggregated into large communities and later, nucleated towns. As a result, tens of thousands of pueblo rooms were built and abandoned.

In this chapter I discuss post-Chacoan developments in the region, with a particular emphasis on those predating A.D. 1350. As with other chapters in the volume, this synthesis puts an undue emphasis on the large sites that characterize the latter part of the period in question. Limited information on the small sites is discussed, but a systematic treatment was not attempted.

The Zuni district is used as the foundation for this presentation because it has the most systematic data and because it is the area that I know best. I begin with a brief description of the available data base for the different districts within the region. Next I provide a discussion of chronological assumptions and issues. The sequence of settlement pattern changes for the Zuni and Manuelito districts is then presented in some detail. In subsequent sections I comment on sequences in the other districts and compare them with the Zuni case. The chapter concludes with a discussion of outstanding demographic and interpretive issues.

Although the period of interest here, A.D. 1150 to 1350, is sometimes referred to as the Pueblo III period, this label does not conform to typical usage for the Cibola area. Occupation of the large nucleated towns (ca. A.D. 1275–1540) is generally referred to as a Pueblo IV (not Pueblo III) phenomenon. To avoid compounding the confusion, use of the Pecos Classification is avoided in this chapter, and I use the term "post-Chacoan" to refer to the time after A.D. 1150.

Archaeological Districts

For this volume, the Cibola region (figure 9.1) is an area bounded on the north by the Rio Puerco of the West, on the east by the continental divide, and on the west by a line from Winslow south to the Mogollon Rim. The southern boundary is formed by the Mogollon Rim and a rather arbitrary line drawn to include much of the drainage of the upper Little Colorado River but excluding the Fence Lake and Quemado areas to the south and east (see Lekson, chapter 11). Although the cultural justification for any of these boundaries might be questioned, the exclusion of the Fence Lake and Quemado areas seems most problematic. During the period of concern, developments there appear to be very closely related to those of the Zuni district.

For purposes of discussion, the 9,180 mi² (23,500 km²) Cibola region has been divided into the five districts for which there is some archaeological information, plus a catchall "elsewhere" category for which systematic data are almost wholly lacking (figure 9.1). Despite problems with the data, it is clear that between A.D. 1150 and 1350 there were major differences in population density in different parts of the region. It is not clear, however, to what extent the *sequence* of post-Chacoan cultural developments was similar in form and timing throughout the region. With available information, it is often impossible to distinguish real differences in the past from apparent differences resulting from uneven and noncomparable data and differing assumptions and interpretations. The following sections provide summaries of the data by district.

Zuni District

The Zuni District encompasses 1,758 mi² (4,500 km²) of the Zuni River drainage, including all of the present-day Zuni Indian Reservation, the El Morro Valley to the east, and a substantial area south and west of the reservation. Major tributaries of the Zuni River are Jaralosa and Venadito Draws and the Rio Nutria and the Rio Pescado. This area has a reasonably well-established cultural sequence for the period from A.D. 1100 to 1400.

Survey coverage includes a thorough large-site reconnaissance (Kintigh 1985). Spier (1917) systematically discussed most of the large pueblos on the New Mexico side of the border. In the 75 years since Spier's survey of this area, only two additional sites with more than 100 rooms have been reported in the archaeological literature (Anyon 1988). Although Spier's (1918) survey to the south and west is less intensive, it seems to be fairly complete with respect to the large sites.

Scattered intensive surveys have been conducted within the district, mainly in the eastern portions. Notable are numerous intensive surveys by the Zuni Archaeology Program (e.g., Fowler 1980; Kintigh 1980; Holmes and Fowler 1980), the Yellow House Survey (Hunter-Anderson 1978), the Cibola Archaeological Research Project (Watson, LeBlanc, and Redman 1980; Stone 1992), and my recent surveys on the Hinkson Ranch and near Heshotauthla (Stone 1992; Kintigh and Duff

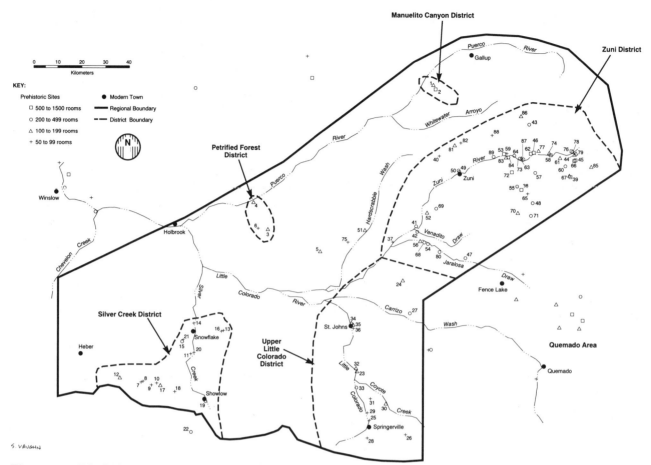

Figure 9.1.   District boundaries and distribution of large (> 50 rooms) Puebloan settlements in the Cibola region, A.D. 1150 to 1350. Site numbers correspond to those listed in the appendix for the Cibola region. Quemado area sites are discussed by Lekson (chapter 11).

1993). Beeson (1966) did a more extensive survey west and south of the reservation that recorded a large number of sites.

There has been comparatively little excavation of relevant sites. Recent excavations include those by Woodbury (1956; Woodbury and Woodbury 1956) at Atsinna, by Watson, LeBlanc, and Redman (1980) at several El Morro Valley sites, Woodall's and Saitta's excavations at the Pettit site (Linthicum 1980; Saitta 1987), Zier's (1976) excavations near Heshotauthla, the Zuni Archaeology Program's work on Jones Ranch Road (Anyon, Collins, and Bennett 1983), the Vogt Ranch near Ramah, and my own work at the Hinkson site (Kintigh, Howell, and Duff 1995) and at Heshotauthla (Kintigh 1991).

Manuelito Canyon District

Manuelito Canyon was surveyed by Weaver (1978) and was recently restudied by Fowler, Stein, and Anyon (1987), but otherwise little systematic work has occurred there. It includes about 59 mi² (150 km²) drained by a tributary of the Puerco River of the West.

Upper Little Colorado District

The Upper Little Colorado District includes the Arizona portion of the Little Colorado River drainage, from its headwaters in the White Mountains to its confluence with Carrizo Wash. Major tributaries are Coyote Creek and Nutrioso Creek. As drawn, this district includes 1,172 mi² (3,000 km²).

Although we have considerable knowledge of large post-Chacoan sites in this

area, the sequence of settlement pattern changes is not as well understood as in the Zuni district. Spier's (1918) reconnaissance of the large sites in this district, though less thorough than his Zuni work, still located most of the known large sites.

Researchers from Harvard University's Upper Gila Expedition surveyed (it is not clear how intensively) along Nutrioso Creek and around Springerville, Arizona (Danson 1957). Danson's report presents useful tables of sites but unfortunately provides no site location maps or other locational information. The Field Museum did an extensive survey of the Little Colorado Valley from Springerville to St. Johns (Martin, Rinaldo, and Longacre 1961:147–64; Martin et al. 1962: 148–67). An intensive sample survey was conducted as a part of the Little Colorado Planning Unit study (Plog 1978,

The Cibola Region in the Post-Chacoan Era   133

1981a, 1981b; Hantman 1989). We have completed our intensive survey of Lyman Lake State Park (Duff and Kintigh 1993). The work of the Upper Gila Expedition, the Little Colorado Planning Unit Study, and my own reconnaissance along the upper Little Colorado in 1983 indicate that the tributary drainages and uplands are poorly known. Despite the lack of work in those areas, Bruce Donaldson suggests that there are probably few unreported sites with more than 50 rooms.

Excavations include those by Paul Martin and his colleagues at Table Rock Pueblo (Martin and Rinaldo 1960) and Hooper Ranch Pueblo (Martin, Rinaldo, and Longacre 1961; Martin et al. 1962), and DeGarmo's (1975) excavation at Coyote Creek Pueblo. Recent excavations have been undertaken at Casa Malpais by Louis Berger and Associates, the Raven Ruin by the White Mountain Archaeological Center (Cunkle 1993) and at Rattlesnake Point Pueblo by Arizona State University.

Silver Creek District

The 585 mi² (1,500 km²) Silver Creek District includes the drainage of Silver Creek upstream (south) of Snowflake as well as the mountainous area along the Mogollon Rim beyond Pinedale toward Heber. Within this area, major tributaries of Silver Creek include Showlow Creek and Cottonwood Wash.

Hough (1903) and Spier (1918) did reconnaissance surveys of this area (Hough also did some excavation). More recently, survey was done by the Field Museum around Snowflake (Martin, Rinaldo, and Longacre 1961:147–64; Martin et al. 1962: 148–67; Longacre 1964) and in the Hay Hollow Valley to the east (Plog 1974). An intensive survey near Pinedale was done by Lightfoot (1984; Lightfoot and Most 1989).

Fewkes (1904) excavated at the Fourmile and Pinedale Ruins. Haury excavated at the Showlow and Pinedale Ruins and sunk a few tests into the Bailey Ruin (Haury and Hargrave 1931). Field Museum archaeologists excavated extensively at sites in the Hay Hollow Valley east of Snowflake, including Broken K Pueblo (Martin, Longacre, and Hill 1967; Hill 1970). The University of Arizona has recently undertaken excavations at Pottery Hill and the Bailey Ruin (Mills et al. 1994).

Petrified Forest

The 59 mi² (150 km²) Petrified Forest District is relatively well known within the boundaries of the national park, but the surrounding areas are poorly known. There has been substantial intensive survey and some recent excavation and testing within the park (Burton 1993a, 1993b; Jones 1983, 1986, 1987; Stewart 1980; Wells 1988). The major excavations of late prehistoric contexts have been at the Puerco Ruin (Burton 1990); in addition, Hough excavated in the cemeteries at the Stone Axe Ruin (1903:320–25). Jones (1993) provides a recent synthesis.

Elsewhere

As can be seen in figure 9.1, nearly all of the known large A.D. 1150 to 1350 sites are within one or another of the districts discussed here. Systematic information on the other areas is almost entirely lacking. We probably are aware of almost all of the "really large" nucleated pueblos (with 100 or more rooms) in the region, but undoubtedly there are many unreported pueblos with from 50 to 100 rooms, and countless smaller sites, both within and outside the defined districts.

Chronological Issues

For the most part, archaeologists working in the Zuni District do not assign temporal phases and avoid use of the Pecos Classification periods. The use of Pecos Classification time periods seems to introduce needless ambiguity into our discussions and into the literature. To some, the Pueblo III period denotes a developmental, Great Pueblo (Roberts 1935) stage, the dates for which may vary from place to place. By Pueblo III others mean a (usually unspecified) range of calendar years. In informal usage around Zuni, the Pueblo III period usually refers to the time from about A.D. 1150 to 1275. Typically, either absolute dates or ceramic assemblages are used to identify time periods (table 9.1).

In compiling these settlement data, tree-ring dating was used to the extent possible. Of course, most sites are dated based on tree-ring dated ceramic types and assemblages. Table 9.1 lists the ceramic complexes and their associated dates as they are used by this author. There is, however, considerable variation in the dates applied to these types and assemblages. Fowler (1989) provides a widely recognized alternative. In the eastern part of the region, the period from A.D. 1150 to 1350 started with the introduction of Wingate Polychrome and ended with the introduction of Matsaki Buff Ware types. This chronology should also apply, with minor additions, to the Manuelito and upper Little Colorado Districts (see Stein and Fowler, chapter 8).

Of some importance for an understanding of the regional dynamics is a bifurcation of the White Mountain Red Ware tradition some time around A.D. 1300. Wingate Black-on-red and Wingate Polychrome (which date before about A.D. 1200) and St. Johns Polychrome (which dates before about A.D. 1300) were common throughout the region. At about A.D. 1300, a Zuni polychrome sequence characterized by Kwakina Polychrome, Heshotauthla Polychrome, and Zuni glazed white wares (Woodbury and Woodbury 1966) developed within the Zuni District. Along the Mogollon Rim (i.e., the Silver Creek District), there arose a similar tradition, characterized by the Pinedale red ware types and Fourmile Polychrome. Upper Little Colorado sites exhibit both of these traditions, as well as Hopi ceramics, and Gila and Tonto Polychromes. Ceramics from the Petrified Forest include White Mountain Red Ware traditions as well as Winslow area and Hopi ceramics.

There are enough excavated sites with tree-ring dates in the region to make attributions to this period on ceramic criteria relatively secure. There is, however, less agreement on occupation spans and the contemporaneity of sites. Most archaeologists assume relatively short occupation spans (probably 50 years or less) for the smaller pueblos and communities, although there is not a great deal of hard information on this topic. Using available tree-ring data and associations (complexes) of tree-ring dated ceramic types, I have argued (Kintigh 1985, 1990) that in the Zuni district, most of the large nucleated settlements also have relatively short occupations, on the order of 25 to 75 years. Exceptions in the form of longer occupations are found at Atsinna, Heshotauthla, and Pueblo de los Muertos. Hantman (1983) also argues that occupations of most pueblos were relatively short. On the other hand, using what he considers to be an innovative methodology, Upham (1987) seems to argue that many of these large pueblos have very long occupations, on the order of a century or more (see also Upham 1982, 1988).

Everyone seems to agree that virtually the entire region was occupied at about A.D. 1150; there is some argument on the dates at which various areas were abandoned. To my knowledge the latest tree-ring date in the region (other than at historic Zuni sites) is A.D. 1384 from the Showlow Ruin (Haury and Hargrave 1931; Robinson and Cameron 1991). There is little (if any) hard evidence that any population remained in the region after A.D. 1400, with the exception of the nine protohistoric Zuni villages on an 18.6-mile (30-km) stretch of the Zuni River (including modern Zuni Pueblo). It should be noted that post-A.D. 1350 ceramic changes, particularly those involving Zuni buff ware types, are not well dated in absolute terms.

Table 9.1   Ceramic Complexes for the Zuni and Upper Little Colorado Districts

Year	Ceramic Types
600–850	*White Mound Black-on-white*, **Lino Gray** (White Mound post-dates 700)
850–1050	**Kiatuthlanna Black-on-white, Red Mesa Black-on-white**, Lino Gray, neckbanded gray, clapboard corrugated gray
1050–1100	Red Mesa Black-on-white, **Gallup Black-on-white, Escavada Black-on-white, Puerco Black-on-white**, *Puerco Black-on-red*, indented corrugated gray
1100–1175	Gallup Black-on-white, Escavada Black-on-white, Puerco Black-on-white, **Reserve Black-on-white**, *Puerco Black-on-red*, **Wingate Black-on-red**, indented corrugated gray
1175–1225	*Gallup Black-on-white, Escavada Black-on-white, Puerco Black-on-white*, Reserve Black-on-white, Puerco Black-on-red, Wingate Black-on-red, **Wingate Polychrome**, indented corrugated gray
1200–1275	*Reserve Black-on-white*, **Tularosa Black-on-white**, *Wingate Polychrome*, **St. Johns Black-on-red**, St. Johns Polychrome, indented corrugated gray
1250–1275	Tularosa Black-on-white, St. Johns Black-on-red & Polychrome, *Springerville Polychrome*, indented corrugated gray
1275–1300	Tularosa Black-on-white, St. Johns Black-on-red, St. Johns Polychrome, *Springerville Polychrome*, **Kwakina Polychrome**, *Pinedale Black-on-red, Pinedale Polychrome*, indented corrugated gray
1300–1325	*Tularosa Black-on-white*, Pinedale Black-on-white, *St. Johns Black-on-red, St. Johns Polychrome*, Kwakina Polychrome, **Heshotauthla Glaze-on-red, Heshotauthla Polychrome**, *Pinedale Black-on-red, Pinedale Polychrome, Gila Polychrome*, indented corrugated gray, indented corrugated buff
1325–1350	Pinedale Black-on-white, Heshotauthla Glaze-on-red, Heshotauthla Polychrome, Kwakina Polychrome, **Fourmile Polychrome**, Gila Polychrome, **Pinnawa Glaze-on-white**, *Pinnawa Red-on-white*, indented corrugated gray, indented corrugated buff
1350–1375	Kwakina Polychrome, Heshotauthla Glaze-on-red & Polychrome, Fourmile Polychrome, Gila Polychrome, **Tonto Polychrome**, Pinnawa Glaze-on-white, Pinnawa Red-on-white, **Kechipawan Polychrome**, indented corrugated buff
1375–1400	Kwakina Polychrome, Heshotauthla Glaze-on-red & Polychrome, Fourmile Polychrome, Gila Polychrome, Tonto Polychrome, Pinnawa Glaze-on-white, Pinnawa Red-on-white, Kechipawan Polychrome, **Matsaki Brown-on-buff, Matsaki Polychrome**, indented corrugated buff, *black ware*
1400–1630	Matsaki Brown-on-buff, Matsaki Polychrome, indented corrugated buff, black ware
1630–1680	Matsaki Brown-on-buff, Matsaki Polychrome, **Hawikuh Glaze-on-red, Hawikuh Polychrome**, indented corrugated buff, black ware

Note: Types that may be present in small or trace quantities are listed in italics. At least one of the types shown in bold must be present to make an assignment to a particular group. Brown wares (not included here) may appear in most assemblages, especially in southern parts of the district. Hopi types may also occur in the Upper Little Colorado District after A.D. 1250 and in the Zuni District after 1350.

Chronological Summary of Settlement Patterns

For each of the districts under consideration, the sequence of settlement patterns is discussed, with a particular emphasis on the large communities.

Zuni and Manuelito Districts

The Chacoan Era: A.D. 1050 to 1150. Prior to A.D. 1150 typical sites were small; the overwhelming majority had fewer than 20 rooms. Room blocks were either dispersed or only loosely clustered along the edges of canyons. Compact residential communities in the sense used here (more than 50 rooms in room blocks within a stone's throw of one another), if they exist, are not archaeologically as distinctive as they are for subsequent periods. Although there are Chacoan outliers in the area, like much of the San Juan Basin, we do not have clear evidence of well defined communities associated with them.

Within the Zuni and Manuelito Districts (and west along the Puerco River to the Petrified Forest area) there are Chacoan great houses with associated great kivas. Among these, the best known is Village of the Great Kivas, which was excavated by Roberts (1932; Fowler, Stein, and Anyon 1987). The Village of the Great Kivas has a great house, two great kivas, and an associated room block with 20 rooms (which may post-date A.D. 1150). Although there are a number of other room blocks in the general vicinity, it does not appear to have a closely associated residential community.

Kin Hocho'i, in Manuelito Canyon, has a great house, great kiva, roads and a formal berm, but fewer than 20 residential rooms (Fowler, Stein, and Anyon 1987; Stein and Fowler, chapter 8). Roger Anyon reports that there was a substantial contemporaneous population density in the vicinity but without further investigation, it is not clear whether it should be considered a compact residential community.

Despite heightened interest in these Chacoan outliers, we simply do not have a good sense of the spatial scale at which the key social and economic units were operating at that time. We need to know how residential settlements were distributed with respect to the Chacoan structures. Were the outliers located within existing, dispersed clusters of pueblos or did they "attract" settlements to a general area? Alternately, were the outliers isolated, did they "repel" local settlement, or was there no evident spatial relationship?

A.D. 1150 to 1250. Intensive survey in the Zuni district suggests that during this period, room blocks were situated typically (but not exclusively) along the edges of canyons at the bases of mesa slopes. At any given time, distributions of occupied sites were quite patchy. Some canyons, or portions thereof, were fairly densely occupied, others nearby apparently were completely vacant. It appears that sites were more closely packed than during the previous century and they became increasingly so during this century (Kintigh 1990).

In the period from A.D. 1150 to 1250 there was a diversity of settlement sizes from small dispersed pueblos to quite large communities. Typical room blocks had from 4 to 40 rooms; the larger ones often had kiva depressions. Room blocks were sometimes dispersed, were often loosely clustered, and sometimes formed large compact clusters.

Although there were truly "dispersed" pueblos, throughout this time period room blocks were frequently within a few hundred meters of one or more ceramically contemporaneous pueblos. In some cases, these pueblos formed compact clusters that fall within the definition of community used here. It is not intuitively obvious whether there is a meaningful distinction between these "communities" and less tightly clustered strings of pueblos (Castellón 1991).

At the core of some of these well-defined communities is an impressive great house and great kiva; others have a great kiva; still others lack both classes of structures (Fowler, Stein, and Anyon 1987; Fowler and Stein 1992; Kintigh, Howell, and Duff 1994). Unlike the Chacoan period, neither great houses nor great kivas appeared in the absence of compact residential communities. Great houses seem always to have had associated great kivas but great kivas did occur in the absence of great houses.

Barth Well and the Bob Place sites were substantial communities, lacking great houses and great kivas, that apparently predated A.D. 1200. The Badger Springs Community and the community including Spier's Site 81 date to about the same time.

Each of these sites has a great house and a great kiva, and each is located in the midst of a community composed of a linear concentration of several room blocks. Slightly later in time, pueblo clusters surrounding Spier's Site 83 and LA 11530 (with about 150 and 65 rooms, respectively) seem to have lacked great houses and great kivas. The communities that include CS 56 and the Jaralosa site included a great kiva and more than 100 rooms (in several room blocks) but no apparent great house.

A number of other communities in the area, including the Hinkson site, Atsee Nitsaa, Los Gigantes, and Garcia Ranch, also had great houses. Instead of Chaco-style great kivas, however, these sites had very large, unroofed, circular structures that I refer to as "large, open, great kivas." This style of great kiva is a separate semisubterranean, circular structure 20 to 35 m in diameter that is unroofed and has a broad earthen bench (Fowler, Stein, and Anyon 1987; Kintigh, Howell, and Duff 1995; McGimsey 1980). Although it seems likely that these large, open great kivas replaced the Chaco-style roofed great kivas during this time period, the chronology is not sufficiently secure to strongly support this inference.

The Hinkson site great house had pecked and ground masonry and an above-ground kiva within the room block. It is associated with a large (530-room) residential community and has evident roads and a berm surrounding the great house-great kiva complex. On recent reexamination, the Scribe S site, with an estimated 410 rooms, may have had a large, open great kiva but there does not appear to have been a great house.

Questions critical to understanding changes in demography and social integration remain unanswered. We need to understand the social implications of great house–oriented communities and of the patchy distribution of sites occupied during this time. That is, did inhabitants of individual room blocks participate to differing degrees in larger scale (pueblo cluster, valley, or supravalley) economic, political, and religious systems? In particular, we need to know whether different levels of social integration are represented by the "communities," the less densely packed linear arrangements of room blocks, and even more dispersed pueblos. Duff (1993; Kintigh, Howell, and Duff 1995) recently made a considerable contribution to this question. Although his research suggests that near the Hinkson site the relevant scale of community integration was at least a 9 kilometer radius around the great house, we are not yet sure how much larger closely interacting communities might have been.

If new social forms are indicated by the compact residential communities (as seems likely to me) we need to know when they arose. We also need to know the role of the great house sites in the social system and the extent to which the people from the dispersed pueblos interacted with those in the great house settlements. We also have no idea whether communities were in competition, alliance, or simple co-existence with each other. The patchy distribution of sites on the landscape suggests that, from the standpoint of a catchment analysis, the landscape was not "filled up."

Problems of chronology persist. In particular, answering the questions posed here will require a dating system that is sufficiently precise to infer contemporaneity. We need to know when the great house-oriented communities with large, open great kivas appeared. It is not clear whether sites of this type were occupied early in this hundred-year period or whether they only appear after A.D. 1200. The surface assemblages of these sites are typically dominated by St. Johns Polychrome, Tularosa Black-on-white, and gray indented corrugated ceramics. At the Hinkson site, St. Johns Polychrome occurs in the construction fill of the open great kiva indicating its construction after about A.D. 1200. The presence of sub-glazed St. Johns pottery at the site along with a very few sherds of Kwakina Poly-

chrome sherds coupled with an absence of later types suggests that occupation of the Hinkson site ended about A.D. 1275.

A.D. 1250–1375. It appears that soon after A.D. 1250, people began to build very large nucleated pueblos. These pueblos generally have a single room block surrounding a plaza and usually have a planned layout; most are oval, rectangular, or trapezoidal (Kintigh 1985). Planning has been argued most convincingly by Watson, LeBlanc, and Redman (1980) for Pueblo de los Muertos, which was established with the planned and essentially simultaneous construction of several hundred rooms. Several early nucleated towns have large, open great kivas outside the room blocks (e.g. Box S, Kluckhohn, and probably Cienega). By A.D. 1300 and perhaps earlier, small pueblos (either within community clusters or dispersed across the landscape) seem to have disappeared completely. Between A.D. 1250 and 1400, at least 28 large pueblos containing a total of more than 13,000 rooms were built and abandoned in the Zuni District alone.

As noted previously, I have argued that these pueblos had relatively short occupations of 25 to 75 years and perhaps less (Kintigh 1985). Interestingly, approximately contemporaneous construction and abandonment seem to have occurred within the same general area. Population movements of more than tens of kilometers are not indicated. For what it is worth, I have attributed these short occupations to a lack of adequate social integration.

With a few exceptions in the Zuni District, these nucleated towns are located in areas of higher elevation (6,600–7,600 ft, 2,000–2,300 m), including the eastern part of the Zuni Indian Reservation and the El Morro Valley. The topographic situations of most of these sites suggests that people relied primarily on runoff irrigation for cultivating crops. Through the fourteenth century, sites became more strongly associated with springs and the

Zuni River (Kintigh 1984, 1985), though the locations of most would also favor runoff agriculture.

In the Zuni area, a number of the very large pueblos (e.g., Pueblo de los Muertos, Heshotauthla, Atsinna, Cienega) seem to overlie smaller structures, and sparse scatters of late twelfth-century ceramics occur on several other large sites. Although it is not clear whether there is a continuity of occupation between the small and large pueblos, it is fairly clear that the later settlements were constructed on a much larger scale.

After A.D. 1375. It appears that by about A.D. 1400, the entire Cibola region, other than the area near Zuni Pueblo itself, had been abandoned. To the north and west, every place except the Hopi Mesas had been abandoned.

At about this time there was a major shift of population at Zuni to the protohistoric towns, along the Zuni river from Ojo Caliente to a few kilometers upstream of modern Zuni. Nine protohistoric Zuni sites with a total of 4,000 rooms were built starting some time in the mid-to-late fourteenth century. (These are not included in the appendix or on figure 9.1.) The fifteenth-century towns were restricted to areas of lower elevation (6,230–6,400 ft, 1,850–1,900 m) that had, at most, a sparse occupation through the thirteenth century.

Unlike the earlier towns, these pueblos apparently were unplanned but had very long occupations, in several cases lasting well into the seventeenth century. Site locations suggest that this population shift was associated with a change in agricultural strategy from a focus on runoff water control to riverine and spring-fed irrigation (Kintigh 1984, 1985).

Upper Little Colorado District

Settlement patterns prior to A.D. 1275 in the upper Little Colorado district are not well understood, but this area appears to have a sequence generally similar to that in the Zuni District. The Upper Gila Expedition reported six villages with great kivas that they date from Pueblo II-III through Pueblo III-IV times. It is not clear how these villages fit into the settlement system. To my knowledge, post-Chacoan great houses and great house-oriented communities are not reported for this area, but the sites have not been examined with an eye toward recognizing that architectural form.

As at Zuni, nucleated towns were built along the upper Little Colorado River after A.D. 1250. Unlike the Zuni district, these nucleated towns were generally smaller and were restricted to areas favorable for riverine irrigation (in this case, from the Little Colorado River) and obvious plazas were not characteristic. Some of these locations (especially near the modern town of St. Johns, Arizona) appear to be notably *un*suitable for runoff agriculture. Bandelier (1892:386) reports remains of prehistoric irrigation canals in this area. Ceramics and a single tree-ring date from Table Rock Pueblo (Martin and Rinaldo 1960) indicate that occupation of the area continued until late in the fourteenth century.

The demography and social dynamics in evidence are not well understood. Based on a re-analysis of population relative to storage, carrying capacity, and the degree of social integration in the Springerville area, Hantman (1989) has argued against Lightfoot's (1978) interpretation of a social and economic hierarchy reflected by a settlement hierarchy.

Silver Creek District

For the Silver Creek district, Lightfoot (1984) argues that from A.D. 1100 to 1250 smaller pueblos in the Pinedale area were clustered around 40- to 80-room pueblos with great kivas. For the Snowflake area, he sees pueblos of 30 to 65 rooms clustered around the 120-room (at that time) Fourmile Ruin (with great kivas and plazas),

with smaller pueblos evenly spaced along Cottonwood Wash. Although Lightfoot has revised his initial formulation, he still maintains that there was a settlement hierarchy reflecting a decision-making hierarchy (Lightfoot and Most 1989).

As Lightfoot recognizes (Lightfoot and Most 1989:401), the notion of a settlement hierarchy is predicated on the contemporaneity of sites of various classes. Yet occupations of even the very small pueblos in his survey area are dated to a minimum of 150 years (Lightfoot 1984: 130–34; cf. Lightfoot and Most 1989). Lightfoot's analysis (1984:125–29) was based on correlations of design attributes with corrugated-plain ware ratios (assumed to be temporally sensitive), leading to the definition of three chronological groupings of sites that span 575 years (A.D. 900–1475). If sites were occupied for only short periods, the temporal resolution of his analysis would be insufficient to show contemporaneity. In any event, these inferences must also be considered in light of the generally accepted (and tree-ring dated) ceramic chronologies for the area that date the polychrome types (and hence the sites containing them) later than the purportedly subordinate sites lacking polychromes. The reconstructions presented throughout this chapter are based on the standard ceramic chronology.

Until a convincing argument for contemporaneity of the site types is made, I remain skeptical of Lightfoot's interpretation of a settlement hierarchy formed by clusters of smaller pueblos, which lack polychrome ceramics, around larger pueblos, which sport polychrome wares. If Lightfoot is right (see also, Upham, Lightfoot, and Feinman 1981), we must reevaluate the sequences for other areas as well.

There is also some argument about the date at which nucleated pueblos with 100 or more rooms were first constructed in the Silver Creek District. I believe that the data are consistent with a sequence like that at Zuni in which these towns postdate A.D. 1250. Haury's investigations led

him to postulate two temporal components at the Showlow Ruin (Haury and Hargrave 1931:13–17). The first, of uncertain size, is associated with St. Johns Polychrome, with tree-ring dates after A.D. 1204. The second occupation, clearly associated with the massive pueblo, dates roughly from 1364 to some time after 1384. The Pinedale Ruin shows earlier ceramics; its major construction dates to the "last decades of the thirteenth century" (Haury and Hargrave 1931:73–74), with construction ending by A.D. 1330.

Petrified Forest

In some ways, the Petrified Forest seems more closely associated with the Winslow and Hopi areas than those considered here. In broad outline, however, settlement patterns probably parallel those found within the Zuni, Manuelito, and Upper Little Colorado Districts. Stein has reported Chacoan great houses from the Arizona–New Mexico border, west along the Puerco to the Petrified Forest. Sites dating to the late twelfth century are very small but common (Burton 1990:18–19). To the extent that there is a post-A.D. 1250 population, it apparently aggregated in larger settlements about A.D. 1275, as elsewhere in the region.

Demographic Inferences

Population

Conventional wisdom is that the Cibola region experienced slow growth through Archaic and early Basketmaker times; in later Basketmaker and Pueblo periods, growth accelerated, peaking some time between A.D. 1100 and 1400. Both in-place growth and in- and outmigration are argued to account for these changes.

Longacre's (1964) curve for the upper Little Colorado River Valley shows a population peak at about A.D. 1400, followed by a precipitous decline. For the entire upper Little Colorado region, his data show that the population peaked at about A.D. 1200, and then went into a gradual decline.[1] Plog (1974) argues that the Hay Hollow Valley population peaked earlier, at about A.D. 1100.

Despite these and other ambitious efforts (e.g., Euler 1989), in my view, we do not have sufficient information to warrant even relative statements about population trends (much less absolute population sizes), for the region as a whole or for any districts therein. Although problems in making demographic inferences are reasonably well known (Nelson, Kohler, and Kintigh 1995; Powell 1989), it appears that they are frequently disregarded.

Systematic survey is sparse for this region, and at least in the Zuni area great variability in settlement density of nearby areas is indicated. For example, Fowler's (1980) survey of Cheama Canyon shows a high settlement density from A.D. 800 to 1100, but little occupation thereafter. Our survey only 6.2 miles (10 km) to the east, in the canyon immediately south of the site of Heshotauthla, revealed little evidence of occupation prior to A.D. 1000, but high densities through the twelfth and thirteenth centuries. A similar pattern obtains in Miller Canyon, which is about 8 miles (13 km) southeast of Heshotauthla (Kintigh 1980). Only 15.5 miles (25 km) east of Heshotauthla, the El Morro Valley seemingly had a very small population until the early to mid-thirteenth century, but a very large population through the late thirteenth century and well into the fourteenth century. Considerable evidence indicates that this patchiness is "real" and not a consequence of differing assumptions or methodologies.

There are substantial problems in determining site size and density, including the troublesome issue of estimating numbers of contemporaneously occupied structures. For earlier periods, structure (i.e., pit house) visibility is not only low but probably varies strongly with the local environment. The Zuni Archaeology Program's work at Oak Wash has shown that there are major visibility problems, even for quite substantial pueblos. Even with

our comparatively good chronologies, surveys that make a convincing argument for site contemporaneity are rare. Also, we do not have well justified estimates of structure use-life for different time periods (Cameron 1990). Of course, it is not clear how (over time) absolute population related to pit house or room counts.

As my colleagues and I have argued elsewhere (Nelson, Kohler, and Kintigh 1995), there are sufficient indeterminacies in our knowledge of the variables needed to estimate population that extant data can be used to support *drastically* different demographic reconstructions using alternative sets of plausible assumptions.

Although large nucleated towns dating to the late thirteenth century and fourteenth century are certainly impressive, there are thousands of modest pueblos dispersed over large areas that were occupied during the early and mid-thirteenth century. It is not at all clear how the pre- and post-nucleation populations of the region compared to one another.

If, however, one believes (as I do) that from A.D. 1300 on the overwhelming majority of the population was housed in large pueblos, and if one accepts the tree-ring dated ceramic chronology as being approximately correct (as I do), it is possible to draw some conclusions concerning demographic trends very late in prehistory. Because of the inherent appeal and high visibility of large nucleated sites, we probably have a reasonably good idea of the number of rooms dating to 50- or 100-year periods (after A.D. 1300) within the Zuni, Manuelito Canyon, Upper Little Colorado, and Silver Creek Districts.

Using a broad range of assumptions, it is clear that there were not enough fifteenth- or sixteenth-century pueblos to account for the thirteenth- and fourteenth-century populations. With the exception of the Zuni District, the entire Cibola region was apparently abandoned by A.D. 1400 (see also Hantman 1983). It is commonly believed that regional populations migrated either to Zuni or to Hopi. The Zuni District is seen as a major candidate

for inmigration as a result of abandonment of areas outside the region, as well. Yet within the Zuni District there appear to be more contemporaneously occupied fourteenth-century rooms than fifteenth-century rooms (Kintigh 1985). I see no strong evidence that migration was a major factor in the demographic picture for the Zuni District. Whatever happened to the people, region-wide there appears to have been a substantial population decline late in the fourteenth century (Kintigh 1990).

Upham's (1982, 1988) alternative to this view is that the collapse of the fourteenth-century population centers is not indicative of a regional depopulation but of the transformation of large numbers of people into mobile hunters-gatherers (Querechos). He speculates that in the Zuni area alone there were on the order of 10,000 Querechos at the time of Spanish contact. Although I am unaware of any archaeological evidence to support this interpretation, such hunter-gatherers may not have left a distinct archeological signature. Nonetheless, in contrast to earlier periods, intensive archaeological survey rarely locates potsherds diagnostic of the fourteenth through sixteenth centuries except at the known villages.

Finally, the rich oral tradition of the Zuni people (Ferguson and Hart 1985:20–23) provides a perspective on Zuni history, including movements of population, that has been largely neglected by archaeologists for most of this century.

Site Size

At this juncture, I do not believe that it is possible to compare the sizes of pit house villages and pueblos at different periods. Some pit house villages dating between A.D. 800 and 1000 have large numbers of structures and cover enormous areas (tens of acres). Yet at present, we have no idea of their size at any moment in time.

Trends in site size are a bit clearer for puebloan architecture. It appears that the larger unit pueblos (30 rooms and larger) predominantly post-date A.D. 1150. Although the Chacoan great houses are impressive structures, it appears that large, well-defined communities may not appear until after Chaco's collapse. These large communities (with up to 500 rooms), whether associated with great houses or not, appear late in the twelfth century or early in the thirteenth century. Dispersed pueblos seem to continue until the late thirteenth century.

The nucleated pueblos (with from 100 to 1,400 rooms), all seem to post-date A.D. 1250. In the Zuni District, the two largest of these (Kluckhohn and Archeotekopa II) are among the earliest (dating to the late thirteenth century) and appear to have had short occupations (25 years or so). Surface indications suggest that several of the earlier nucleated settlements had large, open great kivas, an architectural form apparently absent from later towns.

Overall, from A.D. 1150 until about A.D. 1300 there was an increasing concentration of population in communities or large pueblos in the Zuni District.

Interpretive Comments

Aggregation, Architecture, and Social Organization

Population aggregation during late prehistoric times is surely one of the most significant processes that occurred in the Southwest. We do not have good explanations for why this aggregation occurred or how it persisted. Although I have suggested that it may have been the result of competition between groups (Kintigh 1994), it is not clear what stimulated this competition. For the Cibola region, however, the evidence is fairly good that it was not simply a density-driven change. Throughout the period when aggregation occurs, there are large and economically attractive sections of the landscape that were unoccupied (although not necessarily unused).

As I have discussed elsewhere (Kintigh 1994; Kintigh, Howell, and Duff 1995), site size and communal architecture are important keys to understanding organizational issues. During the early twelfth century, Chacoan and non-Chacoan sites were, of course, quite distinct architecturally, but we do not really have any idea of the extent of supracommunity social integration at that time.

By the late twelfth century there apparently were (at least) two different organizational forms. There were dispersed villages with no particular evidence for strong supracommunity organization. These sites appear to all have fewer than about 60 rooms; the great majority have fewer than 30 rooms. On the other hand, there were communities and nucleated towns that without exception have more than 100 rooms. By A.D. 1275, these sites range in size up to 1,400 rooms.

I have argued (Kintigh 1994) that the apparent lack of sites with between 60 and 100 rooms is due to a different level of social integration operating at the small villages in contrast to the large communities and towns. Using Johnson's notions of scalar stress (Johnson 1982, 1983), one may argue that corporate decisions in the villages were reached by a consensus of heads of households. However, the size of the population of the communities and towns in the Zuni area would have required some higher-level decision making.

This higher-level decision making may have been associated with strong leaders and ranked societies (i.e., chiefdoms) in what Johnson calls a simultaneous hierarchy. Alternately, such decision making might have been consensual, within what Johnson calls a sequential hierarchy (Johnson 1989). In a sequential hierarchy, decisions were reached by a council of individuals that came from (and in some sense represented) more inclusive social groups, such as lineages or clans. The jury is still out on the nature of the social organization of the communities and nucleated towns and how it evolved over time.

Communal architecture in the post-Chacoan era included great houses, large, open great kivas, and roads at some communities. A few of the nucleated towns have open great kivas and most have central plazas. The nucleated pueblos might themselves, with their planned layout and large size, be thought of as public architecture. It is reasonable to suggest that ceremonies performed in open great kivas and plazas may have played a major integrative role for these prehistoric societies, much as katsina dances, performed in plazas, do today (Adams 1991). I have suggested (Kintigh 1994) that the strong architectural patterning of great houses and associated features, and perhaps of the planned nucleated pueblos, may indicate intercommunity competition.

Land Tenure and Risk-Sharing

Adler (1990, 1994; Varien et al., chapter 7) suggests that a key function played by the community in small-scale societies may have been the allocation of land. Hegmon (1989) has advanced the idea that limited household-level resource sharing is advantageous, but as Anyon (personal communication) has pointed out, access to hunted and gathered resources must also be factored in. Following this line of argument, Duff (1993) proposes that a hunting and gathering resource zone surrounding pueblo communities might explain the patchy site distributions we observe. With these concerns in mind, we need to evaluate different political and economic models using archaeological data and simulations. We need a better sense of what types of systems appear viable, and in whose interests they operated.

Extra-regional Exchange

In the Zuni District, there is not much evidence that large quantities of goods were moved around between A.D. 1150 and 1350. There is little pottery that is clearly intrusive [2] (though definitive analyses have yet to be done) and only very small amounts of marine shell, turquoise, and obsidian. In contrast, the protohistoric Zuni villages occupied after A.D. 1400 consistently have small quantities of Hopi and Salado pottery, and larger proportions of obsidian in the chipped stone assemblages. Although Patricia Crown's (1994) work suggests that the Salado polychromes found at the protohistoric villages were not imported from any great distance, potsherds of Salado types are notably absent from fourteenth-century Zuni area sites. This appears to suggest a change in the organization of regional interaction and an increase in exchanged materials sometime in the late fourteenth or early fifteenth centuries, well after the major population aggregation. In contrast, the fourteenth-century upper Little Colorado sites show substantial ceramic diversity. White Mountain Red Ware types characteristic of the Zuni and Mogollon Rim areas were common and Hopi ceramics also appear.

Adaptational Models

Dean (chapter 3, 1988) has argued for an adaptational model of social change. Until we get a better idea of the nature and timing of the organizational changes that occurred, it will be difficult to assess an adaptational model. There was great variation in the environmental conditions that prevailed as the processes of community formation and nucleation occurred between A.D. 1150 to 1300 and during the abandonment and population movement characteristic of the following century. Notable, of course, are the 25-year Great Drought at the end of the thirteenth century and the 40-year cool, moist period at the beginning of the fourteenth century. Although we cannot rule out the possibility, as indicated previously, it is not obvious that populations reached carrying capacities for farming, except in quite local areas.

Warfare

Haas and Creamer (chapter 14) argue that stress leads to social integration that in turn leads to competition and conflict that in turn increases stress. For the Zuni District, LeBlanc (1978) has been the major proponent of warfare as a cause of late Pueblo social change. There is little evidence, positive or negative, bearing on the argument. A number of burned rooms were found at the Scribe S site, but we do not know how widespread such burning was, nor do we have any sense of what frequency of burned rooms resulted from causes other than warfare. Very few burials have been excavated, but the skeletal evidence of trauma associated with conflict is, so far as I know, not remarkable. If, as LeBlanc suggests, aggregation may be due to fear of possible conflict in the absence of much actual violence, we would not expect much archaeological evidence other than "defensive" architecture to support this idea.

Abandonment

Recent attention has been focused more on aggregation than abandonment, but answers associated with abandonment may also bear on organizational issues associated with aggregation. On a small scale, we do not yet have a good argument, environmental or otherwise, for the canyon-to-canyon patchiness of late prehistoric settlement patterns throughout the region. In the big picture, it is difficult to understand why such highly productive agricultural areas as Richville Valley along the upper Little Colorado River or the areas surrounding Pescado Springs in the Zuni District would ever end up so far from permanent habitations (20 to 70 km).[3]

Concluding Thoughts

Whatever was going on at Chaco apparently had less effect on the southern and western portions of the region, the upper Little Colorado and Silver Creek Districts. The ideas I have advanced concerning competing post-Chacoan communities (following Fowler, Stein, and Anyon 1987) have not yet been evaluated by archaeologists with extensive on-the-ground expertise in these two districts. Nonetheless, during the thirteenth century, larger settlements seem to become more common throughout the region, except perhaps in the Petrified Forest.

There is a widely shared (but not universal) view that throughout the region nucleated settlements appeared sometime between A.D. 1250 and 1300 and that by about A.D. 1300 virtually the entire population of the region was housed in those towns. Settlement persisted in all districts (though probably not in many areas between the districts) until at least the mid-thirteenth century. Finally, it appears that with the exception of a small portion of the Zuni District, the entire region was abandoned by about A.D. 1400.

There has been considerable debate on the relatively direct inferences presented in the preceding paragraph as well as on the higher-level interpretations concerning social integration and hierarchy and the causes of social change. Traditional assumptions and interpretations have been challenged and alternative assumptions, variables, and arguments have been introduced.

Although debates on the more abstract issues will probably continue, I do not believe that the debate will advance very far until we can reach some agreement on more accessible observations of site occupation spans and on the timing of major settlement pattern changes. Great strides could be made with a broader dissemination of data that are already collected and with some thoughtful consideration and analysis.

With this chapter, I have tried to define some important issues and to present one construction on this large data set (much of which I control only poorly). The tabulation (appendix) and map (figure 9.1), along with the discussion expose the foundations of this intellectual edifice. They doubtless reveal its weaknesses to those with better information or insights. I can only urge that my own errors of fact be pointed out and the additional data be published so that a fruitful discussion of the cultural issues can advance in a productive manner.

Acknowledgments

First, I must acknowledge the many archaeologists who, over the last century, have contributed to our systematic knowledge of the prehistory of the Cibola Region. I am indebted to the Crow Canyon Archaeological Center for sponsoring the stimulating conference for which this chapter was originally written. The participants of the conference provided important insights and inspiration that I have attempted to incorporate in this published version. Steve Lekson and Bill Lipe are due special credit for organizing the conference. Michael Adler's valiant editorial efforts are also greatly appreciated. I am grateful to Roger Anyon, Bruce Donaldson, Andrew Duff, T. J. Ferguson, Kent Lightfoot, Barbara Mills, Nan Rothschild, and Brenda Shears for their valuable comments on earlier drafts of this chapter. Linda Gregonis's copy editing resulted in valuable clarification and greater readability of the chapter.

Notes

1. Using Longacre's figures and assuming constant growth for each 200-year interval plotted, regional growth from A.D. 400 to 600 is inferred to be at an annual rate of 0.2 percent, from 600 to 800 at 0.7 percent, from 800 to 1000 at 0.3 percent, and from 1000 to 1200 at 0.1 percent, with a 0.07 percent decline in rooms from A.D. 1200 to 1400.

2. Barbara Mills has suggested that the remarkable stylistic consistency of St. Johns Polychrome over an enormous area may indicate widespread interaction or exchange during the thirteenth century. Tammy Stone's (1992) and Andrew Duff's (1993) ICP analyses indicate local production of St. Johns types near each of three locations within the Zuni District, supporting an interpretation of interaction rather than massive exchange.

3. T. J. Ferguson has rightly pointed out that these areas were not fully abandoned, in the sense that they remained part of the economic sustain-ing area of the protohistoric and historic Zuni (Ferguson and Hart 1985).

References Cited

Adams, E. Charles
  1991   *The Origin and Development of the Pueblo Katsina Cult.* University of Arizona Press, Tucson.

Adler, Michael
  1990   *Communities of Soil and Stone: An Archaeological Investigation of Population Aggregation among the Mesa Verde Anasazi, A.D. 900–1300.* Ph.D. dissertation, Department of Anthropology, University of Michigan, Ann Arbor. University Microfilms, Ann Arbor.
  1994   Population Aggregation and Anasazi Social Landscape: A View from the Four Corners. In *The Ancient Southwestern Community: Models and Methods for the Study of Prehistoric Social Organization*, edited by Wirt H. Wills and Robert D. Leonard, 85–101. University of New Mexico Press, Albuquerque.

Anyon, Roger
  1988   The Late Prehistoric and Early Historic Periods in the Zuni-Cibola Area, A.D. 1400–1680. Paper presented at the November meeting of the New Mexico Archaeological Council, Albuquerque.

Anyon, Roger, Susan M. Collins, and Kathryn Bennett (editors)
  1983   *Archaeological Investigations Between Manuelito Canyon and Whitewater Arroyo, Northwest New Mexico* (2 volumes). Report No. 185. Zuni Archaeology Program, Pueblo of Zuni, New Mexico.

Bandelier, Adolph F.
  1892   *Final Report of Investigations among the Indians of the Southwestern United States, Carried on Mainly in the Years from 1880 to 1885*, Part 2. Papers of the Archaeological Institute of America, American Series No. 4. Archaeological Institute of America, Boston.

Beeson, William J.
  1966   *Archaeological Survey Near St. Johns, Arizona: A Methodological Study.* Unpublished Ph.D. dissertation, Department of Anthropology, University of Arizona, Tucson.

Burton, Jeffrey F.
  1990   *Archaeological Investigations at Puerco Ruin, Petrified Forest National Park, Arizona.* Publications in Anthropology No. 54. USDI, National Park Service, Western Archaeological and Conservation Center, National Park Service, Tucson.
  1993a   *Days in the Painted Desert and the Pertified Forests of Northern Arizona: Contributions to the Archeology of Petrified Forest National Park, 1988–1992.* Publications in Anthropology No. 62. USDI, National Park Service, Western Archeological and Conservation Center, Tucson.
  1993b   *When is a Great Kiva? Excavations at McCreery Pueblo, Petrified Forest National Park, Arizona.* Publications in Anthropology No. 63. USDI, National Park Service, Western Archeological and Conservation Center, Tucson.

Cameron, Catherine M.
  1990   The Effect of Varying Estimates of Pit Structure Use-life on Prehistoric Population Estimates in the American Southwest. *Kiva* 55(2): 155–166.

Castellón, Blas
  1991   *Spatial Distribution and Community Structure in the Zuni Area.* Unpublished Master's thesis, Department of Anthropology, Arizona State University, Tempe.

Crown, Patricia L.
  1994   *Ceramics and Ideology: Salado Polychrome Pottery.* University of New Mexico Press, Albuquerque.

Cunkle, James R.
  1993   *Talking Pots: Prehistoric Pottery Icons of the White Mountains of Arizona.* Golden West Publishers, Phoenix.

Danson, Edward B.
  1957   *An Archaeological Survey of West Central New Mexico and East Central Arizona.* Papers of the Peabody Museum of Archaeology and Ethnology No. 44(1). Harvard University, Cambridge.

Dean, Jeffrey
  1988   A Model of Anasazi Behavioral Adaptation. In *The Anasazi in a Changing Environment*, edited by George J. Gumerman, pp. 25–44. Cambridge University Press, Cambridge.

DeGarmo, Glen D.
  1975   *Coyote Creek, Site 01: A Methodological Study of a Prehistoric Pueblo Population.* Ph.D. dissertation,

Department of Anthropology, University of California at Los Angeles. University Microfilms, Ann Arbor.

Duff, Andrew I. L.
1993   *An Exploration of Post-chacoan Community Organization through Ceramic Sourcing.* Unpublished Master's thesis. Department of Anthropology, Arizona State University, Tempe.

Duff, Andrew I., and Keith W. Kintigh
1993   *An Archaeological Survey of Lyman Lake State Park, Apache County, Arizona.* Submitted to the St. Johns Economic Development Corporation and Lyman Lake State Park, St. Johns, Arizona. Copies available at Department of Anthropology, Arizona State University, Tempe.

Euler, Robert C.
1989   Demography and Cultural Dynamics on the Colorado Plateaus. In *The Anasazi in a Changing Environment,* edited by George J. Gumerman, pp. 192–229. Cambridge University Press, Cambridge.

Ferguson, T. J., and E. Richard Hart
1985   *A Zuni Atlas.* University of Oklahoma Press, Norman.

Fewkes, Jesse W.
1904   Two Summers' Work in Pueblo Ruins. *Annual Report of the Bureau of American Ethnology* No. 22. Smithsonian Institution, Washington, D.C.

Fowler, Andrew P.
1980   *Archaeological Clearance Investigation, Acque Chaining and Reseeding Project, Zuni Indian Reservation, McKinley County, New Mexico.* ZAP-020–78s. Zuni Archaeology Program, Pueblo of Zuni.
1989   Ceramic Types of the Zuni Area. Ms. prepared for NMAC Ceramic Workshop, Silver City, New Mexico.

Fowler, Andrew P., and John R. Stein
1992   The Anasazi Great House in Space, Time, and Paradigm. In *Anasazi Regional Organization and the Chaco System,* edited by David E. Doyel, 101–122. Maxwell Museum of Anthropology Papers No. 5. University of New Mexico, Albuquerque.

Fowler, Andrew P., John R. Stein, and Roger Anyon
1987   *An Archaeological Reconnaissance of West-central New Mexico: The Anasazi Monuments Project.* Submitted to the Office of Cultural Affairs, Historic Preservation Division, State of New Mexico, Santa Fe.

Hantman, Jeffrey L.
1983   *Social Networks and Stylistic Distributions in the Prehistoric Plateau Southwest.* Ph.D. dissertation, Department of Anthropology, Arizona State University, Tempe. University Microfilms, Ann Arbor.
1989   Surplus Production and Complexity in the Upper Little Colorado Province, East-Central Arizona. In *The Sociopolitical Structure of Prehistoric Southwestern Societies,* edited by Steadman Upham, Kent G. Lightfoot, and Roberta A. Jewett, pp. 389–418. Westview Press, Boulder.

Haury, Emil W., and Lyndon L. Hargrave
1931   Recently Dated Pueblo Ruins in Arizona. *Smithsonian Miscellaneous Collections* 82(11).

Hegmon, Michelle
1989   Risk Reduction and Variation in Agricultural Economies: A Computer Simulation of Hopi Agriculture. *Economic Anthropology* 8: 89–121.

Hill, James N.
1970   *Broken K Pueblo: Prehistoric Social Organization in the American Southwest.* Anthropological Papers No. 18. University of Arizona Press, Tucson.

Holmes, Barbara E., and Andrew P. Fowler
1980   *The Alternate Dams Survey, An Archaeological Sample Survey and Evaluation of the Burned Timber and Coalmine Dams, Zuni Indian Reservation, McKinley County, New Mexico.* Zuni Archaeology Program, Pueblo of Zuni, New Mexico.

Hough, Walter
1903   Archaeological Field Work in Northeastern Arizona. The Museum-Gates Expedition, 1901. *United States National Museum, Annual Report for 1901.* Washington, D.C.

Hunter-Anderson, Rosalind L.
1978   An Archaeological Survey of the Yellowhouse Dam Area. Ms. on file, Office of Contract Archaeology, University of New Mexico, Albuquerque.

Johnson, Gregory A.
1982   Organizational Structure and Scalar Stress. In *Theory and Explanation in Archaeology,* edited by Colin A. Renfrew, Michael J. Rowlands, and Barbara Abbott Segraves. Academic Press, New York.
1983   Decision-making Organization and Pastoral Nomad Camp Size. *Human Ecology* 11(2):175–199.

1989   Dynamics of Southwestern Prehistory: Far Outside—Looking In. In *Dynamics of Southwest Prehistory,* edited by Linda S. Cordell and George J. Gumerman, pp. 371–389. Smithsonian Institution Press, Washington, D.C.

Jones, Anne Trinkle
1983   *Patterns of Lithic Use at AZ Q: 1: 42, Petrified Forest National Park, Arizona.* Publications in Anthropology No. 25. USDI, National Park Service, Western Archaeological and Conservation Center, Tucson.
1986   *Pueblo Period Archeology at Four Sites, Petrified Forest National Park.* Publications in Anthropology No. 38. USDI, National Park Service, Western Archaeological and Conservation Center, Tucson.
1987   *Contributions to the Archeology of Petrified Forest National Park, 1985–1986.* Publications in Anthropology No. 45. USDI, National Park Service, Western Archaeological and Conservation Center, Tucson.
1993   *Stalking the Past: Prehistory at the Petrified Forest.* Petrified Forest Museum Association, Petrified Forest National Park, Arizona.

Kintigh, Keith W.
1980   *Archaeological Clearance Investigation of the Miller Canyon and Southeastern Boundary Fencing Projects, Zuni Indian Reservation, New Mexico.* Zuni Archaeology Program, Pueblo of Zuni.
1984   Late Prehistoric Agricultural Strategies and Settlement Patterns in the Zuni Area. In *Prehistoric Agricultural Strategies in the Southwest,* edited by Suzanne K. Fish and Paul R. Fish, pp. 215–32. Anthropological Research Papers No. 34. Arizona State University, Tempe.
1985   *Settlement, Subsistence, and Society in Late Zuni Prehistory.* Anthropological Papers No. 44. University of Arizona Press, Tucson.
1990   Protohistoric Transitions in the Western Pueblo Area. In *Perspectives on Southwestern Prehistory,* edited by Paul E. Minnis and Charles L. Redman, pp. 258–75. Westview Press, Boulder.
1991   *Archaeological Work at Heshotauthla. Zuni History: Victories in the 1990s.* Pueblo of Zuni, Zuni, New Mexico.
1994   Chaco, Communal Architecture, and Cibolan Aggregation. In *The*

Ancient Southwestern Community: Models and Methods for the Study of Prehistoric Social Organization, edited by Wirt H. Wills and Robert D. Leonard, pp. 131–140. University of New Mexico Press, Albuquerque.

Kintigh, Keith W. and Andrew I. L. Duff
1993   The Changing Face of Community: Patterns from the Zuni River Drainage. Paper presented at the 58th Annual Meeting of the Society for American Archaeology, St. Louis.

Kintigh, Keith W., Todd L. Howell, and Andrew I. L. Duff
1995   Post-Chacoan Organizational Developments as Evidenced at the Hinkson Site, New Mexico. *Kiva*, in press.

LeBlanc, Steven
1978   Settlement Patterns in the El Morro Valley, New Mexico. In *Investigations of the Southwest Archaeological Research Group: An Experiment in Archaeological Cooperation*, edited by Robert C. Euler and George J. Gumerman, pp. 45–51. Museum of Northern Arizona, Flagstaff.

Lightfoot, Kent G.
1978   Population Movements and Social Interaction in the Prehistoric Southwest: An Experiment from Springerville, Arizona. In *An Analytical Approach to Cultural Resource Management: The Little Colorado Planning Unit*, edited by Fred Plog, pp. 188–200. Anthropological Research Papers No. 13. Arizona State University, Tempe.
1984   *Prehistoric Political Dynamics: A Case Study from the American Southwest*. Northern Illinois University Press, De Kalb.

Lightfoot, Kent G., and Rachel Most
1989   Interpreting Settlement Hierarchies: A Reassessment of Pinedale and Snowflake Settlement Patterns. In *The Sociopolitical Structure of Prehistoric Southwestern Societies*, edited by Steadman Upham, Kent G. Lightfoot, and Roberta A. Jewett, pp. 389–418. Westview Press, Boulder.

Linthicum, B. Lynn
1980   *Pettit Site Masonry: A Study in Intrasite Social Integration*. Unpublished Master's thesis, Department of Anthropology, Wake Forest University, Winston-Salem.

Longacre, William H.
1964   A Synthesis of Upper Little Colorado Prehistory, Eastern Arizona. In Chapters in the Prehistory of Eastern Arizona, II. *Fieldiana: Anthropology* 55:201–15.

Martin, Paul S., William A. Longacre, and James N. Hill
1967   Chapters in the Prehistory of Eastern Arizona, III. *Fieldiana: Anthropology* 57.

Martin, Paul S., and John B. Rinaldo
1960   Table Rock Pueblo. *Fieldiana: Anthropology* 51(2).

Martin, Paul S., John B. Rinaldo, and William A. Longacre
1961   Mineral Creek Site and Hooper Ranch Pueblo, Eastern Arizona. *Fieldiana: Anthropology* 52.

Martin, Paul S., John B. Rinaldo, William A. Longacre, Constance Cronin, Leslie G. Freeman, Jr., and James Schoenwetter.
1962   Chapters in the Prehistory of Arizona, I. *Fieldiana: Anthropology* 53.

McGimsey, Charles R., III
1980   *Mariana Mesa: Seven Prehistoric Sites in West Central New Mexico*. Papers of the Peabody Museum of Archaeology and Ethnology No. 72. Harvard University, Cambridge.

Mills, Barbara J., Trixi Bubemyre, Doug Gann, Sarah Herr, Chuck Riggs, and Ruth Van Dyke
1993   Report on the 1993 Activities of the University of Arizona Archaeological Field School, Silver Creek Archaeological Research Project, Sitgreaves National Forest. Ms. on file, Department of Anthropology, University of Arizona, Tucson.

Mills, Barbara J., Sarah Herr, Eric Kaldahl, Joanne Newcomb, and Scott Van Keuren
1994   Silver Creek Archaeological Research Project: 1994 Field Report. Ms. submitted to Apache-Sitgreaves National Forests. Copy available at Department of Anthropology, University of Arizona, Tucson.

Nelson, Ben A., Timothy D. Kohler, and Keith W. Kintigh
1995   Demographic Alternatives: Consequences for Current Models of Southwestern Prehistory. In *Understanding Complexity in the Prehistoric Southwest*, edited by George J. Gumerman and M. Gell-Mann. Santa Fe Institute Studies in the Sciences of Complexity, Proceedings Vol. 14. Addison-Wesley, Reading, Massachusetts, in press.

Plog, Fred T.
1974   *The Study of Prehistoric Change*. Academic Press, New York.
1981a   *Cultural Resources Overview: Little Colorado Area, Arizona*. USDA, Forest Service, Southwestern Region, Albuquerque, and Bureau of Land Management, Arizona State Office, Phoenix.
1981b   *Managing Archaeology: A Background Document for Cultural Resource Management on the Apache-Sitgreaves National Forests, Arizona*. Cultural Resources Management Report No. 1. USDA, Forest Service, Southwestern Region, Albuquerque.

Plog, Fred (editor)
1978   *An Analytical Approach to Cultural Resource Management: The Little Colorado Planning Unit*. Arizona State University Anthropological Research Papers No. 13. Forest Service Cultural Resources Report No. 19. Arizona State University, Tempe, and USDA, Forest Service, Albuquerque.

Powell, Shirley
1989   Anasazi Demographic Patterns and Organizational Responses: Assumptions and Interpretive Difficulties. In *The Anasazi in a Changing Environment*, edited by George J. Gumerman, 168–91. Cambridge University Press, Cambridge, England.

Roberts, Frank H. H., Jr.
1932   *Village of the Great Kivas on the Zuni Reservation, New Mexico*. Bureau of American Ethnology Bulletin No. 111. Smithsonian Institution, Washington, D.C.
1935   A Survey of Southwestern Archaeology. *American Anthropologist* 37(1).

Robinson, William J. and Catherine M. Cameron
1991   *A Directory of Tree-ring Dated Prehistoric Sites in the American Southwest*. Laboratory of Tree-Ring Research, University of Arizona, Tucson.

Saitta, Dean
1987   *Economic Integration and Social Development in Zuni Prehistory*. Ph.D. dissertation, University of Massachusetts, Amherst.

Spier, Leslie
1917   *An Outline for a Chronology of Zuñi Ruins*. Anthropological Papers No. 18(3). American Museum of Natural History, New York.
1918   *Notes on Some Little Colorado Ruins*. Anthropological Papers No. 18(4). American Museum of Natural History, New York.

Stewart, Yvonne, G.

  1980   *An Archaeological Overview of Petrified Forest National Park*. Publications in Anthropology No. 10. USDI, National Park Service, Western Archaeological Center, Tucson.

Stone, Tammy T.

  1992   *The Process of Aggregation in the American Southwest: A Case Study from Zuni, New Mexico*. Unpublished Ph.D. dissertation, Department of Anthropology, Arizona State University, Tempe.

Upham, Steadman

  1982   *Polities and Power: An Economic and Political History of the Western Pueblo*. Academic Press, New York.

  1987   Assumptions, Methodology and Social Dynamics in Southwestern Prehistory. *North American Archaeologist* 9(1):79–94.

  1988   Archaeological Visibility and the Underclass of Southwestern Prehistory. *American Antiquity* 53(2): 245–61.

Upham, Steadman, Kent G. Lightfoot, and Gary M. Feinman

  1981   Explaining Socially Determined Ceramic Distributions in the Prehistoric Plateau Southwest. *American Antiquity* 46(4):822–33.

Watson, Patty Jo, Steven A. LeBlanc, and Charles L. Redman

  1980   Aspects of Zuni Prehistory: Preliminary Report on Excavation and Survey in the El Morro Valley of New Mexico. *Journal of Field Archaeology* 7:201–218.

Weaver, Donald E., Jr

  1978   *Prehistoric Population Dynamics and Environmental Exploitation in the Manuelito Canyon District, Northwestern New Mexico*. Unpublished Ph.D. dissertation, Department of Anthropology, Arizona State University, Tempe.

Wells, Susan J.

  1988   *Archeological Survey and Testing at Petrified Forest National Park, 1987*. Publications in Anthropology No. 48.

USDI, National Park Service, Western Archaeological and Conservation Center, Tucson.

Woodbury, Richard

  1956   The Antecedents of Zuni Culture. *Transactions of the New York Academy of Sciences*, series 2, 18:557–63.

Woodbury, Richard, and Nathalie F.S. Woodbury

  1956   Zuni Prehistory and El Morro National Monument. *Southwestern Lore* 21:56–60.

  1966   Decorated Pottery of the Zuni Area. Appendix II of the *Excavation of Hawikuh by Frederick Webb Hodge: Report of the Hendricks-Hodge Expedition*, by Watson Smith, Richard B. Woodbury, and Nathalie F. S. Woodbury, 302–6. Contributions from the Museum of the American Indian, Heye Foundation 20. Museum of the American Indian, New York.

Zier, Christian J.

  1976   *Excavations Near Zuni, New Mexico: 1973*. Research Paper No. 2. Museum of Northern Arizona, Flagstaff.

Chapter 10

The Pueblo III Period in the Eastern San Juan Basin and Acoma-Laguna Areas

John R. Roney

My objective in this chapter is to summarize information about the Pueblo III period for two regions, the eastern San Juan Basin and the Acoma-Laguna area. Although adjacent, these two regions were characterized by different ceramic traditions during Pueblo III times and their culture histories are somewhat different. For these reasons each region is first discussed separately and then major trends are discussed for both regions at the end of the chapter.

As used in this chapter the Pueblo III period spans the interval between A.D. 1150 and 1350 and the Pueblo II period dates between A.D. 900 and 1150. Because most of the information discussed in this chapter is based upon survey data, ceramics are the principal means of recognizing Pueblo III remains. In the eastern San Juan Basin this period is recognized ceramically by a preponderance of McElmo and Mesa Verde Black-on-white pottery (or their local varieties). In the Acoma-Laguna Area, sites of this period are indicated by high frequencies of Tularosa Black-on-white. In both areas Wingate Polychrome and St. Johns Polychrome are also important ceramic indicators of this temporal period. The period ends ceramically with the appearance of Rio Grande and Zuni glaze-painted pottery.

Identifying the Prehistoric Community

In the eastern San Juan Basin, and probably in the Acoma-Laguna area as well, the Pueblo III archaeological record is characterized by discrete groupings of small, ceramically contemporaneous buildings, separated by vast areas containing little or

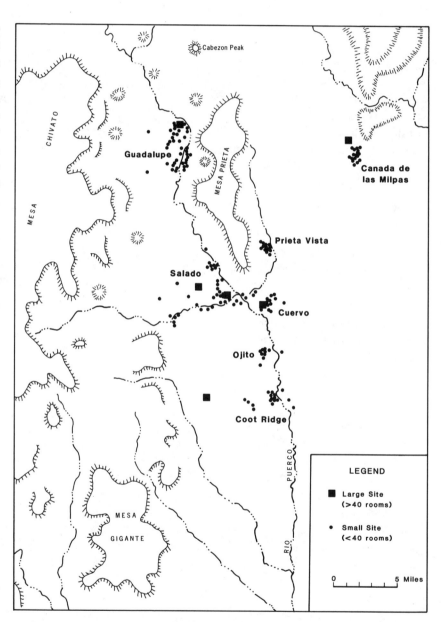

Figure 10.1. Pueblo III period sites and communities in the Middle Rio Puerco Valley, New Mexico (Irwin-Williams and Baker 1991; Peckham 1971, 1987; Bice and Sundt 1972; Sundt et al. 1983).

no evidence of human use. Several such groupings are illustrated in figure 10.1, which was developed with data from the middle Rio Puerco drainage. Many, and perhaps most, of the small buildings are believed to have been residences occupied by individual nuclear or extended families. Groupings of these residential buildings indicate that families were integrated into community-level organizations. This community-level organization was a fundamental aspect of the Pueblo III adaptation and I have placed a great deal of emphasis on description and analysis of individual communities. Figures 10.2 and 10.3 show the locations of these communities within the two study areas, and the range of site sizes within selected communities has been depicted in a series of bar graphs.

All buildings are treated as if they were residential in nature, although it is quite likely that some structures served other functions. For example, some of the one-room buildings may have been field houses, rather than dwellings. The graphs show that kivas or pit structures are often associated with small buildings, however, suggesting that the small buildings were residential. Elsewhere in the Southwest, functional analyses of ceramics from small architectural sites have also generally failed to substantiate their use as seasonal field houses (Plog 1980: 96; Sebastian 1983). Also, I have used the terms "kiva" and "pit structure" interchangeably to reflect ambiguity in interpretation of these circular, subterranean rooms. It is assumed that some of these features served the specialized social and religious functions attributed to kivas, but others were undoubtedly more generalized residential structures.

Analogy with Pueblo II communities suggests that some of the larger buildings may have been used primarily for public purposes. These buildings, here termed "preeminent buildings," are generally 30 rooms or more in size and often occupy prominent locations in the community core, locations that correspond to those

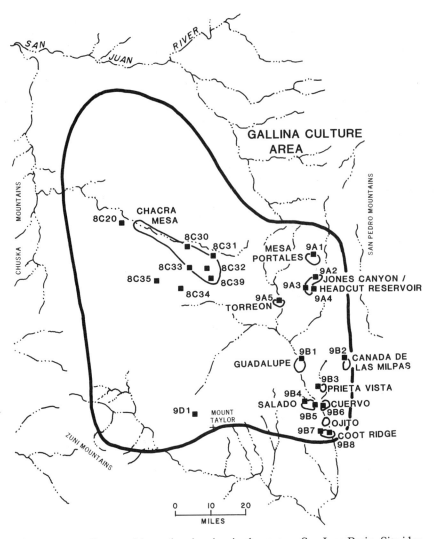

Figure 10.2. Communities and major sites in the eastern San Juan Basin. Site identification numbers correlate with those in the appendix.

of the Bonito-style buildings of Pueblo II times (see also Stein and Fowler, chapter 8). Whenever possible I have included a floor plan of these buildings, as well as floor plans of other buildings that could represent public architecture. The largest buildings are listed in the master data base (appendix), and their locations are shown in figures 10.2 and 10.3.

Another major focus of this chapter is regional organization. For the preceding Pueblo II period, large-scale regional integration is inferred from three data sets: the widespread distribution of relatively uniform ceramic styles, an equally extensive use of distinctive Bonito-style public architecture, and the existence of prehistoric

roads linking at least some outlying sites directly to Chaco Canyon. After the mid-twelfth century Chaco Canyon no longer functioned as a major center of regional integration and the distinctive regional patterns that we associate with Chaco were becoming fragmented. Prehistoric roads were no longer built on a regional scale and public buildings no longer conformed to strict, regionwide architectural conventions. Widespread ceramic style horizons did still exist, but within smaller, sharply bounded geographic areas.

In this analysis I rely heavily upon varying frequencies of decorated ceramic types as a means of inferring supracommunity contemporaneity and organization. Under the information exchange interpretation of stylistic variation developed by Wobst (1977) and Plog (1980), decorated ceramics should signal participation in social networks, and the distributions of major ceramic styles ought to reflect the boundaries of regional social networks. Although detailed stylistic analyses of Pueblo III ceramics are not available, much stylistic information is embedded in the traditional ceramic typologies. Therefore I have attempted to monitor the occurrence and relative frequency of the major ceramic types in contemporaneous sites and communities of the eastern San Juan Basin and Acoma-Laguna area.

Normalized indices of the major wares from various sites and communities (table 10.1) suggest two and possibly three major Pueblo III ceramic traditions: the Mesa Verde tradition that characterizes the eastern San Juan Basin (Mera 1935), the Tularosa tradition that characterizes the western part of the Acoma-Laguna area, and perhaps the Socorro tradition centered on the lower Rio Puerco (see also Lekson, chapter 11).

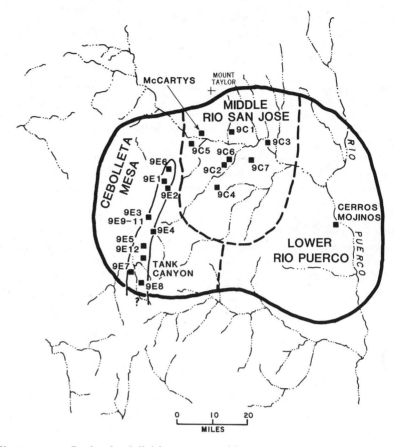

Figure 10.3.   Regional subdivisions, communities, and major sites in the Acoma-Laguna region. Site identification numbers correspond with those in the appendix.

Eastern San Juan Basin

The extent of the eastern San Juan Basin as defined here is shown in figure 10.2. It includes much of the floor of the San Juan Basin proper, the eastern Dutton Plateau and Red Mesa Valley, and the upper and middle Rio Puerco drainage. The area excludes the substantial Mesa Verde tradition settlements along the San Juan River, the lower Chaco Wash, and the eastern slopes of the Chuska Mountains, which are discussed by Stein and Fowler in chapter 8. The eastern San Juan Basin is bounded on the northeast by the distinctive Gallina culture area, on the east by the Rio Grande Valley, and on the south by the distribution of Tularosa tradition sites.

Most major Pueblo III communities in the eastern San Juan Basin have probably been located. This is a bold statement, but it is based upon a considerable amount of systematic and reconnaissance-level sur-

vey in the region. These surveys also show that vast areas of the basin occupied prior to the mid-twelfth century show little or no use during the Pueblo III period.

In the San Juan Basin north of Chaco Canyon, large areas have been surveyed systematically for the Navajo Indian Irrigation Project and in support of proposed energy development projects. Except along the San Juan River and lower Chaco Wash, almost no trace of Pueblo III occupation was found (see Gilpin, Vogler, and Anderson 1984:264–65; Hogan 1982; Huse, Noisat, and Halasi 1978; Kemrer 1982; Kirkpatrick 1980:84–88; Reynolds 1980:5.39–5.42; Sessions 1979; Vierra, Prince, and Powers 1986; Vogler, Gilpin, and Anderson 1983:58–59; Wait and Nelson 1983; Wilson 1979). Pueblo III remains have been documented in Chaco Canyon (Hayes 1981) and on Chacra Mesa (Donaldson 1983; Jacobson and Roney

1985; Swift 1983; Vivian 1960; Vivian and Mathews 1965).

A number of surveys prompted by energy development and federal planning projects to the south of Chaco Canyon and in the Red Mesa Valley have shown that there was little or no Pueblo III occupation in those areas, despite apparently large late Pueblo II populations (see Allan et al. 1976; Ambler 1976; Beal 1976, 1980, 1981, 1984; Doleman 1976; Dulaney and Dosh 1981; Hammack 1985; Harper et al. 1989; Koczan 1978; Miller and Frizell 1980; Powers 1983; Scheick 1981a, 1981b; Whitmore 1979). Other problem-oriented reconnaissance surveys have covered large areas of the San Juan Basin, finding limited or no Pueblo III remains (Kincaid 1983; Marshall et al. 1979; Marshall and Sofaer 1986; Nials, Stein, and Roney 1987; Powers, Gillespie, and Lekson 1983).

The Rio Puerco drainage has been sur-

Table 10.1   Comparison of Ceramic Assemblage

	Mesa Verde Tradition						
	Prieta Vista	Cañada Milpas	Torreon Great Kiva	Headcut Reservoir	Mesa Portales	Chacra Mesa	Chaco Canyon
Decorated as percentage of total	36	40	32	39	14	35	35
Utility as percentage of total	64	60	68	61	86	65	20
McElmo and Mesa Verde Black-on-white as percentage of decorated	53	28	6	87	89	54	20
Other carbon black-on-white as percentage of decorated	38	63	53	—	—	9	—
Tularosa Black-on-white as percentage of decorated	1	—	—	—	—	trace	—
Socorro Black-on-white as percentage of decorated	1	—	—	—	—	trace	—
Other Mineral Black-on-white as percentage of decorated	1	5	3	—	—	5	—
Red ware as percentage of decorated	7	5	3	1	—	4	7
Gray ware as percentage of utility	100	100	99	100	100	100	100
Brown ware as percentage of utility	—	—	1	—	—	—	trace
Corrugated indented as percentage of gray ware	55	48	63	68	63	73	81
Smeared corrugated as percentage of gray ware	42	30	—	—	3	2	—
Sample size (total number)	3004	2431	198	1239	194	7269	4260
Reference	Bice and Sundt 1972	Sundt et al. 1983	Roney notes	Mackey and Holbrook 1978	Roney notes	Jacobson and Roney notes	McKenna 1991

veyed primarily by reconnaissance. Winkler and Davis (1961; Davis 1964) considered much of this country in their wide-ranging search for Mesa Verde phase sites. Over a decade of research by Irwin-Williams has provided a thorough reconnaissance coverage of large areas of the middle Puerco Valley and its tributary, Arroyo Cuervo (Bice and Sundt 1972; Irwin-Williams and Baker 1991). Other important coverage has been supplied by Peckham (1971, 1987), the Albuquerque Archaeological Society (Sundt et al. 1983), Mackey and Holbrook (1978), and the Bureau of Land Management (Wase 1982).

These surveys have resulted in the discovery and documentation of 10 discrete communities and one area of more extensive occupation, Chacra Mesa (figure 10.2 and table 10.2). More detailed descriptions of these communities are provided in the following sections.

Guadalupe Community

The Guadalupe and Salado communities were documented during the Rio Puerco Project, a major long-term program of intensive reconnaissance survey and excavation conducted by Cynthia Irwin-

Table 10.2   Pueblo III Period Communities, Eastern San Juan Basin.

Name	Dates (A.D.)	Number of Buildings	Number of Rooms	Number of Kivas	Largest Site (rooms)	Area (acres)
Guadalupe	800–1325	82	581	?	39	2500
Salado	975–1325	66	914	?	60	4000
Prieta Vista	1220–1240	10	100	1	27	60
Cañada de las Milpas	1225–1325+	50±	400±	0	46	?
Cuervo	1200–1250+	24	208	44	40	2000
Ojito	1150–1200?	13	85	9	15	400
Coot Ridge	1150–1200?	27	222	33	40	1300
Torreon	1150–1325?	18	175	5	50	200
Headcut/Jones Canyon	1150–1300	> 50	?	?	40±	4000±
Mesa Portales	1150–1300?	?	?	?	50±	4000±
Chacra Mesa	1150–1300	> 250	?	?	65	64000?

Williams (Baker 1991b). Because of the length and intensity of this project, it is likely that all architectural sites within the Rio Puerco Project area have been located and recorded. The distribution of sites that made up the Guadalupe Community during the A.D. 1200 to 1250 interval is shown in figure 10.1.

The Rio Puerco Project developed a chronological seriation of 17 ceramic groups spanning the period between ca. A.D. 800 and A.D. 1300. Each site in the project area was attributed to one or more of these ceramic groups (Durand and Hurst 1991), making possible a detailed

analysis of prehistoric population dynamics (Baker 1991a; Baker and Durand 1991). Figure 10.4 shows the total number of rooms occupied during each of the 17 ceramic periods.

The Guadalupe Community was established prior to the ninth century and developed through the early twelfth century into a community consisting of at least 83 separate buildings with a combined total of 664 rooms. A Bonito-style building (Guadalupe Ruin) was established by A.D. 930 and provided a focal point for the community until the demise of the Chacoan system, around A.D. 1130. Decorated

	Tularosa Tradition						Socorro Tradition	
Acoma Tract A	Malpais P III	Cebolla East P III	Cebolla Mesa P III	Cebolla Lake P III	Newton	Calabash	Cerros Mojinos	McCartys
38	42	42	47	42	29	48	49	34
62	58	58	53	58	71	52	51	66
25	—	trace	—	—	—	trace	—	—
—	—	1	—	—	—	—	—	—
24	13	10	19	23	19	30	2	7
trace	trace	3	7	2	8	1	52	36
5	14	19	12	14	17	3	—	—
42	17	22	28	36	20	55	3	28
99	96	99	97	97	62	99	6	69
1	4	1	3	3	38	1	94	31
81	67	98	98	98	99	94	78	88
4	—	—	—	—	—	trace	—	—
9872	901	1019	1215	943	200	7237	1598	2149
Ruppe 1953	Doleman 1989	Marshall 1991	Marshall 1991	Marshall 1991	Marshall and Roney notes	Ruppe 1953	Fenenga and Cummings 1956a	Olson and Wasley 1956

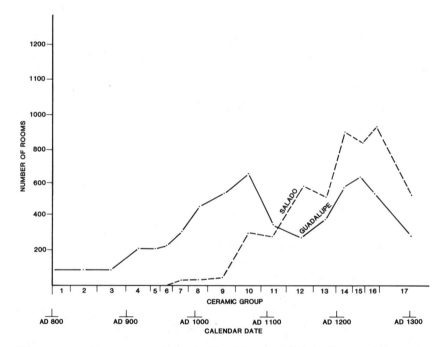

Figure 10.4. Room counts from the Guadalupe and Salado Communities, eastern San Juan Basin (adapted from Baker 1991a).

wares found on these sites include those typical of Pueblo II occupations in the San Juan Basin, including Red Mesa, Gallup, and Escavada Black-on-white.

Between about A.D. 1130 and 1200, room counts suggest a marked population decline compared to the preceding occupation (figure 10.4). Deposits from this period are difficult to find, leading Hurst (1991) to suggest that use of the area may have been seasonal and intermittent, rather than sedentary. Sixty-four sites with a total of 396 rooms evidence some use during this interval, but many of these were earlier buildings that show only minimal use in the latter half of the twelfth century. During this interval, especially the mid-twelfth century, Hurst (1991:219) notes that ceramics show "confusion, technological deterioration, and significantly increased variability."

Between A.D. 1200 and 1250, room counts for the Guadalupe community rose markedly (figure 10.4). Eighty-two sites were occupied with a total of 581 rooms. The largest individual site during this period was the reoccupied Chacoan site, Guadalupe Ruin, which contained 39 rooms (Pippin 1987). Excluding two outlying sites, the Guadalupe Community occupied an area of about 4 mi² (10 km²) at that time.

The final period of occupation in the Guadalupe Community lasted from the mid-twelfth century into the early fourteenth century. During this period the community shrank to 20 buildings with 286 rooms. Ceramic evidence leads Hurst to believe that actual immigrants from the Mesa Verde area either joined or replaced the local population. Sites of this period are often defensive (built atop small, sheer-sided mesa remnants), and the old community center of Guadalupe (that was defensive) was among the last sites to be abandoned.

Baker and Durand (1991) indicate that the average number of rooms per site increased steadily through the Pueblo III period, from 6 rooms per site during the A.D. 1130 to 1200 interval to 14 rooms per site during the interval between A.D. 1260 to 1300. This could represent a tendency toward larger residential units. Alternatively, the change in average number of rooms might be due to the inclusion of one or more sites with nonresidential functions in the sample. A more detailed analysis is needed to more fully address this question.

Salado Community

The Salado Community was also investigated during the Rio Puerco Project. The distribution of architectural units within this community during the A.D. 1200 to 1250 interval is shown in figure 10.1. The detailed ceramic chronology developed for the middle Rio Puerco also applies to this community, and its occupational history (figure 10.4) was reconstructed using the same methods that were summarized for the Guadalupe Community.

Although the Salado Community was not founded until the mid-tenth century, by A.D. 1130 it consisted of 43 buildings with a total of 526 rooms. No Bonito-style building has yet been identified for this community. Current perceptions of Chaco-era communities predict that such a structure should be present in a community of this size, though, and it would be useful to review architectural data from this community in the light of our present knowledge of Bonito-style architecture.

As with the Guadalupe community, the Salado community exhibits a noticeable decline in population between A.D. 1130 and 1200 (figure 10.4). During the later part of this period, however, the Salado population began to grow even as the Guadalupe Community continued to decline. This could reflect a shift in population from one community to the other, and indicates that community-level population changes do not always occur in step with one another within relatively small localities.

Between A.D. 1200 and 1250 the Salado Community population grew rapidly, reaching a maximum expression of 66 sites with a total of 914 rooms (table 10.2 and figure 10.1). Loma Fria, the largest site during this time, included 60 rooms. For this interval the community as a whole occupied an area of about 6.6 mi² (17 km²), with a core of more dense settlement about 200 acres (80 ha) in size.

The spatial extent of the community, number of buildings, and number of rooms all decreased between A.D. 1260 and 1325. Only 20 sites with a total of 541 rooms were occupied, although the largest of these sites had 95 rooms. As at Guadalupe, ceramic evidence suggests

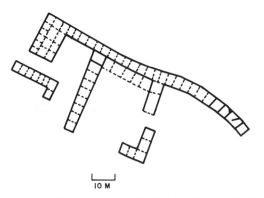

Figure 10.5. Mesa Verde Butte, a site in the Salado Community (9B4 in figure 10.2 and in appendix) (adapted from Davis and Winkler 1959).

that actual population migration from the Mesa Verde area to the Salado Community may have occurred at this time (Hurst 1991). At least some of these latest sites were situated on highly defensive mesa tops.

Baker and Durand (1991) indicate that the average number of rooms per site increased steadily through the Pueblo III period, starting at 12 in the early PIII period and reaching 27 by the end of the period. Mesa Verde Butte is one of the larger late Pueblo III buildings in this community (Davis and Winkler 1959, 1975; Davis 1964:142–44). The site (figure 10.5) is located in a defensive setting on the top of a steep-sided mesa and exhibits the distinctive ladder-type construction also found on Chacra Mesa, at Mesa Pueblo, and in the Cebolleta Mesa subdivision of the Acoma-Laguna area. Ladder-type buildings (Fowler, Stein, and Anyon 1987: 100; Wozniak and Marshall 1991:8.9) were constructed by starting with an exterior wall, followed by a parallel interior wall. Rooms were then created by partitioning the space between the parallel walls with less substantial perpendicular cross-walls. Alternatively, the interior wall was omitted and rooms were tacked onto the more substantial exterior wall. Ladder-type buildings are commonly E or F-shaped, or are in plaza-oriented pueblos. This manner of construction resembles the "spinal" room blocks described by Dean (chapter 3).

Prieta Vista Community

Another exceptionally well documented community is Prieta Vista, a cluster of settlements located in an area investigated by the Albuquerque Archaeological Society (Bice and Sundt 1972) and the Anasazi Origins Project (Irwin-Williams and Baker 1991). Given this level of coverage it is likely that nearly all of the architectural sites in this community have been located.

Prieta Vista is one of the smallest of the Pueblo III communities considered in this chapter. It consists of 10 buildings with a total of about 100 rooms (figure 10.6). The largest building had only 27 rooms and a possible kiva, the only kiva recognized in the entire community (figure 10.7). In total area the Prieta Vista community occupies only about 40 hectares (100 acres).

Prieta Vista seems to have had no predecessor. Diagnostic ceramics lead Bice and Sundt (1972:173–76) to believe that Prieta Vista was occupied between A.D. 1220 and 1240 (table 10.1). Although ceramic information is available from only this one site, Bice and Sundt imply that the other sites in this community were contemporaneous. Bice and Sundt distinguish locally produced McElmo Black-on-white ceramics from varieties that they feel originated in the San Juan Basin proper, but for the purpose at hand I have combined these categories (table 10.1).

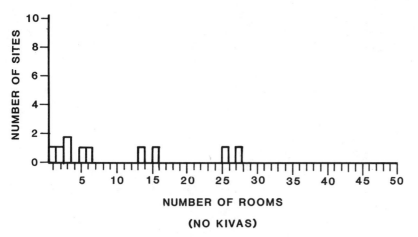

Figure 10.6. Architectural composition of sites in the Prieta Vista Community, eastern San Juan Basin (from Bice and Sundt 1972).

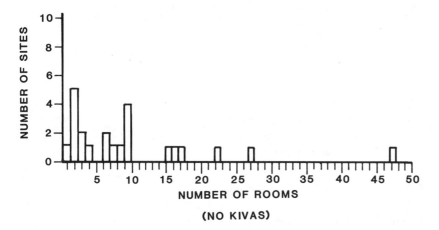

Figure 10.8. Architectural composition of the Cañada de las Milpas Community, eastern San Juan Basin (from Sundt et al. 1983).

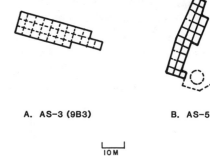

Figure 10.7. Two Pueblo III sites in the Prieta Vista Community. Site identification number in parentheses corresponds with that in figure 10.2 and in the appendix (from Bice and Sundt 1972).

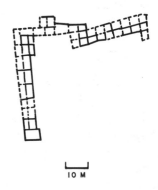

Figure 10.9. AS-8, a Pueblo III settlement in the Cañada de las Milpas Community, eastern San Juan Basin (9B2 in figure 10.2 and in appendix).

Cañada de las Milpas Community

To the northeast of Prieta Vista is the Cañada de las Milpas Community. This group of Pueblo III sites is currently under study by the Albuquerque Archaeological Society and the full extent of the community is not yet known. Richard Bice (personal communication 1989) estimates 50 buildings and 400 rooms for the community as a whole. Only those buildings studied to date have been graphed (figure 10.8) and no kivas have been recognized. The largest building, AS-8 (figure 10.9), includes 48 rooms that define two sides of an informal plaza (Bice and Sundt 1976).

The pottery from 24 recorded sites (table 10.1) suggests that the community was occupied in the mid-thirteenth century, although traces of Rio Grande Glazes, matte-painted polychromes, and biscuit wares indicate that limited use of the area continued into the fourteenth century (Sundt et al. 1983).

Although Cañada de las Milpas is a distinct community, mention should be made of the poorly known Pueblo III occupation along the lower Rio Jemez, just outside the area considered in this chapter. Basal deposits from an excavation at Punamesh Zia yielded a decorated assemblage dominated by Santa Fe Black-on-white, suggesting a date as early as A.D. 1200 (Ellis 1966). Excavations of several other sites in the Zia area indicate beginning dates of about A.D. 1300 (Barnett 1973; Ellis 1966; Mera 1940).

Cuervo Community

The Cuervo Community is one of three Pueblo III communities documented by Peckham (1971, 1987) during a reconnaissance survey along the Middle Rio Puerco immediately south of the Anasazi Origins Project area. The survey was thorough and it is likely that most of the architectural sites in this community have been recorded (figure 10.1).

The Cuervo Community is close to the Salado Community, but the presence of a dense cluster of architectural sites and some spatial separation from the neighboring community (figure 10.1) suggest that it is a distinct community. Twenty-four buildings with 208 rooms and 44 pit structures are present (figure 10.10). In the core of the community is a dense cluster of buildings covering 57 hectares (140 acres). Over half of the buildings and two unusually large kiva depressions are in this cluster. The entire community covers about 3 mi² (8 km²). The largest site in this community core is located on a sheer-sided mesa top and includes about 40 rooms (figure 10.11). Ceramics in the Cuervo community suggest dates between A.D. 1200 and 1250 or later.

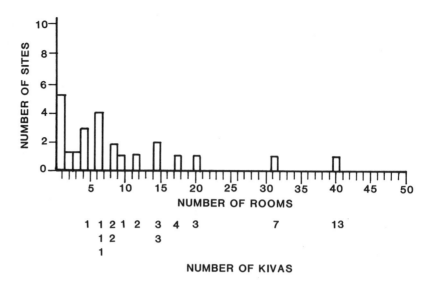

Figure 10.10. Architectural composition of the Cuervo Community, eastern San Juan Basin (from Peckham 1970, 1971, 1987).

Ojito Community

The Ojito Community (figure 10.1) was also documented by Peckham (1971, 1987), and includes 13 buildings with a total of 85 rooms and 9 pit structures (figure 10.12). Over half of the buildings and rooms are concentrated in an 8 hectare (20 acres) area and the entire community occupies about 160 hectares (400 acres). The largest building contained only 15 rooms and no special architectural features were observed. Peckham (personal communication 1989) notes that even though local varieties of McElmo Black-on-white were the dominant decorated ceramic types, Socorro Black-on-white was common, suggesting that the community may date primarily between A.D. 1130 and 1200.

Coot Ridge Community

Peckham's reconnaissance survey (1971, 1987) also located the Coot Ridge community along the middle Rio Puerco (figure 10.1). Twenty-seven buildings with 222 rooms and 33 pit structures were recorded (figure 10.13). The core of this community, an architectural cluster covering 16 hectares (40 acres), contains over half of the buildings, rooms, and pit structures. The second largest building in the community

(figure 10.14B) is in this cluster, but the largest building, which included 40 rooms and one or two informal plazas (figure 10.14A), is somewhat anomalous in that it is located two miles west of the core cluster. Excluding this outlying building, the overall community occupies about 2 mi² (5 km²). As with the Ojito Community, the limited ceramics data seem to indicate an occupation between A.D. 1130 and 1200.

Torreon Community

The largest site in the Torreon Community was originally located by Paul Logsdon, who returned with Stuart Peckham, Rosemary Talley, and Marsha Jackson to record the site. I have subsequently made a brief reconnaissance of the core area of this community (figure 10.2). The area surrounding this concentration of sites has never been surveyed and it is very possible that the overall community is larger than is indicated by present information.

The recorded portion of the Torreon community includes 18 buildings with 175 rooms and five pit structures (figure 10.15), all located within a 65 hectare (160 acre) area. All five pit structures are within the largest building, Logsdon #1, that includes about 50 rooms and a plaza enclosed by a low wall. On a bench below

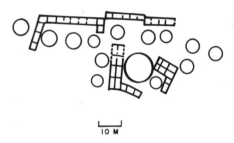

Figure 10.11. LA 10505 (9B6 in figure 10.2 and in appendix), a large settlement in the Cuervo Community, eastern San Juan Basin (adapted from Peckham 1970).

the large site is a large depression and alcove room indicating a probable great kiva.

The dominance of Chaco-McElmo Black-on-white ceramics at the large building and great kiva suggests that both structures were used in the late twelfth century. This impression is reinforced by certain Chacoan attributes of the large building, such as blocked-in kivas and an enclosed plaza. On the other hand, the presence of Heshotauthla Black-on-red indicates that at least some use of the large building persisted until the Pueblo III-Pueblo IV transition. It should also be noted that the tabulated sample (table 10.1) is small and that ceramics found with the great kiva might not be typical of the community as a whole.

Jones Canyon-Headcut Reservoir

Reconnaissance by Winkler and Davis (1961) located a large Pueblo III site in this area. Subsequent work by Mackey and Holbrook (1978) documented the general extent of this community (figure 10.2) and included the excavation of a 10-room pueblo. A large-scale Bureau of Land Management sample survey provided further information (Wase 1982).

Mackey and Holbrook (1978) estimate there are 50 buildings in this community in a 5 mi² (13 km²) area, but it is likely that the community contains more architectural units. No data on numbers of rooms or pit structures are available. Two smaller, plaza-oriented pueblos on steep-sided mesa top locations have been reported (Miller Pueblo and the Headcut Reservoir site) and a third large pueblo is located at Jones Canyon in the northern portion of the community (see the appendix).

Mackey and Holbrook suggest that a few late Pueblo II sites occur in this area, but present evidence implies that the major occupation was during Pueblo III times. Ceramic data from the single excavated site (LA 15927) indicate an occupation between A.D. 1150 and 1230 or so. Peter McKenna and Tom Windes (personal communication 1990) report a similar assemblage from the Jones Canyon site in the northern portion of the community. The presence of St. Johns Polychrome on other sites in this cluster suggest that portions of the community were occupied until late in the thirteenth century.

Gallina tradition sites, recognizable because of their distinctive architecture and ceramics, occur along the Rio Puerco only a few miles west of the Headcut Reservoir Community. The Gallina occupation is supposed to date to approximately the same time as the Headcut Reservoir occupation, but very little is known of the relationship and degree of interaction between the Gallina tradition and the San Juan Anasazi.

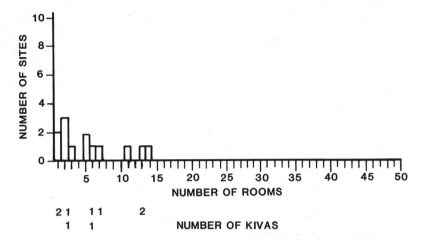

Figure 10.12.   Architectural composition of the Ojito Community, eastern San Juan Basin (from Peckham 1970, 1987).

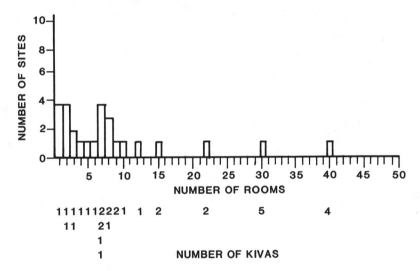

Figure 10.13.   Architectural composition of the Coot Ridge Community, eastern San Juan Basin (from Peckham 1970, 1971, 1987).

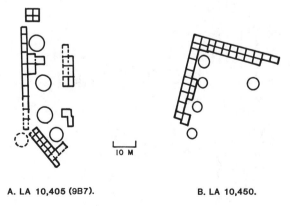

Figure 10.14.   Two sites in the Coot Ridge Community, LA 10,405 (9B7 in figure 10.2 and in appendix) and LA 10,450, eastern San Juan Basin (adapted from Peckham 1970).

Mesa Portales

Ojo Jarido, a large Pueblo III site near Cuba, has been described by Winkler and Davis (1961). Subsequent survey (Sliwinski 1978; Wase 1982) and reconnaissance (Mackey and Holbrook 1978) indicate the presence of a larger, surrounding community although no details about numbers of rooms and pit structures are available. Ojo Jarido includes about 50 rooms and is built on an isolated mesa top. Based on a small ceramic sample (see table 10.1), the occupation at the sites probably spans the interval between A.D. 1200 and 1300. A few late Pueblo II sites may be present in the area, and the survey by Sliwinski (1978) hints that Gallina tradition sites may be intermingled with the San Juan Anasazi sites in the Mesa Portales area.

Chacra Mesa

The largest concentration of Mesa Verde tradition Pueblo III sites within the eastern San Juan Basin is located on Chacra Mesa between Mesa Cortada and Chaco Canyon. Numerous surveys (Donaldson

1983; Hayes 1981; Jacobson and Roney 1985; Marshall and Sofaer 1986; Marshall et al. 1979; Swift 1983; Vivian 1960; Vivian and Mathews 1965; Wait and Nelson 1983) and a handful of site specific investigations (Bradley 1971; Mathien 1991; Phibbs 1974) have contributed to our knowledge of this area. Despite the large amount of survey, promising areas west of Pueblo Pintado and at the eastern end of Chacra Mesa are still virtually unknown. It is likely that the full extent of the Pueblo III occupation of Chacra Mesa has not yet been established. This discussion of Chacra Mesa draws primarily upon investigations at its eastern end, near Reservoir Ruin. In this area we have attempted to collect systematic information about each architectural site (Jacobson and Roney 1985), but it is not known if this area is representative of Chacra Mesa as a whole.

One of the most striking patterns

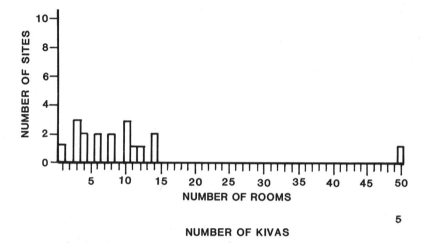

Figure 10.15.   Architectural composition of the Torreon Community, eastern San Juan Basin (from Roney, personal notes).

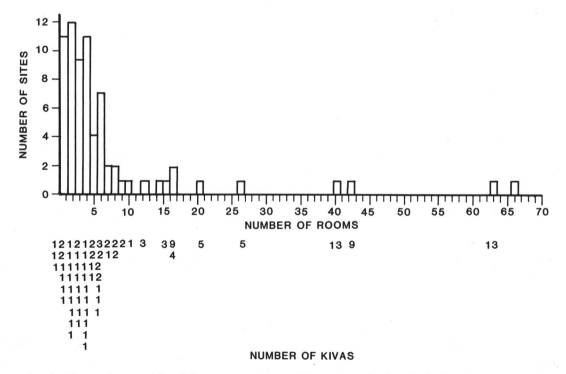

Figure 10.16.   Architectural composition of sites on eastern Chacra Mesa, eastern San Juan Basin (from Jacobson and Roney 1985).

throughout the 67 sites recorded in the Reservoir Ruin vicinity (figure 10.16) is the prevalence of pit structures. Most masonry and jacal structures, including some with only one room, are associated with one or more pit structures. This observation leaves little doubt that these subterranean features were being used as dwellings, rather than for the specialized social and religious purposes usually associated with kivas. Several typical residential units are illustrated in figure 10.17G.

A number of sites on Chacra Mesa exhibit characteristics of public architecture, including formal plazas (figure 10.17B–D, ladder-type construction (figure 10.17E) and "big holes" (figures 10.17 B and C). Big holes are large, circular depressions that resemble unexcavated great kivas, but lack masonry (Fowler, Stein, and Anyon 1987). They have been variously interpreted as reservoirs, barrow pits, and dance plazas. The number of potential public structures on Chacra Mesa indicates that this locality may have been occupied by more than one community.

Several Chacra Mesa sites also have prehistoric roads that are indistinguishable from those built in Chaco Canyon during its heyday. The Chacra Mesa roads are clearly associated with Pueblo III buildings and occur in an area that was unoccupied during the Pueblo II period. One of the roads articulates with Reservoir Ruin, a large site with multiple plazas and a "big hole" (figure 10.17B). This road is marked by a formal pecked groove where it crosses slick rock, similar to those found on Chaco-era roads (Nials, Stein, and Roney 1987:192). Another road leads to a 25-room site that contains a formal plaza (figure 10.17C). Two other roads lead to nondescript residential buildings, one of which seems to have been constructed entirely of jacal (Jacobson and Roney 1985).

A large sample of ceramics from 45 eastern Chacra Mesa sites shows a predominance of McElmo Black-on-white with St. Johns Polychrome the dominant identifiable red ware (table 10.1). These and other temporally sensitive decorated

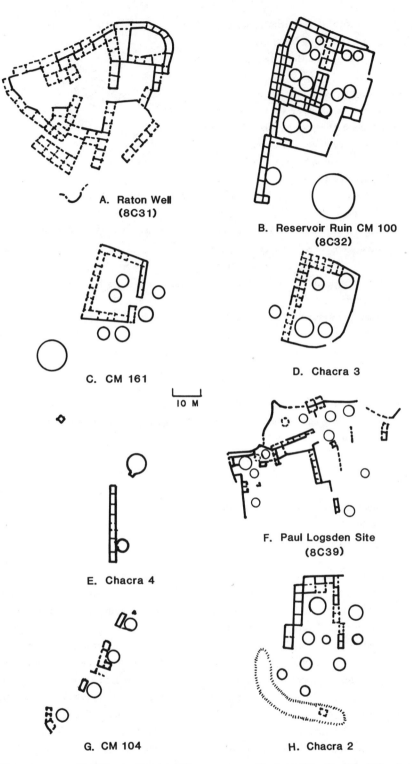

A. Raton Well
(8C31)

B. Reservoir Ruin CM 100
(8C32)

C. CM 161

D. Chacra 3

10 M

E. Chacra 4

F. Paul Logsden Site
(8C39)

G. CM 104

H. Chacra 2

Figure 10.17.   Site plans of major sites on eastern Chacra Mesa. Site identification numbers in parentheses correspond with those in figure 10.2 and appendix (adapted from Jacobson and Roney 1985 [C–H]; Lester et al. 1978 [B]; and Stein and Roney, personal notes [A]).

types indicate that the primary occupation on eastern Chacra Mesa was between
A.D. 1200 and 1300, although some use of
the eastern Chacra Mesa area in the late
twelfth century is also indicated. There is
no evidence of an early twelfth-century
occupation in the eastern Chacra Mesa
area, and no ceramics indicating a post-
A.D. 1300 occupation have been found.

Although the latest types, such as St.
Johns Polychrome and Mesa Verde Black-
on-white, do occur on the larger sites
described here, they also occur in smaller
sites and are not notably prevalent on the
larger sites. This implies that the larger
sites were among the last to be occupied,
but I have seen no ceramic evidence indicating that they were established later than
the majority of the recorded sites. It seems
likely that the large sites are simply a conspicuous element of an overall community
pattern prevalent during the thirteenth
century, rather than representing a wholesale shift into aggregated pueblos late in
the Chacra Mesa occupational sequence.

Chaco Canyon

Little specific architectural information is
available for the Pueblo III occupation in
Chaco Canyon, although McKenna (1991:
131) notes U-shaped pueblos with enclosed plaza kivas and/or blocked-in kivas,
reoccupation of earlier sites without substantial renovation, and an increased use of
talus and cliff edge locations. Hayes (1981:
32) reports 192 structural sites from this
period, a marked decrease from the 350
structural sites of the preceding period.

Windes (1987:383–406) has recently
completed a more detailed reconstruction of population trends for this area
based on resampling of the sites reported
by Hayes. Using total numbers of small
sites occupied during various ceramically
defined intervals, Windes concludes that
Chaco Canyon populations peaked between A.D. 1100 and 1150. He estimates
that 137 sites were occupied at that time,
excluding the great houses. All great house

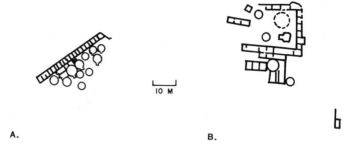

Figure 10.18. Site plans of (A) Mesa Pueblo (8C34 in figure 10.2 and in appendix; adapted from Coleman 1988) and (B) Mesa Tierra (8C20 in figure 10.2 and in appendix; adapted from Marshall et al. 1979).

construction and maintenance ended by
1140, and Windes believes that the 1150
to 1200 interval was one of abandonment
or near abandonment. After A.D. 1200
there was a flurry of new occupation that
Windes believes peaked between A.D. 1220
and 1240.

McKenna (1991) acknowledges that
populations were reduced after A.D. 1150
and that the nature of the Chaco Canyon
occupation changed markedly as new regional centers on the San Juan River
supplanted those of the old Chacoan system. He does, however, stress that there
was continuity between the pre-A.D. 1150
occupation and the post-A.D. 1200 occupation (also see Toll et al. 1980). In his
view the perception of abandonment or
near abandonment between A.D. 1150 and
1200 may be the result of a rapid change
in ceramic assemblages, making the ceramic signature of this interval difficult to
recognize. It is important to note that no
well dated ceramic assemblages from this
period have yet been reported.

Ceramic data from 29SJ633, a recently
excavated Pueblo III site in Chaco Canyon
(McKenna 1991), indicate that Pueblo III
occupations are often contaminated by
the large amounts of material deposited
during the height of occupation in the
canyon. At 29SJ633, only 20 percent of
the decorated assemblage consisted of
either McElmo or Mesa Verde Black-on-
white ceramics, with the latter dominant
(table 10.1).

Other Mesa Verde
Tradition Sites

To the south of Chacra Mesa and Chaco
Canyon are a handful of sites that date
to Pueblo III times but are not associated
with documented communities. These include Mesa Tierra, Kin Nazhin, Mesa
Pueblo, and a reoccupation of the late
Pueblo II Chacoan outlier, El Rito. All
of these sites are relatively large and are
situated in settings that can be considered defensive. These sites all resemble
the preeminent sites in other eastern San
Juan Basin Pueblo III communities.

Mesa Pueblo is a 25-room ladder-type
building (figure 10.18A) that has been excavated over a period of years by R. O.
Coleman (1988). Archaeomagnetic dates
of 1260±43 and 1260±22 have been obtained from two excavated hearths. Both
Dr. Coleman and Jack Moleres, the owner
of the surrounding ranch, state that there
are no smaller ruins in the vicinity (personal communications 1986).

Mesa Tierra (figure 10.18B) and Kin
Nazhin occupy the tops of sheer-sided
mesas. An insufficient amount of survey
has been conducted around either site to
indicate whether or not associated communities exist (Marshall et al. 1979:77–
80).

The El Rito site is a Chacoan outlier with a short and probably minor
thirteenth-century reoccupation (Winkler
and Davis 1961; Powers et al. 1983:216–

25). The Pueblo III occupation was established within a massive, multistory Chacoan building situated on a steep-sided knoll. The building is L-shaped and includes up to 55 rooms, three kivas, and one great kiva. Intensive inventory in the vicinity of El Rito has failed to discover an associated community of smaller Pueblo III sites (Allan et al. 1976; Ambler 1976).

Eastern San Juan Basin Population Trends

Estimating population trends on the basis of sketchy and incomplete data is risky, but initial impressions suggest that the room count curves developed for the Guadalupe and Salado communities (figure 10.4) may hold for the eastern San Juan Basin as a whole. Few sites or communities dating to the mid-1100s have been recognized. A majority of the Pueblo III sites seem to date between A.D. 1200 and 1275 or so. After A.D. 1275 populations drop, followed by the abandonment of the region by A.D. 1300 or 1325.

The possibility of a mid-twelfth-century abandonment or occupational hiatus in this area is an important issue. There are at least two potential explanations of this perceived hiatus. First, there may have been a severe reduction of population in this entire region, brought about either by outmigration or by an excess of deaths over births. Adjacent regions such as the northern San Juan Basin seem to have suffered a similar hiatus, casting doubt on outmigration as a mechanism. Actual reduction of populations is a possibility, however, and the occurrence of clearly defensive sites suggests the intense competition that might have accompanied a period of stress.

Second, McKenna (1991) has suggested that the perceived drop in population in the mid-twelfth century may be due to our inability to recognize the ceramic assemblages that characterize this period. The paucity of chronometric dates and securely dated ceramic assemblages along with the possibility of rapid ceramic change may have archaeologists looking for regional typological consistency that simply did not exist. If so, our perceptions of an occupational hiatus could be exaggerated.

Eastern San Juan Basin Summary

During the late Pueblo II period, Anasazi settlements were widespread in the eastern San Juan Basin. To the north of Chaco Canyon, residential communities are known at Pierre's Ruin, Bis sa'ani, and the Escavada Group. To the south, numerous Chacoan outliers on the basin floor were surrounded by residential communities (e.g., Kin Bineola, Kin Klizhin, Upper Kin Klizhin, Greenlee, Bee Burrow, Indian Creek). Other Chacoan outliers and their associated communities were distributed along the northern base of the Dutton Plateau and in the Red Mesa Valley. There were at least two major communities in the middle Rio Puerco (Guadalupe and Salado), and large-scale construction was occurring in Chaco Canyon (see Marshall et al. 1979; Powers, Gillespie, and Lekson 1983; Lekson 1984).

Several different lines of evidence imply that virtually all of these local communities participated in a system of regional organization centered on Chaco Canyon. Throughout this area there was a remarkable uniformity in decorated ceramics, in particular, Gallup and Escavada Black-on-white. Public architecture within nearly all of these communities conformed to a regional style and can be easily distinguished from residential architecture. Bonito-style architecture, as this complex of building construction and layout traits is known, reached its apogee in the massive constructions of central Chaco Canyon. At least some of the local community centers were linked directly to Chaco Canyon by prehistoric roads.

Dendroclimatic reconstructions indicate that a major drought occurred between A.D. 1130 and 1180. This period of below normal precipitation is most evident in the index of summer precipitation, but is also apparent in the record of springtime precipitation (Powers, Gillespie, and Lekson 1983:282). Although there are indications that important changes in the Chacoan regional system began before the onset of this drought, it is not simply coincidence that system collapse occurred during this interval of climatic stress.

Dramatic changes in settlement distribution coincided with the drought and the demise (or radical reorientation) of the system of regional integration. The Red Mesa Valley, Dutton Plateau, and the entire floor of the San Juan Basin seem to have been abandoned during the latter half of the twelfth century. Of all the Pueblo II communities listed previously, only three continued to be occupied into Pueblo III times, namely Chaco Canyon and the Guadalupe and Salado Communities. Even in those areas populations were greatly reduced and an interval of near total abandonment may have occurred around A.D. 1150. New settlements were established at Torreon and Jones Canyon. Use of Chacra Mesa began between A.D. 1150 and 1200, and it is possible that some of the other middle Rio Puerco communities such as Ojito and Coot Ridge were also occupied at this time.

This change in settlement distribution may have resulted from changes in agricultural strategy made in response to reduced summer precipitation. Lowland areas (below 7,000 ft, 2,121 m) that required a reliance upon dry-land farming were abandoned. New Pueblo III settlements were established in upland settings such as Chacra Mesa, Mesa Portales, and the Jones Canyon-Headcut Reservoir area, where orographic effects enhance summer thunderstorm activity. Lowland settings with either continuing occupation or initial settlement during the Pueblo III period are often characterized by extensive areas of slickrock and other landforms that concentrate rainfall and meltwater, allowing water conservation and diversion. This is true for Chaco Canyon, Torreon, Jones Canyon, and Prieta Vista and is also likely at the Guadalupe, Salado, Cañada de las Milpas, Cuervo, and Ojito Communities.

Despite the disintegration of the Chacoan system of regional organization, local community organization seems to have remained intact and may have assumed increasing importance during the Pueblo III period. These communities generally consist of a community core with dense settlement and an unusually large (preeminent) site, surrounded by an area of more diffuse settlement. Where fairly complete survey coverage is available, communities average about 800 hectares (2,000 acres) in total area while the smaller community core areas contain half or more of the total structures and cover an average of about 40 hectares (100 acres). In terms of room counts, the communities range from 85 to 914 rooms, with an average of about 325 rooms.

Over 90 percent of the individual buildings in the eastern San Juan Basin contain 20 rooms or less, with over 80 percent containing 12 or fewer rooms. Certainly some of these small sites may be field houses or other special purpose buildings. However, the presence of pit houses associated with surface structures of only two rooms indicates that the size of the room blocks is not always a good criterion to distinguish residential sites. Overall the small size of these sites suggests that the basic residential groups were usually individual families.

Preeminent sites in the eastern San Juan Basin range in size from 38 to 66 rooms. Although these were often among the last sites to be abandoned in their communities, there is no strong indication that their initial construction was later than other sites in the same community. Instead they appear to represent the upper size range within their contemporaneous community. Although these preeminent sites may have served as community centers much like the Pueblo II great houses, some of these large Pueblo III sites appear to have

been more residential in function than the great houses. The later sites resemble several unit pueblos and their associated kivas grouped together, sometimes defining informal plazas. Often the preeminent sites exhibit other unique characteristics such as formal interior plazas, "big holes," ladder-type construction, and roads.

Many of the preeminent sites are built on highly defensive mesa tops, and some such as the Paul Logsdon site (figure 10.17F) and El Castillejo on Chacra Mesa are protected by massive defensive walls (see appendix). This suggests conflict, either with other Mesa Verde tradition communities or with groups beyond their own regional interaction sphere, such as those of the Tularosa or Gallina traditions.

The entire eastern San Juan Basin was abandoned by about A.D. 1300 or so. Late polychrome ceramics such as Springerville and Pinedale Polychromes are seldom found in this area and glaze-painted ceramics from either the Zuni or Rio Grande series are also extremely rare or entirely absent. Evidence from the Guadalupe and Salado Communities suggests that abandonment of the area was somewhat gradual, in that the latest occupations that can be recognized ceramically indicate reduced populations.

Acoma-Laguna Area

The second region considered in this chapter is the Acoma-Laguna area (figure 10.3), which extends from Mount Taylor on the north to the Rio Salado in the south, and from the Rio Grande on the east to the Chain of Craters on the west. Information about the Pueblo III occupation in this region is limited and although population levels equaled or exceeded those in the eastern San Juan Basin, fewer individual communities have been investigated. For this reason the discussion of the Acoma-Laguna area is structured according to three subdivisions, namely Cebolleta Mesa, the lower Rio Puerco, and the middle Rio San Jose. Of these, the lower Rio Puerco and the middle Rio San

Jose are poorly documented, while much more research has been conducted in the Cebolleta Mesa subdivision.

Lower Rio Puerco

The Lower Rio Puerco subdivision extends from the vicinity of Interstate 40 southward to the confluence of the Rio Puerco and the Rio Grande. It is bounded on the east by the Rio Grande and on the west by a series of mesas east of Acoma. Major physiographic features include the lower Rio San Jose and Rio Puerco drainages, the Sierra Lucero, Mesa Del Oro, Blue Water Creek, and Gallegos Creek.

Archaeological remains in the lower Rio Puerco are poorly known, but present evidence suggests little sedentary use of the area during the Pueblo III period. Bandelier (1892:309–11) noted ruins in the vicinity of Cerros Mojinos, and later pipeline salvage archaeological investigations revealed a probable Pueblo III community in this area (Fenenga and Cummings 1956a). Hibben (1966) also made passing reference to a pueblo north of Pottery Mound that could be Pueblo III in age. However, subsequent surveys have generally failed to find additional evidence of sedentary Pueblo III communities (Wimberly and Eidenbach 1980; Eidenbach 1982; Lekson and Wandsnider 1983; Elyea 1990). Although this area is generally dry and barren and does not seem likely to have supported much Pueblo III occupation, we should realize that survey coverage is poor and the area could hold surprises.

Cerros Mojinos Community

At present the Cerros Mojinos Community is the only known Pueblo III community in the lower Rio Puerco subdivision (figure 10.3). Sites noted by Bandelier (1892) are probably part of this community. Later data recovery during a pipeline clearance excavated two architectural sites and reported a "dozen-odd similar sites" within a radius of one and a half miles of the excavations (Fenenga 1956; Fenenga and Cummings 1956b). These sites are presumed to represent a contemporaneous community.

The excavated sites include masonry, adobe, and jacal structures containing one to nine rooms as well as a single pit structure, but the extent and character of the remainder of this community are not known. Ceramics from the two sites show a preponderance of Socorro Black-on-white pottery associated with a utility assemblage consisting almost entirely of brown wares (table 10.1).

At least two large Pueblo IV sites are known in the lower Rio Puerco. One of these, Pottery Mound, apparently does not have a Pueblo III period occupation. The other, Hummingbird Pueblo, is poorly documented and it is not known if earlier Pueblo III materials are present at this site. At this point virtually nothing is known about the Pueblo III-Pueblo IV transition in this area.

Middle Rio San Jose

The second subdivision of the Acoma-Laguna area is the middle Rio San Jose (figure 10.3). This subdivision ranges from Mount Taylor in the north to Cebolleta Peak in the south, and from the western rim of Cebolleta Mesa on the west to the vicinity of Mesita on the east. It includes much of the present day Acoma and Laguna Indian Reservations.

This area is known primarily from reconnaissance surveys (Bandelier 1892; Lange and Riley 1966:278–308; Ellis 1974; Winkler and Davis 1961), although a few more intensive surveys have been made in limited areas (Kayser 1971; Broster and Harrill 1982; Broster and Ireland 1982). Excavation data are available from Ruppé's (1953) work at Acoma and from pipeline salvage excavations in the McCarty's community (Olson and Wasley 1956). The middle Rio San Jose was clearly a very important area of Pueblo III occupation, but existing information is limited and major unreported sites and commu-

nities may well exist there. The area is of special interest because it includes a mixture of Mesa Verde, Tularosa, and Socorro tradition sites.

At least four probable Mesa Verde tradition sites are known in the middle Rio San Jose area, including two large defensive sites, Rabbit Butte and Flour Butte, both on the Laguna Reservation (Winkler and Davis 1961). Both sites consist of groupings of small (10- to 15-room) masonry structures arranged in quadrangles atop small, sheer-sided mesas. Winkler and Davis note evidence of occupation during the Pueblo II, III and IV periods. Two additional sites in defensive positions include one on Bug Mesa (L. Rhodes, personal communication 1990) and Shumatzutstya. The latter site has evidence of a Pueblo III occupation as well as Pueblo IV and historic components (anonymous notes, Archeological Records Management System, Museum of New Mexico).

Three large Tularosa tradition sites are known in the middle Rio San Jose subdivision. Mesita Redonda (Bandelier 1892: 318–19) is a major complex that includes over 200 rooms distributed among seven large buildings concentrated in an area only 250 meters in diameter. The largest building is estimated to be 50 or 60 rooms in size. A great kiva, presumably contemporaneous with this occupation, is also present.

Cubero Ruin (Bandelier 1892:314–15) is another major building with a significant Tularosa tradition Pueblo III component. Ceramic and architectural evidence as well as the presence of a sizable late Pueblo II community indicate the site initially might have been a Bonito-style great house. The occurrence of Pueblo III and Pueblo IV ceramics indicates continued use or reoccupation of the site. The later component includes one very large, massive masonry ruin and several smaller adobe units that define an informal plaza. An estimated 120 ground floor rooms are present and portions of the large masonry ruin may have included a second story. Very brief reconnaissance in the immedi-

ate area revealed a number of Pueblo II residential units, but no nearby Pueblo III remains.

A Socorro tradition community has been identified near the Rio San Jose opposite the present day settlement of McCartys. Olson and Wasley (1956:292–323) reported the excavation of two sites in this community, a 10-room masonry pueblo (LA 2639) and a 15-room masonry pueblo (LA 2640). Casual reconnaissance shows a number of other masonry pueblos clustered in this area, at least one of which (LA 98,665) also exhibits a Pueblo III ceramic assemblage dominated by Socorro Black-on-white (table 10.1). Highway salvage excavations a short distance to the east revealed several other sites with late Pueblo II ceramic assemblages dominated by Socorro Black-on-white (Peckham 1962).

Dittert and Ruppé defined a Pueblo III component at Acoma Pueblo. Its size and configuration are not known, although at least 40 rooms are believed to be present. Interestingly, this is the only Pueblo III assemblage reported here that shows a significant mixture of Mesa Verde and Tularosa tradition ceramics.

It is clear that the middle Rio San Jose was an important area of Pueblo III occupation and that sites contain a variety of ceramics from the Mesa Verde, Tularosa, and Socorro traditions. Analogy with findings from the eastern San Juan Basin and the Cebolleta Mesa area suggest that the Pueblo III sites identified in the middle Rio San Jose area might be preeminent sites surrounded by larger dispersed communities. This would indicate that there was a large regional population, but clearly more information is needed to better understand this area.

Many of the Pueblo III sites presently recorded in the middle Rio San Jose area show evidence of Pueblo IV occupation. This indicates that the regional abandonments that are so pronounced across the eastern San Juan Basin and most of the Acoma-Laguna area around A.D. 1300 did not occur in the Middle Rio San Jose.

Cebolleta Mesa

The Cebolleta Mesa subdivision (figure 10.3) includes the western flanks of Cebolleta Mesa, the El Malpais lava flow, the North Plains area, the Chain of Craters, and the eastern flanks of the Zuni Mountains. Of the three subdivisions in the Acoma-Laguna area, the Cebolleta Mesa subdivision is by far the best known archaeologically. Extensive research was initiated in the late 1940s on the flanks of Cebolleta Mesa by Alfred Dittert (1949, 1959) and Reynold Ruppé (1953). Subsequent reconnaissance surveys (Wiseman 1974), systematic sampling (Elyea 1990; Doleman 1989) and three intensive community studies (Wozniak and Marshall 1991; Marshall 1993; Elyea, Hogan, and Wilson 1994) have documented the basic structure of Pueblo III settlement in this subdivision, although much work remains to be done.

Settlement Patterns and Architecture. Puebloan habitation sites are largely restricted to a narrow band along the western slopes of Cebolleta Mesa. The high density of occupation within this band (indicated in figure 10.3) and little use of lands outside this band (USDI, BLM 1990:map 1.9) may be due in part to climatic factors. LeBlanc (1989: 352–54) has argued that during Pueblo III times reduced rainfall, with consequent reductions in productive farmland, forced populations in the Cibola Province as a whole to abandon middle elevations, concentrating along major drainages at lower elevations where irrigation was practical, or at higher elevations (7,000–7,400 ft, 2,121–2,242 m), where rainfall was more abundant. The Cebolleta Mesa data are consistent with this argument, because the narrow band of occupation is a particularly well watered elevational zone between 6,900 and 7,600 ft (2,103–2,317 m).

Within this zone Pueblo I and Pueblo II remains are also widely distributed. On the other hand, Pueblo III habitations seem to be grouped into tight clusters that resemble the community core areas in the

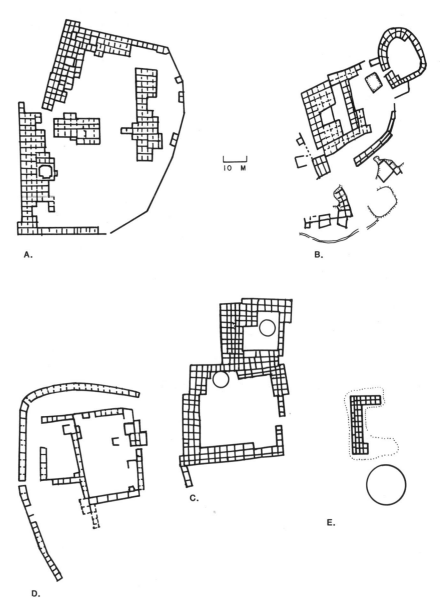

Figure 10.19. Major sites in the Cebolleta Mesa area: A. Calabash Ruin (9E1) (adapted from Ruppé 1953); B. Newton (9E8) (adapted from Stein and Roney, personal notes 1989); C. Rattail Ruin (9E7) (adapted from Roney, personal notes 1991); D. Kowina Ruin (9E2) (adapted from Roney, personal notes, 1994); E. L.V. 4.27-A site (9E5) (adapted from Roney, personal notes 1994; and Dittert 1949).

eastern San Juan Basin and the Scribe S phase settlement pattern described for the El Morro Valley (Watson, LeBlanc, and Redman 1980). Community cores are presumably surrounded by more diffuse distributions of smaller sites. At least five dense concentrations of Pueblo III sites have been documented in the Cebolleta Mesa subdivision: Las Ventanas, Cebollita Canyon (Los Pilares), Cebolla Canyon,

Armijo Canyon (Los Veteados), and Tank Canyon (figure 10.3). Most of the large buildings and dense Pueblo III site concentrations have probably been located by now, although none of the communities has been fully documented.

In their physical layout these community cores comprise a continuum, ranging from loose groupings of sites to fully aggregated pueblos. The best documented

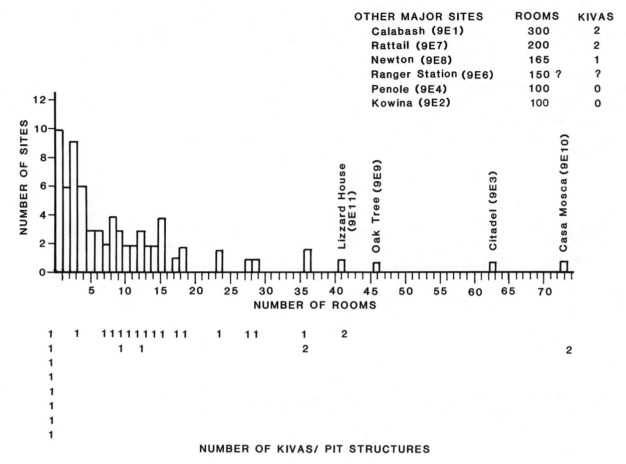

OTHER MAJOR SITES	ROOMS	KIVAS
Calabash (9E1)	300	2
Rattail (9E7)	200	2
Newton (9E8)	165	1
Ranger Station (9E6)	150 ?	?
Penole (9E4)	100	0
Kowina (9E2)	100	0

Figure 10.20. Architectural composition of the Cebolleta Mesa subdivision communities (from Doleman 1989 and Wozniak and Marshall 1991).

community is Cebolla Canyon (Wozniak and Marshall 1991), which consists of 10 to 13 contemporaneous buildings including 165 to 230 rooms. Individual sites are separated by open spaces of 50 to 600 meters none of which appear to have served as plazas areas. In addition to Cebolla Canyon, the Armijo Canyon and Tank Canyon clusters also take the form of loose groupings of individual sites (see Elyea, Hogan, and Wilson 1994).

In other community cores the individual buildings are much closer to one another, with major buildings separated by distances of only 10 to 30 meters. Some of the major buildings are often arranged to define informal plazas, including the Ranger Station site in the Las Ventanas Community and La Mesita Redonda in the middle Rio San Jose subdivision. These aggregations have been

treated as single sites in the Master Database. Finally, in some cases much of the community may have been concentrated into a single large building. Examples of this phenomenon include Calabash Ruin, Newton, and Rattail Ruin (figures 10.19A, B, and C respectively).

The size distribution of large sites in the Cebolleta Mesa area clearly indicates that smaller buildings are very common during the Pueblo III occupation (figure 10.20). There may have been a general trend toward larger residential sites (figures 10.19 and 10.21) in this area through the Pueblo III period, but small sites appear to have been occupied until very late in the Pueblo III sequence.

The final sedentary occupation of the Cebolleta Mesa subdivision is represented at Calabash Ruin (figure 10.19A) and perhaps at the Penole site (9E4). During this

interval most of the Cebolleta Mesa subdivision apparently had been abandoned and almost all of the population was concentrated into one or two large sites. Both of these sites occupy defensive settings and have free-standing walls that enclose portions of the pueblo, a characteristic that can also be interpreted as defensive.

Ceramics. For the most part ceramic assemblages from the Cebolleta Mesa area are attributed to the Tularosa Ceramic tradition (table 10.1). These tabulations contrast sharply with those from contemporaneous eastern San Juan Basin sites in the virtual absence of carbon-painted white wares. Instead, Tularosa Black-on-white pottery comprises between 10 and 30 percent of the decorated assemblage, and less than 1 percent (47 of 7,237) are carbon-painted sherds. In addition to Tularosa Black-on-white and Socorro Black-on-white ceramics, other mineral painted black-on-white wares in these assemblages are dominated by Cebolleta Black-on-white with traces of Red Mesa Black-on-white, Gallup Black-on-white, and Escavada Black-on-white.

Pueblo III period red wares, dominated by St. Johns Polychrome and St. Johns Black-on-red, are common. Pinedale, Wingate, and Fourmile Polychromes are all present, and later types are represented by only a few sherds each, with Kwakina Polychrome completely absent in the Cebolleta Mesa assemblages.

Population Trends. There was little use of the Cebolleta Mesa area during Basketmaker III and early Pueblo I times, but by Pueblo II times populations were growing rapidly. Doleman's (1989) survey suggests a strong peak in occupational intensity during late Pueblo II times (USDI, BLM 1990:figure 13.1). Researchers doing this survey may well have underestimated the Pueblo III occupation because of the extensive inventory strategy used. Pueblo II sites are widely distributed and were frequently encountered in the broad-scale sampling approach required by the project objectives, but the strategy generally missed the highly clustered Pueblo III communities.

Wozniak and Marshall (1991) provide a detailed assessment of one Pueblo III community core, Cebolla Canyon. During the late Pueblo I and early Pueblo II periods this core area contained a series of small, one-to-four-room jacal buildings. After a hiatus in middle Pueblo II times (inferred primarily on architectural evidence), a late Pueblo II community center was established at this location. The community center included a great kiva and Bonito-style building. Wozniak and Marshall believe that there was another brief period of abandonment around A.D. 1150, followed by establishment of the Pueblo III community. This community seems to have remained relatively constant in size between A.D. 1175 and 1325. New buildings

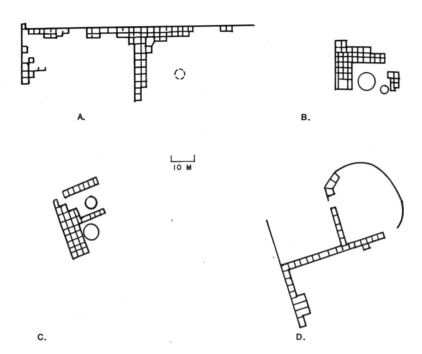

Figure 10.21. Major Pueblo III period sites in the Cebolla Canyon community, Acoma/Laguna region: A. Citadel (9E3); B. Casa Mosca (9E10); C. Lizzard House (9E11); D. Oak Tree (9E9). Site identification numbers correspond with those in the appendix (after Wozniak and Marshall 1991).

were built and others were abandoned, but the overall room count for the core area is estimated at about 200 rooms. Prior to the adoption of glaze-painted ceramics in the fourteenth century the community was abandoned.

Summary. During early Pueblo II times typical Red Mesa Black-on-white was the dominant decorated ceramic type in the Cebolleta Mesa area, suggesting that this area participated in the broad cultural pattern that gave rise to the Chaco regional system. By the mid-eleventh century, however, decorated ceramics in this area began to diverge from those of the Red Mesa Valley and the San Juan Basin. Good examples of Gallup and Escavada Black-on-white pottery are not uncommon in the Cebolleta Mesa area, but local decorated ceramics can be distinguished from these on the basis of paste, slip, and probably decorative style. Despite these beginnings of regional divergence, late Pueblo II community centers still exhibit Bonito-style architecture, linking the Ce-

bolleta Mesa area to Chacoan developments in the greater San Juan Basin.

The effects of the Chacoan system failure during the mid-twelfth century do not appear to have been severe in the Cebolleta Mesa area. There is strong continuity in both ceramics and architecture, and in the Cebolleta Mesa subdivision, there was no major relocation of populations to different environmental settings at this time. The same basic areas were occupied in both Pueblo II and Pueblo III times, although Pueblo III communities may have been more tightly clustered. There are changes in public architecture, but the architecture of residential sites changed very little. Taking all of these factors into account, much less disruption is apparent in this area than in the eastern San Juan Basin.

On the basis of existing information it is not possible to infer major population changes during the Pueblo III period occupation of the Cebolleta Mesa subdivision. Major change occurred between A.D. 1300 and 1325 when large areas were abandoned and the remaining population was concentrated into one or two large, defensive sites. This transition parallels settlement changes in the Zuni area to the west (Kintigh 1985 and chapter 9). Accompanied by the adoption of glaze-painted ceramics, large-scale aggregation and settlement relocations ushered in the Pueblo IV period.

Discussion

Integration

One of the most important themes of this volume is social integration. During the twelfth and thirteenth centuries the Puebloan occupants of the San Juan Basin and Acoma-Laguna areas apparently used at least three levels of integration. The most basic was the family level, indicated by the reliance on small "unit pueblos." These generally consist of 1 to 12 surface rooms, often associated with one or two pit structures. The small size of the buildings indicates they were occupied by individual nuclear or extended families. Through most of Anasazi prehistory these were the basic residential units and probably constituted the basic production units as well. Many discussions of Anasazi prehistory have emphasized these small unit pueblos to the exclusion of higher levels of organization.

Where reasonably complete inventory data are available, it is clear that small residential units do not usually occur in isolation. Pueblo III unit pueblos are commonly found in discrete clusters, rather than being mapped onto the landscape in direct relation to key resources such as surface water or arable land. When detailed chronological data are available these clusters appear to be discrete groupings of contemporaneous residences rather than groupings of sequentially occupied buildings. These clusters normally include a core area with at least one unusually large site (30 rooms or more in size) and a relatively dense cluster of smaller residential buildings. Surrounding the core is an asymmetrical area of more diffuse settlement. This spatial pattern is the result of community-level integration, representing a second, more inclusive level of local social organization for Puebloan populations. Communities can be formally defined in archaeological terms as discrete spatial groupings of ceramically contemporaneous residential units.

During Pueblo III times communities were very well delineated and clearly represent an aspect of organization that was important in the Anasazi adaptation. Data from the eastern San Juan Basin indicate that discrete communities may include anywhere from 85 to almost 1,000 rooms contained in clusters of between 10 and 80 individual buildings. From this perspective the transition from more dispersed unit pueblos to large, aggregated pueblos may not have been as dramatic as is often assumed. The Pueblo III period communities were often comparable in scale to the large, fully aggregated pueblos constructed in this region during and after the fourteenth century, and they were less dispersed than we sometimes assume.

Ceramic data (table 10.1) suggest that multiple communities participated in bounded regional systems that comprise the third and highest level of integration discussed in this chapter. Individual sites can usually be attributed unambiguously to one of three ceramic traditions, based upon the predominant decorated ware (see Mera 1935). In the eastern San Juan Basin the decorated ceramic assemblages are almost always dominated by carbon-painted black-on-white wares that are stylistically identified with the Mesa Verde ceramic tradition. In the western part of the Acoma-Laguna area decorated ceramic assemblages are dominated by mineral-painted wares of the Tularosa tradition. When compared to the Mesa Verde tradition, Tularosa tradition assemblages tend to include more red wares, lower proportions of utility wares, and higher proportions of corrugated sherds. These observations suggest that the distinction between the Mesa Verde and Tularosa traditions involves more than a preference for major decorated wares. Stylistic differences in utility wares, differential access (or need for) White Mountain Red Wares, and systematic differences in vessel sizes or classes may also be involved.

These two ceramic traditions show a strong spatial organization. All the eastern San Juan Basin communities participated in the Mesa Verde tradition, while large contiguous areas of the Acoma-Laguna area were characterized by Tularosa tradition ceramics. Assemblages dominated by Mesa Verde tradition ceramics always have only traces of Tularosa tradition wares. Conversely, Tularosa tradition assemblages usually have no contemporaneous carbon-painted ceramics. Even in areas where the two traditions overlap, such as along the middle Rio San Jose, assemblages from individual sites can nearly always be assigned to one or the other of these two traditions. The only exception in the present data set is Acoma Pueblo, which includes decorated ceramics from both traditions.

The third major ceramic tradition, found on the lower Rio Puerco in the eastern part of the Acoma-Laguna area, is dominated by Socorro Black-on-white pottery. Some communities, such as Cerros Mojinos, seem to be comprised of sites that are entirely dominated by Socorro Black-on-white ceramics. The Socorro tradition does not, however, have the strong spatial integrity that characterizes the Mesa Verde and Tularosa traditions. Low frequencies of Socorro Black-on-white pottery occur in assemblages of the other two traditions, and sites or groups of sites dominated by Socorro tradition ceramics sometimes occur as intrusions in Tularosa or Mesa Verde tradition communities.

The spatial separation between the Tularosa and Mesa Verde traditions implies the existence of a social boundary. At minimum we can infer that there was negligible exchange of decorated white wares across this boundary. If ceramic decorations do signal participation in social networks, we can further infer that at least two broad, regional social networks were operative in the eastern San Juan Basin and Acoma-Laguna areas during the twelfth and thirteenth centuries. Other crude indices of ceramic variation, such as proportions of red wares, proportions of utility wares, and proportions of corrugated gray ware sherds also differ between these two traditions, reinforcing the impression of a real and significant cultural boundary.

Public Architecture

Recognition and description of public architecture is another important issue. Expectations were based upon knowledge of late Pueblo II times, when a community pattern associated with Chaco Canyon prevailed over much of the southern Colorado Plateaus. Relatively small residential sites were loosely clustered around community centers that consisted of a Bonito-style building and often a great kiva. Bonito-style buildings are easily distinguished from residential sites by a suite of architectural characteristics including blocked-in kivas, preplanned layout (as opposed to accretionary growth), massive masonry, unusually large rooms, multistory construction, plazas in front of the building enclosed by low walls, association with great kivas, roads, aureoles, and earthworks, and situation of the buildings upon prominent land forms. These buildings contrast strikingly with contemporaneous unit pueblos and it is clear that they served special, presumably nonresidential purposes within their respective communities. Although regional variation is apparent in this architectural style, there is a remarkable degree of similarity between late Pueblo II community centers over much of the Anasazi culture area. This wide-ranging homogeneity in architectural style is one of the main reasons for inferring that local, village-level integration was rooted in a social, ideological, or political system operating on a regional level of organization during the eleventh and early twelfth centuries.

If this pattern continued into Pueblo III

times, we should expect a consistent set of architectural characteristics among the preeminent sites that were identified in the community descriptions. We would also expect these sites to differ recognizably from ordinary residential sites. A few of the large sites conform to these expectations. Torreon has many of the characteristics of earlier Chaco-era great houses. Jones Canyon and the western portion of the Newton site may also have these characteristics, but for most of the Pueblo III preeminent sites these expectations are not met.

Many of the preeminent sites seem to be residential in nature. This does not imply that they were not the focus of special community functions, but does contrast markedly with the Pueblo II community centers. The residential nature of the later preeminent sites is inferred from several characteristics, including smaller room size, normal patterns of trash disposal (e.g., trash-filled rooms), use of simple or compound masonry, unit pueblo style layout, growth by accretion, and a general absence of distinctive features such as great kivas, blocked-in kivas, roads, aureoles, or earthworks.

Some other large sites combine residential features, such as accretionary growth and domestic patterns of trash disposal with special architectural characteristics. For example, Reservoir Ruin (figure 10.17B) and CM161 on Chacra Mesa (figure 10.17C) include contiguous rooms defining rectangular plazas, "big holes," and prehistoric roads. Calabash Ruin has roads, blocked-in kivas, and an enclosing wall (figure 10.19A), and the Newton site has a probable blocked-in kiva combined with ladder-type construction (figure 10.19B). The reoccupied great houses and sites with defensive walls listed in the appendix are also assumed to have served residential functions, based on evidence of accretionary growth and patterns of refuse disposal.

These observations emphasize major differences between community centers during Chacoan and post-Chacoan times. Following the collapse of the Chacoan

system, community centers were not built in conformity to a homogenous regional architectural style. Particular aspects of the Chacoan architecture, such as roads, plazas, and blocked-in kivas were used occasionally, but were not combined in the highly consistent manner that defines the Bonito style. Indeed, special function community centers may not have been built at all in many communities. Instead unusually large residential structures occupy the physical space in the communities that had previously been reserved for Chacoan buildings.

Pueblo II–Pueblo III Regional Organization

A third important theme is the transition between Pueblo II and Pueblo III period regional organization. As used in this chapter, Pueblo II corresponds to the period when Chaco Canyon dominated much of the Anasazi world. During this era Anasazi communities were widespread in the eastern San Juan Basin and the Acoma-Laguna area. Communities generally consisted of loose groupings of residential pueblos associated with Bonito-style community centers. These community centers are interpreted as local integrative structures that served as a focus of community-level organization. Architectural and ceramic evidence and the existence of prehistoric roads linking some sites suggest that Chaco Canyon was the seat of a regional system of integration that tied local communities into a larger socio-political entity. A degree of regional autonomy in the south is suggested by the emergence of a regional ceramic style (Cebolleta Black-on-white), but it was similar to the Gallup and Escavada styles being used in the San Juan Basin.

The Chacoan regional system of integration faltered in the early twelfth century. No large-scale great house construction occurred in Chaco Canyon after A.D. 1115 and by A.D. 1140 great house construction may have ceased entirely (Lekson 1984:261). In the eastern San

Juan Basin there was a significant reduction in population, accompanied by large scale abandonments in lower elevations and the establishment of new settlements in upland zones and areas conducive to conserving and diverting water for agriculture. These changes were undoubtedly related to climatic variables, including the onset of a severe drought and perhaps changes in seasonality of rainfall and growing season. Population levels seem to have recovered in the early thirteenth century and remained relatively stable until abandonment of the area in the late thirteenth or early fourteenth centuries.

Major changes that accompanied the demise of the Chacoan system include the loss of the regionally consistent Bonito-style architecture and the substitution of large residential buildings for local community centers. More of the larger sites were situated in defensible topographic settings and some had definite defensive constructions. Communities as a whole became more compact and better defined spatially. These changes appear to be related to the deterioration of mechanisms that facilitated regional integration, with a corresponding emphasis upon local, community-level organization.

These disruptions were not so pronounced in the Acoma-Laguna area. Zones of Pueblo II occupation in this area were all in well-watered settings, and the population displacements observed elsewhere in the Cibola region (Kintigh, chapter 9) did not occur in the Acoma-Laguna area. Moreover, ceramics show considerable continuity with preceding Pueblo II period assemblages. Communities did become more compact with well-defined core areas resembling those in the eastern San Juan Basin and Scribe S phase of the Zuni-El Morro area.

Pueblo III–Pueblo IV
Transition

In the eastern San Juan Basin and the Acoma-Laguna area the Pueblo III–Pueblo IV transition was marked by dramatic changes. The entire eastern San Juan Basin was abandoned prior to the adoption of glaze-painted ceramics, with populations presumably moving eastward into the Rio Grande drainage. The reasons for this shift are not understood, but the change was part of a broader regional movement that affected other areas characterized by Mesa Verde tradition ceramics. In the eastern San Juan Basin there are indications that abandonment of some of the communities was gradual. Certain sites, such as Guadalupe Ruin and Loma Fria seem to have been occupied after many other sites in their respective communities had been abandoned.

In the Acoma-Laguna area people moved into large, often defensive sites in the middle Rio San Jose and lower Rio Puerco subdivisions. At the same time the Cebolleta Mesa subdivision was abandoned. Details about this process are not available for the middle Rio San Jose and lower Puerco, but more information has been developed for the Cebolleta Mesa subdivision. In this subdivision there was a marked decline in population by about A.D. 1325. Many communities were abandoned and the remaining population was concentrated into one or perhaps two large, highly defensive sites. After a brief occupation these, too, were abandoned.

Acknowledgments

Many individuals contributed information and ideas that I have drawn upon in this chapter. I especially wish to mention Mike Marshall, Peter McKenna, Stewart Peckham, John Stein, and Tom Windes. Gretchen Obenauf and Patty McLean provided very helpful editorial comments on earlier drafts of the chapter, and Mike Adler's suggestions and encouragement have been much appreciated. Illustrations were prepared by Emilio Montoya. My participation in Crow Canyon Archaeological Center's "Pueblo Cultures in Transition" conference and subsequent work on this chapter were supported by the Bureau of Land Management.

References Cited

Allan, William C., Rory P. Gauthier, Frank J. Broilo, and Richard W. Loose
1976   *An Archaeological Survey near San Mateo, New Mexico: The Keradamex Incorporated Lease.* Office of Contract Archaeology, University of New Mexico, Albuquerque. Submitted to Keradamex, Inc. Copies available from Museum of New Mexico, Laboratory of Anthropology, Santa Fe.

Ambler, J. Richard
1976   *An Archaeological Survey of the San Mateo Mine Area, New Mexico.* Northern Arizona University, Flagstaff. Submitted to Teton Exploration Drilling Co., Inc. Copies available from Museum of New Mexico, Laboratory of Anthropology, Santa Fe.

Baker, Larry L.
1991a   Anasazi Settlement Distribution and the Relationship to Environment. In *Anasazi Puebloan Adaptation in Response to Climatic Stress*, edited by Cynthia Irwin-Williams and Larry L. Baker, pp. 288–322. USDI, Bureau of Land Management, Albuquerque, and Eastern New Mexico University, Portales.
1991b   History of the Puerco River Valley Project. In *Anasazi Puebloan Adaptation in Response to Climatic Stress*, edited by C. Irwin-Williams and Larry L. Baker, pp. 8–32. USDI, Bureau of Land Management, Albuquerque, and Eastern New Mexico University, Portales.

Baker, Larry L., and Stephen R. Durand
1991   Regional Spatial Organization of Anasazi Settlement. In *Anasazi Puebloan Adaptation in Response to Climatic Stress*, edited by Cynthia Irwin-Williams and Larry L. Baker, pp. 323–39. USDI, Bureau of Land Management, Albuquerque.

Bandelier, Adolph F.
1892   *Final Report of Investigations Among the Indians of the Southwestern United States, Carried on Mainly in the Years from 1880 to 1885*, Part II. Papers of the Archaeological Institute of America, American Series 4. Archaeological Institute of America, Cambridge.

Barnett, Franklin
1973   *San Ysidro Pueblos: Two Prehistoric Pueblo IV Indian Ruins in New*

Mexico. Albuquerque Archaeological Society, Albuquerque.

Beal, John D.

1976   *An Archaeological Survey of Two Sections of Land in McKinley County, New Mexico.* School of American Research, Santa Fe. Submitted to Phillips Petroleum Company. Copies available from Museum of New Mexico, Laboratory of Anthropology, Santa Fe.

1980   *Archaeological Survey of 13 Square Miles Adjacent to the Desliz Escarpment, McKinley County, New Mexico, Part I, Survey Results.* School of American Research, Santa Fe. Submitted to Metric Corporation and Santa Fe Mining, Inc. Copies available from Museum of New Mexico, Laboratory of Anthropology, Santa Fe.

1981   *Additional Archaeological Survey Adjacent to the Desliz Escarpment: An Addendum to the Management Document.* School of American Research, Santa Fe. Submitted to Metric Corporation. Copies available from Museum of New Mexico, Laboratory of Anthropology, Santa Fe.

1984   *The Lee Ranch Mine Project: Dimensions of Occupational Persistence.* Report No. 86. School of American Research, Santa Fe.

Bice, Richard A., and William M. Sundt

1972   *Prieta Vista, A Small Pueblo III Ruin in North Central New Mexico.* Albuquerque Archaeological Society, Albuquerque.

1976   *AS-8 Archaeological Salvage Project Progress Report Number One.* USDI, Bureau of Land Management, Albuquerque.

Bradley, Zorro A.

1971   *Site Bc 236, Chaco Canyon National Monument, New Mexico.* USDI, National Park Service, Division of Archaeology, Office of Archaeological and Historic Preservation, Washington, D.C.

Broster, John B., and Bruce G. Harrill (editors)

1982   *A Cultural Resource Management Plan for Timber Sale and Forest Development Areas on the Pueblo of Acoma,* Vol. I. USDI, Bureau of Indian Affairs, Albuquerque.

Broster, John B., and Arthur K. Ireland (editors)

1982   *A Cultural Resource Management Plan for Timber Sale and Forest Development Areas on the Pueblo of*

Acoma, Vol. 2. USDI, Bureau of Indian Affairs, Albuquerque.

Coleman, Robert O.

1988   *A Preliminary Report on Excavations on Casa Morena (Mesa Pueblo), McKinley County, New Mexico.* Record. Dallas Archaeological Society, Dallas.

Davis, Emma Lou

1964   *Anasazi Mobility and Mesa Verde Migrations.* Unpublished Ph.D. dissertation, Department of Anthropology, University of California, Los Angeles.

Davis, Emma Lou, and James Winkler

1959   A Late Mesa Verde Site in the Rio Puerco Valley. *El Palacio* 66:73–84.

1975   Ceremonial Rooms as Kiva Alternatives: SOC-45 and SDV-3. In *Collected Papers in Honor of Florence Hawley Ellis,* edited by Albert H. Schroeder, pp. 47–59. Papers of the Archaeological Society of New Mexico No. 2. Archaeological Society of New Mexico, Albuquerque.

Dittert, Alfred E., Jr.

1949   *The Prehistoric Population and Architecture of the Cebolleta Mesa Region, Central Western New Mexico.* Unpublished Master's thesis, Department of Anthropology, University of New Mexico, Albuquerque.

1959   *Culture Change in the Cebolleta Mesa Region, Central Western New Mexico.* Ph.D. dissertation, Department of Anthropology, University of Arizona, Tucson. University Microfilms, Ann Arbor.

Doleman, William

1976   *Cultural Resources Survey and Inventory for Phillips Petroleum Company Noserock Project, McKinley County, New Mexico.* Museum of New Mexico, Laboratory of Anthropology, Santa Fe.

1989   *El Malpais NCA 1989 Archaeological Survey Final Summary Report.* Office of Contract Archaeology, University of New Mexico, Albuquerque. Submitted to the Bureau of Land Management, Albuquerque District, Albuquerque.

Donaldson, Marcia

1983   *Cultural Resource Inventory along the Proposed Continental Divide Pipeline, Southwestern Colorado and Northwestern New Mexico.* Office of Contract Archaeology, University of New Mexico, Albuquerque.

Dulaney, Alan R., and Steven G. Dosh

1981   *A Class II Cultural Resources Inventory of the Southern Portion of the Chaco Planning Unit, McKinley and Sandoval Counties, New Mexico.* USDI, Bureau of Land Management, Albuquerque.

Durand, Stephen R., and Winston B. Hurst

1991   A Refinement of Anasazi Cultural Chronology in the Middle Rio Puerco Valley Using Multidimensional Scaling. In *Anasazi Puebloan Adaptation in Response to Climatic Stress,* edited by Cynthia Irwin-Williams and L. Baker, pp. 233–54. USDI, Bureau of Land Management, Albuquerque, and Eastern New Mexico University, Portales.

Eidenbach, Peter L. (editor)

1982   *Inventory Survey of the Lower Hidden Mountain Floodpool, Lower Rio Puerco Drainage, Central New Mexico.* Human Systems Research, Tularosa, New Mexico.

Ellis, Florence H.

1966   The Immediate History of Zia Pueblo as Derived from Excavation in Refuse Deposits. *American Antiquity* 31(6):806–11.

1974   *Pueblo Indians II, Archaeologic and Ethnologic Data: Acoma-Laguna Land Claims.* Garland, New York.

Elyea, Janette

1990   *The NZ Project Archaeological Survey Report.* Office of Contract Archaeology, University of New Mexico, Albuquerque.

Elyea, Janette, Patrick Hogan, and C. Dean Wilson

1994   *The Armijo Canyon Archaeological Survey.* Office of Contract Archaeology, University of New Mexico, Albuquerque.

Fenenga, Franklin

1956   Excavations at Site LA 2567. In *Pipeline Archaeology, Reports of Salvage Operations in the Southwest on El Paso Natural Gas Company Projects 1950–1953,* edited by Fred Wendorf, Nancy Fox, and Orian L. Lewis, pp. 233–41. Laboratory of Anthropology, Santa Fe, and Museum of Northern Arizona, Flagstaff.

Fenenga, Franklin, and Thomas S. Cummings

1956a   The Eastern Section of the Permian-San Juan Project. In *Pipeline Archaeology, Reports of Salvage Operations in the Southwest on El Paso Natural Gas Company Projects 1950–1953,* edited by Fred Wendorf,

Nancy Fox, and Orian L. Lewis, pp. 216–26. Laboratory of Anthropology, Santa Fe, and Museum of Northern Arizona, Flagstaff.

1956b   LA 2569: Cerros Mojinos, A Late Pueblo II–Early Pueblo III Village on the Rio Puerco Near Los Lunas, New Mexico. In *Pipeline Archaeology, Reports of Salvage Operations in the Southwest on El Paso Natural Gas Company Projects 1950–1953*, edited by Fred Wendorf, Nancy Fox, and Orian L. Lewis, pp. 242–55. Laboratory of Anthropology, Santa Fe, and Museum of Northern Arizona, Flagstaff.

Fowler, Andrew P., John R. Stein, and Roger Anyon
1987   *An Archaeological Reconnaissance of West-Central New Mexico: The Anasazi Monuments Project*. New Mexico Historic Preservation Division, Santa Fe.

Franklin, Hayward H.
1982   Ceramic Analysis of Nineteen Sites in the Bis sa'ani Community. In *Bis sa'ani: A Late Bonito Phase Community on Escavada Wash, Northwest New Mexico*, edited by Cory D. Breternitz, David E. Doyel, and Michael P. Marshall, pp. 873–934. Papers in Anthropology No. 14. Navajo Nation, Window Rock.

Frisbie, Theodore R.
1973   Field Report: The Newton Site, Catron County, New Mexico. *Awanyu* 1(4):31–6.

Gilpin, Dennis, Lawrence E. Vogler, and Joseph K. Anderson
1984   *Archaeological Survey and Excavation on Blocks I, X, and XI, Navajo Indian Irrigation Project, San Juan County, New Mexico*. Papers in Anthropology No. 25. Navajo Nation, Window Rock.

Hammack, Laurens C.
1985   *Cultural Resource Inventory, Ambrosia Lake, New Mexico Tailings Site*. Complete Archaeological Services Associates, Cortez. UMTRA Archaeological Report 11. Submitted to Jacobs Engineering Group, Inc. Copies Available from Museum of New Mexico, Laboratory of Anthropology, Santa Fe.

Harper, Randy A., Marilyn K. Swift, Barbara Mills, James Brandi, and Joseph C. Winter
1989   *The Casamero and Pierre's Outliers Survey, An Archaeological Class III Inventory of the BLM Lands Surrounding the Outliers*. Office of Contract Archaeology, University of New Mexico, Albuquerque.

Hayes, Alden C.
1981   A Survey of Chaco Canyon. In *Archaeological Surveys of Chaco Canyon, New Mexico*, by Alden C. Hayes, David M. Brugge, and W. James Judge, pp. 1–68. Chaco Canyon Studies, Publications in Archaeology No. 18A. USDI, National Park Service, Washington, D.C.

Hibben, Frank C.
1966   A Possible Pyramidal Structure and Other Mexican Influences at Pottery Mound, New Mexico. *American Antiquity* 31(4):522–29.

Hogan, Patrick
1982   *Overview, Research Design, and Data Recovery Program for Cultural Resources within the Bolack Exchange Lands*. Office of Contract Archaeology, University of New Mexico, Albuquerque.

Huse, Hannah, Bradley A. Noisat, and Judith A. Halasi
1978   *The Bisti-Star Lake Project, A Sample Survey of Cultural Resources in Northwestern New Mexico*. USDI, Bureau of Land Management, Albuquerque, and Eastern New Mexico University, Portales.

Hurst, Winston B.
1991   Typological Analysis of Ceramics from the Middle Rio Puerco of the East. In *Anasazi Puebloan Adaptation in Response to Climatic Stress*, edited by Cynthia Irwin-Williams and Larry L. Baker, pp. 103–32. USDI, Bureau of Land Management, Albuquerque, and Eastern New Mexico University, Portales.

Irwin-Williams, Cynthia, and Larry L. Baker (editors)
1991   *Anasazi Puebloan Adaptation in Response to Climatic Stress, Prehistory of the Middle Rio Puerco Valley*. Museum of New Mexico, Santa Fe. Submitted to Mobil Oil Corporation. Copies available from USDI, Bureau of Land Management, Albuquerque, and Eastern New Mexico University, Portales.

Jacobson, LouAnn, and John R. Roney
1985   Pueblo III Sites on Chaco Mesa, Thematic Group: National Register of Historic Places Inventory, Nomination Form. Document on file, New Mexico Historic Preservation Division, Santa Fe.

Kayser, David W.
1971   *An Archaeological Survey of Mobil Oil Corporation Uranium Lease Areas on the Laguna Indian Reservation, Valencia County, New Mexico*. Museum of New Mexico, Laboratory of Anthropology, Santa Fe. Submitted to Mobil Oil Corporation.

Kemrer, Meade F.
1982   *Archaeological Variability Within the Bisti-Star Lake Region, Northwestern New Mexico*. USDI, Bureau of Land Management, Albuquerque.

Kincaid, Chris (editor)
1983   *Chaco Roads Project, Phase I, A Reappraisal of Prehistoric Roads in the San Juan Basin*. USDI, Bureau of Land Management, Albuquerque and Santa Fe.

Kintigh, Keith W.
1985   *Settlement, Subsistence, and Society in Late Zuni Prehistory*. Anthropological Papers No. 44. University of Arizona Press, Tucson.

Kirkpatrick, David T. (editor)
1980   *Prehistory and History of the Ojo Amarillo*. Report No. 276. New Mexico State University, Las Cruces.

Koczan, Steven
1978   *A Cultural Resource Inventory of a Portion of the Kerr McGee Roca Honda Uranium Claims Northwest of San Mateo, New Mexico*. Museum of New Mexico, Contract Archaeology Section, Project No. 65.41. Copies available from Laboratory of Anthropology, Santa Fe.

Lange, Charles H., and Carroll L. Riley
1966   *The Southwestern Journals of Adolph F. Bandelier, 1880–1882*. University of New Mexico Press, Albuquerque.

LeBlanc, Steven A.
1989   Cibola: Shifting Cultural Boundaries. In *Dynamics of Southwest Prehistory*, edited by Linda S. Cordell and George J. Gumerman, pp. 337–69. Smithsonian Institution Press, Washington, D.C.

Lekson, Stephen H.
1984   *Great Pueblo Architecture of Chaco Canyon, New Mexico*. University of New Mexico Press, Albuquerque.

Lekson, Stephen H., and LouAnn Wandsnider
1983   *East Socorro Class II Survey*. Department of Anthropology, University of New Mexico, Albuquerque. Submitted to USDI, Bureau of Land Management, Socorro Resource

Area. Copies available from USDI, Bureau of Land Management, Albuquerque.

Lester, Curtis, Earl Neller, and Charles A. Hannaford
1978   *Preservation Protection Workbook, Reservoir Site, CM-100, Phase III.* USDI, Bureau of Land Management, Albuquerque.

Mackey, James, and Sally J. Holbrook
1978   The University of California at Santa Barbara's 1977 Archaeological Report on Sites Excavated on Federal Lands. Ms. on file, USDI, Bureau of Land Management, Albuquerque.

Marshall, Michael P.
1991   The Cebolla Canyon Ceramic Analysis. In *The Prehistoric Cebolla Canyon Community: An Archaeological Class III Inventory of 320 Acres of BLM Land at the Mouth of Cebolla Canyon,* by Frank E. Wozniak and Michael P. Marshall, pp. 6.1–6.42. Office of Contract Archaeology, University of New Mexico, Albuquerque.
1993   *Archaeological Investigations in the Cerritos de Jaspé Subunit of the El Malpais Conservation Area, The 1991 BLM Survey.* Office of Contract Archaeology, University of New Mexico, Albuquerque.

Marshall, Michael P., and Anna Sofaer
1986   *Solstice Project Investigations in the Chaco District, 1984–85: The Technical Report.* Museum of New Mexico, Laboratory of Anthropology, Santa Fe.

Marshall, Michael P., John R. Stein, Richard W. Loose, and Judith E. Novotny
1979   *Anasazi Communities of the San Juan Basin.* Public Service Company of New Mexico and Historic Preservation Bureau, Planning Division, Santa Fe.

Mathien, Frances Joan (editor)
1991   *Excavations at 29SJ633: The Eleventh Hour Site, Chaco Canyon, New Mexico.* Reports of the Chaco Center No. 10. USDI, National Park Service, Santa Fe.

McKenna, Peter J.
1991   Chaco Canyon's Mesa Verde Phase. In *Excavations at 29SJ633: The Eleventh Hour Site, Chaco Canyon, New Mexico,* edited by Frances Joan Mathien, pp. 127–37. Reports of the Chaco Center No. 10. USDI, National Park Service, Santa Fe.

Mera, H. P.
1935   *Ceramic Clues to the Prehistory of North Central New Mexico.* Technical Series Bulletin No. 8. Museum of New Mexico, Laboratory of Anthropology, Santa Fe.
1940   *Population Changes in the Rio Grande Glaze-Paint Area.* Technical Series Bulletin No. 9. Museum of New Mexico, Laboratory of Anthropology, Santa Fe.

Miller, John, and Jon Frizell
1980   *The CONOCO-Thoreau Survey: An Archaeological Survey of 2,000 Acres in McKinley County, New Mexico.* Office of Contract Archaeology, University of New Mexico, Albuquerque. Proposal No. 185–56. Submitted to Continental Oil Company. Copies available from Museum of New Mexico, Laboratory of Anthropology, Santa Fe.

Nials, Fred, John Stein, and John Roney
1987   *Chacoan Roads in the Southern Periphery: Results of Phase II of the BLM Chaco Roads Project.* Cultural Resources Series No. 1. USDI, Bureau of Land Management, Santa Fe.

Olson, Alan P., and William W. Wasley
1956   An Archaeological Traverse Survey in West-Central New Mexico. In *Pipeline Archaeology, Reports of Salvage Operations in the Southwest on El Paso Natural Gas Company Projects 1950–1953,* edited by Fred Wendorf, Nancy Fox, and Orian L. Lewis, pp. 256–390. Laboratory of Anthropology, Santa Fe, and Museum of Northern Arizona, Flagstaff.

Peckham, Stewart
1962   *Archaeological Salvage Excavations on Interstate 40 Near McCartys, New Mexico.* Note 11. Laboratory of Anthropology, Santa Fe.
1970   Original unpublished site forms from an archaeological survey of Continental Oil Company uranium lease areas, Bernabe M. Montano Grant, Laguna Indian Reservation, New Mexico. On file, Archaeological Records Management System (ARMS), Museum of New Mexico, Laboratory of Anthropology, Santa Fe.
1971   *An Archaeological Survey of Continental Oil Company Uranium Lease Areas, Bernabe M. Montano Grant, Laguna Indian Reservation, New Mexico.* Submitted to Continental Oil Company. Copies avalable from Museum of New Mexico, Laboratory of Anthropology, Santa Fe.

1987   Not in the Limelight but Never in the Shadow: Preliminary Observations on Prehistoric Sites South of Mesa Prieta, New Mexico. In *Secrets of a City: Papers on Albuquerque Area Archaeology In Honor of Richard A. Bice,* edited by Anne V. Poore and John Montgomery, pp. 87–97. Papers of the Archaeological Society of New Mexico 13. Ancient City Press, Santa Fe.

Phibbs, Donald C.
1974   Preliminary Report on the Excavations of CM156, A Small Unit Pueblo on the Chacra Mesa, New Mexico. Ms. on file, Maxwell Museum of Anthropology, University of New Mexico, Albuquerque.

Pippin, Lonnie C.
1987   *Prehistory and Paleoecology of Guadalupe Ruin, New Mexico.* Anthropological Papers No. 107. University of Utah Press, Salt Lake City.

Plog, Stephen
1980   *Stylistic Variation in Prehistoric Ceramics, Design Analysis in the American Southwest.* Cambridge University Press, New York.

Powers, Robert P.
1983   Preliminary Report on Inventory Survey at Chaco Culture National Historical Park. Ms. on file, USDI, National Park Service, Branch of Cultural Research, Santa Fe.

Powers, Robert P., William B. Gillespie, and Stephen H. Lekson
1983   *The Outlier Survey, A Regional View of Settlement in the San Juan Basin.* Reports of the Chaco Center No. 3. USDI, National Park Service, Albuquerque.

Reynolds, William (editor)
1980   *Final Report of the Cultural Resources Survey of Blocks VI and VII of the N.I.I.P.* Esca-Tech, Costa Mesa, California.

Ruppé, Reynold J., Jr.
1953   *The Acoma Culture Province: An Archaeological Concept.* Unpublished Ph.D. dissertation, Department of Anthropology, Harvard University, Cambridge.

Scheick, Cherie
1981a   *Archaeological Overview for the Rio San Jose Drainage.* Contract Archaeology Report No. 55. Museum of New Mexico, Laboratory of Anthropology, Santa Fe.
1981b   *Investigations into Land Patterning*

in the South Hospah Mine Area, New Mexico. Contract Archaeology Report No. 028. School of American Research, Santa Fe.

Sebastian, Lynne
1983   Anasazi Site Typology and Chronology. In *Economy and Interaction Along the Lower Chaco River*, edited by Patrick Hogan and Joseph C. Winter, pp. 403–19. Office of Contract Archaeology and Maxwell Museum of Anthropology, University of New Mexico, Albuquerque.

Sessions, Steven E. (editor)
1979   *The Archaeology of Southwest Gallegos Mesa: The EPCC Survey Project.* Papers in Anthropology No. 1. Navajo Nation, Window Rock.

Sliwinski, Sophia
1978   *Mesa Portales Triple S Development.* Archeological Resource Service. Copies available from Museum of New Mexico, Laboratory of Anthropology, Santa Fe.

Sundt, William M., Bettie Terry, Beryl McWilliams, and Richard A. Bice
1983   *Report of Archaeological Survey of State of New Mexico Lands along the Cañada de las Milpas.* Albuquerque Archaeological Society. Submitted to New Mexico State Land Office. Copies available from Museum of New Mexico, Laboratory of Anthropology, Santa Fe.

Swift, Marilyn
1983   *An Archaeological Survey of Ninety Miles of Seismic Line near Whitehorse, New Mexico.* San Juan County Museum, Division of Conservation Archaeology. Bloomfield, New Mexico.

Toll, H. Wolcott, Thomas C. Windes, and Peter J. McKenna
1980   Late Ceramic Patterns in Chaco Canyon: The Pragmatics of Modeling Ceramic Exchange. In *Models and Methods in Regional Exchange*, edited by R. E. Fry, pp. 95–118. Society for American Archaeology Papers No. 1. Washington, D.C.

United States Department of the Interior, Bureau of Land Management (USDI, BLM)
1990   El Malpais National Conservation Area General Management Plan, Draft report on file, USDI, Bureau of Land Management, Rio Puerco Resource Area, Albuquerque.

Vierra, Bradley J., Patricia Prince, and Margaret A. Powers
1986   *The Archaeological Resources of the Arch Joint Venture Project along Coal Creek and Denazin Wash, San Juan County, New Mexico.* Studies in Archaeology No. 3. San Juan County Archaeological Research Center, Farmington, New Mexico.

Vivian, R. Gordon, and Tom W. Mathews
1965   *Kin Kletso, a Pueblo III Community in Chaco Canyon, New Mexico.* Technical Series No. 6(1). Southwestern Monuments Association, Globe, Arizona.

Vivian, R. Gwinn
1960   *Archaeology of Chacra Mesa, New Mexico.* Unpublished Master's thesis, Department of Anthropology, University of New Mexico, Albuquerque.

Vogler, Lawrence E., Dennis Gilpin, and Joseph K. Anderson
1983   *Cultural Resource Investigations on Gallegos Mesa: Excavations in Blocks VII and IX, and Testing Operations in Blocks X and XI, Navajo Indian Irrigation Project, San Juan County, New Mexico.* Papers in Anthropology No. 24. Navajo Nation, Window Rock.

Wait, Walter K., and Ben Nelson (editors)
1983   *The Star Lake Archaeological Project.* Southern Illinois University, Carbondale.

Wase, Cheryl L.
1982   *A Class I and Class II Survey of the Rio Puerco Grazing Area.* Ms. on file, USDI, Bureau of Land Management, Albuquerque.

Watson, Patty Jo, Steven A. LeBlanc, and Charles L. Redman
1980   Aspects of Zuni Prehistory: Preliminary Report on Excavations and Survey in the El Morro Valley of New Mexico. *Journal of Field Archaeology* 7(2):201–18.

Whitmore, Jane
1979   *An Archaeological Survey near Prewitt, New Mexico.* School of American Research, Santa Fe. Submitted to Plains Electric. Copies available from Museum of New Mexico, Laboratory of Anthropology, Santa Fe.

Wilson, John P.
1979   *Cultural Resources of the Alamito

Coal Lease Area, Northwestern New Mexico.* Alamito Coal Company, Tucson.

Wimberly, Mark, and Peter Eidenbach
1980   *Reconnaissance Study of the Archaeological and Related Resources of the Lower Puerco and Salado Drainages, Central New Mexico.* Human Systems Research, Tularosa, New Mexico.

Windes, Thomas C.
1987   *Summary of Tests and Excavations at the Pueblo Alto Community. Investigations at the Pueblo Alto Complex, Chaco Canyon, New Mexico, 1975–1979*, Vol. 1. Chaco Canyon Studies, Publications in Archaeology No. 18F. USDI, National Park Service, Santa Fe.

Winkler, James, and Emma Lou Davis
1961   Archaeological Survey in Socorro and McKinley Counties, New Mexico. Ms. on file, Museum of New Mexico, Laboratory of Anthropology, Santa Fe.

Wiseman, Regge N.
1974   *The Malpais Reconnaissance, an Archaeological Inventory and Evaluation of Some Prehistoric Sites in the El Malpais Planning Unit, Socorro District, Bureau of Land Management.* Museum of New Mexico, Santa Fe, Contract No. 52500-CT4-194(N). Submitted to the USDI, Bureau of Land Management. Copies available from Museum of New Mexico, Laboratory of Anthropology, Santa Fe.

Wobst, H. Martin
1977   Stylistic Behavior and Information Exchange. In *Papers for the Director: Research Essays in Honor of James B. Griffin*, edited by C. E. Cleland, pp. 317–42. Anthropological Papers of the Museum of Anthropology No. 61. University of Michigan, Ann Arbor.

Wozniak, Frank E., and Michael P. Marshall
1991   *The Prehistoric Cebolla Canyon Community: An Archaeological Class III Inventory of 320 acres of BLM Land at the Mouth of Cebolla Canyon.* Office of Contract Archaeology, University of New Mexico, Albuquerque.

Chapter 11

Southwestern New Mexico and Southeastern Arizona, A.D. 900 to 1300

Stephen H. Lekson

Southwestern New Mexico is defined here as that part of the state south of U.S. Highway 60 and west of the Rio Grande. Southeastern Arizona is defined as the area below the Mogollon Rim and east of the White Mountain and San Carlos Apache Reservations, which includes Eagle Creek, Blue Creek, and the Gila River through the Safford Valley (figure 11.1).

The "Pueblo II period" is defined as the time from about A.D. 900 to 1150, and "Pueblo III period" spans the years from about A.D. 1150 to 1300. These Anasazi terms are not customarily used in southwestern New Mexico and southeastern Arizona, but I will argue that they are appropriate and useful.

Status of Research

Much of this area was traversed during a remarkable reconnaissance survey by Edward B. Danson (1957) in 1947 through 1949, as part of the Peabody Museum's Upper Gila Expedition. For some districts, Danson's survey remains the primary reference but many districts have seen subsequent research, and are reasonably well known and well-reported. The Mimbres, San Francisco-Tularosa, and Rio Abajo areas have all been extensively surveyed in recent years (see figure 1.1, Districts A, C, and E respectively). The Blue River area (figure 11.1, District B) is less well known and, with the exception of Rice (1975), site data come mainly from Danson. The Safford Valley (figure 11.1, in District B) has received only minimal professional attention (Brown 1973 provides an good summary). Obviously, not all architectural sites have been located

in these districts, but we can have some confidence that most big sites are at least located, if not fully described.

Other districts are either largely unknown or, although partially studied, do not appear to have been occupied during the Pueblo III period. The Plains of San Augustin and the Mogollon Plateau (figure 11.1, District F) are not well surveyed, but it appears that no big Pueblo III sites (and, indeed, few small Pueblo III sites) are present in these areas. The Mogollon Plateau might hold some archaeological surprises, but it probably conceals few if any lost large pueblos. It is my impression that the Mangas Mountains-Datil Mountains area (figure 11.1, District G) is likely to contain Pueblo II and Pueblo III sites. Unfortunately, this area is spottily known. The Lower San Francisco valley and Duncan-Virden valley of the Gila (figure 11.1, District H) are all but unsurveyed.

Settlement Patterns Through Time

The basic Pueblo II settlement pattern in most districts was a cluster of 20 or fewer small (5–7 room) houses (often associated with a pit structure or kiva), a cluster of sites that researchers call a "dispersed community." Because no complete community has been excavated or even tested, the social implications of the term are hypothetical.

During Pueblo II times, the dispersed community pattern characterized the Reserve region (Peterson 1988), the Mimbres area (Lekson 1990, 1992b; but see also Anyon and LeBlanc 1984 and Shafer 1995), the Quemado District (Fowler, Stein, and Anyon 1987), the Rio Abajo

(Marshall and Walt 1984), and perhaps the Blue River (Rice 1975) areas.

In many areas, it appears that the dispersed community pattern continued into the early Pueblo III period. But by the late twelfth century, settlement patterns over almost all of the region changed from somewhat more dispersed residential communities to more compact, aggregated, pueblo-like forms. As discussed later, the shift from dispersed community to pueblo forms did not occur at the same time throughout the region.

San Francisco-Tularosa District

In the San Francisco-Tularosa District, Reserve phase (Pueblo II) dispersed communities were replaced by large, aggregated Tularosa phase (Pueblo III) pueblos (Accola 1981; Berman 1979; Bluhm 1960; Peterson 1988). The Reserve phase is conventionally said to end at A.D. 1150, but resettlement within large aggregated Pueblo III pueblos may not have begun at this time throughout the district. In several areas, there appears to be a continuation of the dispersed community pattern into the late twelfth and early thirteenth centuries. Perhaps the best example is the incompletely understood Apache Creek phase (Berman 1979:56–57). The Apache Creek phase consists of large sites containing small pueblo room blocks, numerous rectangular, masonry-lined pit structures, and a Tularosa Black-on-white ceramic assemblage (apparently without St. Johns Polychrome). The Apache Creek site itself has a great kiva. Presumably, great kivas are present at other sites of this period.

Larger, later Tularosa phase sites of

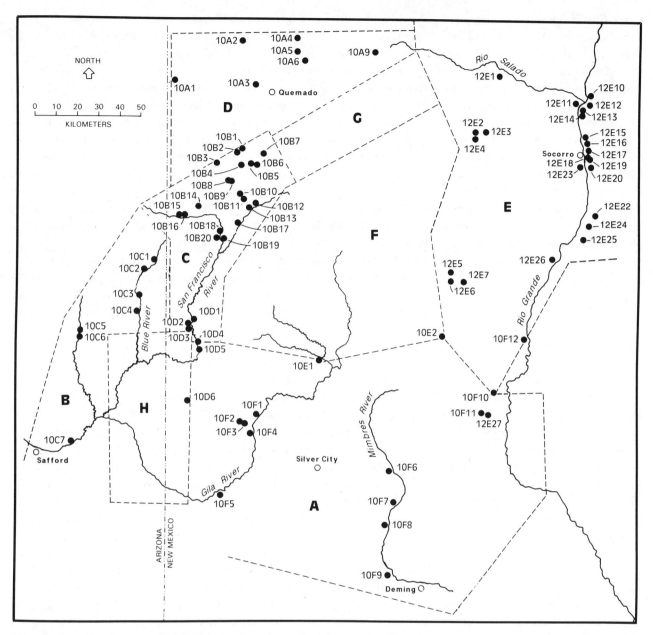

Figure 11.1. Southwestern New Mexico and southeastern Arizona. Districts shown are: (A) Mimbres, (B) Blue River-Safford, (C) San Francisco-Tularosa, (D) Quemado, (E) Rio Abajo, (F) Mogollon Plateau-Plains of St. Augustine, (G) Mangus and Datil Mountains, and (H) Lower San Francisco-Duncan-Virden Valley.

the San Francisco-Tularosa and Blue Districts are compact pueblo-style sites that contain up to 100 rooms but lack internal plazas or other obvious subdivisions. From the surface they appear irregular in plan. The very largest Tularosa site in the San Francisco-Tularosa District (the Delgar group) consists of three of these units (Duff 1897). Great kivas are usually associated with these sites. Some smaller contemporary sites exist in the area, but it

appears that population is almost entirely aggregated into the large settlements.

Quemado District

In the Quemado District, the Pueblo II community pattern was replaced by very large Tularosa phase pueblos sometime after A.D. 1150 (Danson 1957; Fowler, Stein, and Anyon 1987). Tularosa phase is used here to denote sites with a heavy pre-

ponderance of Tularosa Black-on-white pottery. Here, too, the presence of "post-Chacoan Great House" communities during the early Pueblo III period (Kintigh 1994; Fowler, Stein, and Anyon 1987) may mark a transitional stage between the earlier (Pueblo II) dispersed communities and the later (Pueblo III) aggregated pueblos.

Large Tularosa phase pueblos of the Quemado District include sites like those of the San Francisco-Tularosa area and several huge sites (up to 600 rooms) with large, formal internal plazas (see McGimsey 1980). The largest sites date to the middle to late thirteenth century, and are very similar to the very largest Zuni-Acoma area Tularosa phase sites (Kintigh, chapter 9; Roney, chapter 10). (Again, local phase names are subsumed here by "Tularosa.") Great kivas may be present at both types of settlements, but this is far from clear. The later Tularosa phase population appears to have been almost completely aggregated into these very large pueblo-style sites.

Rio Abajo District

I have expanded the Rio Abajo District of the Rio Grande (Marshall and Walt 1984) to include western Socorro and northwestern Sierra Counties in New Mexico. Between about A.D. 1150 and 1300 the Rio Abajo District was an area of mixed but interesting cultural-historical dynamics. In addition to a large apparently local population (discussed later), enclaves of sites with Tularosa Black-on-white and Mesa Verde-like black-on-white pottery appear in isolated pockets of arable land on the eastern slopes of the Black Range (Lekson 1989; Lekson, et al. 1988; Laumbach 1992; Laumbach and Kirkpatrick 1983; Nelson 1986).

In the Rio Abajo proper (i.e., along the Rio Grande in this district), a single phase, the Elmendorf phase, spans the period from A.D. 1000 to 1300 (Marshall and Walt 1984; see also Spielmann, chapter 12). Settlement patterns within the long Elmendorf phase shift from dispersed community forms to much more aggregated, pueblo-like forms at about A.D. 1150. Late Elmendorf phase settlements are few in number, but large in size. The largest site, Piedras Negras, is a highly aggregated, single-story masonry settlement with surrounding (defensive?) walls, as many as 150 rooms and one large, centrally located surface depression that

may indicate a great kiva (Marshall and Walt 1984:107–110).

"Mesa Verde-like" refers here to sites with Mesa Verde, McElmo, and Galisteo-style carbon-painted pottery and massive, pueblo-style aggregated settlements. Two clusters of Mesa Verde-like sites appear as distinct enclaves in the Rio Abajo District: the first and most famous, near Gallinas Springs (northwest of Magdalena) and the second on Palomas Creek (west of Truth or Consequences). The cultural-historical pedigree of these sites is, of course, a matter of controversy (Davis 1964; Lekson 1989; Bertram et al. 1990). In my opinion (reflected by my choice of the term Mesa Verde-like), both of these site clusters stand out like a sore thumb compared to earlier and contemporary sites in this district. Mesa Verde-like sites, ranging in size up to 300 rooms, consist of massively built room blocks of field stone and river cobbles, probably multistoried, that surround interior plazas. Kivas are present, but patterns in the configuration and size of these subterranean structures are not clear.

The third element of the Pueblo III period occupation in this district is the Tularosa phase (Laumbach 1992; Laumbach and Kirkpatrick 1983; Nelson 1993). Tularosa phase sites are, in the main, restricted to the west-central portions of the Rio Abajo District. They range from remarkably large (400-plus rooms) early Pueblo III communities with post-Chaco great houses, such as the Victorio site (Laumbach 1992), to aggregated, pueblo-like, walled (defensive?) sites like the Winston site (Laumbach and Kirkpatrick 1983). It is likely that the more dispersed community settlements like Victorio are earlier than the aggregated pueblo-style sites like Winston.

Safford-Blue Creek District

The Safford District is surprisingly poorly known (Fewkes 1904; Brown 1973, 1974). Recent work by Kyle Woodson, Joseph

Crary, and Robert Neily should improve this situation. There are almost no data from the Pueblo II period sites, some of which appear to contain significant quantities of Mimbres pottery. There is only one well-documented Pueblo III site, the Earven Flat site in the Safford Valley. Earven Flat is a Tularosa phase site with about 170 rooms, two small internal plazas, and no evidence of a kiva (Brown 1973). Little data exist on contemporary settlements in the area, but there do not appear to be any other comparably large Pueblo III sites in the area.

The settlement patterns of the Blue Creek area appear, in general, to parallel the sequence described above for the San Francisco-Tularosa District. Large Tularosa sites such as Blue Post Office site and the Lovelady site are present (Hough 1907; Rice 1975).

Mimbres District

I have argued that many (and perhaps all) Mimbres phase communities of the Pueblo II period (A.D. 900–1150) were initially dispersed and were characterized by numerous small masonry structures surrounding a great kiva and, perhaps, great house (Lekson 1990, 1992a, 1992b, 1993; but see LeBlanc 1986; Shafer 1995). By the middle of the period (about A.D. 1000) community layouts became more nucleated, as indicated by the occupation of pueblo-style villages with 100-plus rooms surrounding central plazas.

The conventional end of the Pueblo II period, A.D. 1150, was a key date in the Mimbres District. In many other districts this date generally marks the change from the more dispersed community pattern to the aggregated pueblo form, but in the Mimbres District this date roughly coincides with an apparent abandonment or cultural discontinuity from Mimbres phase (Pueblo II) occupations to much reduced Black Mountain and El Paso phase (Pueblo III) occupations (Blake, LeBlanc, and Minnis 1986; Lekson 1989, 1992b).

Puebloan settlements in the Mimbres District during the Pueblo III Black Mountain and El Paso phases exhibit an increased use of adobe-wall technology and a greatly diminished use of decorated pottery. A decrease in population levels across the district is also likely. Depending on the estimates used, some researchers argue for a dramatic decrease in the total number of sites and total number of rooms in the post-Mimbres phases (Blake, LeBlanc, and Minnis 1986) while others have proposed a more modest decrease (Lekson 1992b).

The adobe-walled pueblo-style settlements in the Mimbres District occupied during the Black Mountain and El Paso phases generally contain between 25 and 40 rooms each, loosely arranged around a central plaza. The largest sites consist of multiples of such units (Ravesloot 1979; Minnis and LeBlanc 1979; Lekson and Rorex 1987). Later El Paso phase sites include more massively built, multistoried structures surrounding more formally defined interior plazas (Lekson and Rorex 1987). Great kivas, or kivas of any kind, are apparently absent. El Paso phase settlement is part of a much larger, thirteenth- and fourteenth-century, desert system, including and probably centering on developments at Casas Grandes (Schaafsma 1979), a topic that goes well beyond the scope of this chapter.

Intraregional Processes

The transition from the earlier, more dispersed community pattern to larger pueblo-like settlements follows a "sloping horizon" from east to west and, perhaps, from south to north. The shift to pueblo-style aggregated settlements took place first in the Mimbres District about A.D. 1000 to 1050, followed by similar changes in the San Francisco-Tularosa, Quemado, and perhaps the Blue Districts over the next two centuries. This transition occurred even later—in the fourteenth century—to the west, in areas such

as the Grasshopper and Q-Ranch Districts (Reid et al., chapter 6). I believe that this east-west pattern is real, but I have no easy explanation for it. I offer the following ideas only as a tentative model, far from fully developed.

Settlement and land use in the Pueblo II period (A.D. 900–1150) represents the maximum geographic extension of settlement for any time period in the region's prehistory, much like Pueblo II settlement across the southern Colorado Plateaus. Settlements are commonly found along creeks and streams and, significantly, in upland park settings. Later Pueblo III sites are almost never found in upland parks. The extensive Pueblo II settlement pattern probably reflects agricultural strategies dependent upon direct rainfall, collection and diversion of runoff and melt waters, and use of naturally wet areas (Lekson 1993).

Nature provided a limited number of naturally wet "garden spots," including cienegas, upland parks, floodplain constrictions, and other locations that naturally concentrate rainfall and surface flow. Prehistoric agriculturalists could have improved those garden spots and created a few others with varying levels of labor input. Although some rainfall collection and concentration systems required significant amounts of labor to construct (e.g., Peterson 1988), these were low maintenance systems after initial construction. Garden spot agriculture was much less labor-intensive than diversion canal systems on major streams. Canal irrigation systems, such as those used by the Hohokam and Mimbres are expensive to build and maintain.

The Pueblo II adaptation was extensive, but cheap. Not much labor was required to farm with rain. But due to continuing population growth (which appears to be supported by site inventories across much of the region), a threshold was reached where the land-extensive subsistence and settlement strategies of the Pueblo II period no longer worked, and more labor

intensive irrigation strategies were necessary.

Agricultural intensification took the form of canal irrigation on major streams. Within the region considered here, intensification occurred first during the Pueblo II period in the Mimbres District (Herrington 1979; Lekson 1986). Canal irrigation supported an apparently large population until the Mimbres "collapse" at about A.D. 1150, and presumably supported post-Mimbres populations as well (Nelson and LeBlanc 1986). Post-A.D. 1150 site locations in the San Francisco-Tularosa District suggest that canal irrigation was also present, but the discovery and dating of such systems is problematic. A few canal systems have apparently been dated to the Tularosa phase (Kayser 1973), but currently the best evidence for the shift to an increased reliance on canal irrigation in the San Francisco-Tularosa area rests with the concentration of Tularosa phase (Pueblo III) settlement along currently irrigated reaches of major streams (such as the Tularosa, San Francisco, Blue) and the virtual abandonment of previously occupied upland parks.

In the Quemado area, however, this model does not explain the settlement pattern changes between the Pueblo II and Pueblo III periods. Here the earlier Pueblo II occupation of the lower reaches of ephemeral or seasonal drainages gave way to occupations farther up these same drainages (generally to the east) during the Pueblo III period. This movement toward the better watered continental divide (Fowler, Stein, and Anyon 1987) reversed the down-slope trends recorded for the Mimbres and San Francisco-Tularosa Districts.

Concentration of settlements along major streams in the San Francisco-Tularosa area probably reflects agricultural intensification through diversion irrigation. Relocation along permanent streams may also reflect increased concern for access to permanent potable water. Sites in the Quemado District, in the northern San

Francisco-Tularosa area, and around the Gallo Mountains, are built around springs and not on major creeks. Perhaps the Pueblo III riverine focus reflects a concern for domestic water as much as agricultural intensification.

Domestic water was always a consideration in settlement location, but proximity and reliability of drinking water might have become increasingly important with increasing sedentism. Increasing sedentism packs more eggs into fewer baskets, creating a situation where potential causes for site abandonment become less like triggers for normal decision making and more like disasters. Permanent drinking water might thus have been a critically important aspect of site selection, leading, perhaps, to the reduction of the extensive Pueblo II settlement patterns and to more aggregated Pueblo III locations around springs or on permanent streams.

Extraregional Considerations: The Tularosa Horizon

Between about A.D. 1150 and 1350, substantial areas of west-central New Mexico and east-central Arizona were characterized by ceramic assemblages containing large proportions of Tularosa Black-on-white and closely related black-on-white types—especially Pinedale, which Patricia Crown (1994) has recently identified as a slightly later style horizon over much of this area. This ceramic distribution extends from the Tonto Basin (Roosevelt phase) on the west, to the Acoma area (Kowina phase) on the east (see also Roney, chapter 10); from the Zuni region on the north to the Safford Valley on the south. This large spatial distribution has been called the "Tularosa Horizon" (Lekson, Elson, and Craig 1992:figure 3.3). A ceramic horizon need not entail geographic or temporal homogeneity in architecture or settlement pattern, which vary in both time and space within the broad Tularosa area. The term horizon is used only to indicate a wide spatial distribution of a high-visibility archaeological feature of

analytical interest, in this case decorated ceramics.

The eastern and western ends of the Tularosa horizon bump up against other ceramic (and perhaps cultural) traditions: most notably the Elmendorf series on the east (but see discussion of Chupadero Black-on-white that follows), and the early Classic Hohokam and Sinagua series on the west. To the south, the Tularosa horizon meets the bewildering variety of twelfth- and thirteenth-century desert ceramics and architecture, an era and area of heterogeneous, ill-defined ceramic styles and a shift of decorative field from bowl interiors to jar exteriors and greatly reduced use of painted decoration (I have called this age and area "the people who forgot to paint pots"—only half in jest). A number of poorly understood ceramic types may have had localized production in the desert (e.g., El Paso Polychrome on the east, Tanque Verde and San Carlos Red-on-brown on the west), with a confusing overlay of more widely distributed, more visible types (often including minor amounts of Tularosa Black-on-white and St. Johns Polychromes). To the north, the center of the Tularosa horizon is bordered by the depopulated Chacoan core area, the Developmental period populations of the northern Rio Grande on the northeast, and the Tusayan and Kayenta traditions on the northwest.

Tularosa Black-on-white is a legitimate horizon marker across this broad area. Pueblo-like sites with 100 or more rooms and Tularosa Black-on-white and Tularosa-related assemblages mark the scale of the horizon at its peak in the middle to late thirteenth century. The distribution of large sites in which Tularosa is a major part of the ceramic assemblage is extensive, comparable in spatial extent to that of the contemporary Mesa Verde Black-on-white stylistic tradition found 150 miles to the north.

The Tularosa horizon could be expanded to include Roosevelt, Pinedale, Klageto, and Kowina Black-on-white ceramics, which would increase the tem-

poral duration of the horizon, but only slightly expand its geographic extent. Yet another type might be added to the Tularosa group that would significantly expand the spatial extent of the horizon, namely Chupadero Black-on-white. Chupadero Black-on-white ceramics began about the same time as Tularosa Black-on-white, and about A.D. 1350 Chupadero underwent stylistic transformations comparable to the shift from Tularosa to Pinedale Black-on-white or Tularosa to Klageto Black-on-white ceramics (Hayes 1981; Wiseman 1986). If Chupadero Black-on-white pottery was part of the Tularosa complex, the spatial range of the horizon extended much farther to the east across the Rio Grande—and well beyond the limits of this chapter.

Conclusions

Settlement patterns and site plans of southwestern New Mexico and southeastern Arizona Puebloan populations parallel the Anasazi region to the north. This should not surprise us, because settlements in both areas shared similar environments, most specifically the pinyon-juniper and desert grassland zones. It should be remembered that pinyon-juniper, the characteristic vegetation of much of the Colorado Plateau, is not limited to the plateau but, in fact, extends far to the south beyond the plateau proper into the Mogollon uplands. Insofar as "Anasazi" represents an adaptation to that environment, the "Mogollon" of southwestern New Mexico and southeastern Arizona may be expected to mirror that adaptation (Lekson 1993).

What to call it, and why? The history of regional taxonomy in the Southwest is beyond the scope of this chapter. It may be sufficient to note that the battle for the validity of Mogollon was hard-fought and there remains an abhorrence in the Mogollon region for anything suggesting Anasazi "intrusions," "swamping," or "influence" (e.g., LeBlanc 1986). It may be time to lower the old barriers: The similarity of putatively "Mogollon" Pueblo II and Pueblo III period settlement patterns to contemporary patterns to the north is such that it seems pointless to consider either in isolation (Lekson 1992a, 1993). There are important differences, too, but we will learn more by treating the two together than we will by considering "Anasazi" and "Mogollon" as separate research domains.

During the Pueblo II and Pueblo III periods, the cultural boundary between Anasazi and Mogollon is based almost entirely on pottery paste color. Paste color owes at least as much to bedrock geology as to cultural preference, and the Anasazi region is primarily sedimentary while the Mogollon region is predominantly volcanic. Despite the differences in clays, the visible surfaces of Pueblo III pots were strikingly similar. The list of attributes, including corrugated, indented corrugated, black-on-white, and so on, works equally well for Anasazi and post-A.D. 1000 Mogollon assemblages. Therefore I suggest our understanding of settlement dynamics in both areas after A.D. 1000 (or even A.D. 900) stands to gain little and lose a great deal if we maintain the current taxonomic division between Anasazi and upland Mogollon.

Desert Mogollon may have been a different story. The post-Mimbres desert phases (El Paso and Black Mountain phases) began a murky series that led, sequentially if not culturally, to Casas Grandes. Casas Grandes appears to be an ancestral Pueblo site, but its relation to the Pueblo peoples of the pinyon-juniper region is a matter for study, not assertion. Because we have little knowledge of the Casas Grandes region prior to A.D. 1300, I leave its Pueblo II and Pueblo III history to future researchers.

References Cited

Accola, Richard M.
1981   Mogollon Settlement Patterns in the Middle San Francisco River Drainage, West-central New Mexico. *The Kiva* 46(3):155–68.

Anyon, Roger and Steven A. LeBlanc
1984   *The Galaz Ruin, A Prehistoric Mimbres Village in Southwestern New Mexico.* University of New Mexico Press, Albuquerque.

Berman, Mary Jane
1979   *Cultural Resources Overview of Socorro, New Mexico.* USDA, Forest Service, Albuquerque.

Bertram, Jack B., Andrew R. Gomolak, Steven R. Hoaglund, Terry L. Knight, Emily Garber, and Kenneth J. Lord
1990   *Excavations in the South Room Block of Gallinas Springs Ruin (LA 1178).* Submitted to USDA, Forest Service, Cibola National Forest. Chambers Group, Albuquerque.

Blake, Michael, Steven A. LeBlanc, and Paul E. Minnis
1986   Changing Settlement and Population in the Mimbres Valley, Southwest New Mexico. *Journal of Field Archaeology* 13:439–64.

Bluhm, Elaine A.
1960   Mogollon Settlement Patterns in the Pine Lawn Valley, New Mexico. *American Antiquity* 25:538–46.

Brown, Jeffrey L.
1973   *The Origin and Nature of Salado: Evidence from the Safford Valley, Arizona.* Unpublished Ph.D. dissertation, Department of Anthropology, University of Arizona, Tucson.

1974   The Pueblo Viejo Salado Sites and Their Relationship to Western Pueblo Culture. *The Artifact* 12(2):1–53.

Crown, Patricia L.
1994   *Ceramics and Ideology: Salado Polychrome Pottery.* University of New Mexico Press, Albuquerque.

Danson, Edward B.
1957   *An Archaeological Survey of East-Central Arizona and Western New Mexico.* Papers of the Peabody Museum of American Archaeology and Ethnology No. 19. Harvard University, Cambridge.

Davis, Emma Lou
1964   The Magdalena Problem: A Study Which Integrates a New Pottery Variety Within the Mesa Verde Design Tradition. Ms. on file, Laboratory of Anthropology, Santa Fe.

Duff, U. Francis
1897   The Prehistoric Ruins of the Rio Tularosa. *American Geographical Society of New York Bulletin* 29(3):261–70.

Fewkes, Jesse Walter
1904   Two Summers' Work in Pueblo Ruins. *Twenty-second Annual Report of the Bureau of American Ethnology,* part 1. U.S. Government Printing Office, Washington, D.C.

Fowler, Andrew P., John R. Stein, and Roger Anyon
1987   An Archaeological Reconnaissance of West-central New Mexico. Ms. on file, Historic Preservation Division, Office of the State Archaeologist, Santa Fe.

Hayes, Alden C.
1981   *Excavation of Mound 7, Gran Quivira National Monument, New Mexico.* National Park Service Publications in Archaeology No. 16. U.S. Government Printing Office, Washington, D.C.

Herrington, Selma LaVerne
1979   *Settlement Patterns and Water Control Systems of the Mimbres Classic Phase, Grant County, New Mexico.* Unpublished Ph.D. dissertation, Department of Anthropology, University of Texas, Austin.

1982   Water-control Systems of the Classic Mimbres Phase. In *Mogollon Archaeology,* edited by Patrick H. Beckett, pp. 75–90. Acoma Books, Ramona, New Mexico.

Hough, Walter
1907   *Antiquities of the Upper Gila and Salt Rivers in Arizona and New Mexico.* Bureau of American Ethnology Bulletin No. 35. U.S. Government Printing Office, Washington, D.C.

Kayser, David W.
1973   A Prehistoric Water Control System. *El Palacio* 79(3):30–1.

Kintigh, Keith
1994   Chaco, Communal Architecture, and Cibolan Aggregation. In *The Ancient Southwestern Community: Models and Methods for the Study of Prehistoric Social Organization,* edited by Wirt H. Wills and Robert D. Leonard, pp. 131–40. University of New Mexico Press, Albuquerque.

Laumbach, Karl W.
1992   *Reconnaissance Survey of The National Park Service Ojo Caliente Study Area, Socorro County, New Mexico.* Human Systems Research, Tularosa, New Mexico.

Laumbach, Karl W., and David T. Kirkpatrick
1983   *The Black Range Survey: A 2% Archaeological Sample of State Lands in Sierra County, New Mexico.* Cultural

Resources Management Division, New Mexico State University, Las Cruces.

LeBlanc, Steven A.
1983   *The Mimbres People.* Thames and Hudson, London.
1986   Development of Archaeological Thought on the Mimbres Region. In *Emil W. Haury's Prehistory of the Southwest,* edited by J. Jefferson Reid and David E. Doyel, pp. 297–304. University of Arizona Press, Tucson.

Lekson, Stephen H.
1986   Mimbres Riverine Adaptations. In *Mogollon Variability,* edited by Charlotte Benson and Steadman Upham, pp. 181–89. University Museum Occasional Papers No. 15. New Mexico State University, Las Cruces.
1989   An Archaeological Reconnaissance of the Rio Grande Valley in Sierra County, New Mexico. *The Artifact* 27(2):1–102.
1990   *Mimbres Archaeology of the Upper Gila, New Mexico.* University of Arizona Press, Tucson.
1992a   Mimbres Art and Archaeology. In *Archaeology, Art, and Anthropology: Papers in Honor of J. J. Brody,* edited by M. S. Duran and David T. Kirkpatrick, pp. 111–22. The Archaeological Society of New Mexico No. 18. Albuquerque.
1992b   The Surface Archaeology of Southwestern New Mexico. *The Artifact* 30(3): 1–36.
1993   Chaco, Hohokam, and Mimbres: The Southwest in the 11th and 12th Centuries. *Expedition* 35(1):44–52.

Lekson, Stephen H., Mark D. Elson, and Douglas B. Craig
1992   Tonto Basin Culture History. In *Research Design for the Roosevelt Community Development Study,* edited by William H. Doelle, Henry D. Wallace, Mark D. Elson,

and Douglas B. Craig, pp. 21–32. Anthropological Papers No. 12. Center for Desert Archaeology, Tucson.

Lekson, Stephen H., Karl Laumbach, Peter J. McKenna, and David Kirkpatrick
1988   *Reconnaissance Survey of Ojo Caliente, Alamosa Creek, Southwestern Socorro County, New Mexico.* Human Systems Research, Tularosa, New Mexico.

Lekson, Stephen H., and Alan Rorex
1987   *Archaeological Survey of the Cottonwood Spring and Indian Tanks Sites, Dona Ana County, New Mexico.* Human Systems Research, Tularosa, New Mexico.

Marshall, Michael P., and Henry J. Walt
1984   *Rio Abajo: Prehistory and History of a Rio Grande Province.* New Mexico Historic Preservation Division, Santa Fe.

McGimsey, Charles R. III
1980   *Mariana Mesa: Seven Prehistoric Settlements in West-Central New Mexico.* Papers of the Peabody Museum of Archaeology and Ethnology No. 72. Harvard University, Cambridge.

Minnis, Paul, and Steven A. LeBlanc
1979   *The Destruction of Three Sites in Southwestern New Mexico. In Vandalism of Cultural Resources,* edited by Dee Green and Steven LeBlanc, pp. 69–78. Cultural Resources Report No. 28. USDA, Forest Service, Albuquerque.

Nelson, Margaret C.
1986   Occupational History of Palomas Drainage, Western Sierra County, New Mexico. In *Mogollon Variability,* edited by Charlotte Benson and Steadman Upham, pp. 157–68. University Museum Occasional Papers 15. New Mexico State University, Las Cruces.

1993   Changing Occupational Patterns Among Prehistoric Horticulturalists in Southwestern New Mexico. *Journal of Field Archaeology* 20(1): 43–58.

Nelson, Ben A., and Steven A. LeBlanc
1986   *Short-term Sedentism in the American Southwest: The Mimbres Valley Salado.* University of New Mexico Press, Albuquerque.

Peterson, John A.
1988   Settlement and Subsistence Patterns in the Reserve Phase and Mountain Mogollon: A Test Case in Devils Park, New Mexico. *The Kiva* 53(2): 113–27.

Ravesloot, John C.
1979   *The Animas Phase: The Post-Classic Mimbres Occupation of the Mimbres Valley, New Mexico.* Unpublished Master's thesis, Southern Illinois University, Carbondale.

Rice, Glen E.
1975   *A Systematic Explanation of Mogollon Settlement Pattern Changes.* Unpublished Ph.D. dissertation, University of Washington, Seattle.

Schaafsma, Curtis
1979   The "El Paso Phase" and its Relationship to the "Casas Grandes Phenomenon." In *Jornada Mogollon Archaeology,* edited by Patrick H. Beckett and Regge N. Wiseman, pp. 383–88. Historic Preservation Bureau, Santa Fe.

Shafer, Harry J.
1995   Architecture and Symbolism in Transitional Pueblo Development in the Mimbres Valley, Southwestern New Mexico. *Journal of Field Archaeology* 22(1):23–47.

Wiseman, Regge N.
1986   *An Initial Study of the Origins of Chupadero Black-on-White.* Technical Note 2. Albuquerque Archaeological Society, Albuquerque.

Chapter 12

Impressions of Pueblo III Settlement Trends among the Rio Abajo and Eastern Border Pueblos

Katherine A. Spielmann

The region covered in this chapter is quite broad, ranging from the Rio Abajo on the west to the foothills of the Sangre de Cristo Mountains on the east, and south to the middle Pecos in the vicinity of Roswell. It is indicative of the relative lack of research on the Pueblo III period in this area that an archaeologist dealing with protohistoric and historic pueblos has been asked to summarize the current state of knowledge on this earlier period. What I hope to convey here is a general sense of the trends in demographic and settlement patterns through a synthesis of settlement data available largely in published sources. Toward the end of the chapter I briefly examine several models relating to the process of aggregation, and consider those that appear to be most appropriate to the eastern border situation. The conclusions I come to, with regard to pattern identification and explanation, should be considered hypotheses that may be substantiated or refuted by further data from the districts discussed here.

Conclusions concerning the Pueblo III period in the Rio Abajo-eastern border area are hampered by a general lack of research on pre-Pueblo IV occupations in the region. With the exception of the Rio Abajo, the area lacks large-scale, systematic surveys and information on site sizes and kiva counts. Excavations of Pueblo III sites in both areas are few, and chronology is almost universally based on ceramic cross dates. In the entire region, only two suites of radiocarbon dates exist for the Pueblo III period, and both are from southeastern New Mexico. Jane Kelley's project has produced a number of radiocarbon and obsidian hydration dates for the Robinson site, north of Capitan (Stewart, Driver,

and Kelley 1991), and John Speth has obtained radiocarbon and archaeomagnetic dates for Henderson Pueblo east of Roswell (Rocek and Speth 1986). Cordell's (1977a, 1977b) work at Tijeras Pueblo produced a total of 331 tree-ring dates for that site. Hayes (1981) reports no tree-ring dates for the early pueblo at Gran Quivira. In the absence of reliable site size and chronological data from the eastern border area, it is not possible to provide a graph of changing population sizes over time. Figure 12.1 depicts sites greater than 50 rooms that were occupied between A.D. 1100 and 1400 in the study region.

For discussion purposes I have divided the eastern border area into seven districts (see figure 12.1). The following summarizes the settlement and demographic data available from these districts.

Regional Archaeology of the Southern Rio Grande

Middle Pecos-Roswell District

Data concerning Pueblo III occupations in this district are available from Jelinek's (1967) survey of the Middle Pecos, and Kelley's, Speth's and Wiseman's work at sites on tributaries of the Pecos River east of Roswell (Holden 1955; Kelley 1984; Rocek and Speth 1986; Wiseman 1985; Emslie, Speth, and Wiseman 1992). In this area, the early Pueblo III period is subsumed under Jelinek's Late Mesita Negra phase (A.D. 1100–1200), which is characterized by shallow, slab-lined pit houses. None of these sites has been excavated.

Late Pueblo III sites include those identified as McKenzie phase (1200–1350) by Jelinek. These sites contain rectangular,

slab-based surface rooms (jacals), and possibly some adobe surface rooms (structure at site P4C). Jelinek postulated that the area was abandoned by settled farmers after A.D. 1350, and proposed that these farmers may have become bison hunters. More recent research east of Roswell has produced at least one site, Henderson Pueblo, with an occupation dating into the late fourteenth and early fifteenth centuries that shows evidence of both farming and bison hunting.

Bloom Mound, located on the Hondo River east of Roswell, was excavated by the Roswell Archaeological Society between 1938 and 1949 and by Texas Technical College in 1954. Data from these excavations were published by Kelley (1984; Holden 1955). She equated the site with Lincoln phase sites she had worked on in the Sierra Blanca area, which would date the site roughly between A.D. 1200 and 1400. Bloom Mound contained one deep, rectangular, subterranean structure and at least nine adobe surface rooms. Bloom Mound is notable for seven copper bells that were found there. The bells and the macaw found at nearby Rocky Arroyo (Emslie, Speth, and Wiseman 1992) suggest that trading relations to the south may have been more developed than those to the north during Pueblo III times.

Henderson Pueblo, which is within sight of Bloom Mound, was excavated in 1980 and 1981 under the direction of John Speth (figure 12.2). The site is an E-shaped, 50- to 70-room adobe pueblo with one large rectangular subterranean structure (Rocek and Speth 1986; Speth, personal communication 1990). Interestingly, both Kelley and Speth have questioned the ceremonial nature of the subterranean

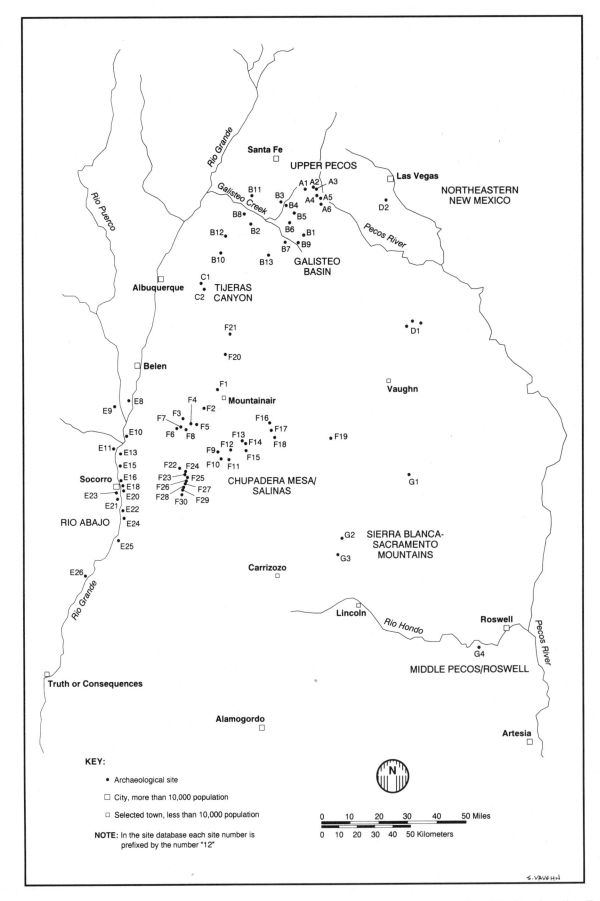

Figure 12.1. Distribution of sites with 50 rooms or more occupied between A.D. 1100 and 1400, southern Rio Grande region. Each site identification number is prefixed by the number 12 in the appendix.

structures at Bloom Mound and Henderson, and thus I do not refer to them as kivas. The radiocarbon and archaeomagnetic dates from the site indicate an occupation between 1250 and 1325, with a possible reoccupation in the late fourteenth and early fifteenth centuries.

The site of Rocky Arroyo, 4 miles east of Henderson Pueblo, was essentially destroyed by local amateurs. Regge Wiseman was able to obtain some data from the site through salvage excavations. The site consists of at least three large, deep rectangular pit rooms and associated midden. Wiseman (1985) dated Rocky Arroyo to approximately A.D. 1300 based on ceramics. More recently, four radiocarbon dates (Emslie, Speth, and Wiseman 1992) place the occupation between A.D. 1250 and 1325.

Sierra Blanca–
Sacramento Mountains District

This district has been divided by researchers (e.g., Kelley 1984) into a northern and a southern component based largely on architectural styles. The significance of these phase designations with respect to other aspects of human behavior (e.g., diet, mobility, social organization, ethnicity) remains unclear (Rocek, personal communication 1994).

In the southern component, the Pueblo III occupation is known as the Glencoe phase. Glencoe phase sites are found on the eastern slopes of the Sacramento and the Sierra Blanca Mountains (Kelley 1984; Spoerl 1985; Rocek 1990, n.d.). The phase is dated roughly between A.D. 900 and 1400, although Rocek (n.d.) has recently obtained three calibrated AMS dates from the Dunlap-Salazar site that range between A.D. 500 and 700. Two calibrated AMS dates from the same site were previously obtained by Stewart, Driver, and Kelley (1991) and document a late tenth-century occupation at the site.

Glencoe sites are open, scattered arrangements of pit houses, with perhaps 5 to 10 pit houses occupied at any one time.

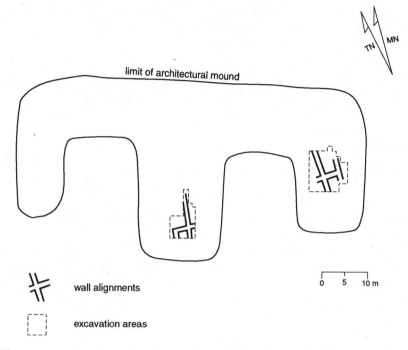

Figure 12.2. Henderson Pueblo near Roswell, New Mexico (from Rocek and Speth 1986:figure 6). Used with permission of the University of Michigan Museum of Anthropology.

No public architecture has been excavated to date in the relatively small Glencoe phase settlements (Kelley 1984:47). Rocek (n.d.) postulates that occupation at these sites was seasonal but recurrent, as the range of dates from Dunlap-Salazar would suggest. The lack of ceremonial structures at these sites is not unusual given that the Glencoe population appears to have occupied small and dispersed settlements (Kelley 1984:47). It is noteworthy that late Glencoe phase sites are contemporaneous with Lincoln phase pueblos in the northern component of this district (see discussion that follows).

The northern component Pueblo III occupations are divided into two phases, Corona and Robinson. Corona phase sites occupy the eastern slopes of the Capitan Mountains and the upper Gallo drainage (Kelley 1984; Ravesloot and Spoerl 1984). These sites are estimated to date between A.D. 900 and 1200, however the radiocarbon dates cluster right around A.D. 900 (Kelley 1984:50; 1991:169). Sites are widely dispersed and are comprised of a scattered arrangement of small jacal units of one to nine rooms. Site sizes range from a single structure to 30 to 40 structures per site. Trash is rather sparse on Corona phase sites, suggesting short-term or seasonal occupation (Kelley 1991).

Lincoln phase sites date between A.D. 1200 and about 1400. They are located from the Upper Gallo drainage to the Hondo drainage. The sites are multiroom pueblos of stone masonry and coursed adobe. Site layout consists either of linear room blocks facing east on a plaza with a square, deep kiva, or an enclosed square around a small plaza with a kiva. The Robinson site, recently excavated by Kelley (1979, 1991; Stewart, Driver, and Kelley 1991) is an example of the latter type. The site contains 200 rooms, with 150 in the enclosed square. No kiva was found in the plaza, but a large rectangular room built into a room block has been identified as a possible kiva. Floral data from the site (Adams 1991) suggest a greater emphasis on corn horticulture than during the Corona phase (Kelley 1991). Based on data from the Dunlap-Salazar site, however, Rocek (1990, n.d.)

has recently questioned whether a shift in emphasis actually occurred with the advent of the Lincoln phase, or whether corn is simply better preserved at the larger, longer-occupied Lincoln-phase pueblos.

To date virtually no transitional sites between the Corona and Lincoln phases have been identified. Although the Corona phase sites date to A.D. 900, researchers in the area do not expect that there was an occupational hiatus (Stewart, Driver, and Kelley 1991), and Lincoln phase sites may contain these "transitional" remains. For example, there is a linear room block at the Robinson site that dates to the early Pueblo III period (Kelley 1991). Aggregation in the Sierra Blanca area was never on the scale of other areas in the Southwest, and Kelley estimates that a maximum of 200 people may have occupied Robinson at any one time (Kelley 1991:175).

Chupadera Mesa-Salinas District

In the late 1960s, T. Caperton (1981) conducted a survey as part of the National Park Service's Mound 7 excavation project at Gran Quivira. The area he covered ranged from Abo Pass on the northwest to the foothills of the Gallinas Mountains on the southeast. Sites were located through interviews with local ranchers. The Pueblo III occupation in this area includes pit house, jacal, and early masonry sites. Dates for these sites are based on ceramic cross dates.

Pit house period sites were occupied between A.D. 800 and 1200; Caperton provides no data on site layouts and sizes. Ice (1968) excavated two pit houses and four surface structures at Gran Quivira that appear to have been roughly contemporaneous. Ceramics in these structures indicate that they date to roughly the late thirteenth century. If this dating is correct, then the transition to aggregated masonry pueblos may have been quite rapid in the Salinas District (Tainter and Levine 1987).

Jacal period sites were occupied between A.D. 1100 and 1350. Some jacal structures occur on pit house sites (e.g.,

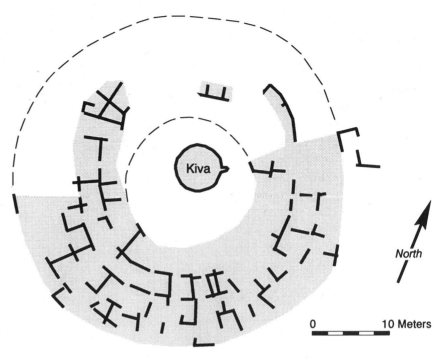

Figure 12.3. Ground plan for the early glaze period occupation of Gran Quivira. This is the only known circular site layout for Salinas area sites of this time period.

Kite site; see Rautman 1990); other jacals are associated with early masonry structures (e.g., Montezuma's Ruin). Ten jacal-only sites were located by Caperton (1981). The jacal sites contain between 1 and 10 rooms per dwelling and up to 50 rooms per village. Rooms are arranged most commonly in I- or L-shaped blocks on a north-south axis. The room blocks were not grouped around plazas. Caperton found several architecturally transitional half jacal, half masonry structures on sites in the southern portion of his survey area, near Gran Quivira.

The density and distribution of jacal sites is vastly under-represented by the current archaeological record. One of the local ranchers who grew up in Mountainair noted that many of the bean fields cultivated in the 1940s had been covered with the upright slab footings characteristic of jacal structures (Jerry Shaw, personal communication 1993). These slabs were removed from the fields to facilitate cultivation, and now only artifact scatters document the existence of these sites.

Early Masonry period sites date from the late thirteenth through mid-fifteenth

century. These sites share a common village plan: rectangular units arranged around a central plaza, some with outlying houseblocks (like Robinson). A kiva is often located in the central plaza, but may occur outside. The early glaze ware pueblo at Gran Quivira is an exception to the quadrangular pattern (figure 12.3), being the only circular pueblo known in the Salinas area. It did have a kiva in the central plaza, and is estimated to have been about 200 rooms in size (Hayes 1981).

In 1986 archaeologists from Eastern New Mexico University revisited 10 of 34 glaze period sites documented by Mera (1940) on the west side of Chupadera Arroyo (Montgomery and Bowman 1989). The sites on which they focused their efforts were located southwest of Chupadera Mesa and east of the Sierra de los Pinos. Based on ceramic dating, the occupations at all 10 sites began in the fourteenth century, although Mera noted pit houses at LA 1069. These plaza-oriented, masonry pueblos range in configuration from C-shaped room blocks with kivas in the plaza (LA 1070, 1076) to 16 room blocks arranged around three plazas (LA 1072).

Although the majority of the ceramics identified during Montgomery and Bowman's (1989) survey dates to Glaze A times (A.D. 1300–1425), LA 1070, 1072, 1073, 1075, and 1076 produced small samples of later glaze wares that indicate they were occupied to some degree until after the introduction of Glaze E, between about A.D. 1525 and 1600. Thus, the Chupadera Arroyo area contains an additional, relatively unknown concentration of post-fourteenth century occupation in central New Mexico. I should note that Montgomery and Bowman's room counts in the data base may appear somewhat high in comparison to counts for other sites in the Salinas area due to their assumption that there were three-storied room blocks at many of the sites.

Galisteo Basin District

Cordell (1979:56), citing Lang (1977) suggests that there is a scarcity of Pueblo II occupation in the Galisteo Basin, indicating a possible hiatus in occupation. Early Pueblo III sites appear scarce as well, although by A.D. 1200 agricultural communities had been established in the basin. These communities contained both pit houses and pueblo-style dwellings. Population in the basin appears to have increased considerably after around A.D. 1250, and most Pueblo III sites were established between about 1280 and 1320 (Stuart and Gauthier 1981:99). These late Pueblo III sites are aggregated villages of masonry and adobe rectangular room blocks grouped around plazas. Sites include Piedra Lumbre, Largo, and Paa-ko (Lambert 1954).

The fourteenth century witnessed continued growth in late Pueblo III villages. By around A.D. 1330 there was a change in settlement location, as many early sites were abandoned, and new sites established where water may have been more reliable. Large pueblos were founded beginning ca. A.D. 1350 on Galisteo Creek and its tributaries (Cordell 1979:58). Estimates of site sizes for the early glaze period oc-

cupations are virtually nonexistent. Reed (1954) did suggest, however, that the early glaze period building at San Marcos, which dates to the mid- to late fourteenth century based on ceramics, contained over 100 rooms.

Tijeras Canyon District

There was no substantial Pueblo III occupation in the area until near the end of the thirteenth century. The early Pueblo III sites that have been located through survey are limited activity sites, possibly suggesting seasonal use (Blevins and Joiner 1977; Anschuetz 1986). By A.D. 1250 the first year-round use of the canyon developed as small villages were established (e.g., Dinosaur Rock and Coconito) that contained pit houses, jacal, and/or adobe surface rooms. This initial occupation was followed relatively quickly around A.D. 1300 by a dramatic change in population and site size in the canyon. Small sites appear to have been abandoned, and two large sites established, Tijeras and San Antonio (Cordell 1977a).

Several seasons of work at Tijeras Pueblo have provided detailed data on the growth of that site (Cordell 1977a, 1977b, 1980). Early Tijeras Pueblo consisted of approximately 200 adobe rooms in room blocks loosely arranged around a central plaza containing a large kiva. The pueblo grew by accretion, with almost continuous building between A.D. 1313 and 1368. It was partially abandoned in late fourteenth century, and a new, smaller pueblo was built over the earlier one (Cordell 1977b).

Upper Pecos District

No sites have been identified in the Upper Pecos drainage that date between A.D. 900 and 1200. The most recent dated pit houses were occupied in the early to mid-ninth century, and there is virtually no evidence of jacal construction in this district (Nordby 1981:7 and personal communication 1991). Whether this lack of sites is an indication of a hiatus in occupation

similar to that suggested for the Galisteo Basin or is simply the result of lack of research in the area is unknown at this time.

Between roughly A.D. 1200 and 1400 the prevailing settlement pattern in the upper Pecos was one of a few large masonry or adobe pueblos, and numerous dispersed one- to two-room sites (Nordby, personal communication 1991). Two sites, Forked Lightning and Dick's Ruin, were probably built in the early thirteenth century. Forked Lightning is a straggling accretion of over 100 rooms constructed of coursed adobe. It contained two round subterranean kivas and five above-ground kivas. Dick's ruin was L-shaped, also over 100 rooms in size, and built of coursed adobe (Kidder 1958). These two sites continued to be occupied into the late fourteenth century.

By A.D. 1300 there were several large masonry pueblos in the valley: Pecos itself (Black-on-White ruin), Rowe, Hobson-Dressler, and an unnamed ruin near Pecos (Nordby 1981:9). Rowe Ruin was organized as three joined quadrangular room blocks (Guthe 1917). Early Pecos Pueblo was comprised of low, straggling buildings around large rectangular plazas (Kidder 1932). Later in the fourteenth century Arrowhead Ruin and Loma Lothrop were built (Holden 1955). Arrowhead Ruin is arranged around a central plaza with a kiva.

Northeastern New Mexico

The following information is largely from Stuart and Gauthier (1981:303–9). There has been relatively little published research conducted in this area, but I include it in this discussion to call attention to the easternmost extent of Pueblo III occupation in the Pueblo world. Four areas were identified by Stuart and Gauthier that contained relatively high densities of Pueblo III sites. Three are in the eastern foothills of the Sangre de Cristo Mountains, and the fourth is along Pintada Draw, west-southwest of Santa Rosa, New Mexico.

The Pintada Canyon sites are intriguing; unfortunately, no work has been done there. The Laboratory of Anthropology files list sites ranging from large adobe pueblos to one- to two-room jacal structures. These have been dated from Pueblo III to early Pueblo IV times based on ceramic assemblages.

The Watrous Valley, Tecolote, and Cimarron areas all have somewhat extensive Pueblo III occupations consisting of multiple room block sites. The Tecolote site (LA 296) contains 10 room blocks. In the Watrous area up to five room blocks have been documented at a single site.

The Cimarron area is the most thoroughly researched of the three due to activities of the Philmont Scout Ranch, which have been summarized by Glassow (1980). The early Pueblo III period, the Ponil phase (A.D. 1100–1250), is characterized in this area by villages with multi-room structures. Glassow's (1980) data document a dramatic population growth during the subsequent Cimarron phase, from A.D. 1200 to 1300. Cimarron phase sites were constructed usually of adobe but also of masonry, and tended to be more restricted to lowland settings than the preceding Ponil phase sites. Site size appears fairly small, with the largest site containing only three concentrations of building rubble. By the beginning of the fourteenth century all northeastern New Mexico habitation sites appear to have been abandoned.

Rio Abajo

All of the following information is taken from Marshall and Walt (1984) who conducted an 80 percent survey of land immediately bordering the Rio Grande from above the Rio Puerco south to below Milligan Gulch. The Pueblo III period, or late Elmendorf phase (A.D. 1100–1300), developed out of the early Elmendorf phase (A.D. 950/1000–1100) pattern of nucleated villages of noncontiguous jacal structures and pit houses. The dates for both phases are approximate due to the lack of temporal differentiation in local ceramics and reliance on trade wares for dating. Very few intrusive wares are found on early Elmendorf phase sites, and thus the lack of intrusive wares, particularly White Mountain Red Wares, determines the dates for this phase. The temporal boundaries of the late Elmendorf phase are based on the presence of temporally sensitive White Mountain Red Wares found on the sites.

Late Elmendorf sites are dominated by masonry pueblos roughly organized around plazas, although isolated hamlets and smaller nucleated villages continue to be occupied. The masonry pueblos are located in more elevated settings than the hamlets. Jacal construction continues to some degree at all types of sites. Pit rooms tend to occur in plazas and may be kivas.

Marshall and Walt (1984) estimate that roughly 5 percent of the population lived in small sites. Most pueblo sites are 22 to 54 rooms in size, with the largest being 150 rooms. These sites are similar in size to early Elmendorf sites. Thus, the settlement data suggest that although more of the Rio Abajo population lived in larger sites in Pueblo III than in Pueblo II times, the size of these aggregated settlements did not increase. Based on these data I suggest that no significant organizational change with regard to settlement structure in the Rio Abajo occurred during the Pueblo III period.

Marshall and Walt (1984:97) suggest that even though there was a 76 percent increase in the number of rooms from the early Elmendorf phase, this may be more a factor of visibility than population growth. Moreover, there is little ceramic evidence of outside contact during this time. Consequently, they do not posit an immigration of people into the area during the late Elmendorf phase.

The lack of midden at late Elmendorf sites suggests short-term occupation, and the phase itself may have been short. Sites are defensively located, causing Marshall and Walt to postulate social unrest as the cause for site relocation and the increase in aggregation during Pueblo III times.

In the early fourteenth century, with the advent of Glaze A ceramics, there was a marked increase in population in the Rio Abajo, and a dramatic change in settlement structure and pattern. Marshall and Walt (1984:135) postulate a sevenfold increase in population at this time. Fourteenth-century site layouts characteristically have room blocks tightly clustered around a single plaza containing a kiva. They averaged 96 ground floor rooms in size, with a range of 60 to 122 rooms, roughly twice the size of late Elmendorf settlements. Occupation of the area expanded to include the west bank of the Rio Grande. During the fourteenth century, sites were distributed at regular intervals along the Rio Grande on both banks.

Hypothesized Temporal Trends

Based on the data discussed previously, which are summarized in figure 12.4, I tentatively propose the following trends in settlement patterning for the period A.D. 1100 to 1400 in the eastern border area. First, the preceding Pueblo II as well as the early Pueblo III settlement patterns seem to be different in the northern and southern parts of the area, with the exception of the foothills east of the Sangre de Cristo Mountains. The southern districts (middle Pecos, Sierra Blanca, Salinas) are distinguished by an indigenous, highly dispersed population that at least seasonally occupied pit house and jacal settlements. The northern districts (Galisteo, Tijeras, Pecos, and I would guess, Pintada Canyon) appear to have been used intermittently, as evidenced by limited activity sites, but no habitation sites were occupied in these districts until roughly A.D. 1200. The exception is the Cimarron area where Pueblo II habitations have been documented. Although the "ethnic" significance of the distinction between brown ware and gray ware ceramic traditions has yet to be established, it is noteworthy that the brown ware districts (which include northeastern New Mexico) exhibit Pueblo II habitations, while gray ware districts do not.

Despite these differences in preceding patterns of occupation, regional changes that occurred between A.D. 1200 and 1300 appear similar throughout the eastern border area, particularly given the rough dating (largely ceramic) available for each district. By mid-Pueblo III times (ca. A.D. 1200–1250), most districts in both the north and south display quite a diversity in architecture, including pit houses, jacals, and masonry and/or adobe pueblos. And by the end of the thirteenth century, a number of pueblos greater than 100 rooms in size were established in every part of this region, with the exception of the Las Vegas-Philmont Scout Ranch area east of the Sangre de Cristo Mountains that appears to have been abandoned around A.D. 1300. In many districts (e.g., Salinas, Sierra Blanca, Galisteo) the prevailing village form was a quadrangular arrangement of room blocks around a central plaza, often with a single kiva in the plaza. This settlement pattern tends to persist throughout the fourteenth century.

Although we have been asked to limit our discussion to roughly A.D. 1100 to 1350, it seems relevant to point out a second period of aggregation that developed out of the first in the eastern border area during the fifteenth century. Very few of the quadrangular pueblos occupied at the time of the Pueblo III-Pueblo IV transition continue well into the fifteenth century. The Roswell and Sierra Blanca Districts and northeastern New Mexico lack evidence of habitation after the early fifteenth century. In the Salinas area, only 7 of 19 known pueblos continued to be occupied. At Pecos, six pueblos were reduced to one by roughly A.D. 1450. Cordell (1979) notes a similar shift in population in the Galisteo Basin. Moreover, in those pueblos that do persist into the protohistoric period, there is evidence of extensive rebuilding. Gran Quivira, Pueblo Colo-

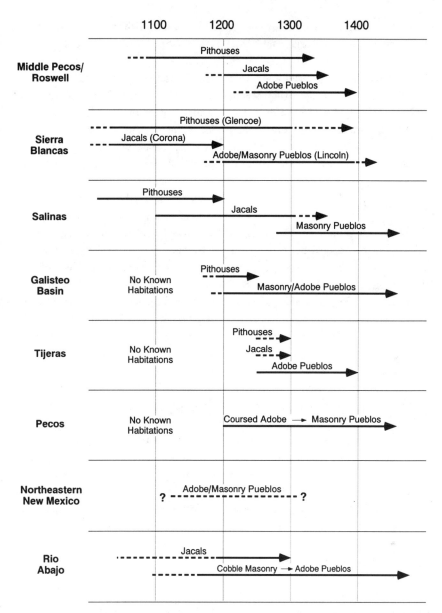

Figure 12.4. Architectural trends between A.D. 1100 and 1400 by district, southern Rio Grande region.

rado (Salinas version), San Marcos, and Pecos all show evidence of earlier pueblos (with black-on-white and early glaze wares) beneath fifteenth- and sixteenth-century room blocks. Thus, a process that began in the Pueblo III period continued in this area well into the Pueblo IV period.

The eastern border area may be profitably compared with the Rio Abajo, where population aggregation began much earlier, during Pueblo II times, and continued into the Pueblo III period. The mixture of jacal, pit house, and pueblo architecture occurs there in Pueblo II rather than Pueblo III times. During the Pueblo III period, most of the local population moved into somewhat plaza-oriented masonry pueblos. More precise dating of this period in the Rio Abajo is important for understanding the rapidity and nature of aggregation there. If the late Elmendorf phase is indeed short, as Marshall and Walt (1984: 97) hypothesize, and dates to the latter portion of the Pueblo III period, then the move to masonry pueblos, and greater aggregation in the Rio Abajo would have been contemporaneous with aggregation in the eastern border area and would date to the late thirteenth and early fourteenth centuries throughout the region. The larger plaza-oriented Rio Abajo pueblos of the fourteenth century are similar in layout to those in the eastern border area.

Explanations

Explaining the process of aggregation in this region is hampered not only by our fuzzy understanding of aggregation in general, but also by the lack of specific information on Pueblo II and Pueblo III settlement systems. Moreover, a single model probably will not account for all of the districts and regions discussed here. What follows are my impressions concerning which models are likely to be useful in understanding aggregation in this area.

During the conference several models were discussed, some of which appear to be applicable to the area and others perhaps not. Those that I consider here are the warfare (Haas and Creamer), competitive emulation (Lipe), adaptation (Dean, also aspects of Kohler), and land tenure and use rights (Adler 1992) models.

Warfare has been postulated as a causal factor in aggregation in the Rio Abajo (Marshall and Walt 1984) and Salinas Districts (Caperton 1981) based on the fact that Pueblo III sites in these regions tend to be situated on prominences. At least for the Salinas area, I find this model difficult to accept, as it fails to specify against whom defense is needed, and why. Conflict with immigrant populations has been ruled out in the Rio Abajo, because outside immigration is not postulated to have taken place until after A.D. 1300. Also, given that "defensive" early masonry pueblos in the Salinas area were built directly at locations of earlier jacal structures, one would have to argue that the jacals, too, were located for defensive purposes (see Tainter and Levine 1987 for such an argument).

In contrast to the warfare model, I have argued (Spielmann and Eshbaugh 1989) that early masonry site location in the Salinas District has more to do with the fact that wild resources formed a significant component of the Pueblo III diet. Sites were situated in upland locations to facilitate the exploitation of these resources. Jane Kelley (1991; see also 1984:60) has made a similar argument for the Sierra Blanca area. In the Rio Abajo, masonry sites are not found in the same locations as the earlier jacal hamlets. Defense may have been more of an issue in this area, though data other than the "defensibility" of the site location need to be marshalled to support the warfare hypothesis. At this point it is not possible to resolve the issue, and the explanations (wild resources vs. warfare) are not mutually exclusive.

The competitive emulation model, although suitable for other areas of the Southwest, is simply not applicable for those portions of the eastern border area that contained a highly dispersed Pueblo II occupation. The small scale of aggregation in these districts does not warrant this form of competition. The model may explain the rapid shift to aggregated pueblos in the northern portion of the study area (Galisteo, Tijeras, Pecos), although I would argue that the land tenure model is equally applicable there (see later discussion).

At this point I tend to favor a combination of the adaptation and land use models, with the expectation that adaptive changes were in response to low frequency environmental change rather than demographic change. Let me first discuss demography.

The data concerning demographic change in the eastern border area are extremely slim. Thus, it is difficult to determine whether the aggregation we witness in the late thirteenth century involves only local populations or also immigrants. Even in the best-documented Pueblo III district, the Sierra Blanca area, the data are equivocal. As mentioned previously, there are virtually no dated sites

that fall between A.D. 900, the beginning of the Corona phase, and A.D. 1200, the beginning of the Lincoln phase and aggregated pueblos (Stewart, Driver, and Kelley 1991). Thus, it is impossible to say whether the Lincoln pueblos represent only Corona peoples or inmigration as well. In the Salinas District, the destruction of jacal sites in the wake of expanding twentieth century agricultural production suggests that there was a much more sizeable pre-aggregation population in this area than had been assumed. In the Rio Abajo, Marshall and Walt are fairly certain that there is little immigration during Pueblo III. In the absence of any contradicting information, I will be conservative and assume that there was little or no immigration into the southern portion of the study area during Pueblo III.

Immigration, when it occurs in the Rio Abajo, dates to the Pueblo IV period. Likewise, Baldwin (1983; cited in Montgomery and Bowman 1989:39) has argued that immigration into the Salinas District occurred early in the fourteenth century, based on the rapid demise of the Chupadero Black-on-white ceramic tradition at Abo and Quarai and its replacement with Glaze A wares. The southern Salinas Pueblos, Gran Quivira and its neighbors, did not participate in this ceramic transformation.

In the northern portion of the eastern border area, obviously, the process of aggregation was different. The Galisteo Basin, Tijeras Canyon, Pecos, and even the Cimarron area appear to witness dramatic increases in population in the late thirteenth century that can best be accounted for by immigration. These populations may have emigrated from areas that had already experienced aggregation and thus were largely replicating a pre-existing organization.

Environmentally, there do appear to be some intriguing patterns with regard to temporal and spatial distributions of rainfall that suggest to me aggregation could have been caused in the southern portion of the region, at least in part, by stress on crop production among dispersed populations who then aggregated in areas more favorable for crop production. Two sources of data—dendroclimatology and modern weather station records—support this argument. The tree-ring sequences are those developed for the Gran Quivira and Santa Fe areas (Dean and Robinson 1977; Rose, Dean, and Robinson 1981:figure 34). The Gran Quivira tree-ring sequence dates from A.D. 1200 to 1600. The two series track each other remarkably closely from A.D. 1200 until the 1380s.

The Santa Fe series documents annual rainfall at or below average for much of the latter half of the twelfth century (Rose, Dean, and Robinson 1981:figure 34). Between A.D. 1195 and 1210, however, Gran Quivira and Santa Fe experience very high rainfall. This high is followed by three periods of relative drought (almost two standard deviations below the mean) in the 1220s, 1250s, and 1280s. These dry periods may correspond roughly in date to the periods of aggregation that have been identified.

After three decades of above average rainfall in the 1290s to 1310s, precipitation again dropped close to two standard deviations below the mean in the 1340s. This is roughly the time of relocation of pueblos in the Galisteo Basin, and perhaps the abandonment of Quarai in the Salinas District. Finally, there is a fairly long period of drought in the 1390s to early 1400s in the Gran Quivira area, which may correspond to the period of site abandonment mentioned earlier. It also may have had an effect on farming in the Sierra Blancas, leading ultimately to the abandonment of that area by farmers in the early fifteenth century.

Information on the spatial distribution of rainfall in central New Mexico is provided by Rautman (1990:90–93), who analyzed weather data from 34 stations. The Galisteo Basin is the only district of interest here that is not represented by these stations. Rautman compared mean precipitation and the standard deviation around this mean from each station with

the regional mean and standard deviation. Of interest here is the fact that virtually all areas with mean precipitation values above the regional mean experienced Pueblo III aggregation, and virtually all areas with precipitation values below the mean have no Pueblo III occupation. The strength of this pattern is borne out in the Pintada Canyon area, where the nearest weather station (Palma) was the only station in that portion of New Mexico to experience precipitation above the mean.

Standard deviation data further distinguish between those areas that remained occupied into the fifteenth century and those areas that were abandoned. Specifically, Santa Fe, Pecos, Mountainair, and Gran Quivira are characterized by lower standard deviations, while Tijeras, Las Vegas, Palma (Pintada Canyon area), and the Sierra Blanca stations' standard deviations are greater than the mean standard deviation for the region.

In sum, the tree-ring data suggest that the initial period of aggregation in the eastern border area of the Southwest was preceded by about 15 years of relatively high rainfall, but was characterized by several periods of drought. Rautman's precipitation data indicate that Pueblo III populations occupied areas of relatively high mean rainfall. There may be a causal relationship between locations of aggregation and rainfall, but research must be done in specific districts to determine what local paleoclimatic conditions were in Pueblo III times, and whether the choice of specific Pueblo III site locations appears to have been constrained by agricultural needs.

As drought continued into the late 1390s and early 1400s, those areas with less predictable rainfall were abandoned, and those with more predictable rainfall increased in population size. Again, it is tempting to read some sort of causal connection into this correlation between climate and settlement pattern. However, more specific information is necessary to evaluate the strength of this association. For example, simulations of corn pro-

duction under climatic regimes in areas abandoned, and under regimes in areas experiencing growth would be very useful in assessing the degree to which the scale of precipitation variability experienced in the eastern border area significantly affects corn production.

Although subsistence stress may have been causal in moving people to better watered areas in some portions of the eastern border area, the establishment and maintenance of land use rights are likely to have been extremely important in the process of aggregation. Adler's land tenure-use rights model (1992) is elegant in its formulation, and relevant to understanding aggregation in the eastern border area. The necessity of legitimizing access to high quality agricultural land may have had a profound effect on the choice of the aggregated site location. For example, in the Sierra Blanca and Salinas Districts, aggregated pueblos were constructed on sites that had earlier jacal structures. Prior use rights may also have determined who moved into the relatively unoccupied northern districts. For example, during early Pueblo III, use of Tijeras Canyon appears to have been sporadic, while later in Pueblo III there were sizeable villages in the canyon. Perhaps descendants of people who hunted and collected in the area were the founders of Tijeras and San Antonio pueblos. Moreover, it is likely that concern over maintaining (defending?) use rights to increasingly limited areas of productive agricultural land dictated a settlement pattern of aggregated pueblos, rather than dispersed hamlets in areas favorable for cultivation. Demonstrating that this was the case unfortunately will be difficult.

Concluding Thoughts

The eastern border area did not experience aggregation until late in the Pueblo III period. In fact, the real heyday of much of this area was during the Pueblo IV period, when sizeable pueblos with multiple room blocks were established at some of the Glaze A pueblo locations, and strong

ties were developed with the Rio Grande
pueblos and with the Plains. Many of these
population centers persisted into the historic period and were missionized by the
Spaniards. These more monumental sites,
made even more visible by their Spanish
churches, have been the focus of most archaeological attention.

Interestingly, despite the relative wealth
of Pueblo IV data, the process of aggregation during the Pueblo IV period has rarely
been addressed in the eastern border area.
With the exception of Pecos, we have virtually no information on the processes
of growth at the large, Pueblo IV sites.
These pueblos as archaeological sites contain up to 26 separate room blocks, and
the sequence of occupation for these room
blocks over time is essentially unknown.
When that lack of knowledge is multiplied
by the number of pueblos in each district,
Pueblo IV aggregation becomes as enigmatic as the beginnings of this process in
Pueblo III times. And Kidder was told the
Southwest was a "sucked orange!"

This preliminary sketch is meant in
part to bestir those who are more knowledgeable than I in the Pueblo III archaeology of each of these districts. I look
forward to enlightenment about existing data and interpretations not discussed
here, and to new information that will be
forthcoming from the ongoing work of researchers in these areas. Would that there
were more of them!

Acknowledgments

Many people were very generous with information they possessed on the various
districts I have covered here. I would like
to thank Linda Cordell, Tom Rocek, Jane
Kelley, and Phil Shelley for sending me
publications and manuscripts. Tim Seaman and Rosemary Talley at the Lab of
Anthropology were very helpful in providing printouts of site information, and
checking on references. Unfortunately, I
did not have the time to pursue these
data further. John Speth, Jane Kelley,

Mike Adler, and two anonymous reviewers
offered helpful comments on the manuscript. Finally, I would like to thank Steve
Lekson and Bill Lipe for hosting one of
the most stimulating conferences I have
attended, and Mike Adler for making the
effort to bring these papers to publication.

References Cited

Adams, Karen R.
1991   Domesticated and Native Plants Re-
        covered From Robinson Pueblo and
        Other Regional Sites in the Capitan
        Area of New Mexico. In Mogollon V,
        edited by Patrick Beckett, pp. 220–
        28. COAS Publishing and Research,
        Las Cruces.
Adler, Michael
1992   Land Tenure Systems and Pre-
        historic Land Use: Perspectives
        from the American Southwest.
        Paper presented at the 57th Annual
        Meeting of the Society for American
        Archaeology, Pittsburgh.
Anschuetz, Kurt F.
1986   Pueblo III Subsistence, Settlement,
        and Territoriality in the Northern
        Rio Grande: The Albuquerque
        Frontier. Paper presented at the
        October New Mexico Archaeological
        Council, Albuquerque.
Baldwin, Stewart J.
1983   A Tentative Occupation Sequence
        for Abo Pass, Central New Mexico.
        COAS New Mexico Archaeology and
        History 1:12–18.
Blevins, Byron B., and Carol Joiner
1977   The Archaeological Survey of Tije-
        ras Canyon. Archaeological Report
        No. 18, pp. 124–68. USDA Forest
        Service, Southwestern Region,
        Albuquerque.
Caperton, Thomas J.
1981   An Archaeological Reconnaissance
        of the Gran Quivira Area. In Contri-
        butions to Gran Quivira Archaeology,
        edited by Alden C. Hayes, pp. 3–
        14. Publications in Archaeology
        No. 17. USDI, National Park Service,
        Washington, D.C.
Cordell, Linda S.
1977a   The 1975 Excavation of Tijeras
        Pueblo, Cibola National Forest, New
        Mexico. Archaeological Report No. 18,
        pp. 1–23. USDA Forest Service,
        Southwestern Region, Albuquerque.
1977b   The 1976 Excavation of Tijeras
        Pueblo, Cibola National Forest,
        New Mexico. Archaeological Re-
        port 18, pp. 169–200. Albuquerque:
        USDA Forest Service, Southwestern
        Region.
1979   A Cultural Resources Overview
        of the Middle Rio Grande Valley,
        New Mexico. USDA, Forest Service,
        Albuquerque Southwestern Region.
1980   Tijeras Canyon: Analyses of the Past.
        Maxwell Museum of Anthropology
        and the University of New Mexico
        Press, Albuquerque.
Dean, Jeffrey S., and William J. Robinson
1977   Dendroclimatic Variability in the
        American Southwest, A.D. 680 to 1970.
        Final Report to the National Park
        Service, Contract CX1595-5-0241.
        Laboratory of Tree-Ring Research,
        University of Arizona, Tucson.
Emslie, Steven D., John D. Speth, and Regge N.
Wiseman
1992   Two Prehistoric Puebloan Avifaunas
        from the Pecos Valley, Southeastern
        New Mexico. Journal of Ethnobiology
        12:83–115.
Glassow, Michael A.
1980   Prehistoric Agricultural Development
        in the Northern Southwest. Ballena
        Press, Socorro.
Guthe, Carl E.
1917   The Pueblo Ruin at Rowe, N.M. El
        Palacio 4 (IV):33–39.
Hayes, Alden C.
1981   Excavation of Mound 7. Publications
        in Archaeology No. 16. National
        Park Service, Washington, D.C.
Holden, Jane
1955   A Preliminary Report on the Bloom
        Mound. Texas Archaeological Society
        Bulletin 26:165–81.
Ice, R. J.
1968   A Report of the 1964 Excavations
        at Gran Quivira. Ms. on file, USDI,
        National Park Service, Southwest
        Region, Santa Fe.
Jelinek, Arthur J.
1967   A Prehistoric Sequence in the Middle
        Pecos Valley, New Mexico. Museum
        of Anthropology Anthropologi-
        cal Papers No. 31. University of
        Michigan, Ann Arbor.
Kelley, Jane H.
1979   The Sierra Blanca Restudy Project.
        In Jornada Mogollon Archaeology:
        Proceedings of the First Jornada
        Conference, ed. by Patrick Beckett
        and Regge N. Wiseman, pp. 107–32.
        New Mexico State University, Las
        Cruces.

1984   *The Archaeology of the Sierra Blanca Region of Southeastern New Mexico.* Museum of Anthropology Anthropological Papers No. 74. University of Michigan, Ann Arbor.

1991   *An Overview of the Capitan North Project. Mogollon v,* compiled by Patrick Beckett, pp. 166–76. COAS Publishing and Research, Las Cruces.

Kidder, Alfred V.
1932   *The Artifacts of Pecos.* Robert S. Peabody Foundation, Phillips Academy. Yale University, New Haven.

1958   *Pecos, New Mexico: Archaeological Notes.* Phillips Academy, Andover, Massachusetts.

Lambert, Marjorie F.
1954   *Paa-ko: Archaeological Chronicle of an Indian Village in North Central New Mexico,* Parts 1–5. Monograph No. 25. School of American Research, Santa Fe.

Lang, Richard W.
1977   *Archaeological Survey of the Upper San Cristobal Arroyo Drainage, Galisteo Basin, Santa Fe County, New Mexico.* Contract Program, School of American Research, Santa Fe.

Marshall, Michael P., and Henry J. Walt
1984   *Rio Abajo: Prehistory and History of A Rio Grande Province.* New Mexico Historic Preservation Program, Santa Fe.

Mera, H. P.
1940   *Population Changes in the Rio Grande Glaze Paint Area.* Technical Series No. 9. Laboratory of Anthropology, Santa Fe.

Montgomery, John, and Kathleen Bowman
1989   *Archaeological Reconnaissance of the Chupadera Arroyo Drainage, Central New Mexico.* Agency for Conservation Archaeology Report. New Mexico Historic Preservation Office, Santa Fe.

Nordby, Larry
1981   The Prehistory of the Pecos Indians. *Exploration: Pecos Ruins.* School of American Research, Santa Fe.

Rautman, Alison E.
1990   *The Environmental Context of Decision-Making: Coping Strategies among Prehistoric Cultivators in Central New Mexico.* Unpublished Ph.D. dissertation, Department of Anthropology, University of Michigan, Ann Arbor.

Ravesloot, John, and Patricia Spoerl
1984   The Jicarilla Mountains: Pre-Lincoln Phase Settlement in the Northern Jornada Mogollon Periphery. In *Recent Research in Mogollon Archaeology,* edited by Steadman Upham, Fred Plog, David G. Batcho, and Barbara E. Kauffman, pp. 179–92. University Museum Occasional Paper No. 10. New Mexico State University, Las Cruces.

Reed, Erik K.
1954   San Marcos Pueblo Excavations 1940. *El Palacio* 61:323–43.

Rocek, Thomas R.
1990   Examining the Pithouse to Pueblo Transition: The Dunlap-Salazer Site, LA 51344, in South-Central New Mexico. Paper presented at the 55th Annual Meeting of the Society for American Archaeology, Las Vegas, Nevada.

n.d.   Diet, Mobility, and Demography: Insights into the Pithouse-to-Pueblo Transition from the Dunlap-Salazar Site (LA 51344), Lincoln County, New Mexico. Ms. on file, Department of Anthropology, University of Delaware, Newark.

Rocek, Thomas R., and John D. Speth
1986   *The Henderson Site Burials.* Museum of Anthropology Technical Report 18. University of Michigan, Ann Arbor.

Rose, Martin R., Jeffrey S. Dean, and William J. Robinson
1981   *The Past Climate of Arroyo Hondo New Mexico Reconstructed from Tree Rings.* School of American Research Press, Santa Fe.

Spielmann, Katherine A., and David C. Eshbaugh
1989   *Salinas Archaeological Survey.* Report submitted to the USDA Forest Service, Cibola National Forest.

Spoerl, Patricia
1985   Mogollon Utilization of the Sacramento Mountains of Southcentral New Mexico. In *Views of the Jornada Mogollon: Proceedings of the Second Jornada Mogollon Archaeology Conference,* edited by Colleen M. Beck, pp. 33–40. Contributions in Anthropology No. 12. Eastern New Mexico University, Portales.

Stewart, Joseph D., Jonathon C. Driver, and Jane H. Kelley
1991   The Capitan North Project: Chronology. In *Mogollon v,* compiled by Patrick Beckett, pp. 177–90. COAS Publishing and Research, Las Cruces.

Stuart, David E, and Rory P. Gauthier
1981   *Prehistoric New Mexico: Background for Survey.* Historic Preservation Bureau, Santa Fe.

Tainter, Joseph A., and Frances Levine
1987   *Cultural Resources Overview: Central New Mexico.* USDA, Forest Service, Albuquerque.

Wiseman, Regge N.
1985   Bison, Fish, and Sedentary Occupations: Startling Data from Rocky Arroyo (LA 25277), Chaves County, New Mexico. In *Views of the Jornada Mogollon,* edited by Colleen M. Beck, pp. 30–32. Contributions in Anthropology No. 12. Eastern New Mexico University, Portales.

Chapter 13

Pueblo Cultures in Transition: The Northern Rio Grande

Patricia L. Crown, Janet D. Orcutt, and Timothy A. Kohler

When Europeans first entered the northern Rio Grande region in the sixteenth century, it was one of the most populous portions of the American Southwest. Yet archaeological investigations reveal that this was not always the case; prior to the thirteenth century, the northern Rio Grande harbored a surprisingly small population. Two issues have framed most examinations of population in this area: Where did the people occupying the northern Rio Grande come from, and how do these populations relate to the linguistic groups found in the sixteenth century (Ford et al. 1972; Reed 1949)? Although these issues continue to be of interest, their resolution will depend on accurate paleodemographic profiles—so far unavailable—for each district within the region. In this chapter we present some preliminary efforts toward building such a framework for the period from A.D. 1100 to 1400.

Studies of population dynamics in the northern Rio Grande are limited by the unevenness of the available data. Most excavations have concentrated on the large pueblos in the region, and many of these excavations have not been reported in complete form. Survey coverage has been spotty, destruction of sites through agriculture and development likely, and subfloor excavation of large sites minimal. Information on community settlement patterns and nonresidential use of the areas is lacking except in isolated pockets where research has fleshed out the prehistoric landscape. Although we are specifically interested here in large residential sites, accurate information on smaller sites is important to our reconstructions of population size and aggregation. Thus, caution must be exercised in evaluating

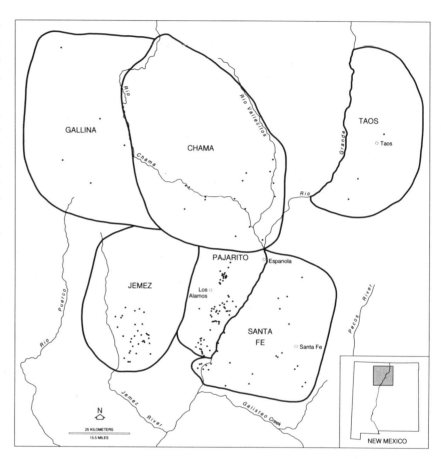

Figure 13.1. Districts of the northern Rio Grande discussed in the text.

any portraits of settlement growth and development for this region.

Many portions of the northern Rio Grande remained sparsely inhabited until after A.D. 1250. Population increased dramatically during the Pueblo III–Pueblo IV transition (A.D. 1250–1350) in the northern Rio Grande, with much of the population occupying large pueblos. With the exception of the Gallina District, communities changed in similar ways throughout the area, with trends toward population aggregation, construction of massive room blocks fronting formal plazas, agricultural intensification, and increased spacing be-

tween sites. The causes for this patterning are explored in this chapter. We begin by defining the "districts" in the area and the basic chronology. We then review evidence for population change throughout the area and examine evidence for changes in food production, community patterns, and extraregional interaction that may relate to shifting population dynamics. Finally, we interpret the patterning found on a broader scale.

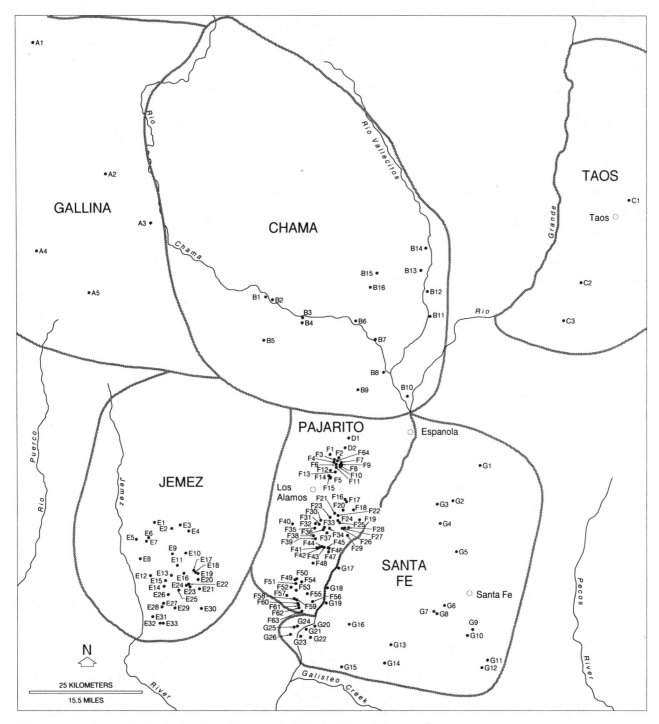

Figure 13.2.   Large sites in the districts; all site numbers begin with 11 (see appendix).

Districts of the Northern Rio Grande

As defined for this volume, our portion of the northern Rio Grande was restricted to an area bounded by the Colorado border on the north, the Galisteo Basin on the southeast, the southern extreme of the Pajarito Plateau on the southwest, the western reaches of the Jemez River on the west, and the Sangre de Cristo Mountains on the east. Elevation in this area varies from 5,000 to over 13,000 feet (1,524–3,963 m), and this variability is reflected in the presence of five life zones: Upper Sonoran, Transition, Canadian, Hudsonian, and Arctic-Alpine (Wetherington 1968:14). The fertile Rio Grande bottom land lies in a trough between parallel ranges of mountains: the Sangre de Cristo range on the east and San Juan-Jemez Mountains on the west.

The northern Rio Grande region subsumes six districts: the Taos, Gallina, Chama, Pajarito, Santa Fe, and Jemez Districts (figures 13.1 and 13.2). These divisions are based on a combination of geographic and ethnohistorical criteria, and except for the Gallina, were generally recognized in Bandelier's day (1892).[1] Each district exhibits relatively uniform developments and is characterized by homogeneous material culture and settlement patterns.

Chronology

The chronological sequence in common use in the northern Rio Grande was devised by Wendorf (1954, altered slightly by Wendorf and Reed 1955). This sequence includes five periods: Preceramic (15,000 B.C.–A.D. 600), Developmental (A.D. 600–1200), Coalition (A.D. 1200–1325), Classic (A.D. 1325–1600), and Historic (A.D. 1600–present). In some districts, these periods have been broken down into shorter phases. The chronology, by district, is presented in table 13.1.

Tree-ring dates are available for many of the large, excavated sites, but sites found on survey are dated using ceramic types. With the exception of the Gallina District, ceramic changes occur broadly over most of this area, and it is probably accurate to assume rough temporal synchroneity for sites with similar ceramic assemblages. The ceramics of the Gallina District differ from the remainder of the northern Rio Grande, as does the general sequence. Unfortunately, few tree-ring dates are available for the area, so that developments in this district are poorly documented.

The sequence devised by Wendorf and Reed (1955) also encompasses changes in settlement patterns that occur more or less contemporaneously over the region. During the Developmental period, much of the area remained unoccupied, but where sedentism occurred, occupation was in pit houses. The Coalition witnessed a shift toward surface structures in small pueblos, with greater aggregation into sites with massed room blocks late in the period. Finally, during the Classic period, populations moved into still larger sites generally situated around plazas.

Although the trends in settlement patterns and material culture must be viewed as highly generalized, they do define the broad shifts seen over much of this area. The Gallina area stands out as the exception, both in terms of settlement patterns and ceramics. We now review the population trajectory in greater detail for each of the districts.

Population Dynamics in the Northern Rio Grande Region

We compare interpolated population curves for each of the six districts.[2] These reveal considerably different trends for the various areas. Curves estimating aggregation as the percentage of the population living in sites of over 50 rooms are presented as well. In contrast to the population curves, the aggregation curves reveal fairly consistent patterning in the northern Rio Grande region. Regardless of population size prior to A.D. 1250, between A.D. 1250 and 1350 populations in all districts either aggregated into large pueblos, or (as in the case of the Gallina District) abandoned the area. The large sites (> 50 rooms) in the districts are listed in the appendix and the data quality ratings for the districts are shown in table 13.2.

There are two issues of importance raised by these curves that will be ad-

Table 13.1 Rio Grande Chronology

Years A.D.	Taos	Chama	Gallina	Rio Grande
1400				
	Vadito Phase	Biscuit A Phase		Classic
1350			Unoccupied	
1300	Talpa Phase	Wiyo Phase		Coalition
1250				
	Pot Creek Phase			
1200				
1150		Unoccupied, no permanent villages	Gallina Phase	
1100	Valdez Phase			Developmental
1050				
1000				

Note: Elliott (1982) uses the Pecos Chronology for the Jemez District. In some areas of the Gallina District, the phases are divided into Rosa phase (A.D. 800–1050), Capulin phase (A.D. 1050–1100), and Llaves Phase (A.D. 1100–1275).

dressed in the remainder of the chapter. First, what accounts for the population dynamics in each region, internal growth and decline, or population movement? Second, what additional processes (environmental change, conflict) accompany the population shifts documented? Obviously we cannot address these issues completely in the space allotted here, but we can provide a brief overview of recent research on these topics. We approach these issues first by reviewing each of the districts in greater detail.

Taos District

As defined by Wetherington (1968:73), the Taos District is bounded by the Rio Grande to the west, the Sangre de Cristo Mountains to the east, Red River to the north, and the Rio Pueblo to the south. Elevation ranges from 6,000 to 13,000 feet (1,829–3,963 m). The area is drained by the Rio Grande and its major tributaries.

The Taos District is characterized by sedentary occupation by A.D. 1000 in dispersed pit house hamlets with one to four structures. Small circular kivas and aboveground storage structures appear around A.D. 1150 (Green 1976).

By A.D. 1200, the first unit pueblos appear, with a maximum of 18 single-story rooms in U-shaped room blocks surrounding courtyards with or without kivas. In two cases, multiple room blocks suggest the beginnings of "modular villages" (Jeançon 1929; Wetherington 1968). Kivas apparently do not occur in "units" with less than 15 rooms. Dry-farming features (Woosley 1986) are also believed to appear at this time.

By A.D. 1250, all of the population had aggregated in two to three pueblos. Two excavated sites, Pot Creek (Wetherington 1968) and Picuris (Dick et al. n.d.), were multistoried pueblos with up to 300 ground-floor rooms. These modular aggregates consist of "unit" room blocks with 10 to 35 rooms, most with associated small kivas, grouped around a larger

Table 13.2 District Data Ratings

District	Name	Data Rating[a]	Comments
A	Gallina District	III	Many small sites known from several small surveys. Definition of "community" different here from other districts.
B	Chama District	II	Large sites well known, portions intensively surveyed, large portions destroyed by farming.
C	Taos District	II	Large sites well known, extent of occupation in smaller sites unknown. Portions intensively surveyed by Woosley (1986), data currently unavailable.
D, F	Pajarito District	I	Area is well known because of recent sample surveys (Hill and Trierweiler 1986; Powers 1988) aimed at recording the range of site types present and concerned with demographic and settlement patterns. Dating is relatively good.
E	Jemez District	III	Large sites well known, range of site sizes and site types poorly known. Recent surveys in connection with timber sales have recorded numerous field houses in the vicinities of the large sites. Dating resolution is poor.
G	Santa Fe District	II	Large sites well known, some survey of areas that allow reconstruction of demographic and settlement patterns. Dating resolution is fair.

Note:

a. Data rating is a subjective ranking that takes into account the extent of survey coverage, availability of data for future research, and level of data resolution for recorded sites in each region. Level I is very good to excellent, Level II is moderate, and Level III is fair to poor. This rating is not a judgment of any single survey or research project undertaken in any region, but simply the present utility of the current data in the district from a regional perspective.

central plaza. Aggregation may have involved only local population, although the adjacent Cimarron District was abandoned at this time (Glassow 1984), and some immigration from that area may have occurred. Regardless of the cause, no major population change is apparent with aggregation (figure 13.3; Wetherington 1968:82). Architectural changes included construction of larger rooms, decreasing access into and between rooms, and construction of multistoried room blocks with storage rooms entered only through hatches from second-story habitation rooms. These shifts are believed to be associated with a shift to extended families in response to greater travel distance to fields, and greater control of access to private as well as communal facilities (Crown and Kohler 1994).

In the decade of A.D. 1310 to 1320, Pot Creek Pueblo witnessed a building surge of a magnitude to suggest immigration (Crown 1991). Because there are no known sites abandoned at this time in the Taos District, it is likely that people arrived from outside of the district. This influx of population was accompanied by further enclosing of the plaza area with room blocks and construction of the first big kiva at the site in A.D. 1318. Pot Creek was abandoned about A.D. 1320.

Perhaps as a consequence of this abandonment, Cornfield Taos was built (Ellis and Brody 1964), and the old pueblo at Picuris was razed and new room blocks constructed by A.D. 1350. The new pueblo at Picuris was not modular, and kivas were no longer associated with distinct room blocks, but were located in central plazas (Dick et al. n.d.). These changes in site structure were probably tied to the need for more integrative facilities and a changing decision-making hierarchy in response to increased population levels. Excavations at Cornfield Taos were too limited to determine the site layout (Ellis and Brody 1964).

It appears then that the Taos District witnessed gradual population growth from A.D. 1000 to 1310, with slowly increasing aggregation (figure 13.3). After A.D. 1250, aggregation in this area apparently involved all district occupants, with no supporting "hinterland" settlements, and consequently no site hierarchy. The reasons for such complete aggregation are not clear. Extant models argue that aggregation was tied to management of agricultural land and water resources (Glassow 1984; Woosley 1986). The large aggregated pueblos are located at 7,400 feet (2,256 m) elevation, adjacent to alluvial fans formed by drainages disgorging from the foothills of the Sangre de Cristos. Glassow (1984) has argued that populations may have aggregated in these locales in response to deteriorating climate in lower elevations. Although this may explain why populations would move to the Taos District, it does not explain why they would aggregate.[3]

Population levels in the Taos District remained low in all time periods. Between A.D. 1250 and 1350, three large pueblos were occupied, each with an estimated 150 habitation rooms at any point in time, in an area of approximately 1,370 mi² (3,552 km²). Although detailed studies have not been carried out, there is no evidence that population had reached carrying capacity by A.D. 1250, or that resource depletion encouraged aggregation. Although aggregation may have facilitated land and water management, this does not seem to have been a determinant of aggregation. Taos District pueblos are located near arable land, but large tracts of arable land remained unoccupied and apparently unused.[4]

We would tentatively conclude that the aggregation in this district was not tied to population pressure, resource depletion, or a desire for proximity to the best agricultural land. Furthermore, although Taos District populations interacted with surrounding populations, there is no evi-

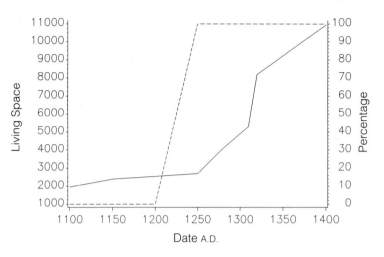

Figure 13.3. Taos District population (square meters of living space; solid line) and percentage of the population aggregated (dashed line).

dence that these interactions affected the sequence of aggregation in any direct manner. Levels of exchanged items remained low in all time periods, at least until the fifteenth century, when exchange with Plains populations may have increased (Spielmann 1983). The possibility remains that aggregation was an indirect competitive response to increasing population levels and the establishment of aggregated pueblos outside of the Taos District to the south.

Chama District

The Chama District comprises an area bounded by the San Juan hills on the north, the confluence of the Rio Grande and the Rio Chama on the south, the Jemez Mountains on the west, and the Rio Grande on the east. The district is drained by the Rio Chama and its major tributaries.

No permanent habitation sites are known to have existed in the Chama District before A.D. 1250 to 1300, although recent intensive survey in the Rio del Oso Valley, which drains into the lower Chama, suggests that the extent of thirteenth-century occupation may be underestimated (Anschuetz 1994). After A.D. 1250 to 1300, increasingly large and complex

pueblos were built until A.D. 1550, when the area was abandoned. Most early pueblos (A.D. 1250–1350) have 20 to 100 rooms in a rectangle surrounding a central plaza with a single kiva, but Tsiping has over 400 rooms, six enclosed plazas, and multiple small and big kivas. The sites exhibit both planned and accretional growth (Hibben 1937; Luebben 1953; Peckham 1959). By A.D. 1400, 2 of these early pueblos were abandoned, but 12 additional pueblos were built. The sites exhibit homogeneity in ceramic, architectural, and artifactual traits, suggesting a homogeneous population. Most sites consist of multiple room blocks surrounding plazas with central kivas. The total number of kiva depressions at sites tends to increase through time. Big kivas may occur at seven of the sites. In addition, ritual use of rooms in room blocks is indicated by painted wall plaster, niches, and kiva-like features (Beal 1987:141). Through time, room size increased and became more standardized, the number of stories increased, room function became more specialized, and variability in the number and type of ritual structures increased (Beal 1987; Maxwell 1990). It has been suggested that there was a shift from floodplain horticulture to dry farming after A.D. 1400 (Beal 1987:19). Extensive farming features have been documented over much of the Chama area that were constructed to conserve water through combinations of rock-bordered grids, cobble-step terraces, gravel-mulched plots, ditches, and perhaps mini-reservoirs (Anschuetz 1994). Gravel-mulched fields may have served in part to extend to the north the area in which cotton could be cultivated (Dean 1991). Researchers interpret this sequence in various ways, including a need to aggregate for defense (Hewett 1906; Hibben 1937; Mera 1934), immigration of people moving from upland areas (Wendorf 1953: 94), immigration of people from the Western Anasazi region (Reed 1949; Riley 1952; Wendorf and Reed 1955), immigration of an amalgamation of people from the San Juan and Gallina areas (Beal 1987: 113), the need to pool labor for irrigation (Ellis 1975a), and the need to maximize use of arable land (Dougherty 1980).

In the absence of evidence for permanent habitation sites before A.D. 1250, immigration must account for the construction of the fairly substantial pueblos in the area after that date. The occurrence of initially planned settlements suggests that immigrant populations moved as groups from areas where aggregated communities already existed. Current archaeological evidence does not, however, permit us to evaluate the source for these migrant populations.

Recent attempts to quantify population growth after the initial occupation of the area (Maxwell 1990) indicate an overall annual population growth rate of .024, higher than has been estimated for either Chaco Canyon (.0078; Hayes 1981) or the Mimbres area (.003; Blake, LeBlanc, and Minnis 1986), but comparable to the growth rate estimated for the early fourteenth century in the Santa Fe District (.0293; Collins 1975:333). Although growth rates this high have been documented in some developing nations, these results suggest a continuing influx of population from outside the area through the early fifteenth century. Maxwell (1990) argues that the total population increase

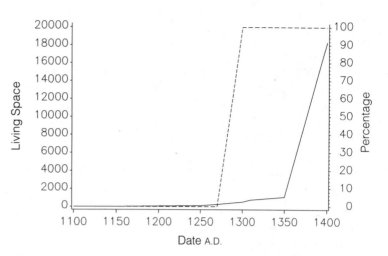

Figure 13.4. Chama District population (square meters of living space; solid line) and percentage of the population aggregated (dashed line).

can be accounted for by an annual immigration of 7 to 13 people; however, his estimate is based on the .024 intrinsic rate of growth over the 300-year period from A.D. 1200 to 1500. As documented in figure 13.4, the growth rate is actually considerably higher in some portions of this period and lower in others. For instance, Maxwell (1990:table 4) estimates the annual growth rate for A.D. 1350 to 1425 at .038, suggesting a much higher rate of immigration for this time period than either earlier or later. The planned layout and synchronous construction of many of the villages in the Chama between A.D. 1350 and 1425 also argues for the immigration of communities, not just households. We would argue then that the population curve for the Chama area represents a continuing immigration of people from outside of the area, beginning in the mid-to late thirteenth century, increasing during the late fourteenth century and continuing into the early fifteenth century.

Several excavated sites reveal evidence suggesting conflict. Three of the earliest sites have surrounding palisades or masonry walls. The dramatic setting of Tsiping, high on a steep mesa, offers clear defensive advantages. Excavations at Te'ewi, Pesedeuinge, Riana, Palisade, Leafwater, and Tsama revealed burned

room blocks, unburied skeletal remains, or mass interments in nontraditional burial locales (Beal 1987:147).

Gallina District

The Gallina District is bounded by the El Vado dam on the north, the San Pedro Mountains on the south, the Rio Chama on the east and the upper reaches of the San Juan drainage to the west (Langenfeld and Baker 1988:1).

The Gallina area exhibits a distinct archaeological complex by the late eleventh century (Dick 1985). Gallina phase sites (A.D. 1100–1300) consist of small communities of individual pit and surface structures, some with associated towers. Many dispersed pit houses may occupy the same mesa, but these have generally been assigned separate site numbers, making definition of community patterns difficult. It is not clear whether sites with large numbers of surface structures were contemporaneous communities or are the result of sequential occupation of structures with short use-lives. In at least one community, researchers argue that only 61 percent of the structures were occupied contemporaneously (Dick 1985:7), and that the structures had an average use-life of 12 years. Nevertheless, the dispersed character of Gallina structures may mask truly cohesive communities (Langenfeld and Baker 1988). No Gallina sites recorded in the New Mexico Historic Preservation Division's Archaeological Records Management (ARMS) files contained over 50 structures, but we included several of the largest documented sites in the appendix. The population and aggregation curves (figure 13.5) are highly speculative due to the lack of complete survey coverage and difficulty of estimating site size.

After A.D. 1200, a few sites with contiguous-walled structures were present, particularly as cliff dwellings (Pattison 1968). Towers are generally dated after A.D. 1200 as well. The function of these towers has not been established, but it has been suggested that they were used for defense, storage (Mackey and Green 1979), or communications (Ireland 1984; Ellis 1988:31). Diversity in tower forms indicates that they might have served all three functions (Langenfeld and Baker 1988).

Throughout the sequence, clearly ceremonial structures are exceedingly rare. Sipapus are sometimes found in subfloor contexts in dwellings (Ellis 1988:37–39) and a possible kiva has been reported from a site dating to the last half of the thirteenth century (Ellis 1988:40–41). Dick (1985:15) interprets a large pit house (7.5 m in diameter) on Huerfano Mesa as a council house.

The changes in settlement structure appear to signal increasing community integration or a need for defense (Beal 1987: 99). Burned structures and skeletal evidence for violent deaths also suggest conflict, particularly between A.D. 1240 and 1280 (Beal 1987:104; although see Cordell 1979b:143). In an alternative view, Dick (1985:13) argues that burned structures on Huerfano Mesa were deliberately set on fire by their inhabitants. Gallina phase settlements were apparently abandoned rapidly between A.D. 1270 and 1300 (Dick 1985), perhaps due to a deteriorating environment (Mackey and Holbrook 1978). There is little evidence for interregional exchange in Gallina sites.

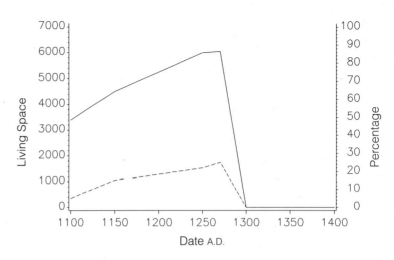

Figure 13.5. Gallina District population (square meters of living space; solid line) and percentage of the population aggregated (dashed line).

In general, the Gallina sequence appears to represent in situ population growth, with little outside influence, followed by rapid population decline (figure 13.5). Researchers have argued that Gallina populations moved southward along the west flank of the Nacimiento Mountains to relocate in the Jemez area (Reiter 1938) or they moved down the Chama to locate in the large, late aggregated Chama villages (Beal 1987). If Gallina populations did migrate to one of these areas, there is no clear continuity in community structure. The particular characteristics of Gallina settlement patterns, including dispersed, isolated structures and towers, do not appear in any northern Rio Grande districts during the late thirteenth and early fourteenth centuries. This suggests that Gallina populations may have moved into existing aggregated pueblo communities.

Jemez District

The Jemez District is bounded by the Jemez Mountains and Sierra de los Valles on the east, the Valle San Antonio on the north, the Sierra Nacimiento on the west, and just south of Jemez Pueblo on the south. This is a mountainous, rugged location with elevations ranging from ap-

proximately 5,700 to over 11,000 feet (1,738–3,354 m). The area is drained by the Jemez River and its major tributaries.

Though Archaic use of the Jemez area is documented (Elliott 1982), the spectacular pueblo ruins of the fourteenth through sixteenth centuries have been the focus of archaeological investigations. At least 11 of these pueblos contain between 200 and 650 rooms, and 4 have more than 1,000 rooms. Unfortunately, chronological control is poor, due in part to the long time range of Jemez Black-on-white ceramics. Consequently almost all of the sites recorded have been assigned to the A.D. 1300 to 1600 period. Most of the surface ceramic data are lists of the types present, but contain no counts, thus hampering our ability to reevaluate site dates. The presence of glaze wares in particular could help us narrow down the time ranges assigned to the sites; however, without counts from systematic surface collections, this is difficult to do with any confidence. The most common glaze ware types appear to be D, E, and F; Glaze A also is present but possibly rare, and Glaze C also has been identified. If the majority of the Jemez pueblos date to the Glaze D through F periods, or if the major occupations of the pueblos occurred during these periods, this puts the primary occupation of the Jemez District in the late fifteenth century through the sixteenth century.

Population was reconstructed for the Jemez District by assigning room counts for each site to 50-year periods. Because almost every site was dated to the A.D. 1300 to 1600 period, the resulting population curve shows little variation after A.D. 1300 (figure 13.6). Based on the presence of late glaze wares, it is probable that figure 13.6 shows population peaking too early. Population aggregation was high after A.D. 1300, especially given the 50-room characterization for "big sites." The range in pueblo sizes is large and it is possible that some kind of site hierarchy may have existed; however, without better temporal control it is not possible to identify contemporaneous sites. Figure 13.7 shows the number of sites and percentage of rooms in different size groups, beginning with 50 rooms and increasing in 100-room increments. There appear to be at least three groups of site sizes with most sites having fewer than 450 rooms. Larger sites are rare but as a group contain the highest percentage of rooms. Basically, figure 13.7 reinforces the fact that Jemez District pueblos were very large and that a high percentage of the population was aggregated.

Pajarito District

The 270 mi² (700 km²) Pajarito Plateau ranges in elevation from 5,000 to 10,000 feet (1,525–3,049 m) and is characterized by rugged canyon and mesa topography. The area is defined by Santa Clara Canyon on the north, Cochiti Canyon on the south, the Jemez Mountains on the west, and the Rio Grande on the east. The prehistoric occupation of the area stretches back at least to late Archaic or early Basketmaker II times. The Anasazi occupied the plateau from approximately A.D. 1150 to 1600 with population reaching a peak in the late thirteenth century (figure 13.8). The geographic area can be divided into the northern and southern plateaus, using Frijoles Canyon as the dividing line (Hewett 1953:41; Lange, Riley, and Lange 1975:

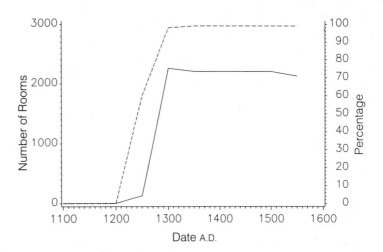

Figure 13.6. Jemez District population (number of rooms; solid line) and percentage of the population aggregated (dashed line).

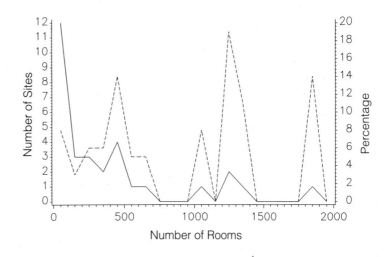

Figure 13.7. Jemez District distribution of rooms among sites (solid line) and the percentage of rooms in different pueblo size classes (dashed line).

57). Cultural developments were different in the two areas, especially after A.D. 1250.

In the Early Coalition period (A.D. 1150–1250), population size and aggregation were relatively low (figure 13.8). Habitation sites were small, averaging less than 10 rooms (Preucel 1988:139), however some population aggregates were present. Population densities in the northern and southern areas appear to have been equal (figure 13.9) and, although population was slightly more aggregated in the south (figure 13.10), there was little difference between the two areas.

Major changes in population size and aggregation occurred during the Late Coalition period (A.D. 1250–1325). The Late Coalition period was characterized by larger communities, usually consisting of a U-shaped room block around a plaza, often with a kiva in the plaza, or "plaza pueblos" with four room blocks enclosing a central plaza with kivas in the plaza and outside the room blocks. There was a population explosion during this period that may have been the result of immigration (figure 13.8). The annual growth rate from the Early to the Late Coalition period was approximately .013, or 1.3 percent, probably higher than what could be sustained through in situ growth (Hassan 1978:84). Although it is difficult to establish contemporaneity among sites in either period, the Late Coalition sites have similar ceramic assemblages, indicating substantial overlap in occupation, if not contemporaneity.

The population increase during the Late Coalition period was greater and aggregation was much more marked in the north (figures 13.9 and 13.10). Plaza and U-shaped pueblos abounded in the north, especially in the higher elevations ranging to 7,400 feet (2,256 m), but were scarce in the south.

The Early Classic period (A.D. 1325–1400) was characterized by major changes in population size, population aggregation, and settlement location (Kohler 1993; Orcutt 1993). Population decreased on the Pajarito Plateau in general (figure 13.8); however, this decrease was confined to the northern plateau (figure 13.9). As a result of major population relocation from the higher to lower elevations (Orcutt 1991), population increased in the south. Population aggregation reached a peak during the Early Classic period with approximately 85 percent of the population in larger sites (figure 13.8). Despite the sharp decline in population size in the north, the northern and southern populations were both highly aggregated (figure 13.10).

Figure 13.11 illustrates changes in population size within Bandelier National Monument, which is mostly on the southern Pajarito Plateau, though some survey has occurred north of Frijoles Canyon (Powers 1988). Population is plotted by decade using site dates instead of the time periods. This reconstruction supports the trends discussed previously, including the peak of population in the Late Coalition period, the population decline at the end of the Late Coalition period, and the increase of population in the south during the Early Classic period. The Bandelier curve indicates that periods of population increase often were followed by plateaus

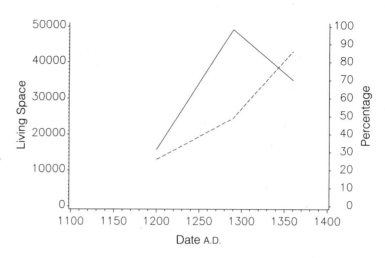

Figure 13.8. Pajarito District population (square meters of living space; solid line) and percentage of the population aggregated (dashed line).

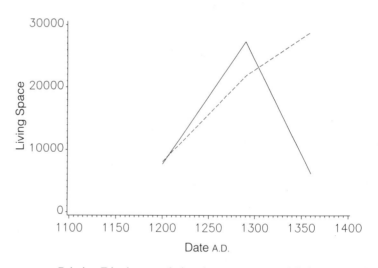

Figure 13.9. Pajarito District population (square meters of living space) for the northern (solid line) and southern (dashed line) Pajarito Plateau.

where population increased slowly or was stable, and it also shows fluctuations during the Late Coalition period that are not represented in the other Pajarito curves.

The major changes in population size, population aggregation, and settlement locations on the Pajarito Plateau probably were the result of several factors, including climatic and floodplain fluctuations, resource depletion, and competition over agricultural land. High water tables and aggraded floodplains coupled with short-term fluctuations in moisture availability

led to settlement in higher elevations during the Early and Late Coalition periods (Orcutt 1991). As people moved into the area during the Late Coalition, population density increased in the higher elevations and aggregation resulted, possibly to minimize conflict over resources (Orcutt, Blinman, and Kohler 1990). The population decline in the Early Classic should have eased the pressure on resources; however, this overlaps with a major degradation in floodplain conditions that began in A.D. 1290 or 1300 and did not improve until A.D. 1450 or 1460 (Dean et al. 1985: figure 1A). Although reconstructions of floodplain conditions are based on chronostratigraphic information from northeastern Arizona, these sequences are generally applicable for drainage systems throughout the Southwest (Karlstrom 1988:64). The changes may not have been exactly contemporaneous but it is probable that floodplain degradation, characterized by soil formation, less runoff and erosion, and more stable valley slopes, did affect the Pajarito Plateau. Combined with a long drought from A.D. 1338 to 1352 (Orcutt 1991:figure 6), dry farming in the higher elevations may have become too risky, and with the best agricultural land on or near the floodplains (Plog et al. 1988:261), the higher elevations may have become less desirable. Conflict over resources because of these environmental changes probably was exacerbated by resource depletion in the higher elevations due to decades of high population density (Kohler and Matthews 1988). Populations reorganized in new settlements at lower elevations, became more aggregated than before, and relied more on agriculture to support the larger communities.

Santa Fe District

The Santa Fe District extends from just below the confluence of the Rio Chama and Rio Grande on the north, east to the foothills of the Sangre de Cristo Mountains, west to the Rio Grande (White Rock Canyon) and across the Rio Grande in the vicinity of Cochiti Pueblo, and south approximately halfway between the Santa Fe River and Galisteo Creek (Cordell 1979a: 53; Dickson 1979:6). Elevations range from 5,200 to 7,300 ft (1,585–2,226 m).

Ellis (1975b) has summarized the existing information about the Pueblo II occupation of the Santa Fe District. She concludes that most people lived in surface structures, usually of jacal, in small clusters associated with a small subterranean kiva or kiva built into the house block. One site in the Tesuque Valley, anomalously

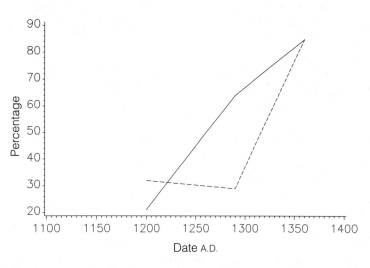

Figure 13.10. Pajarito District percentage of the population aggregated for the northern (solid line) and southern (dashed line) Pajarito Plateau.

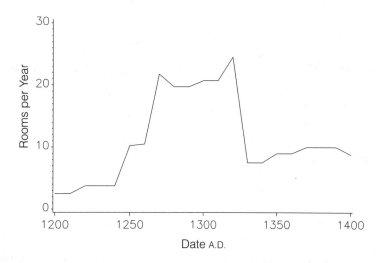

Figure 13.11. Population (rooms built per year) by decade in Bandelier National Monument (Pajarito District) based on data from the 1987 to 1989 National Park Service survey.

large by local standards, contained at least 120 surface rooms, 8 small kivas, and a great kiva (Stubbs 1954). This early aggregation apparently was short-lived and is poorly understood.

Population and aggregation are reconstructed for two recent surveys in the Santa Fe District. The first is Dickson's (1979) 130 mi² (337 km²) transect running in a 5-mile-wide band between Arroyo Hondo Pueblo and Cochiti Pueblo, of which 62 percent was surveyed

(Dickson 1979:17–19). Dickson (1979:19) supplemented his survey data with survey records for known sites in his unsurveyed areas. The second survey for which population and aggregation are reconstructed is the Pajarito Archaeological Research Project's (PARP) survey of the Caja del Rio Plateau (Hill and Trierweiler 1986), which overlaps Dickson's survey area on the south, but extends farther north and not as far to the east.

Population size and aggregation were

calculated separately for each of the two areas. Population and temporal data for Dickson's (1979:table 5) sites were modified to reflect the temporal sequence used for the Pajarito Plateau and the Caja, and were updated, when applicable, with excavation data. In portions of the Santa Fe District, occupation extended back to the Archaic Period, and this is true of the Arroyo Hondo and Caja survey areas. The Anasazi occupation in the Arroyo Hondo transect began ca. A.D. 600 but population remained low until the thirteenth century. From a relatively low population in the Early Coalition, population increased dramatically between A.D. 1200 and 1300 (figure 13.12). At an annual growth rate of .01, or 1 percent, immigration may have contributed to this increase. Population continued to grow into the mid-thirteenth century but at a much slower rate (.001) (see Collins 1975:333, for an alternate calculation of higher growth rates for the Late Coalition and Early Classic periods). Aggregation was high, even in the Early Coalition period, and by the Late Coalition and Early Classic periods, 80 to 90 percent of the population was aggregated (figure 13.12).

The population trajectory for the Caja is similar to that for the Arroyo Hondo transect, except for an apparent absence of Early Coalition habitations or field houses on the Caja (Preucel, Trierweiler, and Larson 1986). The population on the Caja grew rapidly in the thirteenth century and reached a peak in the mid-fourteenth century (figure 13.13). The growth rate from the Early to Late Coalition periods cannot be calculated because of zero population for the former; however, growth obviously was rapid and probably resulted from immigration. For the period from the Late Coalition to Early Classic periods, the growth rate of .005, or .5 percent, is slightly higher than for the same period in the Arroyo Hondo transect. Population aggregation was close to 100 percent on the Caja (figure 13.13) with the population concentrated in four large pueblos.

Population in the Arroyo Hondo and

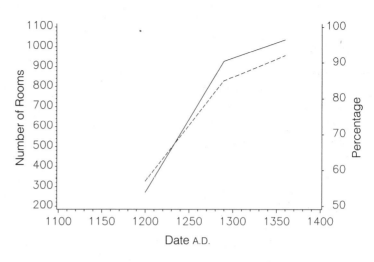

Figure 13.12. Santa Fe District population (number of rooms; solid line) and percentage of the population aggregated (dashed line) for the Arroyo Hondo survey area.

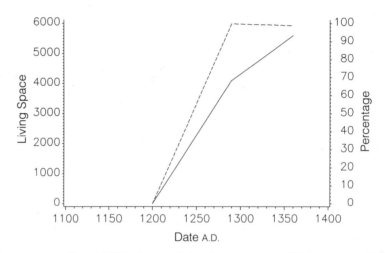

Figure 13.13. Santa Fe District population (square meters of living space; solid line) and percentage of the population aggregated (dashed line) for the Caja del Rio survey area.

Caja areas increased at the same time that population declined on the Pajarito Plateau. Because of the high degree of aggregation, it is possible that people arrived in groups and established aggregated villages similar to those from which they had emigrated. Reasons that these areas would have been attractive may relate to the availability of large areas of previously unexploited territory near arroyos, canyons, and rivers.

It is difficult to say whether the Arroyo Hondo and Caja surveys are representative of population and aggregation trends in the entire Santa Fe District. Cutting dates, and "v" dates, which are "probably cutting dates" (Ahlstrom 1985:614), for large sites in the Santa Fe District were plotted to see whether growth periods at these large sites fit with the population curves. The tree-ring dates indicate four periods of building: A.D. 1120s to 1140s, A.D. 1260s to 1280s, A.D. 1310s to 1330s, and A.D. 1360s to 1380s (figure 13.14). These building periods indicate successively more building, perhaps indicating that the population curve satisfactorily represents population growth in the district.

Discussion

Comparison of all of the population and aggregation figures reveals a number of interesting patterns. Population increased in all areas up to the late thirteenth century. During the period from A.D. 1270 to 1300, population size peaked in the Pajarito District and the Gallina District was abandoned. After A.D. 1300, occupation continued in the other districts, and major increases in population occurred in all districts except the Pajarito. The Chama District received a major population influx after A.D. 1350. With more precise dating, a similar trend might characterize the Jemez District.

Aggregation occurs in all districts between A.D. 1250 and 1300 regardless of population size or growth rate. In some districts, aggregation occurs at low population levels and precedes major population growth (Chama), while in others aggregation continues despite population decline (Pajarito). By A.D. 1300, the majority of sites in all districts have more than 50 rooms. Indeed, with the exception of the Pajarito District, virtually all habitation sites in the northern Rio Grande are over 50 rooms in size by A.D. 1300.

We now explore broader processes that might account for the patterning observed earlier. These processes include environmental change and conflict.

Environmental Change

We are fortunate that a detailed reconstruction of precipitation exists for Arroyo Hondo Pueblo within the Santa Fe District (Rose, Dean, and Robinson 1981). Furthermore, Orcutt (1991) reviews the implications of low- and high-frequency environmental variation for settlement changes on the Pajarito Plateau. Although we must be cautious in applying these data to all districts of the northern Rio Grande, they do provide a baseline for discussions

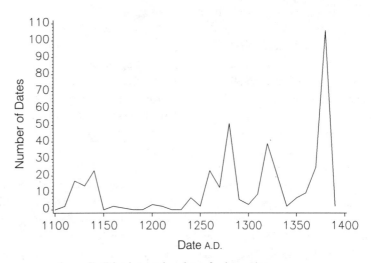

Figure 13.14.   Santa Fe District cutting dates for large sites.

of population change and environmental shifts in this area.

In general, three major periods are of interest. First is the period from A.D. 1250 to 1300, when the Gallina District was abandoned, population size peaked in the Pajarito District, and major settlements appeared in the Santa Fe District. Second, the period from A.D. 1300 to 1350 is characterized by population increase in the Taos District, continued population growth in the Santa Fe District, and population decline in the Pajarito District. Finally, the temporal span between A.D. 1350 and 1400 is of interest due to the dramatic population increase in the Chama District and continued population growth in the Taos District. Without better temporal control, we can only generalize about population growth in the Jemez District, focusing on the A.D. 1300 to 1400 period as the time during which the major occupation of this area may have developed. Whether the Jemez population peaked prior to A.D. 1400 is not known.

The abandonment of the Gallina District coincides with the Great Drought in the Southwest (A.D. 1276–1299), and, as discussed previously, Mackey and Holbrook (1978) found local evidence for a deteriorating environment during this time period. The Arroyo Hondo data indicate that the Great Drought was less severe in

the northern Rio Grande than in areas to the west (Rose, Dean, and Robinson 1981: 106). Analysis of the Palmer Drought Severity Index (PDSI) reconstructed for the northern Rio Grande (Rose, Robinson, and Dean 1982) indicates a moderately severe drought during this period (Orcutt 1991:figure 3). At approximately this same time, there was a population explosion on the Pajarito Plateau. Population reached a peak during this period, people moved into higher elevations than had been occupied previously, and population was significantly more aggregated than before. Population grew in the Santa Fe District with the establishment of major habitation sites, many of which were near perennial water sources. Populations abandoning areas to the west because of the drought may have found the northern Rio Grande a relatively desirable area, an interpretation borne out by the evidence from western areas (Varien et al., chapter 7), in part because population density was low and suitable settlement locations were abundant.

The period following the Great Drought, from A.D. 1300 to 1335, was highly favorable in terms of precipitation (Rose, Dean, and Robinson 1981: 106), a conclusion also borne out by the PDSI (Orcutt 1991:figures 3 and 6). Favorable conditions may have encouraged further settlement by populations from the west. Low-frequency variation in floodplain conditions indicates a period of degradation on the Colorado Plateaus beginning around A.D. 1290 or 1300 (Dean et al. 1985:figure 1A) that may have affected populations on the Pajarito Plateau in the early part of the fourteenth century (Orcutt 1991). It was during this interval of degradation and low water tables that the Pajarito population probably began to abandon the higher elevation aggregated communities for even larger communities in the lower elevations. This settlement reorganization on the Pajarito Plateau, which occurred between approximately A.D. 1310–1325 and A.D. 1400, was accompanied by a decrease in population size. Population in the Santa Fe District continued to grow during this period, possibly because former occupants of the Pajarito District moved into the region. The Taos District experienced growth during this period as well, with what has been interpreted as a major population increase between A.D. 1310 and 1320 (Crown 1991). Although the Santa Fe and Taos Districts had existing populations, their relatively low population densities may have made them attractive to migrants.

The period of floodplain degradation gave way to a long period of stable low water tables and degraded floodplains that persisted until about A.D. 1450 (Dean et al. 1985:figure 1A). Given these conditions, the most favorable agricultural locations would be in or near the floodplains (Plog et al. 1988:261). This may explain the choice of lower elevations on the Pajarito Plateau during this time period; although there would have been less precipitation than in the higher elevations, the latter may not have provided sufficient moisture to continue dry farming, and there would have been a lack of suitable floodplain fields to support the population. For a population dependent on agriculture, the lower elevations provide wider floodplains, deeper soil, a longer growing season, and the option to irrigate (Hunter-Anderson 1986; Orcutt 1981). This also may explain

the rapid population movement into the Chama area.

Between A.D. 1335 and 1400 there was high variability in precipitation, including a long drought between approximately A.D. 1335 and 1355, and shorter droughts approximately every 10 years (Orcutt 1991:figure 6). These climatic factors may have led to additional population movements or restructuring of the existing populations. Schwartz (1981:xiv) and Creamer (1993:138) argue that Arroyo Hondo Pueblo was virtually abandoned by A.D. 1335 to 1345; a second occupation of the pueblo began in the A.D. 1360s and 1370s during a period of high precipitation. Although population growth continued in the Santa Fe District, little construction occurred during the A.D. 1335 to 1355 drought. The Pajarito population continued to decline in this period, but the Chama and (possibly) Jemez districts experienced large increases in population that probably were the result of immigration. Some of those immigrants may have come from the reorganization of settlements within the northern Rio Grande area and from areas to the west. Population movement correlates well with known environmental changes in the northern Rio Grande. Although we speculate here on the impact that such environmental change may have had on population movement, we do not have appropriate data to demonstrate this relationship.

Competition and Conflict

Disputes and conflict over territory can increase as population density increases, and we contend that aggregation provides a strategy that can minimize that conflict and provide a stable means for distributing people across the landscape and equalizing their access to resources (Carneiro 1970; Haas 1982; Hunter-Anderson 1979; G. Johnson 1982, 1989; Johnson and Earle 1987; Kohler 1989; Orcutt, Blinman, and Kohler 1990). Conflict does not necessarily imply warfare; it can range from disagreements between individuals or households to warfare between villages. Larger aggregates are at an advantage in warfare (Johnson and Earle 1987:158–59), but aggregation also offers the means to cope with lesser conflict through social controls imposed on the group. The potential advantages of aggregation, including formal controls on internal conflict, risk management through within-aggregate sharing, defense against other aggregates, and labor availability, often outweigh the costs to the family-level economy when population density is high (Johnson and Earle 1987: 101, 196, 202).

Population density is a critical factor in assessing potential conflict situations. Density relative to resources can increase even if population is stable or declining if resource productivity is declining more rapidly (Graber 1990). Resource productivity is affected by changes in environmental variables (e.g., precipitation, temperature, floodplain conditions) and human manipulation of the environment that depletes critical resources (Dickson 1987; Graber 1990; Kohler and Matthews 1988). Dickson (1987:715) notes that some forms of circumscription can be the result of "anthropogenic environmental destruction," setting in motion a cycle of increased competition over land, environmental destruction, a net decrease in arable land, and "more constricting and circumscribed agricultural environments." That such a circumstance could have existed in the Santa Fe, Pajarito, Chama, and Jemez districts of the northern Rio Grande would not be unusual with periodically very dense populations.

At the present time, it is not possible for us to quantify resource and population levels to identify critical periods that may have affected conflict and aggregation in the northern Rio Grande. Evidence of physical conflict has been found in the Chama and Gallina areas but nothing conclusive exists for the Pajarito, Santa Fe, or Jemez Districts, although there is some evidence for violent deaths prior to aggregation in the Taos area. For the latter four areas, characteristics of settlement location (mesa tops) and site layout (walled plazas, fewer entries) may indicate a perceived need for defense.

Conclusions

Population density is undoubtedly closely tied to environmental change and relative resource availability within the northern Rio Grande, and between the northern Rio Grande and adjacent areas, but at the present time we do not have the means to quantify these relationships. A fuller account of aggregation and intergroup competition and conflict awaits more complete survey and excavation data. Until that day, we must settle for the unsatisfying assertion that the balance between population and resources is a likely source of the conflict that we see in the northern Rio Grande, and the record of settlement size and location.[5]

Aggregation occurred in all areas regardless of specific trends in population growth rates and size in the A.D. 1250 to 1300 period. In some areas, aggregation appears to have grown out of already existing patterns among the indigenous population, but in other areas, initial occupation occurs in aggregated form, suggesting movement of aggregated communities from elsewhere. As discussed previously, aggregation can have a wide variety of benefits for a population. Once aggregated settlements appeared in one portion of the northern Rio Grande, a "domino effect" may have encouraged aggregation elsewhere. In the vocabulary of evolutionary ecology, we interpret this to suggest that aggregation may be an important aspect of an evolutionarily stable strategy for these populations that can successfully "invade" dispersed communities, but cannot be successfully invaded by a dispersed strategy. Among the many potential advantages of aggregation that we discussed, those that are most important in conferring this putative competitive edge have yet to be determined. In any event, aggregation occurred rapidly and by A.D. 1300 virtually all inhabitants of the northern Rio Grande occupied large, aggregated settlements.

Acknowledgments

The authors thank Tim Maxwell for making his unpublished paper on Chama District population growth available.

Notes

1. Although Bandelier (1892) lumped the southern portions of our Santa Fe District with the Galisteo Basin as the "country of the Tanos," he considered the northern portions of our Santa Fe district, the neighboring northern Pajarito, and the Chama to be ancestral to the Tewa.

2. The population data are expressed as square meters of living space or number of rooms, depending on the data available. It was not possible to use the same units of measurement across all districts. The population curve for the Taos District is based primarily on data from Pot Creek Pueblo extrapolated to other sites in the area. The data used for the Chama District population curve are taken from Tim Maxwell's (1990) paper on population growth in this area. The curve for the Gallina area is highly speculative and derived primarily from data presented in Dick (1985) and in the ARMS files. The numbers presented should be considered gross approximations, although the shape of the curve may represent general trends.

3. Greiser et al. (1990) have recently argued that ditch irrigation was widespread in the twelfth and thirteenth centuries near small sites located along lower stream courses that are presently predominantly dry, and that increased aridity after A.D. 1250 resulted in decreased stream flow, which required farmers to move upstream to secure irrigable water. However, both the identification and the dating of these ditches are highly controversial. No undisputed prehistoric irrigation ditches have been documented near the aggregated site of Pot Creek Pueblo.

4. No known habitation sites dating between A.D. 1250 and 1350 occur in close proximity to the rich agricultural land farmed today along the Rio Pueblo de Taos and the lower reaches of the Rio Grande del Rancho (from Talpa to the confluence with the Rio Grande).

5. With additional data, we speculate that we could address these issues more fully if we could construct curves relating resource harvest rates to their value to the individual consumer (see Smith 1988:235); to estimate stochastic variation in harvests for the spectrum of major subsistence resources; to determine acquisition, transport, and storage costs for resources; to estimate variable degrees of knowledge about the distributions of particular resources; and to accomplish all this in specific spatial and temporal contexts that are well characterized. Once this is accomplished, we can estimate pay-off matrixes for various strategies and let iterated game theory that begins with the individual help us to determine optimal or at least evolutionarily stable configurations for population in space. The fine-grained environmental and economic analyses called for by this program would in all likelihood not be sufficient to account for the full range of settlement changes that we see in this record; but a subset of this program has proven very helpful in understanding the history of aggregation and dispersion in some other portions of the Southwest (Kohler and Van West 1994).

References Cited

Ahlstrom, Richard V. N.
1985   *The Interpretation of Archaeological Tree-Ring Dates*. Ph.D. dissertation, University of Arizona, Tucson. University Microfilms International, Ann Arbor.

Anschuetz, Kurt F.
1994   Earning a Living in the Cool, High Desert: Transformations of the Northern Rio Grande Landscape by Anasazi Farmers to Harvest and Conserve Water. Paper presented in the 1994 Southwest Symposium, Tempe.

Bandelier, Adolph F.
1892   *Final Report of Investigations among the Indians of the Southwestern United States, Carried on Mainly in the Years from 1880 to 1885*, Part 2. Papers of the Archaeological Institute of America, American Series No. 4. Archaeological Institute of America, Cambridge, Massachusetts.

Beal, John D.
1987   *Foundations of the Rio Grande Classic: The Lower Rio Chama River A.D. 1300–1500*. Report prepared for Office of Cultural Affairs, Historic Preservation Division, State of New Mexico, Santa Fe.

Blake, Michael, Steven A. LeBlanc, and Paul E. Minnis
1986   Changing Settlement and Population in the Mimbres Valley, Southwest New Mexico. *Journal of Field Archaeology* 13:439–64.

Carneiro, Robert L.
1970   A Theory of the Origin of the State. *Science* 169:733–38.

Collins, Susan H.
1975   *Prehistoric Rio Grande Settlement Pat-*

terns and the Inference of Demographic Change. Unpublished Ph.D. dissertation, Department of Anthropology, University of Colorado, Boulder.

Cordell, Linda S.
  1979a   *Cultural Resources Overview: Middle Rio Grande Valley*. USDA, Forest Service, Southwest Region, and USDI, Bureau of Land Management, Albuquerque. U.S. Government Printing Office, Washington, D.C.
  1979b   Prehistory, Eastern Anasazi. In *Southwest*, edited by Alfonso Ortiz, pp. 131–51. Handbook of North American Indians, William C. Sturtevant, general editor. Smithsonian Institution, Washington D.C.

Creamer, W.
  1993   *The Architecture of Arroyo Hondo Pueblo, New Mexico*. School of American Research Press, Santa Fe.

Crown, Patricia L.
  1991   Evaluating the Construction Sequence and Population of Pot Creek Pueblo, Northern New Mexico. *American Antiquity* 56:291–314.

Crown, Patricia L., and Timothy A. Kohler
  1994   Community Dynamics, Site Structure, and Aggregation in the Northern Rio Grande. In *The Ancient Southwestern Community: Model and Methods for the Study of Prehistoric Social Organization*, edited by Wirt H. Wills and Robert D. Leonard, pp. 103–18. University of New Mexico Press, Albuquerque.

Dean, Glenna
  1991   *Pollen Analysis of Archaeological Samples from Basketmaker and Anasazi Features at LA 75287 and LA 75288, Abiquiu West Project, Rio Chama Valley, New Mexico*. Technical Series Report No. 6302. Castetter Laboratory for Ethnobotanical Studies, University of New Mexico, Albuquerque.

Dean, Jeffrey S., Robert C. Euler, George J. Gumerman, Fred Plog, Richard H. Hevly, and Thor N. V. Karlstrom
  1985   Human Behavior, Demography, and Paleoenvironment on the Colorado Plateaus. *American Antiquity* 50:537–54.

Dick, Herbert W.
  1985   The Anatomy of a Dispersive Gallina Village. Paper presented at the Archeological Society of New Mexico, Santa Fe.

Dick, Herbert W., Daniel Wolfman, Curt F. Schaafsma, and Marianne Wolfman
  n.d.   Introduction to Picuris Archaeology. Ms. on file, Fort Burgwin Research Center, Taos.

Dickson, D. Bruce, Jr.
  1979   *Prehistoric Pueblo Settlement Patterns: The Arroyo Hondo, New Mexico, Site Survey*. Arroyo Hondo Archaeological Series, vol. 2. School of American Research Press, Santa Fe.
  1987   Circumscription by Anthropogenic Environmental Destruction: An Expansion of Carneiro's (1970) Theory of the Origin of the State. *American Antiquity* 52:709–16.

Dougherty, Julia D.
  1980   *An Archaeological Evaluation of Tsiping Ruin*. Cultural Resources Report No. 1. USDA, Forest Service, Santa Fe National Forest, Santa Fe.

Elliott, Michael L.
  1982   *Large Pueblo Sites Near Jemez Springs, New Mexico*. Cultural Resources Report 3. Santa Fe National Forest, Santa Fe.

Ellis, Florence Hawley
  1975a   Highways to the Past. *New Mexico Magazine* 53:18–40.
  1975b   Life in the Tesuque Valley and Elsewhere in the Santa Fe Area During the Pueblo II Stage of Development. *Awanyu* 3(2):27–49.
  1988   *From Drought to Drought: An Archaeological Record of Life Patterns as Developed by the Gallina Indians of North Central New Mexico A.D. 1050 to 1300*. Sunstone Press, Santa Fe.

Ellis, Florence H., and J. J. Brody
  1964   Ceramic Stratigraphy and Tribal History at Taos Pueblo. *American Antiquity* 29(4):316–27.

Ford, Richard I., Albert H. Schroeder, and Stewart L. Peckham
  1972   Three Perspectives on Puebloan Prehistory. In *New Perspectives on the Pueblos*, edited by Alfonso Ortiz, pp. 19–40. University of New Mexico Press, Albuquerque.

Glassow, Michael
  1984   Explaining Variations in Agricultural Settlement Systems in Northeastern New Mexico. In *Prehistoric Agricultural Strategies in the Southwest*, edited by Suzanne K. Fish and Paul R. Fish, 199–214. Anthropological Research Papers No. 33. Arizona State University, Tempe.

Graber, Robert B.
  1990   Areal Decrease, Density Increase,

and Circumscription: A Mathematical Note. *American Antiquity* 55:546–49.

Green, Ernestine L.
  1976   *Valdez Phase Occupation near Taos, New Mexico*. Publication No. 10. Fort Burgwin Research Center, Taos.

Greiser, Sally T., T. Weber Greiser, and David Putnam
  1990   Prehistoric Irrigation in the Taos Valley, New Mexico. Paper presented at the 55th Annual Meeting of the Society for American Archaeology, Las Vegas.

Haas, Jonathan
  1982   *The Evolution of the Prehistoric State*. Columbia University Press, New York.

Hassan, Fekri A.
  1978   Demographic Archaeology. In *Advances in Archaeological Method and Theory*, Vol. 1, edited by Michael B. Schiffer, pp. 49–103. Academic Press, New York.

Hayes, Alden C.
  1981   A Survey of Chaco Canyon Archaeology. In *Publications in Archaeology, Chaco Canyon Studies*, edited by Alden C. Hayes, David M. Brugge, and W. James Judge, pp. 1–68. USDI, National Park Service, Washington, D.C.

Hewett, Edgar L.
  1906   *Antiquities of the Jemez Plateau, New Mexico*. Bureau of American Ethnology Bulletin No. 32. U.S. Government Printing Office, Washington, D.C.
  1953   *Pajarito Plateau and Its Ancient People*, revised by Bertha Dutton. University of New Mexico Press, Albuquerque, and the School of American Research, Santa Fe.

Hibben, Frank
  1937   *Excavations of the Riana Ruin and Chama Valley Survey*. Anthropological Series No. 2(1). University of New Mexico, Albuquerque.

Hill, James N., and W. Nicholas Trierweiler
  1986   Prehistoric Responses to Food Stress on the Pajarito Plateau, New Mexico: Technical Report and Results of the Pajarito Archaeological Research Project, 1977–1985. Final report to the National Science Foundation. Ms. on file, Department of Anthropology, University of California, Los Angeles.

Hunter-Anderson, Rosalind D. L.
  1979   Explaining Residential Aggregation

in the Northern Rio Grande: A Competition Reduction Model. In *Adaptive Change in the Northern Rio Grande Valley*, pp. 169–75. Archeological Investigations in Cochiti Reservoir, New Mexico, Vol. 4, edited by Jan V. Biella and Richard C. Chapman. University of New Mexico, Office of Contract Archeology, Albuquerque.

1986   *Prehistoric Adaptation in the American Southwest*. Cambridge University Press, Cambridge.

Ireland, Arthur K.
1984   A Potential Gallina Communications System. In *A Cultural Resource Management Plan for Timber Sale and Forest Development Areas on the Jicarilla Apache Indian Reservation*, edited by J. B. Broster and Arthur K. Ireland, pp. 117–24. USDA, Forest Archeological Program and USDI, Bureau of Indian Affairs, Albuquerque.

Jeançon, Jean A.
1929   Archaeological Investigations in the Taos Valley, New Mexico During 1920. *Smithsonian Miscellaneous Collections* 81(12). Smithsonian Institution, Washington, D.C.

Johnson, Allen W., and Timothy Earle
1987   *The Evolution of Human Societies: From Foraging Group to Agrarian State*. Stanford University Press, Stanford.

Johnson, Gregory A.
1982   Organizational Structure and Scalar Stress. In *Theory and Explanation in Archaeology: The Southampton Conference*, edited by Colin Renfrew, Michael J. Rowlands, and Barbara A. Segraves, pp. 389–421. Academic Press, New York.

1989   Dynamics of Southwestern Prehistory: Far Outside–Looking In. In *Dynamics of Southwest Prehistory*, edited by Linda S. Cordell and George J. Gumerman, pp. 371–89. Smithsonian Institution Press, Washington, D.C.

Karlstrom, Thor N. V.
1988   Alluvial Chronology and Hydrologic Change of Black Mesa and Nearby Regions. In *The Anasazi in a Changing Environment*, edited by George J. Gumerman, pp. 45–91. Cambridge University Press, Cambridge.

Kohler, Timothy A. (editor)
1989   *Bandelier Archaeological Excavation Project: Research Design and Summer 1988 Sampling*. Reports of Investigations No. 61. Washington State University, Department of Anthropology, Pullman.

Kohler, Timothy A.
1993   Shohakka Pueblo and the Early Classic Period in the Northern Rio Grande. In *Papers on the Early Classic Period Prehistory of the Pajarito Plateau, New Mexico*, edited by Timothy A. Kohler and Angela R. Linse, pp. 1–10. Reports of Investigations 65. Washington State University, Department of Anthropology, Pullman.

Kohler, Timothy A., and Meredith Matthews
1988   Long-Term Anasazi Land Use and Forest Reduction: A Case Study from Southwest Colorado. *American Antiquity* 53:537–64.

Kohler, Timothy A., and Carla Van West
1994   The Calculus of Self Interest in the Development of Cooperation: Sociopolitical Development and Risk among the Northern Anasazi. Ms. on file, Santa Fe Institute, Santa Fe, New Mexico.

Lange, Charles H., Carroll L. Riley, and Elizabeth M. Lange
1975   *The Southwestern Journals of Adolph F. Bandelier 1885–1888*. University of New Mexico Press, Albuquerque.

Langenfeld, Kristin, and Larry L. Baker
1988   Site Variability in Tanques Canyon, New Mexico and its implications for Largo-Gallina Community Structure. Paper presented at the 53rd Annual Meeting of the Society for American Archaeology, Phoenix.

Luebben, Ralph A.
1953   Leaf Water Site. In *Salvage Archaeology in the Chama Valley, New Mexico*, compiled by Fred Wendorf, pp. 9–33. Monograph No. 17. School of American Research, Santa Fe.

Mackey, James C., and Roger C. Green
1979   Largo-Gallina Towers: An Explanation. *American Antiquity* 44:144–54.

Mackey, James C., and Sally J. Holbrook
1978   Environmental Reconstruction and the Abandonment of the Largo-Gallina Area, New Mexico. In *Journal of Field Archaeology* 5:29–49.

Maxwell, Tim D.
1990   Prehistoric Population Change in the Lower Rio Chama Valley, Northwestern New Mexico. Ms. in possession of author.

Mera, H. P.
1934   *A Survey of the Biscuit Ware Area in Northern New Mexico*. Technical Series Bulletin No. 6. Laboratory of Anthropology, Museum of New Mexico, Santa Fe.

Orcutt, Janet D.
1981   *Changing Settlement Locations on the Pajarito Plateau, New Mexico*. Ph.D. dissertation, University of California, Los Angeles. University Microfilms, Ann Arbor.

1991   Environmental Variability and Settlement Changes on the Pajarito Plateau, New Mexico. *American Antiquity* 56:315–32.

1993   Villages, Field Houses, and Land Use on the Southern Pajarito Plateau. In *Papers on the Early Classic Period Prehistory of the Pajarito Plateau, New Mexico*, edited by Timothy A. Kohler and A. R. Linse, 87–104. Reports of Investigations No. 65. Washington State University, Department of Anthropology, Pullman.

Orcutt, Janet D., Eric Blinman, Timothy A. Kohler
1990   Explanations of Population Aggregation in the Mesa Verde Region Prior to A.D. 900. In *Perspectives on Southwestern Prehistory*, edited by Charles L. Redman and Paul E. Minnis, pp. 196–212. Westview Press, Boulder.

Pattison, Natalie B.
1968   *Nogales Cliff House: A Largo-Gallina Site*. Unpublished Master's thesis, Department of Anthropology, University of New Mexico, Albuquerque.

Peckham, Stewart
1959   *The Palisade Ruin, LA 3505: Archaeological Salvage Excavations Near the Abiquiu Dam, Rio Arriba County, New Mexico*. Report prepared in cooperation with the National Park Service, Region 3, United States Department of the Interior, Santa Fe. School of American Research, Santa Fe, and the Museum of New Mexico, Albuquerque.

Plog, Fred, George J. Gumerman, Robert C. Euler, Jeffrey S. Dean, Richard H. Hevly, and Thor N. V. Karlstrom
1988   Anasazi Adaptive Strategies: The Model, Predictions, and Results. In *The Anasazi in a Changing Environment*, edited by George J. Gumerman, pp. 230–76. Cam-

bridge University Press, Cambridge, England.

Powers, Robert P.

1988   Final Archeological Research Design for a Sample Inventory Survey of Bandelier National Monument. Ms. on file, National Park Service, Branch of Cultural Research, Santa Fe, New Mexico.

Preucel, Robert W.

1988   *Seasonal Agricultural Circulation and Residential Mobility: A Prehistoric Example from the Pajarito Plateau, New Mexico*. Ph.D. dissertation, University of California, Los Angeles. University Microfilms, Ann Arbor.

Preucel, Robert W., W. Nicholas Trierweiler, and Beverly M. Larson

1986   Appendix 2: Summary of Site Survey Data. In *Prehistoric Responses to Food Stress on the Pajarito Plateau, New Mexico: Technical Report and Results of the Pajarito Archaeological Research Project, 1977–1985*, by James N. Hill and W. N. Trierweiler. Final report to the National Science Foundation. Department of Anthropology, University of California, Los Angeles.

Reed, Erik K.

1949   Sources of Upper Rio Grande Pueblo Culture and Population. *El Palacio* 56(4):163–84.

Reiter, Paul

1938   *The Jemez Pueblo of Unshagi, New Mexico, with Notes on the Earlier Excavations at "Amoxiumqua" and Giusewa*. Bulletin No. 326, Monograph Series No. 1(5). University of New Mexico, Albuquerque.

Riley, Carroll L.

1952   San Juan Anasazi and the Galisteo Basin. *El Palacio* 59(3):77–82.

Rose, Martin R., Jeffrey S. Dean, and William J. Robinson

1981   *The Past Climate of Arroyo Hondo, New Mexico, Reconstructed from Tree Rings*. Arroyo Hondo Archaeological Series, Vol. 4. School of American Research Press, Santa Fe.

Rose, M. R., William J. Robinson, and Jeffrey S. Dean

1982   *Dendroclimatic Reconstruction for the Southeastern Colorado Plateau*. Final report to Division of Chaco Research, National Park Service, Albuquerque.

Schwartz, Douglas W.

1981   Foreword. In *The Past Climate of Arroyo Hondo, New Mexico, Reconstructed from Tree Rings*, by Martin R. Rose, Jeffrey S. Dean, and William J. Robinson, pp. ix–xv. Arroyo Hondo Archaeological Series, Vol. 4. School of American Research Press, Santa Fe.

Smith, Eric A.

1988   Risk and Uncertainty in the 'Original Affluent Society': Evolutionary Ecology of Resource-Sharing and Land Tenure. In *Hunters and Gatherers 1: History, Evolution, and Social Change*, edited by T. Ingold, D. Riches, and J. Woodburn, 222–51. Berg, Oxford.

Spielmann, Katherine

1983   Late Prehistoric Exchange Between the Southwest and Southern Plains. *Plains Anthropologist* 28:257–72.

Stubbs, Stanley A.

1954   Summary Report on an Early Pueblo Site in the Tesuque Valley, New Mexico. *El Palacio* 61(2):43–5.

Wendorf, Fred

1952   Excavations at Cuyamungue. *El Palacio* 59(8):265–66.

1953   *Salvage Archaeology in the Chama Valley, New Mexico*. Monograph No. 17. School of American Research, Santa Fe.

1954   A Reconstruction of Northern Rio Grande Prehistory. *American Anthropologist* 56:200–27.

Wendorf, Fred, and Erik K. Reed

1955   An Alternative Reconstruction of Northern Rio Grande Prehistory. *El Palacio* 62(6):131–73.

Wetherington, Ronald K.

1968   *Excavations at Pot Creek Pueblo*. Paper No. 6. Fort Burgwin Research Center, Taos.

Woosley, Anne I.

1986   Puebloan Prehistory of the Northern Rio Grande: Settlement, Population, Subsistence. *Kiva* 51:143–64.

Chapter 14

The Role of Warfare in the Pueblo III Period

Jonathan Haas and Winifred Creamer

Because we have already succeeded in irritating most archaeologists in the Southwest with the seemingly preposterous idea that warfare played a central role in the Kayenta area during the Pueblo III period (Haas and Creamer 1993), we thought it would be interesting to take the idea even further. Basically we argue in this chapter that warfare was endemic throughout the northern Southwest in the thirteenth century, and that any explanations of settlement, political relations, and abandonment must incorporate warfare as a central causal variable.

Following a short discussion of various types of warfare, we argue that the aggregation seen throughout much of the Anasazi area in the thirteenth century was largely a defensive measure taken in response to the threat of warfare; the move toward political centralization and consolidation was an adaptive response to a prolonged pattern of intergroup conflict. As a result, the ultimate abandonment of the Four Corners region can be attributed to a complex interaction between the people and their environment under conditions of war. In arguing for the importance of warfare, we are not denying the (overriding) importance of environmental variables in influencing patterns of human behavior in the Anasazi area during the late Pueblo III period (A.D. 1200–1300). In fact, Anasazi warfare arose as a response to a pattern of environmental degradation (Haas and Creamer 1993).

The kind of warfare we are talking about is relatively simple "tribal" warfare that would have consisted primarily of small scale sporadic raiding with limited physical contact (see Redmond 1994). The objectives of such raids would be wife-stealing, limited acquisition, and general destruction of an enemy's resources. Staged, formal "battles" are less likely in tribal warfare; consequently, low numbers of fatalities result (Haas and Creamer 1993; Service 1971). Although some would want to refer to such conflict as "raiding" or some other term, they certainly fit the term "war" as it is commonly applied as an analytical concept in the anthropological literature. Based upon his comparison of different kinds of definitions of warfare, Ferguson (1984:5) offers a broad definition that recognizes warfare as "organized, purposeful group action, directed against another group that may or may not be organized for similar action, involving the actual or potential application of lethal force."

Ethnohistoric Information on Pueblo Warfare

Before turning to the evidence for the causes and effects of warfare in the Pueblo III period, we would first like to offer an indication of the nature of warfare among the Pueblo people as manifested in the ethnographic and ethnohistoric records. The image of the peaceful Pueblos, although popular in the public eye, has not had much support in the anthropological literature for a long time. Ellis (1951:177) has pointed out that "the Pueblo Indians of the Southwest enjoy a reputation for peacefulness which, in the main, they have appeared to deserve because in historic times they were more peaceful than Plains peoples and the Apache," but she goes on to state:

Examination of the history, traditions, formal social organization, and family life in the various Pueblo communities suggests not only some appreciable differences between degrees of peacefulness today but likewise a definite underlying stratum of personal aggression, apparently related primarily to the competition so thoroughly decried by all (Ellis 1951:177).

Part of the problem in assessing the role of warfare among Pueblo societies is that colonial period reductions in population, forced resettlement, religious proselytization, and imposition of Spanish government operated collectively to end previous warlike Pueblo traditions. Relatively little information has been collected on warfare among Pueblo groups in the early historic or protohistoric period, and its role has not been clearly established.

There does appear to have been a regular pattern of warfare among Pueblo groups before the arrival of Europeans in 1540. The chronicles of Coronado's expedition in 1540 to 1542 relate numerous accounts of Pueblo warriors and tales of warfare, though is it not immediately clear from these accounts whether the warfare was internecine between Pueblo groups or between Pueblo and nomadic groups from the Plains (Hammond and Rey 1940). For example, Castañeda, the chief chronicler of the Coronado expedition, in referring to what was probably the area of the Galisteo Basin, south of present-day Santa Fe, noted:

Farther on there was another large pueblo completely destroyed and leveled. The patios [plazas] were covered with numerous stone balls as large as jugs of one *arroba*. It looked as if the stones had been hurled from catapults or guns with which an enemy had destroyed the pueblo. All that we could find out about it was that sixteen years before some people called Teyas had come in large numbers to that land and had destroyed those pueblos. They besieged Cicuye [Pecos] but could not take it because it was strong (Hammond and Rey 1940:257–58).

Based on this and other accounts, Nelson concluded that by the time of Coronado's travels, four of the eight large pueblos in the Galisteo Basin had been destroyed by attack from other Indian groups (Nelson 1914:14).

Later reports are similar. In 1591, Gaspar Castaño de Sosa reported "two villages abandoned but very few days previously on account of war, as the Indians who were with us gave us to understand by signs; and we saw clearly that it was so, from the many dead bodies. In these villages were much maize and stores of beans" (Bandelier 1892:123).

These reports of intensive warfare in the Pueblo area show that destructive conflicts appear to have occurred prior to and at the time of European contact. That at least some warfare was internecine, involving attack on historically known pueblos by other Puebloan groups is made clear in Bandelier's remarks about the ruins of Kuapa:

The village of Kua-pa was once attacked by the Tehuas [Tewas] and captured. The survivors retreated to the Potrero Viejo; the Tehuas pursued, but their attack upon the lofty cliff signally failed. They were defeated and driven back across the Rio Grande, many of them are said to have perished in that river, and the Tehuas never troubled the Queres again. In consequence of these hostilities, the survivors established themselves on the potrero [high cliff] for a short time, whence they de-

scended to settle where Cochiti stands today (Bandelier 1892:165–66).

The ability of the Pueblos to wage war is further illustrated by the Pueblo Revolt of 1680, when most of the pueblos formed an alliance to wage war on all foreigners. The Indian forces overwhelmed the Spanish and forced a small surviving party out of New Mexico (Sando 1979). When Europeans returned to the region in the 1690s they systematically "pacified" the Indians of the area, who were already very reduced in numbers. It is of significance to our argument that during this period of pacification following the revolt, the Pueblo people quite often retreated to high, inaccessible, mesa-top locations.

Throughout the eighteenth and nineteenth centuries, foreign rulers and clergy emphasized norms of cooperation with colonial laws, conversion to Catholicism, and suppressed intertribal conflicts (Woodbury 1959:126). During this same time, however, there are repeated reports of the skill, bravery, and aggressiveness of the Pueblo warriors (Jones 1966).

Ethnographic reports of Pueblo groups in the twentieth century record strong traditions of warfare, including warrior cults, the office and activities of village War Chief, and ceremonialism accompanying warfare. "Warfare was an important activity in the past and war associations are found in every pueblo. Indeed, among the Tanoans there is a counterpart women's organization—the Women's Scalp Association" (Dozier 1970:81). Fox (1967:66) noted for Cochiti, for example, that membership in the War Society initially included any man who had killed another man and been purified by the society (1967:66). Ellis also talks about war societies in Santa Ana Pueblo, in which "[the War] Society would have died out, as in most other pueblos, if the Santa Anans had not arranged to permit men to become 'Animal Opi' [Animal Warrior] after having killed certain types of animals: a similar situation exists in Zuni, Cochiti,

and (previously unreported) in Jemez" (Ellis 1951:185).

A similar pattern is found in the western Pueblos with widespread occurrence of war chiefs, war gods, and warrior societies at Hopi and Zuni (Eggan 1950). There are also Hopi myths and traditions of extensive conflict and war between villages, with villages being burned and all the people killed (Courlander 1982, 1987; Voth 1905).

Given a clear historic pattern of warfare among the historic pueblos, it is reasonable to ask when this pattern emerged in the evolutionary trajectory of Pueblo peoples. There are at least some indications that the substantial fourteenth-century immigration into the Rio Grande Valley following the abandonment of the Four Corners region was accompanied by a continuation of this pattern of warfare. Although no one has looked systematically at site locations or patterns of violence, some major sites occupied in the early fourteenth century are strategically placed in defensible positions and protected by defensive measures. The site of Tsiping, for example, in the lower Chama drainage, is situated on a high mesa with a steep escarpment on three sides, and a wall across the fourth side. The only access to the site is through a carefully carved zigzag entry guarded by a parapet walkway. Without canvassing all the data on Pueblo IV period warfare, it nevertheless seems that warfare was an established tradition among the Pueblos of the northern Southwest in late prehistoric and early historic times. Pushing back further in time, the available evidence indicates the start of a pattern of endemic warfare in the northern Southwest dates to the thirteenth century, just prior to the abandonment of the Four Corners region.

In the mid-1980s we spent several years in the Long House Valley-Tsegi Canyon area of northeast Arizona investigating the beginnings of warfare and the relationship between warfare and tribalization among the Kayenta Anasazi. We will not present the voluminous data from that project recently summarized in our monograph (Haas and Creamer 1993). Instead we would like to bring in some broad insights gained from this research that are not presented in the monograph.

Warfare and Site Location

At the beginning of the Kayenta Warfare project, we worked with the Long House Valley survey data generated by Jeff Dean, Lex Lindsay, and Bill Robinson (1978; Effland 1979). These data showed an interesting pattern of aggregation during the Pueblo III period. In the early twelfth century there was an even distribution of small sites spread across the valley floor. Between about A.D. 1150 and 1250, the sites remained mostly small, but concentrated in the northern half of the valley. Between A.D. 1250 and 1300 the settlement system was transformed with the emergence of five large, aggregated pueblos of 75 to 400 rooms. Each of these five "focal" sites (see also Dean, chapter 3) was surrounded by a group of 2 to 10 smaller sites, all generally within 500 m or less of the focal site. It might be argued that these smaller "satellite" sites were in fact not really separate sites at all, but merely separate architectural blocks of a single community. In some instances this clearly seems to be the case, because the satellites are separated from the focal sites by only 50 to 100 m. In all cases, there is relatively uninterrupted ceramic debris, all dating to the Tsegi phase (A.D. 1250–1300), linking all the sites in a cluster.

In addition, it is possible that the smaller sites were not fully contemporaneous with the larger sites. The ceramic assemblages from the focal and satellite sites are roughly the same and imply contemporaneity. But hard dates are somewhat more ambiguous. We have tree-ring dates from only one focal site, Long House Pueblo, and all cluster in the late A.D. 1260s to 1270s. Tree-ring dates from two satellite sites range from the 1240s through the early 1270s. These dates do

not preclude the possibility that the satellites were abandoned in the 1270s and the people moved into the focal sites as part of the process of aggregation. In other words, what appears to be a two-tiered site size hierarchy may be an artifact of inadequate dating rather than a reflection of an actual settlement pattern. This possibility must be considered for other kinds of Pueblo III period site distribution patterns in which multiple site types are thought to be contemporaneous with one another.

Putting aside the possibility that the satellites and focal sites may not have been fully contemporaneous, we nevertheless see in the Long House survey data the appearance of large, aggregated villages in the latter half of the thirteenth century. In this sense, Long House Valley looks like many other parts of the northern Southwest at this same time. In field checking these five sites, it quickly became apparent that all are located in elevated and defensible positions. This was not a particularly new revelation, as Lindsay (1969) noted the elevated location of large, late Kayenta sites 25 years ago. Also, Jeff Dean commented (personal communication 1983) that while mapping Long House Pueblo, he and Lindsay had noted that access into the site was limited to two side ramps and that the site could be described as defensive.

In fact, we were hard pressed to explain the entire Long House Valley settlement system in the late thirteenth century except as part of a deliberate, coordinated defensive strategy on the part of the valley residents. Perhaps the strongest indication of this defensive strategy is an entire site cluster—Organ Rock Pueblo and its satellites—that is located on top of an isolated sandstone block with sheer walls rising up over 150 m. Access is only by way of a single crack in the rock up a combination of stairs and hand-and-toe holds. There is no cultivable land on top and no water. It makes no sense for people to live up there unless they were absolutely convinced of the need for protection.

Although the Long House Valley data seemed to point to defense as an extremely important variable in site location in the thirteenth century, those data alone did not confirm a state of endemic warfare. Three of the focal sites are simply on hilltops, and although in defensible locations they did not appear to have overtly defensive features. So we turned to the surrounding area to see what the settlement pattern looked like in the neighboring valleys. Earlier, based largely on casual surveys, Dean (1969:193) had stated that the population of the Klethla Valley to the west "declined sharply after A.D. 1250" and that Monument Valley, to the northeast "was almost completely abandoned by 1250." We were also told informally that there appeared to have been a similar population decline in the Kayenta Valley immediately to the east. Dean accordingly reasoned that the aggregation seen in Tsegi Canyon (and presumably the Long House Valley area) was due to population immigration from the surrounding valleys. Thus, there was some doubt that we would find much when we looked for a similar pattern of defensibly located focal-type sites in the valleys on either side of Long House Valley. Nevertheless, we initiated surveys in these two valleys to see what was there.

The surveys in the Klethla and Kayenta Valleys (up to the edge of Monument Valley) were guided by a computer program set up by Ken Kvamme (1993). The program pinpointed topographic features that shared similar characteristics to the loci of the focal sites in Long House Valley. The survey crews then went out and looked at a large sample of the targeted defensible locations, as well as at a smaller sample of control plots in nondefensible locations. The survey results did not confirm the idea of a sharp population decline in the valleys surrounding Long House Valley in the thirteenth century. These surrounding valleys were not abandoned, nor did they witness population declines. If anything the population in these valleys increased in the latter half of the thirteenth century. The reason these valleys looked abandoned is that the sites were almost all large pueblos of 50 to 200 rooms, perched up on top of inaccessible rocks and mesa tops. They were in places that did not fit the patterns that often emerge from traditional settlement pattern studies. You might look for shrines on these hilltops, but habitation did not seem likely. It got so that one of the best indicators of site location was when the survey crews were unable to find an access route to the top of a particular topographic feature. In each such case, a second effort revealed a skinny crack in the rock or steep trail up the cliff side, and a pueblo on top invariably dating to A.D. 1250 to 1300.

In one case the crews were working in an area surveyed some years previously as part of a cultural resource management survey. The earlier survey had recorded a large Pueblo II period site at the base of a sheer rock outcrop in a major wash in the Klethla Valley area. Nothing was recorded on top of the outcrop. Maybe this was because the survey crews did not have a reason to look on top or maybe it was because they could not find a way up. Our crew found a treacherous route up and recorded a large, late, Pueblo III period pueblo. In another case at the mouth of Tsegi Canyon a major site of over 200 rooms was discovered on top of an isolated sandstone butte about 200 m high. Access was up a long dune, through a crack and across a narrow saddle, which had two prehistoric walls cutting across it. From a survey standpoint the interesting thing about this site is that the Rainbow Bridge-Monument Valley expedition headquarters was almost at the base of the butte, and yet there is no record of them ever having found the pueblo on top.

In one last example, one of the focal sites we recorded was behind the large Basketmaker site of Juniper Cove, excavated (but largely unreported) in the 1910s by Byron Cummings (1953). On a visit to this site a senior southwestern archaeologist, who had been visiting Juniper

Cove since the 1950s, commented "You know, I've been coming to this site for 30 years and we always knew there was a Tsegi phase [A.D. 1250–1300] site around here somewhere, but we never could find it" (Lex Lindsay, personal communication 1986). The reason is that the site, a two-story focal pueblo of over 80 rooms, was on the very top of one of the pointed flat-irons along the eastern edge of Skeleton Mesa (see Haas and Creamer 1993:68–69) This is a location that simply does not fit most traditional ideas of major habitation site location.

No criticism of any kind of earlier surveys is intended by these anecdotes. It is, however, important to point out that at least in the Kayenta region, an area that has been heavily explored by professional archaeologists for at least 70 years, the sites from the late thirteenth century do not fit the traditional, environmentally based pattern of Anasazi settlement in the Southwest. They are not near water, they are not near cultivable land, nor are the located near transportation routes. They are all very selectively placed in defensible locations. At times, the efforts people made were extraordinary. They lived up on top of steep cliffs, up to 250 m high, with no immediate source of water and with potential fields down on the flats 500 m away. Whenever slides of these sites are shown to cultural anthropologists working with warring peoples or to archaeologists working in other world areas where warfare is an accepted part of the local prehistory, they are struck by the extreme defensive posture taken by the Kayenta people (see, for example, Haas and Creamer 1993: 64, 75).

The insight to be gained from these survey data is that unless a deliberate and selective effort is made to survey a non-random sample of topographically defensible locations, we are not likely to know if we have a true picture of aggregation and settlement during the Pueblo III period.

It can be (and has been) argued that even if we accept the notion that the Kayenta were afraid of someone and en-

gaged in war at some level, this does not really apply to the entire Anasazi area. Nor is it particularly relevant to the Pueblo III period as a whole. This line of reasoning often includes the rationale that this was a particular historical event in a particular geographic location. This reasoning leads to our next insight.

Endemic Warfare

In looking across the Kayenta region, the settlement pattern data indicate that some level of warfare was endemic throughout. To date, everywhere we have looked in northeastern Arizona, we have consistently found sites located in extraordinarily defensive positions in the late Pueblo III period. In the Glen Canyon area, for example, Lindsay et al. (1969: 231) report on excavations of a thirteenth-century community of sites on Segazlin Mesa, also referred to as "Lost Mesa." The primary access route into this mesa-top community is protected by "Guardian Pueblo," a site consisting of a solid face of rock walls and rooms. In the Tsegi Canyon system we found that in the thirteenth-century occupation of rock shelters there was deliberate selection of inaccessible shelters. They were not selectively located near cultivable land or water sources; they were selectively located in caves with limited and treacherous access. The pattern is consistent and impossible to ignore. The Kayenta Anasazi were at war and they took explicit and fairly dramatic steps to protect themselves and their resources from outside attack.

An obvious question is, "who were they fighting with?" Ambler and Sutton (1989) have argued, without evidence from surveys or excavations, that "Numic speakers" were responsible for the predation on the Kayenta. Although some have argued that hunters and gatherers could not have been strong enough to have threatened settled village horticulturalists, Ambler and Sutton discount this argument by citing historic examples of such predation. To some extent their arguments are mitigated by the fact that modern and historic patterns of raiding by nomadic groups have all been heavily influenced by the presence of the horse and other large, rideable beasts; nevertheless, such a possibility cannot be ruled out without further study. At the same time, one would think that if nomadic raiders did play a dominant role in affecting the behavior of the Anasazi they would have left behind some evidence in the archaeological record. Perhaps some of our amorphous Archaic and Basketmaker II sites are the camps of Numic speakers. If so, they have certainly defied detection over the past century.

Alternatives to the Numic-speaker hypothesis include the possibility that the Kayenta people were fighting with each other, or that they were fighting with Anasazi from other areas. We looked explicitly for evidence of the former in the course of our survey and excavations, with ambiguous results at best. There is some evidence of spatial gaps between clusters of communities, but this spatial data is accompanied by evidence of economic exchange across this gap (see Green 1993; Lucius 1993; Stoltman, Burton, and Haas 1992). The economic data do not obviate the possibility that these separated communities may have been raiding each other, but neither do the spatial data constitute a solid basis for inferring intercommunity conflict. This is a question that needs to be explored further.

Turning from the possibility of internecine Kayenta warfare to warfare between the Kayenta and their neighbors, we have found an interesting pattern of anecdotal data over the past 10 years. A substantial body of evidence shows defensive site location and accompanying conflict in almost every nook and cranny of the Anasazi world during late Pueblo III times. Excavations by the Crow Canyon Archaeological Center at Sand Canyon Pueblo in southwest Colorado have uncovered evidence of heavy burning, human remains on the floors of houses, and smashed artifacts in rooms (Bradley 1992). Sand Canyon Pueblo is located on an outcrop of land

with steep sides around part of the site and a wall protecting the rest. Though alternative explanations might be constructed (see Lipe 1992), Occam's Razor would seem to demand warfare be explicitly considered and ruled out as a possible explanation of this pattern. Elsewhere, we have sites like Balcony House at Mesa Verde, which almost everyone agrees was defensive. There are the enigmatic towers at Hovenweep, which somehow do not seem defensive because they are not up on mesa tops, but which nevertheless would have been impregnable to attack.

Elsewhere in the northern Southwest, such as in Canyon de Chelly, thirteenth-century settlement patterns show a distinct shift in residence from the comfortable, but open, canyon-floor shelters to the high, inaccessible caves etched out of the middle canyon walls (McDonald 1976). It is no coincidence that the remote and isolated balcony at White House, which most Southwest archaeologists have looked upon at one time or another as an interesting challenge, was built in the latter half of the thirteenth century (Morris 1969). The same is true of the numerous other isolated, inaccessible shelters such as Three Turkey Ruin or Ledge Ruin. Rafting down the San Juan River, one is struck by the fact that the sites that can be entered only with climbing gear and nerves of steel all date to the thirteenth century. Moving over to the Hopi region, a recent tour of Homol'ovi IV found us being shown around a pueblo initiated in the late 1200s and perched on top of a lone rock knoll.

The pattern of defensively situated sites appearing in the mid-thirteenth century is not limited to the Kayenta area, but is a panregional pattern found across the northern Southwest. This should not be surprising, given that the development of raiding and warfare in the Kayenta region clearly appears to have been induced by environmental degradation during the twelfth and thirteenth centuries. Because the other culture areas were suffering similar conditions, it might well be

expected that they would have similar responses. Furthermore, it also is reasonable to hypothesize that if one area is at war, there will be rippling repercussions for other areas. After all, by moving into one of these remote defensive sites a community becomes a tough target for raiding. It would then be easier for a raiding party to look around for more exposed prey. Given the distances traveled by raiding parties in modern ethnographic examples in the Amazon or Africa (Chagnon 1983 and personal communication; Katsuyoshi and Turton 1979; Whitehead 1988), the entire northern Southwest is well within the potential range of raiding parties from any one Anasazi area to any of the others.

The insight to be gained here is that warfare was probably a fact of life in the late Pueblo III period throughout the Anasazi area. It certainly may have varied in intensity across time and space. But the Anasazi entered a cycle of regional conflict and raiding in the thirteenth century, and if we ever want to understand the workings of virtually all aspects of Anasazi culture at the time, this cycle of conflict and raiding is going to have to be taken into consideration. Sand Canyon Pueblo may have witnessed a ceremonial abandonment, but we would venture to guess that it was a short ceremony in advance of a burning arrow.

Warfare and Aggregation During the Pueblo III Period

The final insight we offer from the Kayenta Warfare Project relates to the previous one. If warfare was endemic in the Anasazi area, what was its effect on Anasazi culture? There are obviously myriad possible answers to this question, but we focus on one aspect of the broader cultural system, albeit an aspect that is near and dear to the hearts of many archaeologists.

One of the clearest patterns emerging in the Pueblo III period is aggregation. In fact we were asked by the organizers of the present symposium to identify "big Pueblo III period sites," and such big sites have long been a hallmark of the period

(Kidder 1924). Aggregation, whether in the Pueblo III period or at other times has held the interest of many of us in southwestern archaeology. This is probably due to the fact that aggregation is so visible in the archaeological record and the "big" sites have attracted a disproportionate share of the research effort. In addition to the historical focus on big sites, a great deal has been made of the social processes accompanying aggregation, and much of the current debate about the nature of political systems in the transition between the Pueblo III and Pueblo IV periods revolves around aggregation.

In the Kayenta region, the appearance of the aggregated pueblos is clearly associated with the assumption of a defensive posture on the part of the population in the middle of the thirteenth century. We have found a few defensively positioned small sites dating to the immediately preceding decades of the first half of the thirteenth century. But it is the second half of the century that witnessed the transformation of the settlement system, as aggregation and defensive posturing went hand-in-hand. Correlation does not mean causation, but we have come to the conclusion that the aggregation must have been partially a result of the conflict. There just does not seem to be an alternative and parsimonious explanation for why the Kayenta people moved together in unison into large villages that were regularly placed in defensive positions.

Again, we must ask whether what applies to the Kayenta applies elsewhere as well. Are there not other kinds of explanations that might be applied to aggregation in other areas that would account for local patterns of aggregation? Some might want to argue from a post-processual standpoint that the Anasazi made the uniquely human decision to move into aggregated villages for ceremonial or aesthetic reasons. It might thus be inappropriate for us to look too hard for "rational" or positivist explanations. Although we acknowledge that people do not always respond "logically" to their environment, it does seem

unlikely that the Anasazi in the Kayenta area and elsewhere rose up as one and made the decision sometime in the thirteenth century that living in larger villages would be somehow aesthetically desirable. One need only consider the health and sanitation problems accompanying aggregation to rule out such ideological explanations. A visit to Inscription House or any of several other south-facing cliff dwelling in the summer gives an idea of how unpleasant pueblo aggregation can be. It seems equally unlikely that a synchronous, panregional pattern would be caused by many local, idiosyncratic factors. If everybody did roughly the same thing at roughly the same time, it seems reasonable to look at the possibility that they were making a common and probably interrelated adaptive response to common environmental and cultural conditions.

Aside from humanistic interpretations, southwestern archaeologists have often turned to environmental and cultural models in trying to explain aggregation (see, for example, Orcutt, Blinman, and Kohler 1990). Not meaning to oversimplify their arguments, in the most general terms they hold that people banded together in larger communities in order to more effectively exploit limited resources or resource zones. The explanations rarely include a consideration of the possible role of warfare in inducing aggregation. In commenting in a symposium on the Dolores Project some years ago, Tim Earle observed that in the Southwest, "warfare seems to be a dirty word."

This unwillingness to consider the causal role of warfare in the evolving settlement strategies is all the more puzzling in that warfare offers a highly parsimonious, if perhaps only partial, explanation of why people would have banded together into physically larger communities. The phrase "united we stand, divided we fall" although trite also seems glaringly obvious for Pueblo III period settlement. What better reason for the Anasazi to aggregate into large villages with poor sanitation than because there was safety

in numbers? Large villages are not an efficient way to exploit shrinking resources in a hostile environment. The pattern of aggregation does not fit a maximization model, and it is not a particularly adaptive strategy in the face of the twelfth and thirteenth century conditions of increased erosion and lower overall precipitation. Even if populations were forced to cluster around remnant zones of cultivable land and water sources, such circumstances do not necessarily induce all people to live in one village.

Kohler and Van West (1996) develop a model of aggregation arising as a result of food-sharing during times of agricultural abundance. Van West (chapter 15) offers a reconstruction of past land productivity that makes it appear there were no shortages of land and resources prior to or during the period of aggregation. She goes on to argue that abandonment of the northern Southwest is a result of the development of aggregation and attendant social relations to a degree that did not allow for disaggregation. In her view, despite the availability of adequately productive land, the population was unable to disperse. Presumably, both kin and sodality relations were so strong that people either stayed in aggregated settlements or completely vacated the region. Van West's data are very elegant and persuasively argued, but other kinds of data would indicate that additional variables must be considered to address questions of aggregation and abandonment.

We know from archaeological data collected outside the American Southwest, for example, that periods of population increase and aggregation can be followed by thorough disaggregation of population clusters (Culbert 1988; Fash and Stuart 1991:168; Kristiansen 1982). There are also archaeological data from the northern Southwest to suggest that aggregation occurred only after economic conditions were already in decline, as indicated by high incidence of malnutrition in skeletal remains starting in the twelfth century and intensifying in the thirteenth century (Ryan 1977). Although potential land productivity provides valuable insights, it may not be an accurate gauge of the actual resources that were available to a group of people at any given point in time. At least for the Kayenta region, where admittedly no one has attempted to reconstruct land productivity, aggregation and abandonment took place within the context of significant shortages of resources. It would be interesting to examine skeletal evidence of nutrition for the Mesa Verde area where Van West has provided such excellent information on potential land productivity.

Faced with conflict, raiding, or predation of some sort, however, aggregation is an eminently logical choice. The advantages of sheer numbers coupled with increased defensive capabilities (in terms of defending a village site) would outweigh the disadvantages of poor sanitation, crowding, and increased distance to fields.

The Kayenta data point to a pattern of correlation between aggregation and warfare, and raise the prospect of a cross-cultural causal relationship between these same two phenomena. The insight here is that any causal model that does not at least consider the potential role of warfare in the Pueblo III pattern of aggregation is destined to be incomplete. Similarly, we feel that it will be difficult to generate full explanations of other patterns of behavior in the late Pueblo III period, such as increased ceremonialism (an increase in the number of kivas, and the rise of the Katsina cult), interregional interaction, and ultimately abandonment, without factoring in an endemic pattern of regional warfare.

Conclusions

In offering these insights, we are not trying to say that warfare was the overriding factor influencing all behavior and the evolution of the Anasazi cultural systems in the Pueblo III period. Quite to the contrary, we have argued throughout our work that we see the environment as playing the dominant causal role. We fully agree with Gumerman and associates (Gumerman 1988) in their argument for the importance of the environment in influencing the behavior of the Anasazi. The difference between our model and Van West's is also not a disagreement over productive capacity, but we believe that successful systems modeling requires some analog of warfare as input along with environmental data. In our view, conditions of environmental stress first lead to malnutrition and eventually to the pattern of warfare, which invokes aggregation. Environment is the big player in all of this. Warfare is just the vehicle of change. What we have learned in the post-processual era of archaeological thought, however, is that human strategies for dealing with environmental forces are multifaceted. People respond in different ways to similar environmental pressures, depending on specific historic circumstances and even specific human decisions. Warfare is but one possible response to conditions of environmental stress. Once the conflict option is chosen, however, even if it is by but one group in one area, it will have a chain reaction effect. Here we appeal to George Gumerman's example of the "tit-for-tat" response to the prisoner's dilemma (Axelrod 1983; Axelrod and Hamilton 1981; Gumerman and Dean 1989).

During the twelfth and thirteenth centuries, the Anasazi people were faced with deteriorating environmental conditions and suffered from increasing malnutrition (see, for example, Ryan 1977). Integrative social networks that served to distribute resources across the landscape in times of shortage would have continued to function until there were no resources in the system at all, a result of panregional environmental problems.[1] Faced with such conditions, raiding one's neighbors (near or far) would have been one option available to the Anasazi. Not the only option certainly, but one option. Under these circumstances, however, the decision by one group to raid another village to obtain resources for hungry kith and kin would have initiated a cycle of warfare. In a "tit-for-tat" model, the cycle of conflict would gain its own momentum once initiated. Over the long term, such a strategy might very well be counterproductive and maladaptive, but the modern world is very convincing of the fact that humans do not always make rational decisions.

If we are ever to understand the complex and dynamic patterns of human behavior in the Pueblo III period, we must begin factoring warfare into all of our equations. Not to do so would be like trying to understand the modern American economy without considering the military. But just as American economists do not all study the military, all southwestern archaeologists should not be studying warfare. We do, however, have to stop turning a blind eye to warfare, and consider more fully its potential role in the evolution of the Anasazi culture in the Pueblo III period.

Acknowledgments

We would like to thank the Harry Frank Guggenheim Foundation for its support of our research on warfare and conflict in the Southwest.

Note

1. The panregional environmental problems that we refer to include a decrease over time in available productive land due to erosion, increase in population and need for food, and a gradual decrease in the productivity of cultivable land over time in the Kayenta area. Van West (chapter 15) presents a model of soil productivity that suggests there was land available throughout the thirteenth century with adequate productive capacity to feed the regional population in even the worst of times. She lists a number of factors that could limit the utilization of productive land, however, including "perceptions of risk and uncertainty for the success of future harvests." We believe that perception of risk, or fear, had a much greater impact on people than Van West suggests. The onset of malnutrition prior to aggregation, for example (Ryan 1977), suggests that people were far more constrained in their choices of where to plant than the distribution of productive land on a map indicates.

References Cited

Ambler, J. Richard, and Mark Q. Sutton
  1989 The Anasazi Abandonment of the San Juan Drainage and the Numic Expansion. *North American Archaeologist* 10(1):39–53.

Axelrod, Robert
  1983 *The Evolution of Cooperation*. Basic Books, New York.

Axelrod, Robert, and William D. Hamilton
  1981 The Evolution of Cooperation. *Science* 211:1390–96.

Bandelier, Adolph F.
  1892 *Final Report of Investigations among Indians of the Southwestern United States, carried on mainly in the years from 1880 to 1885*, Part 2. Papers of the Archaeological Institute of America, American Series No. 4. Cambridge University Press, New York.

Bradley, Bruce A.
  1992 Excavations at Sand Canyon Pueblo. In *The Sand Canyon Archaeological Project: A Progress Report*, edited by William Lipe, pp. 79–97. Occasional Papers No. 2. Crow Canyon Archaeological Center, Cortez, Colorado.

Chagnon, Napoleon
  1983 *Yanamamo: The Fierce People*, 3rd Edition. Holt, Rinehart and Winston, New York.

Courlander, Harold C.
  1982 *The Fourth World of the Hopi*. University of New Mexico Press, Albuquerque.
  1987 *Hopi Voices*, recorded, transcribed, and annotated by Harold C. Courlander. University of New Mexico Press, Albuquerque.

Culbert, Patrick
  1988 The Collapse of Classic Maya Civilization. In *The Collapse of Ancient States and Civilizations*, edited by Norman Yoffee and George L. Cowgill, pp. 69–101. University of Arizona Press, Tucson.

Cummings, Byron
  1953 *First Inhabitants of Arizona and the Southwest*. Cummings Publication Council, Tucson.

Dean, Jeffrey S.
  1969 *Chronological Analysis of Tsegi Phase Sites in Northeastern Arizona*. Papers of the Laboratory of Tree-Ring Research, No. 3. University of Arizona, Tucson.

Dean, Jeffrey S., Alexander J. Lindsay, Jr., and William Robinson
  1978 Prehistoric Settlement in Long House Valley, Northeastern Arizona. In *Investigations of the Southwestern Anthropological Research Group: An Experiment in Archaeological Cooperation: The Proceedings of the 1976 Conference*, edited by Robert C. Euler and George Gumerman, 25–44. Museum of Northern Arizona, Flagstaff.

Dozier, Edward P.
  1970 *The Pueblo Indians of North America*. Holt, Rinehart and Winston, New York.

Effland, Richard W.
  1979 *A Study of Prehistoric Spatial Behavior: Long House Valley, Northeastern Arizona*. Ph.D. dissertation, Department of Anthropology, Arizona State University, Tempe. University Microfilms, Ann Arbor.

Eggan, Fred
  1950 *Social Organization of the Western Pueblos*. University of Chicago Press, Chicago.

Ellis, Florence Hawley
  1951 Patterns of Aggression and the War Cult in Southwestern Pueblos. *Southwestern Journal of Anthropology* 7(2):177–201.

Fash, William L., and David Stuart
  1991 Dynastic History and Cultural Evolution at Copan, Honduras. In *Classic Maya Political History*, edited by T. Patrick Culbert, pp. 147–79. Cambridge University Press, Cambridge.

Ferguson, R. Brian
  1984 Introduction: Studying War. In *Warfare, Culture, and Environment*, edited by R. Brian Ferguson, pp. 1–81. Academic Press, Orlando.

Fox, Robin
  1967 *The Keresan Bridge: A Problem in Pueblo Ethnography*. Oxford University Press, Oxford.

Green, Margerie
  1993 Analysis of Lithic Materials. In Stress and Warfare Among the Kayenta Anasazi of the 13th Century, edited by Jonathan Haas and Winifred Creamer. *Fieldiana: Anthropology*, n.s., 21:181–200. Field Museum of Natural History, Chicago.

Gumerman, George J. (editor)
  1988 *The Anasazi in a Changing Environment*, Cambridge University Press, New York.

Gumerman, George J., and Jeffrey S. Dean
  1989 Prehistoric Cooperation and Competition in the Western Anasazi Area. In *Dynamics of Southwest Prehistory*, edited by Linda S. Cordell and George J. Gumerman, pp. 99–148. Smithsonian Institution Press, Washington, D.C.

Haas, Jonathan, and Winifred Creamer (editors)
  1993 Stress and Warfare Among the Prehistoric Kayenta Anasazi of the Thirteenth Century. *Fieldiana: Anthropology*, n.s., 21. Field Museum of Natural History, Chicago.

Hammond, George P., and Agapito Rey
  1940 *Narratives of the Coronado Expedition, 1540–1542*. University of New Mexico Press, Albuquerque.

Jones, Oakah L., Jr.
  1966 *Pueblo Warriors and Spanish Conquest*. University of Oklahoma Press, Norman.

Katsuyoshi, F., and David Turton (editors)
  1979 *Warfare among East African Herders*. Senri Ethnological Studies, No. 3. National Museum of Ethnology, Osaka.

Kidder, Alfred V.
  1924 *An Introduction to the Study of Southwestern Archaeology, with a Preliminary Account of the Excavations at Pecos*. Papers of the Phillips Academy Southwestern Expedition No. 1. Yale University Press, New Haven.

Kohler, Timothy A., and Carla R. Van West
  1996 The Calculus of Self Interest in the Development of Cooperation: Sociopolitical Development and Risk among the Northern Anasazi. In *Evolving Complexity and Environmental Risk in the Prehistoric Southwest*, edited by Joseph A. Tainter and Bonnie Bagley Tainter. Addison-Wesley, Reading, Massachusetts, in press. Ms. 1993.

Kristiansen, Kristian
  1982 The Formation of Tribal Systems in Later European Prehistory: Northern Europe, 4000–5000 B.C. In *Theory and Explanation in Archaeology: The Southampton Conference*, edited by Colin Renfrew, Michael J. Rowlands and Barbara Abbott Segraves, pp. 241–80. Academic Press, New York.

Kvamme, Kenneth L.
1993   Computer Methods: Geographic Information Systems. In Stress and Warfare Among the Kayenta Anasazi of the 13th Century, edited by Jonathan Haas and Winifred Creamer. *Fieldiana: Anthropology*, n.s., 21:171–80. Field Museum of Natural History, Chicago.

Lindsay, Alexander J., Jr.
1969   *The Tsegi Phase of the Kayenta Cultural Tradition in Northeastern Arizona.* Ph.D. dissertation, Department of Anthropology, University of Arizona. University Microfilms, Ann Arbor.

Lindsay, Alexander J., Jr., J. Richard Ambler, Mary Anne Stein, and Philip M. Hobler
1969   *Survey and Excavations North and East of Navajo Mountain, Utah, 1959–1962.* Bulletin No. 45. Glen Canyon Series No. 8. Museum of Northern Arizona, Flagstaff.

Lipe, William D.
1992   Summary and Concluding Comments. In *The Sand Canyon Archaeological Project: A Progress Report*, edited by William D. Lipe. pp. 121–334. Occasional Papers No. 2. Crow Canyon Archaeological Center, Cortez, Colorado.

Lucius, William
1993   Temper Analysis of Ceramics. In Stress and Warfare Among the Kayenta Anasazi of the 13th Century, edited by Jonathan Haas and Winifred Creamer, *Fieldiana: Anthropology*, n.s., 21:201–11. Field Museum of Natural History, Chicago.

McDonald, James A.
1976   *An Archeological Assessment of Canyon De Chelly National Monument.* Publications in Anthropology No. 5. USDI, National Park Service, Western Archaeological and Conservation Center, Tucson.

Morris, Don
1969   Stabilization records, Upper White House ruin. Ms. on file, USDI, National Park Service, Western Archaeological and Conservation Center, Tucson.

Nelson, Nels C.
1914   *Pueblo Ruins of the Galisteo Basin, New Mexico.* Anthropological Papers No. 15, Part 1. American Museum of Natural History, New York.

Orcutt, Janet D., Eric Blinman, and Timothy A. Kohler
1990   Explanation of Population Aggregation in the Mesa Verde Region Prior to A.D. 900. In *Perspectives on Southwestern Prehistory*, edited by Paul E. Minnis and Charles L. Redman, pp. 196–212. Westview Press, Boulder.

Redmond, Elsa M.
1994   *Tribal and Chiefly Warfare in South America.* Memoirs of the Museum of Anthropology No. 28. University of Michigan, Ann Arbor.

Ryan, Dennis J.
1977   *The Paleopathology and Paleoepidemiology of the Kayenta Anasazi Indians in Northeastern Arizona.* Ph.D. dissertation, Department of Anthropology, Arizona State University, Tempe. University Microfilms, Ann Arbor.

Sando, Joe
1979   The Pueblo Revolt. In *Southwest*, edited by Alfonso Ortiz, pp. 194–97. Handbook of North American Indians, Vol. 9, William C. Sturtevant, general editor. Smithsonian Institution Press, Washington, D.C.

Service, Elman
1971   *Primitive Social Organization: An Evolutionary Perspective.* Random House, New York.

Stoltman, James B., James H. Burton, and Jonathan Haas
1992   Chemical and Petrographic Characterizations of Ceramic Pastes: Two Perspectives on a Single Data Set. In *Chemical Characterization of Ceramic Pastes in Archaeology*, edited by Hector Neff, pp. 85–92. Prehistory Press, Madison, Wisconsin.

Voth, Henry
1905   *Traditions of the Hopi.* Publication No. 96, Anthropological Series No. 8. Field Museum of Natural History, Chicago.

Whitehead, Neil
1988   *Lords of the Tiger Spirit.* Foris Publications, Providence, Rhode Island.

Woodbury, Richard B.
1959   A Reconsideration of Pueblo Warfare in the Southwestern United States, *Actas del 33 Congreso Internacional de Americanistas*, Tomo 2:124–33. Editorial Lehmann, San Jose, Costa Rica.

Chapter 15

Agricultural Potential and Carrying Capacity in Southwestern Colorado, A.D. 901 to 1300

Carla R. Van West

In the American Southwest, archaeologists have used environmental data to make inferences about the causes of culture change and the distribution of prehistoric populations since the early decades of the twentieth century (e.g., Bryan 1925; Douglass 1929; Fewkes 1904). In recent years, the paleoenvironmental record from which these inferences are derived has been significantly refined. Reconstruction of past environments has been based on the analysis of geomorphological, palynological, macrobotanical, faunal, and dendrochronological remains (e.g., Betancourt and Van Devender 1981; Dean 1969; Gumerman 1988; Karlstrom 1988; Mackey and Holbrook 1978; Petersen 1988). Each specialty has its strengths and limitations as well as an appropriate level of temporal and spatial resolution (Cordell 1984:35–45; Dean 1988), but underlying all paleoenvironmental studies is the principle of uniformitarianism, which assumes that the processes responsible for the variation in the natural world observed today also operated in the past. Of all these sources of information, the greatest reliance is currently placed on tree-ring data to retrodict the effective environments of past populations because of the high temporal resolution and relative ease with which these data can be calibrated with various environmental parameters, such as precipitation, temperature, streamflow, fire histories, and soil moisture.

The research described in this study is based on dendroclimatic data. Its goals are to reconstruct a local expression of high-frequency variation in regional climate, as has been modeled by tree-ring data (Dean 1988; see also Dean et al. 1985; Euler et al. 1979), and to observe the effect of this variation on the distribution and productivity of arable land farmed by dryland agricultural techniques and the regional potential human carrying capacity. An approach pioneered by Rose and his colleagues (Rose, Dean, and Robinson 1981; Rose, Robinson, and Dean 1982) was further developed to reconstruct soil moisture values and potential agricultural yield for specific soils in given elevational settings on an annual basis during the late occupation of the Mesa Verde area, from A.D. 901 to 1300. Further, the study was undertaken at a rather high level of spatial resolution (10 acres, 4 hectares) for a moderately large study area (701.1 mi²; 1,816 km²) in the southwestern portion of Colorado. This was made possible by the use of Geographic Information Systems (GIS) technology and newly available environmental data in the form of recently mapped soil distributions, Digital Elevational Models (DEMs), and quantified productivity values for individual soil types (data on file with the U.S. Soil Conservation Service in Cortez; Burns 1983). The method results in the production of maps depicting the dynamic character of the annual potential agricultural environment and the estimation of annual values of total maize productivity. These in turn form the basis for estimates of the population size and density able to be sustained by such yield. The data generated by the model make it possible to study the relationship between the location, abundance, and predictability of potential prehistoric crop yields and the known location of prehistoric settlements and their populations. They also make it possible to evaluate an issue of long standing in the northern Southwest: whether climatic variability was severe enough to disrupt agriculture and promote the abandonment of the northern San Juan region toward the end of the thirteenth century. Thus, this chapter sheds some light on the issues of central importance to this volume by firmly addressing one of the factors commonly invoked in archaeological explanations of site establishment, site abandonment, and population movement across the Anasazi world: namely climatic variation and its effect on obtaining a secure subsistence.

Methods

Conceptually, the model incorporates five logical elements (figure 15.1). First, it reconstructs soil moisture conditions for each soil type in the study area as they existed on July 1 of each year in the reconstructed sequence (A.D. 901–1970). This is accomplished by calculating Palmer Drought Severity Indexes (PDSIs; Palmer 1965) for the month of June for specific soils of the study area within the period of instrumented weather records (defined by the availability of appropriate monthly temperature and precipitation records), quantifying the relationship between PDSI values and historic tree-ring width values, and retrodicting prehistoric PDSI values with the pre-instrumented and prehistoric portion of the tree-ring record. Second, it translates the soil moisture conditions as expressed by PDSI values into predicted crop yields, first as production in beans (the same genus and species grown by the Anasazi are still grown in southwestern Colorado in great abundance by contemporary Anglo Americans) and finally as production in maize. In this way, PDSI values (here used as a proxy for climate)

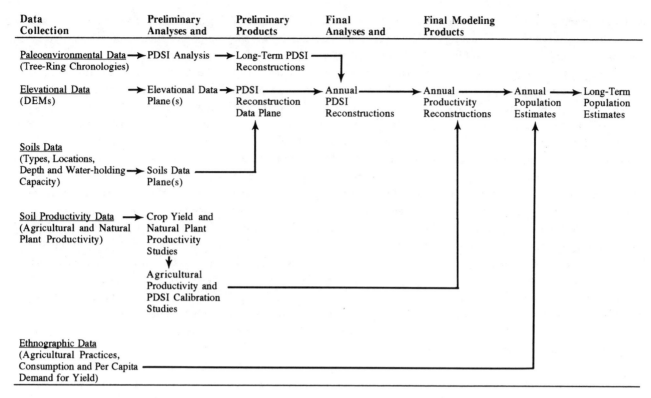

Data Collection	Preliminary Analyses and	Preliminary Products	Final Analyses and	Final Modeling Products

Figure 15.1. The conceptual model for reconstructing agricultural potential and human carrying capacity (PDSI = Palmer Drought Severity Index).

are made meaningful by their "translation" into agricultural yield, an entity that is more interpretable and useful from an archaeological perspective. Third, it calculates the total productivity of the agricultural habitat on a year-by-year basis and provides an estimate of the maximum annual food supply from this basic staple of Pueblo subsistence, maize. Fourth, it estimates the maximum annual population size and density that could have been supported by a net annual maize supply after the gross supply has been adjusted to reflect land use practices, normal harvest loss, rates of seed retention, and certain assumptions about agricultural demand (i.e., annual per person consumption rates and potential rates of storage) have been made. Finally, it examines the entire 400-year sequence (A.D. 901–1300) of yield and population values and identifies sustainable population levels over time, expressed as maximum, critical, and optimal carrying capacity values.

A number of assumptions underlie the

model. Most basic of all is the recognition that this reconstruction is, in fact, a theoretical model, and as such, is a much simplified representation of a multivariate, dynamic, real-world phenomenon. It is simplified so that the phenomenon under investigation—the potential productivity of arable land in southwestern Colorado—can be evaluated on the basis of measures identified by the model. Thus, not every factor thought to affect the outcome of successful harvests has been included directly in the construction of the model (e.g., the potential effect of nutrient depletion on arable soils or the erosion of topsoil by winds and destructive sheet wash), although some have been considered at a later point in the modeling process and have been included indirectly (e.g., crop loss due agricultural pests and predators or the practice of fallowing fields).

The model presumes that the primary prehistoric agriculture technology in southwestern Colorado was dryland farming. Although floodplains, alluvial fans,

and arroyo bottoms of ephemeral drainages may have been used for farming by some prehistoric farmers in the study area, it is the rolling hills and swales of deep mesa-top aeolian soils that served as the principal loci for agriculture. Precipitation in the form of rainfall and snowmelt provide the water needed to make a potentially arable soil productive. Water-harvesting techniques, such as the placement of fields down slope of natural watersheds, or the deliberate redirecting of runoff to downslope fields by means of rock terraces, brush walls, or earthen berms, are not specified but are assumed to have been used during the 400 years being considered. Likewise, soil retention and erosion control features, in the form of rock, brush, and earthen walls and checkdams are assumed to have been used, but their location and timing of use are likewise not specified.

The model assumes that the most critical variables that account for the greatest amount of variation in preindustrial dryland agricultural production are arable soil quality, soil moisture, and adequate growing season length. Arable soil quality is measured on a number of dimensions, but texture, depth, water-holding capacity, natural plant productivity, and, where available, the reported productivity of cultivated crops, are among the most telling attributes. Soil moisture is largely a function of soil texture and water-holding potential, coupled with precipitation, evaporation, and runoff. It can be estimated by the Palmer Drought Severity Index, which requires data on water-holding capacities of each subsurface layer, total depth of the soil profile, and a source of information on precipitation and temperature for that specific soil and its location. Adequate growing season length in this portion of the American Southwest is predominantly a function of elevation, as it is mediated through the adaptive capability of the plant to withstand temperature extremes. In this study, elevation is used as a proxy for the general zone in which the number of growing days is sufficient to grow and mature a crop of maize. Cold air drainage (Adams 1979) is generally not a problem in this model because the vast majority of arable soils occur on uplands areas less vulnerable to this factor.

The model further assumes that maize was the major crop of the prehistoric Pueblo Southwest, and that 80 percent of all farmland was devoted to its production (Hack 1942; Hough 1930). Maize provided at least 50 to 60 percent of daily caloric needs and was a critical economic resource.

Finally, the model makes no assumption about the distribution of arable land and the distribution of population in the study area. I presume that agricultural populations monitored their crops during the growing and harvesting season, but exactly where populations resided, how long they resided in a given place, and why individual sites are located where they are, are left as empirical problems meant to be solved on a case-by-case basis.

Several steps were taken in operational-izing the model: First, a study area and a unit of analysis were established. The study area was defined by a set of 12 contiguous 7.5 minute quadrangle maps for which commercially available USGS 7.5 minute Digital Elevational Models (DEMs) and Soil Conservation Service (SCS) soil maps were also available (figure 15.2). The 701.1 mi² (1,816 km²) study area is located in southwestern Colorado about 22 mi (35 km) north of the New Mexico border and immediately east of the Utah border. The modern settlements of Cahone and Dolores, Colorado are located near its northern and eastern margins, respectively, and the Sleeping Ute Mountain and the Utah state line mark its southern and western margins. A grid of 200 by 200 m (4 ha) cells or "pixels" were superimposed on this space. This pixel size represents the smallest unit of analysis. Given the size of the study area, it represents a compromise between the desire for high spatial resolution and the time it takes to manually locate and record environmental data.

Second, the mapped locations of soil types depicted on aerial photographs by the Cortez SCS were recorded for all 45,400 cells (200 rows by 227 columns) now included in the study area. This was accomplished with the assistance of 7.5 minute orthophoto quad sheets also available for the area. In addition, information on soil depth, available water capacity, natural plant productivity, and recorded agricultural productivity were recorded for the 98 mapped soil types in the study area. A total of 36,759 cells representing 568 mi² (1,470 km²) had complete soils information.

Third, the 98 mapped soil types were reduced to 11 classes based on the quantity of water held in the upper and lower soil layers (0 to 6 inches, and 6 inches to the recorded soil depth, respectively), and a representative soil type was selected to represent the class. It was not known what the optimal number of classes would be, but it was clear that a reduced number of classes was desirable for analytic purposes. A graphic depiction of the soil types as a plot of upper layer soil moisture against lower layer soil moisture suggested eleven groupings, and this number was used in the absence of other criteria.

Fourth, five weather stations at contrasting elevations in and around the study area, each of which exhibited a minimum of 30 years of joint monthly precipitation and temperature records, were used to calculate the monthly PDSI values of the eleven soil classes for the length of their instrumented recording periods. The five stations were, from lowest to highest: Bluff, Utah (4,315 ft; 1,315 m) and Cortez (6,212 ft; 1,893 m), Ignacio (6,460 ft; 1,969 m), Mesa Verde (7,115 ft; 2,169 m), and Fort Lewis (7,600 ft; 2,317 m), Colorado. The five weather stations were used to model the effects of altitude on climatic variation for soils within contrasting elevational zones. The PDSIS are temporally sensitive and climatically integrative measures of stored soil moisture. They are calculated by means of a hydrological accounting method. Water supply to a given soil is modeled by adding precipitation derived from a new month to the balance of water estimated for the previous month. Water demand from a given soil is modeled by removing available moisture through potential evapotranspiration (which requires temperature data) and local rates for local recharge and runoff. Thus, the PDSI incorporates the effects of the previous month's water surplus or deficit, and as such, considers the effect of time. The process is iterative and results in an integrative value that reflects the combined effects of past and present patterns of precipitation and temperature on soil moisture—factors that are major components of the successful production of dryland crops.

PDSIS were calculated for every month of each year for the instrumented historic period. Values for the month of June, which reconstructs soil moisture as they would have existed every year on July 1—the driest time in the productive cycle immediately preceding the arrival of summer monsoons—were correlated with tree-

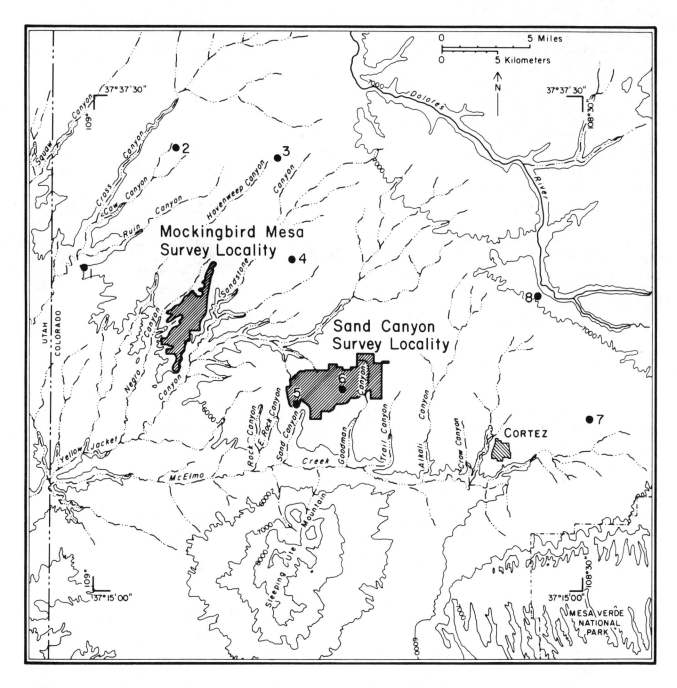

Figure 15.2. Location of the study area (within the grid marks), the Sand Canyon and Mockingbird Mesa Localities, and the eight tree-ring dated sites used in this study. Sites illustrated are: (1) DCA site, (2) Lowry Ruin, (3) Norton House, (4) Aulston Pueblo, (5) Sand Canyon Pueblo, (6) Mustoe Ruin, (7) Wallace Ruin, and (8) Escalante Ruin.

ring data for the same set of historic years. The tree-ring data, which were used as the predictor variables, took the form of eigenvector amplitudes or factor scores created from a principal components analysis performed on seven expanded tree-ring chronologies from northwest New Mexico and southwest Colorado (Van West 1990:83) and represented the period from A.D. 901 to 1970. These data were provided by Rose (Rose, Robinson, and Dean 1982). This calibration of instrumented PDSI values was verified by a series of statistical tests, and a final set of calibration equations or transfer functions was applied to the full length of the tree-ring series, which included both the instrumented and pre-instrumented periods. The result of the above steps was the creation of 55 long-term (A.D. 901–1970) reconstructions of PDSI, one for each combination of elevational stratum and soil moisture group.

Fifth, GIS technology was used to assign the appropriate reconstruction to each 9.9 acre (4 ha) cell in the 701.1 mi² (1,816 km²) study area for the period of greatest interest, A.D. 901 to 1300, and to depict the state of farmland at the driest point in the yearly agricultural cycle as a series of 400 maps. In this study, two GIS systems were used, one a mainframe system (VICAR-IBIS) and the other a PC-based system (EPPL7). VICAR was used to log in, verify, correct, and mosaic the DEMS, whereas EPPL7 was used to store, process, and display much of the subsequent data.

Sixth, each reconstructed annual PDSI value was re-expressed in terms of potential bean and maize yield, based on a number of regression analyses that determined the historical relationship between the yield of these two crops and soil moisture values. Again, GIS technology was used to relate each pixel's PDSI value to its appropriate yield estimate and to produce the 400 maps and 400 tables of values that summarized per pixel class yield.

Seventh, the tabular output generated by EPPL7 was uploaded to a mainframe system and processed with a statisti-

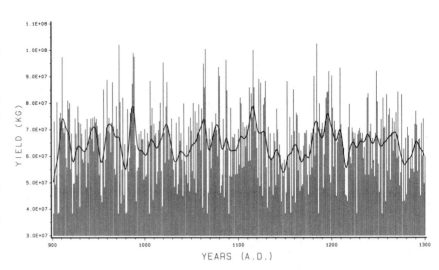

Figure 15.3. Maize production in the study area, A.D. 901 to 1300. The vertical needles represent annual maize yield. The undulating line represents the weighted mean yield value.

cal analysis package, SAS (CMS-SAS Rel. 5.18, Washington State University Computer Center), for further analysis. The annual per-pixel estimates of maize productivity were summed to derive a single annual value of potential gross yield for each of the 400 years being investigated. Only pixels that produced above a pre-defined threshold (approximately equal to 448 kg/ha or 400 lbs/ac or 7.1 bu/ac) were allowed to contribute to the gross yield for a given year, thereby simulating Anasazi selection for the better producing soils in the study area. Thus, the annual estimates of total productivity used in my study reflect this modification to potential gross yield (figure 15.3).

Eighth, three different estimates of sustainable maximum population size were calculated on a yearly basis, one for a population growing and storing the equivalent of one, two, or three years of maize after harvest. Further, carrying capacity estimates for longer periods of time were also generated, in some cases, for periods as short as 10 years and, in others, cases, for periods as long as the full length of the time series (i.e., 400 years). These estimates were of three kinds (adapted from

Hassan 1981:166–68): a "maximum carrying capacity" value reflecting the average production of the period under consideration (represented by the periodic mean); a "critical carrying capacity" value determined by the worst year in a period (represented by the periodic minimum); and an "optimal carrying capacity zone" reflecting a population size generally living below the limits imposed by the productive environment (represented by a range of values equal to 20 percent to 60 percent of the periodic mean).

These data were subsequently analyzed in a variety of ways to address questions at three geographic scales. The first study was conducted at the scale of the 568 mi² (1,470 km²) study area for which complete soils and elevation data were available (and inferred for the full 701.1 mi² [1,816 km²] study area). A second study was undertaken at a smaller spatial scale using two intensively surveyed archaeological localities within the study area. A final study on yet a smaller scale was based upon small-radius catchments surrounding eight tree-ring dated sites within the study area (see figure 15.2). What follows is a brief summary of the original full-length analysis reported first in Van West (1990, 1994a) and later described in a series of papers (Kohler and Van West 1996; Van West 1994b, 1995; Van West and Kohler 1995; Van West and Lipe 1992).

Results

The first study was intended to determine the maximum population that could be sustained in the study area over the 400-year period, given different scenarios for harvested yield, food storage time, and type of carrying capacity estimate. If only a few hundred or a few thousand people could be supported by meager maize production in the study area, this result would strengthen the argument that climatic variation (i.e., extended and/or severe drought) was among the prime causes for the final abandonment of the region. This turned out not to be the case (table 15.1). The long-term minimum value (the 400-year "critical carrying capacity," which was equivalent to 60 percent of the long-term mean, the 400-year "maximum carrying capacity") for a population annually harvesting and storing a two-year supply of maize is approximately 31,000 people at an aggregate density of 8.2 people/mi² (21.2 people/km²). This is comparable to what Rohn (1989:166) estimated for regional population levels during the thirteenth century based upon archaeological survey in the region. A more conservative estimate of consumption and demand using a goal of harvesting and storing a three-year supply still results in a high estimate of 17,000 people at a density of 4.3 people/mi² (11.1 people/km²).

Examination of the annual maps during periods of pronounced low, moderate, and high productivity further indicated that there was considerable variation in the distribution of the most productive and predictable farm lands across the study area. In some years, there were large, connected patches of arable land, and in others the patches were smaller and more scattered. Despite periods of pronounced

Table 15.1   Carrying Capacity Estimates at Three Levels of Storage for A.D. 901 to 1300 for the 568 mi² (1470.36 km²) Study Area

Storage Level	Maximum Carrying Capacity	Critical Carrying Capacity	Optimal Carrying Capacity
POP1YR (persons per km²)	88 ± 19	52 (59%)	18−35−53
POP1YR (number of persons)	131,473 ± 28,222	77,439	26,295−52,589−78,884
POP2YR (persons per km²)	35 ± 7	21 (60%)	7−14−21
POP2YR (number of persons)	53,246 ± 11,429	31,363	10,649−21,298−31,948
POP3YR (persons per km²)	19 ± 4	11 (58%)	4−8−11
POP3YR (number of persons)	28,752 ± 6172	16,936	5750−11,501−17,251

Notes

Maximum Carrying Capacity = Mean Value ± Standard Deviation

Critical Carrying Capacity = Minimum Value

Optimal Carrying Capacity = 20%−40%−60% of Mean Value

Population values are truncated integers.

Percent of Maximum Carrying Capacity (% of mean values) is rounded to the nearest whole number.

For an in-depth discussion of level of carrying capacity and potential levels of demand or storage modeled in the original study, see Van West 1990 or Van West 1994.

POP1YR, POP2YR, and POP3YR = Estimated value of the maximum number and density of people who could be supported by annual yield for a population requiring one year (POP1YR), two years (POP2YR), or three years (POP3YR) of maize in storage at the end of harvest.

temporal and spatial variation in yield, the estimates suggest that a sizeable population could have been supported at all times within the 400-year period if either one of two conditions could have been met. Either the producers (and the consumers) must move to or have access to the productive lands, or the necessary products of production—the food and other crops—must be made available to the consumers through household-level food sharing, community level redistribution, and intercommunity level exchange. That either or both of these conditions were met probably depended greatly on a number of factors, including population size, demand for agricultural products, the history of land use and resource depletion, perceptions of risk and uncertainty for the success of future harvests, access to consistently productive farmland, systems of land tenure, established patterns of aggregated settlement, and in-place systems for food distribution. Although it is not my intent to take on these topics in this chapter (but see Hegmon 1989; Kohler and Van West 1996; and Van West and Lipe 1992 for exploration of some of these issues), it

is probably fair to say that high frequency climatic variation was never so extreme in the study area that decreased agricultural production can be cited as the sole or even primary cause for the thirteenth-century depopulation of southwestern Colorado.

What is perhaps more likely is that a complex set of conditions were in operation and included highly variable yields from year-to-year and place-to-place as well as an overall trend toward reduced productivity. These contributed to a heightened perception of uncertainty in making a secure living. As modeled by Van West and Kohler (1995) and Kohler and Van West (1996), the appropriate social response should have been dispersion across the landscape and contraction of the local food-sharing networks. But the cumulative effect of hundreds of years of living on the land, which changed the distribution of economic resources, and elevated population levels resulted in a physical environment that was not conducive to this type of disaggregation. Thus, interacting populations were forced to leave the region not so much because they collectively could not achieve certain absolute levels of food pro-

Table 15.2 Comparison of Population Values for the Study Area, Sand Canyon Survey Locality, and Mockingbird Mesa Survey Locality, A.D. 901 to 1300

	Study Area		Sand Canyon Locality		Mockingbird Mesa Locality	
	POPKM	POPNUM	POPKM	POPNUM	POPKM	POPNUM
Area (km²)	1470.36	1470.36	26.08	26.08	17.96	17.96
TOTPROD(kg)	64,925,217 ± 13,936,845	64,925,217 ± 13,936,845	1,779,087 ± 337,524	1,779,087 ± 337,524	801,336 ± 204,994	801,336 ± 204,994
C.V.	21.5	21.5	19.0	19.0	25.6	25.6
POP1YR						
Mean and S.D.	88 ± 19	131,473 ± 28,222	137 ± 26	3602 ± 683	89 ± 23	1622 ± 415
Range	52–141	77,439–207,382	93–198	2437–5174	46–142	834–2553
POP2YR						
Mean and S.D.	35 ± 7	53,246 ± 11,429	55 ± 10	1458 ± 276	36 ± 9	656 ± 168
Range	21–57	31,363–83,989	37–80	987–2095	18–57	337–1034
POP3YR						
Mean and S.D.	19 ± 4	28,752 ± 6172	29 ± 5	787 ± 149	19 ± 5	354 ± 90
Range	11–30	16,936–45,354	20–43	532–1131	10–31	182–558

Notes:

TOTPROD = the total mean productivity of maize. This value is rounded to the nearest whole number.

C.V. = coefficient of variation, the ratio of the standard deviation to the mean multiplied by 100. This value is rounded to the nearest tenth.

POP1YR = ((TOTPROD × .324)/160)/area.

POP2YR = (((TOTPROD × .324) × .81)/320)/area.

POP3YR = (((TOTPROD × .324) × .6561)/480)/area.

See Van West 1990 for how these formulae were derived.

POPKM = Estimated population density per km²

POPNUM = Estimated total population for area

duction, but rather because time-honored patterns of social intercourse could not be carried out in a physical world that was increasingly unpredictable (see Dean 1994 for a discussion of a 200-year breakdown in the long-term climatic patterns of the Southwest from ca. A.D. 1250 to 1450). This heightened unpredictability was also fueled by a social environment that probably lacked the strong social sanctions necessary to hold potentially noncooperating populations together.

The second study was undertaken to compare the theoretical expectations generated by the model with estimates of population generated from archaeological survey data. Two intensively surveyed localities within the study area were used (figure 15.2). One is a 10.0 mi² (25.9 km²) area within the Sand Canyon Project boundary investigated by Crow Canyon Archaeological Center (Adler 1988, 1990, 1992; Van West 1986; Van West, Adler and Huber 1987). The other is a 6.9 mi² (17.9 km²) area on the nearby but slightly

lower Mockingbird Mesa surveyed by the Bureau of Land Management in the early 1980s (Fetterman and Honeycutt 1987; Schlanger 1985). The goals of this study were several: first, to see how closely population levels would covary with climatic variation as it is measured by potential agricultural productivity; second, to assess whether populations ever exceeded the productive capacity of their respective domains; and third, to further document the result of the larger-scale study indicating some areas within the study area were more productive and predictable than others.

Both survey areas were digitized and processed by the GIS using the same model that had been developed for the study area as a whole. The results of this study are presented in table 15.2 and figures 15.4 and 15.5. Data from the upland Sand Canyon survey area allowed Adler (1988, revised slightly in Adler 1992) to make momentary population estimates for several ceramically distinct periods, one based

on a 20-year habitation site use-life and the other based on a 50-year site use-life. Similarly, data from the Mockingbird Mesa survey permitted Schlanger (1985) to estimate the size of a population based on a 20-year site use-life for each of her ceramically defined periods. Estimates for a 50-year site use-life were not made by Schlanger. Presently, Crow Canyon archaeologists believe that the 50-year site use-life figure is unrealistically long, and actual habitation site use-lives are more in the range of 10 to 20 years (Adler and Varien 1994; Schlanger 1985). Therefore, the data from the productive uplands (6,200–7,100 ft; 1,890–2,164 m) in the Sand Canyon locality suggest that population never exceeded what the local agricultural landscape could support. In contrast, on the nearby, lower (6,000–6,480 ft; 1,829–1,975 m) Mockingbird Mesa population probably exceeded the productive limits of the area at least twice, once during the A.D. 980 to 1025 period and again during the A.D. 1175 to 1250

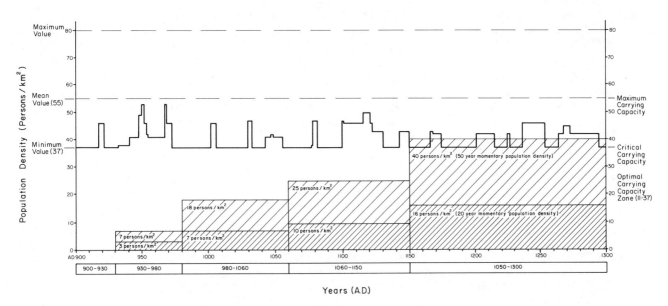

Figure 15.4. Comparison of estimates of carrying capacity for the Sand Canyon Survey Locality, A.D. 901 to 1300, generated by the model with estimates derived from archaeological survey in the locality.

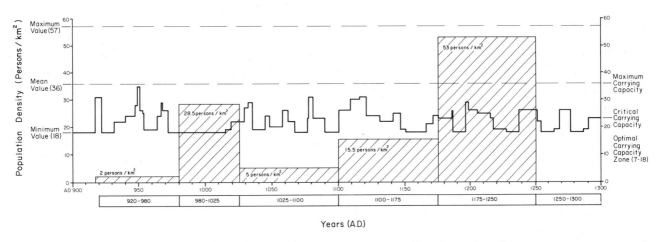

Figure 15.5. Comparison of estimates of carrying capacity for the Mockingbird Mesa Survey Locality, A.D. 901 to 1300, generated by the model with estimates derived from archaeological survey in the locality.

period. Adler's data suggest a gradual increase in population size through time, whereas Schlanger's data suggest a twice-repeated pattern of population overshoot and collapse when human demand exceeded agricultural supply.

This comparative study indicates that estimates of population size and climatic variability do not covary in any predictable way. Different places, even within a restricted study area such as the one defined here, have contrasting population and land use histories. The study also shows that in the past, as in the present, certain places were more productive and predictable than others during certain times. The long-term carrying capacity values derived for the Mockingbird Mesa area were much like that of the study area as a whole, although it is somewhat less predictable than the study area, as seen by its slightly larger coefficient of variation. In contrast, the Sand Canyon survey locality was clearly superior to both Mockingbird Mesa and the overall study area; the maximum and critical carrying capacity values are higher and the coefficient of variation is lower, indicating that it was more predictable from year-to-year. The analysis shows clearly that the geographic scale of analysis is important in assessing where the most productive and predictable areas are in any region and determining the patterning of site use and local abandonments within a region. Inappropriately defined survey boundaries and the lack of precision in dating surface artifact assemblages and architecture might be accentuating the trends seen in these

Table 15.3.   Summary of Population Values (POPKM) for Eight Tree-ring Dated Sites, A.D. 901 to 1300

		5MT8371 (DCA)	5MT8839 (Norton)	5MT2433 (Aulston)	5MT3834 (Mustoe)
	Occup. dates	A.D. 935–950	A.D. 1029–1048	A.D. 1030–1050	A.D. 1173–1231
	Area (km²)	7.88	7.88	7.88	7.88
	TOTPROD (kg)	350,669 ± 104,956	653,070 ± 99,827	500,847 ± 115,085	553,196 ± 108,069
	C.V.	29.9	15.3	23.0	19.5
	Maximum value	57	94	77	80
Maximum CC	Mean Value	35 ± 10	67 ± 10	51 ± 12	56 ± 11
Critical CC	Minimum Value	9 (26%)	49 (73%)	32 (63%)	39 (70%)
Optimal CC	60% of Mean	21	40	31	34
	40% of Mean	14	26	20	22
	20% of Mean	7	13	10	11

Notes

Estimates are given as population density values, persons per km², for a population annually growing and storing a two-year supply of maize.

TOTPROD = the total mean productivity of maize. This value is rounded to the nearest whole number.

C.V. = Coefficient of Variation, the ratio of the Standard Deviation to the Mean multiplied by 100. This value is rounded to the nearest tenth.

data, but it seems reasonable to posit that these patterns are real and that they will be consistent with patterns found in other parts of the study area.

The third study was undertaken at a relatively small geographic scale, the level of the individual site catchment. The purposes of the study were twofold. First, it investigated the relations between agricultural productivity and site establishment, longevity, and abandonment. Second, it was set up to observe whether there are any notable differences between the locations of small and large sites in the study area. It is summarized here in greater length than the other two studies simply because it has not been reported in any detail outside of the original report (Van West 1990:248–319).

Catchments were defined as being an eight-pixel cell radius (1 mile [1.6 km] radius incorporating a 3.04 mi² [7.88 km²] area) around the cell containing the archaeological site. The radius distance chosen was one of convenience and amounted to the incorporation of an area approximately one mile from the center of the site. In two instances, the site was near the margin of the study area, and only a portion of the radius was incorporated into the analysis; however, the use of population density values rather than absolute population values makes it possible to compare

all sites. Sites selected for this study were drawn from data on file in 1990 for the Colorado "V" quadrangle at the Laboratory of Tree-Ring Research. Of the 46 sites with tree-ring dates in the study area, only nine met the minimal criteria of having at least two cutting dates and one cluster of dates, and two of these nine were combined as a single site (table 15.3). For the most part, the earliest cutting date from a site was used as the beginning occupation date (table 15.3), unless other information indicated otherwise. The last date, regardless of its status as a cutting date or noncutting date, was used as the end date of the site occupation if no other data provided cause to extend the occupation. Four sites were small hamlets with fewer than 10 rooms and no large-scale public architecture: the DCA site (5MT8371; Dykeman 1986); Norton House (5MT8839; Fuller 1987; Kuckelman 1988); Aulston Pueblo (5MT2433; Kane 1975; Morris 1986); and Mustoe Ruin (5MT3834; Gould 1982). The remaining four were larger hamlets or villages with 25 to 400 rooms, evidence of community integrative structures, and each probably was a focus of ritual activity in its own community. These sites include Wallace Ruin (5MT6970; Bradley 1974, 1984, 1988b), which incorporated its neighbor, Ida Jean Ruin (5MT1566; Brisbin and Brisbin 1973); Lowry Ruin (5MT1566;

Martin 1936; White and Breternitz 1976); Escalante Ruin (5MT2149; Hallasi 1979; White and Breternitz 1979); and Sand Canyon Pueblo (5MT765; Adams 1985; Bradley 1986, 1987, 1988a, 1992; Kleidon and Bradley 1989). Though the sample of sites does not cover the entire 400-year study period, the eight sites used are reasonably representative of the occupational history of the study area.

The GIS program was again used to identify the catchment of each site and the model was run for the full 400-year period. Maximum, critical, and optimal carrying capacity values for a population attempting to grow and store two years of maize were calculated for each site for the full 400 years and also for the period of time when the site was believed to be occupied. These values were compared to assess whether the time of site establishment was better, worse, or the same as that for that location through time and to assess whether site occupants were responsive to changes in local productivity. Further, they were compared to conditions in both the Mockingbird Mesa survey locality, the Sand Canyon survey locality, and the study area as a whole, to assess whether prehistoric farmers reacted to differential productivity across space. In addition, each catchment was ranked by the number of years when productivity

5MT6970 (Wallace)	5MT1566 (Lowry)	5MT2149 (Escalante)	5MT765 (Sand Canyon Pueblo)
A.D. 1045–1125	A.D. 1086–1120	A.D. 1124–1138	A.D. 1252–1274
4.32	7.88	6.72	7.88
297,798 ±	409,875 ±	291,075 ±	459,114 ±
53,732	102,360	53,857	92,902
18.0	25.0	18.5	20.2
78	68	58	71
56 ± 10	42 ± 10	34 ± 6	47 ± 9
37 (66%)	26 (62%)	24 (70%)	10 (21%)
34	25	20	28
22	17	14	19
11	8	7	9

Percent given is percent of mean value. This is rounded to the nearest whole number.
All population values are truncated integers and are given as population density per kilometer.

remained especially high (here used as a measure of sustained predictability) and also when the minimum population density for a population annually growing and storing two years of maize was particularly high (here used as a measure of sustained productivity).

Table 15.3 presents the long-term population density values for all eight sites. Although it is perhaps unwise to suggest general trends on the basis of only eight sites, it is instructive to compare the catchment data as an exercise in pattern recognition. The median site-use life for the small hamlets is 20.5 years compared to 29 years for the focal-place villages. Of the four small hamlets, Norton House is clearly located in the potentially most productive and most predictable catchment. This is indicated by the relatively high long-term mean (i.e., the maximum carrying capacity), and the relatively low coefficient of variation. Based on the mean population density value for each catchment, the ranking for the hamlets is, from highest to lowest, Norton, Mustoe, Aulston, and the DCA site. Of the four focal-place villages, Wallace has the highest long-term mean population density, followed by Sand Canyon, Lowry, and Escalante. It is interesting to note that of the two contemporary hamlets, Norton and Aulston, the former is by far the more attractive as a locale for potentially high maize yields and population densities, but both were occupied for approximately the same number of years (21 and 20, respectively). Similarly, of the three partially contemporaneous village sites, Wallace Ruin (occupied 81 years) is potentially more productive than Lowry (occupied 35 years) and both Wallace and Lowry are markedly more capable of sustaining higher population densities than Escalante (occupied 15 years). If the dates used to bracket the major Chacoan components present at these sites are reasonably correct, then Wallace's productive primacy may be a factor in its early establishment and enduring presence in the Mesa Verde region.

The mean population value for the four hamlets as a group is 20.5±5.0 people per mi² (53.0±12.9 people/km² [c.v. 24.3]), whereas the mean for the four villages is 17.4±3.4 people per mi² (45.0±8.8 people/km² [c.v. 19.6]). Likewise, the mean minimum population density for the small hamlets is 12.5±6.5 people per mi² (32.4±17.0 [c.v. 52.7] people/km²) and the mean minimum population density for the focal place villages is 9.4±4.3 people per mi² (24.3±11.1 [c.v. 45.8] people/km²). These statistics suggest that the small hamlets were located in catchments that were more productive and more capable of sustaining higher minimum population levels than those for the focal place villages. Although this is an admittedly small sample, these data might indicate that the agricultural potential of a residential location and its immediate environs was a stronger factor in site selection for inhabitants of small farming sites than it was for inhabitants of larger settlements that possessed integrative functions for a local community. Further, seven of the eight sites (the only exception being the Mustoe site) were dated to a time period that is considered among the best for their particular catchments. Collectively, then, these data seem to indicate that Anasazi farmers had developed a keen awareness of and selection for locations and time intervals of high agricultural productivity.

Conclusions

The "paleoproduction" model described previously and the results of three studies conducted at differing spatial scales have several important implications for the study of culture change in the A.D. 1100 to 1300 period in the northern Southwest. First among these is that explanations for the changes that we see in settlement patterns and social organization at the end of the thirteenth century cannot be based solely on the disruptive consequences of environmental fluctuations on the prehistoric economy. In the 701.1 mi² (1,816 km²) study area used here, an area considered to be the heartland of the Mesa Verde Anasazi and one of the "bread baskets" of the prehistoric Pueblo world, there was enough land of sufficient productivity to support many thousands of people even during five decades of notable dryness and low productivity in the mid-twelfth century and again during the last quarter of the thirteenth century. Whether a significant proportion of this land was depleted of important nutrients (Kohler 1990; Matson, Lipe, and Haase 1988), had been lost to natural forces of erosion, or lost through poor land use practices, is currently unknown. Also unknown is how land was used and controlled by various populations, but it is suspected that socially defined limits on access to predictably productive land or its produce may be an important variable in determining the number of people that could be supported at any given time (Adler 1990; Kohler 1989). Nevertheless, there was a great deal of arable land, and one must wonder why there was not at least a reduced and dispersed but stable population that could have remained when a significant proportion of the population either left the area or dwindled in place (see Adams and Adams 1993 for a discussion of possible Puebloan occupation of the Four Corners area during the early fourteenth century).

Second, if archaeologists are going to use paleoenvironmental reconstructions as a theoretical basis for understanding distributions of material traits, settlements and population aggregates, then we need to build temporally and spatially high-resolution reconstructions that are locally relevant to particular study areas. Relatedly we must take care not to uncritically apply regional models (e.g., Dean 1988; Dean et al. 1985) that may obscure the importance of high-frequency variation to local populations. The most useful local reconstructions of the effective environments of particular populations need to account for a plethora of factors. These include the differential effects of elevation and temperature on available soil moisture, groundwater, and surface water supplies; the variability in the location and quality of critical economic resources such as arable land, water, native plants and animals, fuel wood and timber; the suite of feasible agricultural techniques used and under what environmental conditions they could be successful; the proportion of the subsistence needs met by agricultural products; and the history of land use (Adler 1990; Burns 1983; Cordell 1972, 1975; Darsie 1982; Kohler 1989; Kohler and Matthews 1988; Kohler et al. 1986; Speth and Scott 1989).

Third, the use of Geographic Informations Systems technology for this study was essential to the construction of this model, and probably should be an essential tool for examining the broad patterns of settlement in regions as large as that taken on in this volume. The high temporal resolution afforded by tree-ring data and the ability to record a variety of spatial attributes thought to be important in the distribution of human populations can be harnessed and controlled through GIS. It will become an empirical problem to determine what type of environmental attributes are associated with site locations; how settlements thought to be contemporaneous do cluster; what kinds of distances, vistas, and sustaining areas are characteristic of certain sites or communities; and how these characteristics change through time given locally relevant reconstructions of past environments. Models can be made "dynamic" by virtue of the time-depth and annual variability recorded in tree-rings, and various scenarios incorporating the effects of anthropogenic changes (e.g., wood depletion, loss of arable land, increasing control of various territories by individual communities) can be simulated. These theoretical results can then be compared to the archaeological record to test for incongruences or concordances. Such explorations could result in the refinement of models that account for the changes we see in the archaeological record and shed light on the nature of (pre)historic occupation and land use in the northern Southwest.

In conclusion, it would seem that the forces of change that we see in the Pueblo III period are many and complex. Apparently, these causes fall in the sociopolitical realm of human cultural systems as much as they fall in the environmental realm. If the study reported here does nothing else, it forces us to consider the complicated interactions of climatic variation, environmental opportunities and limitations, predictability structure, and human behavior in issues of culture change and stability. We certainly strive to understand why things happened the way they did in prehistory, but studies of this kind also allow us an opportunity to learn about our own relationship and responsibility to the environment and the resilience of our social, cultural, and economic systems in accommodating an ever-changing world.

Acknowledgments

I would like to thank Bill Lipe and Steve Lekson for the opportunity to participate in the PIII Conference. The forum provided me an opportunity to present some of the preliminary results of my doctoral dissertation research. That it was received well and stimulated some animated discussion was most gratifying. I would also like to acknowledge Sigma-Xi, The Scientific Research Society, who awarded me a grant-in-aid of research for archaeological field work in southwestern Colorado in 1986 and the Wenner-Gren Foundation for Anthropological Research, who awarded me a predoctoral grant (#4799) in 1987 to partially defer the costs of data analysis. The Laboratory of Tree-Ring Research, University of Arizona, Tucson, paid the computing costs associated with the dendroclimatologic-based reconstructions of Palmer Drought Severity Indices and generously provided support personnel to assist me with processing of the data from 1987 through 1989. The Department of Anthropology, Washington State University, awarded me money to cover computing costs while in residence in Pullman, from 1989 to 1990.

References Cited

Adams, E. Charles
1979   Cold Air Drainage and Length of Growing Season on the Hopi Mesa. *The Kiva* 44: 285–97.
1985   *Annual Report of Test Excavations at 5MT765, Sand Canyon Pueblo, and Archaeological Survey in T36N, R18W, Sections 12 and 24, and T36N, R16W, Sections 29 and 30.* Crow Canyon Archaeological Center, Cortez, Colorado. Submitted to Office of the State Archaeologist, Colorado Historical Society, Denver.
Adams, E. Charles, and Jenny L. Adams
1993   Thirteenth Century Abandonment

of the Four Corners: A Reassessment. Paper presented at the 1993 Annual Meeting of the American Anthropological Association, Washington, D.C.

Adler, Michael A.
1988   *Archaeological Survey and Testing in the Sand Canyon Pueblo/Goodman Point Ruin Locality, Montezuma County, Colorado, 1987 Field Season.* Crow Canyon Archaeological Center, Cortez, Colorado. Submitted to USDI, Bureau of Land Management, San Juan Resource Area, Durango, and Office of the State Archaeologist, Colorado Historical Society, Denver.
1990   *Communities of Soil and Stone: An Archaeological Investigation of Population Aggregation among the Mesa Verde Anasazi, A.D. 900–1300.* Unpublished Ph.D. dissertation, University of Michigan, Ann Arbor.
1992   The Upland Survey. In *The Sand Canyon Archaeological Project: A Progress Report*, edited by William D. Lipe, pp. 11–23. Occasional Paper No. 2. Crow Canyon Archaeological Center, Cortez, Colorado.

Adler, Michael A., and Mark D. Varien
1994   The Changing Face of the Community in the Mesa Verde Region A.D. 1000–1300. In *Proceedings of the Second Anasazi Symposium, 1991*, compiled by Art Hutchinson and Jack E. Smith, pp. 87–101. Mesa Verde Museum Association, Mesa Verde National Park.

Betancourt, Julio L., and Thomas R. Van Devender
1981   Holocene Vegetation in Chaco Canyon, New Mexico. *Science* 214: 656–58.

Bradley, Bruce A.
1974   Preliminary Report of Excavations at Wallace Ruin, 1969–1974. *Southwestern Lore* 40(3 and 4):63–71.
1984   The Wallace Ruin and the Chaco Phenomenon. In *Insights Into the Ancient Ones*, 2d edition, edited by Joanne H. Berger and Edward F. Berger, pp. 122–127. Interdisciplinary Supplemental Educational Programs, Cortez, Colorado.
1986   *1985 Annual Report of Test Excavations at Sand Canyon Pueblo (5MT765).* Crow Canyon Archaeological Center, Cortez, Colorado. Submitted to USDI, Bureau of Land Management, San Juan Resource Area, Durango, and Office of the

State Archaeologist, Colorado Historical Society, Denver.
1987   *Annual Report of Excavations at Sand Canyon Pueblo (5MT765), Montezuma County, Colorado, 1986 Field Season.* Crow Canyon Archaeological Center, Cortez, Colorado. Submitted to USDI, Bureau of Land Management, San Juan Resource Area, Durango, and Office of the State Archaeologist, Colorado Historical Society, Denver.
1988a   *Annual Report on the Excavations at Sand Canyon Pueblo, 1987 Field Season.* Crow Canyon Archaeological Center, Cortez, Colorado. Submitted to USDI, Bureau of Land Management, San Juan Resource Area, Durango, and Office of the State Archaeologist, Colorado Historical Society, Denver.
1988b   Wallace Ruin Interim Report. *Southwestern Lore* 54(2): 8–33.
1992   Excavations at Sand Canyon Pueblo. In *The Sand Canyon Archaeological Project: A Progress Report*, edited by William D. Lipe, pp. 79–98. Occasional Paper No. 2. Crow Canyon Archaeological Center, Cortez, Colorado.

Brisbin, Joel M., and Charlotte J. Brisbin
1973   Contribution to the Sites Being Excavated in the North McElmo Drainage Area of Southwestern, Colorado. Ms. on file, Crow Canyon Archaeological Center, Cortez, Colorado.

Bryan, Kirk
1925   Dates of Channel Trenching (Arroyo Cutting) in the Arid Southwest. *Science* 62: 338–44.

Burns, Barney T.
1983   *Simulated Anasazi Storage Behavior Using Crop Yields Reconstructed From Tree-Rings: A.D. 652–1968, 2 vols.* Unpublished Ph.D. dissertation, University of Arizona, Tucson.

Cordell, Linda S.
1972   *Settlement Pattern Changes at Wetherill Mesa, Colorado: A Test Case for Computer Simulation in Archaeology.* Unpublished Ph.D. dissertation, University of California, Santa Barbara.
1975   Predicting Site Abandonment at Wetherill Mesa. *The Kiva* 40: 189–202.
1984   *Prehistory of the Southwest.* Academic Press, New York.

Darsie, Richard F., III
1982   *Prehistoric Agricultural Potential and Site Location in the Dolores River Valley, Southwest Colorado.* Unpublished Master's thesis, Washington State University, Pullman.

Dean, Jeffrey S.
1969   *Chronological Analysis of Tsegi Phase Sites in Northeastern Arizona.* Laboratory of Tree-Ring Research Papers No. 3. University of Arizona, Tucson.
1988   Dendrochronology and Paleoenvironmental Reconstruction on the Colorado Plateaus. In *The Anasazi in a Changing Environment*, edited by George J. Gumerman, pp. 119–67. Cambridge University Press, Cambridge.
1994   Environmental Change and/or Human Impact: The Case of the Colorado Plateau. Paper presented at the 1994 Southwest Symposium, Arizona State University, Tempe.

Dean, Jeffrey S., Robert C. Euler, George J. Gumerman, Fred Plog, Richard H. Hevly, and Thor N. V. Karlstrom
1985   Human Behavior, Demography, and Paleoenvironment on the Colorado Plateaus. *American Antiquity* 50: 537–54.

Douglass, Andrew E.
1929   The Secret of the Southwest Solved by Talkative Tree-Rings. *National Geographic Magazine* 54:737–70.

Dykeman, Douglas D.
1986   *Excavations at 5MT8371, An Isolated Pueblo II Pithouse Structure in Montezuma County, Colorado.* Studies in Archaeology No. 2. Division of Conservation Archaeology, San Juan County Museum Association, Farmington, New Mexico.

Euler, Robert C., George J. Gumerman, Thor N. V. Karlstrom, Jeffrey S. Dean, and Richard H. Hevly
1979   The Colorado Plateaus: Cultural Dynamics and Paleoenvironment. *Science* 205: 1089–1101.

Fetterman, Jerry, and Linda Honeycutt
1987   *The Mockingbird Mesa Survey.* Cultural Resource Series No. 22. USDI, Bureau of Land Management, Denver.

Fewkes, Jesse, W.
1904   Two Summers' Work in Pueblo Ruins. In *Twenty-Second Annual Report of the Bureau of American Ethnology 1900–1901*, pp. 3–196. Smithsonian Institution, Washington, D.C.

Fuller, Steven L.

1987   *Cultural Resource Inventories for the Dolores Project: The Dove Creek Canal Distribution System and Dawson Draw Reservoir.* Four Corners Archaeological Project Report no. 7. Complete Archaeological Service Associates, Cortez, Colorado. Submitted to USDI Bureau of Reclamation, Upper Colorado Region, Salt Lake City.

Gould, Ronald R.

1982   *The Mustoe Site: The Application of Neutron Activation Analysis in the Interpretation of a Multi-Component Archaeological Site.* Unpublished Ph.D. dissertation, University of Texas, Austin.

Gumerman, George J. (editor)

1988   *The Anasazi in a Changing Environment.* Cambridge University Press, Cambridge, England.

Hack, John T.

1942   *The Changing Physical Environment of the Hopi Indians of Arizona.* Papers of the Peabody Museum of American Archaeology and Ethnology, Vol. 35, No. 1. Harvard University, Cambridge.

Hallasi, Judith A.

1979   Part II: Archaeological Excavation at the Escalante Site, Dolores, Colorado, 1975 and 1976. In *The Archeology and Stabilization of the Dominguez and Escalante Ruins,* pp. 197–425. Cultural Resources Series No. 7. USDI, Bureau of Land Management, Denver.

Hassan, Fekri A.

1981   *Demographic Archaeology.* Academic Press, New York.

Hegmon, Michelle

1989   Risk Reduction and Variation in Agricultural Economies: A Computer Simulation of Hopi Agriculture. *Research in Economic Anthropology* 11: 89–121.

Hough, Walter

1930   Ancient Pueblo Subsistence. *Proceedings of the 23rd International Congress of Americanists, 1928,* pp. 67–69. Science Press Printing, Lancaster, Pennsylvania.

Kane, Allen E.

1975   Archaeological Resources in the Great Cut–Dove Creek Area. Dolores Project: Report of the 1974 Season. Ms. on file, USDI, Bureau of Land Management, Anasazi Heritage Center, Dolores, Colorado.

Karlstrom, Thor N. V.

1988   Alluvial Chronology and Hydrologic Change of Black Mesa and Nearby Regions. In *The Anasazi in a Changing Environment,* edited by George J. Gumerman, pp. 45–91. Cambridge University Press, Cambridge.

Kleidon, James, and Bruce A. Bradley

1989   *Annual Report of the 1988 Excavations at Sand Canyon Pueblo (5MT765).* Crow Canyon Archaeological Center, Cortez, Colorado.

Kohler, Timothy A.

1989   Chapter 1: Introduction. In *Bandelier Archaeological Excavation Project: Research Design and Summer 1988 Sampling,* edited by Timothy A. Kohler, pp. 1–12. Department of Anthropology Reports of Investigations No. 61. Washington State University, Pullman.

1990   Prehistoric Human Impact on the Environment in the Upland North American Southwest. Paper presented at the 1990 Annual Meeting of the American Association for the Advancement of Science, New Orleans.

Kohler, Timothy A., and Meredith H. Matthews

1988   Long-term Anasazi Land Use and Forest Reduction: A Case Study from Southwestern Colorado. *American Antiquity* 53: 537–64.

Kohler, Timothy A., Janet D. Orcutt, Eric Blinman, and Kenneth L. Petersen

1986   Anasazi Spreadsheets: The Cost of Doing Agricultural Business in Prehistoric Dolores. In *The Dolores Archaeological Program: Final Synthetic Report,* compiled by David A. Breternitz, Christine K. Robinson, and G. Timothy Gross, pp. 525–38. USDI, Bureau of Reclamation, Engineering and Research Center, Denver.

Kohler, Timothy A., and Carla R. Van West

1996   The Calculus of Self Interest in the Development of Cooperation: Sociopolitical Development and Risk among the Northern Anasazi. In *Evolving Complexity and Environmental Risk in the Prehistoric Southwest,* edited by Joseph A. Tainter and Bonnie Bagley Tainter. Addison-Wesley, Reading, Massachusetts, in press. Ms. 1993.

Kuckelman, Kristin A.

1988   Excavations at Norton House (Site 5MT8839), A Pueblo II Habitation. In *Archaeological Investigations on*

South Canal, Vol. 2, pp. 373–403. Four Corners Archaeological Report No. 11. Complete Archaeological Service Associates, Cortez, Colorado. Submitted to USDI, Bureau of Reclamation, Upper Colorado Region, Salt Lake City.

Mackey, James C., and Sally J. Holbrook

1978   Environmental Reconstruction and the Abandonment of the Largo-Gallina Area, New Mexico. *Journal of Field Archaeology* 5:29–49.

Martin, Paul S.

1936   *Lowry Ruin in Southwestern Colorado.* Anthropological Series Vol. 23, No. 1. Field Museum of Natural History, Chicago.

Matson, R. G., William D. Lipe, and William R. Haase, III

1988   Adaptational Continuities and Occupational Discontinuities: The Cedar Mesa Anasazi. *Journal of Field Archaeology* 15:245–64.

Morris, James N.

1986   *Monitoring and Excavation at Aulston Pueblo (Site 5MT2433), A Pueblo II Habitation Site.* Four Corners Archaeological Project Report No. 6. Complete Archaeological Service Associates, Cortez, Colorado. USDI, Bureau of Reclamation, Upper Colorado Region, Salt Lake City.

Palmer, Wayne C.

1965   *Meterological Drought.* Research Paper No. 45. U.S. Department of Commerce, Office of Climatology, U. S. Weather Bureau, Washington, D.C.

Petersen, Kenneth L.

1988   *Climate and the Dolores River Anasazi.* Anthropological Papers No. 113. University of Utah Press, Salt Lake City.

Rohn, Arthur H.

1989   Northern San Juan Prehistory. In *Dynamics of Southwest Prehistory,* edited by Linda S. Cordell and George J. Gumerman, pp. 149–77. Smithsonian Institution Press, Washington, D.C.

Rose, Martin R., Jeffrey S. Dean, and William J. Robinson

1981   *The Past Climate of Arroyo Hondo, New Mexico, Reconstructed from Tree-Rings.* Arroyo Hondo Archaeological Series, Vol. 4. School of American Research Press, Santa Fe.

Rose, Martin R., William J. Robinson, and Jeffrey S. Dean

1982   *Dendroclimatic Reconstruction for the*

Southeastern Colorado Plateau. Final
Report to Dolores Archaeological
Project and Division of Chaco Re-
search. Laboratory of Tree-Ring
Research, University of Arizona,
Tucson.

SAS Statistical Analysis Package

1984   1986 CMS-SAS Release 5.18, Washington State University Computer
Center (01545002), Pullman.

Schlanger, Sarah H.

1985   *Prehistoric Population Dynamics in the
Dolores Area, Southwest Colorado.*
Unpublished Ph.D. dissertation,
Washington State University,
Pullman.

Speth, John D., and Susan L. Scott

1989   Horticulture and Large-Mammal
Hunting: The Role of Resource De-
pletion and Constraints of Time and
Labor. In *Farmers as Hunters: The
Implication of Sedentism,* edited by
Susan Kent, pp. 71–79. Cambridge
University Press, Cambridge.

Van West, Carla R.

1986   *Cultural Resource Inventory for the
1985 Field Season in the Crow Canyon
and Sand Canyon Areas, Montezuma
County, Colorado.* Crow Canyon
Archaeological Center, Cortez,
Colorado. Submitted to USDI, Bureau
of Land Management, San Juan
Resource Area, Durango, and Office
of the State Archaeologist, Colorado
Historical Society, Denver.

1990   *Modeling Prehistoric Climatic Variability and Agricultural Production
in Southwestern Colorado: A GIS
Approach.* Unpublished Ph.D. dissertation, Washington State University,
Pullman.

1994a   *Modeling Prehistoric Agricultural
Productivity in Southwestern Colo-
rado: A GIS Approach.* Reports of
Investigations No. 67. Washington
State University, Pullman.

1994b   Reconstructing Prehistoric Climatic
Variability and Agricultural Pro-
duction in Southwestern Colorado,
A.D. 901–1300: A GIS Approach. In
*Proceedings of the Second Anasazi
Symposium, 1991,* compiled by
A. Hutchinson and Jack E. Smith,
pp. 25–33. Mesa Verde Museum
Association, Mesa Verde National
Park.

1995   The Heuristic Value of Estimates of
Prehistoric Agricultural Production:
A Case Study from Southwestern
Colorado. In *Interpreting Southwest-
ern Diversity: Underlying Principles
and Overarching Patterns,* edited by
Paul R. Fish and J. Jefferson Reid.
Anthropological Research Papers.
Arizona State University, Tempe, in
press. Ms. 1992.

Van West, Carla R., and Timothy A. Kohler

1995   A Time to Rend, A Time to Sew:
New Perspectives on Northern
Anasazi Sociopolitical Development
in Later Prehistory. In *Anthropology,
Space, and Geographic Information
Systems,* edited by Mark Aldenderfer
and Herbert D. G. Maschner. Oxford
University Press, Oxford, in press.
Ms. 1992.

Van West, Carla R., and William D. Lipe

1992   Modeling Prehistoric Climate and
Agriculture in Southwestern Colorado. In *The Sand Canyon Archaeological Project: A Progress Report,*
edited by William D. Lipe, pp. 105–
19. Crow Canyon Archaeological
Center, Cortez, Colorado.

Van West, Carla R., Michael A. Adler, and Edgar
K. A. Huber

1987   *Archaeological Survey and Testing in
the Vicinity of Sand Canyon Pueblo,
Montezuma County, Colorado, 1986
Field Season.* Crow Canyon Archaeo-
logical Center, Cortez, Colorado.
Submitted to Bureau of Land Man-
agement, San Juan Resource Area,
Durango, and Office of the State
Archaeologist, Colorado Historical
Society, Denver.

White, Adrianne S., and David A. Breternitz

1976   *Stabilization of Lowry Ruins.* Cul-
tural Resource Series No. 1. USDI,
Bureau of Land Management,
Denver.

1979   Stabilization of Escalante Ruin
5MT2149 and Dominguez Ruin
5MT2148, Dolores, Colorado. In
*The Archeology and Stabilization of
the Dominguez and Escalante Ruins.*
Cultural Resource Series No. 7.
USDI, Bureau of Land Management,
Denver.

Chapter 16

Big Sites, Big Questions: Pueblos in Transition

Linda S. Cordell

This volume and the conference from which it developed concern a time of dramatic change across much of the northern Southwest. The period under discussion is the interval from A.D. 1150 to 1350. The changes that occurred and were explored by the conference have been stated concisely by Lipe and Lekson (1990) as follows: (1) the effects of the decline of Chaco, (2) the development of aggregated settlements outside the San Juan Basin, (3) the dramatic shrinkage of the geographic area occupied by Puebloan populations, (4) changes in community layouts from dispersed to aggregated to plaza-oriented villages, (5) the development of new patterns of material and information exchange, and, ultimately, (6) development of katsina ceremony and kiva complex resembling the historic Pueblo pattern.

As conference discussants, David Wilcox and I were asked to comment on individual presentations, synthesize information about Pueblo III for the region as a whole, and indicate directions for future research. This was no small request. Conference participants presented their data by district so that rather than correlating details from twelve major areas, the discussants were confronted with trying to organize information from 50 different districts. In order to begin to approach this daunting task, I review and comment on what I see as the salient characteristics of the Pueblo III period in light of the six major changes iterated by Lipe and Lekson (1990) and listed here. I discuss the effects of the decline of Chaco and the development of aggregated communities in some detail. Changes in settlement layout, territorial shrinkage, new patterns of inte-

gration, and the development of Pueblo Indian ideological systems are touched on far more briefly. The bias in my coverage of these issues reflects the amount of discussion each topic engendered during the conference rather than my personal interests among them.

Reflections on Integration: Disintegration of the Chaco System

As noted, the "Pueblo Cultures in Transition" conference focused on the period from A.D. 1150 to 1350. The precision with which the years are specified is at once unusual in the world of archaeology and an acknowledgment of the level of detail with which southwesternists work. Between A.D. 1130 and 1180 a period of severe drought struck the Colorado Plateaus; this is the same time during which the Chacoan system appears to have disintegrated. Using the year A.D. 1150 as the beginning of the Pueblo III period recognizes the potentially widespread importance of a real event in Anasazi history; the end of building and probably, for 100 years, of occupation in Chaco Canyon. This is no small event given Chaco's role as a major center of activity, population, and exchange. The date is not an arbitrary archaeological construct such as a phase boundary drawn when a certain ceramic type makes up 50 percent of the pottery assemblage. Prior to A.D. 1150, specifically between about A.D. 1020 and 1150, much of the northern Southwest is thought to have been tied to or influenced by events centered in Chaco Canyon.

There is scholarly disagreement in interpreting how the Chacoan system was

organized and how it functioned (see Judge 1989, 1991; Lekson 1991; Lekson et al. 1988; Vivian 1990). The Pueblo III Conference had the opportunity to explore ideas about the limits of Chacoan influence in different areas by examining the extent of repercussions, if any, with the end of building in Chaco Canyon. In addition, current research (Fowler, Stein, and Anyon 1987; Stein and Fowler, chapter 8; Varien et al., chapter 7) suggests that some ideological aspects of the Chacoan system, as reflected in site locations and architecture, may have persisted beyond A.D. 1150 and served as a means of integrating people in newly established aggregated communities.

The geographic areas and districts represented at the conference were not equally influenced by Chaco. In order to evaluate the intensity of interaction with Chaco, it might be useful to be able to rank the influence of Chaco with respect to increasing amounts of apparent connectivity. For example, from lowest to highest these might be (1) no apparent interaction, (2) presence of Chacoan trade goods, (3) presence in Chaco of raw materials from the region, (4) presence in Chaco of finished items from the region, (5) production in the region of some local version of Chacoan-style ceramics (such as Mancos Black-on-white at Mesa Verde), (6) presence of Chacoan outliers in the region, and (7) presence of Chaco outliers linked to Chaco Canyon with one or more roads. Presumably, each higher order indicator of interaction would subsume most or all of those of lower order.

There are difficulties in applying even such a rudimentary scheme as the seven indicators listed. For example, the second indicator is currently not useful. According to Toll (1991:80) "there are no durable goods that can be identified specifically as having come from central Chaco Canyon." A further difficulty is the problem of determining the source locations for most biotic materials, especially foodstuffs and wood for building that were transported within the system, although some progress along these lines is being made (see Durand, Rose, and Shelley 1993; Shelley 1988; Toll 1991). Even with items that are durable and most confidently assigned to a geographic origin, such as obsidian, the relative frequency with which a particular source occurs in Chaco changes over time (Toll 1991).

Despite these difficulties, a rough sorting of the areas represented in this volume suggests boundaries of interaction with Chaco. The areas that lack Chacoan outliers would seem to have had the least connectivity to the Chacoan system. These areas include the northern and southern Rio Grande, the Southeast Mogollon Uplands, the Southwest Mogollon Uplands, the Middle Little Colorado (the Hopi Buttes, Moenkopi, Hopi Mesas, and Silver Creek Districts), Southwest Utah and the Arizona Strip, and possibly the Salado District. There is some doubt about the Salado District, because Roney (chapter 10) indicates that he suspects the presence of a Chacoan outlier there. Most of the Kayenta area also appears to have been outside the Chacoan sphere and to be devoid of Chacoan outliers, except for the Chacoan great house and great kiva at Teec Nos Pos (Stein and Fowler, chapter 8).

As expected, none of these areas show a high level of exchange-based interaction with Chaco. Brown and red wares from the Mogollon region do occur in low frequencies in Chaco Canyon, particularly during the tenth century. At that time too, a small amount of obsidian from Red Hill was brought into Chaco (Toll 1991: 95). The turquoise found in Chaco is generally considered to have come from the Cerrillos mines south of Santa Fe. Al-though turquoise occurs throughout the sequence in Chaco, it is most abundant in contexts dating between A.D. 920 and 1120, when Chaco was at its height. Finally, Jemez obsidian from the northern Rio Grande region was imported into Chaco. During the eleventh century the Jemez source becomes numerically dominant over other obsidian sources and appears to peak numerically in the twelfth century (Toll 1991).

Reciprocally, although some Chacoan-style ceramics and, in some cases, imports from the San Juan Basin area, occur in most of these surrounding regions, they do not overshadow local assemblages. Imports appear in sufficiently low frequencies to classify them as trade items. Nevertheless, there are differences among the disconnected areas with regard to ceramic style and other characteristics. It is my impression that in the Rio Grande area, particularly the Northern Rio Grande, south to about Albuquerque, ceramic styles show a greater affiliation to Chaco than contemporaneous styles found in the Mogollon or Kayenta and far western Anasazi areas. Of particular note are the Red Mesa-like types of the tenth century and Kwahe'e Black-on-white ceramics of the eleventh century. It is debatable whether these stylistic similarities indicate real interactions with Chaco or are simply "pan-Anasazi" styles that can be found across the northern Anasazi region (Wheat 1983). However, I think it is suggestive of specific interactions with Chaco that both obsidian and turquoise, apparently, were obtained from the Northern Rio Grande area. That this connectivity between the Rio Grande and Chaco probably did not involve integration into the same political or ideological systems is supported by Toll's statement in regard to turquoise:

The quantity of turquoise in Chaco is considerable. In terms of volume, however, there is little doubt that the population would have been quite capable of acquiring and transporting all the turquoise in Chaco themselves, probably with a great deal less energy expenditure than was invested in the import of ceramics and timber (Toll 1991:83).

As a group, the areas that lack outliers contrast markedly in connectivity to Chaco to the areas that do have outliers. This observation extends to a lack of synchronicity with events in the Chaco core. For example, the date of A.D. 1150 that marks the end of the Chacoan system is not correlated with any changes in the Rio Abajo, most of the Mogollon Highlands, the Northern Rio Grande, or the far west. Anasazi settlement of the northern Southwest does shrink geographically beginning at about A.D. 1150, but in those areas that are abandoned, such as the far west, abandonment occurs somewhat gradually and seems to be related to the same climatic changes that spelled the end for Chaco. Although I think it is safe to conclude that the areas without Chacoan outliers were functionally outside the Chacoan system and were little influenced by Chaco, I suspect that the Chacoan system did not integrate the remaining areas, those with outliers, equally.

Among the areas where Chacoan outliers are known to occur, the greatest connectivity would seem to be with the Chuska Mountains on the west and south to Narbona Pass. The Chuskas seem to have been the source area for much of the imported Chacoan ceramics found in the central canyon and possibly for some of the timber used for construction. The Chuska slopes and Narbona Pass also provided some lithic raw materials brought into the canyon. Because Chaco Canyon itself lacked significant wood resources during the height of its occupation, it seems reasonable that ceramic manufacturing, which obviously requires wood for firing, may have been done routinely at a remote location with abundant wood such as the Chuskas. It is possible that the activities involved in obtaining timber for building, cherts for stone tools, ceramic manufacturing, and hunting were imbedded in structured interactions with communities in the Chuskas or by residents of Chaco in formal use of the Chuskas. In order to explore these kinds of possibilities, we must know a great deal more about the outliers than we now do.

We should have a better understanding of the nature of the contact between Chaco and the outliers. Conference participants pointed out a variety of empirical problems related to Chacoan outliers that should be resolved before we can address the degree of connectivity these areas had with Chaco. We need to know approximate temporal placement of the known outliers and that placement must be determined independently from the architectural configuration that identifies them as outliers in the first place. John Stein's contribution to this volume is an important beginning in this regard, and additional information is available in the outlier studies (Marshall et al. 1979; Powers, Gillespie, and Lekson 1983). Currently, we do not know if the outliers were built or inhabited by people from Chaco Canyon, by local people emulating Chacoan architecture, or both. Clearly, resolution of this question will require well-designed excavation research strategies. We must also be aware of the likelihood that the answer to this question (and others) will be different for different outliers (see Mobley-Tanaka 1990).

We cannot assume that Chacoan outliers that are surrounded by local communities were functionally equivalent to those that were isolated. Only in a few instances, such as for Bis sa' ani (Breternitz, Doyel, and Marshall 1982) and the great houses reported by Varien and others (chapter 7) in the Mesa Verde region, do we know the temporal relationship between the great houses and the surrounding settlements. In fact, for the two instances just mentioned, the temporal relationships differed. At Bis sa' ani, the construction of the surrounding community residences and great house seem to be contemporary, whereas the dispersed communities preceded the great houses in the Mesa Verde region. It is not to be expected that all Chacoan outliers

were functionally equivalent even in the same settings. It is to be expected that there are differences in function through time as well. These are all important questions that require continued research efforts. They are particularly germane to the question of whether or not some aspect of Chacoan ideology, as reflected in the great house, was retained and became central to post-Chaco community organization in some areas (Fowler, Stein, and Anyon 1987) or whether great house morphology represented a pan-Anasazi, or at least geographically widespread, architectural form separate from Chaco (Mobley-Tanaka 1990).

Finally, with respect to Chaco, as Lekson (1991) acknowledges, it is the road system that gives coherence to what the Chacoan system was—and in fact to the probability that there was a system. The system has not been well-documented through distribution analyses of goods, raw materials, or surrogate measures of information exchange and interaction. Some (e.g., Wheat 1983) are reluctant to define a system at all for this reason. Some (e.g., Toll 1991) would define the system more conservatively than would others (e.g., Lekson 1991).

Because we suspect that road construction was primarily late in the development of the Chacoan system, at a minimum we need to refine our expectations and propose that there will be differences in what the "system" might have looked like throughout the period during which it existed. We should also note that for conservative or nonconservative outlier counts, the full extent of connecting roadways has not been established. Although we know that in some cases, modern land modification negates the possibility of ever confirming or disconfirming the prior existence of the full extent of most of the roads, there are methods that we can use to increase our confidence in the extensions of road systems that we know about (see Lekson 1991). This area of inquiry should not be neglected.

In sum, we should expect the decline

of Chaco to have differentially affected the regions represented in this volume if for no other reason than their having varying degrees of connectivity to the canyon. At a minimum, those areas that lack Chacoan outliers probably should manifest fewer effects of the collapse of Chaco than those with outliers. For the areas with Chacoan outliers, it is important that we know more about the extent of the roads associated with outliers and the relative dating of all the recorded outliers. It is crucial that we establish the relationship between the occupants of outliers and the residents of the surrounding dispersed communities. Finally, we should address measures of connectivity between Chaco Canyon, its resource areas, and its outliers.

Population Aggregation: All Big Sites are Not Equal

The second major change that characterized the Pueblo III period was the development of aggregated settlements outside the San Juan Basin. The topic of population aggregation is an enduring one in southwestern archaeology. Yet, issues relating to population aggregation transcend the Southwest, archaeology, and anthropology. For example, aggregation is an area of study in biological ecology and in historical demography. Most of the conference participants discussed population aggregation in their specific case and in the broader, more theoretical, sense. In contrast to a previous generation of southwesternists for whom population aggregation was understood to have developed naturally among those with a secure food supply (Haury 1962), the current view is that living in aggregated settlements is socially difficult and economically inefficient. A component of this view is an underlying conviction that the natural environment of the Anasazi Southwest is generally too harsh and the climate too unpredictable to provide resources adequate to sustain very large communities for long periods of time. The perspective is also, in part, conditioned by the knowledge that for most of southwestern prehistory small, dispersed settlements were the most common pattern (e.g. Plog, Effland, and Green 1978) and that many large, aggregated sites were not continually occupied for the long periods of time that signal a successful adaptation (Cordell 1984:330–350, 1994; Graves, Holbrook, and Longacre 1982; Smith, Woodbury, and Woodbury 1966).

As is so often true, Julian Steward's (1955) thoughts on aggregation were seminal. Steward (1955) described how ecological and economic factors (among which he included population density, the relative abundance of the food supply, and the method of agricultural production), made the concentration of population possible, but he believed that cultural historic forces of a nonecological order were also necessary for aggregation to occur. For the Southwest, he pointed to warfare and a need for defense. Harold Colton (1960) was also among those who discussed difficulties for aggregated populations, specifying the dangers of poor sanitary conditions and epidemic diseases.

More recently, some archaeologists turned to locational geographers (e.g., Chisholm 1962; Haggett 1966; and see Smith 1976) who argue that with a uniform distribution of resources, the most efficient settlement strategy is for households to be evenly and equidistantly located one from another. Along these lines, Kohler (1989) points out that with a mixed agricultural and hunting and gathering subsistence base, food producers incur substantial costs when they live in aggregated settlements. Assuming a uniform distribution of resources, each doubling of the population approximately doubles the average distance to fields. Certainly in no part of the southwestern landscape are resources uniformly distributed. Nevertheless, distributions that are evenly dispersed with respect to a localized resource (such as hamlets along a river) might be expected to occur more often than the large aggregated villages that developed

in the Anasazi area in the thirteenth and fourteenth centuries.

The locational geographers argue that aggregation occurs, despite its inherent inefficiency, if diverse field types are dispersed irregularly on the landscape and farmers must position themselves so that they can cultivate more than one type of field. The geographers also note that aggregation takes place if the key resource is highly localized and requires great investment of labor (i.e., hand irrigation from a very deep well). They also note that aggregation comes about for reasons of defense.

In a discussion that has been very influential in southwestern archaeology, William Longacre (1966) considered aggregation a social effort to sustain populations, through cooperation, in the face of increasing economic uncertainties brought about by climatic deterioration. The benefits of aggregation that he noted are the ability to bring more labor together for cooperative tasks and to redistribute food efficiently. Subsequently, a number of investigators in the Southwest linked aggregation to agricultural intensification (e.g. Woosley 1988) or specifically to irrigation (e.g. Ellis 1976).

One view of the relationship between aggregation and environmental stress that differs from Longacre (1966) was proposed by Plog (1983; Plog et al. 1988) and others (Dean et al. 1985). Plog suggested that systems of social alliances among settlements offset resource shortfalls brought on by periods of high spatial variability in rainfall. These alliances centered on larger sites and were characterized by agricultural intensification, extensive exchange networks, and increased social stratification. As systems like these are costly to maintain, it is claimed that they developed when overall regional population densities were so high that mobility for groups of people was inhibited. This model therefore predicts aggregation coincident with periods of high interlocal environmental differences and increased population densities.

Dean's (1988) model of Anasazi behav-

ioral adaptation was favored by a number of conference participants when they considered population aggregation in their region. This model considers three variable classes; environmental, demographic, and behavioral that together, and with other variable classes, interact to define the adaptive system at any point in time. The environmental variables important to his model are low frequency processes (LFP) that have periodicities that are longer than a human generation and high frequency processes (HFP) characterized by shorter periodicities. Demographic and behavioral variability are also described in low and high frequency terms, although these are not defined in the same way as the environmental processes (see Dean 1988). In this context, however, I note that population aggregation is considered a possible high frequency behavioral response to stress defined in both environmental and demographic terms. In A.D. 1150:

> many areas were abandoned, and large settlements and high population densities developed in the localities that remained inhabited. These twelfth-century changes coincide with a regional population maximum, one of the secondary LFP depositional hiatuses identified by Karlstrom, and severe and protracted HFP dendroclimatic drought. These correspondences suggest that by A.D. 1150 population was sufficiently close to systemic limits that a secondary LFP hydrologic perturbation, coupled with an HFP drought, reduced the carrying capacity enough to create systemic stresses that triggered major adaptive responses (Dean 1988:42).

Data and discussions from the conference are relevant to some evaluation of all the models of aggregation discussed here. At the conference, Jonathan Haas (Haas and Creamer, chapter 14; Haas and Creamer 1993) was the major proponent of warfare and defense underlying the formation of aggregated villages. His supporting data derive primarily from survey in the Kayenta area, and he suggests that

Anasazi warfare arose largely as a response to a pattern of environmental degradation. Reid and others (chapter 6) provide supporting evidence, suggesting that raiding may have been an important factor in the Grasshopper district where all three aggregated villages show evidence of burning. In the Turkey Creek District, they suggest that aggregation occurred specifically to protect stored resources.

Others at the conference found the evidence for warfare more equivocal. Some participants referred to models in which potential competition and defensive considerations are more important than actual warfare. In these models it is argued that with increasing population density, aggregated communities and the threat of attack foster the maintenance of interstitial "buffer zones" that may be exploited for game and other wild resources (e.g., Hunter-Anderson 1979). Or it may be argued that once a community has solved various internal social problems and retained an aggregated pattern–for whatever initial reason—that village would be a highly effective competitor for resources or in warfare (Carneiro 1970). Nevertheless, for the central and southern Rio Grande areas, Kate Spielmann (chapter 12) finds no evidence that would implicate warfare as a processes underlying aggregation. Kintigh (chapter 9) states that for the Cibola area, there is little evidence one way or the other with regard to warfare.

Others at the conference accentuated one or another of the models or factors rather than addressing warfare and defense specifically. For the southeast Mogollon highlands, Lekson (chapter 11) links instances of aggregation to intensified agriculture, particularly canal irrigation in some districts, although not in others. Even though the minimal aggregation in the far western area addressed by Lyneis (chapter 2) seems to be considerably different in being smaller scale than the aggregation reported for other areas, Lyneis observes small scale intensification

of agriculture accompanying population build up.

Crown, Orcutt, and Kohler (chapter 13) note good correlations between population and environmental changes in the Northern Rio Grande. Spielmann (chapter 12) suggests that data from the Rio Abajo generally support Dean's (1988) behavioral model. In the southern portion of the Rio Abajo, stress on crop production among dispersed populations may have encouraged movement to areas more favorable for farming. The tree-ring data from the eastern border area of the Southwest suggest that initial aggregation was preceded by about 15 years of relatively high rainfall but that aggregation continued through several periods of drought (Spielmann, chapter 12).

There is certainly a measure of artificiality in examining each proposed cause of aggregation against the comments made in the contributions to this volume. Most authors follow Dean in viewing aggregation as a complex social response to environmental and social variables. Yet, some notion of density dependence, of regional population build up reaching some threshold, or just of regional population increase, is an important component of all the models of aggregation discussed. Notions of density dependence and carrying capacity are also crucial aspects of Adler's (1992 and chapter 7) discussion of land tenure. In fact, density dependence is simply another form of the population pressure arguments that have become the panacea for all prehistoric ills that have been re-evaluated since Boserup (1965).

Two separate discussions that emerged from the conference are of central importance because of the tremendous weight given to density-dependent situations. These are in Van West's (chapter 15) presentation on southwestern Colorado and Crown, Orcutt, and Kohler's (chapter 13) chapter on the Northern Rio Grande. Van West reports results from simulations of crop production for her study area in southwestern Colorado indicating that for

the area as a whole, a sizable population (of about 31,000, or 8.1 people/mi² [21 people/km²]) could have been supported throughout the full 400 years of Anasazi occupation. Within her area, some localities were less productive than others, and at times there were shortfalls in harvests. Nevertheless,

climatic factors affecting agricultural productivity were not causing sufficient shortfalls in crop yield, at the scale of the 701.1 mi² (1,816 km²) study area, to have led to an unavoidable abandonment of the study area. If prehistoric populations could have dispersed to favored locations in the late thirteenth century, there would have been sufficient productive land to grow food for many thousands of people. Apparently other limiting factors or social considerations came into play (Van West and Kohler 1992).

Many years ago, my own crude simulations of Mesa Verde settlement patterns and productivity, which were largely impressionistic for want of data (Cordell 1972, 1975, 1981), resulted in conclusions that were essentially the same. Van West's model and simulations are truly impressive for their complexity, precision, accuracy and sophistication. Her results are well-founded and should be considered when density dependence is invoked as a causal agent underlying aggregation.

Density dependence is also addressed in Crown, Orcutt, and Kohler's chapter (13) on the Northern Rio Grande. For the six districts examined, the authors find that aggregation occurs between A.D. 1250 and 1300 regardless of population size in the district or population growth rate! In this case, the archaeological data seem to be providing a natural laboratory suggesting a lack of correlation between aggregation and population pressure. The results are certainly unexpected and important for that reason alone.

In sum, questions about the conditions under which humans form aggregated settlements transcend the parochial interests of southwestern archaeology. Nevertheless, data from the Southwest are relevant for the continued evaluation of a variety of current theoretical models. There is some empirical support for arguments that invoke warfare or defense, as well as for those that point to agricultural intensification and to behavioral adaptations to environmental perturbations under conditions of regional precontact population maxima. None of these are universally supported by the data presented in this volume. It is certainly possible that aggregation may be a solution to more than one kind of problem. On the other hand, the results reported by Van West (chapter 15) and the data reported by Crown and others (chapter 13) suggest that we may wish to further refine our ideas about behaviors associated with aggregation and with population pressure. For example, when we identify aggregation in the archaeological record of the Southwest we are generally looking at big architectural sites with many rooms separated by empty spaces on the landscape where there had previously been small, dispersed settlements throughout. We need to know more about what behavioral changes are reflected by the change. Have the size of units of production or consumption changed (Adler 1994), with larger sites representing a larger group organized in these basic tasks? Has residential mobility decreased, in which case small dispersed sites may have been only seasonally occupied or occupied over a very few years while large sites were occupied over longer time spans? Has the amount of stored food increased, so that the ratio of habitation rooms to store rooms is very different in small sites compared to large sites? Has the amount of resource pooling increased (Van West and Kohler 1992)? Under what set of conditions are these behaviors likely to persist long enough for us to see them archaeologically?

Changes in Community Layouts: Site Plans of Big Sites

The third change characterizing the Pueblo III period according to Lipe and Lekson is the dramatic shrinkage of the geographic area occupied by Puebloan populations, but I defer this topic to the next section. The fourth Pueblo III change listed by Lipe and Lekson (1990) involves changes in community configuration from dispersed to aggregated to plaza oriented villages. Little of the discussion during the conference concerned dispersed settlements, except as the common condition prior to A.D. 1150. It is important to note that although in some areas aggregation appeared to be a rather gradual process (see Varien et al., chapter 7), it was also generally reported as being complete where it did occur. That is, in the Rio Grande, Cibola, southwest and southeast Mogollon Mountains, and Hopi areas, once aggregation occurred, small dispersed settlements were no longer part of the settlement system. There is little support then for one recent model of late prehistoric adaptations in the Southwest.

The model is proposed in slightly different forms; one by Stuart and Gauthier (1981), the other by Upham (1982, 1984). In both cases, it is argued that two kinds of residential patterns were contemporary over long periods of time. One pattern, termed either resilient or efficient, is characterized by greater mobility and more dependence on hunting and gathering than the other "power" (Stuart and Gauthier 1981) pattern that is viewed as sedentary and predominantly agricultural. It is the latter that is responsible for the big sites. Smaller or more ephemeral settlements are expected to have been used or occupied at the same time as the big sites and to reflect the resilient or efficient strategy. None of the conference participants documented examples of a dual pattern of this sort for his or her area.

One formulation of the dual pattern model (see Stuart 1982), however, refers specifically to hunters and gatherers regionally coexisting with horticulturists. The expected pattern of sites then is that "limited activity loci" or lithic scatters will have been deposited at the same time that pueblos were occupied and that different groups would be responsible for each type of site. The conference did not address limited activity loci or lithic scatters. Rather, the remarks (e.g., Kintigh, chapter 9) referred to those small residential sites that were to have reflected groups with minimal dependence on horticulture or the settlements of people at the lowest rung in a settlement hierarchy, and these are not documented for the region. Most of the conference discussion focused on big sites and was devoted to documenting and trying to understand the site plans of post-Chacoan aggregated sites. At a minimum, it is important to describe the potentially varied forms and locations of the aggregated sites. Did any of these seem to represent an attempt to reinstate a Chaco or Chaco-like system or do they reflect new mechanisms of social integration?

One of the exciting new developments in southwestern archaeology is the recognition of a pattern of post-Chaco great houses, and what Kintigh (chapter 9) refers to as "large, open great kivas." This pattern, described by Fowler, Stein, and Anyon (1987) for sites along the Chuska spine, may represent an attempt to bring Chaco back to life in only slightly modified form. We would like to know just how widespread this pattern was. Other patterns of aggregated settlements include what appear to be architectural agglomerations of previously dispersed households with no formal supra-household architectural features. Another pattern is what Roney (chapter 10) refers to as "ladder structures" and Dean (chapter 3) terms "spine buildings," in which two very long parallel walls are erected first and cross-walls then subdivide sections into rooms. Finally, some configurations of aggregated settlements seem to indicate the development of new integrative features for the entire village, such as formal plazas surrounded by massed room blocks (see Adams 1991 and chapter 4). The conference provided the opportunity to discuss the spatial and temporal distributions of these forms as a beginning toward understanding why they came about.

As noted, it is through the work of Fowler, Stein, and Anyon (1987) that we are in a position to recognize a post-Chacoan signature that is potentially important to our understanding of population aggregation in some portions of the post-Chacoan Pueblo world. Yet, it is important that we learn the variability represented in that signature and that we refrain from assuming the range of variability and the ways in which the post-Chacoan structures related to the Chaco system.

Variation in the post-Chacoan signature is noted by Kintigh (chapter 9) for the Zuni and Manuelito districts, where between A.D. 1200 and 1275 there are sites with both great houses and large, unroofed great kivas. Kintigh finds that between A.D. 1275 and 1400, there are very large, planned pueblos at which the large, open great kivas have been moved to areas outside the room blocks. The change in architectural form and possibly in the location of the kivas may be significant. We will, however, hinder future attempts to understand the nature of, and reasons for, changes in the location of large, open great kivas in other districts if we simply label the Chacoan or post-Chacoan great house-kiva complex as such and assume that these are all part of a singular Chacoan system. Although I argue against labels that assume greater homogeneity than seems warranted, we still need a working vocabulary that is descriptive and understandable. Lacking such a vocabulary, I am not entirely sure that the "big holes" John Roney (chapter 10) describes for the Chacra Mesa district are the same as the large, unroofed great kivas of the Manuelito Plateau and Chuska Spine, although I suspect they are.

In looking at the social landscape of

post-Chaco population aggregation, Kintigh (chapter 9) notes that there is no region-wide political subordination after A.D. 1150. In part for this reason, Kintigh (1994) finds aspects of Colin Renfrew's (Renfrew and Cherry 1986) characterization of peer polity interaction relevant. Peer polity interaction attempts to explain the existence of particular architectural forms or public symbols at many places within a region where there is no over-arching political authority. Although primarily concerned with situations involving chiefdoms and states, such interactions also might apply to instances of lesser organizational complexity (Renfrew and Cherry, 1986). According to Renfrew, when increased organizational complexity is recognized in one political unit, other units within the area will undergo the same transformations at about the same time. These changes may be accompanied by monuments and intensification of production, among other things. The term peer polity interaction refers to the processes that underlie and are responsible for these simultaneous changes. Peer polity interactions are of different sorts, including competition, warfare, competitive emulation, symbolic entrainment, and increased flow in the exchange of goods. The use of the term peer polity interaction is a signal that the processes operate among societies without one or more of them exercising hegemony over others.

Kintigh (1994) suggests that the processes of competitive emulation and symbolic entrainment might both be relevant to understanding post-Chacoan aggregation in the Cibola area and possibly elsewhere in the Chaco "extended core," an area that might include the Mesa Verde District. Competitive emulation refers to instances in which one group imitates another group by building a particular kind of public structure in order to maintain its own prestige. Symbolic entrainment describes situations in which a fully developed symbolic system will likely be adopted when it comes into contact with a less-developed one with which it does

not conflict in a major way. The well-developed system carries with it an assurance and prestige that a less-developed symbolic system may not share (Renfrew and Cherry 1986). Further thought should be given to the possibility that aspects of the "defunct" Chacoan ideological system were appropriated through symbolic entrainment and that these are manifested in the architectural forms we see as post-Chacoan great houses and large, open great kivas.

Outside those areas that had been part of the Chaco extended core, presumably those districts without roads, outliers, or other material and social ties to Chaco where post-Chacoan great houses were built, this particular form of competitive emulation or symbolic entrainment might not be expected to occur. For instance, in the Rio Abajo, Spielmann's (chapter 12) data appear to rule out competitive emulation as a process underlying the development of aggregated villages because there were apparently no models available to emulate. That is, there are no post-Chacoan great house communities in that region.

The post-Chaco pattern in the Mesa Verde region may, in fact, contrast with that in the Cibola area, and be contrary to the expectations of a peer polity interaction model. In the Mesa Verde district, the large, aggregated sites show a return to modularity (Varien et al., chapter 7) suggesting either less or more ephemeral impact of the Chacoan system than appears to be the case in the Cibola region or than one might suppose. Although I have no reason to challenge either the Cibola or Mesa Verde data, I note that knowing the dates during which great houses in each area were constructed is crucial to the argument. In neither area is the dating of these structures ideal.

Whether or not post-Chacoan great houses are part of their specific regional record, most of the volume contributors with appropriate data indicate that the initial construction of plaza-oriented aggregated villages generally dates to the late thirteenth and fourteenth centuries, and that this pattern of village layout seems to derive from a southern, or desert, pattern rather than one with origins in the San Juan region (Adams, chapter 4; Lekson, chapter 11; Spielmann, chapter 12). Elsewhere Adams (1991) documents the early Pueblo IV distribution of plaza-oriented villages in the Southwest and discusses the potential relationship between plazas and the development of katsina ceremonialism, which he sees originating in the U.S. Southwest in the central Cibola and Middle Little Colorado areas. Subsequent to the conference, Patricia Crown (1994) published her analysis of the Salado Polychromes, from which she infers a slightly older religious manifestation that she calls a "Southwest regional cult." In my view, much of Adams's (1991) detailed argument is compelling and not contradicted in any way by data presented at the conference. Nevertheless, it is true that neither the origins or ideology associated with Katsina rituals was examined in detail during the conference, either for lack of time or because the attendees concurred that the ritual complex constitutes a later, Pueblo IV, phenomenon.

There was perhaps less discussion than I would have liked of the differences between Roney's ladder structures (chapter 10), Dean's spine buildings (chapter 3), and the modular building described by Varien and others (chapter 7). It seems to me that the different kinds of building reflect very different sorts of labor organization and planning. Constructing ladder-spine structures seems to require the acquiescence, if not the cooperation, of all domestic units in a village, whereas construction of modules does not. In addition, it seems to be that the ladder-spine structures reflect planning for village growth through immigration (Cordell 1984, 1989). A line of rooms can be added in order to accommodate additional groups of people. On the other hand, basic village spatial reorganization may be required if a plaza-oriented village incorporates a substantial number of people at once. Both plaza and ladder villages occur in the northern and central Rio Grande area, and it is frequently the ladder villages that prevail over time reflecting an accommodation to the instability of the late precontact villages. This suggestion might be a focus of future discussion. One reason that it was not discussed at the conference may be that we have too little excavation data to begin to evaluate how labor was organized in constructing the large villages, except perhaps for Grasshopper Pueblo (Reid et al., chapter 6) and Pot Creek Pueblo (Kulisheck, Adler, and Hufnagle 1994).

Aggregation occurs at different scales, a circumstance that can be confusing. In southwestern Utah and the Arizona Strip, for example, room counts at some sites qualify them as aggregated settlements according to the conference definition of big sites consisting of at least 50 rooms. For example, the Main Ridge at "Lost City" consists of 124 rooms (Lyneis 1992). C-shaped and circular sites on the Western Plateaus may have 50 to 75 rooms. These sites, which date to the Pueblo II period, seem to be of a very different order from big sites elsewhere. As Lyneis (chapter 2) points out, a large room count does not necessarily mean a large aggregated population. In the far west region most of the rooms in the large sites were used as small storage spaces, meaning sites with 50 or more rooms often seem to have housed no more than three to five families.

In southwestern Utah and the Arizona Strip, aggregation that is in any sense comparable to other Anasazi areas did not occur. This raises the problem of using numbers of rooms as criteria for defining big sites. I have no easy solution for this. I personally find Steward's (1955) use of the ratio of kivas to rooms useful, but obviously this does not work in areas that lack kivas. Another possibility is to use the "Kintigh Gap," or the apparent lack of sites that have between 60 and 90 rooms (Kintigh 1994).

Kintigh's (1994) suggestion is useful for those situations in which rooms may be used as a proxy for households rather than situations in which there are an abundance of specialized rooms such as storerooms or public spaces. The measure is actually derived from a consideration of Johnson's (1989) ideas of scalar stress. Johnson notes that the number of basal units in decision-making hierarchies rarely exceeds 15 and is generally about 6. When it becomes necessary to integrate more basal units, some form of hierarchy (Johnson argues that it will be either sequential or simultaneous) develops that will enable the incorporation of an additional set of about 6 to 15 basal units. Kintigh (1994) therefore would expect an aggregated settlement to consist of more than one set of basal units. There should not be an incremental increase in the number of basal units. Kintigh's preliminary evaluations confirm a gap in the number of rooms at sites consisting of a single set of basal units and larger sites (the gap between 60 and 90 rooms). An aggregated site might be defined as one that consists of more than one set of basal units.

There are interesting data, from very different sources, that seem to support Johnson's expectations. Adler (1990) notes that cross-culturally the primary access group varies from one to fifteen, but averages about nine households. From simulation experiments, Hegmon (1989) argues that risk-sharing among more than about nine families is not an advantageous strategy. Finally, the utility Reid and others (chapter 6) find in Jorgensen's (1980) cross-culturally derived categories of political-economic-territorial units may be related to the "magic numbers" that predominate in cross-cultural studies. These examples may in fact reflect pan-human thresholds in the ability to process information (Kosse 1990). These observations do not resolve the difficulty of how we define aggregation. Rather, they suggest that it is important to for us to continue to try to identify not only the basal units represented in archaeological situations (see Reid and others, chapter 6) but also the ways in which the size and number of basal units changed at large sites.

To summarize, although representing a low level of intellectual activity, we should work toward standardizing our observations about big sites. Most of the conference participants view site layout as a means of access to inferences about the more interesting features of social organization in the broadest sense. It appears that after Chaco's heyday, there were areas in which post-Chacoan great houses and unroofed great kivas were built. The architectural "signatures" of these sites need to be rigorously compared throughout the region and the sites themselves need to be dated. In many areas lacking the post-Chacoan great houses, aggregation occurred anyway, indicating that a Chacoan or post-Chacoan model for aggregated communities was not necessary for their development. In the areas without post-Chacoan great houses, the pattern of aggregated sites may have been largely modular, as in the Kayenta area, or ladder-form, as in the Eastern San Juan Basin and parts of the Rio Grande drainage. In the Northern Rio Grande area there are also sites with rather small plazas that seem to constitute a third form. We need much better data on the relative order of the occurrence of these different architectural configurations for all the areas concerned.

In areas with post-Chacoan great houses, such as the Cibola and Mesa Verde areas, the post-Chacoan structures are later replaced by large sites with modular plans. This suggests that Chacoan ideology may have had less influence on subsequent aggregation than previously thought. We clearly need better chronological control over the post-Chacoan great houses and the modular aggregates. We also need to be able to recognize architectural forms that inform on the composition and combination of basal units in aggregated settlements.

We have all noted that large sites are also often occupied longer than are small sites. It is also true that sometimes the entire configuration of the large sites is changed during the occupation. In my experience at Tijeras Pueblo (Cordell 1980)

and at Rowe Ruin the final layout of the site was not at all similar to its original plan. At Tijeras, the original pueblo consisted of several spatially separate room blocks loosely arranged around a great kiva. The later occupation consisted of a large plaza, open to the east-southeast with room blocks on three sides. At Rowe, an early adobe-walled pueblo underlay and extended south of a series of three plazas surrounded by masonry room blocks. If previous site organization is not examined, the final buildings at big sites may manifest a degree of organization or planning that can misleadingly suggest in-migration of a large group, rather than spatial reorganization of the existing population. Distinguishing among the different organizational modes of large sites will require examination of existing survey records, additional survey, testing, and excavation programs.

Abandonments: The Continuing Mystery

It is fascinating to me that what most lay persons would consider the biggest question of the Pueblo III period, namely regional abandonment, is not one of the major changes listed by Lipe and Lekson (1990). In fact, abandonment was discussed by the conference but as I hope the title of this section indicates, it is considered a part of larger issues of organization and change. Most of the conference participants were careful to differentiate the abandonment of sites, localities and regions (cf. Cordell 1984:312–20) in their discussions.

On the lowest, or site, level, abandonment is sometimes, reasonably, viewed as the immediate consequence of aggregation. If a locally dispersed population moves into one aggregated settlement, a great many small settlements are abandoned. This situation has been discussed in detail. Abandonment of a single site is, however, frequently part of a pattern of local abandonments. The abandonment of localities is most often perceived as behav-

ioral adjustment to environmental processes (cf. Dean 1988). In most cases, these seem to be either a move up or down in elevation, or up or down stream, following the patterns outlined by Stuart and Gauthier (1981). These patterns are now very well documented for the northern Southwest, and they probably underlie other local or more broadly regional changes in settlement location as well. These patterns might be seen as a shifting background that may obscure other patterns of interest.

Despite the regularity of these movements, two cautionary observations made at the conference should be considered. First, Dean (chapter 3) warns that the hydrological curves underlying our interpretations of aggrading vs. degrading streams and, concomitantly, raised versus lowered water tables are derived from alluvial situations. Therefore, a pattern of aggrading streams, interpreted as a higher water table, occurs at low elevations at the same time that degradation is occurring at higher elevations. We should therefore be careful to determine whether or not the higher elevation areas are showing behavior that is the opposite of what would be predicted from the regional hydrologic curves (i.e., Karlstrom 1988). Second, from the widely separated areas of the Mesa Verde-Northern San Juan and the southeastern Mogollon, Varien and others (chapter 7) and Lekson (chapter 11) document situations in which the final movement of aggregated settlements is apparently toward reliable sources of water rather than toward arable land. How prevalent this pattern is throughout the larger Southwest should be determined.

The matters of regional abandonments and territorial shrinkage seem to have engendered less discussion than they might have. In some cases, notably the far west (Lyneis, chapter 2), it appears as though abandonment was rather gradual (occurring over about 200 years) and most likely related to the same climatic deterioration that underlay the decline of Chaco. This evaluation seems entirely reasonable.

Many of the localities involved could not be successfully farmed by Mormon settlers of the mid-nineteenth century or by later groups. Yet, acknowledging the likelihood of having isolated a probable cause, the conference did not really address the problems of the apparent disappearance of archaeologically defined ethnic groups such as the Virgin Anasazi (see Lyneis, chapter 2). Perhaps, that too is a matter for a future conference.

The abandonment of specific sites and entire regions was examined from the perspective of the new patterns of community organization and material and information exchange that developed at the end of the Pueblo III period. As the conference participants noted, it seemed more valuable to concentrate on these as "pull" factors rather than to dwell on "push" factors such as great droughts or long-term erosion. It was noted that many local abandonments and the retraction of Anasazi settlement from the far west occurred over a period of many years and could be related to environmental changes. At the same time, the abandonments of the thirteenth and fourteenth centuries reflected a more general instability of large, aggregated settlements, particularly in environmental settings that were marginal or risky for horticulture. Finally, in a few areas, aggregated settlements seem to have solved whatever organizational problems had plagued earlier big settlements. These settlements may have become the nucleus for previously dispersed populations as well as centers for those who were leaving failed aggregated villages. Although not discussed in detail, it appears as though the plaza-oriented villages that Adams (1991) would associate with the development of katsina ceremonialism represent the final, successful, form of aggregated village.

The way that regional abandonment occurred in various areas is not clear at this time. Lyneis (chapter 2) suggests that one expected result of regional abandonment would be a wave or bulge of population in surrounding areas as populations retreated

from a region. She indicates that there are not enough data to evaluate this pattern for the far west. On the other hand, it appears as though the Northern Rio Grande does support a wave model. If the minor distortions of moving up and down in elevation in response to local environmental changes are taken into account, then the "wave" moves through the Pajarito Plateau, Chama Valley and finally into the Rio Grande Valley.

Shifting the emphasis to pull factors is entirely reasonable at this time. There seem to be a great many issues and problems surrounding pull factors that need to be resolved. On the other hand, at least one central question raised at the conference, and some minor ones as well, were not resolved. The central question is whether or not there were as many people in the Southwest in A.D. 1450 as there had been in A.D. 1150. In area after area, there seem to be too few protohistoric villages to account for previous population maxima, either at A.D. 1150 or somewhat later. There was a general agreement that we must know more, through excavation, of different abandonment behaviors. I think we must also resolve whether or not periods of significant depopulation through warfare, disease or other sources of large-scale mortality were part of the prehistoric pattern.

As indicated previously, there are also remaining difficulties in tracing populations such as the Virgin Anasazi and many others. In order to begin to understand some of the twisted ethnic threads, I think we need to explore a variety of models about how populations migrate. One suggestion is to explore the literature of demographic history, exemplified by the writings of Daniels (1990) and others.

A Few Last Words

The focus on big sites and aggregated populations marks the reversal of a 20-year trend in Anasazi archaeology. During the early heyday of traditional southwestern archaeology, researchers had generally confined their activities to the large

sites. Beginning in the 1970s, that situation changed, a reflection of two considerations. First, it was apparent that small sites greatly outnumbered large sites throughout the period before European contact, yet the small sites had been ignored by archaeologists. There was a shift to work on small sites in order to rectify this neglect. Second, by the late 1970s, most fieldwork was being conducted in the context of cultural resources management, a research realm that generally avoids excavation and testing of large sites and undertakes surveys in areas not necessarily known to contain large sites. In returning to examine the big sites, the "Pueblo Cultures in Transition" conference had the opportunity to discover gaps in our knowledge of these settlements. I suspect to everyone's surprise but no one's complete astonishment, the big sites were found to be an underdeveloped resource (Lipe and Lekson 1990).

Throughout the chapters in this volume, there are mentions of specific gaps in our data. Much of the far west is obviously under-studied but so too are large parts of more central areas that are outside national parks and monuments. The area surrounding Petrified Forest is a good example. It is almost shocking to note that the area around Mesa Verde is another. Clearly, there is a fair amount of basic survey and mapping that needs to be done.

Quite obviously too, chronological control for the Chaco system, the post-Chaco revisionists, and the many large sites discussed needs to be refined. Maps of site ground plans and test excavations that will enable some evaluation of sequences of building at big sites are also critical. As noted, we need excavations that will address the diversity of abandonment behaviors to help us to understand possible situations of cultural homogeneity and heterogeneity in big sites. In all of the preceding, there is a need for better and more refined models to accompany basic field work. It is clear that A. V. Kidder was, and still is, correct about the southwestern archaeological record, particularly that for big sites. The Southwest is not a "sucked orange" (Kidder 1958:322), but I refrain from guessing the amount of juice left in the orange.

References Cited

Adams, E. Charles
1991   *The Origin and Development of the Katsina Cult.* University of Arizona Press, Tucson.

Adler, Michael
1990   *Communities of Soil and Stone: An Archaeological Investigation of Population Aggregation among the Mesa Verde Anasazi, A.D. 900–1300.* Ph.D. dissertation, Department of Anthropology, University of Michigan. University Microfilms, Ann Arbor.
1992   Land Tenure Systems and Prehistoric Land Use: Perspectives from the American Southwest. Paper presented at the 57th Annual Meeting of the Society for American Archaeology, Pittsburgh.
1994   Population Aggregation and Anasazi Social Landscape: A View from the Four Corners. In *The Ancient Southwestern Community: Models and Methods for the Study of Prehistoric Social Organization,* edited by Wirt H. Wills and Robert D. Leonard, pp. 85–101. University of New Mexico Press, Albuquerque.

Boserup, Ester
1965   *The Conditions of Agricultural Growth: The Economics of Agrarian Change Under Population Pressure.* Aldine, Chicago.

Breternitz, Cory D., David E. Doyel, and Michael P. Marshall
1982   *Bis sa'ani: a late Bonito Phase Community on Escavada Wash, Northwest New Mexico.* Papers in Anthropology No. 14. Navajo Nation, Window Rock.

Carneiro, Robert L.
1970   A Theory of the Origin of the State. *Science* 169:733–38.

Chisolm, Michael
1962   *Rural Settlement and Land Use.* Methuen, London.

Colton, Harold S.
1960   *Black Sand.* University of New Mexico Press, Albuquerque.

Cordell, Linda S.
1972   *Settlement Pattern Changes at Wetherill Mesa, Colorado: A Test Case for Computer Simulation in Archaeology.* Unpublished Ph.D. dissertation, Department of Anthropology, University of California, Santa Barbara.
1975   Predicting Site Abandonment at Wetherill Mesa. *The Kiva* 40(3): 189–202.
1980   The Setting. In *Tijeras Canyon: Analyses of the Past,* edited by Linda S. Cordell, pp. 1–11. Maxwell Museum of Anthropology and University of New Mexico Press, Albuquerque.
1981   The Wetherill Mesa Simulation, A Retrospective View. In *Simulating the Past,* edited by Jeremy Sabloff, 119–41. University of New Mexico Press and the School of American Research, Albuquerque.
1984   *Prehistory of the Southwest.* Academic Press, Orlando.
1989   Northern and Central Rio Grande. In *Dynamics of Southwest Prehistory,* edited by Linda S. Cordell and George J. Gumerman, pp. 293–336. Smithsonian Institution Press, Washington, D.C.
1994   Introduction: Community Dynamics of Population Aggregation in the Prehistoric Southwest. In *The Ancient Southwestern Community, Models and Methods for the Study of Prehistoric Social Organization,* edited by Wirt H. Wills and Robert Leonard, pp. 79–84. University of New Mexico Press, Albuquerque.

Crown, Patricia L.
1994   *Ceramics and Ideology: Salado Polychrome Pottery.* University of New Mexico Press, Albuquerque.

Daniels, Roger
1990   *Coming to America: A History of Immigration and Ethnicity in American Life.* Harper Collins, Princeton, New Jersey.

Dean, Jeffrey S.
1988   A Model of Anasazi Behavioral Adaptation. In *The Anasazi in a Changing Environment,* edited by George J. Gumerman, pp. 25–44. Cambridge University Press, Cambridge, England.

Dean, Jeffrey S., Robert C. Euler, George J. Gumerman, Fred Plog, Richard H. Hevly, and Thor N. V. Karlstrom.
1985   Human Behavior, Demography, and Paleoenvironment on the Colorado Plateau. *American Antiquity* 50: 537–54.

Durand, Stephen R., Martin R. Rose, and Phillip Shelley
1993   Techniques for Identifying Tree Source Areas. Paper presented at the 57th Annual Meeting, Society for American Archaeology, St. Louis.

Ellis, Florence Hawley
1976   Datable Ritual Components Proclaiming Mexican Influence in the Upper Rio Grande of New Mexico. In *Collected Papers in Honor of Marjorie Ferguson Lambert,* edited by Albert H. Schroeder, pp. 85–108. Papers of the Archaeological Society of New Mexico No. 3. Albuquerque.

Fowler, Andrew P., John R. Stein, and Roger Anyon
1987   *An Archaeological Reconnaissance of West-central New Mexico: the Anasazi Monuments Project.* Submitted to the Office of Cultural Affairs, Historic Preservation Division, Santa Fe.

Graves, Michael W., Sally J. Holbrook, and William J. Longacre
1982   Aggregation and Abandonment at Grasshopper Pueblo: Evolutionary Trends in the Late Prehistory of East-Central Arizona. In *Multidisciplinary Research at Grasshopper Pueblo, Arizona,* edited by William A. Longacre, Sally J. Holbrook, and Michael W. Graves, pp. 110–21. University of Arizona Press, Tucson.

Haas, Jonathan, and Winifred Creamer
1993   Stress and Warfare among the Kayenta Anasazi of the Thirteenth Century. *Fieldiana: Anthropology,* n.s., 21. Field Museum of Natural History, Chicago.

Haggett, Peter
1966   *Locational Analysis in Human Geography.* St. Martin's Press, New York.

Haury, Emil W.
1962   The Greater American Southwest. In *Courses Toward Urban Life,* edited by Robert J. Braidwood, pp. 106–31. Wenner-Gren Foundation for Anthropological Research, New York.

Hegmon, Michelle
1989   Risk Reduction and Variation in Agricultural Economies: A Computer Simulation of Hopi Agriculture. In *Research in Economic Anthropology,* edited by Barry L. Issac, pp. 89–122. JAI Press, Greenwich, Connecticut.

Hunter-Anderson, Rosalind
1979   Explaining Residential Aggregation in the Northern Rio Grande: A Competition Reduction Model. In *Adaptive Change in the Northern Rio Grande Valley*, 169–76. Archaeological Investigations in Cochiti Reservoir, New Mexico, Vol. 4, edited by Jan V. Biella and Richard C. Chapman. Office of Contract Archaeology, University of New Mexico, Albuquerque.

Johnson, Gregory A.
1989   Dynamics of Southwestern Prehistory: Far Outside—Looking In. In *Dynamics of Southwest Prehistory*, edited by Linda S. Cordell and George J. Gumerman, pp. 371–89. Smithsonian Institution Press, Washington, D.C.

Jorgensen, Joseph G.
1980   *Western Indians*. W. H. Freeman, San Francisco.

Judge, W. James
1989   Chaco Canyon-San Juan Basin. In *Dynamics of Southwest Prehistory*, edited by Linda S. Cordell and George J. Gumerman, pp. 209–62. Smithsonian Institution Press, Washington, D.C.
1991   Chaco: Current Views of Prehistory and the Regional System. In *Chaco & Hohokam: Prehistoric Regional Systems in the American Southwest*, edited by Patricia L. Crown and W. James Judge, pp. 11–30. School of American Research Press, Santa Fe.

Karlstrom, Thor N.V.
1988   Alluvial Chronology and Hydrologic Change of Black Mesa and Nearby Regions. In *The Anasazi in a Changing Environment*, edited by George J. Gumerman, pp. 45–91. Cambridge University Press, Cambridge, England.

Kidder, Alfred V.
1958   *Pecos, New Mexico: Archaeological Notes*. Papers of the Peabody Foundation for Archaeology, vol. 5. Phillips Academy, Andover, Massachusetts.

Kintigh, Keith W.
1994   Chaco, Communal Architecture, and Cibolan Aggregation. In *The Ancient Southwestern Community: Models and Methods for the Study of Prehistoric Social Organization*, edited by Wirt H. Wills and Robert Leonard, pp. 131–40. University of New Mexico Press, Albuquerque.

Kohler, Timothy
1989   *Bandelier Archaeological Excavation Report: Research Design and Summer 1988 Sampling*. Papers of Investigations No. 61. Department of Anthropology, Washington State University, Pullman.

Kosse, Krisztina
1990   Group Size and Societal Complexity: Thresholds in the Long-Term Memory. *Journal of Anthropological Archaeology* 9:275–303.

Kulisheck, Jeremy, Michael Adler, and John Hufnagle
1994   Diversity and Continuity in Classic and Protohistoric Villages of the Taos District, Northern New Mexico. Paper presented at the 59th Annual Meeting of the Society for American Archaeology, Anaheim.

Lekson, Stephen H.
1991   We Get The Southwest That We Deserve: Different Approaches to Southwest Archaeology. Paper presented at the Second Anasazi Symposium, Mesa Verde National Park.

Lekson, Stephen H., Thomas C. Windes, John R. Stein, and W. James Judge
1988   The Chaco Canyon Community. *Scientific American* 256(7):100–109.

Lipe, William, and Stephen Lekson
1990   Pueblo Cultures in Transition: Report of a Conference. Paper presented at the 55th Annual Meeting of the Society for American Archaeology, Las Vegas.

Longacre, William A.
1966   Changing Patterns of Social Integration: A Prehistoric Example from the American Southwest. *American Anthropologist* 68(1):94–102.

Lyneis, Margaret
1992   *The Main Ridge Community at Lost City: Virgin Anasazi Architecture, Ceramics, and Burials*. Anthropological Papers No. 117. University of Utah Press, Salt Lake City.

Marshall, Michael P., John R. Stein, Richard W. Loose, and Judith E. Novotny
1979   *Anasazi Communities of the San Juan Basin*. Public Service Company of New Mexico, Albuquerque, and New Mexico Historic Preservation Bureau, Santa Fe.

Mobley-Tanaka, Jeannette L.
1990   Intracommunity Interactions at Chimney Rock: The Inside View of the Outlier Problem, In *The Chimney Rock Archaeological Symposium*, edited by J. McKim Malville and Gary Matlock, pp. 37–42. General Technical Report No. RM-227. USDA Forest Service, Rocky Mountain Forest and Range Experiment Station, Fort Collins.

Plog, Fred
1983   Political and Economic Alliance on the Colorado Plateau, A.D. 400–1450. *Advances in World Archaeology* 2:289–330.

Plog, Fred, Richard Effland, and Dee F. Green
1978   Inferences Using the SARG Data Bank. In *Investigations of the Southwestern Anthropological Research Group: An Experiment in Archaeological Cooperation, Proceedings of the 1976 Conference*, edited by Robert C. Euler and George J. Gumerman, pp. 139–48. Museum of Northern Arizona, Flagstaff.

Plog, Fred, George J. Gumerman, Robert C. Euler, Jeffrey S. Dean, Richard H. Hevly, and Thor N.V. Karlstrom
1988   Anasazi Adaptive Strategies: The Model, Prediction, and Results. In *The Anasazi in a Changing Environment*, edited by George J. Gumerman, pp. 230–76. Cambridge University Press, Cambridge.

Powers, Robert P., William B. Gillespie, and Stephen H. Lekson
1983   *The Outlier Survey: A Regional View of Settlement in the San Juan Basin*. USDI, National Park Service, Albuquerque.

Renfrew, Colin, and John F. Cherry
1986   *Peer Polity Interaction and Sociopolitical Change. New Directions in Archaeology*. Cambridge University Press, New York.

Shelley, Phillip H.
1988   Hypotheses of Intraregional Technological Specialization and Exchange. Paper presented at the 53rd Annual Meeting of the Society for American Archaeology, Phoenix.

Smith, Carol A.
1976   Regional Economic Systems: Linking Geographical Models and Socioeconomic Problems. In *Economic Systems, Regional Analysis*, Vol. 1, edited by Carol A. Smith. Academic Press, New York.

Smith, Watson, Richard B. Woodbury, and Natalie F. S. Woodbury
1966   *The Excavation of Hawikuh by Frederick Webb Hodge*. Museum of the American Indian, Heye Foundation, New York.

Steward, Julian H.

1955   Lineage to Clan: Ecological Aspects of Southwestern Society. In *Theory of Culture Change*, by Julian H. Steward, pp. 151–72. University of Illinois Press, Urbana. Originally published 1937, *Anthropos* 32: 87–104.

Stuart, David E.

1982   Power and Efficiency: Demographic Behavior, Sedentism, and Energetic Trajectories in Cultural Evolution. In *The San Juan Tomorrow, Planning for the Conservation of Cultural Resources in the San Juan Basin*, edited by Fred Plog and Walter Wait, pp. 127–62. USDI, National Park Service, Southwest Region, Santa Fe.

Stuart, David E., and Rory P. Gauthier

1981   *Prehistoric New Mexico: Background for Survey*. New Mexico Historic Preservation Bureau, Santa Fe.

Toll, H. Wolcott

1991   Material Distributions and Exchange in the Chaco System. In *Chaco & Hohokam: Prehistoric Regional Systems in the American Southwest*, edited by Patricia L. Crown and W. James Judge, pp. 77–108. School of American Research Press, Santa Fe.

Upham, Steadman

1982   *Polities and Power: An Economic and Political History of the Western Pueblo*. Academic Press, New York.

1984   Adaptive Diversity and Southwestern Abandonment. *Journal of Anthropological Research* 40:235–56.

Van West, Carla R., and Timothy A. Kohler

1992   A Time to Rend, A Time to Sew: New Perspectives on Northern Anasazi Sociopolitical Development in Later Prehistory. Paper presented at The Anthropology of Human Behavior Through Geographic Information and Analysis Conference, Santa Barbara.

Vivian, R. Gwinn

1990   *The Chacoan Prehistory of the San Juan Basin*. Academic Press, San Diego.

Wheat, Joe Ben

1983   Anasazi Who? In *Proceedings of the Anasazi Symposium*, edited by Jack E. Smith, pp. 11–15. Mesa Verde Museum Association, Mesa Verde National Park.

Woosley, Anne I.

1988   Population Aggregation and the Role of Large Pueblos in the Northern Rio Grande. Paper presented at the 53rd Annual Meeting of the Society for American Archaeology, Phoenix.

Chapter 17

Pueblo III People and Polity in Relational Context

David R. Wilcox

As an invited conference, the meeting held at Crow Canyon Archaeological Center in the spring of 1990 to discuss the Pueblo III period was necessarily somewhat restrictive. By asking people knowledgeable about the archaeology of a series of particular regions to come together to share their data and ideas, the organizers effected a pooling of information that provided all participants with something new to think about, thus giving everyone an opportunity to move ahead in the common effort to understand southwestern prehistory. Methodologically, the importance of this process is that the empirical data from many areas was systematically transferred to a common theoretical domain where it can be subjected to a new kind of scientific study. What at first glance may seem like little more than a lot of dots on maps are indeed the foundation for the erection of new models of social, economic and political process, theoretical regions long thought to be beyond the reach of archaeology. No doubt the conferees join in hoping that the publication of the resulting chapters and maps will go far toward reigniting the sense of excitement experienced during the proceedings.

In the following discussion I first examine the research contexts within which the traditional topics of village aggregation, regional interaction, and abandonment have been studied in the Southwest. I propose that the approach to these topics should be rethought, and I argue in particular that we must develop a greater appreciation for macroregional networks of interaction and exchange in our attempts to understand Puebloan prehistory. As a case in point I discuss the development and transformation of the Chacoan re-gional system from a macroregional perspective. I conclude with a consideration of late prehistoric interaction networks that enmeshed the American Southwest in macroregional systems stretching from the Pacific Coast to the Great Plains.

The Pueblo III Period and Its Research Context

In its beginnings, southwestern archaeology focused primarily on artifacts and architecture, its cultural classifications often being based on propositions about both kinds of data. The "Pueblo III period," for example, when this terminology was first adopted at the 1927 Pecos Conference, was inferred to refer to a stage of culture growth characterized by aggregation into large pueblo sites when certain kinds of black-on-white pottery were made (Kidder 1927). It was soon learned that the correlation of pottery and architectural form was not so simple (Kluckhohn and Reiter 1939; Morris 1939), and pottery proved to be much superior as a chronological indicator. "Pueblo III" has since become a term simply for the period between A.D. 1150 and 1300 (but see Kintigh, chapter 9).

The development of dendrochronology (Haury 1935), and later radiocarbon dating, made possible the independent dating of both artifacts and architecture (Dean 1978). This in turn made possible the refinement of spatial distribution studies in relatively narrow time intervals. First glimpsed by Julian Steward (1937) in the Southwest, this approach was developed shortly after World War II and was eagerly adopted in the 1950s by a wide spectrum of leading archaeologists (Willey 1956). K. C. Chang's (1958) seminal paper and subsequent work (Chang 1967, 1968) held significant promise for southwestern studies (Dean 1969; Rohn 1965, 1977; Wilcox 1975), but the controversies swirling around what was styled the "New Archaeology" deflected much attention from these initiatives.

Organized efforts to coordinate the development of southwestern archaeology in the last two decades emphasized the environment as a causative factor (Dean et al. 1985; Euler et al. 1979; Gumerman 1988) or a nonrelational approach to settlement data (Plog and Hill 1971; see also Sullivan and Schiffer 1978). The resulting models treat the humans who occupied the prehistoric cultural landscapes of the Southwest as animals helplessly subject to the forces of environmental change or demographic densities (Dean et al. 1985). The possibility that the prehistoric people had social organizations, economic organizations, political organizations or ideas that affected what they did, is not seriously considered. The reason for this is scientific rigor; the insistence, with which we may agree, that adequate empirical grounds be found for postulating such processes and testing theoretical propositions.

To solve this problem we must reexamine the roots of archaeological logic and archaeological metaphysics, the ways in which we construct arguments and concepts (Clarke 1973). Most discussions of such matters have long focused primarily on artifacts, and a monothetic logic of an entity and its qualities has been assumed necessary (Dunnell 1971; Fritz and Plog 1970; Spaulding 1960). Relational logic provides an alternative approach to archaeological theory construction. The idea that relations are observable in the archaeological record and that relational logic can also be used to construct archaeological concepts is only slowly being recognized (Butzer 1982; Krause and Thorne 1970; Wilcox 1975; Wilcox, McGuire, and Sternberg 1981:147–56). This is particularly pertinent to the research and data discussed in each of the chapters of this volume. Dots on a map form a graph; when lines are added they can symbolize relations and all graphs can be studied using graph theory, the mathematics of relations (Hage and Harary 1983). "Because it is essentially the study of relations, graph theory is eminently suited to the description and analysis of a wide range of structures that constitute a significant part of the subject matter of anthropology, as well as of the social sciences generally" (Hage and Harary 1983:2). Graphs can also be expressed as matrices and thus can be explored using matrix algebra. Both graph theory and matrix algebra can be pursued using computers, making the study of large, complex data sets practical.

The switch to thinking relationally instead of statically in terms of an essentialist logic of qualities and entities makes possible the modeling of behavioral processes without undue dependence on ethnographic analogy. Thus freed, archaeological arguments can formulate postulates about change and differences between two time periods far more effectively than can analogical arguments. The outcomes of behavior specified by relations should produce classes of observable data in the archaeological record that permit the direct testing of relational propositions (Wilcox 1975).

Although both artifacts and architecture can be defined as relational sets, architecture is perhaps more readily understood that way (Hillier and Hanson 1984) and has, in fact, long been so understood in southwestern archaeology. T. Mitchell Prudden's concept of a "unit-type" pueblo is a relational set, consisting of a small room block, a "kiva," and a trash midden ordered in space from north to south.

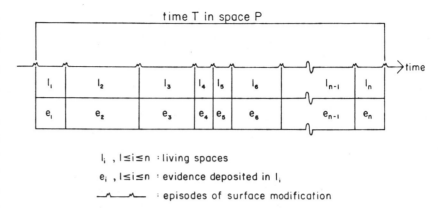

Figure 17.1.   Schematic representation of living-surface model.

Prudden (1903) further recognized that large Pueblo III sites such as Goodman Point Ruin are sets of aggregated "unit-type" pueblos—hence his choice of terminology (Lipe and Hegmon 1989; Wilcox 1976).

Less abstractly, Prudden (1903) also had another fundamental insight: He recognized that the occupants of his unit-type pueblos were comparable social groups and that the comparative study of the domains of their domestic activities provided a way for archaeologists to understand something important about social organization. K. C. Chang (1958, 1967) has elaborated on this idea. Chang points out that, by treating settlements rather than artifact collections as the primary focus of archaeological attention, and by recognizing that "the people who lived there" are an empirical unit of study that can be compared to other groups, archaeologists have a kind of direct access to prehistoric human behavior.

In my own attempts to operationalize these ideas I have defined a formal set-theoretic concept of the "living surface" (Wilcox 1975), a theoretical domain that models the actual surfaces on which all human behavior is conducted (figure 17.1). Such surfaces form the settings or domains in which all behavior occurs. They can be studied at the scale of the room floor, the room block, the settlement, the locality, the region, or the macroregion. Living surfaces are a key concept in what Clarke (1973) called "depositional

theory" in that all physical traces of past behavior enter the archaeological record through the membrane of a living surface. Of central importance in the translation of empirical data into these living-surface domains are chronology and behavioral boundaries.

Dean (1969) has made a useful distinction between "classificatory" and "absolute" contemporaneity, the former characterizing what we know when speaking of archaeological phases or components and the latter referring to what we know (or claim to know) when speaking of behavior in instantaneous temporal terms. If the elements of a set co-occur for a certain interval, we may properly say that they are absolutely contemporaneous over that interval. The living surface concept (Wilcox, McGuire, and Sternberg 1981: 147–56) identifies such sets and by distinguishing between daily activity and the domains in which those activities were conducted, it provides the archaeologist a framework for getting at some aspects of domestic routines. In this way, it has been possible to discriminate the domains of household-like social units, suprahouseholds, etc. (Wilcox 1975, 1991b; Wilcox, McGuire, and Sternberg 1981).

Social boundaries are relations or relational sets that differentiate one social group, or their domains, from others. Prudden's (1903) recognition of the replication of unit-type sets in Pueblo III sites was the first clear example of the formal specification of a social boundary in southwestern archaeology. Rohn (1965) and Dean (1969), among others, have demonstrated much more fully how such inferences can be drawn without any reliance on ethnographic analogy. At higher levels, progress has been slower, but Rohn (1977) has again led the way, showing how a concept of "community" can be meaningfully defined. Several of the chapters in this volume usefully take up this concept and suggest some provocative elaborations ("socially negotiated space"; see Varien et al., chapter 7).

From a Hohokam perspective it is interesting to note that in southern Arizona what has been viewed as a "site" is behaviorally comparable to what are only now being called "communities" in the Anasazi area, where small pueblos (elements of communities) have most frequently been called "sites." What follows from this is the surprising finding that Hohokam and Anasazi communities were much more similar than site-based comparisons have implied. Both consisted of household or suprahousehold domains spaced about 160 to more than 650 feet (50 to 200+ meters) apart that have unique use histories that are often shorter than the occupation interval of the community. The spatial scale of these communities, as much as 450 to 1,300 acres in the Hohokam case (Turney 1929), and perhaps as much as 2,000 acres in some Anasazi cases (see Roney, chapter 10), and their centuries-long durations, are facts that should redefine the debates about aggregation and sedentism (see Varien et al., chapter 7).

The identification of behavioral boundaries on regional or macroregional scales is still one of the least studied problems in southwestern archaeology. Most work on this issue has examined ceramic distributions, and the standard terminology for higher-level groupings (Hohokam, Western Anasazi, Eastern Anasazi, etc.) is based on macro-patterns in the ceramic data. The apparent correlation of ceramic-type distributions with late prehistoric-early protohistoric ethnic-political groups (Ford, Schroeder, and Peckham 1972)—

if viewed from a boundary perspective—is a provocative indication of how we can go beyond cultural materials to society and polity on the regional level. Studies of site clustering (Jewett 1989; Upham 1982) also point in this direction, although Kintigh's (chapter 9) cautions regarding this approach merit close consideration.

The first step toward a comprehensive, regional, or macroregional approach to the study of southwestern societies and polities is to think in terms of the people living in communities interacting with one another as close or distant neighbors. It was from this perspective that I suggested redefining the Hohokam concept as a "regional system" (Wilcox 1979, 1980) and similar approaches can be taken to the Mimbres and Chacoan regional systems (Crown and Judge 1991; Lekson 1986a, 1986b; Neitzel 1994; Wilcox 1988, 1992, 1993). More abstractly, communities are nodes in a matrix and as such our goals should include attempts to measure the nature of transfers of matter, energy, and information (MEI) among such nodes (see Blanton et al. 1984; Crown, Orcutt, and Kohler, chapter 13). Understanding changes in a regional matrix depends on two assumptions. First, no single node is a closed system. Second, each node has a transition probability associated with it that is a function of the inputs and outputs of MEI that determine its viability. Organization internal to a node and organization linking it to others affect these transition probabilities. If, for example, a set of neighboring settlements form a polity within which endogamy is the rule, exchanges between this polity (super-node) and others would be considerably affected (Wilcox 1984). Exchanges might still take place, but the social and political mechanisms supporting the exchanges would be different from those in a simple domestic economy.

A widely held working assumption has been that public architecture in southwestern sites (ballcourts, great kivas, great houses, plazas) indicate group transactions between households, suprahouseholds, so-

dalities, or communities and the distributional study of these social arenas has been the basis for models of regional interaction (Lekson 1991; Wilcox 1991b, 1991c; Wilcox and Sternberg 1983). More recently, analyses have been directed toward discriminating subsets of "regional systems" that may be meaningfully viewed as polities (McGuire 1991; Wilcox 1991a, 1991b, 1994). The evidence for human conflict in the Southwest, of which there is a surprising amount (Haas and Creamer 1992 and chapter 14; Wilcox and Haas 1994), is also of great interest because its patterns and parameters assist archaeologists in distinguishing the boundaries of polities. The relations of intervisibility, empty space (Mera's [1935] "no-man's lands"), clustering of defensively organized settlements, and other data all merit much greater systematic study across all of the Southwest and beyond.

Chaco in Regional Context

Once we have put dots on a map, what can we do next? Clearly, the next step is to find ways to study the relations among those dots (nodes) and to express those relations as lines that connect subsets of the dots. Figure 17.2 illustrates one direction such analyses can take. Surely one of the critical measures of human interaction between communities in the Southwest, where there were no draft animals before A.D. 1540, is the distance a person with a pack can go on foot in a day. Robert Drennan (1984) has suggested that this parameter is 22 miles (36 kilometers), a figure supported by other data (Platt 1979; for a more sophisticated approach to mapping these relationships, see Gorenflo and Gale 1990). A related idea would be how far people can run in a day (see Osler and Dodd 1979), which affects estimates of the threat radius a community can exert on its neighbors. Bourke (see Porter 1986) reports that Apaches in the rugged Sierra Madres could run 50 miles in a day, day after day. By Drennan's measure, 11 miles (18 km) is the distance a person on foot

244   Wilcox

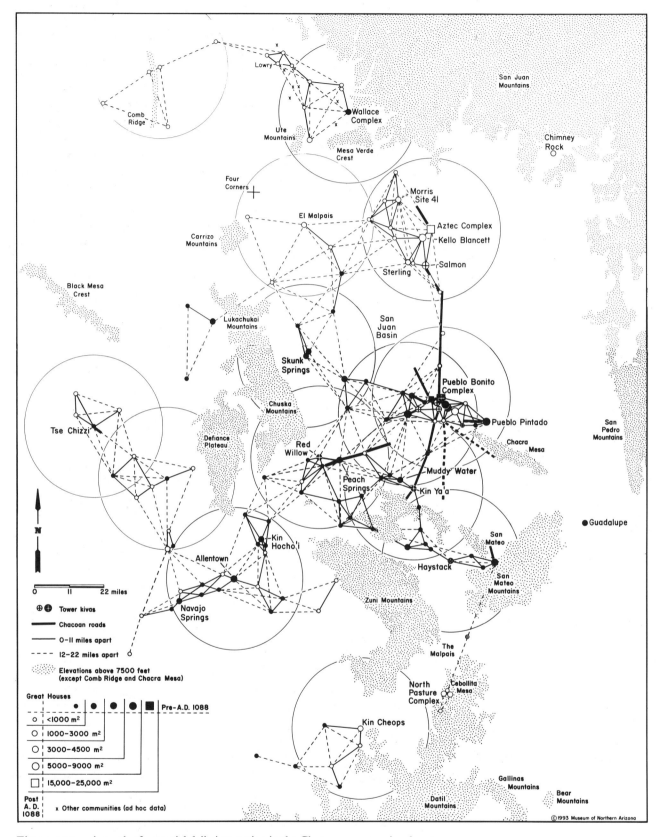

Figure 17.2.   A graph of potential daily interaction in the Chacoan macroregional system.

with a pack can go and come back in a day (see also Johnson 1987:115). This parameter thus defines the outer limit of the potential for daily intercourse between communities.

In figure 17.2 I have assembled data on 150 Chacoan or Chaco-like great house sites, coded them into two temporal classes (before and after Salmon Ruin was first built in A.D. 1088) and five size classes, and displayed them with circles of 22-mile radius around the largest of the nodes in each local area. Nodes that are 11 miles or less apart are connected with a solid line and those that are 12 to 22 miles apart are connected with a dashed line. The earlier image of a "Chacoan regional system" is thus reconceptualized in terms of the potentials for daily neighbor-to-neighbor interactions. Figure 17.3 gives the rank-order sizes of the measured great houses. Based upon these data, I propose that a macroregional peer-polity system had emerged in this portion of the Southwest by the early twelfth century, and thus that Chaco was not simply a "regional system" (cf. Lekson 1991; Neitzel 1994; see Wilcox 1994, 1995b).

On the basis of these and other data I have constructed a general model of the evolution of the Chacoan polities (Wilcox 1993, 1994, 1995a). Two points about those inferences are of methodological interest here. First, there is a strong pattern of interconnectivity between the circles south and west of Chaco Canyon, the solid-line subgraphs in that area, and the pattern of roads with tower kivas (signaling devices) at their ends (integrating the same set). Second, and in contrast, the circles centered on Allantown and Aztec are discrete from the interconnected Chaco system to the south and west, respectively. By the early twelfth century, when these patterns had fully come about, I infer from these (and other) data that the set of tightly interconnected nodes centered on Chaco Canyon was a single polity surrounded by "peer" polities that were (by then) comparably organized, but were far enough away or strong enough to re-

sist the threats posed by the larger Chaco polity (figure 17.3). Indeed, the construction of roads, tower kivas, and walls around the fronts of the Chaco Canyon great houses during the early twelfth century (Judd 1959; Lekson 1984) indicates that their occupants were by then fearful of the neighboring polities. Many new questions and research directions are opened up by this peer-polity model.

Macroregional scales of analysis must also be rethought from a relational perspective, even though this may force us to become truly southwestern archaeologists, not only regional specialists. That interactions across regional boundaries occurred is certain; what has yet to be done is to achieve a general systemic understanding of the significance of such exchanges of MEI. Figure 17.4 presents an atemporal summary of ballcourt and great-house distributions in relation to a series of proposed long-distance exchange routes, with 5-day circles (of 110-mile radius) added as a standard reference. As a heuristic device, this image provides a point of reference for many issues relevant to a discussion of the Pueblo III period. It should also be carefully noted that all ballcourt and great-house sites that were known when the map was constructed are shown, new ones continue to be discovered, and much more remains to be learned about the construction and use histories of each. Figure 17.4 serves to emphasize the largely disjunct nature of the ballcourt and great-house distributions, but other maps will have to be prepared to portray the evolution of these "systems" in relation to one another and to their other neighbors.

Let us begin with Wupatki. Located at the far northeastern edge of the ballcourt network, it has the only masonry court in the system and one of the latest, probably dating in the period A.D. 1150 to 1225, based on tree-ring dates and predominant ceramics (Fairley and Geib 1989; Robinson, Harrill, and Warren 1975; Wilcox 1995b). The pueblo's masonry has long reminded observers of Chacoan styles (Stanislawski 1963) and it is, in fact, orga-

nizationally, a great house in the midst of a dispersed small-house community (see Downum and Sullivan 1990; Fowler and Stein 1992). In the sense of a node that connected two distinct networks, I infer that Wupatki was a "gateway" community (see Hirth 1978; Lyneis 1984) between the Chacoan and Hohokam regional systems during the first generation or so of the Pueblo III period. In short, with the construction of Wupatki and its ballcourt, most of the Southwest became integrated into a single macroregional system.

This brings us to the great question of the Chacoan chronology. As Varien et al. (ch. 7) and Roney (ch. 10) make clear, the ceramic chronology and independent dating for the mid-twelfth century are still weak. Against the arguments of Tom Windes (1987), I would join others (Blinman and Wilson 1989; Stein and McKenna 1988) in arguing for continuity of occupation in many important Chacoan great houses well after A.D. 1130. This happened, however, not only at Aztec and Salmon but also in the Chaco Canyon great houses (Wilcox 1993, 1994). The facts are that construction in Chaco Canyon ceased once Aztec was built (about A.D. 1130), but construction dates are not necessarily a good measure of abandonment dates. If one reads Judd's (1954, 1959, 1964) and Pepper's (1920) descriptive reports using the framework provided by Lekson (1984; see also Lekson 1983) to order their data, empirical support for continued occupation of the largest great houses is found. Great Kiva A in Pueblo Bonito, for example, which Lekson (1984) found was built some time after A.D. 1085, had 17 floors in it (Judd 1964:135, 203). Similar continuity of occupation is seen in many parts of these structures, and the uppermost pottery includes Mesa Verde Black-on-white, which was not made until after A.D. 1175 (Morris 1939) or 1200 (Breternitz et al. 1974). Windes's (1985) Chaco-McElmo type, the latest painted pottery assemblage in Pueblo Bonito and Pueblo del Arroyo, includes repeated examples of Flagstaff Black-on-white de-

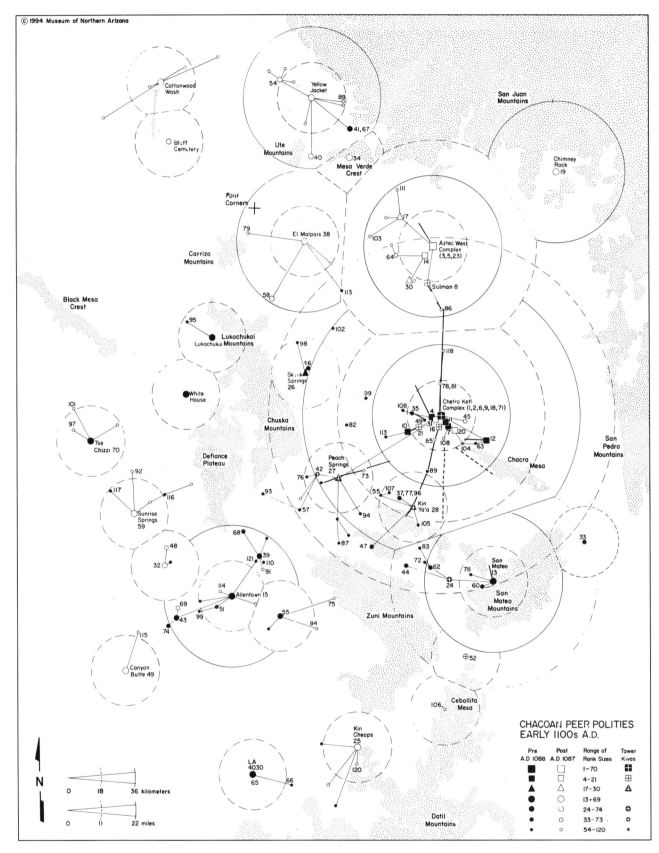

Figure 17.3.   The rank-order structure of the Chacoan macroregional system.

Figure 17.4. Long-distance connectivity in the far west and the southwestern macroregional system.

signs (Phil Geib, personal communication 1994), which post-date A.D. 1150 (Fairley and Geib 1989; see also Blinman and Wilson 1989).

The rich assemblages of artifacts found on Pueblo Bonito's uppermost floors, then, date not to A.D. 1130 but more likely to the end of the twelfth century (see also Vivian and Reiter 1960), meaning that the Chaco polity continued to be a major player until at least the beginning of the thirteenth century. It was thus a contem-

porary of Wupatki. The implications of this proposition are profound, necessitating that we make the resolution of these chronological issues a high priority for future research. One of the tasks worth doing in this connection would be a complete reanalysis of Judd and Pepper's data, putting them into Harris matrices (Harris 1979) as much as possible and constructing a detailed, dynamic series of map-pictures of the changing site and activity structure of these important buildings.

Where Wupatki came from is also a key issue. The predominance there of Alameda Brown Ware led Colton (1946) to interpret it as a Sinagua site. However, almost all of its brown ware is of one type, Sunset Red, which in the 1930s was observed to be more highly polished, well slipped, and made using a coil-and-scrape technique (MNA site files, where it is called Flagstaff Red). It thus may have been made by Kayenta rather than Sinagua potters. I thus infer that Wupatki was a southern Kayenta site built as part of an organized, politically motivated intrusion into the Flagstaff area by people from the northern drainages of the Little Colorado River valley (Wilcox 1995b). Wupatki's Chaco-style architecture is accountable by this intrusion, because it probably derives from Chaco-like great houses that were already being built in sites like Tse Chizzi that have a predominance of Kayenta pottery during the 11th century. (Gilpin 1989; see figures 1 and 2). In his dissertation on Wupatki artifacts, Stanislawski (1963) recognized the site's Chacoan connections and the role of this connection in the emergence of the historic Hopi. Adams (chapter 4) and Dean (chapter 3) underestimate the importance of these political and economic processes in their evaluations of Western Anasazi archaeology.

The excellent chapter by Dean (chapter 3; see also Gumerman and Dean 1989) stresses the disjunction between Kayenta and Chaco, emphasizing the intriguing fact that virtually no Chaco pottery is found in Kayenta sites (whether he includes sites like Tse Chizzi on the southeastern flank of Black Mesa is unclear). There is, however, a striking correlation that bears closer study: the Kayenta expansion (Lyneis, chapter 2) to the north, northwest, and west, which brought Kayenta populations into direct contact with Mesa Verde, Fremont, Virgin Anasazi, and Cohonina neighbors, began about A.D. 1050, just at the time when their eastern and southeastern neighbors were integrating (or being integrated into) the advancing Chacoan great-house macroregional system. Dean's failure to consider the political variables that may have been involved in Kayenta area dynamics needs to be remedied by anthropologically sounder models. As Aristotle some time ago noted (see Snodgrass 1980), polity can be achieved both in aggregated settlements (the polis) and in networks of widely dispersed homesteads (the ethnos; see also Kelly 1985).

The Macroregional Approach to Prehistoric Change

Figure 17.4 also poses the perennial question of how far we have to go to include all the relevant interactions that were central to the macroregional processes involving the Southwest. Must we become American archaeologists as well as southwestern archaeologists? I believe we must. All explanations require a discrimination of both internal and external factors, together with a weighing of their relative importance. Lyneis (chapter 2) presents an elegant and tightly argued "internal" (regional) model that can be used to illustrate this position. Her model contrasts with a preliminary exploration of mine (Wilcox 1992) that stressed the involvement of the Kayenta populations in large-scale exchange systems and the possible importance of the Old Spanish Trail route, an idea suggested to me by Phil Geib (see also Lyneis 1992; Rafferty 1991). I would now reformulate the problem along macroregional lines as follows (Wilcox 1994, 1995a): Basketmaker period networks formed a broad east-west series of neighbors from southern Nevada to the upper San Juan River. Connectivity with peoples in the Mohave Desert and California to the west brought quantities of *Haliotis* and *Olivella* shell deep into the Southwest (Gumerman and Dean 1989). The breakup of the contiguity of these networks coincides with the emergence of the first true villages (Wilshusen 1990) and where these villages are found is right along the best pedestrian route across the northern Colorado Plateau (later called the Old Spanish Trail). Regional "tribal" groupings had begun to form even in Basketmaker II times (Dean, chapter 3; Matson 1991) but those regional boundaries became much sharper by the Pueblo I period, when wide no-man's lands opened up and distinct cultural traditions became apparent (Hegmon 1990). The Kayenta expansion reintegrated many of these "tribal" networks and the "gateway" vil-

lage community at the Coombs site was probably a key political mechanism regulating the new kinds of interactions that emerged. But that new macro-network proved fragile and it soon disintegrated, resulting in a stepwise process of macroregional abandonment and ecological replacement by hunter-gatherers.

To understand this macroregional scale I think we must include close analyses of the southern Fremont populations, the Saratoga Springs culture centered in Death Valley, the Antelope Valley and Chumash areas farther west in California, and the Mohave on the Colorado River (figure 17.4). The Pacific shell and southwestern pottery in the Antelope Valley and Saratoga Springs sites (Warren 1984) are what remain from repeated interactions between these people and their neighbors to the west and east. Such interactions may have been critical to their survival, and, indeed, the Saratoga Springs culture disappears shortly after the abandonment of the lowland Virgin sites in the mid-twelfth century (Warren 1984). Intertribal conflict to control the exchange flows generated by such contact may have escalated after A.D. 1100. A surge by the Mohave in the south and the Paragonah Fremont in the north for control of the trans-Mohave Desert traffic may have squeezed out the lowland Virgin groups. Of related interest is the fact that Mesa Verde groups expanded westward to the Canyonlands of the Colorado River in the early thirteenth century (Varien et al., chapter 7) after the Kayenta-Virgin gateway to the Mohave Desert (the Main Ridge Village and related settlement system) was abandoned and during the period of population growth at Paragonah Village (Dodd 1982), making Paragonah Village the western gateway to the Mohave Desert (Meighan 1956). Changing patterns of connectivity like this may be highly informative about the changing political contexts of human decision making in the Southwest, but to see them, we must position ourselves so we can see "the big picture" of macroregional relationships in the far west and western Mexico as a continuous relational field (see Lesser 1961).

We come, finally, then, to the difficult question of Southwest-Mesoamerica connections (Mathien and McGuire 1986). We know with certainty that copper bells from West Mexico (and probably scarlet macaws) came into the Southwest during early Pueblo III times. Several bells and 42 macaws were found at Wupatki (Fewkes 1900; Hargrave 1970; Stanislawski 1963). Thirty macaws were found in Pueblo Bonito, and in two inner rooms their guano was on the uppermost floors (Judd 1964). I infer that macaws at Wupatki came there from Chaco, which received them from West Mexico via the Mimbres area (see Creel and McKusick 1994; Wilcox 1993, 1994).

During middle Pueblo III times, in the late twelfth and early thirteenth centuries, these connections within the southwestern macroregional system disintegrated. A period of radical restructuring of local societies rapidly ensued in all parts of the Southwest. In southern Arizona, room blocks were built on the Hohokam platform mounds, and the mounds were enclosed by high compound walls ca. A.D. 1250 (Gregory 1987, 1991). In the north, a dense new network of tightly nucleated villages developed along an east-west axis from the middle Verde Valley along the southern reaches of the Colorado Plateaus, into the Rio Grande Valley and beyond onto the western Plains. In the latter area, by the late thirteenth century, aggregated hamlets of the Antelope Creek phase contain *Olivella* said to come from the Pacific (Lintz 1991). A new long-distance exchange structure thus emerged that was probably critically important in facilitating the colonization and settlement of the Rio Grande Valley, providing also a "pull" on communities in the northern Colorado Plateau that had become increasingly isolated and contentious. It should come as no surprise, therefore, that during the middle and late

thirteenth century whole communities began to move southward and eastward out of the northern San Juan country (Lekson, chapter 11; Reid et al., chapter 6; and Crown, Orcutt, and Kohler, chapter 13; see also Haury 1958), taking up positions where they could participate in the new exchange structure.

What Fowler, Stein, and Anyon (1987) have aptly called "walled towns" became a general settlement form all along this east-west axis by late Pueblo III times. The famous late thirteenth-century cliff dwellings of Kiet Siel, Cliff Palace, Poncho House, and Mummy Cave are analogous forms. These sites are a new kind of node in the social matrix of southwestern communities. Their appearance is marked within a generation or so by the shift from high kiva-to-room ratios to the domestic domain noted by Kidder in his notes on Pecos (Kidder 1958; see also Adams 1983; Lipe 1989). This new type of domestic domain was constructed by partitioning the large room blocks that faced the plaza into sets of rooms characterized by both up-and-down and back-and-forth doorway access, but not lateral access. It was this kind of domestic domain that the Spaniards called "houses" in the later sixteenth century (Hammond and Rey 1966). The spread of what archaeologists call the "katsina cult" (Adams 1991, chapter 4; Schaafsma and Schaafsma 1974) apparently indicates the development of a new ecumenical ideology that helped integrate these walled towns. Reorganization of the division of labor and new forms of economic exchanges are also likely, if as yet poorly documented (see Wilcox 1991a).

In the basin-and-range country to the south, two very different macroregional structures developed in the late thirteenth and early fourteenth centuries (Wilcox 1991a, 1994). Also integrated along an east-west axis, the Salado and later Paquimé macroregional systems somehow facilitated the colonization and development of rich agricultural areas on their eastern margin in northwestern Chi-

huahua. The Phoenix Basin may have been the largest, integrated polity of the Salado macroregion, but it appears to have been devastated by severe flooding in A.D. 1356 and 1358 (Gregory 1991). Beginning in the mid-fourteenth century, Casas Grandes (Paquimé), achieved a macroregional ascendancy more or less coincident with the decline of the Phoenix Basin polity. It also had many more Mesoamerican-like ideological forms than we see in the northern Southwest (Di Peso 1974; for a corrected version of the chronology of the Medio period, see Dean and Ravesloot 1993).

Although I think we are a long way from a good understanding of any of these events, it does seem clear that the story of the Pueblo III period cannot be understood until archaeologists make a serious effort to compare and contrast the emergence of the northern and southern macroregional structures, define the internal and external mechanisms that drive macroregional systems, examine the sources of political interactions and mutual influences, and set all of that into the context of contemporary events in California, the Great Basin, the Rocky Mountains, the Plains, and northern and western Mexico. We may dispute what Charles Di Peso (1974) proposed as a specific model of Paquimé development (Mathien and McGuire 1986; McGuire 1980; Wilcox 1991a), but there is no getting around the fact that he was right about the scale at which we must model the interaction of prehistoric societies in the Southwest.

More than anything else, the Pueblo III Conference at Crow Canyon was important because it succeeded in bringing together into a single corpus the basic data currently available on a huge series of Pueblo III sites. By transferring these data to a single map, a new foundation has been created for future studies of Pueblo III social, economic and political dynamics. It is a good beginning, but, as I have sought to show, there still is much to be done to achieve anything approaching a comprehensive understanding. Adding relations to the dots on the map is here recommended as a highly fruitful approach. To take full advantage of that strategy, the curricula of our undergraduate and graduate schools must also be changed to include training in abstract algebra, graph theory, matrix analysis, and network theory. Doing so will not only greatly enrich our discipline, it also will generate a new scientific revolution in archaeological theory and method that all those who wish to put people back into archaeological history should warmly support.

Acknowledgments

First thanks go both to Bill Lipe and Steve Lekson, who asked me to be a general discussant at the PIII conference at Crow Canyon, and to the other participants for making it such a fine experience. The staff of the Crow Canyon Archaeological Center also deserve much credit for smoothly handling the logistics of the meetings. Special thanks also goes to Michael Adler for his encouragement and efforts to pull this volume together. Many people over the last 25 years have contributed to the development of the ideas expressed in my discussion. Of special note recently are Bill Lipe, Phil Geib, Dennis Gilpin, Margaret Lyneis, Helen Fairley, and Miranda Warburton who have helped me to learn much about the archaeology of the Colorado Plateaus. Jodi Griffith of the MNA Exhibits Department drafted the figures. For all errors or excesses of interpretation, I alone am responsible.

References Cited

Adams, E. Charles
    1983   The Architectural Analogue to Hopi Social Organization and Room Use, and Implications for Prehistoric Northern Southwest Culture. *American Antiquity* 48(1):44–61.
    1991   *The Origin and Development of the Pueblo Katsina Cult.* University of Arizona Press, Tucson.

Blanton, Richard E., Stephen A. Kowalewski, Gary Feinman, and Jill Appell
    1984   *Ancient Mesoamerica, A Comparison of Change in Three Regions.* Cambridge University Press, Cambridge, England.

Blinman, Eric, and C. Dean Wilson
    1989   Mesa Verde Region Ceramic Types. Paper presented at the NMAC Ceramic Workshop, Red Rock State Park, New Mexico.

Breternitz, David A., Arthur H. Rohn, Jr., and Elizabeth A. Morris (compilers)
    1974   *Prehistoric Ceramics of the Mesa Verde Region.* Ceramic Series No. 5. Museum of Northern Arizona, Flagstaff.

Butzer, Karl
    1982   *Archaeology as Human Ecology.* Cambridge University Press, Cambridge.

Chang, Kwang-chih
    1958   Study of the Neolithic Social Grouping: Examples from the New World. *American Anthropologist* 60:298–334.
    1967   *Rethinking Archaeology.* Random House, New York.
    1968   *Settlement Archaeology.* National Press, Palo Alto.

Clarke, David
    1973   Archaeology: The Loss of Innocence. *Antiquity* 47:6–18.

Colton, Harold S.
    1946   *The Sinagua: A Summary of the Archaeology of the Region of Flagstaff, Arizona.* Bulletin No. 22. Museum of Northern Arizona, Flagstaff.

Creel, Darrell G., and Charmion McKusick
    1994   Prehistoric Macaws and Parrots in the Mimbres Area, New Mexico. *American Antiquity* 59(3):510–24.

Crown, Patricia L., and W. James Judge (editors)
    1991   *Chaco & Hohokam, Prehistoric Regional Systems in the American Southwest.* School of American Research Press, Santa Fe.

Dean, Jeffrey S.
    1969   *Chronological Analysis of Tsegi Phase Sites in Northeastern Arizona.* Papers of the Laboratory of Tree-Ring Research No. 3. University of Arizona, Tucson.
    1978   Independent Dating in Archaeological Analysis. In *Advances in Archaeological Method and Theory,* Vol. 1, edited by Michael B. Schiffer, pp. 223–55. Academic Press, New York.

Dean, Jeffrey S., Robert C. Euler, George J. Gumerman, Fred Plog, Richard H. Hevly, and Thor N. V. Karlstrom
    1985   Human Behavior, Demography, and Paleoenvironment on the Colorado Plateaus. *American Antiquity* 50(3): 537–54.

Dean, Jeffrey S., and John C. Ravesloot
    1993   The Chronology of Cultural Interaction in the Gran Chichimeca. In *Culture and Contact, Charles C. Di Peso's Gran Chichimeca,* edited by Anne I. Woosley and John C. Ravesloot, pp. 83–103. University of New Mexico Press, Albuquerque.

Di Peso, Charles C.
    1974   *Casas Grandes, a Fallen Trading Center of the Gran Chichimeca,* Vol. 2. Northland Press, Flagstaff.

Dodd, Walter A., Jr.
    1982   *Final Year Excavations at the Evans Mound Site.* Anthropological Papers No. 106. University of Utah Press, Salt Lake City.

Downum, Christian E., and Sullivan, Alan P., III
    1990   Settlement Patterns. In *The Wupatki Archeological Inventory Survey Project: Final Report,* compiled by Bruce A. Anderson, 5.1–5.90. Professional Paper No. 35. USDI, National Park Service, Southwest Regional Office, Division of Anthropology, Southwest Cultural Resources Center, Santa Fe.

Drennan, Robert D.
    1984   Long-Distance Transport Costs in Pre-Hispanic Mesoamerica. *American Anthropologist* 86(1): 105–12.

Dunnell, Robert C.
    1971   *Systematics in Prehistory.* Free Press, New York.

Euler, Robert C., George J. Gumerman, Thor N. V. Karlstrom, Jeffrey S. Dean, and Richard Hevly
    1979   The Colorado Plateaus: Cultural Dynamics and Paleoenvironment. *Science* 205:1089–1101.

Fairley, Helen C., and Phil R. Geib
    1989   Data Gaps and Research Issues in Arizona Strip Prehistory. In *Man, Models and Management, An Overview of the Archaeology of the Arizona Strip and the Management of Its Cultural Resources,* by Jeffrey H. Altschul and Helen C. Fairley, pp. 219–44. Statistical Research, Tucson.

Fewkes, Jesse Walter
    1900   Pueblo Ruins Near Flagstaff, Arizona, A Preliminary Notice. *American Anthropologist,* n.s., 2: 422–50.

Ford, Richard I.; Albert H. Schroeder, and Stewart L. Peckham
    1972   Three Perspectives on Puebloan

Prehistory. In *New Perspectives on the Pueblos*, edited by Alfonso Ortiz, pp. 19–39. University of New Mexico Press, Albuquerque.

Fowler, Andrew P., and John R. Stein
1992   The Anasazi Great House in Space, Time, and Paradigm. In *Anasazi Regional Organization and the Chaco System*, edited by David E. Doyel, pp. 101–22. Anthropological Papers no. 5. Maxwell Museum of Anthropology, Albuquerque.

Fowler, Andrew P., John R. Stein, and Roger Anyon
1987   An Archaeological Reconnaissance of West-Central New Mexico, The Anasazi Monuments Project. Ms. on file, Zuni Archaeological Program, Zuni, New Mexico.

Fritz, John M., and Fred T. Plog
1970   The Nature of Archaeological Explanation. *American Antiquity* 35: 405–12.

Gilpin, Dennis
1989   Great Houses and Pueblos in Northeastern Arizona. Paper presented at the Pecos Conference, Bandelier National Monument.

Gorenflo, L. J., and Nathan Gale
1990   Mapping Regional Settlement in Information Space. *Journal of Anthropological Archaeology* 9: 240–74.

Gregory, David A.
1987   The Morphology of Platform Mounds and the Structure of Classic Period Hohokam Sites. In *The Hohokam Village: Site Structure and Organization*, edited by David E. Doyel, pp. 183–210. American Association for the Advancement of Science, Glenwood Springs, Colorado.
1991   Form and Variation in Hohokam Settlement Patterns. In *Chaco & Hohokam: Prehistoric Regional Systems in the American Southwest*, edited by Patricia L. Crown and W. James Judge, pp. 159–94. School of American Research, Santa Fe.

Gumerman, George J. (editor)
1988   *The Anasazi in a Changing Environment*. Cambridge University Press, Cambridge, England.

Gumerman, George J., and Jeffrey S. Dean
1989   Prehistoric Cooperation and Competition in the Western Anasazi Area. In *Dynamics of Southwest Prehistory*, edited by Linda S. Cordell and George J. Gumerman, pp. 99–

148. Smithsonian Institution Press, Washington, D.C.

Haas, Jonathan, and Winifred Creamer
1992   Demography of the Protohistoric Pueblos of the Northern Rio Grande, A.D. 1450–1680. In *Current Research on the Late Prehistoric and Early History of New Mexico*, edited by Bradley J. Vierra and Clara Gualtieri, pp. 21–28. Special Publication No. 1. New Mexico Archaeological Council, Albuquerque.

Hage, Per, and Frank Harary
1983   *Structural Models in Anthropology*. Cambridge University Press, Cambridge.

Hammond, George P., and Agapito Rey (translators and editors)
1966   *The Rediscovery of New Mexico, 1580–1594: The Explorations of Chamuscado, Espejo, Castaño de Sosa, Morlete, and Leyve de Bonilla y Humana*. University of New Mexico Press, Albuquerque.

Hargrave, Lyndon L.
1970   *Mexican Macaws, Comparative Osteology and Survey of Remains from the Southwest*. Anthropological Papers No. 20. University of Arizona Press, Tucson.

Harris, Edward C.
1979   *Principles of Archaeological Stratigraphy*. Academic Press, New York.

Haury, Emil W.
1935   Tree-rings, the Archaeologist's Time-Piece. *American Antiquity* 1(2): 98–108.
1958   Evidence at Point of Pines for a Prehistoric Migration from Northern Arizona. In *Migrations in New World Culture History*, edited by Raymond H. Thompson, pp. 1–8. University of Arizona Bulletin No. 29(2). Social Science Bulletin No. 27. University of Arizona, Tucson.

Hegmon, Michelle Michal
1990   *Style As a Social Strategy: Dimensions of Ceramic Stylistic Variation in the Ninth Century Northern Southwest*. Unpublished Ph.D. dissertation, University of Michigan, Ann Arbor.

Hillier, Bill, and Julienne Hanson
1984   *The Social Logic of Space*. Cambridge University Press, Cambridge.

Hirth, Kenneth
1978   Interregional Trade and the Formation of Prehistoric Gateway

Communities. *American Antiquity* 43(1):35–45.

Jewett, Roberta A.
1989   Distance, Integration, and Complexity: The Spatial Organization of Pan-Regional Settlement Clusters in the American Southwest. In *The Sociopolitical Structure of Prehistoric Southwestern Societies*, edited by Steadman Upham, Kent G. Lightfoot, and Roberta A. Jewett, pp. 363–88. Westview Press, Boulder.

Johnson, Gregory A.
1987   The Changing Organization of Uruk Administration on the Susiana Plain. In *The Archaeology of Western Iran*, edited by Frank Hole, pp. 107–40. Smithsonian Institution Press, Washington, D.C.

Judd, Neil M.
1954   The Material Culture of Pueblo Bonito. *Smithsonian Miscellaneous Collections*, Vol. 124. Washington D.C.
1959   Pueblo del Arroyo, Chaco Canyon, New Mexico. *Smithsonian Miscellaneous Collections*, Vol. 138(1). Washington D.C.
1964   The Architecture of Pueblo Bonito. *Smithsonian Miscellaneous Collections*, Vol. 147(1). Washington D.C.

Judge, W. James
1989   Chaco Canyon-San Juan Basin. In *Dynamics of Southwest Prehistory*, edited by Linda S. Cordell and George J. Gumerman, pp. 209–62. Smithsonian Institution Press, Washington, D.C.

Kelly, Raymond C.
1985   *The Nuer Conquest, The Structure and Development of an Expansionist System*. University of Michigan Press, Ann Arbor.

Kidder, Alfred V.
1927   Southwestern Archaeological Conference. *Science* 66:489–91.
1958   *Pecos, New Mexico: Archaeological Notes*. Papers of the Robert S. Peabody Foundation for Archaeology, Vol. 5. Meriden, Connecticut.

Kluckhohn, Clyde, and Paul Reiter (editors)
1939   *Preliminary Report on the 1937 Excavations, Bc 50–51, Chaco Canyon, New Mexico*. University of New Mexico Bulletin, Anthropological Series No. 3(2). University of New Mexico, Albuquerque.

Krause, Richard, and Robert M. Thorne
1970   Toward a Theory of Archaeological

Things. *Plains Anthropologist* 16(54): 245–57.

Lekson, Stephen H. (editor)

1983   *The Architecture and Dendrochronology of Chetro Ketl.* Reports of the Chaco Center No. 6. USDI, National Park Service, Division of Cultural Research, Albuquerque.

Lekson, Stephen H.

1984   *Great Pueblo Architecture of Chaco Canyon, New Mexico.* University of New Mexico Press, Albuquerque.

1986a   The Mimbres Region. In *Mogollon Variability*, edited by Charlotte Benson and Steadman Upham, pp. 147–56. University Museum Occasional Papers No. 15. New Mexico State University, Las Cruces.

1986b   Mimbres Riverine Adaptations. In *Mogollon Variability*, edited by Charlotte Benson and Steadman Upham, pp. 181–90. University Museum Occasional Papers No. 15. New Mexico State University, Las Cruces.

1991   Settlement Patterns and the Chaco Region. In *Chaco & Hohokam, Prehistoric Regional Systems in the American Southwest*, edited by Patricia L. Crown and W. James Judge, pp. 31–56. School of American Research Press, Santa Fe.

Lesser, Alexander

1961   Social Fields and the Evolution of Society. *Southwestern Journal of Anthropology* 17(1):40–48.

Lintz, Christopher

1991   The Historical Development of a Culture Complex: The Basis for Understanding Architectural Misconceptions of the Antelope Creek Focus. In Current Trends in Southern Plains Archaeology, edited by Timothy G. Baugh. *Plains Anthropologist* 31(114:2):111–28.

Lipe, William D.

1989   Social Scale of Mesa Verde Anasazi Kivas. In *The Architecture of Social Integration in Prehistoric Pueblos*, edited by William D. Lipe and Michelle Hegmon, pp. 53–72. Occasional Paper No. 1. Crow Canyon Archaeological Center, Cortez, Colorado.

Lipe, William D., and Michelle Hegmon

1989   Historical Perspectives on Architecture and Social Integration in the Prehistoric Pueblos. In *The Architecture of Social Integration in Prehistoric Pueblos*, edited by William D. Lipe

and Michelle Hegmon, pp. 15–34. Occasional Paper No. 1. Crow Canyon Archaeological Center, Cortez, Colorado.

Lyneis, Margaret M.

1984   The Western Anasazi Frontier: Cultural Processes Along a Prehistoric Boundary. In *Exploring the Limits, Frontiers and Boundaries in Prehistory*, edited by Suzanne P. DeAtley and Frank J. Findlow, pp. 81–92. BAR International Series 223.

1992   Social Complexity among the Lowland Virgin Anasazi. *The Kiva* 57(3):197–212.

McGuire, Randall H.

1980   The Mesoamerican Connection in the Southwest. *The Kiva* 46(1–2):3–38.

1991   On the Outside Looking In: The Concept of Periphery in Hohokam Archaeology. In *Exploring the Hohokam: Prehistoric Desert Dwellers of the Southwest*, edited by George J. Gumerman, pp. 347–82. University of New Mexico Press, Albuquerque.

Mathien, Frances Joan, and Randall H. McGuire (editors)

1986   *Ripples in the Chichimec Sea.* Southern Illinois University Press, Carbondale.

Matson, R. G.

1991   *The Origins of Southwestern Agriculture.* University of Arizona Press, Tucson.

Meighan, Clement W.

1956   Excavations at Paragonah: A Summary. In *Archeological Excavations in Iron County, Utah*, by Clement W. Meighan, Norman E. Coles, Frank D. Davis, Geraldine M. Greenwood, William M. Harrison, and E. Heath, pp. 1–22. Anthropological Papers No. 25. University of Utah Press, Salt Lake City.

Mera, H. P.

1935   *Ceramic Clues to the Prehistory of North Central New Mexico.* Technical Series, Bulletin No. 8. Laboratory of Anthropology, Santa Fe.

Morris, Earl H.

1939   *Archaeological Studies in the La Plata District; Southwestern Colorado and Northwestern New Mexico.* Publication No. 519. Carnegie Institution of Washington, Washington D. C.

Neitzel, Jill E.

1994   Boundary Dynamics in the Chacoan Regional System. In *The Ancient Southwestern Community*, edited

by Wirt H. Wills and Robert D. Leonard, pp. 209–40. University of New Mexico Press, Albuquerque.

Osler, Tom, and Ed Dodd

1979   *Ultra-Marathoning, The Next Challenge.* World Publications, Mountain View, California.

Pepper, George H.

1920   *Pueblo Bonito.* Anthropological Papers, Vol. 27. American Museum of Natural History, New York.

Platt, Colin

1979   *The English Medieval Town.* Paladin, Granada, London.

Plog, Fred, and James N. Hill

1971   Explaining Variability in the Distribution of Sites. In *The Distribution of Prehistoric Population Aggregates*, edited by George J. Gumerman, pp. 7–36. Anthropological Reports No. 1. Prescott, Arizona.

Porter, Joseph C.

1986   *Paper Medicine Man, John Gregory Bourke and his American West.* University of Oklahoma Press, Norman.

Prudden, T. Mitchell

1903   The Prehistoric Ruins of the San Juan Watershed in Utah, Arizona, Colorado, and New Mexico. *American Anthropologist* n.s., 5(2):224–88.

Rafferty, Kevin

1991   The Virgin Anasazi and the Pan-Southwestern Trade System, A.D. 900–1150. *Kiva* 56(1):3–24.

Robinson, William J., Bruce G. Harrill, and Richard L. Warren

1975   *Tree-Ring Dates from Arizona H-I, Flagstaff Area.* Laboratory of Tree-Ring Research, University of Arizona, Tucson.

Rohn, Arthur H.

1965   Postulation of Socio-economic Groups from Archaeological Evidence. In *Contributions of the Wetherill Mesa Archeological Project*, compiled by Douglas Osborne, pp. 65–69. Memoirs of the Society for American Archaeology No. 19.

1977   *Cultural Change and Continuity on Chapin Mesa.* Regents Press of Kansas, Lawrence.

Schaafsma, Polly, and Curtis F. Schaafsma

1974   Evidence for the Origin of the Pueblo Katchina Cult as Suggested by Southwestern Rock Art. *American Antiquity* 39:535–45.

Snodgrass, Anthony

1980   *Archaic Greece, The Age of Experi-*

ment. University of California Press, Berkeley.

Spaulding, Albert
1960   Statistical Description and Comparison of Artifact Assemblages. In *The Applications of Quantitative Methods in Archaeology,* edited by Robert F. Heiser and Sherbourne F. Cook, pp. 60–72. Publications in Anthropology No. 28. Viking Fund, New York.

Stanislawski, Michael B.
1963   *Wupatki Pueblo: A Study in Cultural Fusion and Change in Sinagua and Hopi Prehistory.* Unpublished Ph.D. dissertation, Department of Anthropology, University of Arizona, Tucson.

Stein, John R., and Peter J. McKenna
1988   *An Archaeological Reconnaissance of a Late Bonito Phase Occupation Near Aztec Ruins National Monument, New Mexico.* National Park Service, Southwest Cultural Resources Center, Division of Anthropology, Santa Fe.

Steward, Julian H.
1937   Ecological Aspects of Southwestern Society. *Anthropos* 32:87–104.

Sullivan, Alan P., and Michael B. Schiffer
1978   A Critical Examination of SARG. In *Investigations of the Southwestern Anthropological Research Group, The Proceedings of the 1976 Conference,* edited by Robert C. Euler and George J. Gumerman, pp. 168–78. Museum of Northern Arizona, Flagstaff.

Turney, Omar
1929   *Prehistoric Irrigation in Arizona.* Arizona Historian, Phoenix.

Upham, Steadman
1982   *Polities and Power.* Academic Press, New York.

Vivian, R. Gordon, and Paul Reiter
1960   *The Great Kivas of Chaco Canyon and Their Relationships.* Monographs No. 22. School of American Research and Museum of New Mexico, Santa Fe.

Warren, Claude N.
1984   The Desert Region. In *California Archaeology,* by Michael J. Morratto, pp. 339–430. Academic Press, New York.

Wilcox, David R.
1975   A Strategy for Perceiving Social Groups in Puebloan Sites. *Fieldiana: Anthropology* 65:120–59.
1976   How the Pueblos Came to be as They Are: The Problem Today. Ms,

Preliminary Exam Paper, on file, Arizona State Museum Archives, University of Arizona, Tucson.
1979   The Hohokam Regional System. In *An Archaeological Test of Sites in the Gila Butte-Santan Region, South-Central Arizona,* by Glen Rice, David Wilcox, Kevin Rafferty, and James Schoenwetter, pp. 77–116. Anthropological Research Paper No. 18. Arizona State University, Tempe.
1980   The Current Status of the Hohokam Concept. In *Current Issues in Hohokam Prehistory: Proceedings of a Conference,* edited by David Doyel and Fred Plog, pp. 236–42. Anthropological Research Paper No. 23. Arizona State University, Tempe.
1984   Multi-Ethnic Division of Labor in the Protohistoric Southwest. In *Collected Papers in Honor of Harry L. Hadlock,* edited by Nancy L. Fox, pp. 141–56. Papers of the New Mexico Archaeological Society No. 9. New Mexico Archaeological Society, Albuquerque.
1988   Rethinking the Mogollon Concept. *The Kiva* 53(2):205–09.
1991a   Changing Contexts of Pueblo Adaptations, A.D. 1250–1600. In *Farmers, Hunters and Colonists: Interaction Between the Southwest and the Southern Plains,* edited by Katherine A. Spielmann, pp. 128–54. University of Arizona Press, Tucson.
1991b   Hohokam Social Complexity. In *Chaco & Hohokam, Prehistoric Regional Systems in the American Southwest,* edited by Patricia L. Crown and W. James Judge, pp. 253–76. School of American Research Press, Santa Fe.
1991c   The Mesoamerican Ballgame in the American Southwest. In *The Mesoamerican Ballgame,* edited by Vernon Scarborough and David R. Wilcox, pp. 101–28. University of Arizona Press, Tucson.
1992   The Changing Structure of Macroregional Organization in the North American Southwest: A New World Perspective. Ms, on file, Museum of Northern Arizona Library, Flagstaff.
1993   The Evolution of the Chacoan Polity. In *The Chimney Rock Symposium,* edited by J. McKim Malville and Gary Matlock, pp. 76–90. USDA, Forest Service, Rocky Mountain Forest

and Range Experiment Station, Fort Collins.
1994   Three Macroregional Systems in the North American Southwest and Their Relationships. Paper presented at the Advanced Seminar on "Great Towns and Regional Polities: Cultural Evolution in the U.S. Southwest and Southeast," Amerind Foundation, Dragoon, Arizona.
1995a   The Diversity of Regional and Macroregional Systems in the American Southwest. In *Proceedings of the 26th Chacmool Meetings.* Department of Archaeology, University of Calgary, Alberta, Canada, in press.
1995b   The Wupatki Nexus: Chaco-Hohokam-Chumash Connectivity, A.D. 1150–1225. In *Proceedings of the 25th Chacmool Conference.* Department of Archaeology, University of Calgary, Calgary, Alberta, in press.

Wilcox, David R., and Jonathan Haas
1994   The Scream of the Butterfly: Competition and Conflict in the Prehistoric Southwest. In *Themes in Southwest Prehistory,* edited by George J. Gumerman, pp. 211–38. School of American Research, Santa Fe.

Wilcox, David R., Thomas R. McGuire, and Charles Sternberg
1981   *Snaketown Revisited.* Arizona State Museum Archaeological Series No. 155. University of Arizona, Tucson.

Wilcox, David R., and Charles Sternberg
1983   *Hohokam Ballcourts and Their Interpretation.* Arizona State Museum Archaeological Series No. 160. University of Arizona, Tucson.

Willey, Gordon R. (editor)
1956   *Prehistoric Settlement Patterns in the New World.* Publications in Anthropology No. 23. Viking Fund, New York.

Wilshusen, Richard H.
1990   *Early Villages in the American Southwest: Cross-Cultural and Archaeological Perspectives.* Unpublished Ph.D. dissertation, University of Colorado, Boulder.

Windes, Thomas C.
1985   Chaco-McElmo Black-on-white from Chaco Canyon with an Emphasis on the Pueblo del Arroyo Collection. In *Prehistory and History in the Southwest, Collected Papers in Honor of Alden C. Hayes,* edited by Nancy L. Fox, pp. 19–42. Papers

of the Archaeological Society of
New Mexico No. 11. Archaeo-
logical Society of New Mexico,
Albuquerque.

1987   *Summary of Tests and Excavations
at the Pueblo Alto Community*. In-
vestigations at the Pueblo Alto
Complex, Chaco Canyon, New
Mexico, 1975–1979, Vol. 1. Chaco
Canyon Studies, Publications in
Archeology No. 8F. USDI, National
Park Service, Santa Fe.

Mapping the Puebloan Southwest

Compiled by Michael Adler and Amber Johnson

The master data table has been compiled from 12 regional maps and site lists. The site information for each region was presented by participants in the "Pueblo Cultures in Transition" conference in 1990, and in most cases, has been updated for this publication. The primary challenge in compiling the master data table has been to include all of the data pertinent to the regional syntheses without sacrificing the overall utility of the data base.

Although the organizers of the conference provided participants with guidelines for the types of site information to be included in their data summaries, participants were not always able to collect these data. As a result, the data included here include only those variables for which data was nearly always available. Due to publication limitations, a complete bibliography for site-specific references could not be included. The bibliographic information is available in an electronic format. Information on how to access this information is supplied later in the appendix.

Site Selection Criteria

Following Lipe and Lekson (1990), the participants in the Pueblo III conference compiled data on big sites, which were arbitrarily designated as those sites containing more than 50 rooms that had significant occupations during the Pueblo III period. Not all the data included here meet the site size or date of occupation criteria. Several contributors to the volume have included sites that fall below the 50-room cutoff, particularly when the sites figure into important explanatory contexts on the regional or district levels. For

example, Lyneis (chapter 2), Pilles (chapter 5), and Reid and others (chapter 6), note that few Anasazi sites in their regions ever attained the arbitrary 50-room count, but these smaller sites are still important for understanding the process of population aggregation across those regions during the twelfth and thirteenth centuries. Dean (chapter 3) also includes a number of smaller Kayenta sites to point out the small-scale nature of population aggregation in certain parts of the Kayenta region prior to its abandonment during the thirteenth century.

Users should also be aware that some authors have extended their discussions to include occupations between A.D. 1100 and 1400. The Pueblo III period as defined (A.D. 1150–1350) was intended to serve as a fuzzy boundary to guide the overall scope of the conference proceedings. Inclusion of sites occupied during the 50 years on either side of the Pueblo III period allows more realistic perspectives of the Pueblo II antecedents and protohistoric developments that frame the Pueblo III period.

Site Identification

The first four columns of data are for site identification. The first column contains an alphanumeric code (or numeric, in the case of the Cibola region sites identified by Kintigh) that keys into the site identification labels on each of the regional maps in chapters 2 through 13. Column 2 identifies the subarea or district within which the site is located. Column 3 includes the most commonly used site name. Column 4 lists the most commonly used regional, state, or federal site identification number.

Site Size

The fifth column contains estimates of room counts. Methods of arriving at the room count are discussed by many of the authors in the regional summary chapter. These counts are, for the most part, approximate, and are presented here only as best guesses of room counts on each site. In those cases where the authors feel the estimates are low or based on incomplete information, a "+" sign follows the estimate. It should be noted that these room counts are not accurate for all components of a multicomponent site, but are an approximation of the maximal extent of the site during the Pueblo III period.

Due to the great interregional variability in settlement patterns in the Southwest during this period, these guidelines make more sense in some regions than in others. As already noted, few of the sites mapped in the Virgin Anasazi (Lyneis), Sinagua (Pilles), and southwestern Mogollon uplands (Reid et al.) regions have more than 50 rooms, particularly when one realizes that "rooms" in these sites might be small storage enclosures appended onto the larger domestic rooms or any of a variety of domestic pit structures. In other words, these data should be handled with care. It is clear that the arbitrary 50-room criterion for "big sites" does limit the broad use of this database for regional population estimates or settlement pattern syntheses. Given that there is a clear trend toward a greater degree of residential aggregation during the Pueblo III and Pueblo IV periods, there is some consolation in the fact that, through time, the "big site" perspective becomes increasingly useful for regional population estimates. At the same time the authors in volume all stress that "big site" data will remain only partially useful without accompanying information on the small sites of the Pueblo III period.

Data on site size are not available for all sites in the master data table. In those cases where the site met the size criterion but lacked dependable size estimates, the site was included with the hope that future regional archaeological syntheses would provide the missing data.

Kiva Counts

Column 6 includes kiva counts in those cases where such structures exist and have been counted or estimated. The overall usefulness of this category is limited at this point due to the fact that subterranean structures are not ubiquitous across the Pueblo world between the eleventh and fourteenth centuries, and where they are present, archaeologists must contend with the difficulties involved in counting unexcavated kivas and the spottiness of kiva counts both within and between regions. These problems should come as no surprise to veterans of southwestern archaeology. The ongoing ambiguity surrounding the identification of kivas is reflected in the regional data compilations. For the Northern Rio Grande, Kayenta, and Mesa Verde regions, kiva counts in the master data table represent all kivas (no matter how great or small). The data for the San Juan Basin include only great kivas, bi-wall structures, and tower kivas. These data are most useful as indications of the presence and relative number of such features on sites across the various Pueblo regions.

Occupation Dates

Column 7 is the estimated date of initial occupation or reoccupation of the site, and column 8 is the estimated ending date for the site occupation. Participants were asked to use calendar dates instead of, or in addition to, the traditional Pecos Classification. In most cases, these dates correspond to regional chronological phases that are based upon ceramic and architectural criteria. Authors were asked to make an educated guess regarding site occupation dates for all sites, but in some cases, no estimate could be made. In many cases, estimates have been included with some reservation on the part of the author(s). Where a range of dates (e.g. 1100–1300) is given, these dates are used as the beginning and ending dates, respectively. Where only an ending date is given (e.g. –1300), the authors were unable to estimate the initial occupation of the site.

Site Layout and Architecture

Column 9 includes data on site layout characteristics. The availability of site layout data is variable across the regions, and in many cases this column has been left empty. Site layout is included in the database for sites where obvious features such as plaza, courtyard, great house, great kiva, and cliff dwelling are visible. These terms are explained at more length in the chapters where the data are summarized.

The Master Map

A single map, showing the location and relative densities of large settlements across the Pueblo world between A.D. 1150 and 1350, has been included in the volume (figure 1.1). Space limitations prevented the use of site identification labels on this map, but the map still provides the first compilation of its type in the Southwest. This master map, dubbed the "measle map" for obvious reasons, was originally compiled by Steve Lekson at the close of the Pueblo III conference, and was later redrafted by Amber Johnson, Mike Adler, and Staso Forenbaher. The map integrates data from over two dozen smaller maps. It should be noted that the precision with which sites are located on the master map is directly proportional to the precision with which sites are located on each regional map. Although each original regional map was to be drawn at a scale of 1:50,000, some participants were forced to resort to different scales. In addition, parts of some districts were included in two different regional maps. In cases where a site showed up on two overlapping regional maps, the final location of the site on the master map represents the location agreed upon by the compilers of the two original maps.

Electronic Version of the Pueblo III Data

A primary reason for the Pueblo III conference and this publication is the broader dissemination of regional archaeological interpretations and the supporting settlement data. Limitations on space and resources prevent the publication of all site data, including dating criteria and bibliographic references.

These data are available in an electronic format from the volume editor and Crow Canyon Archaeological Center. Requests for these data must be accompanied by two 1.44 MB floppy disks and sufficient return postage. Plans have also been made to make these data available "on-line" though an Internet node so that interested persons can download the data from a remote host. Because plans have not yet been finalized, the location of the on-line data can be obtained from the volume editor. Given the potential that specific site locational data might be used by those unscrupulous few who wish to illicitly collect or dig on these sites, none of these data sources list specific site location data. Specific locational data for most of the archaeological sites listed in this volume are available to qualified professionals from State Historic Preservation Offices in the Southwest.

Southwestern Utah, the Arizona Strip, and Southern Nevada

Site ID	District	Site Name	State/Federal Site Number	Rooms	Kivas	Begin Date	End Date	Architectural Layout
1B1	Western Plateaus	Mecca site	AZ B:1:68	90+		1000	1050	4 plazas
1D1	Lower Muddy	Mesa House		80+		1125	1150	single courtyard
1D2	Lower Muddy	Main Ridge	26CD-2148	190+		1050	1075	small courtyard group
1D3	Lower Muddy	House 47		50+		1100	1150	courtyards

Sinagua Region

Site ID	District	Site Name	State/Federal Site Number	Rooms	Kivas	Begin Date	End Date	Architectural Layout
2A2	Wupatki	East Mesa	NA373	25		1150	1250	massed room block
2A3	Wupatki	Citadel	NA355	51		1150	1250	unknown
2A4	Wupatki	Crack-in-Rock Pueblo		22	1	1150	1250	plaza; clustered rooms
2A5	Wupatki	North Mesa	NA656	22		1150	1250	clustered rooms
2A7	Wupatki	Middle Mesa	NA352	24		1150	1250	unknown
2A8	Wupatki	Juniper Terrace	02–19	59	1	1070	1300	courtyard
2A9	Wupatki	North Arrowhead Tank	WS830	25		1150	1250	massed room block
2A10	Wupatki	Wupatki	NA405	102	7	1087	1213	courtyard
2A11	Wupatki	Campground Ruin	NA2222	33		1150	1250	plaza
2B1	Flagstaff	Elden Pueblo	NA142	65	3	1070	1275	massed room block
2B2	Flagstaff	Sunset Pueblo	02–1819	22		1150	1250	massed room block
2B3	Flagstaff	Turkey Hill Pueblo	02–120	35	1	1100	1300	massed room block
2B4	Flagstaff	New Caves	02–3760	34	3	1100	1250	massed room block
2B5	Flagstaff	Cosnino Caves	02–486	21		1150	1275	cavate
2B6	Flagstaff	Ridge Ruin	NA1785	30	3	1100	1250	courtyard
2B7	Flagstaff	South of Winona	02–712	50		1150	1300	massed room block
2B8	Flagstaff	Marozas Citadel	02–2461	43	2	1070	1300	massed room block
2B9	Flagstaff	Old Caves Pueblo	02–270	50	1	1250	1400	massed room block
2B12	Anderson	Nuvakwewtaqa Southwest	07–21A	20	1	1150	1400	plaza
2B13	Anderson	Nuvakwewtaqa North	07–20	20	1	1100	1400	massed room block
2B14	Anderson	Nuvakwewtaqa Southeast	07–21B	20	2	1150	1400	massed room block
2C1	Verde Valley	Honanki	06–58	30		1150	1300	massed room block
2C2	Verde Valley	Polles Mesa TNF 122	TNF 122	20		1150	1400	plaza
2C3	Verde Valley	Polles Mesa TNF 40	TNF 40	25		1150	1400	unknown
2C4	Verde Valley	Cane Springs	TNF 324	20		1150	1400	massed room block
2C5	Verde Valley	Hatalacva	NA1263	28		1150	1400	clustered rooms
2C6	Verde Valley	Tuzigoot	NA1261	43	3	1000	1400	clustered rooms
2C7	Verde Valley	Sugarloaf	06–78	20		1150	1400	plaza
2C8	Verde Valley	Bridgeport Ruin	06–74	32	1	1150	1400	massed room block
2C9	Verde Valley	Polles Mesa	NA6362	31		1150	1400	massed room block
2C13	Verde Valley	Riordan Canyon	01–302	25		1150	1400	massed room block
2C14	Verde Valley	Ruin Point	01–70	50	1	1150	1300	unknown
2C18	Verde Valley	Cornville Ruin	06–43	20		1150	1400	plaza
2C19	Verde Valley	Verde Ruin	01–58	20	3	1150	1400	massed room block
2C20	Verde Valley	Montezuma Castle A	01–640	20	1	1150	1400	massed room block
2C21	Verde Valley	Oak Creek Ruin	06–41	24	2	1150	1400	massed room block
2C23	Verde Valley	Talbot Ranch Ruin	01–26	20	1	1150	1400	massed room block
2C24	Verde Valley	Jackson Ranch Ruin	01–43	21	2	1150	1400	massed room block
2C30	Verde Valley	John Heath Ruin	01–68	20	2	1150	1400	plaza
2C31	Verde Valley	Wingfield Mesa	01–67	50		1150	1400	plaza
2C32	Verde Valley	Mindeleff's Cavate Lodge Pueblo	01–266	20	1	1150	1400	massed room block
2C33	Verde Valley	Clear Creek Ruins	01–05	70	4	1150	1400	massed room block
2C34	Verde Valley	Clear Creek Bridge	V:5:39	20		1150	1400	unknown
2C35	Verde Valley	Bull Pen Ranch	NA2448	20		1150	1400	unknown
2C37	Verde Valley	Boulder Canyon	01–255	20	1	1150	1400	massed room block

Sinagua Region (*continued*)

Site ID	District	Site Name	State/Federal Site Number	Rooms	Kivas	Begin Date	End Date	Architectural Layout
2C39	Verde Valley	Doran Castle	01–100	20	1	1150	1400	massed room block
2C42	Verde Valley	Bull Run	NA3518	20		1150	1400	massed room block
2C43	Verde Valley	Brown Springs	NA5348	20	1	1150	1400	massed room block
2C44	Verde Valley	Verde Hot Springs	01–499	20		1150	1400	massed room block
2C49	Verde Valley	East Verde Ruin	NA3514	20		1150	1400	massed room block

Note: Both kivas and community rooms are included in the "kivas" column in those cases where surface remains indicate the presence of these architectural spaces (see Pilles, chapter 7). The absence of data means that no surface indications of these structures were visible, and is not an indication that the structures are not present on the site.

Kayenta Region

Site ID	District	Site Name	State/Federal Site Number	Rooms	Kivas	Begin Date	End Date	Architectural Layout
3A1	Navajo Canyon–White Mesa	Inscription House		85	2	1200	1300	courtyard
3A2	Navajo Canyon–White Mesa		AZ D:5:9–1			1200	1300	plaza
3A3	Navajo Canyon–White Mesa		AZ D:5:19			1150	1300	
3B1	Rainbow Plateau	Upper Desha Pueblo		25	1	1250	1300	plaza
3B2	Rainbow Plateau	Segazlin Mesa		90	6	1250	1300	courtyard
3B3	Rainbow Plateau	Red House		50	3	1200	1300	plaza
3B4	Rainbow Plateau	Terrace Ruin		20	1	1200	1300	courtyard
3B5	Rainbow Plateau	Yellow House		50	3	1200	1300	plaza
3B6	Rainbow Plateau		AZ D:2:93	25	2	1200	1300	plaza
3B7	Rainbow Plateau	Pottery Pueblo		100	5	1200	1300	courtyard
3B8	Rainbow Plateau	Neskahi Village		18	1	1250	1300	plaza
3B9	Rainbow Plateau	Thumb Rock Pueblo		25	1	1250	1300	plaza
3B10	Rainbow Plateau		AZ D:2:236	70	2	1200	1300	plaza
3B11	Rainbow Plateau		AZ D:2:1	50	2	1200	1300	plaza
3B12	Rainbow Plateau		AZ D:2:2			1200	1300	
3C1	Shonto Plateau		NA 8839	40	3	1250	1300	plaza
3C2	Shonto Plateau	Begashibito Canyon		50	0	1250	1300	plaza
3D1	Klethla Valley	Shonto Canyon	UVK 80	20		1200	1300	
3D2	Klethla Valley	Little Thief Rock	UVK 92	50	0	1200	1300	
3D3	Klethla Valley	Thief Site	UKV 77	50		1250	1300	pit house
3D4	Klethla Valley	Kin Klethla	UKV 115	70		1200	1300	pit house
3D5	Klethla Valley	Valley View	UKV 75	50	2	1200	1300	plaza
3E1	Long House Valley		NA 11980	45	1	1250	1300	plaza
3E2	Long House Valley		NA 11958	40	4	1100	1300	plaza
3E3	Long House Valley	Long House		350		1000	1300	plaza
3E4	Long House Valley	Camp Cemetery		46	3	1075	1300	plaza
3E5	Long House Valley	Pottery Hill		80	0	1000	1300	plaza
3E5	Long House Valley	LHV 12	NA 10614	20	1	1150	1300	courtyard
3E6	Long House Valley	Tower House		60	2	1150	1300	plaza
3E7	Long House Valley	LHV 404	NA 12225	40		1200	1300	plaza
3E7	Long House Valley	LHV 410	NA 12231	10	2	1150	1250	plaza
3E7	Long House Valley	LHV 405	NA 12226	5		1200	1300	plaza
3E7	Long House Valley	LHV 408	NA 12229	10	1	1150	1300	plaza
3E8	Long House Valley		NA 12230	50	1	1200	1300	plaza
3F1	Tsegi Canyon	Kiet Siel		150	7	1150	1300	courtyard
3F2	Tsegi Canyon	Twin Caves Pueblo		50	2	1250	1300	courtyard
3F3	Tsegi Canyon	Batwoman House		50		1250	1300	courtyard
3F4	Tsegi Canyon	Betatakin		120	3	1250	1300	courtyard
3F5	Tsegi Canyon	Wildcat Canyon Ruin				1250	1300	
3F6	Tsegi Canyon	Six Foot Ruin		50	1	1250	1300	plaza
3G1	Kayenta Valley	Kin Po		50	1	1250	1300	plaza
3G2	Kayenta Valley	Happy Valley				1250	1300	courtyard

Kayenta Region (*continued*)

Site ID	District	Site Name	State/Federal Site Number	Rooms	Kivas	Begin Date	End Date	Architectural Layout
3G3	Kayenta Valley	Tachini Point		40	2	1175	1300	plaza
3G4	Kayenta Valley		RB568	85	3	1200	1300	courtyard
3G5	Kayenta Valley	Rabbit Ears		30		1250	1300	courtyard?
3G5	Kayenta Valley	Parrish Creek		60	1	1250	1300	plaza
3G6	Kayenta Valley	Moki Rock		150	3	1200	1300	plaza
3G7	Kayenta Valley	Moqui Overlook		25	1	1200	1300	plaza
3H1	Laguna Creek-Chinle Wash	Kits'iil		100		1200	1300	
3H2	Laguna Creek-Chinle Wash	Poncho House	MORSS 36	100	3	1200	1300	courtyard
3H3	Laguna Creek-Chinle Wash	Tsegi Ho Chong		45	10	1250	1300	courtyard
3J1	Interior Black Mesa	Fat House		100		1250	1300	plaza
3J2	Interior Black Mesa	DJW Sites		40		1200	1300	plaza
3J2	Interior Black Mesa	Cliff Dwelling		40		1250	1300	courtyard
3J3	Interior Black Mesa	Kitisili		50		?	1300	plaza
3J4	Interior Black Mesa	Covered Spring		80		1250	1350	plaza
3J5	Interior Black Mesa		AZ-J-58-2	100		1200	1300	plaza

Note: Kiva counts indicate the total number of large and small kivas at each settlement based on surface indications.

Hopi Region

Site ID	District	Site Name	State/Federal Site Number	Rooms	Kivas	Begin Date	End Date	Architectural Layout
4A1	Moenkopi	Red Lake	D:7:	20		1100	1250	
4A2	Moenkopi	Moenave	NA 812	20		1100	1250	
4A3	Moenkopi	Castle Rocks	NA 48	35		1100	1250	
4A4	Moenkopi	Old Moenkopi	NA 1119	30		1350	1830	
4A5	Moenkopi	Posewlelena	C:16:8	20		1100	1250	
4A6	Moenkopi	Tutukmola	C:16:	10		1100	1250	
4A7	Moenkopi	Coal Mine Canyon	D:13:	10		1100	1250	
4A8	Moenkopi	Tohnali Spring	C:16:	10		1100	1250	
4A9	Moenkopi	Salt Spring	I:3:	35		1100	1250	plaza
4B2	Hopi Mesa	Lamb Springs	D:16:	55		1100	1250	
4B3	Hopi Mesa	Mcenany	J-58-48	40		1100	1250	
4B4	Hopi Mesa	Pinon	NA 851	100		1100	1250	
4B5	Hopi Mesa	Dinnebito	J-61-39	60		1100	1300	
4B6	Hopi Mesa	Hoyapi	NA 837	150		1250	1400	
4B7	Hopi Mesa	Kwaituki	NA 489	200		1250	1300	
4B8	Hopi Mesa	Oraibi	NA 828	500		1250	present	
4B9	Hopi Mesa	Huckovi	NA 872	300		1250	1300	plaza
4B11	Hopi Mesa	Chumalisko	NA 1163	100		1250	1325	
4B12	Hopi Mesa	Chukovi	NA 1132	250		1300	1500	
4B13	Hopi Mesa	Sikyatki	NA 814	500		1275	1530	
4B14	Hopi Mesa	Kuchaptevela	NA 1699	500		1250	1690	
4B15	Hopi Mesa	Lamehva	NA 1707	150		1200	1400	
4B16	Hopi Mesa	Old Mishongnovi	NA 871	400		1250	1690	
4B18	Hopi Mesa	Old Shunopavi	NA 868	500		1250	1690	plaza
4B20	Hopi Mesa	Lululongturqui	NA 1056	60		1250	1300	
4B21	Hopi Mesa	Kokopnyama	NA 1019	250		1275	1400	
4B22	Hopi Mesa	Nesuftanga	NA 1048	100		1250	1400	
4B23	Hopi Mesa	Pink Arrow	J:4:1	100		1275	1350	
4B24	Hopi Mesa	Chakpahu	NA 1039	250		1250	1500	
4B25	Hopi Mesa	Kawaika-a	NA 1001	500		1250	1530	
4B26	Hopi Mesa	Awatovi	NA 820	800		1250	1700	
4C1	Hopi Buttes	Bidahochi	NA 1054	250		1300	1350	
4C2	Hopi Buttes	Bidahochi Southeast	NA 1052	150		1300	1350	

Hopi Region (*continued*)

Site ID	District	Site Name	State/Federal Site Number	Rooms	Kivas	Begin Date	End Date	Architectural Layout
4C3	Hopi Buttes	Bidahochi Southwest	P-48–2	100		1250	1300	
4C4	Hopi Buttes	Malpais Springs	J:12:	36		1050	1250	
4E1	Middle Little Colorado	Homol'ovi IV	NA 2212	150		1260	1285	
4E2	Middle Little Colorado	Homol'ovi III	NA 4089	50		1280	1300	
4E3	Middle Little Colorado	Homol'ovi II	NA 953	1000		1330	1400	
4E4	Middle Little Colorado	Homol'ovi I	NA 952	500		1280	1400	
4E5	Middle Little Colorado	Cottonwood Creek	NA 926	50		1280	1350	
4E6	Middle Little Colorado	Chevelon	NA 1026	500		1280	1400	
4E7	Middle Little Colorado	Jackrabbit	P:3:23	150		1280	1350	

Note: Estimates of numbers of kivas were not consistently available, so these data have not been included.

Cibola Region

Site ID	District	Site Name	State/Federal Site Number	Rooms	Kivas	Begin Date	End Date	Architectural Layout
1	Manuelito	Atsee Nitsaa	LA1507	150		1150	1250	compound
2	Manuelito	Big House	LA1379	500		1200	1325	
3	Petrified Forest		AZ Q:2:22	100		1275	1375	
4	Petrified Forest	Puerco Ruin	AZ Q:1:22	125		1250	1350	
5	Petrified Forest	Seven Springs	AZ Q:3:70	175		1175	1300	
6	Petrified Forest	Wallace Tank	AZ Q:2:21	50		1275	1375	
7	Silver Creek		AZ P:11:130	50		1100	1250	
8	Silver Creek		AZ P:11:133	50		1250	1300	
9	Silver Creek		AZ P:11:42	60		1100	1250	
10	Silver Creek		AZ P:11:83	80		1100	1250	
11	Silver Creek		AZ P:12:135	50		1100	1250	
12	Silver Creek	Bailey	AZ P:11:1	150		1250	1300	
13	Silver Creek	Broken K	HHV 188	95		1150	1280	
14	Silver Creek	Flake Ruin	AZ P:8:1	50		1100	1300	
15	Silver Creek	Fourmile	AZ P:12:4	450		1100	1400	
16	Silver Creek	HHV 201	HHV 201	80		1100	1250	
17	Silver Creek	Pinedale	AZ P:12:2	150		1275	1330	
18	Silver Creek	Pottery Hill	AZ P:12:12	60		1225	1275	
19	Silver Creek	Showlow	AZ P:12:3	200		1325	1400	
20	Silver Creek	Shumway	AZ P:12:6	54		1300	1375	
21	Silver Creek	Spier 212		52		1150	1250	
22	Silver Creek	Tundastusa	AZ P:16:3	300		1250	1350	
23	Upper Little Colorado	Baca Pueblo	AZ Q:11:74	100		1300	1385	
24	Upper Little Colorado	Bean Patch Community	AZ Q:8:12	100		1175	1275	
25	Upper Little Colorado	Casa Malpais	AZ Q:15:3	86		1250	1300	
26	Upper Little Colorado	Donaldson		50		1150	1250	
27	Upper Little Colorado	Garcia Ranch Community	AZ Q:8:5	300		1175	1325	
28	Upper Little Colorado	Greenwood Site		70		1200	1275	
29	Upper Little Colorado	Hooper Ranch	AZ Q:15:6	60		1200	1375	
30	Upper Little Colorado	Knight		120		1175	1250	
31	Upper Little Colorado	Oscar's		60		1275	1325	
32	Upper Little Colorado	Rattlesnake Point	AZ Q:11:118	100		1325	1385	
33	Upper Little Colorado	Raven	AZ Q:11:48	335		1275	1385	
34	Upper Little Colorado	Spier 175	AZ Q:7:7	175				
35	Upper Little Colorado	Spier 176		125		1325	1385	
36	Upper Little Colorado	Table Rock	AZ Q:7:5	80		1325	1385	
37	Zuni		AZ Q:4:159	80		1050	1200	
38	Zuni	Archeotekopa II	NM:13:D:103	1412		1250	1300	
39	Zuni	Atsinna	LA99	875		1275	1385	

Cibola Region (*continued*)

Site ID	District	Site Name	State/Federal Site Number	Rooms	Kivas	Begin Date	End Date	Architectural Layout
40	Zuni	Badger Springs Community						
41	Zuni	Barth Well Community	LZ 215–17...	313		1100	1200	
42	Zuni	Bob Place Community	LZ 222	204		1100	1200	
43	Zuni	Box S	LA5538	473		1225	1290	
44	Zuni	CS 56 Community	CS 56	145		1200	1250	
45	Zuni	Cienega	LA425	500		1275	1375	
46	Zuni	Day Ranch	NM:12:Z2:82	574		1250	1300	
47	Zuni	Fort Atarque	LA55637	200		1175	1300	
48	Zuni	Fort Site	NM:13:D:101	216		1250	1300	
49	Zuni	Halona:wa North	NM:12:K3:1	200		1300	present	
50	Zuni	Halona:wa South	NM:12:K3:172	375		1275	1340	
51	Zuni	Hardscrabble	AZ Q:3:9–10 ?	114		1175	1275	
52	Zuni	Heshoda Yala:wa	AZ:15:H:16	150		1225	1290	
53	Zuni	Heshotauthla	LA15605	875		1275	1385	
54	Zuni	Hinkson Ranch Community	LA11439	445		1175	1275	
55	Zuni	Jack's Lake	NM:12:I3:21	245		1250	1300	
56	Zuni	Jaralosa Community	LA3993	120		1175	1275	
57	Zuni	Kay Chee	NM:12:I3:29	255		1225	1275	
58	Zuni	Kluckhohn	LA424	1142		1275	1310	
59	Zuni	LA11530 Community	LA11530	65		1200	1285	
60	Zuni	Lookout	LA1551	300		1250	1300	
61	Zuni	Los Gigantes Community	LA56159	120		1175	1275	
62	Zuni	Lower Deracho	NM:12:I3:110	609		1225	1275	
63	Zuni	Lower Pescado	NM:12:I3:6	180		1325	1375	
64	Zuni	Lower Pescado Village	NM:12:I3:109	420		1300	1375	
65	Zuni	Miller Ranch	NM:13:D:41	60		1200	1275	
66	Zuni	Mirabal	LA426	743		1275	1325	
67	Zuni	North Atsinna	LA430	180		1275	1325	
68	Zuni	Ojo Bonito	LA11433	225		1300	1385	
69	Zuni	Ojo Caliente Community		250				
70	Zuni	Ojo Hallado Community						
71	Zuni	Ojo Pueblo	LA27612	222		1250	1300	
72	Zuni	Pescado Canyon	NM:12:I3:140	723		1225	1275	
73	Zuni	Pescado West	NM:12:I3:4	445		1325	1375	
74	Zuni	Pettit Site	LA1571	125		1225	1275	
75	Zuni	Prospect	AZ Q:3:52	75		1175	1300	
76	Zuni	Pueblo De Los Muertos	LA1585	880		1275	1375	
77	Zuni	Ramah School	NM:12:A3:17	186		1275	1325	
78	Zuni	Scribe S Community	NM:12:G3:4	410		1225	1275	
79	Zuni	Spier 142		165		1250	1300	
80	Zuni	Spier 170		200		1300	1385	
81	Zuni	Spier 61	NM:12:X2:55	122		1225	1275	
82	Zuni	Spier 62 Community		93		1175	1275	
83	Zuni	Spier 81	LA82742	163		1150	1200	
84	Zuni	Spier 83 Community	LA82693	369		1150	1250	
85	Zuni	Tinaja	LA427	163		1250	1300	
86	Zuni	Upper Nutria Village	NM:12:S2:60	180		1275	1340	
87	Zuni	Upper Pescado	LA9108	405		1300	1375	
88	Zuni	Village of Great Kivas	LA631	80		1000	1225	
89	Zuni	Yellowhouse	NM G:14:2	425		1275	1325	

Note: Site identification numbers correspond with those on figure 9.1. Estimates of numbers of kivas were not consistently available, so these data have not been included.

Arizona Mountain Mogollon Region

Site ID	District	Site Name	State/Federal Site Number	Rooms	Kivas	Begin Date	End Date	Architectural Layout
6B1		Forestdale	AZ P:16:9	40		1200	1300	
6C1			S-259	80				
6D1		Kinishba	AZ V:4:1	800		1200	1400	
6E1			S-225	50		1250	1300	
6F1			48–33	115		1200	1300	
6F2			S-238	135		1300	1400	
6G1			86–13	60		1250	1300	
6H1		Turkey Creek	AZ W:9:123	335	1	1240	1300	
6H2		Point of Pines	AZ W:10:50	800		1275	1400	
see map		Q Ranch	AZ P:13:13	200		1275	1400	
see map		Grasshopper	AZ P:14:1	500		1275	1400	

Note: District names have not been assigned because the authors of this chapter do not use district distinctions. Site names and identification numbers refer to the sites included in Figure 6.1.

Mesa Verde Region

Site ID	District	Site Name	State/Federal Site Number	Rooms	Kivas	Begin Date	End Date	Architectural Layout
7A1	Piedra		5AA8	45+	4	1090	1135	great house
7A2	Piedra	Chimney Rock Pueblo	5AA83	45+	2	1090	1135	great house
7A3	Piedra	Chimney Rock Lower Mesa		175	0	1090	1135	great kiva
7C1	Mesa Verde	Battleship Rock Cluster		75+	13+	1175	1225	
7C2	Mesa Verde	Site 34	5MV34	50	5	1150	1250	
7C3	Mesa Verde	Far View House	5MV808	50	5	1100	1200	great house?
7C4	Mesa Verde	Bowman's Pueblo		100+	15+	1225	1275	
7C5	Mesa Verde	Mug House	5MV1229	94	8	1225	1275	
7C6	Mesa Verde	Spring House	5MV1406	55	2	1250	1270	
7C7	Mesa Verde	Ruin 16	5MV1241	50	5	1225	1275	
7C8	Mesa Verde	Long House	5MV1200	150	22	1250	1280	
7C9	Mesa Verde	Spruce Tree House	5MV640	114	8	1235	1275	cliff dwelling
7C10	Mesa Verde	Kodak House	5MV1212	60	7	1225	1275	
7C11	Mesa Verde	Double House	5MV1385	75	5	1225	1275	
7C12	Mesa Verde	Cliff Palace	5MV625	220	23	1250	1280	cliff dwelling
7C13	Mesa Verde	Square Tower House	5MV650	200	7	1250	1280	cliff dwelling
7C14	Mesa Verde	Oak Tree House	5MV523	55	7	1235	1275	cliff dwelling
7C15	Mesa Verde	Hoy House	5MV2150	60+	6	1130	1250	cliff dwelling
7C16	Mesa Verde	Lion House	5MV2156	46+	6	1130	1250	cliff dwelling
7C17	Mesa Verde	Site 20½	5MV1449	48	3	1225	1275	cliff dwelling
7C18	Mesa Verde	Kiva Point	5MT2767	100+	8	1150	1200	
7D1	Dolores Valley	Escalante Ruin	5MT2149	25	2	1130	1180	great house
7D2	Dolores Valley	Reservoir Ruin	5MT4450	40+	7+	1050	1125	great house, great kiva
7E1	McElmo-Yellow Jacket	Miller Pueblo	5MT875	80+	16	1225	1275	
7E2	McElmo-Yellow Jacket	Yellow Jacket	5MT5	600+	130+	1075	1250	great house, great kiva
7E3	McElmo-Yellow Jacket		5MT1647	200+	40	1225	1275	
7E4	McElmo-Yellow Jacket		5MT4421	100	14	1150	1250	great kiva
7E5	McElmo-Yellow Jacket		5MT10581	50	8	1175	1225	
7E6	McElmo-Yellow Jacket	Rohn 84	5MT121	100	9	1200	1250	
7E7	McElmo-Yellow Jacket	Stevenson Site	Rohn Y68	150	20	1200	1250	
7E8	McElmo-Yellow Jacket	Rohn 150	5MT207	75	12	1200	1250	
7E9	McElmo-Yellow Jacket	Bass Pueblo	5MT136	100+	18+	1150	1250	
7E10	McElmo-Yellow Jacket	Big Spring Ruin	5MT7088	150+	30+	1250	1280	
7E11	McElmo-Yellow Jacket	Uncle Albert Porter Site	5MT123	80+	13+	1100	1225	great house, great kiva
7E12	McElmo-Yellow Jacket	Woods Canyon Pueblo	5MT11842	250	50	1250	1280	
7E13	McElmo-Yellow Jacket	Griffey Site	Rohn Y-149	150	20	1200	1250	

Mesa Verde Region (*continued*)

Site ID	District	Site Name	State/Federal Site Number	Rooms	Kivas	Begin Date	End Date	Architectural Layout
7E14	McElmo-Yellow Jacket	Easter Ruin	5MT3793	125	20+	1250	1275	road?
7E15	McElmo-Yellow Jacket	Hibbetts Pueblo	5MT7656	100	16	1250	1280	
7E16	McElmo-Yellow Jacket		5MT4700	80+	11+	1200	1250	
7E17	McElmo-Yellow Jacket		5MT1541	60+	9	1150	1250	
7E18	McElmo-Yellow Jacket	Seven Towers Ruin	5MT1000	175	43	1250	1280	
7E21	McElmo-Yellow Jacket	Mustoe Community		45	8+	1150	1250	great kiva?
7E23	McElmo-Yellow Jacket	Goodman Point Pueblo	5MT604	350+	80	1225	1275	biwall, great kiva
7E24	Four Corners	Hovenweep: Horseshoe-Hackberry		100	20	1250	1300	
7E26	McElmo-Yellow Jacket	Sand Canyon Pueblo	5MT765	400+	100	1250	1280	biwall, great kiva
7E28	McElmo-Yellow Jacket	Casa Negra	5MT3925	60	4	1100	1150	road
7E29	McElmo-Yellow Jacket		5MT6359	50	6	1225	1275	
7E30	McElmo-Yellow Jacket	Ida Jean Ruin		50+	2+	1125	1150	great kiva
7E31	McElmo-Yellow Jacket	Haynie Ruin		50+	5+	1100	1275	great house
7E32	McElmo-Yellow Jacket	Wallace Ruin	5MT6970	124	7	1075	1125	great house
7E33	McElmo-Yellow Jacket	Hovenweep Square Tower		50+	8	1225	1280	
7E34	McElmo-Yellow Jacket	Castle Rock Pueblo	5MT1825	60	12	1200	1280	
7E35	McElmo-Yellow Jacket	Cannonball Ruin	5MT338	90	15	1250	1280	
7E36	McElmo-Yellow Jacket	Mitchell Springs		140+	23+	1200	1275	triwall, great kiva
7E37	McElmo-Yellow Jacket	Morley-Kidder 1917		100	11+	1225	1275	
7E38	McElmo-Yellow Jacket	Mud Springs	5MT6878–88	150+	30+	1200	1250	triwall
7F1	Ute Mountain	Yucca House	5MT4359	200+	40+	1080	1275	2 great kivas, great house
7F2	Ute Mountain	Moqui Spring Pueblo	5MT4474	150+	20+	1250	1280	great kiva, road?
7F3	Ute Mountain	Cowboy Wash Pueblo	5MT7740	40+	9	1225	1275	
7G1	Montezuma Valley	Montezuma Creek Ruin II	42SA836	175+	17+	1075	1125	
7G2	Montezuma Valley	Montezuma Creek Ruin I	42SA822	75	4	1075	1125	great house
7G3	Montezuma Valley	Ansel Hall Site		200+	36	1080	1150	great house
7G4	Montezuma Valley	Monument West Hill Ruin		200	40	1100	1200	
7G5	Montezuma Valley	Brewer Pueblo		50+	14+	1250	1300	
7G6	Montezuma Valley	Monument Main Ruin		300+	76	1200	1250	
7G7	Montezuma Valley	Monument Middle Ruin		150	30	1200	1250	
7G8	Montezuma Valley	Berkley Bryant Site		200+	45+	1250	1300	
7G9	Montezuma Valley	Alkali Mesa Canyon Ruin	42SA4998	50	7+	1250	1300	
7G10	Montezuma Valley	Ten-acre Ruin	42SA15206	275+	40	1150	1250	
7G11	Montezuma Valley	Coalbed Village	42SA920	125+	20	1200	1300	walled
7G12	Montezuma Valley	James A. Lancaster Ruin	5MT4803	350+	60+	1075	1300	
7G13	Montezuma Valley	Finley Farm-Charnel House-Ray Ruin		50+	5+	1175	1225	
7G14	Montezuma Valley	Brew's Site #1	42SA1	85	14	1200	1250	
7G15	Montezuma Valley	North Lowry Great House	5MT839	65+	14	1100	1250	great house
7G16	Montezuma Valley	Pigg Site	5MT4802	150	25	1175	1225	roads
7G17	Montezuma Valley	Lowry Ruin	5MT1566	50	7	1080	1150	great house
7G18	Montezuma Valley	Five-acre Ruin		120	20	1200	1250	
7G19	Montezuma Valley	Casa Del Valle		50+	7+	1180	1250	
7G20	Montezuma Valley	Little Cow Canyon Pueblo	5MT834–5	200+	30+	1225	1275	
7G21	Montezuma Valley	Herren Farms Complex	5MT2516	250+	50	1150	1250	
7G22	Montezuma Valley	Beartooth Ruins	5MT2299	300+	50	1175	1275	
7G23	Montezuma Valley	Upper Squaw Point Village	5DL860	50	6	1080	1150	great house
7G24	Montezuma Valley	Brewer Well Site	5DL506	60+	7+	1250	1280	
7G25	Montezuma Valley	Cottonwood Ruin		80	12+	1250	1280	
7G26	Montezuma Valley	Papoose Canyon Pueblo		50+	6+	1250	1280	
7G27	Montezuma Valley	Ruin Canyon Rim Pueblo	5MT10438	45	7	1225	1275	
7G28	Montezuma Valley	Lower Squaw Mesa Village		75+	14+	1175	1225	
7G29	Montezuma Valley	Cow Mesa 40		50	7+	1250	1280	
7G30	Montezuma Valley	Spook Point Pueblo		50	7+	1250	1300	
7G31	Montezuma Valley	Pedro Point	5MT4575	40	11	1250	1300	
7G32	Montezuma Valley	Nancy Patterson Village	42SA2110	260	25+	1200	1300	

Mesa Verde Region (*continued*)

Site ID	District	Site Name	State/Federal Site Number	Rooms	Kivas	Begin Date	End Date	Architectural Layout
7H1	Four Corners		42SA18100	50	7+	1150	1250	
7H2	Four Corners		42SA6670	85+	18+	1050	1125	
7H3	Four Corners		42SA6671	100	15	1200	1250	
7H4	Four Corners		42SA7123	55	7	1150	1250	
7I1	Cottonwood	Red Knob Complex	42SA259	175+	25+	750	1250	
7I2	Cottonwood	Edge of the Cedars	42SA?	75+	12+	1075	1125	
7I3	Cottonwood	Cottonwood Falls Site		75	8	1080	1150	great house
7I4	Cottonwood	Arch Canyon Site	42SA5271	50+	7+	1080	1150	great house
7I5	Cottonwood	Ruin Spring Ruin		75+	9+	1250	1300	
7I6	Cottonwood	Radon Spring Ruin		60+	7+	1250	1280	
7I7	Cottonwood	Parker Site		75+	10+	1200	1250	
7I8	Cottonwood	Mule Canyon Site		45+	7	1150	1200	
7I9	Cottonwood	Gravel Pit Site		75+	7+	1200	1250	
7I10	Cottonwood	Decker Ruin		60+	9	1200	1250	
7I11	Cottonwood	Bluff Cemetery Site		50	2	1080	1150	great house
7J1	Canyonland	Fable Valley Pueblo		75	12	1075	1125	
7K1	Cedar Mesa	Et Al. Site	42SA18431	20	2	1100	1150	great house, great kiva, roads
7M1	Escalante	Coombs Site	42GA34	70+	10+	1125	1175	

Note: Kiva counts indicate the total number of large and small kivas at each settlement based on surface indications.

San Juan Basin and Peripheries

Site ID	District	Site Name	State/Federal Site Number	Rooms	Kivas	Begin Date	End Date	Architectural Layout
8A1	Middle San Juan-Lower Chinle	Mouth of Comb Wash	42-SA-5647			1150	1250	great house
8A2	Middle San Juan-Lower Chinle	Promontory Ruin		50	10#	1150	1300	cliff dwelling
8A3	Middle San Juan-Lower Chinle	Aneth Terrace	DCA 78-3			700	1300	compound
8A4	Middle San Juan-Lower Chinle	Pancho House	NA 2660	200		500	1300	cliff dwelling
8A5	Middle San Juan-Lower Chinle	Waterfall Ruin				1150	1300	cliff dwelling
8A6	Middle San Juan-Lower Chinle	Ford House			25	1150	1300	cliff dwelling
8B1	Totah	Kello Blancett	LA59/967	200		1080	1130	great house
8B2	Totah	Holmes Great Kiva	NM-A-1-29			1200	1300	great kiva
8B3	Totah	Twin Towers	NM-A-1-45	50	0	1150	1300	walled compound
8B4	Totah	Bulldozer Pueblo	F.N. #33					
8B5	Totah	San Juan Biwall	NM-A-1-11					
8B6	Totah	Canal Creek Great Kiva	NM-A-1-12					
8B7	Totah	El Malpais	LA685	14	2	1100	1200	great house
8B8	Totah	Tse Taak'a		200	1	1150	1300	compound
8B9	Totah	Aztec West	LA45	400	1	1110	1120	great house
8B10	Totah		CGP 652	25		1200	1300	compound
8B11	Totah	West Water	LA13112	400		1150	1225	compound
8B12	Totah	Fruitland Pueblo	LA8620	80	2	1150	1250	compound
8B13	Totah	Hogback	LA11594	10		900	1250	great house
8B14	Totah	Squaw Springs-Morris 40	LA1988	20	2	1000	1200	great house
8B15	Totah	Upper Barker Draw	LA2519/20	60		900	1300	great house
8B16	Totah	Morris 41	ENMU 5098	500	2	600	1300	great house
8B17	Totah	Holmes Group	LA1898	500	3	1150	1250	great house
8B18	Totah	Morris 39 Building 1	LA1897	300	4	600	1300	great house
8B19	Totah	Jackson Lake	LA1921	49	1	1150	1200	great house
8B20	Totah		LA2513	49	3	1250	1300	compound
8B21	Totah	Old Fort	ENMU 5033			800	1300	
8B22	Totah	Shannon Bluff	LA8619	150	1	800	1300	compound
8B23	Totah	Aztec East-Earl Morris	LA45		3	1115	1300	great house
8B24	Totah	Aztec North	LA5603	50	2	1100	1150	great house

San Juan Basin and Peripheries (*continued*)

Site ID	District	Site Name	State/Federal Site Number	Rooms	Kivas	Begin Date	End Date	Architectural Layout
8B25	Totah	Salmon	LA8846	200		1085	1110	great house
8B26	Totah	Flora Vista	LA2514	400		1250	1300	great house
8B27	Totah	Old Indian Race Track	LA9050		1	1150	1300	
8B28	Totah	Gillentine Complex	LA6226		1			great house
8B29	Totah	East Mesita	LA5626		2			great house
8B30	Totah	Tonache Tower	NA-A-1-8	50		1150	1300	compound
8C1	Central Basin	Twin Angels	LA5642	17				great house
8C2	Central Basin	Champignon	LA36639	10		925	1300	pinnacle
8C3	Central Basin	Pueblo Bonito and Core				920	1130	great house
8C4	Central Basin	Fajada Butte		40		1175	1250	pinnacle
8C5	Central Basin	East Chaco				1200	1300	pinnacle
8C6	Central Basin	Pueblo Pintado	LA574	40		1200	1300	reoccupied great house
8C7	Central Basin	Bis Sa' Ani	LA17286-7	37	1	1080	1140	great house
8C8	Central Basin		LA8500	20	0	1200	1300	
8C9	Central Basin	Raton Well	LA14354	65	0	1200	1325	terraced
8C10	Central Basin	Reservoir Ruin	LA15278	63	13*	1200	1300	walled
8C11	Central Basin	El Castillejo	LA51145	42	9*	1200	1300	pinnacle
8C12	Central Basin	Mesa Pueblo		25	10*	1200	1325	pinnacle
8C13	Central Basin	Kin Nazhin		50		1200	1300	pinnacle
8C14	Central Basin	Paul Logsden	LA50055	40	11*	1200	1300	
8D1	Chuska	Naschitti	LA8532	50		1200	1300	compound
8D2	Chuska	Tohatchi Well	LA4470	30		1150	1300	compound
8D3	Chuska	Red Willow-Los Rayos	LA51141		2	850	1200	great house
8D4	Chuska	Deer Springs	LA47858					great house
8D5	Chuska	Beautiful Mountain		100	1	1150	1300	compound
8D6	Chuska	Twin Lakes	LA51140		1	1150	1250	great house
8D7	Chuska	To Dil Hil Dry Lake	LA7575	100		1150	1300	compound
8D8	Chuska	Cemetery Ridge	LA7551	12	3	850	1200	great house
8D9	Chuska	Kin Lizhin	LA7000	45	4	850	1250	great house
8D10	Chuska	Crumbled House	LA7070-7080	300		1250	1300	compound
8D11	Chuska		LA14779		1	1150	1250	great house
8E1	Canyon de Chelly	Antelope House		90	5	1140	1270	cliff dwelling
8E2	Canyon de Chelly	White House		20	2	1045	1300	great house
8E3	Chuska	Many Farms		75		1100	1325	compound
8E4	Canyon de Chelly	Mummy Cave		180	1	1275	1300	cliff dwelling
8E5	Canyon de Chelly	Salina Springs		200		1050	1275	compound
8F1	Tusayan	Hogay		50	0	1200	1275	compound
8F2	Tusayan	Bear Springs North and South		120		1130	1300	compound
8F3	Tusayan	Lululongtuqui		60		1250	1300	compound
8F4	Tusayan	Eighteen Mile Ruin		30		1150	1300	compound
8F5	Tusayan	Eagle Crag		100	0	1150	1300	compound
8G1	Defiance	Kin Tiel		675	1	1250	1300	terraced
8G2	Defiance	Chechibikhin				1200	1300	
8G3	Defiance	Kinlichee		75	2	1050	1250	great house
8G4	Defiance	Wide Reed		150		1250	1300	compound
8G5	Defiance	Black Rock Gaddy				1150	1275	
8G6	Defiance	Cornfields		275		1150	1250	walled
8G7	Defiance	Sunrise Springs		50	2	1100	1250	great house
8G8	Defiance	Klagetoh		35		1150	1300	compound
8H1	Painted Desert	Adamana	Spier 206	125		1250	1300	compound
8H2	Painted Desert	Canyon Butte Ruin 4		65		1250	1300	compound
8H3	Painted Desert	Canyon Butte Ruin 3		22		1250	1300	compound
8J1	Rio Puerco West	Tseyatoh	LA40394	40	1	1150	1200	great house
8J2	Lobo Mesa	Muddy Water Complex	LA10959	45	1	1000	1200	great house
8J3	Rio Puerco West	Taylor Spring				1200	1300	compound
8J4	Rio Puerco West	Chambers Ranch		40	2	1000	1300	great house

San Juan Basin and Peripheries (*continued*)

Site ID	District	Site Name	State/Federal Site Number	Rooms	Kivas	Begin Date	End Date	Architectural Layout
8J5	Rio Puerco West	Fenced up Horse Group	LA16279-B	150	1	1150	1250	great house
8J6	Rio Puerco West	Rocky Point	AZ-K-15:2		1	1150	1250	great house
8J7	Rio Puerco West	Emigrant Spring		75		1200	1300	compound
8J8	Rio Puerco West	Fort Wingate	LA2690	53	1	950	1250	great house
8J9	Rio Puerco West	Isham		50		1250	1300	compound
8J10	Rio Puerco West	Springstead			1	1150	1250	great house
8J11	Rio Puerco West	Lupton Butte	M 6					walled
8J12	Rio Puerco West	Big House-Naat'a'anii	LA1379	500	2	1250	1300	compound
8J13	Rio Puerco West	Atsee Nitsaa	LA1507	20	1	1150	1250	compound
8J14	Rio Puerco West	Fenced-up Horse Tower			1			tower
8K1	Lobo Mesa	Peach Springs	LA10770	30	1	900	1175	great house

Note: Except for those indicated with * or #, all kiva counts for the San Juan Basin refer to the total number of great kivas, biwall structures, and tower kivas. Those counts indicated by * are discussed by Roney in chapter 10; he prefers to include both large and small kivas. The site indicated by # uses a kiva count supplied by Varien and others in chapter 7.

Eastern San Juan Basin, Acoma-Laguna Region

Site ID	District	Site Name	State/Federal Site Number	Rooms	Kivas	Begin Date	End Date	Architectural Layout
9A1	Upper Puerco	Mesa Portales	LA4568	50	0	1200	1300	
9A2	Upper Puerco	Jones Canyon		40		1150	1200	
9A3	Upper Puerco	Miller Pueblo	LA98366	50		1200	1300	
9A4	Upper Puerco	Headcut Reservoir	LA59019	50		1200	1300	
9A5	Upper Puerco	Torreon	LA51967	50	5	1150	1325	
9B1	Middle Puerco	Guadalupe Ruin	LA2757	40	6	930	1325	
9B2	Middle Puerco	AS-8	LA13197	48	8	1250	1300	plaza
9B3	Middle Puerco	AS-3	LA5010	27	1	1215	1235	
9B4	Middle Puerco	Mesa Verde Butte	LA57614	60	0	1250	1300	
9B5	Middle Puerco	Loma Fria		95		1240	1275	plazas
9B6	Middle Puerco	Cuervo	LA10505	40	14	1130	1300	
9B7	Middle Puerco	Coot Ridge	LA10405	40	4	1130	1300	plaza
9C1	Acoma	Cubero	LA494	175		1100	1400	
9C2	Acoma	Rabbit Butte				1200	1300	
9C3	Acoma	Shumatzutstya	LA413	40		1200	1400	
9C4	Acoma	Acoma	LA112	40		1250	present	
9C5	Acoma	La Mesita Redonda		230	1+	1150	1325	
9C6	Acoma	Flour Mesa				1200	1300	
9C7	Acoma	Bug Mesa				1200	1300	
9D1	El Rito	El Rito	LA13831	55		1250	1275	plaza
9E1	El Malpais	Calabash	LA1331	367	2	1200	1350	plaza
9E2	El Malpais	Kowina	LA1334	86	1	1200	1350	plaza
9E3	El Malpais	Citadel	LA11651	62	1	1200	1250	
9E4	El Malpais	Penole	LA11677	100	0	1100	1325	plaza
9E5	El Malpais	LV4:27-A		50	0	1200	1350	
9E6	El Malpais	Ranger Station		150		1200	1300	
9E7	El Malpais	Rattail Ruin	LA68112	200	1	1150	1325	
9E8	El Malpais	Newton	LA13422	165	1	1200	1325	
9E9	El Malpais	Oak Tree	LA1337	40	0	1250	1325	
9E10	El Malpais	Casa Mosca	LA1341	72	2	1275	1325	
9E11	El Malpais	Lizzard House	LA11672	40	2	1225	1325	
9E12	El Malpais	Dittert Site	LA11723	40	1	1150	1300	

Note: Kiva counts are estimated only when researchers found surface indications of buried pit structures; totals include large and small kivas.

Southwestern New Mexico and Southeastern Arizona

Site ID	District	Site Name	State/Federal Site Number	Rooms	Kivas	Begin Date	End Date	Architectural Layout
10A1	Quemado	Goesling	LA4026	200		1150	1350	
10A2	Quemado	Cerro Prieto	LA48656	100		1150	1350	
10A3	Quemado	Largo Gap	LA3918	40		1150	1350	
10A4	Quemado	Veteado	LA44918			1250	1350	
10A5	Quemado	Horse Camp Mill	D-616	500		1200	1350	
10A6	Quemado	Trechado Spring	D-190	500		1200	1350	
10A9	Quemado	Newton	LA13422	150		1200	1350	
10B1	San Francisco-Tularosa	Demetrio	D-196	50		1150	1350	
10B2	San Francisco-Tularosa	Jewett Gap		50		1150	1200	
10B3	San Francisco-Tularosa	7 Trough Springs	D-78	100		1200	1350	
10B4	San Francisco-Tularosa		FS 364	50		1200	1350	
10B5	San Francisco-Tularosa	Costilla Springs	D-37 (?)	50		1150	1350	
10B6	San Francisco-Tularosa	Gallita (Gallo) Springs	D-38	75		1200	1350	
10B7	San Francisco-Tularosa	Armijo Springs				1200	1350	
10B8	San Francisco-Tularosa	East Camp	D-99	40		1150	1350	
10B9	San Francisco-Tularosa	Bishop's Ranch	Hough 121	50		1150	1350	
10B10	San Francisco-Tularosa		D-412	75		1150	1350	
10B11	San Francisco-Tularosa		A			1150	1350	
10B12	San Francisco-Tularosa		WNMT 41			1150	1350	
10B13	San Francisco-Tularosa	Apache Creek		75		1150	1200	
10B14	San Francisco-Tularosa	Spur Ranch	Hough 77	50		1150	1350	
10B15	San Francisco-Tularosa	Luna A	Hough 70	50		1150	1350	
10B16	San Francisco-Tularosa	Brush Springs	D-97?	50		1150	1200	
10B17	San Francisco-Tularosa	Delgar		300		1150	1350	
10B18	San Francisco-Tularosa		B	50		1150	1350	
10B19	San Francisco-Tularosa	Higgins Flat		30		1150	1350	
10B20	San Francisco-Tularosa	Hudson Ranch		50		1150	1350	
10C1	Blue River-Safford	Blue				1150	1300	
10C2	Blue River-Safford	Foote Canyon		100		1250	1350	
10C3	Blue River-Safford	Lovelady				1150	1300	
10C4	Blue River-Safford	Hough #37		50		1150	1300	
10C5	Blue River-Safford	C (Willow and Eagle)				1150	1300	
10C6	Blue River-Safford	Double Circle				1300	1400	
10C7	Blue River-Safford	Earven Flat		170		1150	1300	
10D1	Duncan-Virden Valley	WS Ranch		100		1150	1350	
10D2	Duncan-Virden Valley		C	40		1150	1350	
10D3	Duncan-Virden Valley	Across from WS Ranch				1300	1400	
10D4	Duncan-Virden Valley	Glenwood				1150	1350	
10D5	Duncan-Virden Valley	Pleasanton				1300	1400	
10D6	Duncan-Virden Valley	Mule Creek				1300	1400	
10E1	Mogollon Plateau	Gila Cliff Dwellings		40		1285	1285	
10E2	Mogollon Plateau	Cuchillo Negro		75		1200	1350	
10F1	Mimbres	Kwillelykia		200		1350	1450	
10F2	Mimbres	Dinwiddie		50		1300	1450	
10F3	Mimbres		LA34774	90		1300	1400	
10F4	Mimbres	Ormand		100		1300	1450	
10F5	Mimbres	Fortenberry	LA8706			1300	1450	
10F6	Mimbres	Disert	Z:5:10	70		1350	1450	
10F7	Mimbres	Montoya	Z:5:112	40		1150	1300	
10F8	Mimbres	Walsh	Z:5:80	125		1150	1300	
10F9	Mimbres	Black Mountain	LA49	300		1150	1300	
10F10	Mimbres	Palomas	LA45157	50		1250	1350	
10F11	Mimbres		LA3948	40		1300	1450	
10F12	Mimbres		LA50519	50+		1300	1450	

Northern Rio Grande

Site ID	District	Site Name	State/Federal Site Number	Rooms	Kivas	Begin Date	End Date	Architectural Layout
11A1	Gallina	La Jara	LA14318	42	1	1000	1200	
11A2	Gallina	Rattlesnake Point	LA35648	21		1150	1250	
11A3	Gallina	Castle of the Chama	LA9053	24		1100	1300	
11A4	Gallina		LA1708	41		1000	1275	
11A5	Gallina	Las Trincheras	LA10702	25		1100	1300	
11B1	Chama	Riana	LA920	23		1335	1350	
11B2	Chama	Palisade	LA3505	48		1312	1320	
11B3	Chama	Buena Vista	LA6610	52	0	1375	1450	
11B4	Chama	Buena Vista II	LA6611	62		1375	1450	
11B5	Chama	Tsiping	LA301	400		1275	1400	
11B6	Chama	Tsama	LA908 909	600		1250	1500	
11B7	Chama	Leafwater-Kap	LA300	175		1275	1400	
11B8	Chama	Te'ewi	LA252	500	0	1250	1500	
11B9	Chama	Pesedeuinge-Torreon	LA299	300		1350	1450	
11B10	Chama	Yuque-Yunque	LA59	400		1250	1610	
11B11	Chama	Ponsipa'akeri	LA297	900		1250	1550	
11B12	Chama	Nute'	LA298			1350	1500	
11B13	Chama	Pose'uinge	LA632	600		1300	1550	
11B14	Chama	Hupobi	LA380	450		1300	1550	
11B15	Chama	Sapawe	LA306	1000	0	1300	1550	
11B16	Chama	Ponyi Pakuen	LA307	350		1350	1450	
11C1	Taos	Cornfield Taos	LA3932			1350	1450	
11C2	Taos	Pot Creek Pueblo	LA260	300		1250	1320	
11C3	Taos	Picuris	LA127	400		1250	Present	
11D1	Pajarito	Puye	LA47			1250	1590	
11D2	Pajarito		LA180	123		1250	1325	
11E1	Jemez		LA24792	75		1300	1600	
11E2	Jemez	Nanishagi	LA541	450		1300	1600	
11E3	Jemez	Unshagi	LA123	300		1300	1620	
11E4	Jemez		LA24553	75		1300	1600	
11E5	Jemez	Tovakwa-Mera's LA484	LA484	1850		1300	1600	
11E6	Jemez	Mera's LA483	LA483	300		1300	1600	
11E7	Jemez	Kiashita	LA484	50	0	1300	1600	
11E8	Jemez	Kwastiyukwa	LA482	1250		1300	1600	
11E9	Jemez	Totaskwinu	LA479	300		1300	1600	
11E10	Jemez	Seshukwa	LA303	1100	0	1300	1600	
11E11	Jemez	Wabakwa	LA478	1400		1300	1600	
11E12	Jemez		LA44000	250		1300	1600	
11E13	Jemez		LA135	350		1300	1600	
11E14	Jemez		LA24789	75		1300	1600	
11E15	Jemez		LA44001	100		1300	1600	
11E16	Jemez		LA5920	475		1300	1600	
11E17	Jemez	Kiatsukwa	LA132 133	600		1300	1700	
11E18	Jemez		LA386	150		1300	1600	
11E19	Jemez		LA385	75		1300	1600	
11E20	Jemez	Pejunkwa	LA130	1300		1300	1600	
11E21	Jemez		LA5918	525		1300	1600	
11E22	Jemez		LA137	75		1300	1600	
11E23	Jemez	Boletsakwa	LA136	250		1300	1600	
11E24	Jemez		LA128	150		1300	1600	
11E25	Jemez		LA64452	60		1300	1600	
11E26	Jemez		LA398	450		1300	1600	
11E27	Jemez		LA65155	100		1300	1600	
11E28	Jemez		LA65153	100		1300	1600	
11E29	Jemez		LA403	75		1300	1600	
11E30	Jemez	Guacamayo	LA189	400		1300	1600	

Northern Rio Grande (*continued*)

Site ID	District	Site Name	State/Federal Site Number	Rooms	Kivas	Begin Date	End Date	Architectural Layout
11E31	Jemez		LA373	100		1250	1350	
11E32	Jemez		LA258	100		1300	1600	
11E33	Jemez		LA248	75		1300	1600	
11F1	Pajarito		LA52300	60				
11F2	Pajarito		LA21691A	80				
11F3	Pajarito		LA21422	100				
11F4	Pajarito		LA21430	90				
11F5	Pajarito		LA12700F	100				
11F6	Pajarito		LA21455	55				
11F7	Pajarito		LA21601	100				
11F8	Pajarito		LA21440	50				
11F9	Pajarito		LA21605	130				
11F10	Pajarito		LA52347	50				
11F11	Pajarito		LA29764	88				
11F12	Pajarito		LA21475	100				
11F13	Pajarito		LA12700C	50				
11F14	Pajarito		LA12700D	257				
11F15	Pajarito		LA12700E	150				
11F16	Pajarito	Otowi	LA169	450				
11F17	Pajarito		29A	100				
11F18	Pajarito		LA42	65				
11F19	Pajarito	Navawi	LA257	200				
11F20	Pajarito		LA12609	120				
11F21	Pajarito		LA4607	75				
11F22	Pajarito		LA12830	100		1200	1500	
11F23	Pajarito		LA21690	50				
11F24	Pajarito		LA4616	65				
11F25	Pajarito		LA4619	70				
11F26	Pajarito		LA350	50				
11F27	Pajarito		LA351	200				
11F28	Pajarito	Tshirege	LA170	600		1400	1680	
11F29	Pajarito		LA355	300				
11F30	Pajarito		LA4682	60				
11F31	Pajarito	Phermex	LA4665	150				
11F32	Pajarito		LA12655	50				
11F33	Pajarito		LA12664C	50				
11F34	Pajarito		LA12718	50				
11F35	Pajarito		LA4693	75				
11F36	Pajarito		LA4708	100				
11F37	Pajarito		LA21389	250				
11F38	Pajarito		LA3783	70				
11F39	Pajarito	Burnt Mesa	LA60372	65				
11F40	Pajarito	Water Canyon	LA545	50				
11F41	Pajarito		LA3769	60				
11F42	Pajarito		LA3759	66				
11F43	Pajarito		LA3848	60				
11F44	Pajarito		LA3765	55				
11F45	Pajarito	Long House	LA82	220				
11F46	Pajarito	Tyuonyi	LA82					
11F47	Pajarito	Frijolito	LA78	75				
11F48	Pajarito	Yapashi	LA250	350				
11F49	Pajarito		LA29837	80				
11F50	Pajarito		LA29798	70				
11F51	Pajarito		LA29804	50				
11F52	Pajarito		LA29819	55				
11F53	Pajarito		LA21259	125				

Northern Rio Grande (*continued*)

Site ID	District	Site Name	State/Federal Site Number	Rooms	Kivas	Begin Date	End Date	Architectural Layout
11F54	Pajarito	San Miguel	LA370	102				
11F55	Pajarito		LA12211	100				
11F56	Pajarito		LA9781	50				
11F57	Pajarito	Pueblo Canada	LA35	400		1450	1650	
11F58	Pajarito		LA9862	250				
11F59	Pajarito		LA9865	65				
11F60	Pajarito	Kuapa II	LA3444	800		1300	1500	
11F61	Pajarito		LA9831	150				
11F62	Pajarito	Kuapa I	LA3443	425				
11F63	Pajarito		LA3662	250				
11F64	Pajarito		LA21427					
11G1	Santa Fe	Cundiyo	LA31	50		1335		
11G2	Santa Fe	Nambe	LA17			1350	Present	
11G3	Santa Fe		LA835	120		600	1150	
11G4	Santa Fe	Cuyamunge	LA38	54		1200	1700	
11G5	Santa Fe	Tesuque Williams I	LA6560	40		1200	1300	
11G6	Santa Fe	Arroyo Negro	LA114	65		900	1150	
11G7	Santa Fe	Agua Fria School House	LA2					
11G8	Santa Fe	Pindi	LA1	175		1000	1400	
11G9	Santa Fe	Upper Arroyo Hondo	LA76	50				
11G10	Santa Fe	Arroyo Hondo	LA12	1100	0	1350		
11G11	Santa Fe	Pueblo Alamo	LA8	70		1200		
11G12	Santa Fe	Chamisa Locita	LA4	300		1300	1400	
11G13	Santa Fe	La Cieneguilla	LA16					
11G14	Santa Fe	La Cienega	LA3	140				
11G15	Santa Fe	La Bajada	LA7	450				
11G16	Santa Fe	Los Aguajes	LA5	166				
11G17	Santa Fe	Caja Del Rio North	LA174	250				
11G18	Santa Fe		LA12579	300				
11G19	Santa Fe	Caja Del Rio South	LA5137	400				
11G20	Santa Fe	Pueblo Del Encierro	LA70	198				
11G21	Santa Fe		LA247	100				
11G22	Santa Fe		LA249	200				
11G23	Santa Fe		LA331	75				
11G24	Santa Fe		LA6455	50				
11G25	Santa Fe		LA6462	75				
11G26	Santa Fe	Cochiti	LA126	138		1250	Present	

Note: Kiva counts indicate the total number of large and small kivas at each settlement based on surface indications.

Lower Rio Grande

Site ID	District	Site Name	State/Federal Site Number	Rooms	Kivas	Begin Date	End Date	Architectural Layout
12A1	Pecos	Arrowhead	LA251	81+		1300	1500	
12A2	Pecos	Loma Lothrop	LA277			1300	1500	
12A3	Pecos	Pecos	LA625	100+		1200	1830	
12A4	Pecos	Forked Lightning	LA672	100+		1100	1200	
12A5	Pecos	Dick's Ruin	LA276	100+		1220	1230	
12A6	Pecos	Rowe	LA108			1200	1500	
12B1	Galisteo	Pueblo Largo	LA183	480+		1275	1475	
12B2	Galisteo	San Lazaro	LA91/92			1275	1675+	
12B3	Galisteo	Galisteo	LA26			1275+	1700+	
12B4	Galisteo	Las Madres	LA25	47+		1275+	1370+	
12B5	Galisteo	Colina Verde	LA309			1275+	1300+	

Lower Rio Grande (*continued*)

Site ID	District	Site Name	State/Federal Site Number	Rooms	Kivas	Begin Date	End Date	Architectural Layout
12B6	Galisteo	San Cristobal	LA80			1375+	1675+	
12B7	Galisteo	Pueblo She	LA239			1300+	1600+	
12B8	Galisteo	Piedra Lumbre	LA309	150+		1250+	1330+	
12B9	Galisteo	Pueblo Colorado	LA62			1275+	1600+	
12B10	Galisteo	Paako	LA162	253		1200	1425	
12B11	Galisteo	San Marcos	LA98	100+		1300+	1675+	
12B12	Galisteo	Tonque	LA240			1425+	1500+	
12B13	Galisteo	Pueblo Blanco	LA40			1400	1600	
12C1	Tijeras	San Antonio	LA24			1300+	1600+	
12C2	Tijeras	Tijeras	LA581	200		1300	1425	
12D1	Pintada	Pintada Canyon Pueblo				1300	1450	
12D2	Pintada	Tecolote Pueblo	LA296					
12E1	Rio Abajo	La Jara Peak	LA786	75		1300	1400+	
12E2	Rio Abajo	Gallinas Springs	LA1178	300+		1250	1350	
12E3	Rio Abajo		SOC-36	70		1250	1350	
12E4	Rio Abajo		SOC-37	75		1250	1350	
12E5	Rio Abajo		LA1131	80		1300	1400	
12E6	Rio Abajo		LA1134	55		1300	1400	
12E7	Rio Abajo		LA2292	85		1300	1400	
12E8	Rio Abajo	Abeytas Pueblo	LA780	250+		1300+		
12E9	Rio Abajo	Hidden Mountain	LA415	122		1300+		
12E10	Rio Abajo	Sevilleta	LA774	175+		1300+		
12E11	Rio Abajo	Cerro Indio	LA287	117		1300+		
12E12	Rio Abajo	Canoncitos	LA 5094	65		1100	1300	
12E13	Rio Abajo	Piedras Negras	LA2004	155		1100	1300	
12E14	Rio Abajo	San Acacia	LA 1999	60		1300	1400	
12E15	Rio Abajo	Veranito Pueblo	LA6422	54		1100	1300	
12E16	Rio Abajo	Pueblito Pueblo	LA761	125+		1300+		
12E17	Rio Abajo	Tio Bartolo	LA31736	65		1000	1100	
12E18	Rio Abajo	Pueblo Presilla	LA31720	115		1300+		
12E19	Rio Abajo	Presilla Del Sur	LA31741	50+		1100	1300	
12E20	Rio Abajo	Las Canas Group	LA755	200		1300+		
12E21	Rio Abajo	Pargas Pueblo	LA31746	175+		1300+		
12E22	Rio Abajo		LA758	100		1300+		
12E23	Rio Abajo		LA282	175+		1300+		
12E24	Rio Abajo	Qualacu	LA757	150+		1300+		
12E25	Rio Abajo	San Pasqual	LA487	500+		1300+		
12E26	Rio Abajo	San Felipe		250+		1300+		
12E27	Rio Abajo		LA50766	50		1150	1300	
12F1	Salinas	Quarai	LA95			1300+	1600+	
12F2	Salinas		LA9009			1200+	1300+	
12F3	Salinas	Abo	LA97			1300+	1600+	
12F4	Salinas		LA503			1200+	1300+	
12F5	Salinas		LA9007			1200+	1300+	
12F6	Rio Abajo	Tenabo	LA200			1300+	1600+	
12F7	Salinas		LA2541			1300+		
12F8	Salinas		LA2548			1200+	1400+	
12F9	Salinas		LA9021			1200+	1300+	
12F10	Salinas		LA9014			1200+	1300+	
12F11	Salinas		LA9016			1200+	1300+	
12F12	Salinas	Montezuma's Ruin	LA197			1200+	1300+	
12F13	Salinas	Kite Site	LA199			1200+	1300+	
12F14	Salinas	Gran Quivira	LA120	200		1300	1670+	
12F15	Salinas	Pueblo Pardo	LA83			1300+	1600+	
12F16	Salinas	Pueblo Blanco	LA51			1300+	1600+	
12F17	Salinas	Pueblo Colorado	LA476			1300+	1500+	

Lower Rio Grande (continued)

Site ID	District	Site Name	State/Federal Site Number	Rooms	Kivas	Begin Date	End Date	Architectural Layout
12F18	Salinas	Pueblo de la Mesa	LA2091	100		1300+	1400+	
12F19	Salinas		LA2045			1220+	1300+	
12F20	Salinas	Tajique	LA381					
12F21	Salinas	Chilili	LA847					
12F22	Salinas		LA1069	136		1300	1400	
12F23	Salinas		LA1070	450		1350	1400+	
12F24	Salinas		LA1071	85		1350	1400+	
12F25	Salinas		LA1072	414		1300	1515+	
12F26	Salinas		LA1073	591		1350	1515+	
12F27	Salinas		LA1074	97		1300	1400+	
12F28	Salinas		LA1075	1462		1350	1600+	
12F29	Salinas		LA1076	864		1300	1515	
12F30	Salinas		LA1181	690		1270	1400+	
12G1	Sierra Blanca	Hiner		120		1200	1400+	
12G2	Sierra Blanca	Robinson	LA46326	200		1150+	1400+	
12G3	Sierra Blanca	Phillips		49+		1100	1400+	
12G4	Sierra Blanca	Henderson	LA1549	60+		1250+	1400+	

Note: Kiva counts indicate the total number of large and small kivas at each settlement based on surface indications.

Contributors

E. Charles Adams — Arizona State Museum, University of Arizona, Tucson

Michael A. Adler — Department of Anthropology, Southern Methodist University, Dallas

Bruce A. Bradley — Crow Canyon Archaeological Center, Cortez, Colorado

Winifred Creamer — Department of Anthropology, Northern Illinois University, DeKalb

Linda S. Cordell — University Museum, University of Colorado, Boulder

Patricia L. Crown — Department of Anthropology, University of New Mexico, Albuquerque

Jeffrey S. Dean — Tree Ring Laboratory, University of Arizona, Tucson

Andrew P. Fowler — Victor, New York

Jonathan Haas — Field Museum of Natural History, Chicago

Amber Johnson — Department of Anthropology, Southern Methodist University, Dallas

Keith W. Kintigh — Department of Anthropology, Arizona State University, Tempe

Timothy A. Kohler — Department of Anthropology, Washington State University, Pullman

Stephen H. Lekson — Crow Canyon Archaeological Center, Cortez, Colorado

William D. Lipe — Department of Anthropology, Washington State University, Pullman

Margaret M. Lyneis — Department of Anthropology, University of Nevada, Las Vegas

Barbara K. Montgomery — Department of Anthropology, University of Arizona, Tucson

Janet D. Orcutt — Southeast Regional Office, National Park Service, Santa Fe

Peter J. Pilles, Jr. — Coconino National Forest, Flagstaff, Arizona

J. Jefferson Reid — Department of Anthropology, University of Arizona, Tucson

John R. Roney — Archaeology Department, Bureau of Land Management, Albuquerque

Katherine A. Spielmann — Department of Anthropology, Arizona State University, Tempe

John R. Stein — Navajo Nation Historic Preservation Department, Window Rock, Arizona

Ian M. Thompson — Crow Canyon Archaeological Center, Cortez, Colorado

John R. Welch — Fort Apache, Arizona

Mark D. Varien — Crow Canyon Archaeological Center, Cortez, Colorado

Carla R. Van West — Statistical Research, Inc., Tucson

David R. Wilcox — Museum of Northern Arizona, Flagstaff

María Nieves Zedeño — Department of Anthropology, University of Arizona, Tucson

Index

Page references in italics refer to figures, and those in boldface type refer to tables.

About the Editor

Michael A. Adler is Associate Professor of Anthropology at Southern Methodist University and Director of Archaeology Field Programs at SMU's Fort Burgwin Research Center, near Taos, New Mexico. He received his Ph.D. in 1990 from the University of Michigan, Ann Arbor, with his dissertation research focusing on population aggregation in the Mesa Verde region of southwestern Colorado between A.D. 900 and 1300. His current research interests include village formation and community organization among food-producing societies and archaeological approaches to prehistoric social organization. He pursues these interests on regional and site-specific levels in the American Southwest, as well as through cross-cultural research.